An Historical Encyclopedia
of the Arab–Israeli
Conflict

AN HISTORICAL ENCYCLOPEDIA OF THE ARAB–ISRAELI CONFLICT

Edited by Bernard Reich

Joseph E. Goldberg, Associate Editor
Stephen H. Gotowicki, Military Editor
Sanford R. Silverburg, Bibliographic Editor
Mark Daryl Erickson, Assistant Editor

Greenwood Press
Westport, Connecticut

Library of Congress Cataloging-in-Publication Data

An historical encyclopedia of the Arab–Israeli conflict / Bernard
  Reich, editor-in-chief.
     p. cm.
  Includes bibliographical references and index.
  ISBN 0–313–27374–X (alk. paper)
    1. Jewish-Arab relations—1949- —Encyclopedias. 2. Israel-Arab
  conflicts—Encyclopedias. I. Reich, Bernard.
  DS119.7.A67218   1996
  327.5694017'4927—dc20   95–6684

British Library Cataloguing in Publication Data is available.

Library of Congress Catalog Card Number: 95–6684
ISBN: 0–313–27374–X

First published in 1996

Greenwood Press, 88 Post Road West, Westport, CT 06881
An imprint of Greenwood Publishing Group, Inc.

Printed in the United States of America

The paper used in this book complies with the
Permanent Paper Standard issued by the National
Information Standards Organization (Z39.48–1984).

10 9 8 7 6 5 4 3 2 1

Contents

Preface

The Arab–Israeli conflict continues to preoccupy much of the world, as it has for most of the period since World War II. It has been vigorously and hotly debated and has been the subject of a substantial, if generally highly partisan, literature. It has been the focus of the policies of the parties and their partisans, the theme of journalists and authors, and the core of policies of small and large powers, and it has been at the center of the activities and objectives of the superpowers. Despite this attention, the conflict has not generated much dispassionate analysis. Now, in a single reference book we provide detailed information about every aspect of this complex and controversial regional and international conflict. This volume, the work of a number of scholars and students of varying backgrounds, interests, disciplines, and perspectives, covers the whole range of the conflict with a focus on the period since the adoption of the Palestine partition plan in November 1947 and the consequent first Arab–Israeli War up to the Israel–Palestine Liberation Organization (PLO) Declaration of Principles and subsequent agreements, as well as the Israel–Jordan Peace Treaty and implementation process.

No other book, in any language, contains the comprehensive coverage provided by this, the first encyclopedia of the Arab–Israeli conflict. It offers a new and focused perspective on the events and individuals in the history and evolution of the Arab–Israeli conflict prepared by a group of scholars under the general editorship of Bernard Reich of The George Washington University.

This is a tool designed to fill a gap in the reference literature by providing detailed and comprehensive information about the important political, military, and diplomatic events, organizations, personalities, institutions, places, agreements, treaties, documents, concepts, military operations, conflicts, and groups that are part of the Arab–Israeli conflict. The encyclopedia is designed to include in a single source the references that the student and scholar, the journalist, and the general reader will find useful in understanding this continuing conflict and the myriad factors that have shaped and still affect its content, evolution, and future.

Hundreds of entries of varying lengths are alphabetically arranged and supply detailed information. They are cross-referenced to facilitate the tracing of related topics and trends. Entries are followed with appropriate references to the literature for the reader who wishes to pursue the subject further.

A work of this sort requires a large number of choices. The primary period of focus is the one since the partition plan of Palestine adopted by the United Nations in November 1947. Nevertheless, material from earlier periods is included. Several techniques were used to construct the final list of entries. A form of reputational analysis was employed in which the major works on the subject were surveyed to determine the subjects that were considered significant for the evolution of the conflict. Also, specialists from the academic and policy communities as well as journalists and students in the United States and abroad, some of them authors of the entries that follow, were queried about the appropriateness and relative weight of the terms to be included and were asked to identify potential subjects. They reacted to an initial list and made the suggestions that contributed to the compilation of the ultimate roster of subjects. Ultimately, the editor made the final selection based on more than thirty years of investigation into, and teaching about, the subject. Each entry contains essential facts and seeks to present them in an objective manner. Each entry is signed by the writer, except in the case of those written by the editor, where no author is indicated.

A brief bibliography of works follows each item and provides sources for further research and information and generally is limited to works in English that will be useful to the reader.

The Arabic and Hebrew languages pose problems of transliteration and of spelling in English. Rather than getting involved in lengthy and cumbersome processes of transliteration, about which even linguists are not in full accord, we have chosen to use the transliteration generally utilized in works on the region and in the media, that is, the most common and widely and generally accepted usage. Thus, the reader will find Yasser rather than Yasir and Nasser rather than Nasir as the preferred rendition in this volume. Diacritical marks have been omitted. With Arab names the last name is used as the family name, and the entry is in alphabetical order accordingly (e.g., Saddam Hussein is located under Hussein). Kings and princes (emirs, sheiks) are listed by their first names (e.g., King Farouk under Farouk). The Arabic al or Al is disregarded in the alphabetical listing.

Foreign words and terms have been defined in parenthetical phrases in the text where employed, and, thus, we have omitted a glossary. To facilitate the use of the volume and to provide a context for the reader, a chronology of important events has been constructed.

The subject matter of this volume is among the most controversial subjects of contemporary international relations and evokes passionate responses and arouses intense emotions. We have tried to steer clear of these by including authors with a wide range of positions and perspectives on the issues in question. In all cases, the authors were enjoined to keep in mind that this volume is designed as a reference work of factual material, not an additional volume to "make points" and win arguments concerning the conflict or to further endorse or support a particular position or party. Each entry was subjected to editorial review by several other individuals to help assure that the work contained the essential factual information while excluding, to the greatest extent possible, an author's bias.

We trust that this work will be a useful addition to the literature and will provide both students and scholars with basic information, definitions, and descriptions of critical elements in the Arab–Israeli conflict and serve as a basic research tool containing generally hard-to-find factual information.

Acknowledgments

My interest in the Arab–Israeli conflict owes its origins to my mentor, Professor R. K. Ramazani of the University of Virginia, who first convinced me that the study of Middle East politics was a worthwhile endeavor. More than three decades have passed since that introduction to the region and to this particular conflict. In that time I have researched and discussed this topic in more than fifty countries on five continents and in hundreds of forums in the United States. I have also visited the area and the participants on dozens of occasions and have lived on both sides of the Arab–Israeli fence of hostility in a region that now shows some signs of conciliation. The thousands of hours of discourse on this subject have convinced me of the need for a work such as this one and also have informed its content.

This volume results from a substantial effort over a long period during which a number of individuals made particularly valuable contributions. The list of entries was originally devised as a result of discussions with and questions by students in courses on the Arab–Israeli conflict at The George Washington University and the Defense Intelligence College and was refined in response to suggestions by colleagues at these and other institutions of higher learning as well as by those involved in the policy process in the United States and abroad. Joe Goldberg was a cooperative co-editor of this work, and his contribution is far greater than the entries which bear his signature. He reviewed and edited the entire volume and offered invaluable suggestions for its improvement. Sandy Silverburg, a bibliographical wizard, provided numerous helpful suggestions and the bibliographical entries reflect his knowledge of the subject and of the massive literature on the Middle East and on this conflict. Steve Gotowicki ensured the accuracy of the military entries. Mim Vasan was, as always, instrumental in ensuring that the project moved from concept to reality. Mark Erickson has earned the title of Assistant Editor through diligent effort at all stages of this work. Nevertheless, the book would have been impossible without the constant help and support of my wife, to whom it is dedicated.

Bernard Reich
Washington, D.C., June 1995

Abbreviations and Acronyms

AIPAC	American Israel Public Affairs Committee
ALF	Arab Liberation Front
ANO	Abu Nidal Organization
CIA	Central Intelligence Agency
DFLP	Democratic Front for the Liberation of Palestine
DMZ	demilitarized zone
DOP	Declaration of Principles, Israel-PLO (1993)
ECM	Electronic countermeasures
EU	European Union
GCC	Gulf Cooperation Council
IDF	Israel Defense Forces
IRM	Islamic Resistance Movement
JNF	Jewish National Fund
LEHI	Lohamei Herut Yisrael (Fighters for the Freedom of Israel)
MAHAL	Mitnadvei Hutz Laeretz (foreign volunteers)
MAPAI	Mifleget Poalei Eretz Yisrael (Land of Israel Workers Party, Israel Workers Party)
MAPAM	Mifleget Poalim Hameuhedet (United Workers Party)
MNF	Multinational Force
NATO	North Atlantic Treaty Organization
NAHAL	Noar Halutzi Lohaim (Fighting Pioneering Youth)
NRP	National Religious Party

NUG	National Unity Government
OAPEC	Organization of Arab Petroleum Exporting Countries
OPEC	Organization of Petroleum Exporting Countries
PA	Palestinian Authority
PCC	Palestine Conciliation Commission
PDFLP	Popular Democratic Front for the Liberation of Palestine
PECDR	Palestinian Economic Council for Development and Reconstruction
PFLP	Popular Front for the Liberation of Palestine
PFLP-GC	Popular Front for the Liberation of Palestine—General Command
PFLP-SOG	Popular Front for the Liberation of Palestine—Special Operations Group
PIJ	Palestinian Islamic Jihad
PLA	Palestine Liberation Army
PLF	Palestine Liberation Front
PLO	Palestine Liberation Organization
PNC	Palestine National Council
PPSF	Palestine Popular Struggle Front
PSF	Popular Struggle Front
RAFI	Reshimat Poalei Yisrael (Israel Labor List)
SAM	Surface-to-air missiles
SFM	Sinai Field Mission
SHABAK	Sherut Bitahon Klali, Shin Bet (General Security Services)
SLA	South Lebanese Army
SSM	Sinai Support Mission
UAR	United Arab Republic
UIA	United Israel Appeal
UJA	United Jewish Appeal
UN	United Nations
UNDOF	United Nations Disengagement Observer Force
UNDP	United Nations Development Program
UNEF	United Nations Emergency Force
UNGA	United Nations General Assembly
UNIFIL	United Nations Interim Force in Lebanon
UNOGIL	United Nations Observation Group in Lebanon
UNRWA	United Nations Relief and Works Agency for Palestine Refugees

UNSC	United Nations Security Council
UNSCOP	United Nations Special Committee on Palestine
UNTSO	United Nations Truce Supervision Organization
UPA	United Palestine Appeal
US	United States
USSR	Union of Soviet Socialist Republics
WOJAC	World Organization of Jews From Arab Countries
WZO	World Zionist Organization
ZAHAL	Zvah Haganah Leyisrael—Israel Defense Forces

A

A-4 SKYHAWK. The A-4 Skyhawk aircraft is a subsonic attack bomber renowned for its light weight, heavy ordnance load, fuel efficiency, and ease of maintenance. The Skyhawk can carry nearly its own weight in ordnance, and, besides being able to carry nuclear and conventional bombs, it can carry air-to-surface and air-to-air rockets, Sidewinder missiles, torpedoes, electronic countermeasures pods, and other specialized ordnance. The maximum speed of the Skyhawk is 685 mph. The aircraft's maximum range with external fuel tanks is over 2,000 miles. The original aircraft came armed with two 20mm cannons, while newer versions have two 30mm cannons. There is also a two-seat version called the Skyhawk TA-4F. The aircraft was originally developed for the U.S. Navy by McDonnell Douglas in 1956.

Israel originally purchased forty-eight Skyhawks in 1967. Eighty A-4s were provided to Israel during the U.S. emergency military airlift at the time of the Yom Kippur War* in 1973. Altogether, Israel has acquired over 300 Skyhawks.

The Skyhawk was a workhorse for the Israeli air force (IAF) during the War of Attrition,* the Yom Kippur War, Operation Litani,* and the War in Lebanon.* The A-4 is especially adept in providing close air support to ground troops. In the Yom Kippur War, the A-4 flew more sorties than all other Israeli combat aircraft combined and on October 14, 1973, helped Israeli forces repel the main Egyptian force in the Sinai Peninsula.* This proved to be a decisive turning point in the war.

For further information see: Victor Flintham, *Air Wars and Aircraft* (New York: Facts on File, 1990); *Jane's All the World's Aircraft 1975–1976;* Bryce Walker, *Fighting Jets* (Alexandria, VA: Time-Life Books, 1984); Ehud Yonay, *No Margin for Error* (New York: Pantheon Books, 1993).

Nolan Wohl

ABBAS, MAHMUD (Known as ABU MAZEN) (b. Safed, Palestine,* 1935). He studied at Damascus and Moscow Universities and became a member of the Fatah* Central Committee. He was elected a member of the Executive Committee of the Palestine Liberation Organization* (PLO) in 1980. He was the PLO official who negotiated the agreement with the Israeli delegation in the Oslo talks* in the spring and summer of 1993. He signed the Declaration of Principles* (DOP) for the PLO in Washington in September 1993.

Abu Mazen wrote a book published in Arabic under the title *The Path to Oslo,* which was issued in Amman, Jordan, at the beginning of January 1995. In the book, a number of revelations stunned the political establishment in Israel. He claimed that the Labor Party* held secret talks with the PLO before the 1992 elections, when contacts with the organization were still illegal under Israeli law. According to Abu Mazen, the contacts were aimed at toppling the Likud Party* in the forthcoming Israeli Knesset* elections. He says they were started two months before the election by Efraim Sneh, on instructions of Yitzhak Rabin* and Said Kanan for PLO chairman Yasser Arafat.* Abu Mazen said that Sneh asked the PLO to thwart the peace talks in Washington under the Likud government by making demands, such as a freeze on all settlement activity in the territories. In this way, the talks would explode, and the Likud would be pushed into a corner before the elections. In response, Sneh and other Labor Party ministers strongly denied Abu Mazen's claims. Sneh confirmed that he had met with Said Kanan in April 1992 but denied that they had discussed torpedoing the talks in Washington. The PLO said that there was no truth to the statements contained in the Abu Mazen book regarding coordination between the Labor Party and the PLO as part of an effort to influence the 1992 Israeli Knesset election.

ABBAS, MOHAMMED ABUL (ABU ABBAS, ABUL ABBAS, or MUHAMMAD ABBAS ZAYDAN) (b. near Haifa, 1947). Abbas's family moved to Syria* and also lived in the Yarmuk refugee camp in Jordan. He studied at the University of Damascus, where he earned a degree in Arabic literature and English.

In the 1960s, Abbas joined the Popular Front for the Liberation of Palestine* (PFLP) led by George Habash.* In 1965, he broke with the PFLP and joined Ahmed Jibril's* splinter organization, the Popular Front for the Liberation of Palestine—General Command* (PFLP-GC). While with Jibril's PFLP-GC, Abbas fought with the PFLP-GC and Sunni militia against the Christian Maronites in Beirut in 1975. Because of disagreements with Syria over its policies during the Lebanese Civil War, he left the PFLP-GC to found his own organization, the Palestine Liberation Front* (PLF), in 1976.

In February 1983, while still a member of Fatah,* Abbas was elected to the Palestine Liberation Organization* (PLO) Executive Committee. On September 28, 1991, Abbas was dropped from the Palestine National Council.*

Abbas and the PLF have conducted numerous terrorist attacks. In March and

April 1981, two air attacks against Israel were foiled. On March 7, 1981, a motorized hang-glider attack originating from southern Lebanon attempting to destroy an oil refinery near Haifa was stopped, and on April 16, 1981, a hot-air balloon was shot down.

Abbas has been identified as the mastermind of the seizure of the *Achille Lauro,** an Italian cruise liner, in October 1985. Leon Klinghoffer,* a wheel-chair-bound American, was murdered, and his body was thrown overboard. Egyptian authorities negotiated the hijackers' surrender on October 10. U.S. fighter jets forced the Egyptian airliner carrying Abbas and his associates to Tunisia to land at a North American Treaty Organization (NATO) air base in Sicily, where they were placed in Italian custody. Efforts by the United States to have Abbas extradited for trial were rejected by Italy, and he was released and went to Yugoslavia on October 12, 1985. An Italian court convicted Abbas in absentia for his involvement in the *Achille Lauro* incident, and he was sentenced to life imprisonment.

The Palestine Liberation Front, under Abbas's command, is believed to receive much of its funding from Iraq.* Abbas himself has been known to travel under an Iraqi passport.

Joseph E. Goldberg

ABDELSHAFI, HEIDAR (b. Gaza City, 1919). A physician who was among the founders of the Palestine Liberation Organization* (PLO), he served as president of the Red Crescent in the Gaza Strip.* He was the chief Palestinian delegate to the Madrid Peace Conference* and negotiator in the initial Washington rounds* of the peace talks with Israel. After the signing of the Declaration of Principles* (DOP) in September 1993, he criticized the agreement for failing to address the issue of Jewish settlements* in the occupied territories,* and he was among those who challenged Yasser Arafat* to shift his leadership style and allow more democracy and dissent within the ranks of the PLO and among the Palestinians.

Nancy Hasanian

ABDULLAH IBN HUSSEIN (b. Mecca, 1882; d. Jerusalem,* 1951). The second son of Sherif Hussein* of Mecca,* Abdullah sought to fulfill his father's dream of a unified Arab world under Hashemite leadership. The Mandate* period after World War I saw Abdullah and his younger brother Feisal* as sovereigns over Transjordan* and Iraq,* respectively, but, at the end of World War II, they were no closer to enlarging the Hashemite dynasty. Abdullah's annexation of the West Bank* was a step toward his Greater Syria* scheme, but his leadership in the Arab world was contested.

Abdullah was educated in Constantinople while living with his family (1891–1908). He returned to Mecca after the Young Turk's Revolution and served as a member of the Ottoman Parliament as the deputy from Mecca in 1912. When Sherif Hussein launched the Great Arab Revolt* in June 1916, Abdullah aided his father in external relations and commanded some forces, although T. E. Lawrence* did not consider him a military equal of Feisal.

At a congress of Syrian nationalists in March 1922, Feisal was proclaimed King of Greater Syria. This did not complement France's plans for its new Syria/Lebanon* Mandate, and it sought to remove Feisal from power. With the professed intention of assisting his brother and leading an armed band, Abdullah moved toward Amman via Maan in November 1920, Karak the following January, and entered Amman on March 9, 1921.

Britain decided to negotiate with Abdullah and to preempt any moves toward Syria. In discussions with Winston Churchill,* then secretary of state for colonial affairs, on March 27, 1921, Abdullah recognized the validity of Britain's Mandate in Palestine. In return, Britain limited Palestine's* eastern boundaries at the Jordan River* and recognized Abdullah as the Emir of Transjordan—the East Bank.* This territorial arrangement was formalized in Churchill's 1922 White Paper* on Palestine and confirmed in Article 25 of the Palestine Mandate as approved by the League of Nations on September 16, 1922.

After Transjordan's nominal independence on May 15, 1923, Abdullah grappled with two interrelated issues—his dependency on Britain and Palestine's future. Since Transjordan's founding, Abdullah was constrained by his financial and military reliance on Britain. However, their relationship evolved through a series of treaties that granted Abdullah increasing freedom to act. Formal independence was established by treaty on March 22, 1946, and the next month Abdullah proclaimed himself king of the Hashemite Kingdom of Transjordan.

This fueled Abdullah's lobbying for his Greater Syria plan, composed of Transjordan, Syria, Lebanon, and Palestine. During the opening session of Parliament on November 11, 1946, Abdullah stated that Greater Syria was a basic principle of Transjordan's foreign policy. Such statements and the publication of a White Paper (May 1947) about Greater Syria did not endear him to other Arab leaders. The new Arab League* had discussed the subject (March 1947) and did not back Abdullah's intentions, despite Abdullah's assertions that a Greater Syria would resolve the Jewish–Arab problem in Palestine.

Abdullah was naturally concerned about Mandatory Palestine's future status and its impact on his ambitions. By the time of the 1937 Peel Report,* which recommended partition of Palestine into separate Jewish and Arab states, Abdullah had consolidated his internal situation sufficiently so that he could devote more attention to the issue. While not considered hostile to Jewish immigration to Palestine, Abdullah's objections to partition strengthened when it became clear that Britain was determined to terminate the Mandate and leave Palestine. Abdullah objected to the United Nations partition plan,* as did the Arab League (December 17, 1947), due to its implications for his own goals.

Amid increasing Arab belligerence, Abdullah held two secret meetings with Golda Meir.* At the first meeting in November 1947, Abdullah proposed that Transjordan annex the Arab areas of Palestine and asked about likely Jewish opinion if Transjordan were to completely annex Palestine and create semiautonomous Jewish regions. This idea was rejected, and during the second meeting in May 1948, with war seemingly inevitable, Abdullah asked whether the Jews would postpone independence and accept Palestine's annexation as well as representation in Parliament. Falling well short of the Israeli state envisioned in the partition plan,* Abdullah's proposal was rejected.

Abdullah joined the Arab League's rejection of the partition plan and their subsequent resolution (February 8, 1948) to use all means possible to prevent the establishment of a Jewish state, but Arab League unity did not extend much beyond these platforms. Each state sought its own aims, and when Abdullah maneuvered an appointment as commander in chief of the Arab armies on May 14, 1948, it meant nothing. The next day, Abdullah's Arab Legion* joined the Arab attack against the new Jewish state.

At war's end, the legion occupied the predominantly Arab areas of Palestine—later, the West Bank*—and the eastern areas of Jerusalem. On December 1, 1948, at a Palestinian Congress in Jericho,* composed mostly of sympathetic delegates, Abdullah was proclaimed king of Palestine. Following the April 3, 1949, Israeli–Jordanian armistice, Abdullah announced the annexation of the West Bank and proclaimed himself the king of the Hashemite Kingdom of Jordan.

The annexation was formalized on April 24, 1950, during Parliament's opening session (with equal delegates from both banks of the Jordan River), but officially it was not to "prejudice a final settlement of Palestine's just cause." This was nominally in line with the Arab League's policy (April 12, 1948) that Arab armies in Palestine are considered temporary. To further placate the strenuous Arab opposition, King Abdullah renounced a drafted nonaggression treaty with Israel that dealt with territorial exchanges and Transjordan's annexation of the West Bank. Nearly fifteen months later, on July 20, 1951, Abdullah was assassinated by a Palestinian outside the al-Aksa Mosque* in Jerusalem, in part, because of Jordan's secret negotiations with Israel. He had two sons, Talal and Nayif.

King Abdullah wrote *Mudhakkirati* (Amman, Jordan: n.p., 1945), abridged and translated by Philip Graves and G. Khuri as *Memoirs of King Abdullah of Transjordan* (London: Jonathan Cape, 1950) and *al-Takmilah* (Amman, Jordan: n.p., 1951), and published in English as *My Memoirs Completed* (London: Longman, 1978).

For further information see: Alec Kirkbride, *A Cackle of Thorns* (London: John Murray, 1956); Benjamin Shwadran, *Jordan: A State of Tension* (New York: Council for Middle East Affairs Press, 1959); Mary C. Wilson, *King Abdullah, Britain and the Making of Jordan* (Cambridge: Cambridge University Press, 1987); Mary C. Wilson, "Abdullah Ibn Hussein," in Bernard Reich, ed., *Political Leaders of the Contemporary Middle East and North Africa* (Westport, CT: Greenwood Press, 1990), pp. 24–32.

Paul S. Robinson, Jr.

ABED, HANI (d. Gaza Strip,* November 2, 1994). A senior member of Islamic Jihad* who was killed in November 1994 in the Gaza Strip when a bomb attached to his car exploded. Abed was reportedly involved in the killing of two Israel Defense Forces* (IDF) soldiers at the Erez crossing from Gaza* to Israel on May 20, 1994. Israel was accused of killing Abed, and Islamic Jihad leaders vowed retaliation. A crowd at his funeral prevented Palestine Liberation Organization* (PLO) chairman Yasser Arafat* from participating in the funeral service.

ABED-RABBO, YASSER (b. Jaffa, 1945). Educated in Egypt,* Jordan,* and Lebanon.* Member of the Palestine Liberation Organization* (PLO) Executive Committee since 1977. He joined the Democratic Front for the Liberation of Palestine.* Later he split with Hawatma* over support for Arafat's* evolving approach toward Israel in the late 1980s and 1990s.

ABU ADNAN. See **ABDELKARIM HAMAD KAIS.**

ABU ALA. See **AHMED SULEIMAN KARIA.**

ABU ALAA. See **AHMED SULEIMAN KARIA.**

ABU AMMAR. See **YASSER ARAFAT.**

ABU DAOUD. See **MOHAMMED DAOUD AUDEH.**

ABU IBRAHIM. See **15 MAY ORGANIZATION.**

ABU IYAD. See **SALAH KHALAF.**

ABU JIHAD. See **KHALIL AL-WAZIR.**

ABU LUTUF. See **FAROUQ KADDOUMI.**

ABU MARWAN. See **HAKAM BALAOUI.**

ABU MAZEN. See **MAHMUD ABBAS.**

ABU MEIZER, ABDEL MUHSEN (d. Damascus, April 3, 1992). In the early 1960s, he was appointed chief editor of the official newspaper of Syria's ruling Baath Party. He held several leadership positions in the Palestine Liberation Organization* (PLO) and held a seat for many years on the Palestine National Council.* He broke away from PLO chairman Yasser Arafat* and joined the newly formed Palestine National Salvation Front in the 1980s.

Joseph E. Goldberg

ABU NIDAL (b. Jaffa, 1937). Real name is Sabri al-Banna.* His nom de guerre was taken in honor of his eldest son, Nidal. He was the youngest of seven children of a prosperous citrus grower in Jaffa. He became a refugee in the wake of the independence of Israel. He said that his family moved to Gaza.* He studied engineering at Cairo University and then worked in Saudi Arabia for ARAMCO. He joined Fatah* after the June 1967 war.* In 1973, he formed his own small, radical, and secretive organization, the Fatah Revolutionary Council.* The organization and its members were essentially mercenaries rather than ideologically committed to a particular political perspective. Originally, he worked for Iraqi intelligence and later for Syria.* Later, he shifted his primary base of operations to Libya. His terrorist organization has had a variety of targets, which have included Saudi diplomats and a Syrian minister, as well as Israeli and Jewish targets. The latter included strikes in Rome and Vienna as well as a synagogue in Istanbul. In 1982, the organization attempted to kill the Israeli ambassador, Shlomo Argov,* in London. Nidal was also active in striking Palestinian targets. Palestine Liberation Organization* (PLO) officials were often targeted as traitors to the Palestinian revolution. Abu Nidal has claimed to be the true defender of the Palestinian revolution, which he claims has been betrayed by Yasser Arafat* and Fatah. He has a particular hatred as well for Jordan* and King Hussein* and views them as "bourgeois and pro-imperialist." In January 1991, his group killed Abu Iyad,* Arafat's deputy.

In 1974, he broke with Yasser Arafat over Arafat's decision to begin to limit the PLO's role in international terrorism and look to the diplomatic front in the struggle against Israel. The PLO accused Abu Nidal of plotting to kill Arafat and sentenced him, in absentia, to death. Abu Nidal and his followers found protection and sponsorship successively with Iraq,* Syria, and Libya.

For further information see: Yossi Melman, *The Master Terrorist: True Story of Abu Nidal* (New York: Adama Books, 1986); Aaron David Miller, "Sabri Khalil Al-Banna," in Bernard Reich, ed., *Political Leaders of the Contemporary Middle East and North Africa: A Biographical Dictionary* (Westport, CT: Greenwood Press, 1990), pp. 65–71; Patrick Seale, *Abu Nidal: A Gun for Hire* (New York: Random House, 1992); Matti Steinberg, "The Radical Worldview of the Abu-Nidal Faction," *Jerusalem Quarterly,* no. 48 (Fall 1988): 88–104.

Joseph E. Goldberg

ABU NIDAL ORGANIZATION (ANO). An international terrorist organization led by Sabri al-Banna.* It also has been known as Fatah Revolutionary Council,* Arab Revolutionary Council, Arab Revolutionary Brigades, Black September,* and Revolutionary Organization of Socialist Muslims. It split from the Palestine Liberation Organization* (PLO) in 1974. In June of that year, the Palestinian National Council* accepted a policy of "intermediate steps," which would accept a "Palestinian state on any portion of liberated territory." Sabri al-Banna rejected the idea and severed his relationship with the PLO. He founded the Fatah Revolutionary Council, which became known as the Abu

Nidal Organization. It has carried out a large number of terrorist attacks in more than twenty countries. It tends to target the United States, the United Kingdom, France,* Israel, moderate Palestinians, the PLO, and various Arab countries, depending, to a large extent, on its current sponsor. Among its major targets were the Rome and Vienna airports in December 1985 and the Neve Shalom synagogue in Istanbul. In 1990 and 1991, there were substantial intraorganizational attacks and assassinations. It was headquartered in Iraq between 1974 and 1983 and in Syria* from 1983 to 1987 and subsequently in Libya, with a presence in Lebanon* and other states.

For further information see: Matti Steinberg, "The Radical Worldview of the Abu-Nidal Faction," *Jerusalem Quarterly,* no. 48 (Fall 1988): 88–104.

Joseph E. Goldberg

ABU RUDEIS. Oil fields located in the southwestern portion of the Sinai Peninsula.* The Israeli return of the oil fields and the Mitla* and Gidi* Passes was considered by Egyptian president Anwar Sadat* to be the minimum concession necessary to bring about an Egyptian movement toward peace. However, before relinquishing its hold on Abu Rudeis, Israel demanded assurances that an alternative and secure supply of oil for the country's energy needs would be found. As a result of the Sinai II* agreements signed on September 1, 1975, it was agreed that Israel would withdraw from the oil fields within two weeks of the signing of the protocol for implementation of the agreement. The protocol was signed by both parties on September 23, 1975. Israel realized that the oil fields of Abu Rudeis were important not only for its economy but also for military preparedness. Nevertheless, Israeli leaders decided that the Sinai II agreement was an opportunity to bring about peace. This belief, coupled with U.S. assurances for military, political, and economic support, convinced the Knesset* to approve Sinai II Accords by a vote of seventy to forty-three, with seven abstentions.

David Salzberg

ABU SAID. See **KHALID AL-HASSAN.**

ABU SHARIF, BASSAM (b. Jordan,* 1947). He studied at American University of Beirut. For many years, he was a member of the Popular Front for the Liberation of Palestine,* and he took part in its hijacking of three airliners to Jordan in 1970. His face and hands were disfigured in 1972 by a parcel bomb, thought to have been sent by Israelis, that blew up in his Beirut office. He switched affiliations in 1987 and has since been a political adviser to Yasser Arafat.*

ABU YUSIF. See **MUHAMMAD AL-NAJJAR.**

ABU ZABAL. On February 12, 1970, Israeli air force jet aircraft bombed the Egyptian National Metal Products Factory in Abu Zabal, a small village located about fifteen miles northeast of Cairo, killing an estimated eighty civilians and injuring at least the same number. The attack occurred at the height of Israel's deep-penetration raids* and was the first known Israeli strike on a civilian industrial target outside the Suez Canal zone.* The attack was carried out by two American-made F-4 Phantom jet aircraft.* Israel officially stated that the attack on the factory was accidental and that the target of the raid had been an Egyptian air force arms depot located less than one mile away.

The attack and Israel's policy of deep-penetration raids were criticized by the major powers, and the attack was one of the last of such raids to be carried out. Because of the involvement of American-made aircraft, the incident played a role in the U.S. decision, announced on March 23, 1970, to hold in abeyance consideration of further aircraft sales to Israel.

For further information see: Yaacov Bar-Siman-Tov, *The Israeli–Egyptian War of Attrition, 1969–1970* (New York: Columbia University Press, 1980); Bernard Reich, *Quest for Peace: United States–Israel Relations and the Arab–Israeli Conflict* (New Brunswick, NJ: Transaction Books, 1977); Jonathan Shimshoni, *Israel and Conventional Deterrence* (Ithaca, NY: Cornell University Press); United Arab Republic, Ministry of National Guidance, State Information Service, ''Israeli Air Attack on the National Metal Products Factory at Abu Zaabal, Cairo, Thursday, February 12, 1970'' (n.p., n.d.).

Noah L. Dropkin

ABUL ABBAS. See **MOHAMMED ABUL ABBAS.**

ACHILLE LAURO. The *Achille Lauro,* an Italian cruise ship, was on a Mediterranean cruise when, on the evening of October 7, 1985, four members of the Palestine Liberation Front* (PLF) seized control of the ship as it left Alexandria, Egypt.* The operation was masterminded by Mohammed Abbas,* also known as Abul Abbas. The PLF issued a statement in Nicosia, Cyprus, in which it asserted that the terrorists boarded the ship to enter Israel at Ashdod, where the *Achille Lauro* was to make a port call, and were to attack Ashdod in retaliation for the Israeli air raid on Palestine Liberation Organization* (PLO) headquarters in Tunis on October 1, 1985. On October 7, the PLF demanded that Israel release fifty Palestinians being held in prison. Failure to comply with this demand would result in the execution of hostages, beginning with American passengers. The PLF threatened to blow up the ship if any rescue attempt was made. The *Achille Lauro*'s captain later testified that one of the Palestinian hijackers came to the captain's bridge, gave him the passport of Leon Klinghoffer,* a sixty-nine-year-old crippled American, and told him that Klinghoffer had been killed. A ship steward testified that he had been ordered to dump Klinghoffer's body and wheelchair into the sea.

The *Achille Lauro* was refused port rights in both Syria* and Cyprus. Anchored off Port Said, Egypt, the hijackers, in negotiations with the Italian and West German ambassadors, agreed on October 9 to surrender to Egyptian authorities, who had promised them safe passage. Despite a U.S. request to turn the hijackers over to Italy or the United States, the Egyptians placed the four hijackers and two Palestinian officials, one of whom was Abbas, on an Egyptian Boeing 737 for a flight to Tunisia. Four U.S. F-14 fighter planes based on the aircraft carrier USS *Saratoga* forced the airliner to land at a North Atlantic Treaty Organization (NATO) air base in Sicily. NATO troops surrounded the plane, and the hijackers were taken into custody. Egypt insisted that Abbas and another Palestinian were guests of their country and should be released. Italy allowed Abbas and the other Palestinian officials to fly to Yugoslavia on an Egyptian airliner on October 12, despite the U.S. request that Abbas be extradited and tried for hostage-taking, piracy, and conspiracy to participate in both offenses. The Italian decision to allow Abbas to leave led to an Italian–U.S. dispute that eventually contributed to the collapse of Italian prime minister Bettino Craxi's government. Italy charged the four hijackers with murder, kidnapping, hijacking, and possession of arms and explosives. Three of them were tried and convicted and given prison sentences. Abbas was tried in absentia and given a life sentence. Abdulrahim Khaled, the second Palestinian sentenced to life in prison in absentia, was arrested on March 5, 1991, in Athens when Greek police thwarted a plan to bomb the Barclays Bank in Athens. Italy requested and was granted extradition of Khaled. Because Abbas was known to be closely associated with Yasser Arafat,* and Arafat had forsworn international terrorism in 1975, the incident called into question whether the PLO could be accepted as a trustworthy body for future negotiations. Abbas led the only faction of the Palestine Liberation Front that had remained loyal to Arafat after the PLO had been forced out of Lebanon* in 1983. Arafat had Abbas elected to the PLO Executive Committee in November 1984. The U.S. interception of the Egyptian airliner was an embarrassment to Egyptian president Hosni Mubarak,* and relations between the two states were strained. On October 9, 1985, the United Nations Security Council unanimously condemned the ''unjustifiable and criminal hijacking'' of the *Achille Lauro*.

For further information see: Antonio Cassese, *Terrorism, Politics, and Law: The Achille Lauro Affair* (Princeton, NJ: Princeton University Press, 1989); Gregory V. Gooding, ''Fighting Terrorism in the 1980's: The Interception of the Achille Lauro Hijackers,'' *Yale Journal of International Law* 12 (Winter 1987):158–79; Neil C. Livingstone and David Halevy, *Inside the PLO* (New York: William Morrow, 1990); Jeffrey D. Simon, *The Implications of the Achille Lauro Hijacking for the Maritime Community* (Santa Monica, CA: Rand Corporation, [1986]); U.S. Congress, House of Representatives, Committee on Foreign Affairs, *Aftermath of the Achille Lauro Indicent: Hearing and Markup* (Washington, DC: Government Printing Office, 1986).

Yasha Manuel Harari

ACRE PRISON. Acre (or Akka) is an ancient port city that was known during the Crusades era as St. Jean d'Acre, located on the northern end of the Bay of Carmel, across from Haifa. The fortress barracks of Acre were built by the Crusaders and restored by the Turks and withstood Napoleon's artillery. For centuries the barracks have been used as a prison.

Acre Prison gained notoriety in 1920, when Vladimir Jabotinsky* was imprisoned there. In the spring of 1920, Jabotinsky, a Russian-Jewish journalist who had organized the Jewish regiment in Allenby's army, formed the Jewish Self Defense Corps in Jerusalem, ostensibly to protect Jews from Arab rioters. When rioting broke out on April 4, Jabotinsky offered the services of the corps to the military governor, who declined his offer. Jabotinsky was subsequently arrested by the British police and charged with carrying a weapon and with distributing arms to a self-defense group. He was brought before a closed military court-martial, sentenced to fifteen years' imprisonment, and incarcerated in Acre Prison.

The outrage at Jabotinsky's incarceration in Acre Prison was skillfully used by the Zionists to stir up opposition to the British military rule in Palestine.* On July 8, 1920, almost immediately after his arrival in Palestine, Sir Herbert Samuel,* a British Jew who was appointed the first high commissioner of Palestine, released Jabotinsky from prison and granted him amnesty.

Over a quarter of a century later, the fortress barracks were still being used as a prison. On April 16, 1947, the British executed Dov Gruner in Acre Prison. Gruner was a member of the Irgun* and had been wounded and captured during a raid in which the Irgun took a number of weapons from a police station.

To revenge the execution of Gruner, the Irgun (including Menachem Begin*), with the help of the Stern gang,* on May 4, 1947, blasted their way into Acre Prison, liberating forty-one alleged terrorists and more than 200 common criminals. Three members of the Irgun were captured by the British during the attack on Acre Prison and were condemned to death.

The Zionists used the execution of Gruner and three individuals who were captured during the attack to rally worldwide support against British rule in Palestine. As a result of the events in 1920 and 1947, Acre Prison became a symbol of the resistance by the British military in Palestine to the creation of a Jewish homeland.

Richard G. R. Schickele

ADMINISTERED AREAS. See **OCCUPIED TERRITORIES.**

ADWAN, KAMAL (d. April 10, 1973). A Fatah* leader who was killed in Beirut during an Israeli raid. Adwan became an associate of Yasser Arafat* in Kuwait in the mid-1950s. He was a member of the Palestine Liberation Organization* (PLO) General Secretariat and was a spokesman for Fatah. He served as chief operations officer of Fatah and Black September* commander of all activities inside Israeli-controlled territory.

Joseph E. Goldberg

AFULA. A city in Israel that was the site of a terrorist attack on April 6, 1994, after, and in response to, the Hebron Massacre.* A Palestinian terrorist affiliated with HAMAS* detonated a car bomb near a bus stop in Afula, killing seven

Israelis. In response, the president of the United Nations Security Council, New Zealand's ambassador Colin Keating, spoke as follows:

The Members of the Security Council view with shock and outrage the attack on Israeli civilians on a passenger bus in the town of Afula on April 6, 1994. The Members condemn this act of terror and extend sincere condolences to the wounded and the families of those who lost their lives. Terrorist acts must not be allowed to divert the parties' efforts to continue and intensify the peace process, or to delay the implementation of the Declaration of Principles.*

AGRANAT COMMISSION OF INQUIRY. In November 1973, the government of Israel appointed a five-member Commission of Inquiry to investigate the events leading up to the hostilities (including information concerning the enemy's moves and intentions), the assessments and decisions of military and civilian bodies in regard to this information, and the Israel Defense Forces'* deployments, preparedness for battle, and actions in the first phase of the fighting in connection with the Yom Kippur War.* The commission was composed of Supreme Court Chief Justice Shimon Agranat, Justice Moshe Landau of the Supreme Court, State Comptroller Yitzhak Nebenzahl, and two former chiefs of staff of the Israel Defense Forces, Yigael Yadin* and Haim Laskov. The commission issued an interim report in April 1974, which focused primarily on events prior to the outbreak of hostilities and the conduct of the war during its early stages. Among its findings were that prime minister Golda Meir* and defense minister Moshe Dayan* were not responsible for Israel's lack of preparation for the Yom Kippur War and that faulty intelligence analysis was the primary failure. Lieutenant General David Elazar* resigned as chief of staff of the Israel Defense Forces, and Major General Yitzhak Hofi was named as his temporary replacement. The commission's report also called for a new director of military intelligence to replace Major General Eliahu Zeira and for the reassignment of three other intelligence officers.

The full report was made public in January 1995. It reaffirmed the conclusion that the intelligence establishment and the government fell victim to a mistaken conception that Egypt* and Syria* were incapable of starting a war in 1973. Thus, there was difficulty in accepting facts that did not fit the conception.

For further information see: Dan Ofry, *The Yom Kippur War* (Tel Aviv: Zohar, 1974).

AGREED COMMON AGENDA. See **COMMON AGENDA.**

AIDE-MÉMOIRE OF 1957. A document provided by the United States to Israel in February 1957 as part of the reassurances that led to Israel's withdrawal from the Sinai Peninsula* and the Gaza Strip* after the Sinai War* that appeared to guarantee Israel's right of passage through the Strait of Tiran.* This led to a controversy in the spring of 1967, when President Gamal Abdul Nasser* of

Egypt* announced the blockade of the strait, and Israel sought U.S. reassurances that the action would not stand.

The aide-mémoire from Secretary of State John Foster Dulles to Ambassador Abba Eban of February 11, 1957, provided, inter alia:

With respect to the Gulf of Aqaba and access thereto—the United States believes that the Gulf comprehends international waters and that no nation has the right to prevent free and innocent passage in the Gulf and through the Straits giving access thereto. We have in mind not only commercial usage, but the passage of pilgrims on religious missions which should be fully respected. . . . In the absence of some overriding decision to the contrary, as by the International Court of Justice, the United States, on behalf of vessels of United States registry, is prepared to exercise the right of free and innocent passage and to join with others to secure general recognition of this right.

AIPAC. See **AMERICAN ISRAEL PUBLIC AFFAIRS COMMITTEE.**

AL-AKSA MOSQUE. Umar ibn Abd al-Khattab, the second caliph of the Islamic Empire, built a plain wooden structure in which Muslims could pray at the southern end of Herod's platform after his army took Jerusalem* in 638. In 715, during Umayyad rule, the Caliph el-Walid demolished the wooden structure and built a large decorated mosque with fifteen prayer aisles capable of holding 3,000 people. Earthquakes damaged the mosque in 748, 774, and again in 1033. The present-day structure is a result of renovations made in 1218 based on the eleventh-century design.

Muslims consider the al-Aksa Mosque to be the third holiest site in Islam after Mecca and Medina. The Koran tells of Mohammed's midnight journey in the opening verse of Sura 17: ''Glory be to Him who carried His servant by night from the holy shrine to the distant shrine, the precincts of which We have blessed, that we might show him some of our miraculous signs.'' Classical Muslim commentators have concluded that the ''distant shrine'' of this passage refers to Jerusalem because at that time no mosque existed farther away from Mecca than the one at Jerusalem. During the nineteenth century, Jerusalem, under Ottoman* rule, suffered a deterioration of municipal order, and the Temple Mount* and al-Aksa likewise fell into disrepair.

Under the Palestine Mandate,* care of al-Aksa fell to Emir Abdullah* of Transjordan.* Jordan's* control lasted until June 10, 1967, when Israel gained possession of East Jerusalem* in the Six Day War* and unified the Old and New Cities of Jerusalem while allowing King Hussein* to remain custodian of the Temple Mount.

Israeli Defense Minister Moshe Dayan* ordered the removal of the Israeli flag from the minaret of al-Aksa Mosque the day after fighting stopped in the Old City. He also sought to assure Muslim and Christian dignitaries that all their rights would be respected as in the past and convinced the government to allow unrestricted traffic throughout Jerusalem within weeks. The w*aq*f, which administers the Mount, allows free access to all religions and nationalities, though not for religious activities and not during times of Muslim prayer.

The Temple Mount and surrounding areas embody profound significance for all three monotheistic religions, making their administration an international concern.

In 1969, an Australian sheep shearer set fire to the al-Aksa Mosque for unknown reasons. For political reasons it took until 1988 to begin repairs on the damaged mosaics and delicate wood carvings.

Some evangelical Christians and ultra-Orthodox Jews believe Muslim control of the Temple Mount area is the last impediment to the coming of the Messiah. The biblical conditions for the Messiah's return are a Jewish nation in Israel, a Jewish city of Jerusalem, and the rebuilding of the Temple.* On January 27, 1984, Israeli security forces discovered eighteen grenades and thirteen pounds of explosives on the Temple site. They believe that financial support for the continuing violence directed at the Mount comes from evangelical Christian sources in America.

In another instance evangelical Christians complained of harassment by Muslim authorities when they tried to sing in large groups on the Mount in the late 1980s.

An incident that gained international attention occurred in October 1990, when Israeli soldiers opened fire on stone-throwing Palestinians near the Mount who said they had come to protect al-Aksa and al-Quds* from attacks by Jewish zealots threatening to raze the site.

In the 1994 peace negotiations between Prime Minister Yitzhak Rabin and Yasser Arafat,* neither Jerusalem nor the Haram al-Sharif* nor Noble Sanctuary was discussed, although Arafat has stated publicly that he considers it the capital of a future Palestinian state.

Both Yasser Arafat and King Hussein claim the right to serve as custodians of the Muslim holy sites in Jerusalem, and Saudi Arabia quietly asserts its claim as well, although Israel has stated that it recognizes only the legitimacy of King Hussein.

For further information see: Albert Hourani, *A History of the Arab Peoples* (Cambridge: Harvard University Press, 1992); F. E. Peters, *Jerusalem, the Holy City in the Eyes of Chroniclers, Visitors, Pilgrims, and Prophets from the Days of Abraham to the Beginnings of Modern Times* (Princeton, NJ: Princeton University Press, 1985).

Erin Z. Ferguson

AL-AKSA MOSQUE INCIDENT (1990). An event at the al-Aksa Mosque* between approximately 3,000 Palestinian protestors and 200 Israeli security personnel in the ancient walled city of Jerusalem* in October 1990. The "Movement of the Faithful to the Temple Mount and the Land of Israel" and their leader, Gershon Salomon, organized a march to the Temple Mount* in October 1990 (as it had done on previous Jewish holidays) to draw attention to its view that the two mosques on the Temple Mount (or Haram al-Sharif*) should be demolished to make way for the reconstruction of the Temple* that once stood on that site. With each march, the Islamic leadership had been staging counterdemonstrations. In October 1990, the situation turned into riots and a battleground in which Palestinian youths and Israeli police clashed in the fiercest, bloodiest, and deadliest single clash in the twenty-three years of Israeli control of Jerusalem. Some worshipers and tourists at the Western (Wailing) Wall* were injured by stones thrown by Palestinian youths. At least 19 Arabs were killed, and more than 140 were wounded; some Israeli police and civilians as well as tourists were also hurt.

The First Temple, built by King Solomon, was destroyed by the Babylonians in the tenth century B.C.; a replacement, constructed by King Herod, was demolished by the Romans in A.D. 70. Both were located on the same thirty-five-acre site where the Islamic mosques of the Dome of the Rock* and al-Aksa* were built in the seventh and eighth centuries A.D. Both mosques exist there today. A retaining wall of the Temple, located on the southwestern edge of the plateau, just below the al-Aksa Mosque, known as the Western Wall or the Wailing Wall, is what remains of the Temple and is considered the holiest site of the Jewish faith. According to Scripture, a Third Temple will one day be established on the same site where the first two were located.

While many Jewish religious groups believe the Third Temple may be constructed only following the return of the Messiah, some, such as the Temple Mount Faithful, call for the razing of the Islamic mosques and the immediate construction of a Third Temple.

The Temple Mount Faithful caused considerable concern in the Arab community when they attempted prior cornerstone layings in 1988 and 1989. Gershon Salomon petitioned city officials for a permit to conduct the ceremony again in 1990. The request was denied. For the day of their derailed ceremony (the Feast of the Tabernacles), Temple Mount Faithful members were allowed to ascend the Temple Mount, known as Haram al-Sharif (or Noble Sanctuary) to Muslims, in police-escorted pairs.

On October 4, 1990, Adnan Husseini, director of the Jerusalem Islamic Administration Authority, was informed by city officials that the Temple Mount Faithful would not be allowed to carry out their cornerstone ceremony. But Temple Mount Faithful leaflets, which called for persons to witness the laying of "the cornerstone of the Third Temple," were circulated. Also on October 4, the Palestinian newspaper *Al Fajr* called for Muslims to organize against the Temple Mount Faithful ceremony. On October 5, Sheik Mohammed Hussein, al-Aksa's chief cleric, issued a call for "Muslims to come and protect the mosque." The declaration was issued to some 20,000 Muslims who attended prayers three days before the clash. More than 3,000 arrived at al-Aksa by 5 A.M. on the morning of October 8.

As crowds within the compound grew, Israeli police feared potential rioting and prevented all Temple Mount Faithful members from entering the compound. When the crowds did not dissipate, the police spread word that Temple Mount

Faithful would not be permitted to conduct its cornerstone laying. According to reports, the news apparently did not spread, or the protestors did not believe it.

A small group of young Palestinians began to throw rocks at police at approximately 10:40 A.M. The police confronted the group with tear gas and rubber bullets. At that point the attention of the larger crowd was drawn to the small skirmish. The crowd, angered at the tear-gas firing, charged the vastly outnumbered police. The police were forced to retreat through the Mugrahbi gate of the compound. An Arab police clerk and janitor were trapped by the demonstrators in a small police station located in the compound. The retreating police, aware of the two left behind and the emerging moblike situation, called for reinforcements. The lives of the two police employees were spared, but the demonstrators sacked and burned the station.

With the destruction of the police post, the Palestinian group turned to the vicinity of the Western Wall, where some 10,000 Jewish worshipers and tourists remained after morning prayers. A barrage of rocks and bottles was thrown in their direction. Eleven people were injured before worshipers and tourists scattered for cover.

For some fifteen minutes, according to eyewitness accounts, the plaza beside the Western Wall was empty. During this interval police reorganized into a force of some 200 and reentered the compound, using tear gas, rubber bullets, and live ammunition. According to some reports, the shooting by the Israeli security forces continued for some thirty to forty minutes. When the firing stopped, 21 Palestinians were dead, and over 125 were wounded.

The Israelis claimed that the Palestinians had orchestrated the event by attacking the Israeli police and Jewish worshipers at the Western Wall to draw attention away from Saddam Hussein's* invasion and occupation of Kuwait and to Israel's continued occupation of Jerusalem and the West Bank* and Gaza Strip.* Palestinians argued that the Israeli police perpetrated a massacre on a peaceful crowd that had gathered to resist an attempt by Jewish extremists to desecrate a Muslim holy site.

Apparently, the tragedy began with what had become routine Palestinian stone throwing at the Israeli police, who responded with tear gas. As the Palestinians charged the vastly outnumbered police, the police withdrew. Later, stones were thrown at Jewish worshipers below the mosque area near the Western Wall. When the police returned, they began firing into the Palestinian crowds.

The United Nations (UN) sent a delegation to investigate. Israel officially denounced the United Nations' decision and noted that it would not receive the UN delegation. The United States noted that it was concerned that Israel rejected the inquiry and that it might divert attention from the Iraqi* invasion of Kuwait and might further affect the already tense relations between the United States and Israel.

Israel was widely condemned for its use of excessive force in quelling the disturbances. The United States sponsored United Nations Security Council Resolution 672* on October 12, which condemned ''especially the acts of violence

committed by the Israeli security forces resulting in injuries and loss of life.''
Palestinian and Israeli accounts of the incident vary widely. The U.S. action
came at a time when the Bush administration was attempting to construct and
sustain a United Nations coalition against Iraq in response to its invasion of
Kuwait in August 1990.

For further information see: Joel Brinkley, ''How Passion and Grief Brought Grief to
Jerusalem,'' *New York Times,* October 15, 1990; Sabra Chartrand, ''19 Arabs Killed in
Battle with Jerusalem Police,'' *New York Times,* October 9, 1990.

Robert Crangle, Jr.

ALAMI, MUSA (b. 1867; d. Amman, 1984). Musa Alami was born into a prominent Jerusalem* family. His father served as mayor of Jerusalem from 1906 to
1909 and represented the Jerusalem District in the Ottoman* Parliament from
1914 to 1918. Alami studied law at the American University of Beirut and later
joined the Legal Department of the Palestine government. Although an Arab
nationalist, he was not an activist. Related to the Husseini* family, he took a
political position close to theirs. He was a representative of the Arab community
in talks held with Jewish leaders before and during the Arab rebellion* in Palestine in the 1930s. He had discussions with David Ben-Gurion* in the 1930s
to ''bridge the gap'' between Zionist* and Arab aspirations. Ben-Gurion proposed that unlimited Jewish immigration be allowed into Palestine* and Transjordan* in return for Palestine's being part of a Pan-Arab federation. No
agreement was reached. Alami was removed from government service in 1937
because of his alleged involvement with the leadership of the Arab rebellion,
and he went into exile to Syria* and Iraq.* He returned to Palestine in 1941.
The Arab League* appointed him as part of the Palestinian delegation to the
Preparatory Conference of Alexandria in October 1944 and to the foundation of
the Arab League in March 1945. He was the first Palestinian delegate to be
elected to the Arab League in 1945. In 1945, Alami was appointed to the newly
reformed Arab Higher Committee,* but he resigned to work on the Palestinian–
Arab Information project, which engaged in propaganda dissemination in London, Washington, Beirut, and Jerusalem. He also initiated the ''Constructive
Scheme,'' which promoted Palestinian–Arab land development to prevent the
sale of Arab lands to Jews. Both of these projects ended in 1948 with the war
of that year. After 1967, he lived in London.

He wrote *The Lesson of Palestine ('Ibrat Filastin),* which was published in
1949. Alami was one of the first Arab intellectuals to suggest that the primary
reason for the Arab defeat in the 1948–49 war was the lack of unity among the
Palestinians and among the Arab states. He believed that the British were to
blame for the Balfour Declaration* and stated that the Mandate system was
biased toward the Jews. Dividing the battle for Palestine into two phases, Alami
described where the Arabs went wrong. In the first phase, from the passage of
United Nations (UN) Resolution 181* to Israel's declaration of independence,
he believed that the burden of defense was on the Palestinian community. He

recognized that the Jews were unified in their command and that their aim was solely to win. On the other hand, the Palestinians were not unified; their leadership was scattered and had diverse aims in battle. In the second phase of the battle, which began as the Arab armies invaded the new state of Israel, Alami accused the Arab states of disunity and lack of a unified command and a unified policy objective. In addition he blamed them for their lack of seriousness in winning the war and their pursuit of individual ambitions. They did not consider the war as a means to save the Palestinians but as a vehicle to gain the territory for themselves. The Arab states, he noted, failed to see the far-reaching implications of their unpreparedness. The Jews, on the other hand, took advantage of the Arabs' disunity.

Stressing the need to remedy the problems that caused their defeat in the war, Alami stated that the Arabs needed to correct the inefficiencies within their governments. The remedies could be found in the modernization of government, organizational reforms for internal and external policies, and raising the standard of living within the Arab states. Furthermore, he added that the people should demand rights for all and improve the system of education for everyone.

Alami indicated that the Arabs would not be strong until they were united in their foreign policies, defense policies, and defense forces. He also stated that the freedom from internal oppression should be granted, in addition to freedom of belief, speech, press, and political groups. Also mentioned was the need to provide social services for men and women and that women should be granted the same privileges as men. Only with all of these reforms did Alami believe that the unity needed to confront Israel could be achieved.

For further information see: Musa Alami, ''The Lesson of Palestine,'' *Middle East Journal* 3 (October 1949): 373–405; Geoffrey Furlonge, *Palestine Is My Country: The Story of Musa Alami* (London: John Murray, 1969).

                                                    Susan L. Rosenstein and Joseph E. Goldberg

ALEXANDRIA CONFERENCE. During World War II, a number of steps were taken to create an Arab League* to foster the unity and cooperation of the independent Arab states. These culminated in the Alexandria Conference, at which the Pact of the League of Arab States* was signed. A general conference on Arab unity was held in Alexandria, Egypt,* from September 25 to October 7, 1944. The conference adopted a text that stated that the signatories had decided to create a league of independent Arab states to coordinate their political plans and to ensure their cooperation with each other. On March 22, 1945, the heads of state of Iraq,* Saudi Arabia, Lebanon,* Syria,* Transjordan,* Egypt, and Yemen and observers from Palestine and the Maghreb met in Alexandria and signed the Covenant of the League of Arab States,* thus bringing the Arab League into existence. The covenant was a modified version of the provisions established in the October 1944 Protocol of Alexandria, which had laid the foundation for the Arab League.

The reasons for the formation of the Arab League, as stated in the preamble of the covenant, are

to affirm the close connections and numerous ties which link the Arab States, and being desirous of maintaining and establishing these connections on the foundations of respect for the independence and sovereignty of those states, and in order to direct their efforts towards the general good of the Arab States, the improvement of their circumstances, the security of their future, and the realization of their hopes and aspirations, and in response to Arab public opinion in all quarters of the Arab World.

The covenant emphasizes the sovereignty of each of the member states and anticipates a policy of political coordination and economic, social, and cultural cooperation rather than a move toward a united federation of Arab states. Each of the member states is strictly enjoined to abstain from interfering in the domestic affairs of the other members of the league and to respect the existing regimes in the other league states.

The stated objectives of the Arab League are ''to strengthen the ties between the participant states, to coordinate their political programs in such a way as to effect real collaboration between them, to preserve their independence and sovereignty, and to consider in general the affairs and interests of the Arab countries.''

In signing the 1944 Protocol of Alexandria, the precursor to the Pact of the Arab League, the Arab states finally recognized the 1939 MacDonald White Paper and the guarantees that it made regarding the rights of the Palestinians.

For further information see: Boutros Boutros-Ghali, *The Arab League: 1945–1955* (New York: Carnegie Endowment for International Peace, 1954); Muhammad Khalil, *The Arab States and the Arab League: A Documentary Record,* 2 vols. (Beirut: Khayats, 1962).

Mark Daryl Erickson

ALF. See **ARAB LIBERATION FRONT.**

ALI, GENERAL KAMAL HASAN (b. 1921). He was a battalion commander of Egyptian forces in Israel's War of Independence* and between 1962 and 1967 led the Egyptian force in Yemen. General Ali served as a commander of the Egyptian Armored Brigade in the Six Day War.* Afterward he moved up rapidly in the military hierarchy, becoming major general and chief of staff in the Armored Corps in 1970. In 1972, Ali was promoted to director of the Armored Corps and in 1975 joined the government as assistant minister of war and chief of intelligence. In 1978, he became minister of defense and military production, replacing General Gamassy,* and was promoted to commander in chief of the armed forces. He was an active participant in the peace negotiations with Israel leading to the Egypt–Israel Peace Treaty.* In May 1980, General Ali assumed the offices of deputy prime minister and minister for foreign affairs. Following the assassination of President Anwar Sadat,* Ali was retained in both posts by President Hosni Mubarak* in October 1981. In July 1984, he became prime minister but resigned in September 1985 because of ill health.

ALIYA (Derived from the Hebrew word for "ascent" or "going up"). The immigration of Jews from the Diaspora* to the Holy Land* (Palestine* and, later, Israel). Jewish immigration to, and settlement in, the Land of Israel is a central concept in Zionist* ideology, and the ingathering of the exiles was the primary objective of the Zionist movement. However, even before the founding of the Zionist movement, there was immigration to Eretz Israel,* the Holy Land. Throughout Jewish history prior to the modern political Zionist movement, small numbers of Jews had always migrated to the Holy Land, in keeping with the Jewish religion's concept that to live and die in the Holy Land was an important precept. Immigrating to the Holy Land was an important activity, and over the centuries Jews migrated to Eretz Israel and lived in the four holy cities: Jerusalem,* Safed, Tiberias, and Hebron.* With the practical and political Zionism of the nineteenth century, beginning in the 1880s, the numbers of Jewish immigrants to Palestine grew dramatically, but they also varied in number, depending on practical conditions both in their countries of origin and in Palestine (and, later, Israel).

Immigration to Palestine traditionally has been divided into five major phases or *aliyot* (waves of immigration) between the 1880s and World War II. During the First Aliya (1882–1903), some 20,000 to 30,000 individuals immigrated to Palestine, primarily groups organized by the Hovevei Zion* and Bilu* movements in Russia and Romania. Some arrived on their own, mostly from Galicia. The Second Aliya* (1904–14) involved some 35,000 to 40,000 young pioneers, mostly from Russia. In the Third Aliya (1919–23), some 35,000 young pioneers immigrated to Palestine from Russia, Poland, and Romania. The Fourth Aliya (1924–31) involved mainly middle-class immigrants from Poland, numbering some 88,000. The Fifth Aliya (1932–38) consisted of some 215,000 immigrants, mainly from Central Europe. During World War II (1939–45), immigration to Palestine continued both legally and illegally (Aliya Bet*) and totaled some 82,000. After World War II (1945) until the independence of Israel in May 1948, there were severe British Mandatory* restrictions on Jewish immigration to Palestine, but some 57,000 Jews arrived. After Israeli independence, the flow of immigrants to Palestine grew dramatically as Israel allowed free immigration, and whole communities opted to move to the Holy Land.

For further information see: Sergio Dellapergola, "Aliya and Other Jewish Migrations: Toward an Integrated Perspective," in Uriel Schmelz and Gad Nathan, eds., *Studies in the Population of Israel in Honor of Roberto Bachi* (Jerusalem: Magnes Press, 1986), pp. 172–209; S. N. Eisenstadt, *The Absorption of Immigrants: A Comparative Study Based Mainly on the Jewish Community in Palestine and the State of Israel* (London: Routledge and Paul, 1954); Shmuel Ettinger and Israel Bartal, "The First Aliyah: Ideological Roots and Practical Accomplishments," in Lee I. Levine, ed., *The Jerusalem*

Cathedra (Jerusalem: Izhak Ben-Zvi Institute, 1982), pp. 197–227; Dan Giladi, "The Economic Crisis during the Fourth Aliya, 1926–1927," *Zionism* 1 (1975):157–92; Yosef Gorni, "Changes in the Social and Political Structure of the Second Aliya between 1904 and 1940," *Zionism* 1 (1975):49–101; Leon Rubinstein, *The First Swallows: The Dawn of the Third Aliya* (New York: Cornwall Books, 1986); Justin McCarthy, *The Population of Palestine: Population Statistics of the Late Ottoman Period and the Mandate* (New York: Columbia University Press, 1990); Erich Gerschon Steiner, *The Story of the Patria* (New York: Holocaust Library, 1982).

ALIYA BET. A term for the illegal immigration of Jews into Palestine* under the British Mandate* in defiance of official British restrictions.

Article 6 of the Palestine Mandate stated that Britain must "facilitate Jewish immigration under suitable circumstances." However, the British administration did not allow sufficient numbers of Jews into the country to satisfy the Yishuv,* especially as the pressure to escape Nazi persecution was increasing in Europe and the Jews of Palestine were determined to increase immigration to ensure the Jewishness of their desired state. The British, at times, drastically halted or cut Jewish immigration to Palestine, and, as a result, an effort was initiated to bring Jews into the country illegally.

In 1934, the Hehalutz movement began the first efforts to bring Jews to Palestine secretly by sea. Operations were suspended, however, until 1937, when Betar* and the Revisionist Movement* began the Af al Pi ("in spite of") operation. Its success led Hehalutz to resume its efforts, canceled earlier due to initial failure and lack of experience. In 1938, the Mossad for Aliyah Bet was established by the Haganah* as Hitler's regime was threatening Jews in Germany. In May 1939, the British published the White Paper* that restricted Jewish immigration at a time when the Jews of Europe were increasingly endangered. This energized the efforts of Aliyah Bet.

During and after World War II, densely packed ships sailed to Palestine in the hopes of escaping British patrol boats. Intercepted vessels were taken by the British, and the refugees were sent to detention camps in Atlit and Cyprus.

The most famous "illegal" ship was the *Exodus 1947*,* which carried 4,515 refugees and was turned away from Palestine by the British. These refugees were then returned to a British internment camp in Germany. The *Exodus 1947* became a symbol of world outrage at the British policy of barring survivors of Hitler's camps from reaching their homeland.

From 1934 to 1948 some 115,000 immigrants came to Eretz-Yisrael in Aliyah Bet operations, and another 51,500 were interned in Cyprus after 1946 and arrived in Israel after its independence.

For further information see: Ehud Avriel, *Open the Gates! A Personal Story of "Illegal" Immigration to Israel* (London: Weidenfeld and Nicolson, 1975); Ze'ev Venia Hadari, *Second Exodus: The Full Story of Jewish Illegal Immigration to Palestine, 1945–1948* (London: Valentine Mitchell, 1991); Ze'ev Venia Hadari and Zeev Tsahor, *Voyage to Freedom: An Episode in the Illegal Immigration to Palestine* (London: Vallentine,

Mitchell, 1985); Gershon Shafir, *Land, Labor and the Origins of the Israeli–Palestinian Conflict, 1882–1914* (New York: Cambridge University Press, 1989).

David Salzberg

ALLA, ABU. Chairman of the Palestinian Reconstruction and Development Council,* negotiator for the Palestine Liberation Organization* (PLO), and chief executive officer (CEO) of SAMED (the economic institution of the PLO). Abu Alla (Ahmad Quray) has been at the very heart of Israeli–PLO negotiations since the two sides first made secret contacts in 1993.

Since the signing of the Israel–PLO Declaration of Principles* (DOP), Abu Alla stepped into the forefront of the Israeli–PLO negotiations. Having played a crucial role in the Palestinian delegations to the secret Oslo* meetings and the public bilateral peace talks, Abu Alla has been in close contact with Israeli Foreign Ministry director general Uri Savir,* and in those negotiations the Israelis and Palestinians made considerable progress toward security agreements concerning the occupied territories* and the Palestinian police, who took over immediately after the withdrawal of the Israeli army from Gaza* and Jericho.* As early as February 11, 1994, the two sides signed agreements that specified details on several issues, such as Palestinian powers under autonomy and other technical points. This document was signed by Abu Alla and Uri Savir, as well as by Foreign Minister Shimon Peres* of Israel and PLO chairman Yasser Arafat.* The sides did come to an agreement on security in late March 1994, after the PLO agreed to come back to the negotiating table, following a one-month withdrawal from the bilateral talks in the wake of the Hebron Mosque Massacre* of February 25, 1994. The agreement established a joint Israeli–Palestinian police unit that would train a select group of officers from the Israeli army and the newly trained Palestinian force, to patrol together, in groups of two vehicles, one Israeli and one Palestinian, ensuring joint policing over the Gaza Strip* and Jericho areas.

Furthermore, Abu Alla has negotiated with Israeli finance minister Avraham Shohat, and they discussed an economic program that would establish an understanding and a form of economic cooperation between Palestinians and Israelis.

In the wake of the Hebron Massacre, Abu Alla was instrumental in getting the PLO talking to the Israelis again when he stressed that, although it was an important step in the right direction for Israel to outlaw such groups as Kach* and Kahane Chai,* more security for the Palestinians was needed, specifically, more security measures around the Mosque of Ibrahim* and the location of settlers.

Yasha Manuel Harari

ALLAF, MOWAFFAK (MUWAFFIQ, MUAFAK) (b. Damascus, Syria,* May 17, 1927). He was educated at the Faculty of Law at Syrian University. He joined the Syrian diplomatic corps and served in a variety of posts beginning as a commercial attaché at the Syrian Embassy in Cairo in 1950. He served from 1968 to 1974 as ambassador of Syria to the United Nations office in Geneva and from 1975 to 1978 as ambassador to the United Nations in New York. From 1978 to 1982, he was deputy director general of the United Nations office in Geneva, and, from 1982 to 1987, he was director general of the United Nations office in Vienna. He served as the head of the Syrian delegation to the Washington rounds* of the Israeli–Syrian bilateral peace talks that followed the Madrid Peace Conference.*

Yasha Manuel Harari

ALLENBY BRIDGE. The Allenby Bridge, also known as the King Hussein Bridge* in Jordan,* was the primary point of contact between Israel and the occupied West Bank* and Jordan. Named for the British General Sir Edmund Allenby, who captured Jerusalem* (December 9, 1917) and Jericho* (February 1918) from Ottoman* forces as commander of the Egyptian Expeditionary Force during World War I, the bridge spans the Jordan River* just north of the Dead Sea.* Originally one of five bridges crossing the river, it connected Jaffa on the Mediterranean Sea coast to Amman 110 miles away in Jordan.

The Allenby Bridge serves several roles relating to security, politics, and economics. Its strategic value was demonstrated during the 1948 war* when Transjordan's Arab Legion* crossed the bridge on May 15, took positions around Ramallah, Latrun, and Bethlehem* in predominantly Arab regions of Mandatory Palestine,* and attacked the Sheikh Jarrah quarter of Jerusalem four days later. The bridge lay behind the front line after Transjordan's annexation of the West Bank but regained its former military significance when Israel took control of the area during the Six Day War;* Jerusalem lay only thirty miles away, Jericho six miles, and Amman forty-three miles.

The Allenby Bridge has possessed symbolic and real political and economic importance since the 1967 war, when it became the link among Israel, the Palestinians, and Jordan and lent its structure to the open bridges policy.* Contact between the West Bank and Jordan has meant a flow of goods and people in both directions, depending on the enforced policies of the day. West Bank agricultural products travel to Jordan and beyond while consumer goods are trucked from Jordan; Jordanian and West Bank Palestinians must cross the bridge with their permits in order to visit relatives on the other side; and tourists pass over to visit sites on the opposite bank.

Paul S. Robinson, Jr.

ALLIANCE OF PALESTINIAN FORCES. The Alliance of Palestinian Forces consists of Palestinian factions opposed to the Gaza-Jericho Agreement* reached between Israel and the Palestine Liberation Organization* in Oslo, Norway. The factions began meeting in September 1993 to discuss the possibility of upgrading their coalition, which was initially formed in 1992. On December 30, 1993, the groups met in Damascus to discuss an organizational draft for the alliance, which originated with four Palestinian groups based in that city: the Democratic Front for the Liberation of Palestine,* the Popular Front for the Liberation of Palestine—General Command,* the Palestinian Popular Struggle Front,* and the Palestine Liberation Front.* In addition to these four organizations, the alliance consists of the Islamic Resistance Movement (HAMAS*), Fatah—the Uprising, the Islamic Jihad Movement,* Vanguards of the Popular Liberation War,* and the Revolutionary Communist Party. They believe that the Oslo agreement will recognize Israeli occupation without creating an Arab and Islamic homeland. The alliance rejects the agreement. Their alternative is continued jihad until the balance of power changes. They claim that Yasser Arafat* no longer speaks for, or expresses the will of, the Palestinian people, and therefore his positions are no longer binding.

Joseph E. Goldberg

ALLON, YIGAL (Formerly Paicovitch) (b. Kfar Tabor (Mesha), Lower Galilee, October 10, 1918; d. 1980). He received an education at local schools, graduating in 1937 from the Kadourie Agricultural School. He later studied at Hebrew University and St. Antony's College, Oxford. In 1937, Allon became a founding member of Kibbutz Ginnosar. During the Arab riots of 1936–39 in Palestine,* he served in the underground defense forces commanded by Yitzhak Sadeh.* In 1941, Allon helped found the Palmach,* a commando unit that assisted in Allied operations in Syria and Lebanon. In 1942, he headed an underground intelligence and sabotage network in Syria* and Lebanon.* The following year, Allon became the deputy commander of Palmach, and in 1945 he became its commander, a post he retained until 1948. In this capacity he directed sabotage against civil and military installations of the British Mandatory* government and supported Aliya Bet,* the illegal immigration of Jews into Palestine. Toward the end of Israel's War of Independence,* he commanded the Southern Front and drove the Arab armies out of the Negev.*

After Prime Minister David Ben-Gurion* dissolved the Palmach, Allon entered politics. In 1954, he was elected to the Knesset* and served as minister of labor from 1961 to 1967. In June 1967, he participated in the inner war Cabinet, which helped to plan the strategy of the Six Day War.* He was also the author of the "Allon plan."* In July 1968, he became deputy prime minister and minister for immigrant absorption. From 1969 to 1974, he served as deputy prime minister and minister of education and culture, and from 1974 to 1977 he was deputy prime minister and minister of foreign affairs.

For further information see: Yigal Allon, "The Arab–Israeli Conflict: Some Suggested Solutions," *International Affairs* 40 (April 1964): 205–18; Yigal Allon, *Shield of David: The Story of Israel's Armed Forces* (London: Weidenfeld and Nicolson, 1970); Yigal Allon, *The Making of Israel's Army* (London: Valentine, Mitchell, 1970).

ALLON PLAN. A proposal developed by Yigal Allon* to establish peace and secure borders for Israel after the Six Day War.* Essentially, it called for the return of the densely populated areas in the West Bank* and Gaza Strip* to Arab control as well as a return of most of the Sinai Peninsula* to Egypt.* Israel would retain control of the Jordan River* valley and mountain ridges, where it could establish settlements and early-warning systems (of radar and other devices) to provide warnings against attacks from the east. There would be changes along the armistice lines, and Israel would retain Jerusalem* and the Gush Etzion* area. Other specifics were included in the detailed plan. The plan was never adopted as Israel's official policy, but Labor*-led governments until 1977 pursued their settlement* construction policy, using the plan as their guideline.

Allon argued that settlements should be confined to strategic necessities for the territorial defense of a country that lacks strategic depth. He felt that the interests of the Arab side should also be taken into consideration and thus recommended that new settlements should be located only in strategic areas and not in heavily Arab-populated areas. This left open options for territorial compromise. Allon suggested that his plan's "map" was based on a number of principles: the Jordan River to the Dead Sea* and the line that bisects the Dead Sea along its middle had to form Israel's eastern border—a political border. The almost uninhabited tract of land, with one flank resting on the mountain ridge, with the Jordan valley and the shore of the Dead Sea lying in between, should be joined to the state of Israel and come under its sovereignty. This strip, which is about fourteen kilometers wide and about twenty-four kilometers long from the shore of the Dead Sea to Hebron,* makes up approximately a third of the West Bank. His argument was based on the security value of an area that could not be pierced by a mechanized and armored land force. The river, an excellent antitank barrier, the topographical steps between the river and the foothills, and the series of hills and high mountains with few passes through them make the defensive system impenetrable. At the same time, it is an excellent base for an Israeli counterattack against enemy forces, if such should be concentrated east of the river. Control of the Judean desert by Israeli forces will help to guarantee the safety of Jerusalem against any guerrilla force. And, of course, there is the historical importance of this region. Allon argued that

the idea of this plan is, of course, to seek a compromise which takes into consideration both needs, ours and the Arabs, including the Palestinian community, to provide Israel with defensible borders that can be defended by ourselves, and by their mere existence the chance of averting other wars would grow. Secondly, to keep Israel by and large as a Jewish state in character, of course, with a considerable Arab minority which we have always had, in which they are treated as equal citizens.

The Israeli Cabinet discussed the Allon Plan a number of times but took no vote on it. This could be attributed to the fact that the government was divided on the issues and also because it would preclude certain matters in the negotiations with the Arabs. Nevertheless, the plan formed something of an unofficial guideline for the government's decisions concerning the placement of settlements. The plan was never formally adopted as a security or settlement policy, though it served as the basis for the settlement programs in the occupied territories* during the first years of Israeli administration of the territories.

Allon's plan is mainly pragmatic. It does not contain any decision on the annexation of Judea and Samaria,* but it also does not bar an annexation in the distant future if matters continued without any peaceful arrangement.

It could be implemented immediately and does not leave a vacuum in the absence of an Israeli presence. It creates conditions for the formation of a new Israeli policy within the borders of western Israel, without Israel's being accused of either unilateral annexation or of barring the way to any peace agreement whatsoever, be it by means of establishing a Palestinian state joined by treaty with Israel and Jordan or by the return of part of the populated areas that were conquered in Judea and Samaria to Jordanian rule in the framework of a duly subscribed peace agreement.

For further information see: Yigal Allon, "Israel: The Case for Defensible Borders," *Foreign Affairs* 55 (October 1976):38–51; Yigal Allon, "The West Bank and Gaza within the Framework of a Middle East Peace Settlement," *Middle East Review* 12 (Winter 1979–80):15–18; "Interview: Yigal Allon: 'Everyone Gives You Advice,' " *Newsweek* (international ed.), May 24, 1976, p. 52.

Matthew Dorf

ALTALENA. Altalena means "lever" in Italian and was Revisionist* leader Zeev Jabotinsky's* literary name. In 1947, this name was given to an American World War II destroyer purchased by Etzel's* political and information arm in the United States. It planned to use the ship to bring to Palestine* and, later, Israel arms and trained European Jewish immigrants who would take part in the emerging nation's struggle with its Arab neighbors. About 100 days prior to the British* withdrawal from Palestine, Menachem Begin,* the Etzel commander, sent a letter to central Etzel headquarters in the Diaspora,* located in Paris, with a request for a large arms purchase and its immediate delivery to Israel. Begin felt these weapons would help protect the young state against Arab hostilities that were expected following the British withdrawal. A day after Israel's declaration of independence, Begin met with Yisrael Galili and Levi Eshkol,* both of whom were Prime Minister Ben-Gurion's* close associates, to discuss the distribution of weapons brought aboard the ship among the three underground organizations that at that time operated in the Yishuv.* The negotiations between Begin and the Haganah* representatives soon broke off after the sides could not reach agreement.

The *Altalena* left the port of Marseilles on the night of June 11, 1948, loaded with weapons and 850 passengers, mostly Holocaust* survivors who were trained by Etzel. The first cease-fire of the War of Independence* came into effect on the same day. Begin himself did not know that the ship had left the port, learning about its departure only from a BBC broadcast. Fearing it could break the cease-fire without consent of the central Israeli government, he tried to communicate with the ship to delay its arrival in Israel. Communication with the ship was problematic, and no foreign port was willing to host the ship in the interim. Begin then again consulted with Eshkol and Galili and told them about the ship and its cargo. It was agreed to let the immigrants and arms land on an undisclosed Israel shore, near Kfar Vitkin. As the ship approached the shores of Israel, Etzel and Haganah representatives again met to discuss the future of the weapons it carried. In these negotiations, the Etzel commander claimed that their units who joined the newly formed Israel Defense Forces* (IDF) received little or no weaponry. Etzel representatives, therefore, requested that 20 percent of the weapons on the ship be slated for Etzel's forces in Jerusalem,* which at that time was an independent international city in which Etzel was fighting outside the IDF framework. Galili acceded to Etzel's desire to move the weaponry to Jerusalem; however, he refused to specify whether the weapons would be delivered to Etzel forces or whether Haganah-oriented units would incorporate them. The negotiations broke off after several days and on June 19, Galili told Ben-Gurion that Etzel was planning a revolt, or at least a declaration of an independent state in Jerusalem.

As a result of the suspicions strongly held by Ben-Gurion and Galili, the government decided to blockade the beach where the *Altalena* was to land and sent two corvettes to intercept it. As the corvettes were unable to stop the large destroyer, the *Altalena* reached the shores of Netanya. Learning about the blockade, Begin's main concern was quickly unloading the ship before United Nations (UN) observers discovered its weapons and seized them. On the morning of June 21, the government gave Begin an ultimatum: surrender the ship's cargo and appear at a meeting at the IDF Central Command within ten minutes. Because Begin suspected that he would be arrested at that meeting, he rejected the ultimatum. Instead, he decided to board the ship himself and sail toward Tel Aviv, where Etzel had widespread support. Begin believed that after reaching Tel Aviv, he would meet with IDF representatives to negotiate the distribution of the weaponry without being under the shadow of the threat of arrest and under the pressures of ultimatums. This belief rested on the assumption that the IDF would not dare attack the ship in front of the city's citizens because Tel Aviv was generally a community sympathetic to the Revisionists.

IDF forces opened fire on the ship near the Tel Aviv shore. After being hit by an artillery shell, the ship began to burn. The hundred people still aboard were forced to abandon ship and, as many of the survivors claimed, swam to shore as IDF units continued to fire upon them. Upon reaching shore, several Etzel leaders were arrested and imprisoned without trial for an extended period.

Traditional explanations for the government's action emphasize their fear that Etzel was planning a revolution and did not respect democracy. Such a revolution was not, in fact, planned.

Many Etzel members also criticized Begin for being indecisive, which caused confusion. When the IDF opened fire, Begin decided to prevent further bloodshed and ordered his units not to fire in response. He maintained that Jews should not kill each other. Further, Begin refused to fight the nascent Israeli government as it prepared for the next round of warfare with its neighbors. Such a challenge, he believed, would threaten the very survival of the state.

Following the *Altalena* incident, Begin and his associates understood that the time had passed for the continued operation of an independent underground. He organized his forces into a political party and placed all Etzel units under centralized IDF control.

For further information see: Menachem Begin, *The Revolt* (New York: Nash, 1981); J. Bowyer Bell, *Terror out of Zion: Irgun Zvai Leumi, Lehi, Palestine Underground, 1929–1949* (New York: St. Martin's Press, 1977); Samuel Katz, *Days of Fire* (Garden City, NY: Doubleday, 1968); Zeev Schiff and Eytan Haber, eds., *Israel, Army and Defense: A Dictionary* (Jerusalem: Zmora, Bitan and Modan, 1976); Yonatan Shapiro, *Chosen to Command: The Road to Power of the Herut Party* (Tel Aviv: Am Oved, 1989).

David Wurmser

AMAL. Afwaj al-Muqawama al-Lubnaniya, the Shiite Lebanese Resistance Detachments, is best known by its Arabic acronym AMAL, which means "hope." AMAL was founded by Imam Musa al-Sadr in 1975 during the Lebanese Civil War as a means of protecting the Shiite Muslim community in Lebanon.* Born in Qum, Iran, Sadr studied in Najaf, Iraq,* and in 1958 moved to Tyre, Lebanon, to replace their mufti, who had died. A year after he moved to Tyre, Imam Sadr established a vocational training institute in southern Lebanon, which served as a means of spreading his influence among the young Shiites. The Imam's political movement, "Movement of the Deprived" (Harakat al-Mahrumin), established in 1974, worked closely with the Lebanese National Movement of Kamal Jumblatt in the early 1970s, but he broke from the front over his dissatisfaction with Syria's* entry into Lebanon. Sadr believed that the Palestine Liberation Organization's* (PLO) use of southern Lebanon to shell Israel and Israeli retaliation for these attacks left the Shiite community vulnerable and without defense. Despite his sympathy for the Palestinian cause, his dissatisfaction with the PLO and his belief that the Palestinians were also terrorizing the Lebanese population led to poor relations between the two populations. To protect the community, he created a militia, AMAL, associated with the Movement of the Deprived. Ironically, Fatah* provided the initial training for AMAL. In August 1978, the Imam disappeared in Libya while visiting Gaddafi. He was succeeded by Nabih Berri, a Shiite lawyer who had emerged as an AMAL leader.

AMAL's headquarters was located in Baalbek. Like Imam Sadr, Berri also accepted Syrian support and has attempted, at the same time, to maintain an independent and moderate course. This has been complicated by the fragmented nature of the Shiite community in Lebanon. The success of Ayatollah Khomeini's revolution in Iran and the establishment of Hezbollah* as a Shiite Lebanese force under Iranian influence created a direct challenge to AMAL's leadership of the Shiites. Both Hezbollah and AMAL were viewed by tribal and clan leaders in Lebanon as a challenge to their authority as well. Disagreement over Berri's moderation led Abbas Mussawi* to break away from AMAL in June 1982 and create his own militia, Islamic AMAL. Mussawi believed that Berri's policies were too secular.

When Israel invaded Lebanon in 1982 to destroy the PLO infrastructure established in the south, Berri's AMAL came to the support of the Palestinians. Yet, when the PLO attempted to reestablish its state within a state in 1985, AMAL opposed its actions. Fighting between the PLO and AMAL began in 1985, but Berri and his militia were not successful, and the PLO returned to Tyre and Sidon. In 1987, AMAL forces placed the Palestinian refugee camp, Burj al Barajinah, under siege for five months. AMAL's attempt to prevent the PLO from using southern Lebanon as a staging ground for attacks on Israel has led to increased tension between AMAL and its former allies, the Druze militia under Walid Jumblat and the Maronite Lebanese Forces under the leadership of Elie Hobeika.

The most significant challenge to AMAL's leadership of the Shiite community remains Hezbollah. Although both organizations are willing to use force, Hezbollah wishes to establish an Islamic regime similar to that established in Iran, while AMAL wishes to reform Lebanon to bring about greater Shiite influence but not establish an Islamic regime. AMAL is willing to live in a multisectarian state free of outside influence—whether Iranian, Syrian, or Israeli. Because Syria has been an ally of Iran, it finds itself in a somewhat difficult political situation.

For further information see: Elaine C. Hagopian, *Amal and the Palestinians: Understanding the Battle of the Camps: Viewpoints* (Belmont, MA: Association of Arab-American University Graduates, 1985); Augustus R. Norton, *Amal and the Shia: Struggle for the Soul of Lebanon* (Austin: University of Texas Press, 1987).

Joseph E. Goldberg

AMBASSADOR'S TALKS. A reference to the informal talks in Washington between the Israeli ambassador to the United States, Itamar Rabinovich,* and the Syrian ambassador to the United States, Walid Mualem.* At the end of 1994, there was an expansion of the process when the Israeli and Syrian military chiefs of staff (Ehud Barak* and Hikmat Shihabi*) and accompanying officers (including Prime Minister Rabin's* military secretary, Major General Danny Yatom) joined in the process in secret meetings in Washington. After a brief hiatus, they were resumed in the spring of 1995.

AMER, ABDEL HAKIM (b. Istal, Minia Province, Egypt,* 1919; d. Cairo, Egypt, September 14, 1967). He was born to the son of the head of the village, Sheikh Ali Amer, and graduated from the Egyptian Military Academy in 1938 and was commissioned in 1939. He became friends with Gamal Abdul Nasser* when the two were stationed in Khartoum together. In May 1948, Amer graduated from the Egyptian Staff College, and shortly thereafter he fought with the Egyptian army in the 1948 war* with Israel. As a major in the Egyptian army, Abd el

Hakim Amer was a member of the Free Officers group, which carried out the successful coup d'état in Egypt on July 23, 1952. Prior to the coup he was a staff officer for General Mohammed Naguib and later his aide-de-camp. Amer was promoted from the rank of major to brigadier in 1953 and to lieutenant general in 1957. He was made marshal in 1958. On September 1, 1954, following Nasser's overthrow of Naguib, Amer was appointed minister of war. He survived a scandal that revealed that a smuggling ring was operating from his office. In 1956, he was Egyptian minister of defense and commander in chief.

Amer was among the original group of Free Officers who led the 1952 revolution and was reputed to be Gamal Abdul Nasser's closest confidant and companion in the pre- and postrevolutionary period. Within the Revolutionary Command Council, Amer's position was promoted by Nasser, who secured for Amer the title of commander in chief from General Naguib in June 1953.

Amer became minister of war in 1954. Amer's powerful position within the military helped Nasser survive politically the resignation, reinstatement, and eventual house arrest of General Naguib during 1954, as Nasser emerged as ruler of Egypt.

The 1956 Suez War* heightened the importance of the military and, with it, General Amer. With the formation of the United Arab Republic* by Egypt and Syria* in February 1958, Amer was appointed chief coordinator of the Northern Region (Syria), in addition to serving as field marshal, vice president of Syria, and minister of defense. In October 1959, he was made governor of Syria. In September 1961, Amer was expelled from Syria following the seizure of Damascus by Syrian army units opposed to continuing the link between their country and Egypt. Amer continued to serve as minister of war in Egypt until March 1964, when he resigned to become first vice president and deputy commander in chief.

In late October 1959, Amer was appointed Nasser's proconsul in Syria. He was one of two Egyptian vice presidents in the United Arab Republic. Amer's relations with Abdul Hamid al-Sarraj, a pro-Syrian Nasserist who was the mastermind of a military coup in Syria that made unity with Egypt possible, were antagonistic. When the Syrian revolution of September 28, 1961, took place, the Syrian mechanized forces surrounded Amer's residence to present their demands. Ultimately, the revolt led to the secession of Syria from the United Arab Republic on October 10, 1961. He led Egyptian forces in Yemen in support of the left-wing revolutionaries. In 1964, he was appointed first vice president and deputy commander of the armed forces.

In September 1957, Amer was appointed to the Executive Committee of the National Union. But by 1961, when he returned from Syria, there was reputedly a growing rift between Nasser and Amer over the increasing socialism of government policy and, more important, over the strength and autonomy of Amer himself.

In 1966, Nasser named Amer chairman of the politically controversial Committee for the Liquidation of Feudalism, which was charged with investigating the holdovers of prerevolutionary social and political practices in the country-side.

Egypt's humiliating defeat in the Six Day War* was the cause of his downfall, as he was considered responsible for much of the military failure during the conflict. The Egyptian military's lack of preparedness, despite a series of provocative actions by both sides in the months preceding the outbreak of hostilities, left most of Egypt's aircraft destroyed on the ground in the first hours of the conflict. The fighting was therefore dominated by Israel's control of the air. Amer, together with the Egyptian Minister of War, Shams al-Din Badran, and those associated with them in the High Command and in the Egyptian officer corps, was forced to resign in June. Badran and Amer requested that an investigation be conducted on the decisions leading to the war, but this was rejected. It was said that Amer attempted to stage a coup in order to regain the support of the Egyptian Army, but he failed. Along with a number of other officers, Amer was arrested on August 26, 1967, and charged with involvement in a plot to overthrow Nasser. His suicide was announced on September 14, 1967.

Joseph E. Goldberg

AMERICAN EMERGENCY COMMITTEE FOR ZIONIST AFFAIRS. See **AMERICAN ZIONIST COUNCIL.**

AMERICAN ISRAEL PUBLIC AFFAIRS COMMITTEE (AIPAC). The American Israel Public Affairs Committee (AIPAC) was formally established on March 22, 1954, to replace the American Zionist Committee for Public Affairs. AIPAC was created to coordinate and direct the actions of the American Zionist movement to improve the friendship and goodwill between the United States and Israel. It is a registered lobbying organization acting on behalf of American–Israeli relations. In the process of carrying out its mandate, AIPAC has been a source of information about Middle Eastern affairs that affect U.S.–Israeli relations for both Congress and the executive branch. Its research papers as well as formal briefs and testimony before congressional committees are supported by a professional staff.

For further information see: David H. Goldberg, *Foreign Policy and Ethnic Interest Groups: American and Canadian Jews Lobby for Israel* (New York: Greenwood Press, 1990); Edward Tivnan, *The Lobby: Jewish Political Power and American Foreign Policy* (New York: Simon and Schuster, 1987).

Joseph E. Goldberg

AMERICAN ZIONIST COMMITTEE FOR PUBLIC AFFAIRS. See **AMERICAN ISRAEL PUBLIC AFFAIRS COMMITTEE.**

AMERICAN ZIONIST COUNCIL. In 1939, fourteen American Zionist organizations established an Emergency Committee for Zionist Affairs to educate the American public on the importance of establishing a Jewish homeland in Palestine.* Because of the conflict in Europe, it was uncertain whether the World Zionist Executive housed in London and Jerusalem* would be able to operate effectively. The Emergency Council for Zionist Affairs, located in the United States, would be more likely to function in wartime. The organization was renamed the American Emergency Committee for Zionist Affairs in 1942, the American Zionist Emergency Council in the fall of 1942, and the American Zionist Council in 1949. In its early years, there was a reluctance by its leadership to engage in public action. The objective of establishing a Jewish homeland was to be sought through the British Mandate.* Though reluctant to alienate the British, Rabbi Abba Hillel Silver began to organize the American Jewish community into a mass political movement as early as 1943. Silver's intention was to cultivate support for the creation of a Jewish state within the non-Jewish, as well as Jewish, communities in the United States. Civic organizations, churches, and members of Congress were contacted on behalf of the Zionist cause. With the independence of Israel, the American Zionist Council (AZC) committed itself to lobbying the U.S. government for American economic aid to the Jewish state. Under the guidance of AZC's chief lobbyist, I. L. Kenen, the organization was able to influence the adoption of pro-Israeli statements in both Democratic and Republican Party platforms. In 1953, the American Zionist Council became concerned that, though they were lobbying on behalf of American Jewish organizations to influence American Middle Eastern policy, they were being investigated for acting on behalf of a foreign government. Kenen had not registered as a foreign agent. It was decided to establish a new lobbying organization, the American Zionist Council of Public Affairs, formed in 1954, which later changed its name to the American Israel Public Affairs Committee (AIPAC).*

Joseph E. Goldberg

ANDERSON MISSION. Robert B. Anderson (1910–89) served as secretary of the navy in 1953 and 1954, as deputy secretary of defense in 1954 and 1955, and as secretary of the treasury of the United States from 1957 to 1961.

In 1956, he undertook a secret and ambitious peace mission to Cairo and Jerusalem* for President Dwight D. Eisenhower.* Anderson was then deputy secretary of defense. Eisenhower had great confidence and trust in Anderson and therefore chose him for this mission.

The mission was to develop a rapprochement between Israel and Egypt* in meetings with Egyptian president Gamal Abdul Nasser* and Israeli prime minister David Ben-Gurion.* If an agreement was reached, the United States would guarantee the two countries' borders and would aid Egypt in its efforts to build the Aswan Dam and would help Israel to compensate Palestinian refugees.* Anderson was to convince both leaders that peace was in the interest of both Israel and Egypt. Anderson was to be assisted by State Department and Central Intelligence Agency (CIA) officials since he had limited background in Middle East affairs. The mission was conducted in the strictest secrecy, as Anderson's only U.S. contacts were with CIA agents in Israel and Egypt, thereby bypassing the U.S. ambassadors in those countries.

The first meeting was with Nasser in Cairo on January 19, 1956. Nasser refused to accept Israel's frontiers as permanent, nor did he agree to peace with Israel. Nasser argued that a quick settlement was not possible, stated that a solution to the refugee problem had to be implemented first, and insisted on the return to Egypt of basically the entire Negev* from "Dahahirya about 10 miles southwest of Hebron* to Gaza.*" He refused to hold direct negotiations with Israel, characterizing such an idea as "political suicide."

On January 23, 1956, Anderson met with Ben-Gurion and Moshe Sharett.* Ben-Gurion felt that Nasser was unwilling to make peace due to his exorbitant demands, his alignment with the USSR, and the Czech arms deal.* Ben-Gurion was willing to meet Nasser face-to-face, but, if not, he seemed willing to institute low-level talks as well. Israel feared that Nasser was playing for time until his army had mastered the new Soviet weaponry it had received. Ben-Gurion saw this as a threat to Israel's security and asked for U.S. arms to offset Soviet shipments to Egypt.

Anderson flew back to Cairo to try to get Nasser to agree to face-to-face negotiations, but he refused for fear of being assassinated.

For several weeks Anderson went back and forth, with no result. Each side would not accept the other's demands. On February 10, Anderson returned to Washington to report on the failure of the mission. However, Eisenhower and John Foster Dulles* sent him back to try again. On March 6, Anderson held two secret meetings with Nasser and discussed a new proposal—rather than face-to-face negotiations with Israel, Nasser could meet with an American Jewish citizen under the auspices of the Israeli government. Final decisions on these proposed negotiations were to be decided by the leadership of both Israel and Egypt. Nasser refused; he would only agree to mediation through the United States. Anderson proposed resettling the refugees outside the Middle East with U.S. grants. With regard to territorial continuity, Anderson proposed an east–west corridor across the Negev, with an overpass over the north–south highway to Eilat. Again Nasser refused, adding, in fact, that even if Israel accepted his demands, Egypt would not sponsor a settlement; this, he felt, should be left to the United States or United Nations (UN). Thus, Anderson left Cairo empty-handed.

On March 9, Anderson went to Jerusalem. Israel's leaders continued to worry about the influx of Soviet arms and Nasser's aggressive intentions. They were most concerned about preparing for the next war and again requested arms from the United States.

The Anderson mission failed because the problems between Israel and Egypt appeared to be insoluble, as leaders from both countries stuck to their positions and mistrusted one another. Nasser wanted Israel to give up territory and take in the refugees before making peace. Israel wanted negotiations without pre-conditions, which Nasser refused to consider—thus, the stumbling block to the mission. The result of the Anderson mission was to convince Eisenhower of Nasser's intransigence, and the president began to consider ways to develop a plan to isolate Egypt, remove Soviet influence from the region, and prevent aggression against Israel.

For further information see: Isaac Alteras, *Eisenhower and Israel: US–Israeli Relations, 1953–1960* (Gainesville: University Press of Florida, 1993).

David Salzberg

ANGLO-AMERICAN COMMITTEE OF INQUIRY. A committee of British and American representatives appointed in November 1945 to study the question of Jewish immigration to Palestine* and the future of the British Mandate.* After numerous meetings and hearings in the region and elsewhere, it issued a report on April 20, 1946. The recommendations included the immediate issuing of 100,000 immigration certificates for Palestine to Jewish victims of Nazi and Fascist persecution. Although U.S. president Harry S Truman* accepted much of the report, especially the recommendation concerning Jewish immigration, the British government did not accept it. The Palestine problem was turned over to the United Nations.

On November 4, 1945, Ernest Bevin* proposed an Anglo-American Committee of Inquiry, and Truman agreed. The committee consisted of six British and six American members. It held hearings and heard proposals from representatives of the Jews and Arabs in a number of world cities. Its report was issued on May 1, 1946. It unanimously recommended that 100,000 Jews be immediately admitted to Palestine, but there was no agreement on Palestine's future. It rejected the creation of a Jewish or an Arab state but suggested a form of unitary state and proposed continuation of the Mandate for the time being. See also MORRISON-GRADY COMMITTEE.

For further information see: Anglo-American Committee of Inquiry on Jewish Problems in Palestine and Europe, *A Survey of Palestine* (Jerusalem: Government Printer, 1947); Great Britain, Parliamentary Papers, *Report of the Anglo-American Committee of Enquiry regarding the Problems of European Jewry and Palestine,* Lausanne, April 20, 1946, Command 6808 (London: His Majesty's Stationery Office, 1946); Amikam Nachmani, *Great Power Discord in Palestine: The Anglo-American Committee of Inquiry into the Problems of European Jewry and Palestine, 1945–1946* (London: Frank Cass, 1987); Allen H. Podet, *The Success and Failure of the Anglo-American Committee of Inquiry, 1945–1946: Last Chance in Palestine* (Lewiston, NY: Edwin Mellen Press, 1986).

AQABA. A city located at the northern end of the Gulf of Aqaba* and at the southern end of Jordan,* Aqaba is the kingdom's only port. It is located only a few kilometers from the Israeli port of Eilat.*

AQABA, GULF OF. See GULF OF AQABA.

AL-AQSA MOSQUE. See AL-AKSA MOSQUE.

ARAB BOYCOTT OF ISRAEL. The Arab League,* then comprising Egypt,* Lebanon,* Syria,* Transjordan,* Iraq,* Yemen, and Saudi Arabia, formally initiated the Arab boycott of Israel (then the Jewish community of Palestine*) on December 2, 1945. Resolution 16 of the Council of the Arab League stated that

Jewish products and manufactured [goods] in Palestine shall be [considered] undesirable in the Arab countries; to permit them to enter the Arab countries would lead to the realization of the Zionist political objectives. [It called upon all Arab] institutions, organizations, merchants, commission agents and individuals . . . to refuse to deal in, distribute, or consume Zionist products or manufactured goods. . . . Accordingly . . . every State of the League should . . . take measures which they consider fit . . . in order to prevent these products and manufactured [goods] from entering [these] countries regardless of whether they have come from Palestine or by any other route.

In February 1946, a Permanent Boycott Committee was established. When Israel was established in May 1948, this concept was applied to Israel, and the Arab League banned all commercial and financial transactions between Israel and the Arab states. In 1951, the Arab League opened a Central Boycott Office in Syria to systematize the boycott. In December 1954, the Arab League adopted a codification of the boycott rules.

The boycott is divided into three elements: primary, secondary, and tertiary boycotts. The primary boycott prohibits direct economic, political, and cultural relations with Israel by Arab League member states. The secondary boycott is a boycott of any company that trades with Israel or has contributed to Israel's strength. A blacklist maintained by the Central Boycott Office in Damascus is used to enforce the secondary boycott. The tertiary boycott bans trade with companies that do business with blacklisted companies. Arab states boycott businesses that deal with boycotted companies. It also includes the arts, culture, and information. A list is also maintained by the Central Boycott Office.

On October 1, 1994, the Cooperation Council of the Arab States of the Gulf (the Gulf Cooperation Council—GCC), consisting of Bahrain, Kuwait, Oman, Qatar, Saudi Arabia, and United Arab Emirates, issued a statement in which they noted that they "seriously recognize the importance of a review of the provisions of the Arab boycott of Israel so as to take into consideration progress achieved and substantive future requirements of the peace process." They also stated: "Concerning the application of the Arab boycott of Israel, necessary measures have been taken with a view to protecting the mutual interests of the GCC and its trading partners. As a result of these measures and for all practical purposes, secondary and tertiary boycotts are no longer a threat to the interests of these partners." The GCC members also noted that the matter would have to be addressed by the Arab League since it was enacted by that body.

For further information see: Dan S. Chill, *The Arab Boycott of Israel: Economic Aggression and World Reaction* (New York: Praeger, 1976); Marwan Iskandar, *The Arab Boycott of Israel* (Beirut: Research Center, Palestine Liberation Organization, 1966); Leila Meo, Audrey Shabbas, and Fuad K. Suleiman, *The Arab Boycott of Israel* (Detroit,

MI: Association of Arab-American University Graduates, 1976); Terence Prittie and Walter Henry Nelson, *The Economic War against the Jews* (London: Corgi Books, 1979); Aaron J. Sarna, *Boycott and Blacklist: A History of Arab Economic Warfare against Israel* (Totowa, NJ: Rowan and Littlefield, 1986).

ARAB FRONT FOR STEADFASTNESS AND CONFRONTATION. See **STEADFASTNESS FRONT.**

ARAB HIGHER COMMITTEE. On April 25, 1936, six Palestinian political parties and clan leaders joined together to form a coalition known as the Arab Higher Committee, under the leadership of Hajj Amin al-Husseini,* the mufti of Jerusalem. The Higher Committee acted as the major spokesman for the Palestinian national movement from 1936 until the end of the Palestine Mandate* in 1948.

The Arab Higher Committee was the first executive body of the Palestinian national movement to function smoothly. The committee was led by a ten-man executive organ under the presidency of the mufti of Jerusalem and included both Muslim and Christian members. The committee enabled the individual parties to coordinate their efforts in the 1936 Arab Revolt.* Soon after its formation, the committee announced that the purpose of the 1936 Arab uprising was to force an end to Jewish immigration into Palestine, to stop the transfer of land from Arabs to Jews, and to force the British to replace the Mandate with a national government. The creation of the committee and the fact that it iterated specific objectives for the Arab uprising helped to turn a spontaneous and unorganized movement into an organized campaign of civil disobedience and violence that threatened the British position in Palestine.

Following several acts of violence in September 1937, the British government enacted stringent emergency regulations designed to end the uprising and dissolve any organization conducting activities ''inimical to the Mandate.'' These regulations abolished both the Supreme Muslim Council and the Arab Higher Committee, and five members of the committee were arrested, charged with ''moral responsibility'' for acts of terrorism, and deported to the Seychelles Islands. Hajj Amin al-Husseini escaped the British and slipped into Damascus, where he reestablished the Arab Higher Committee, though it had relatively little impact in Palestine itself.

In 1944, the Arab states were in the process of creating the Arab League* and supported the idea of re-creating a true Arab Higher Committee in Palestine, made up once again of local parties and notables, but followers of al-Husseini in Damascus vetoed the idea. However, in June 1946, following the release of Hajj Amin al-Husseini's nephew Jamil al-Husseini from a British prison camp in Rhodesia, the Arab Higher Committee moved back to Palestine. The committee, this time led by Jamil al-Husseini, became a vocal and inflexible opponent of any United Nations solution to the Palestine Mandate problem that included the creation of a Jewish state. The committee succeeded in becoming the preeminent Palestinian organization by co-opting its rivals, and it exerted decisive influence on the Arab League in everything associated with Palestine.

The committee boycotted all meetings of the United Nations Special Committee on Palestine (UNSCOP*) and therefore deprived the United Nations group of any chance to hear an official Palestinian voice in deciding what to do with Palestine. This contrasted sharply with the Zionists,* who offered their services and provided lengthy testimony to the Special Committee on Palestine.

Israel's War of Independence* effectively ended the relevance of the Arab Higher Committee to any action on the Palestine question and the Arab–Israeli conflict, though Hajj Amin al-Husseini continued to make periodic statements in the name of the committee, until his death in 1974, from his exile in Damascus and Beirut.

Mark Daryl Erickson

ARAB LEAGUE. See **LEAGUE OF ARAB STATES.**

ARAB LEGION. The Arab Legion is the forerunner of Jordan's* armed forces. Officially formed at the birth of the emirate of Transjordan* in 1923, its roots start in 1921 as a British-organized force to contain conflicts along the Syrian border and to control Bedouin raiding within the emirate. First commanded by Captain F. G. Peake, who had served with Amir Abdullah* during the Great Arab Revolt,* the legion was led by British officers and depended on Britain for money and supplies. This relationship mirrored the various stages of Transjordan's independence from Britain and continued beyond World War II.

In October 1920, Peake received permission from the British high commissioner in Jerusalem* to enlist 100 men to maintain order in the capital, Amman, and to secure the road to Palestine* and another 50 men to assist the British official in Karak. One year later, a new Transjordan Frontier Force was organized as a mobile force with 250 recruits from Palestine, with duties largely devoted to suppressing tax revolts. In 1923, all security forces were merged with the Reserve Mobile Forces and were known as the Arab Legion. Growing gradually, Peake's force grew to 1,500 in 1926.

Early armed encounters occurred along the Saudi Arabian border in the summer of 1922 and 1924 as the Wahhabi allies of Abdul Aziz, the Saudi king, tried expanding the territory of the emerging Saudi state. The Transjordan force was overmatched, and the Wahhabi's massive defeats by Royal Air Force (RAF) air power prompted Britain and King Abdul Aziz to sign the 1925 Hadda treaty establishing security relations along the Transjordanian–Saudi frontier.

A separate Transjordan Frontier Force was organized in April 1926 with recruitment largely from Palestine and was responsible for safeguarding the Syrian and Saudi frontiers/borders. Although the legion was nominally the state's armed forces, it performed mostly police duties, and internal turmoil steadily increased. In 1930, Captain John Bagot Glubb* was assigned to create a more armylike Desert Mobile Force as an elite bedouin unit within the legion capable of long-range mobility to stop intertribal raiding. The specific recruitment of bedouins for this unit was a reversal of earlier policies to exclude bedouins—ironically, those considered most supportive of the Hashemites'* anti-Turkish revolt.

The close relationship with Britain continued; in 1939, Glubb was appointed the commander of the Arab Legion, and Britain continued its maintenance. The legion's size increased as recruitment efforts tended to follow periods of trouble and protest within the emirate. The increasing probability of war motivated Glubb to emphasize the legion's army aspects, although it was undersized when the war began—about 1,600 men in 1939 and only 800 combat-ready. During World War II, Britain modernized the legion, and units served guard duty in Palestine, freeing British troops for other battlegrounds. Some units participated in campaigns in Iraq* and Syria,* but the bulk of the legion remained outside the battlefronts. At war's end the legion stood at 8,000 men, with another 2,000 executing police functions.

By the 1948 Arab–Israeli War,* the legion's strength was down to 6,000 men, and Glubb was still in command. In a prelude to the war, legion forces stationed in Palestine began to shell four settlements of the Etzion bloc between Hebron* and Jerusalem and a week later captured those positions. On May 15, 1948, the Arab Legion crossed over the Damia and Allenby Bridges* from Transjordan, fanned out, and, by May 18, held the areas around Ramallah, Bethlehem,* and Latrun*—the latter being an important link between Jerusalem and the new Jewish state. Using armored cars and artillery, the legion began to assault the northern Sheikh Jarrah quarter in Jerusalem on May 19 and forced its surrender on May 28. The legion withstood Israeli counterattacks on May 25 and June 9; by the 1949 armistice,* the Arab Legion occupied the West Bank* and East Jerusalem.* Britain continued to assist the legion after the war and considered the 12,000-man force (1950) too small to adequately execute its responsibilities both in Jordan and the newly annexed West Bank. By 1953, the legion's size had grown to 17,000–20,000.

When King Hussein* ascended the throne in 1952, he faced increasing internal disorder and pressure from Britain for him to align himself with its Near East policies and to join the new Turkish–Iraqi defense agreement. Under pressure from Arab states and his own population, Hussein dismissed General Glubb as the legion's commander in March 1956. Strictly speaking, the Arab Legion continued to serve as Jordan's army, and Glubb's departure did not produce dramatic changes. Already strongly identified with the Hashemite regime since its foundation and tax revolt activities, the "nationalization" of the legion placed Jordanians in positions formerly held by British officers, while Britain continued its support.

For further information see: Uriel Dann, "The Beginnings of the Arab Legion," *Middle Eastern Studies* 5 (October 1969): 181–91; John Bagot Glubb, *The Story of the Arab Legion* (London: Hodder and Stoughton, 1948); John Bagot Glubb, *A Soldier with the Arabs* (London: Hodder and Stoughton, 1957); Peter Gubser, *Jordan: Crossroads of Middle Eastern Events* (Boulder, CO: Westview Press, 1983); James D. Lunt, *Glubb*

Pasha, A Biography: Lieutenant-General Sir John Bagot Glubb, Commander of the Arab Legion, 1939–1956 (London: Harvill Press, 1987); Benjamin Shwadran, *Jordan: A State of Tension* (New York: Council for Middle East Affairs Press, 1959); P. J. Vatikiotis, *Politics and the Military in Jordan: A Study of the Arab Legion, 1921–1957* (New York: Praeger, 1967); Peter York, *Bedouin Command with the Arab Legion, 1953–56* (London: W. Kimber, 1956); Peter York, *The Arab Legion* (London: Osprey, 1972).

Paul S. Robinson, Jr.

ARAB LIBERATION ARMY. The Arab Liberation Army was created in December 1947 with the purpose of assisting Palestinian forces in Palestine.* Organized, trained, and armed by Syria,* it was led by Fawzi el-Kaukji and consisted almost entirely of Arab irregulars or volunteers from Syria, Lebanon,* and Iraq.*

The Arab Liberation Army initially entered Palestine on January 10, 1948, when it attacked a Jewish settlement: Kfar Szold, which was located 200 yards from the Syrian border. The attack failed, despite the terrain and the Arab superiority of numbers, when the settlers received aid from a British armored unit.

On February 16, 1948, the army targeted Tirat Zvi, an isolated settlement dominated by Arab villages at the foothills of Gilboa in the southern Beisan valley. The Arabs, hoping to surprise the settlers, attacked at dawn, with organized units each carrying out the mission assigned to them, with support established between each unit. However, the settlers were prepared and repelled the Arab Liberation Army with heavy casualties.

After the failed attempt to take Tirat Zvi, the army targeted the settlement of Mishmar Haemek, which was close to Arab Liberation Army bases in the Northern Triangle and also important for Jewish traffic and communications between the Tel Aviv and Haifa areas. Early on April 4, the army opened fire on the settlement with Syrian-supplied field guns, which caused extensive damage to buildings and caused many casualties. The Haganah* could not respond effectively. When the Liberation Army infantry moved, they were stopped just outside the settlement fence. The next morning a cease-fire was negotiated by a British officer. When the cease-fire ended, Haganah forces were ready to counterattack against Arab villages nearby from their positions in Ein Hashofet. In the ensuing battle neither side gained a clear advantage. On April 12, Kaukji tried and failed to take Mishmar Haemek and was forced to retreat for fear of being isolated from his bases of supply. It soon became evident that the Jewish forces were greater in strength and caliber when they seized the offensive, capturing Haifa on April 22, 1948, and controlling Jaffa and most of eastern Galilee by early May 1948.

Kaukji's army had a core of about 2,200 men and was often augmented by local Arabs. While ZAHAL* was not threatened by the Liberation Army in terms of size, strength, or equipment, its locations in Nazareth, Tarshiha, and Tzipori made it possible for Kaukji to link up with other Arab armies and thus constituted a danger in the Galilee. The Liberation Army was involved in the attack on Sejera in Lower Galilee in July, but Kaukji's forces were beaten back.

On the night of October 28, 1948, ZAHAL launched Operation Hiran, the objective of which was to destroy the Liberation Army and gain control of Upper Galilee. The Liberation Army was to be encircled by a pincer movement east and west. Within sixty hours, the operation was completed successfully. The entire Galilee was now under Israeli control, and Kaukji's forces were routed. The Liberation Army suffered from desertions and ceased to be a significant military force from then on.

Several factors contributed to the failure of the Arab Liberation Army and to that of the Arab states in the first Arab–Israeli War.* Despite their larger population, they suffered from organizational and logistical weaknesses. Not only were they poorly trained and organized, but they also lacked the infrastructure, experience, and specialists needed for modern warfare. Whereas the Arabs were initially better armed than the Jewish forces, the United Nations arms embargo left them without an adequate supply of arms and equipment.

A second factor was that prior to the end of the British Mandate,* no Arab government had committed regular Arab armies to assist in the Palestine situation. It had been hoped that the Arab Liberation Army and the Palestine Arab forces would succeed in dealing with the situation without the intervention of regular Arab armies. The decision to commit regular Arab armies was not formally discussed by Arab governments until April 1948 and did not finally occur until May 15, 1948, when the Arab states dispatched some 20,000 to 25,000 troops into Palestine.

A third factor lay in the marked differences of view and rivalry, particularly between King Farouk* of Egypt and King Abdullah* of Transjordan,* regarding the military and political objectives that were to be achieved in Palestine. Such discord hindered the establishment of a coordinated military strategy and a unified military command. The presence of such divisiveness prevented the Arab Liberation Army from making permanent gains prior to the end of the Mandate and during the first Arab–Israeli War.

For further information see: Netanel Lorch, *The Edge of the Sword: Israel's War of Independence, 1947–1949* (New York: G. P. Putnam's Sons, 1961).

Anamika Krishna and David Wurmser

ARAB LIBERATION FRONT (ALF). The Arab Liberation Front was founded in 1969 by the Iraqi* government and controlled by the Baath Party, partly as a response to active Syrian* influence in the Palestinian movement. Although the group is small and not very active, it conducted raids against Israel from Lebanese* territory and is thought to have specialized in bombings. After the 1982 War in Lebanon,* most ALF members retreated to Iraq.

ARAB REBELLION. See **ARAB REVOLT.**

ARAB REFUGEES. See **REFUGEES.**

ARAB REVOLT. The Arab Revolt (or the Great Arab Revolt) began in Palestine*
in April 1936 with acts of violence by a group inspired by Sheikh Izzed Din
al-Qassim,* who was killed by the British in 1935. The Arab Higher Commit-
tee* called for a general strike by Arab workers and government employees, a
boycott of Jewish goods and of sales to the Jews, and attacks on Jews, Jewish
settlements, and British forces. The first stage lasted from April to November
1936. A second stage began after the Peel Commission* proposed the partition
of Palestine. This lasted from September 1937 to January 1939. Among the
principal targets were British officials. Attacks on Jews led to reprisals. The
Haganah* was permitted to arm itself, and there was even cooperation between
the Haganah and the British. Special Jewish units under the direction of Orde
Wingate* were formed to carry out night attacks against various bases.

For further information see: Yehuda Bauer, ''The Arab Revolt of 1936,'' *New Outlook*
9 (August 1966): 49–57 and 9 (September 1966): 21–28; Yehoshua Porath, *The Palestinian Arab National Movement, 1929–1939: From Riots to Rebellion* (London: Frank
Cass, 1977).

ARAB REVOLUTIONARY BRIGADES. See **ABU NIDAL ORGANIZATION.**

ARAB REVOLUTIONARY COUNCIL. See **ABU NIDAL ORGANIZATION.**

ARAB–ISRAELI WARS, ISRAEL'S WAR OF INDEPENDENCE—1948–49. See
WAR OF INDEPENDENCE.

ARAB–ISRAELI WARS, SINAI WAR—1956. See **SINAI WAR.**

ARAB–ISRAELI WARS, SIX DAY WAR—1967. See **SIX DAY WAR.**

ARAB–ISRAELI WARS, WAR OF ATTRITION—1969–70. See **WAR OF AT-
TRITION.**

ARAB–ISRAELI WARS, YOM KIPPUR WAR—1973. See **YOM KIPPUR
WAR.**

ARAB–ISRAELI WARS, WAR IN LEBANON—1982. See **WAR IN LEBA-
NON.**

ARAFAT, YASSER (b. August 4, 1929). Although he claims to have been born
in Jerusalem,* there is evidence that Yasser Arafat was most likely born either
in Gaza* or Cairo, where his father was in business. He spent his early childhood
in Cairo, and then his family moved to Gaza in 1939.

By 1946, Arafat was involved in smuggling arms to Palestine.* In 1952, he
was elected to the presidency of the General Union of Palestinian Students*
(GUPS) at Cairo University, where he received a degree in civil engineering.

In 1948, his family returned to Cairo, where Arafat was sent to a school run by the Muslim Brotherhood,* and in 1950 he returned to Gaza, where he joined a fedayeen* group. In 1951, he entered the Faculty of Engineering at Cairo University. From 1953 to 1955, he was involved in organization and political agitation among Palestinian student groups. He also passed a course in sabotage at an Egyptian* army college and was given the military rank of lieutenant. In 1957, Arafat left Egypt. A year later, he settled in Kuwait, where he was employed as an engineer in the Ministry of Public Works.

In 1962, Arafat moved to Beirut, and, with money he had raised in Kuwait, he opened the first branch of the Fatah* organization. In 1964, he established the headquarters of Fatah in Damascus. It is reported that from a camp in Syria* he led a group of five men on January 1, 1965, in making Fatah's first raid into Israel, attacking a pumping station for the diversion of water from the Jordan River.* In 1968, he transferred his headquarters to Jordan* and established his base near Karameh.* In February 1969, Arafat became chairman of the Executive Committee of the Palestine Liberation Organization* (PLO), and Fatah managed to secure control of a majority of seats in the Palestine National Council.* In September 1970, following the Jordan Civil War,* Arafat left Jordan and established his base in Beirut.*

In 1974, the United Nations (UN) General Assembly voted to invite Arafat to address it. Soon after, the assembly adopted Resolution 3236,* a recognition of Palestinian national and individual rights.

On February 11, 1985, he signed an accord with King Hussein* of Jordan and came to accept the notion of direct negotiation with Israel on the basis of the UN resolution. This represents a dramatic and major shift of the earlier PLO position regarding Israel's existence.

In 1994, he was awarded the Nobel Peace Prize, along with Yitzhak Rabin* and Shimon Peres,* for his efforts in connection with the Declaration of Principles* (DOP).

After the War in Lebanon,* Arafat and his forces were ejected from Beirut, and he took up residence in Tunis.

Yasser Arafat has shown himself to be a consummate politician. In 1990, Arafat and the PLO sided with Saddam Hussein* and Iraq* in its occupation of Kuwait. This action incurred the wrath of the PLO's wealthy Arab patron-states such as Saudi Arabia and Israel. It was widely believed that by siding with the Iraqis, Arafat had marginalized the role of the PLO and had disqualified himself from any future role on the international level.

However, three years later, Arafat was present on the White House lawn as an accepted leader of his people with a role to play.

Following the signing of the Declaration of Principles in September 1993, Arafat's role and leadership were again challenged. Israel and several Arab states questioned his negotiating style and seriousness. Palestinians were divided between those who accused him of autocratic tendencies and those who felt he had been "too soft" in his discussions with the Israelis. His skills as a survivor and a political manipulator were again tested.

Arafat showed skill in playing off the various elements and factors in the negotiations. He warned that if he failed, HAMAS* would be the likely substitute to the PLO. He was able to secure concessions from the Israelis concerning control of the crossing points into Gaza and Jericho,* as well as other concessions regarding the size of the autonomous region around Jericho. Arafat secured Israel's agreement to more than double the original size of this territory. He also continued to insist on movement toward Palestinian independence.

In addition, he faced criticism from fellow Palestinians in the occupied territories* who complained about various factors, including an apparently growing autocratic PLO leadership. There were concerns about the extent to which Arafat sought to control all aspects of activity in the Gaza Strip* and Jericho after the agreement was put into effect. In all of this he had, among other advantages, the benefit derived from the lack of an alternative or viable successor.

For many years he argued that he was married to the revolution. He married Suha Tawil* in 1990, although the marriage was kept secret at that time.

For further information see: Helena Cobban, "Yasser Arafat," in Bernard Reich, ed., *Political Leaders of the Contemporary Middle East and North Africa* (Westport, CT: Greenwood Press, 1990), pp. 44–51; Andrew Gowers and Tony Walker, *Behind the Myth: Yasser Arafat and the Palestinian Revolution* (New York: Olive Branch Press, 1992); Alan Hart, *Arafat: A Political Biography* (Bloomington: Indiana University Press, 1989); Herbert C. Kelman, "Talk with Arafat," *Foreign Policy,* no. 49 (Winter 1982–83): 119–39; Thomas Kiernan, *Arafat, the Man and the Myth* (New York: Norton, 1976); Janet Wallach and John Wallach, *Arafat in the Eyes of the Beholder* (New York: Carol Publishing Group/Lyle Stuart, 1990).

Nancy Hasanian

ARAFAT–HUSSEIN ACCORD (1985). A temporary, yearlong agreement between Palestine Liberation Organization* (PLO) chairman Yasser Arafat* and Jordan's* King Hussein* that established a framework for a joint Palestinian–Jordanian approach to negotiations with Israel. The February 11, 1985, accord included the following principles:

Total Israeli withdrawal from the territories occupied in 1967 in exchange for a comprehensive peace as established in United Nations and Security Council resolutions. Right of self-determination for the Palestinian people: Palestinians will exercise their inalienable right of self-determination—Jordanians and Palestinians will be able to consolidate within the context of the formation of the proposed confederated Arab states and Jordan. Resolution of the problem of Palestinian refugees in accordance with United Nations resolutions. Resolution of the Palestinian question in all its aspects. On this basis, peace negotiations will be conducted under the auspices of an international conference in which the five permanent members of the Security Council and all the parties to the conflict will participate, including the Palestinian Liberation Organization, the sole legitimate representative of the Palestinian people, within a joint delegation (joint Jordanian–Palestinian delegation).

Four months of intra-Palestinian and Palestinian–Jordanian negotiations preceded the February 23, Amman-announced accord. Although the agreement made no specific mention of United Nations Security Council Resolutions 242* or 338,* the Palestinian acknowledgment of Israel's existence and its commitment to the notion of "land for peace"* had never before been openly pronounced.

King Hussein played a determining factor in bringing about the agreement. Arafat's acquiescence on behalf of the PLO was made over the objections of numerous leaders within the organization, including Abu Nidal,* who threatened to kill Arafat for his complicity with the accord.

King Hussein believed that a subtle inclusion of self-determination under a future arrangement with Jordan would be necessary to attract Reagan* administration support. Upon reaching the proposed federation with Jordan, it was assumed that the PLO would be able to assert its own authority. Since self-determination was not an irrefutable precondition, Hussein believed it might avoid the potential for diverting the accord's main focus, Arafat's implied recognition of Israel.

Israeli prime minister Yitzhak Shamir* reacted skeptically to the accord, stating that Israel did "not see the agreement as an opening to peace in the region" and that only after the PLO outrightly accepted Israel's right to exist might real progress be achieved. The United States offered a limited approval of the accord, specifically, the notion of an international conference, and also extended an invitation to the joint Palestinian–Jordanian delegation. But the Reagan administration refused to accept the Palestinian concept of self-determination and sided with the Israeli charge that a tacit acceptance to its right of existence was insufficient.

A number of international terrorist attacks, some of which were traced to the PLO, discredited Arafat's commitments to change. Angered by Arafat's backing out of what he believed would lead to the PLO's acceptance of United Nations Security Council Resolutions 242 and 338, King Hussein dissolved his pact with the PLO on February 19, 1986. In a speech broadcast on Jordanian television, Hussein stated that "I and the Government of the Kingdom of Jordan announce that we are unable to continue to coordinate politically with the PLO leadership until such time as their word becomes their bond, characterized by commitment and constancy." Relations between Jordan and the PLO continued to deteriorate, and, on July 7, King Hussein closed all twenty-five offices of Arafat's Fatah* wing of the PLO. The result of the closings lowered relations between Hussein and Arafat to those previously experienced during the Jordanian–Palestinian Civil War of 1970.

For further information see: Alan Hart, *Arafat, a Political Biography* (Bloomington: Indiana University Press, 1989); David Kimche, *The Last Option: After Nasser, Arafat*

& *Saddam Hussein, the Quest for Peace in the Middle East* (New York: Charles Scribner's Sons, 1991); James Lunt, *Hussein of Jordan, Searching for a Just and Lasting Peace* (New York: William Morrow, 1989); Janet Wallach and John Wallach, *Arafat: In the Eyes of the Beholder* (New York: Carol Publishing Group, 1990).

Robert Crangle, Jr.

ARENS, MOSHE (b. Kovno, Lithuania, 1925). In 1939, Moshe Arens and his family immigrated to the United States, and he served in the U.S. Army during World War II. He secured a B.S. degree from the Massachusetts Institute of Technology. Arens went to Israel at the outbreak of the War of Independence* and served in the Irgun* led by Menachem Begin.* After the war he settled in Mevo Betar but returned to the United States in 1951 and secured an M.A. degree from the California Institute of Technology in aeronautical engineering in 1953. He then worked for a number of years on jet engine development in the United States. In 1957, Arens took a position as an associate professor of aeronautical engineering at the Technion. He joined Israel Aircraft Industries in 1962, where he was vice president for engineering, while continuing his relationship with the Technion. He won the Israel Defense Prize in 1971.

From the outset Arens was active in Herut Party* politics and was elected to the Knesset* in 1974. After the Likud* victory of 1977, he became chairman of the Knesset Foreign Affairs and Defense Committee. Arens voted against the Camp David Accords* but subsequently supported the Egypt–Israel Peace Treaty* as an established fact. He was appointed ambassador to Washington in February 1982. In 1983, following the resignation of Ariel Sharon,* he became defense minister.

Arens was a well-regarded technocrat and was highly praised for his activities as ambassador to Washington. His record as defense minister gained him similar positive reactions. He served as minister without portfolio in the National Unity government,* established in 1984, until he resigned when the government decided to halt production of the Lavi fighter plane. He served again as minister without portfolio from April to December 1988, when he became foreign minister in the Likud-led National Unity government. In 1990, he became defense minister after the National Unity government was dissolved.

He retired from politics after the 1992 Knesset election.

For further information see: Merrill Simon, *Moshe Arens: Statesman and Scientist Speaks Out* (New York: Dean Books, 1988).

ARGOV, SHLOMO (b. 1930). Israel's ambassador to the United Kingdom who was severely wounded in 1982 outside the Dorchester Hotel in London by a Palestinian* gunman who was believed to be a member of the Abu Nidal* group. This was a factor in Israel's decision to launch military strikes against Palestinian positions in Lebanon* in June 1982 known as Operation Peace for Galilee.*

He held a B.A. degree in government from Georgetown University and an

M.A. in international relations from the London School of Economics. He served in the Israeli army from 1947 to 1950 and began his government career in the prime minister's office in 1955. He served in a number of foreign service posts prior to becoming ambassador to the United Kingdom.

ARMISTICE AGREEMENTS. In the spring of 1949, Israel and each of the neighboring states signed an Armistice Agreement terminating the hostilities of Israel's War of Independence.* Iraq,* although a participant in the conflict, refused to do so. The agreements were to end the hostilities and pave the way for peace negotiations, but the latter did not occur. The armistice negotiations were held under the auspices of the United Nations acting mediator for Palestine, Ralph Bunche.*

Egypt signed the Armistice Agreement with Israel on February 24, 1949; Lebanon* on March 23, 1949; Jordan* on April 3, 1949; and Syria* on July 20, 1949.

Each of the agreements was based on several principles: no military or political advantage should be gained under the truce; no changes in military positions should be made by either side after the armistice; and the provisions of the armistices were a consequence of purely military considerations—they were temporary pending the negotiation of more binding arrangements. Each agreement set up a mixed armistice commission to observe and maintain the cease-fire. See also RHODES TALKS.

For further information see: The Arab–Israeli Armistice Agreements, February–July 1949 (Beirut: Institute for Palestine Studies, 1967); Nissim Bar-Yaacov, The Israel–Syrian Armistice: Problems of Implementation, 1949–1966 (Jerusalem: Magnes Press, 1967); David Brook, Preface to Peace: The United Nations and the Arab–Israel Armistice System (Washington, DC: Public Affairs Press, 1964); Shabtai Rosenne, Israel's Armistice Agreements with the Arab States: A Juridical Interpretation (Tel Aviv: Blumstein's Bookstores [for the International Law Association, Israel Branch], 1951).

ARMS CONTROL AND REGIONAL SECURITY. One of the five multilateral negotiations* working groups established as a part of the Madrid Conference peace process.*

ASHRAWI, HANAN MIKHAIL (b. Ramallah, 1946). She is an Anglican Christian and the youngest daughter of Daoud Mikhail, a wealthy physician. Ashrawi graduated from the American University of Beirut and received her Ph.D. in English literature from the University of Virginia in 1981. An English professor at Bir Zeit University in the West Bank* who taught medieval and comparative literature, she was the Palestinian spokesperson in the Madrid-inaugurated peace process.* She became a member of the Palestinian delegation to the Washington talks and the spokesperson for them between 1991 and 1993. She resigned as Palestine Liberation Organization* (PLO) spokesperson in December 1993 and declined to be the minister of information for the Palestinian National Authority,* constructed in 1994. She founded the Palestinian Independent Commission for Citizens' Rights, whose goal is to put civil liberties on the Palestinian agenda.

For further information see: Hanan Ashrawi, *The Side of Peace: A Personal Account* (New York: Simon & Schuster, 1995); Claudia Dreifus, "Hanan Ashrawi: A Separate Peace," *New York Times Magazine,* June 26, 1994, pp. 22–25.

AL-ASIFA (The Storm). Al-Asifa is the military arm of Fatah.* It began operations in January 1965 and used a name distinct from the Palestinian* organization in order to protect Fatah in the event its terrorist attacks failed. Initially, Asifa had strong Syrian* support. Lieutenant Colonel Abd al-Karim al-Jundi, head of Syrian intelligence, aided in its initial organization into a series of cells in which the cell leader alone had association with the strata above it. Membership in Asifa was restricted to Palestinians between twenty and thirty years of age. It is estimated that in its formative period, it numbered only several dozen members, but its membership grew; by late 1966, it had reached about 500, and by 1980 its ranks grew to between 10,000 and 12,000 fighters. Underground training was provided in Algeria, and it established bases in northern Jordan* and Syria. Asifah's first commander was Muhammad Yusuf al-Najjar. Its first attack was on Israel's national water-carrier.

Joseph E. Goldberg

AL-ASSAD, HAFEZ (b. Qardaha, near Latakia, Syria,* 1928 or 1930). His family was from the minority Alawi sect, an offshoot of Shiite Islam. He attended the Syrian Military Academy and studied in France. From 1966 to 1970, he was a member of the regional command of the Baath Party while serving as minister of defense under the Baath leader Salah Jadid.

In 1970, the Syrian army attempted to help the fedayeen* in their attempt to destabilize King Hussein* of Jordan.* Hussein was determined to oust them and began to move militarily in September. The fedayeen requested help from Damascus, but Jordan, and especially Israel, threatened the Syrian army with immediate retaliation if they did not withdraw. The certainty of attack combined with a lack of air cover for the Syrian army, which many believe was purposefully orchestrated by Assad, forced Jadid to call for a humiliating retreat. Assad was able to take advantage of the already unpopular leader's weakened position and staged a coup six weeks later. In June 1971, he established himself as president of the Syrian Arab Republic.

In order to maintain political control at home, to reinforce his Pan-Arabist credentials, and to secure the return of the Golan Heights* to Syrian control, Assad collaborated with Anwar Sadat* in the Yom Kippur War.* By the war's end, Syria lost additional land and suffered heavy casualties.

What Assad could not achieve on the battlefield, he has attempted to achieve through diplomacy and in the United Nations. Assad publicizes his stance against Israel by constantly professing to adhere to the principles adopted at the

Khartoum Summit* in 1967. In addition, the war against Israel is mentioned in the preamble of the Syrian constitution and is considered integral to Syria's identity.

Though Assad supported the Palestine Liberation Organization* (PLO), he did not trust it. He wanted to control it and use it as leverage in Syria's foreign policy. Because of Assad's desire to maintain strict control of many PLO factions, most of them moved into Lebanon,* where they destabilized Lebanon's fragile government and helped to cause a civil war. In early 1976, Assad failed to mediate between the warring factions in Lebanon. In June 1976, Assad ordered the Syrian army into Lebanon, where it pushed the National Movement–PLO forces back, stabilizing Maronite control over their traditional areas. Other Arab states responded by sending supplies to the National Movement. The Syrian army began to serve as an Arab deterrent force, to ostensibly keep the peace but with the real goal of consolidating Assad's control over Lebanon.

After 1973, Assad's strategy shifted from overt confrontation with Israel to mostly covert attempts to destabilize Israel through increasing his support for terrorism. In 1978, Israel invaded and occupied southern Lebanon (Operation Litani*) in response to constant PLO attacks from over the border, but Syria did not retaliate openly. Again in 1981, Israel encouraged Maronite forces to extend their area of control. Assad tried to respond militarily, but Israeli forces shot down Syrian helicopters and bombed Beirut. Before further damage was done, Philip C. Habib,* a veteran American diplomat called upon by President Ronald Reagan,* negotiated a cease-fire. In June 1982, Israel launched an all-out war to chase the PLO and the Syrian forces out of Lebanon and enhance the power of the Maronite forces. Israel succeeded within a few days to remove the PLO presence in Lebanon and overrun Syrian resistance. Only a cease-fire enforced by the United States stopped Israel from expelling Syrian forces from Lebanon and breaking Assad's hold over its government.

Assad has continued to allow terrorist groups to operate in Lebanon, notably the Hezbollah,* which is supported by Iran with Assad's tacit consent. Since the collapse of the Soviet Union, Syria's position has become increasingly marginalized. The separate negotiations for peace with Israel by Anwar Sadat,* Yasser Arafat,* and King Hussein, combined with the loss of Soviet military and financial support, led Assad to reexamine his options and agree to some minor negotiations lacking in substance. He maintains that peace will not be made until Israel withdraws from the Golan Heights.

For further information see: Moshe Ma'oz, *Syria under Assad* (New York: St. Martin's Press, 1986); Moshe Ma'oz, *Asad: The Sphinx of Damascus: A Political Biography* (London: Weidenfeld and Nicholson, 1988); Moshe Ma'oz, "Hafez al-Assad," in Bernard Reich, ed., *Political Leaders of the Contemporary Middle East and North Africa: A Biographical Dictionary* (Westport, CT: Greenwood Press, 1990), pp. 51–64; Charles Patterson, *Hafez al-Assad of Syria* (Englewood Cliffs, NJ: J. Messner, 1991); Patrick Seale, *Asad of Syria: The Struggle for the Middle East* (Berkeley: University of California Press, 1988).

Erin Z. Ferguson

ASWAN DECLARATION. See **ASWAN FORMULA.**

ASWAN FORMULA. On January 4, 1978, during a brief stopover in Aswan, Egypt,* President Jimmy Carter* enunciated what became known as the Aswan Declaration or Aswan Formula. Carter praised Egyptian president Anwar Sadat's* initiative of November 1977, which took him to Jerusalem.* The declaration also stressed the friendship and convergence of goals between the United States and Egypt. Additionally, Carter stressed the need for the Egyptian–Israeli peace negotiations to succeed, which depends on both sides' recognizing the values and beliefs of the other and willingness to compromise.

The most important part of the declaration came when Carter outlined the "principles" or bases that would provide the foundation for the achievement of a "just and comprehensive peace." The first principle is the normalization of relations between Egypt and Israel. The second principle is the withdrawal of Israel from territories it occupied in the Six Day War* and the agreement of all parties to recognize secure and recognized borders as outlined in United Nations Security Council Resolutions 242* and 338.* The third principle, the most controversial, called for "a resolution of the Palestinian problem in all its aspects, . . . recogniz[ing] the legitimate rights of the Palestinian people and enabl[ing] the Palestinians to participate in the determination of their own future." This seemed to go further than any other statement previously made by an American president on the Palestinian question.

Each party to the conflict had its own construction of the statement. For the Egyptians, the declaration seemed to be an endorsement of President Sadat's oft-stated demand for self-determination for the Palestinians. The Israelis interpreted the declaration to mean self-determination for the Palestinians and the creation of a Palestinian state. This was unacceptable to them, as previous statements and policies of the Begin* government clearly stated. The Palestine Liberation Organization* (PLO) criticized the declaration as being too vague and renewed its call for an independent Palestinian state.

In an attempt to clarify what he meant at Aswan, Carter stated that an independent Palestinian state located between Israel and Jordan* would not be advisable for the United States, the Middle East, or the world. An entity or homeland tied at least in federation with Jordan was the most viable option and what he was advocating in the Aswan Declaration.

Fearful of the malaise that seemed to surround the peace negotiations after Sadat's trip to Jerusalem and the failure of the summit talks at Ismaliya to move the process forward, President Carter sought to keep the talks moving by looking for compromise language acceptable to both sides on the issues of peace, withdrawal, and the Palestinians. His use of the word *self-determination* proved inadequate to all parties.

For further information see: William B. Quandt, *Camp David: Peacemaking and Politics* (Washington, DC: Brookings Institution, 1986).

Pamela Rivers

AUDEH, MOHAMMED DAOUD (b. Silwan, May 16, 1937). After graduation from high school, he taught mathematics and physics in Jordan,* where he joined the Communist Party. Audeh moved to Saudi Arabia, where he taught and also studied law. He also worked for the Kuwaiti Ministry of Justice.

In 1965, he joined Fatah* and took the code name Abu Daoud (father of David). He has claimed to have established El Rasid (the Observations), which was Fatah's intelligence department. He was actively involved as the commander of Palestinian militias in the Palestine Liberation Organization* (PLO) conflict with Jordan from 1968 until the intense fighting between the two in September 1970.* He is said to have been wounded in the leg in one of the battles and spent the duration of the conflict recuperating in Damascus. Fatah used him later to cultivate diplomatic support in Europe, North Korea, and China. A senior Fatah member, Abu Daoud was the founder of the Palestinian Black September* group of Fatah. Abu Daoud had been associated with the assassinations of Jordanian prime minister Wasfi al-Tal* on November 28, 1971, and U.S. ambassador Cleo Noel, Jr., in Khartoum on March 1, 1973. He masterminded the September 1972 terrorist attack on the Israeli Olympic team in Munich,* which resulted in the murder of eleven Israel athletes. Daoud was arrested in Paris on January 7, 1977, traveling on a visa issued to Youssef Roji. Both Israel and West Germany requested his extradition, but the French Court released him on January 11, 1977, and he fled to Algeria. Israel held that France had violated its extradition treaty and recalled its ambassador to France, Mordechai Gazit, and issued a vigorous protest to the French ambassador in Tel Aviv, Jean Herly.

Joseph E. Goldberg

AL-AUJA. A demilitarized zone along the Egypt*–Israel frontier over which Israel took control in 1955. As part of the Israeli-Egyptian Armistice Agreement of 1949,* a triangular-shaped demilitarized zone (DMZ) was established along the old Egypt–Palestine* frontier around the Al-Auja oasis, located fifty kilometers southeast of Rafah in the Gaza Strip.* Neither country was allowed to deploy troops there. Although not formally designated as part of Israel, the Al-Auja DMZ was, in the Israeli interpretation of the Armistice Agreement, considered to be under Israeli sovereignty. Egypt felt that the DMZ was no-man's-land and refused to accept Israeli claims of sovereignty. Before 1948, the Azazme and Tarrabin bedouin tribes lived in and around Al-Auja but fled to Sinai* during the fighting. After the war, hundreds of bedouin families returned to Al-Auja, encouraged, in Israel's view, by the Egyptians. In the early and middle 1950s, the Egyptians encouraged and directed bedouin infiltration and migration from within the Al-Auja DMZ in order to challenge Israel's control over the area. There had been a continuous Israeli effort to impose sovereignty over the DMZ, and this can be seen in Israeli efforts to round up and expel the Azazme bedouin tribes from the Al-Auja zone on August 20, 1950. The Azazme had raided other bedouin tribes in the Negev* and sabotaged Israeli

targets and were considered to be "troublemakers." Just as quickly as the
Azazme were expelled, many infiltrated their way back into Israel, thereby forcing the Israel Defense Forces* (IDF) to repeat such round-up and expulsion
operations. In September 1953, IDF Unit 101* expelled some Azazme bedouins
from Al-Auja into Egypt who were considered to be agents of Egyptian intelligence involved in intelligence gathering and acts of sabotage and mining. Citing the need to increase security in the area, the IDF established a NAHAL*
base called Givat Rahel (later known as Ketziot) next to Al-Auja, which Israel renamed Nitzana. Ketziot subsequently became a civilian kibbutz and army base
from which Nahal troops patrolled the DMZ area. In response, Egypt established
three checkposts along the DMZ border. Following the heightened tension along
the Gaza* border as a result of fedayeen* attacks, incidents in the DMZ increased. On September 20, 1955, Moshe Sharett* and David Ben-Gurion* decided to occupy the DMZ until the Egyptians dismantled the checkposts. On
the night of September 20, the IDF moved into the DMZ and dug trenches and
planted minefields. Withdrawal was made contingent on removal of all the
checkposts in the Egyptian limited forces zone, on Egyptian noninterference
with Israeli border marking, and on the Egyptian agreement to observe the cease-
fire in the DMZ and in Gaza. Egypt agreed to withdraw from positions in the
DMZ, and Israel withdrew most of its forces from the area; however, armed
Israelis remained, and Israel increased the number of minefields planted. The
following days saw a number of Egyptian–Israeli strikes and counterstrikes in
the area, all of which underlay the great tensions between the two countries that
ultimately led to the 1956 war.* Until the Suez War* broke out, a de facto
cease-fire remained in effect through the intervention of Dag Hammarskjold*
and Major General E.L.M. Burns,* and de facto Israeli control of the DMZ
continued.

For further information see: Benny Morris, *Israel's Border Wars 1949–1956* (New
York: Oxford University Press, 1993).

David Salzberg

AUSTIN, WARREN (b. Highgate Center, Vermont, November 12, 1877; d. December 25, 1962). He received his Ph.D. from the University of Vermont and
went on to practice law in both St. Albans and Burlington, Vermont. Austin
served Vermont as a Republican senator from 1931 until 1946. He was anti-
New Deal but internationalist in his foreign policy views.

President Harry Truman* appointed Austin as the first U.S. ambassador to
the United Nations (UN) in 1946, a position he held until 1953. He was a firm
believer in the UN as a forum for the mediation of international disputes.

Austin's interest and involvement in the burgeoning Palestine* crisis centered
on his internationalist philosophy. In the early 1940s, he had been an advocate
of a binational state in Palestine,* only to find the idea unpalatable to the State
Department. When the question arose in 1942 about the continuation of the
Mandate,* Austin expressed the wish that the Allies assume the mantle shed by

Britain so as to allow the establishment of a truly free and independent government in the area. Austin firmly believed that only the Western nations could provide such assistance free from the ideological baggage carried by the Eastern bloc. The flaw in Austin's philosophy was his diplomatic naïveté. Nowhere was this more clearly evident than in his public statements on the Palestine situation. He once stated that the Jews and Arabs should learn to settle their differences like good Christian peoples.

During the work of the United Nations Special Committee on Palestine* (UNSCOP), Austin wrote to Secretary of State George Marshall that the United States should advocate a unitary, independent Palestinian state, neither Jewish nor Arab. Further, he advocated that immigration to the state be restricted to the economic absorptive capacity of the state and that a UN trusteeship be established for up to ten years to prepare the state for independence. Unofficially, this became U.S. policy. The UNSCOP plan that emerged advocated a partitioned state. Eventually, this would be the plan supported by the United States.

For further information see: George T. Mazuzan, *Warren R. Austin at the U.N., 1946–1953* (Kent, Ohio: Kent State University Press, 1977).

Pamela Rivers

AUTONOMY. See **AUTONOMY TALKS, INTERIM SELF-GOVERNING ARRANGEMENTS.**

AUTONOMY TALKS. The Camp David Accords* of September 1978 included a proposal for full autonomy for the Palestinian Arabs living in the West Bank* and Gaza Strip.* The details of this autonomy, including the means of its establishment and the powers the Palestinians would have, were to be determined in future negotiations between Egypt* and Israel. After the signing of the Egypt–Israel Peace Treaty* in March 1979, negotiations were held on the autonomy matter. They began in May 1979. The United States participated at the invitation of both Egypt and Israel. Egypt and Israel each put forward ideas and proposals based on its views of the self-governing authority. Over the succeeding months and years the talks were conducted and suspended. Despite the complexity of the problem and the various suspensions of the dialogue, some agreement was reached between the parties on many of the questions relating to election modalities: they defined a list of powers to be transferred to the autonomous body; they reached agreement that autonomy would not encompass external security or foreign policy; and they agreed that some powers would have to be shared. Discord focused on a number of questions, including the role of the inhabitants of East Jerusalem* in the elections for the autonomous body. Egypt sought to extend the powers granted to the autonomous body that Israel argued should be reserved for an independent state.

Ultimately, despite some agreement, the talks did not produce agreement on a document or a process for according autonomy to the Palestinians. See also INTERIM SELF-GOVERNING ARRANGEMENTS.

AL-AWDA (The return). The concept of return to Palestine* by those who had left during the various wars between the Arabs and Israel, especially the Arab–Israeli War of 1948–49.* See also RIGHT OF RETURN.

B

BAB EL MANDEB. Translated from Arabic, *Bab el Mandeb* means the "Gate of Tears" or the "Gate of Lamentations," or, in other words, a dangerous strait, where slave trade and pirate attacks on merchant ships were common practice in the seventeenth, eighteenth, and nineteenth centuries. The Bab el Mandeb separates Arabia from the Horn of Africa and links the Red Sea to the Indian Ocean's Gulf of Aden. It is 37 kilometers wide but is no more than 25.7 kilometers at the narrowest point. Geographically located at the southernmost end of the Red Sea, the Strait of Bab el Mandeb is the sole point of entrance to, and exit from, the Indian Ocean for shipping to and from Israel's southern port of Eilat* and Jordan's port of Aqaba,* a literal gate, from the Arabic word *bab*.

There are several islands within the strait, the largest one being Perim, which divides the Bab el Mandeb into two branches: the eastern, which is 3.25 kilometers wide and 12 to 29 meters deep, and the western or big one (Arab name Daht-al-Mayoum), which is less than 20 kilometers wide and up to 340 meters deep.

Besides Perim, there are small islands located in the strait. One kilometer off the Yemeni coast lies the rocky Djazirat Ruban Island (called the Pilot Island by the English or the Fishermen Island in some other sources). There are several volcanic, cliffy islands (76 to 108 meters high) situated 14 kilometers north of Perim.

The main channel runs through the Bab el Mandeb's eastern branch. The other runs through the wide western branch close to Perim, which thus dominates the entire strait. Coastal defense installations and a small military garrison of the Yemeni army are located on the island.

During the East–West global confrontation, the Bab el Mandeb was assessed by the great powers primarily from a military and geopolitical point of view.

Through this strait and through the Suez Canal* lies the major water route linking Europe and the Mediterranean Sea to the countries of the Indian Ocean basin and the oil-producing states of the Persian Gulf.

For over two decades the Soviet Union had rather strong positions in the Bab el Mandeb area, having acquired military and political advantages in South Yemen, Ethiopia, and Somali. Djibouti as the West's advanced post cannot be compared to Aden, Assab, Berbera, and Massawa. In practical terms, gaining control of the strait has always been a high-priority goal for the Great Powers. Control of Bab el Mandeb provides extremely advantageous military-strategic positioning.

Until its withdrawal from positions east of Suez in the late 1960s, Great Britain* controlled Perim Island. After the British departure, the South Yemen (People's Democratic Republic of Yemen [PDRY])-controlled National Liberation Front (NLF) took control. South Yemen announced that the island would be used to block trade and travel to and from Israel, through the Bab el Mandeb. Soon thereafter, the Soviet Union sent a small fleet to the northwest corner of the Indian Ocean and, in time, added a few larger ships.

Israel's concern has been to guarantee safe passage of all ships to and from Israel through this strait. In 1971, an attack on a tanker bound for Israel, the *Coral Sea,** by a commando unit based on Perim, with the collusion of PDRY leaders, focused attention on this area.

During the second week of the Yom Kippur War,* the strait was closed by Egyptian artillery and ships, defying Israel's long-standing claim that the guarantee of transit through the straits was necessary. An American ship was shelled by an Egyptian destroyer during the hostilities.

For further information see: Mordechai Abir, *Sharm al-Sheikh—Bab al-Mandeb: The Strategic Balance and Israel's Southern Approaches* (Jerusalem: Leonard Davis Institute for International Relations, Hebrew University of Jerusalem, 1974); Mordechai Abir, *Oil, Power and Politics: Conflict in Arabia, the Red Sea and the Gulf* (London: Frank Cass, 1974); Aaron S. Klieman, ''Bab al-Mandab: The Red Sea in Transition,'' *Orbis* 11 (Fall 1967): 758–71.

Yasha Manuel Harari and Yevgeni Kozlov

BAGHDAD SUMMIT MEETING (1978). After the signing of the Camp David Accords,* a majority of Arab leaders met at the (ninth) Summit in Baghdad, Iraq,* November 2–4, 1978, at the initiative of the government of Iraq. The Summit's communique rejected the Camp David Accords on the grounds that they harmed the Palestinian* cause and contravened resolutions of the Algiers and Rabat Summit conferences forbidding unilateral Arab action in settling the Middle East conflict or solving the Palestinian problem. It noted that a solution to the conflict should be based on joint Arab action decided at an Arab Summit. Among the decisions was the relocation of the Arab League's* headquarters from Cairo to Tunis.

''The conference held discussions with deep awareness of Pan-Arab responsibility and common care for the unity of the Arab stand vis-à-vis the dangers and challenges threatening the Arab nation, particularly following the developments resulting from the signing by the Egyptian* Government of the Camp David accords and their effect on the Arab struggle against the Zionist aggression and the interests of the Arab nation.''

The conference affirmed a number of principles, including:

(1) The cause of Palestine is an Arab fateful cause; it is the essence of the struggle against the Zionist enemy. All the sons and countries of the Arab nation are concerned with this cause and are committed to struggle for it and to make all material and moral sacrifices for it. The struggle for the restoration of Arab rights in Palestine and the occupied Arab territories is a Pan-Arab responsibility. . . . (4) In the light of the above principles it is not permitted for any side to act unilaterally in solving the Palestinian question in particular, and the Arab–Zionist conflict in general. . . .

The conference discussed the two agreements signed by the Egyptian Government at Camp David and considered that they harmed the Palestinian people's rights and the rights of the Arab nation in Palestine and the occupied Arab territory. The conference considered that these agreements have taken place outside the framework of collective Arab responsibility and were opposed to the resolutions of the Arab summit conferences, particularly the resolutions of the Algiers and Rabat summit conferences, the Arab League charter and the UN [United Nations] resolutions on the Palestinian question. . . .

The conference decided to call on the Egyptian Government to abrogate these agreements and not to sign any reconciliation treaty with the enemy. The conference hoped that Egypt would return to the fold of joint Arab action and not act unilaterally in the affairs of the Arab–Zionist conflict.

BAKER, JAMES ADDISON, III (b. Houston, Texas, April 28, 1930). Baker received his B.A. from Princeton University in 1952 and his law degree from the University of Texas Law School in 1957. He served in the U.S. Marine Corps. After practicing law, he served as under secretary of commerce in 1975–76 in the Gerald Ford* administration. From 1981 to 1985 he served as the White House chief of staff for President Ronald Reagan.* In 1985, Baker became secretary of the treasury until he resigned in 1988 to become the chairman of George Bush's* presidential campaign. He served as secretary of state from 1989 to 1992, when he resigned to run Bush's unsuccessful reelection campaign.

In his confirmation hearings in January 1989, Baker raised two issues concerning U.S. Middle East policy. He was critical of congressional earmarking of foreign aid, which mandated that significant percentages of it be given to Israel and Egypt,* and of congressional opposition to arms sales to Arab states. In response to a question, Baker said that the Department of State would continue to monitor Palestine Liberation Organization* (PLO) activities to ensure that Yasser Arafat's* pledge to renounce terrorism was being fulfilled. Nevertheless, Baker said that Arafat might not be able to control all of the PLO factions, and for that reason the United States must look at the whole picture and judge PLO actions with good faith.

On April 14, 1989, Baker said that U.S. policy is intended "to reduce tensions, to promote dialogue between Israelis and Palestinians,* and to build an environment that can sustain negotiations on interim arrangements and permanent status." This was conceived by the administration as a step-by-step process to bring about Israeli–Palestinian discussions as a way to facilitate a broader peace.

Responding to administration pressure, Israeli prime minister Yitzhak Shamir* presented an Israeli initiative on May 14, 1989,* in which he proposed that there be "free and democratic elections among the Palestinian Arab inhabitants of Judea,* Samaria,* and the Gaza* district in an atmosphere devoid of violence, threats and terror." The elections would select representatives to conduct negotiations with Israel for a transitional period of self-rule, which would constitute a test for cooperation and coexistence and eventually lead to negotiations for a permanent solution.

In a major policy statement to the American Israel Public Affairs Committee* in Washington, D.C., on May 22, 1989, Baker emphasized that the right mix of principles and pragmatism is required to make progress. He stated that a comprehensive settlement must be based on United Nations Resolutions 242* and 338,* that they must be face-to-face negotiations, that there must be a transitional period between the negotiations and the final settlement because of the complexity of the issues, that there will be no dictation of the final outcome by the United States or any other nation, and that the middle ground to settlement should be self-government for the Palestinians in the West Bank* and Gaza. None of these principles contradicted statements made by American officials. What did create controversy, however, was the cool and calculating style in which he made the presentation. Unlike previous U.S. secretaries of state, Baker showed no emotional involvement with Israel. Further, toward the conclusion of the speech, Baker challenged the Revisionist Zionist dream of Israel when he said, "For Israel, now is the time to lay aside, once and for all, the unrealistic vision of a greater Israel. Israeli interests in the West Bank and Gaza—security and otherwise—can be accommodated in a settlement based on Resolution 242. Forswear annexation. Stop settlement activity. Allow schools to reopen. Reach out to the Palestinians as neighbors who deserve political rights."

What followed from May to September 1989 was disagreement concerning what constituted an atmosphere devoid of violence, who were acceptable negotiating partners, whether residents of the West Bank who had been deported could participate, and whether Arabs residing in East Jerusalem* constituted Arabs living in the territories. In September 1989, Egyptian president Hosni Mubarak proposed a ten-point plan,* and in October Baker also sought to facilitate the negotiations by offering a five-point plan.*

Little progress was made, and, in the spring of 1990, the government in Israel fell on a vote of no confidence. In June 1990, Shamir formed a right-of-center government that suggested more difficulty in pursuing Baker's approach.

In an outburst while testifying on Capitol Hill on June 13, 1990, the secretary of state indicated his frustration with Israel when he declared that Israel can call the White House when it is serious about peace. With emphasis, he slowly recited the telephone number of the White House. On June 28, 1990, Shamir rejected the U.S. proposals for talks based on the question of representation of the Arab delegation.

In August 1990, the crisis generated by Iraq's* invasion of Kuwait diverted Baker from Arab–Israeli issues. After the beginning of the Gulf War,* while appearing before the Senate Foreign Relations Committee on February 6, 1991, Baker outlined the elements of future U.S. policy, defining the new world order.* Included was "the search for a just peace and real reconciliation for Israel, the Arab states and the Palestinians." In the following months Baker traveled to the Middle East eight times to initiate the Madrid Peace Conference* and the ensuing process.

For further information see: Sanford R. Silverburg, "The Bush Administration and the Middle East," *JIME Review,* no. 9 (Spring 1990): 60–71.

Joseph E. Goldberg

BAKER FIVE-POINT PLAN (OCTOBER 1989). See **FIVE-POINT PLAN.**

BAKER PLAN (OCTOBER 1989). See **FIVE-POINT PLAN.**

BALFOUR DECLARATION. The declaration, issued by the British government on November 2, 1917, took the form of a letter from Arthur James Balfour, the foreign secretary, to Lord Rothschild, a prominent British Zionist* leader. Substantial effort by the Zionist organization, with a special role played by Chaim Weizmann,* preceded the government's decision, after lengthy discussion and some division. It stated:

His majesty's government view with favour the establishment in Palestine* of a national home for the Jewish people, and will use their best endeavours to facilitate the achievement of this object, it being clearly understood that nothing shall be done which may prejudice the civil and religious rights of existing non-Jewish communities in Palestine, or the rights and political status enjoyed by Jews in any other country.

The declaration was vague and sought to assuage the fears of prominent Jews in England as well as those of the non-Jewish inhabitants of Palestine. Nevertheless, it engendered much controversy, then and since. Among the problems was the Balfour Declaration's apparent conflict with arrangements made during World War I by the British with the French in the Sykes–Picot Agreement* and with the Arabs concerning the future of the Middle East after the termination of hostilities. Foremost among those was the Hussein–McMahon correspondence,* which the Arabs saw as a promise that an independent Arab kingdom would include all of Palestine, although the British later argued that they had excluded the territory west of the Jordan River* from that pledge. The declaration provided a basis for Zionist claims to Palestine.

See also PUBLIC RESOLUTION NO. 73, 67TH CONGRESS, SECOND SESSION, SEPTEMBER 21, 1922.

For further information see: Arthur James Balfour, *Speeches on Zionism* (London: Arrowsmith, 1928); Blanche Dugdale, *Arthur James Balfour,* 2 vols. (London: Hutchinson, 1936); Rashid Ismail Khalidi, *British Policy towards Syria and Palestine 1906–1914: A Study of Antecedents of the Hussein-the ["sic"] McMahon Correspondence, the Sykes-Picot Agreement, and the Balfour Declaration* (London: Ithaca Press [for The Middle East Centre, St. Antony's College], 1980); Jon Kimche, *The Unromantics: The Great Powers and the Balfour Declaration* (London: Weidenfeld and Nicolson, 1968); Ronald Sanders, *The High Walls of Jerusalem: A History of the Balfour Declaration and the Birth of the British Mandate for Palestine* (New York: Holt, Rinehart and Winston, 1983); Leonard Stein, *The Balfour Declaration* (London: Vallentine, Mitchell, 1961); Mayir Verete, "The Balfour Declaration and Its Makers," *Middle Eastern Studies* 6 (January 1970): 48–76.

AL-BANNA, SABRI. See **ABU NIDAL.**

EL-BANNAH, SABRI. See **ABU NIDAL.**

BAR-LEV, HAIM (b. Vienna, Austria, November 16, 1924; d. Tel Aviv, May 7, 1994). Bar-Lev emigrated to Palestine* in 1939 from Zagreb, Yugoslavia. He graduated from the Mikveh Yisrael agricultural school. While still in school, he joined the Haganah.* He later joined and served in the Palmach* (from 1942 to 1948), and, during the War of Independence,* Bar-Lev commanded a battalion of the Negev Brigade that repulsed the Egyptian attack. In the 1956 Sinai War,* he was a colonel in command of the Armored Corps, and his unit was among the first to reach the Suez Canal.* From 1957 to 1961, Bar-Lev was commander of the Armored Corps. He spent time studying for his M.B.A. at Columbia University in New York and then became commanding officer of the Northern Command in 1962. From 1964 until May 1966, when he went to Paris for advanced military courses, Bar-Lev served as chief of the General Staff Branch Operations of the Israel Defense Forces* (IDF). He returned to Israel in May 1967 and was appointed deputy chief of staff. He was deputy chief of staff to Yitzhak Rabin* during the Six Day War* and became chief of staff of the IDF on January 1, 1968. He remained in that post until he retired in 1971. He was responsible for the building of the Bar-Lev Line* fortifications along the Suez Canal.* Bar-Lev became chief of staff during a period in which the Israel Defense Forces had to convert from an attack-oriented army into a defensive one without forfeiting any of its offensive qualities and capabilities. In response to continuing attacks and the escalation by President Gamal Abdul Nasser* of Egypt in the War of Attrition,* he reversed the war and created the defensive fortifications along the Suez Canal that came to be known as the Bar-Lev Line.

During the Yom Kippur War,* he served as commander of the Egyptian

Front. He was elected in 1973 as a member of Knesset* for the Alignment-Labor Party.* He served as minister of commerce, industry and development between 1972 and 1977. In 1978, he was elected secretary-general of the Labor Party. From 1984 to 1988, he served as minister of police in the National Unity government, and he was reappointed to that post in the government established in December 1988. His last post was as ambassador to Russia, to which he was appointed in 1992.

For further information see: Generals of Israel (Tel Aviv: Hadar, 1968).

BAR-LEV LINE. A defensive system on the east bank of the Suez Canal* constructed by the Israel Defense Forces* during the tenure of Haim Bar-Lev* as chief of staff. The Bar-Lev Line was essentially a series of fortifications and strong points constructed along the Suez Canal to withstand artillery shelling and other weapons and tended to reduce Israeli manpower requirements and potential casualties along the Suez Canal.

It was a defensive network of fortifications along the east bank of the Suez Canal built between January and February 1969. It consisted initially of seventeen *maozim,* or strong points, at ten to thirty-kilometer intervals along the canal, each manned by thirty to ninety soldiers and controlling a front of just under one mile. These were backed by artillery and armored concentrations located farther inland along the artillery and lateral roads. Forward of the strong points, the Israelis built sand ramparts three to ten meters high to block vehicles from crossing and to prevent observation and direct fire from Egyptian forces. Between each position were observation posts and armored patrols with connecting roads linking them together for rapid reinforcement. The strongholds themselves were huge sand bunkers with underground command centers, maintenance facilities, storage areas, underground fuel tanks, and water and communication systems. They were defended by minefields, wire obstacles, and firing ports. Bunkers located in isolated areas or on the anchor points in the north and south were supplemented with extra tank contingents and commanded by field-grade officers. Smaller groupings of tanks were situated along the bank where they had enfilade fire along the canal. In all, the Israel Defense Forces deployed two armored brigades forward along the defensive positions, with one additional brigade to the rear for a total of nearly 300 tanks.

The line was viewed by Egypt* as a permanent, impregnable military presence indicating that the Israelis intended to keep the Sinai.* Subsequently, just after its initial construction, they bombarded it in what has been called the War of Attrition.* Egyptian artillery attacks forced the Israelis to rely on the bunkers for cover. As the Bar-Lev Line became more a series of shelters than fighting positions, Israel's reliance on early warning of an attack across the canal increased.

Believing that the artillery and armored units deployed inland were vulnerable to Egyptian artillery attacks, General Ariel Sharon* constructed a second line of defenses, including eleven fortifications, interior roads, and artificial barriers five to seven kilometers to the rear. Extensive minefields were also laid, along with barbed-wire obstacles and roads across the marshes and lagoons in the north. In all, more than $40 million was spent on the defensive network.

Israeli officers recognized that the Bar-Lev Line was vulnerable to suppression from Egyptian artillery and could not hold against an attack but believed they needed a ground presence to prevent Egyptian commandos from seizing the east bank of the canal and calling for a cease-fire. In order to limit the vulnerability of Israeli troops, the individual contingents were reduced to as low as twenty men in January 1972, with ten of the then-twenty-six *maozim* being closed.

When the Yom Kippur War* began in 1973, those positions where the Israeli troops were suppressed by Egyptian artillery attacks were quickly penetrated, while those positions that were not suppressed held off the first assaults. When the local armored units advanced to support the bunkers, they were ambushed by Egyptian commandos armed with Soviet-made rocket-propelled grenades (RPGs). Lacking sufficient early warning, the Israelis were unable to reinforce the armored units and relieve the fortifications. Those not taken in the initial attack or evacuated were forced to surrender. Following the war there was much domestic criticism within Israel over the ''failure'' of the Bar-Lev Line.

For further information see: Avraham Adan, *On the Banks of the Suez: An Israeli General's Personal Account of the Yom Kippur War* (San Rafael, CA: Presidio Press, 1980); Peter Allen, *The Yom Kippur War* (New York: Charles Scribner's Sons, 1982); Yaacov Bar-Siman-Tov, ''The Bar-Lev Line Revisited,'' *Journal of Strategic Studies* 11 (June 1988): 149–76; Chaim Herzog, *The War of Atonement, October 1963* (Boston: Little, Brown, 1975); Edgar O'Ballance, *No Victor, No Vanquished: The Yom Kippur War* (San Rafael, CA: Presidio Press, 1978).

David J. Abram

BARAK, EHUD (b. Kibbutz Mishmar Hasharon, Palestine,* February 12, 1942). His university education included undergraduate studies in physics and mathematics at Hebrew University and a master's degree from Stanford University in California in systems analysis. He enlisted in the Israel Defense Forces* (IDF) in 1959 and was schooled in various military educational courses and held a number of significant military assignments. He served as director of military intelligence* from 1983 to 1986 and later as deputy chief of staff of the Israel Defense Forces. He became chief of staff in April 1991, a post he retained until his retirement at the end of 1994. He is credited with fighting terrorist and fundamentalist groups opposed to the peace process and especially the Israel–Palestine Liberation Organization* (PLO) Declaration of Principles* and the Cairo Agreement.* During that tenure he became the primary adviser on security issues to Yitzhak Rabin* when he again became prime minister in 1992. He was also responsible for the beginning of the reorientation of the IDF's tasks in response to the changing security situation resulting from the Israel–PLO DOP and the Israel–Jordan Peace Treaty.*

BASEL PROGRAM. See **BASLE PROGRAM.**

BASLE PROGRAM. On August 23, 1897, in Basle (or Basel), Switzerland, Theodor Herzl* convened the first World Zionist Congress, representing Jewish communities and organizations throughout the world. The congress established the World Zionist Organization* (WZO) and founded an effective, modern, political Jewish national movement with the goal, enunciated in the Basle Program (the original official program of the WZO), that "Zionism seeks to establish a home for the Jewish people in Palestine secured under public law." In reality this meant the creation of a Jewish state. Zionism* rejected other solutions to the "Jewish Question"* and was a political response to centuries of discrimination, persecution, and oppression. It sought redemption through self-determination. Herzl argued in *Der Judenstaat*: "Let the sovereignty be granted us over a portion of the globe large enough to satisfy the rightful requirements of a nation; the rest we shall manage for ourselves." For the attainment of the aims of the Basle Program, the congress envisaged the promotion of the settlement of Palestine* by Jewish agriculturists, artisans, and tradesmen; the organization and unification of the whole of Jewry by means of appropriate local and general institutions in accordance with the laws of each country; the strengthening of Jewish national sentiment and national consciousness; and preparatory steps toward securing the consent of governments, which was thought to be necessary to attain the aim of Zionism.

BAZ, OSSAMA EL (b. 1931). He graduated from the University of Cairo in 1952 with a degree in law. He holds a master's degree and a doctorate in law from Harvard University. In 1975, he became director of the Office of the Minister of Foreign Affairs' office. In 1977, he was named the director of the vice president's office.

He was recruited by President Anwar Sadat* in the mid-1970s to be an active player in the peace negotiations team with Israel. In 1981, he was appointed by President Hosni Mubarak* to head his office and be his adviser for political affairs. In that position he has been an instrumental factor in defining Egypt's* role and position in the Arab–Israeli conflict and peace process.

Ahmed Elbashari

BEGIN, MENACHEM (b. Brest-Litovsk, White Russia [later Poland], August 16, 1913; d. Tel Aviv, March 9, 1992). Menachem Begin was born the son of Zeev-Dov and Hassia Begin. He was educated in Brest-Litovsk at the Mizrachi Hebrew School and later studied and graduated in law at the University of Warsaw. After a short association with Hashomer Hatzair, he became a devoted follower of Vladimir Zeev Jabotinsky,* the founder of the Revisionist Zionist Movement.* At the age of sixteen he joined Betar,* the youth movement affiliated with the Zionist Revisionist Movement, and in 1932 he became the head of the Organization Department of Betar in Poland. Later, after a period of service as head of Betar in Czechoslovakia, he returned to Poland in 1937 and, in 1939, became head of the movement there. In 1939, he married Aliza Arnold (d. 1982).

Upon the outbreak of World War II, he was arrested by the Russian authorities and confined in concentration camps in Siberia and elsewhere until his release in 1941. He joined the Polish army and was dispatched to the Middle East, arriving in Palestine* in 1942. After demobilization in 1943, Begin remained in Palestine and assumed command of the Irgun Tzvai Leumi.* For his activities against the British authorities as head of that organization, he was placed on their "most wanted" list and managed to evade capture by living underground in Tel Aviv.

With the independence of Israel in 1948 and the dissolution of the Irgun, Begin founded the Herut (Freedom) Party* and represented it in the Knesset,* since its first meetings in 1949. He became Herut's leader, retaining that position until he resigned from office as prime minister and retired from public and political life in 1983. Herut was known for its right-wing, strongly nationalistic views, and Begin led the party's protest campaign against the reparations agreement with West Germany in 1952. He was instrumental in establishing the Gahal faction (a merger of Herut and the Liberal Party) in the Knesset in 1965. He developed a reputation as a gifted orator, writer, and political leader. Begin remained in opposition in Parliament until the eve of the Six Day War* of June 1967, when he joined the government of National Unity as minister without portfolio. He and his Gahal colleagues resigned from the government in August 1970 over opposition to its acceptance of the peace initiative of U.S. secretary of state William Rogers (Rogers Plan*), which implied the evacuation by Israel of territories occupied in the course of the Six Day War. Later, Gahal joined in forming the Likud bloc* in opposition to the governing Labor Alignment, and Begin became its leader.

After the elections of May 1977, Begin became Israel's first nonsocialist prime minister when the Likud bloc secured the mandate to form the government. He also became the first Israeli prime minister to meet officially and publicly with an Arab head of state when he welcomed Egyptian president Anwar Sadat* to Jerusalem* in November 1977. He led Israel's delegations to the ensuing peace negotiations and signed, with Sadat and U.S. president Jimmy Carter,* the Camp David Accords* in September 1978. In March 1979, he and Egyptian president Sadat signed the Egypt–Israel Peace Treaty,* with Carter witnessing the event, on the White House lawn in Washington. Begin and Sadat shared the 1978 Nobel Peace Prize for their efforts. For Begin and for Israel, it was a momentous but difficult accomplishment. It brought peace with Israel's most populous adversary and significantly reduced the military danger to the existence of Israel by neutralizing the largest Arab army, with which Israel had fought five wars. However, it was also traumatic, given the extensive tangible concessions required of Israel, especially the uprooting of Jewish settlements in Sinai.*

The Knesset election of June 30, 1981, returned a Likud-led coalition government to power in Israel, contrary to early predictions that projected a significant Labor Alignment victory. Menachem Begin again became prime minister, and his reestablished government coalition contained many of the same personalities as the outgoing group and reflected similar perspectives of Israel's situation and of appropriate government policies. He also served as minister of foreign affairs in 1979–80 and as minister of defense from May 1980 to August 1981.

The War in Lebanon,* which occasioned debate and demonstration within Israel, resulted in substantial casualties and led, at least initially, to Israel's increased international isolation and major clashes with the United States. Many of the outcomes were muted over time, but the war left a legacy that continued to be debated long after Begin retired from public life. It was also a factor in Begin's decision to step down from the prime minister's office, but it was a decision he chose, and was not forced, to make.

Within Israel, Begin's tenure was marked by prosperity for the average citizen, although there were indicators (such as rising debt and inflation levels) that this might prove costly in the long term. The standard of living rose, as did the level of expectations. The religious parties enhanced their political power and secured important concessions from a coalition that recognized their increased role in maintaining the political balance and from a prime minister who was, on the whole, sympathetic to their positions.

The relationship with the United States underwent significant change during Begin's tenure. The ties were often tempestuous, as the two states disagreed on various aspects of the regional situation and the issues associated with resolution of the Arab–Israeli conflict. Nevertheless, U.S. economic and military assistance and political and diplomatic support rose to all-time high levels.

Begin's political skills were considerable and apparent. Despite his European origins and courtly manner, he was able, through his powerful oratorical skills, charismatic personality, and political and economic policies, to secure and maintain a substantial margin of popularity over other major political figures, particularly the opposition leaders. At the time of his resignation he was the most popular and highly regarded of Israeli politicians, as the public opinion polls regularly indicated.

Menachem Begin's decision to resign as prime minister of Israel on September 16, 1983, brought to an end a major era in Israeli politics. It was a surprise and a shock to Israelis, notwithstanding Begin's earlier statements that he would retire from politics at age seventy. Although no formal reason for his resignation was forthcoming, Begin apparently believed that he could no longer perform his tasks as he felt he ought to, and he seemed to be severely affected by the death of his wife the previous year and by the continuing casualties suffered by Israeli forces in Lebanon.*

After his retirement from public life, he was a virtual recluse. He rarely went out of his Jerusalem apartment into public except for medical treatment or to put flowers on his wife's grave. As the memory of the War in Lebanon receded, his stature in popular opinion grew once again.

Menachem Begin wrote *White Nights: The Story of a Prisoner in Russia* (describing his wartime experiences in Europe) and *The Revolt* (describing the struggle against the British) and numerous articles.

For further information see: Frank H. Gervasi, *The Life and Times of Menachem Begin: Rebel to Statesman* (New York: G. P. Putnam and Sons, 1979); Eitan Haber, *Menachem Begin: The Legend and the Man* (New York: Dell Books, 1979); Gertrude Hirshler and Lester S. Eckman, *From Fighter to Statesman: Menachem Begin* (New York: Shengold, 1979); Harry Hurewitz, *Menachem Begin* (Johannesburg: Jewish Herald, 1977); Ilan Peleg, *Begin's Foreign Policy, 1977–1983: Israel's Move to the Right* (Westport, CT: Greenwood Press, 1987); Ilan Peleg, "Menachem Begin," in Bernard Reich, ed., *Political Leaders of the Contemporary Middle East and North Africa: A Biographical Dictionary* (Westport, CT: Greenwood Press, 1990), pp. 71–78; Amos Perlmutter, *The Life and Times of Menachem Begin* (Garden City, NY: Doubleday, 1987); Eric Silver, *Begin: The Haunted Prophet* (New York: Random House, 1984); Ned Temko, *To Win or Die: A Personal Portrait of Menachem Begin* (New York: William Morrow, 1987).

BEILIN, YOSSI (b. 1948). He joined the Labor Party* in 1977 after lecturing and doing research in politics at Tel Aviv University. He was appointed Cabinet secretary in 1984 and served as director general of the Foreign Ministry from 1986 to 1988 and as deputy finance minister from 1988 to 1990. Beilin was elected to the Knesset* in 1988. He became deputy minister of foreign affairs under Shimon Peres* in 1992. He has been a close confidant of Peres. He was an active player in the peace process and especially in the Oslo talks* that led to the signing of the Israel–Palestine Liberation Organization* (PLO) Declaration of Principles* in Washington in September 1993.

For further information see: Yossi Beilin, *Israel: A Concise Political History* (New York: St. Martin's Press, 1992).

BEIRUT AIRPORT RAID (Otherwise known as Operation Teshura). On the night of July 22, 1968, three members of the Popular Front for the Liberation of Palestine* (PFLP), headed by George Habash,* attacked an Israeli El Al plane carrying forty-two passengers, twelve of whom were Israeli citizens, traveling from Rome to Tel Aviv. The hijackers forced the plane to land in Algeria, where they released all non-Israeli passengers. On July 29, the terrorists released an Israeli woman and three children. Seven crew members and five Israelis remained hostages in Algiers. Following indirect negotiations with the terrorists, Israel released fifteen Palestinians jailed in Israel in exchange for the remaining hostages, who returned to Israel on August 31. The hijackers went free.

Four months later, the organization, based in Lebanon,* struck again. On December 26, 1968, two members of the PFLP entered the Athens airport and approached an El Al plane about to leave for Milan, Italy. They fired machine guns and threw hand grenades at the loaded plane, killing a passenger.

In retaliation, the Israeli government decided to execute a raid against the Beirut Airport. The decision to carry out such an attack and the plans for it had been made a half-year earlier, but no date had been set for its execution. The decision to execute the raid resulted directly from the terrorist attack on the El Al plane in Athens. Israel argued that it was justified in the Beirut raid since the attackers of an El Al airplane at Athens, where they sought to destroy an El Al aircraft and killed a passenger, had maintained their headquarters in Beirut, where they were allowed to function freely, and it was from Beirut Airport that they had departed for their Athens mission. The Athens incident was the second act of violence in six months by a Beirut-based Palestinian* group directed against the Israel national airline.

The Israeli retaliatory raid took place on December 28, 1968. One hundred and fifty Israeli soldiers, including paratroop units, participated in the attack. Since Israel wanted to draw attention to this operation, all units involved were dressed in Israeli uniforms. The attack began when three Israeli military planes and a helicopter carrying the command element, led by Rafael Eitan,* landed at Beirut Airport. Four Israeli missile-bearing ships waited along Beirut's shores to evacuate soldiers in case ground forces encountered heavy resistance.

Soldiers blew up Lebanese Middle East Airlines planes parked at the airport. Passengers were removed from a plane about to depart, and it, too, was destroyed. The main difficulty Israeli units encountered was in convincing Lebanese airport workers that this was not a Lebanese military exercise but an actual Israeli raid. As a result, Israeli paratroopers had to forcefully evacuate Lebanese technicians from one of the large hangers.

The entire operation on the ground in Beirut lasted twenty-nine minutes. A total of thirteen Lebanese planes were destroyed; one was undamaged when a bomb failed to explode. Israeli forces suffered no casualties and lost no equipment. The successful attack on the Beirut Airport became a model for the Israel Defense Forces (IDF)* for numerous subsequent retaliatory raids.

On December 31, 1968, after considerable debate, the United Nations Security Council unanimously (fifteen to none) adopted a resolution (262) in which it condemned "Israel for its premeditated military action in violation of its obligations under the Charter and the cease-fire resolutions."

Worldwide condemnation, including U.S. disapproval, was expressed at an emergency meeting of the United Nations Security Council on December 31. The late-night emergency session, requested by Lebanon and Israel, ended with a unanimous vote for Israeli censure. Although President Lyndon Johnson* described the Israeli attack as "serious and unwise," the recently concluded American sale of fifty F-4 Phantom jets* to Israel was not reconsidered. Had the American presidency not been between administrations at the time of the attack, the suggestion exists that the U.S. condemnation of Israel might have been more substantive.

For further information see: Yehuda Z. Blum, "The Beirut Raid and the International Double Standard: A Reply to Professor Richard A. Falk," *American Journal of International Law* 64 (January 1970): 73–105; Richard A. Falk, "The Beirut Raid and the International Law of Retaliation," *American Journal of International Law* 63 (July 1969): 415–43; Edward Haley, *Lebanon in Crisis* (Syracuse, NY: Syracuse University

Press, 1979); Tabitha Petran, *The Struggle over Lebanon* (New York: Monthly Review Press, 1987); Itamar Rabinovich, *The War for Lebanon, 1970–83* (Ithaca, NY: Cornell University Press, 1984); Anthony Sampson, *The Arms Bazaar* (New York: Viking Press, 1977); Avner Yaniv, *Dilemmas of Security, Politics, Strategy, and the Israeli Experience in Lebanon* (New York: Oxford University Press, 1987).

Robert Crangle, Jr., and David Wurmser

BEIT LID. The Beit Lid road junction near Netanya was the site of a major terrorist attack against Israel on January 22, 1995. In the terrorist attack, nineteen Israelis (eighteen soldiers) were killed, and sixty-two were wounded. One or more Palestinian* terrorists detonated two bombs near a crowd of Israeli soldiers waiting to return to their bases after weekend leaves. A bomb was placed against the wall of a cafeteria where soldiers had gathered and was activated by remote control. Shortly afterward, one of the terrorists detonated explosives strapped to his body just as people nearby had arrived to assist the injured and as other soldiers attempted to apprehend him. Islamic Jihad* took responsibility for the act. The Israeli Cabinet decided to close the occupied territories, suspend the planned release of additional Palestinian prisoners and the opening of the safe passage routes* between the Gaza Strip* and Jericho,* and continue peace process negotiations.

BEKA (BEQA) VALLEY (al-Biqa in Arabic, meaning "the valley"). It is located in eastern Lebanon,* between Mount Lebanon and the Anti-Lebanon mountains in Syria.* The Orontes River flows through the valley to the north, and the Litani River* to the south. Located in the southeastern part of Lebanon between the Litani River and the Syrian border, the Beka Valley has been an area of conflict. One of Israel's main objectives in the War in Lebanon* was to rid the valley of Palestinian* terrorists. The valley had become a haven for terror training camps and was used to target civilian populations in Israel's Galilee.

In January 1980, the Syrians announced a withdrawal of some of their forces from Beirut and the coastal areas of Lebanon. They were then redeployed along the road from Beirut to Damascus, but the majority were based in the Beka Valley. Syria wanted most to create and preserve a strong defensive position in the valley, which the Syrians had controlled since 1976. The valley is considered strategically crucial to the defense of Damascus. Also, bases in the Beka Valley could be used for offensive deployment against Israel.

Syria was known to have offensive missiles in the valley, and, in 1981, their presence was perceived by Israel as a threat to its security. By June 1982, the Israeli Cabinet decided that it must rid southern Lebanon of the Palestine Liberation Organization's* (PLO) influence and terrorist training camps to secure safety for northern Israel. It was believed that this objective could not be achieved unless the Palestinians were ousted from the Beka Valley. By the third day of the war, Israel outflanked Syrian troops in the valley and continued to destroy Syrian missiles and shoot down Syrian aircraft. In the process Israeli forces came close to Damascus via the Beka Valley.

The Israelis were able to destroy most of the PLO's infrastructure in southern Lebanon, but, by the end of the war, Syria still remained in control of parts of the Beka Valley.

Susan L. Rosenstein

BEN-ELISAR, ELIAHU (Formerly Gottlieb) (b. Radom, Poland, February 2, 1932). He immigrated to Palestine* in 1942. His original family name was Gottlieb, and when he Hebraized his name, he did so by combining the first half of his father's two names (Eliezer Yisrael) to create Ben-Elisar. He was educated in political science and international law at the University of Paris. During that time, he was enlisted by the Mossad,* where he worked until 1965. In 1965, Ben-Elisar left the Mossad to pursue his doctorate at the University of Geneva, where he wrote on the Jewish factor in the foreign policy of the Third Reich. It was published as a book in 1969. He returned to Israel and worked as a correspondent for several European newspapers. He also became involved in Herut Party* political activities and in 1971 began to serve as head of the Information Department of the Herut Movement. He served as director general of Prime Minister Menachem Begin's* office and as Israel's first ambassador to Egypt.* A member of the Knesset* on the Likud list,* Ben-Elisar served as chairman of the Foreign Affairs and Security Committee of the Tenth Knesset.

BEN-GURION, DAVID (Formerly Gruen) (b. Plonsk, Poland, October 16, 1886; d. December 1, 1973). Under the influence of his father and grandfather, he became a committed Zionist* in childhood. In September 1906, he arrived in Jaffa. He was elected to the Central Committee of the Poalei Zion (Workers of Zion) and began organizing workers into unions. In 1910, he joined the editorial staff of a new Poalei Zion paper, *Ahdut* (Unity) in Jerusalem* and began publishing articles under the name Ben-Gurion. He joined a group of young socialist Zionists who went to study at Turkish universities and moved in 1912 to the University of Constantinople, where he earned a law degree with highest honors. In 1914, Ben-Gurion returned to Palestine* and resumed his work as union organizer; but, in 1915, he was exiled by Ottoman authorities. In May 1918, he enlisted in a Jewish battalion of the British Royal Fusiliers and sailed to Egypt* to join the expeditionary force. From 1921 to 1935, Ben-Gurion was the general secretary of the Histadrut* and was instrumental in the founding of the United Labor Party, which eventually became MAPAI.* In the 1920s and 1930s, Chaim Weizmann,* the head of the World Zionist Organization* and chief diplomat of the Zionist movement, ran general Zionist affairs while Ben-Gurion headed Zionist activities in Palestine, where his major rival was Vladimir Jabotinsky.* Convinced that Revisionist Zionists* under Jabotinsky were endangering the drive toward eventual statehood, Ben-Gurion sought to undermine and discredit

Revisionism. In 1935, Ben-Gurion defeated the forces of Chaim Weizmann and was elected chairman of the Jewish Agency Executive,* a post in which he served from 1935 to 1948.

Ben-Gurion assumed responsibility for the defense portfolio in the Zionist Executive in December 1946. The creation of this responsibility was a recognition by the twenty-second Zionist Congress, meeting in Basle, that the British would eventually withdraw from Palestine. The Yishuv realized that British evacuation required preparation for its own defense. Ben-Gurion saw his task as transforming the Haganah* from a security organization into an army capable of protecting Israel from hostile Arab armies. This effort required a reorganization of the Haganah General Staff, an increase in recruitment for the Jewish forces, and the equipment of the force itself. Furthermore, Ben-Gurion was adamant that the Israel Defense Forces* be under civilian control and free of politicalization. On the last issue, he was challenged by the Yishuv's political parties of the Left, especially MAPAM, which had strong influence, if not control, over the Palmach.* On May 26, 1948, Israel's government passed the Israel Defense Forces order establishing its defense forces—an act that reflected Ben-Gurion's guidance.

Recognized as the founder of Israel, Ben-Gurion served as prime minister from 1948 to 1963, except for two years from 1953 to 1955, when he voluntarily retired to Sde Boker in the Negev* to seek respite from the rigors of his long political career and to dramatize the significance of pioneering and reclaiming the desert. In 1955, when Pinhas Lavon* was forced to resign as minister of defense, Ben-Gurion left Sde Boker to become minister of defense in the government headed by Moshe Sharett.* After the election of 1955, Ben-Gurion undertook to form a new government. However, the eruption of the Lavon affair in 1960 brought disarray to MAPAI, and Ben-Gurion's political strength eroded. It was also the period of the Eichmann trial. He resigned as prime minister in June 1963. Ben-Gurion founded a new political party, RAFI, in 1965 and remained in the Knesset* until he resigned in 1970.

Ben-Gurion was a prolific author. Among his many works are *Israel: Years of Challenge* (New York: Holt, Rinehart and Winston, 1963); *The Jews in Their Land* (Garden City, NY: Doubleday, 1966); *Israel: A Personal History* (New York: Funk and Wagnalls, 1971); *Letters to Paula* (London: Vallentine, Mitchell, 1971); and *My Talks with Arab Leaders* (Jerusalem: Keter, 1972).

For further information see: Michael Bar Zohar, *Ben-Gurion, A Biography,* trans. Peretz Kidron (New York: Delacorte Press, 1978); Marver H. Bernstein, "David Ben-Gurion," in Bernard Reich, ed., *Political Leaders of the Contemporary Middle East and North Africa: A Biographical Dictionary* (Westport, CT: Greenwood Press, 1990), pp. 97–108; Barnet Litvinoff, *Ben-Gurion of Israel* (London: Weidenfeld and Nicolson, 1954); Moshe Pearlman, ed., *Ben-Gurion Looks Back in Talks with Moshe Pearlman* (New York: Simon and Schuster, 1964); Robert St. John, *Ben-Gurion* (New York: Doubleday, 1971); Shabtai Teveth, *Ben-Gurion: The Burning Ground 1886–1948* (Boston:

Houghton Mifflin, 1987); Ronald W. Zweig, ed., *Ben-Gurion* (London: Frank Cass, 1991).

Joseph E. Goldberg

BERNADOTTE, COUNT FOLKE (b. 1895; d. Jerusalem,* September 17, 1948). Count Folke Bernadotte was a Swedish diplomat appointed by the United Nations (UN) General Assembly to mediate during the war between the newly established state of Israel and the neighboring Arab states. On May 21, 1948, UN secretary-general Trygve Lie confirmed Bernadotte's appointment to the position of mediator. Prior to his appointment, Bernadotte knew very little about the conflict. He immediately flew to Paris, where he met with colleagues to discuss the conflict and arrived in Egypt* on May 28 to begin his duties.

On May 30, Bernadotte began negotiations for a truce, which was secured by June 9 between Israel and Egypt, Jordan,* Lebanon,* Syria,* and Iraq.* The truce was put into effect on June 11 and was to last until July 9. It stipulated that no additional weapons or troops were to be introduced into the area, Jewish male immigrants of military age were to be held in camps under UN supervision, and the people in Jerusalem were to be allowed only one month's food supplies. Neither side observed these restrictions, and numerous serious truce violations were overlooked, in part, because of the lack of UN manpower to enforce the truce. The Arab armies used the truce to fortify their units with additional manpower. The Israelis were able to significantly strengthen their position by smuggling a substantial number of weapons and integrating several thousand military-aged immigrants into their fighting forces.

Bernadotte wanted to extend the truce and work out a political settlement between the parties. On June 17, he proposed a settlement that was a variation on the November 1947 Partition Resolution.* There was to be a union between an independent, enlarged Transjordan* and an independent Jewish area governed by a Parliament to undertake matters of mutual concern. Unlimited Jewish immigration would be allowed for the first two years, and then decisions on future immigration would be decided by the UN Social and Economic Council. Palestinian Arabs were to be allowed to return to their homes and property. Bernadotte then suggested that the Negev,* included in the Jewish state by the partition plan, would be included in the Arab territory instead. The western Galilee, originally allocated to the Arabs, would be included in the Jewish state, and Jerusalem would be given to the Arab state instead of becoming an international city. Facing bitter resentment from the Arabs and the Jews, his proposal was flatly rejected.

The truce ended on July 8 before it officially expired. The Israeli forces were able to acquire significantly more territory than was allocated to them by the UN partition plan. With more staff and resources at his disposal, Bernadotte was able to impose a second truce on July 18 and to work more seriously for a political settlement.

On September 16, Bernadotte issued his final report, the Second Bernadotte

Plan, which modified his original proposal. He called for two sovereign states, Israel and Transjordan, to divide Mandatory Palestine* between them. Israel would receive all of the Galilee. The Negev, Lod, and Ramle, in addition to Judea and Samaria,* would be incorporated into the Arab state. Haifa port and Lydda Airport would be declared free zones while the holy places and Jerusalem would be placed under UN control. The right of return* for Arab refugees* was also included. Bernadotte also recommended the establishment of a conciliation commission for Palestine and urged that the UN General Assembly place the peaceful settlement of the Palestine question and the refugee problem on the agenda for its third session. Again his proposal was rejected by the disputants. The plan added to the growing resentment of Bernadotte by Israeli leaders.

On September 17, the day after Bernadotte submitted his report to the UN and Israeli and Arab governments, he was assassinated by members of a Jewish extremist group in the Jewish zone of Jerusalem. Because Bernadotte had received many threats from Lohamei Herut Yisrael* (LEHI), it was commonly believed that its members carried out the assassination. The murderers were not found, but many members of the group, as well as others, were arrested. No one was ever convicted of the assassination.

For further information see: Amitzur Ilan, *Bernadotte in Palestine, 1948: A Study in Contemporary Knight-Errantry* (New York: St. Martin's Press, 1989); Kati Marton, *A Death in Jerusalem* (New York: Pantheon Books, 1994); Sune O. Persson, *Mediation & Assassination: Count Bernadotte's Mission to Palestine, 1948* (London: Ithaca Press, 1979).

                                                                        Susan L. Rosenstein

BERNADOTTE PLAN. The Bernadotte Plan, submitted by Count Folke Bernadotte,* United Nations (UN) mediator for Palestine,* to the United Nations in 1948, called on Israel to relinquish control over the southern Negev,* in return for retention of western and Central Galilee. The plan also called for the repatriation of all Arab refugees* who had fled from Palestine during the War of Independence,* the merger of the Arab part of Palestine with Jordan,* and making Haifa an international port. The proposal was opposed by both Jews and Arabs and was rejected by the Political Committee of the United Nations General Assembly in early December 1948. Bernadotte was assassinated on September 17, 1948.

For further information see: Count Folke Bernadotte, *Instead of Arms* (New York: Bonniers, 1948); Count Folke Bernadotte, *To Jerusalem* (London: Hodder and Stoughton, 1951); Louis M. Farshee, "The Bernadotte Plan and Zionist Expansionism," *American-Arab Affairs,* no. 26 (Autumn 1988): 28–39; Mordechai Gazit, "American and British Diplomacy and the Bernadotte Mission," *History Journal* 29 (September 1986):677–96; Joseph Heller, "Failure of a Mission: Bernadotte and Palestine, 1948," *Journal of Contemporary History* 14 (July 1979):515–34; Amitzur Ilan, *Bernadotte in Palestine, 1948: A Study in Contemporary Humanitarian Knight-Errantry* (London: Macmillan, 1990); Sune O. Persson, *Mediation & Assassination: Count Bernadotte's Mission to Palestine in 1948* (London: Ithaca Press, 1979); United Nations, General Assembly, Official Records, Third Session, Supplement No. 11, *Progress Report of the United Nations Mediator on Palestine. Submitted to the Secretary-General for Transmission to the Members of the United Nations* (New York: United Nations, 1949) (Document A/648).

BETAR. Hebrew acronym for "Joseph Trumpeldor Hebrew Youth Society." A Revisionist Zionist youth movement founded in 1923 in Riga, named after Joseph Trumpeldor, and affiliated with the Revisionist Movement.* The movement's ideological mentor was Vladimir Zeev Jabotinsky.* Betar's ideological tenets are Jewish statehood, territorial integrity of the homeland, ingathering of the exiles, the centrality of the Zionist idea, cultivation of the Hebrew language, social justice, military preparedness for defense, national service, and *hadar*— a code of honor and strict personal behavior. Following Israel's War of Independence,* Betar founded agricultural and rural settlements. It also supports a sports society by the same name.

For further information see: Joseph B. Schechtman, *Fighter and Prophet: The Vladimir Jabotinsky Story* (New York: A. S. Barnes, 1961).

BETHLEHEM. A town in the West Bank,* it lies about five miles (eight kilometers) south of Jerusalem* and is the birthplace of Jesus. In Hebrew, Bethlehem means "house of bread." Bethlehem is chiefly a religious shrine with many churches and other religious institutions. Bethlehem was a walled city during the time of King David, who was born there. Christian Crusaders captured it in the first Crusade but later lost it to Turkish Muslims. The Ottoman Turks* gained control of the area in the 1500s. In 1917, during World War I, British forces led by General Allenby took the town. It was part of the West Bank area annexed by Jordan* in 1949. Israel took control of the city during the Six Day War* of 1967.

BEVIN, ERNEST (b. Winsford Somerset, England, March 9, 1881; d. London, April 14, 1951). He was forced to leave school at the age of eleven. He formed a branch of the Dockers' Union in Bristol and was the union's assistant general secretary by the end of World War I. In 1922, Bevin helped form the Transport and General Workers' Union and served as its general secretary until 1940. Winston Churchill* invited Bevin to join his wartime coalition government as minister of labor and national service. Bevin instituted conscription of civilians into defense industries to help the war effort. In the post–World War II Labor government of Clement R. Attlee, Bevin was appointed foreign secretary. He was an active supporter of the creation of the North Atlantic Treaty Organization (NATO). In addition, Bevin inherited the British difficulties in India and Palestine.*

During World War II, the Labor Party issued numerous pro-Zionist* declarations. At the May 1945 Labor Party Election Conference, the party's National Executive confirmed its commitment to its 1944 platform on Palestine, which called for the ending of the White Paper with unlimited Jewish immigration.

The Attlee Cabinet's Palestine Committee was not committed to the partition of Palestine. Attlee perceived the conflict in Palestine as an issue that could be resolved through negotiations. Bevin supposedly said that he risked his political future on solving the Palestine problem. Unable to agree on a policy toward Palestine, the Labor government depended on Bevin's improvisation. Although the British foreign secretary assumed responsibility for Palestine, the colonial secretary retained responsibility for the administration of Palestine on a daily basis.

Bevin proposed a Federal Union of Palestine and Transjordan,* with Abdullah* its king. This was not acceptable to the Zionists. Labor proposed an Anglo-American Committee of Inquiry* to explore alternatives to the conflicting Zionist and Arab demands for Palestine. Bevin wanted the United States to make significant contributions toward solving the Jewish refugee problem arising from the Holocaust.* He hoped that refuge for them could be found outside Palestine. President Harry Truman* insisted, however, that any inquiry should focus on Palestine as a potential home for the Jewish survivors. Bevin announced on November 13, 1945, that an Anglo-American Committee of Inquiry* to investigate the issue would be created. At the same time, the policy of the 1939 White Paper* would continue. By this time the Zionists were convinced that Bevin was an enemy, with many believing that he was anti-Semitic. This view was encouraged by a response that Bevin gave to a press conference in 1945, when he said that Zionist promises for increasing Palestine's natural resources were "eighty percent of propaganda with twenty percent of fact." Bevin attempted to prevent illegal Jewish immigration into Palestine. The most famous interception was the British seizure of the *Exodus** in 1947.

On February 14, 1947, Bevin announced that the Labor government would refer the problem of Palestine to the United Nations, and he continued to press for British withdrawal from Palestine. In February 1948, a Transjordanian delegation visited London and met with Bevin. It is reported that at this meeting Bevin endorsed Abdullah's intention to occupy the Arab areas contiguous with its borders, by saying it appears "the obvious thing to do."

For further information see: Harold Beely, "Ernest Bevin and Palestine," in Derek Hopwood, ed., *Studies in Arab History: The Antonius Lectures, 1978–1987* (London: Macmillan, 1990); Alan Bullock, *The Life and Times of Ernest Bevin,* 3 vols. (London: Heinemann, [1960]–83); Alan Bullock, *Ernest Bevin, Foreign Secretary, 1945–1951* (New York: Norton, 1983); Michael J. Cohen, *Palestine: Retreat from the Mandate: The Making of British Policy, 1936–45* (New York: Holmes and Meier, 1978); Richard H. S. Crossman, *A Nation Reborn: A Personal Report on the Roles Played by Weizmann, Bevin and Ben-Gurion in the Story of Israel* (New York: Atheneum, 1960); Trevor Evans, *Bevin of Britain* (New York: Norton, [1946]); Elizabeth Monroe, "Mr. Bevin's 'Arab Policy,' " in Albert Hourani, ed., *Middle Eastern Affairs, Number Two, St. Antony's Papers No. 11* (Carbondale: Southern Illinois University Press, 1961), pp. 9–48; John T. Murphy, *Labour's Big Three: A Biographical Study of Clement Atlee, Herbert Morrison and Ernest Bevin* (London: Bodley Head, [1948]); Mark Stephens, *Ernest Bevin: Unskilled Labourer and World Statesman, 1881–1951* (Stevenage: Spa Books, 1985); Christopher Sykes, *Crossroads to Israel* (Cleveland: World, 1965); Peter Weiler, *Ernest Bevin* (Manchester: Manchester University Press, 1993); Francis Williams, *Ernest Bevin: Portrait of a Great Englishman* (London: Hutchinson, [1952]).

Joseph E. Goldberg

BILTMORE CONFERENCE (1942). An extraordinary Zionist* conference of some 600 delegates from seventeen countries met at the Biltmore Hotel in New York between May 6 and 11, 1942. The organizers, the Emergency Committee for Zionist Affairs, sought to unite American Jewish organizations behind a program of political activity and fund-raising on behalf of the Zionist cause and to mobilize them for action. See also BILTMORE PROGRAM.

Joseph E. Goldberg

BILTMORE PROGRAM. After World War I, when the British Mandate* replaced Ottoman* rule in Palestine,* the focus of Zionist* political and diplomatic endeavor was Britain. However, during and after World War II, political necessity and reality resulted in a shift in focus on the United States. The Biltmore Program, adopted by the extraordinary Zionist Conference in New York on May 11, 1942, in response to Britain's policy toward the Jewish National Home (particularly the restrictions on land sales and immigration), became the basis for Zionist effort until Israel's independence and was a harbinger of change. The program rejected efforts to restrict Jewish immigration to, and settlement in, Palestine and called for the fulfillment of the Balfour Declaration* and the Mandate, urging that ''Palestine be established as a Jewish Commonwealth.'' The Biltmore Program reflected the urgency of the situation in which the Jewish leadership found itself as a consequence of the Holocaust* and the need to provide for the displaced Jews of Europe.

BILU MOVEMENT. A Zionist* society and movement of Palestinian* pioneers from the nonreligious, Jewish-Russian intellectual leadership, founded in Kharkov in 1882, who spearheaded the First Aliya.* It derived its name from the Hebrew acronym of the biblical verse: ''Bet Yaakov Likhu Vnelha'' (''House of Jacob, come ye and let us go,'' Isaiah 2:5), which served as its slogan. Its aim was the national renaissance of the Jewish people, the development of its productiveness, and its return to agriculture. The society was founded after the pogroms of 1882, and the first group of Bilu settlers in Palestine arrived in July 1882. Although their concrete achievements of establishing settlements were limited, the moral and historical effect of the movement was substantial because the ideals it represented inspired successive generations.

For further information see: Hayyim Hisin, *A Palestine Diary: Memoirs of a Bilu Pioneer, 1882–1887* (New York: Herzl Press, 1976).

BINATIONAL STATE. A concept for resolving the competing claims to Palestine* by Jews and Arabs by creating a binational state. Among the groups that advocated the idea were Brit Shalom* and Ihud.* Among the prominent individuals who advocated the idea were Judah Magnes* and Martin Buber.*

BIRNBAUM, NATHAN (b. Vienna, Austria, 1864; d. Scheveningen, the Netherlands, 1937). The term *Zionism** in its modern context was first used probably by Nathan Birnbaum in an article published in 1886.

Birnbaum studied at the University of Vienna, where he helped found a student organization in 1883. Named Kadima, "eastward" and "forward," the national Jewish fraternity nurtured a love and return to a national Jewish homeland. Like Leon Pinsker, Birnbaum opposed assimilation as a solution for solving political, economic, and social discrimination against Jews. An active writer on the "Jewish problem," Nathan Birnbaum is credited with first using the term *Zionism* publicly on January 23, 1892, in a meeting in Vienna. An early adherent to the ideas of Hovevei Zion* (Lovers of Zion), he publicized the importance of a revival of Jewish nationalism and Jewish settlement in Palestine through the publication in 1885 of the periodical *Selbst-Emanzipation.* Early in the Zionist movement, Birnbaum was a supporter of Theodor Herzl,* and he was a significant contributor to the First Zionist Congress in 1897.* Not satisfied with the objectives of political Zionism as well as disagreeing with Herzl, Birnbaum left the Zionist movement in 1898. His emphasis was placed on developing Jewish national awareness through Jewish cultural development—especially through the use of Yiddish, the popular language used by East European Jews. The use of Yiddish, the language of the Galut, was opposed by most Zionists, who advocated the adoption of Hebrew, the biblical language of the Jewish people. Gradually, Birnbaum's concern with the national-cultural foundations of the Jewish people led him to religious Zionism. He joined Agudat Israel and articulated the ideas of the ultra-Orthodox, who rejected the reestablishment of a Jewish state through human action. In 1917, he published articles calling for the spiritual redemption of the Jewish people in preparation for the coming of the Messiah and the Messiah's creation of a Jewish kingdom. Birnbaum emphasized the importance of Palestine throughout all of his writings: political, cultural, and religious. Residing in Germany, Birnbaum found haven in the Netherlands when the Nazis took control. Among his many writings are *Die Nationale Wiedergeburt des Judischen Volkes in Seinem Lande, als Mittel zur Losung der Judenfrage* (The National Rebirth of the Jewish People in Its Homeland as a Means of Solving the Jewish Problem), 1893, and *Divre Ha'Olim* (Words of the Ascendants), 1917.

Joseph E. Goldberg

BIR ZEIT UNIVERSITY. Bir Zeit was the first institution of higher education in the West Bank* to be granted university status. Originally founded in 1924 as an elementary school, it later became a secondary school, and it offered college-level classes as early as 1961. In 1972, the administration requested of the Israeli authorities permission to upgrade Bir Zeit's status to that of a university. Israel agreed, and in 1973 it began to function as a full-fledged university.

The largest university in the West Bank, Bir Zeit is located near the town of Ramallah and has approximately 1,500 students. Together with the other West Bank and Gaza Strip* universities, Bir Zeit has been accused of being a center of the *intifada.** At various times the universities have been closed by Israeli authorities to reduce violence and disorder. The Palestinians have claimed that the closings were intended as collective punishment. In addition to nurturing a sense of Palestinian nationalism through a variety of cultural activities, the students at Bir Zeit reached out beyond the university to provide a variety of social services to the villages in the West Bank. The Palestine Communist Party provided support for the students.

For further information see: Baruch Kimmerling and Joel S. Migdal, *Palestinians: The Making of a People* (New York: Free Press, 1993); Sammy Khalil Mar'i, ''Higher Education among Palestinians with Special Reference to the West Bank,'' in Gabriel Ben-Dor, ed., *The Palestinians and the Middle East Conflict* (Ramat Gan, Israel: Turtledove, 1978), pp. 433–48.

Joseph E. Goldberg

BLACK SEPTEMBER. Black September refers to the crisis in Jordan* in September 1970 between the Hashemite Kingdom of Jordan and segments of the Palestine Liberation Organization* (PLO), specifically, the Popular Front for the Liberation of Palestine* (PFLP) and the Democratic Front for the Liberation of Palestine* (DFLP). Following Jordan's defeat and loss of the West Bank* to Israel in 1967, several hundred thousand Palestinians entered Jordan. In addition to the financial burden, the loss of the West Bank put an additional strain on Jordan's economy. They also contributed to the internal security problems of Jordan. The conflicting claims of the PLO and Jordan to the West Bank compounded the problems existing as a consequence of the Palestinian* presence and their creation of a structure within Jordan that threatened Palestinian loyalties to King Hussein* and the survival of the Hashemite regime.

Various Palestinian factions used Jordan as a base for operations to conduct attacks in the West Bank and inside Israel. There was also the dissatisfaction of elements of the PLO who perceived a lack of support by the Hashemite regime in the struggle against Israel. King Hussein was particularly concerned about the increasing level of PLO raids and the resulting Israeli reprisals, which threatened to involve Jordan in an undesired war with Israel. The tension between the PLO and Jordan deteriorated into open conflict on September 1, 1970.

Since the creation of the PLO at the 1964 Arab Summit in Cairo, the organization's leadership had been active in recruiting members and nurturing its program and ideology in the Palestinian refugee camps in Jordan. The PLO found a willing audience for its message that the Palestinian cause had been forsaken by the Arab leadership and was able to establish bases for recruitment and training in Jordan.

Politically, the loss of Islam's third holiest city, Jerusalem,* was the hardest burden for King Hussein. Gradually, the various elements of the PLO (Fatah,* PFLP, and DFLP) grew in strength at the expense of the regime. Attempts by King Hussein to curb commando activity were met with virulent propaganda campaigns or were just outright ignored.

Of particular concern to King Hussein was the increasing level of raids conducted by the Palestinians into Israel and the resulting Israeli reprisals. On occasion the Jordanian army fought alongside the Palestinians during the reprisal attacks. King Hussein feared losing control of his kingdom. The situation finally came to a head in September 1970.

A chronology of the major events during the twenty-day crisis follows. On September 1, there is an attempted assassination of King Hussein by leftist elements of the PLO. Fighting breaks out in Amman, Irbid, Zarqa, and Ma'an between government and PLO commandos. Yasser Arafat* attempts to get the leftists to temper their activities due to support for the regime among Palestinians in the East Bank,* Egypt,* and the Arab Legion.* On September 6, members of the PFLP hijack three airliners and force two of them to land at Dawson Airfield, a former Royal Air Force airstrip. A third plane is hijacked to Cairo and destroyed after its passengers are evacuated. On September 9, a British BOAC plane is hijacked by the PFLP and flown to Zarqa. At this point, Arafat joins the extremists. On September 12, all three airliners are destroyed after their passengers are removed to various locations throughout Amman. The destruction of the airliners casts a negative light on the PLO, and Hussein feels compelled to strike back. On September 15, PLO commandos take the city of Irbid and establish a "people's government." In response, King Hussein declares military rule and replaces the civilian Cabinet with one composed primarily of East Bank Palestinian officers. Speculation circulates that the naming of Mohammed Da'ud as prime minister is to disguise the intention of the government to destroy the PLO. On September 16, the Arab Legion surrounds Amman and begins an attack on PLO headquarters within the city. On September 17, some 12,000 Iraqi* troops stationed in Jordan as part of the 1967 Eastern Command agreement between Jordan and Iraq were withdrawn. Earlier, Baghdad had intimated that these troops would be available to aid the PLO. On September 20, Syria* sends 200 tanks into northern Jordan to support the PLO. On September 20–21, Jordanian forces are able to attack and destroy seventy-five of the Syrian tanks, which lack the benefit of Syrian air cover. On September 23, the Syrian force withdraws. On September 24, Nasser,* afraid that Hussein would destroy the PLO, calls on Hussein to cease activity against their forces. Hussein refuses. An Arab League* delegation sent to "mediate" the crisis announces a successful cease-fire between the combatants. On September 25, King Hussein and Yasser Arafat announce a cease-fire.

On September 27, in Cairo, Hussein and Arafat signed a formal cease-fire to end the conflict. Among the major provisions, both parties agreed to uphold the cease-fire; extraordinary measures taken before the cease-fire by both sides would be halted; Jordan reiterated its support for the PLO and its cause; both parties would withdraw from cities; the fedayeen* agreed to recognize the Jordanian civilian police as the only legitimate security authority in Jordan; and all prisoners taken by both sides would be released.

A more formal agreement was signed in Amman on October 13, 1970, which effectively ended the PLO's tenure in Jordan. The PLO was forced to disband all bases, was forbidden to bear arms or wear uniforms, and was forced to obey all Jordanian civil laws. The PLO shifted its bases to Syria and then to Lebanon.*

Subsequently, a Palestinian group composed primarily of dissillusioned members of Fatah was named after this episode. It targeted all enemies of the Palestinian revolution. Its first notable act of terrorism was the assassination of Jordanian prime minister Wasfi Tal* in Cairo on November 28, 1971. This was condemned by the Fatah leadership, but other acts followed. Perhaps the most infamous act was the attack on the Israeli Olympic team at the Munich Olympics* in September 1972.

For further information see: Clinton Bailey, *Jordan's Palestinian Challenge 1948–1983: A Political History* (Boulder, CO: Westview Press, 1984); Michael Bar-Zohar and Eitan Haber, *The Quest for the Red Prince* (New York: William Morrow, 1983); Neville Brown, "Jordanian Civil War," *Military Review* 51 (September 1971): 38–48; Christopher Dobson, *Black September: Its Short, Violent History* (New York: Macmillan, 1974); H. N. Howard, "Jordan in Turmoil," *Current History* 62 (January 1972): 14–19; Bard E. O'Neill, *Armed Struggle in Palestine: A Political-Military Analysis* (Boulder, CO: Westview Press, 1978); Anne Sinai and Allen Pollack, eds., *The Hashemite Kingdom of Jordan and the West Bank: A Handbook* (New York: American Academic Association for Peace in the Middle East, 1977).

Joseph E. Goldberg and Pamela Rivers

BLACK SEPTEMBER 13th. A splinter group from the Palestine Liberation Organization* (PLO) that opposed the Israel–PLO Declaration of Principles* (DOP) (and took its name from the date of the signing of the DOP) and used violence, including Katyusha rocket* attacks on Israel from Lebanon,* to try to subvert the post-DOP peace process.

BLOODY FRIDAY. Friday, November 18, 1994, when Palestinian police shot Islamic militants in the Gaza Strip.* At least 12 were killed, and more than 100 were injured in the massive Islamic rally.

AL-BOGHDADI, ABDULLATIF MAHMOUD (b. Shawa, Dakahlia province, Egypt,* September 20, 1917). Boghdadi entered the Egyptian Military College in 1936 in a class that produced many of the leaders of the Free Officer Corps who led the overthrow of the Egyptian monarchy. He graduated from the Egyptian Air Force Academy in 1939 and became a wing commander. Boghdadi was involved in anti-British activity in 1940–42. An original member of the Free

Officers, he was one of its "Committee of 9." When the Free Officers were transformed into the Revolutionary Command Council, Boghdadi became a member. He also served as the president of a Special Revolutionary Tribunal that tried those held responsible for the Egyptian military's poor performance against Israel in 1948. On June 18, 1953, Boghdadi was appointed minister of war. When the 1956 Suez crisis* developed, he recommended to Gamal Abdul Nasser* that Egypt stand up to the French–British ultimatum of October 30, 1956, to withdraw from the fighting in Suez. Nasser had great confidence in him, as did others who admired Boghdadi's administrative skills. When Syria* joined Egypt to form the United Arab Republic,* he was appointed one of four vice presidents on March 6, 1958. That same year, due to Syrian dissatisfaction, Boghdadi headed a committee to recommend means by which proper representation to offices could be provided. Those recommendations were largely ignored, and the committee was disbanded in October 1959. On October 18, 1961, he was given the additional responsibility of treasury minister. Boghdadi's differences with Nasser centered on the latter's efforts to promote socialism. He opposed Nasser's growing nationalization of Egyptian industry. Though Boghdadi favored land reform, he believed Egypt had to develop a middle class. In 1962, Nasser reorganized the Egyptian defense structure, and Boghdadi became part of a National Defense Committee. He resigned in 1964. In the events leading up to the Six Day War* of 1967, Boghdadi warned Nasser against closing the Gulf of Aqaba* to Israel—an act that he predicted would lead to a war. He did not believe that the Egyptian army could defend itself against Israel. In 1970, Nasser tried to persuade him to return as prime minister, but Boghdadi declined the offer.

Joseph E. Goldberg

BOURGUIBA PROPOSALS. In April 1965, Tunisian president Habib ben Ali Bourguiba criticized the Arab League's* position of denying Israel's legitimate right to exist as a state. He proposed direct negotiations between the Arab states and the Jewish state to discuss the original 1947 United Nations partition plan for Palestine.* In exchange for recognition of Israel by the Arab states, Bourguiba proposed that Israel provide land for the settlement of Arab refugees.* Egypt* and Tunisia withdrew their ambassadors from each other's country because of Egyptian president Gamal Abdul Nasser's* strong condemnation of Bourguiba's position. A Summit of Arab leaders in May 1965, without Bourguiba, rejected his proposals. In October 1966, Tunisia and the United Arab Republic* severed diplomatic relations.

For further information see: Samuel Merlin, *The Search for Peace in the Middle East: The Story of President Bourguiba's Campaign for a Negotiated Peace between Israel and the Arab States* (South Brunswick, NJ: Thomas Yoseloff, 1969).

Joseph E. Goldberg

BOUTROS BOUTROS-GHALI (b. Cairo, November 14, 1922). An Egyptian diplomat, he was appointed secretary-general of the United Nations for a five-year term by the United Nations General Assembly on December 3, 1991. From May 1991 until that time, Boutros-Ghali had been deputy prime minister for foreign affairs of Egypt.* Prior to that, he had served as minister of state for foreign affairs since October 1977, a position in which he was considered the principal architect of Egypt's African policy. He had been a member of the Egyptian Parliament since 1987 and part of the secretariat of the National Democratic Party since 1980. He had also been vice president of the Socialist International, a worldwide organization of social democratic, socialist, and labor parties.

Upon assuming his responsibilities as the sixth secretary-general of the United Nations on January 1, 1992, he began restructuring the organization with the aim of streamlining the bureaucracy and rationalizing the decision-making process. His recommendations for ways to improve the organization's capacity to pursue and preserve peace were published in a report entitled ''An Agenda for Peace.''

Boutros Boutros-Ghali has had a long association with international affairs as a diplomat, jurist, scholar, and published author.

Boutros-Ghali received his Ph.D. in international law and regional organizations from Paris University in 1964. He holds a degree in law from Cairo University. He taught international law and headed the political science department at Cairo University. He has numerous publications in English, French, and Arabic. He was one of the first faculty members at the School of Economics and Political Science established at Cairo University in 1961 and served as a member of the Center for Arab, African, and Asian Studies. Boutros-Ghali accompanied President Sadat* on his journey to Jerusalem* in November 1977 and was one of the major negotiators during the various stages of the Egyptian-Israeli peace talks.

Boutros-Ghali participated in the Camp David* summit talks and played a leading role in negotiating the peace treaty between Egypt and Israel that was signed in March 1979.* When the time came to put words to paper in a peace treaty, Boutros-Ghali—like the rest of the Egyptian lawyers and diplomats at the Foreign Ministry—pushed Anwar Sadat toward taking harder positions in negotiating with the Israelis.

In his meeting with then U.S. president Jimmy Carter,* Boutros-Ghali made the case for linkage.* Meanwhile, President Carter had been urging the Egyptians not to allow the issues of the West Bank* and Gaza Strip* to impede any progress toward an Egyptian–Israeli peace treaty. In contrast to the position of Sadat, who felt that details were minute and could be overcome as long as achieving a lasting peace was the goal, Boutros-Ghali argued the case for some correlation between the treaty negotiation and the Palestinian* question. In particular, he put forward the idea of establishing diplomatic relations in stages that would somehow be related to progress on the West Bank and Gaza. Sadat had orally agreed at Camp David that ambassadors would be exchanged at the time of the interim Israeli withdrawal.

Ahmed Elbashari

BOYCOTT OF ISRAEL. See **ARAB BOYCOTT OF ISRAEL.**

BREZHNEV PLAN. The name given to Soviet proposals for resolving the Arab–Israeli conflict put forward on September 15, 1982, in Moscow by general secretary of the Communist Party of the Soviet Union Leonid Brezhnev during talks with general secretary of the Yemeni Socialist Party (YSP) Ali Nasser Mohammed.

On the basis of the corresponding resolutions of the United Nations (UN) Security Council, Security Council Resolutions 242* (1967) and 338* (1973), the Brezhnev Plan emphasized securing the Palestinians'* rights to self-determination and establishing their own state.

In particular the Brezhnev Plan dealt with:

1. The strict fulfillment of the principle of inadmissibility of seizure of another's territories by aggression and the necessity to return to the Arabs the territories occupied in 1967, namely, the Golan Heights,* the West Bank* of the Jordan,* and the Gaza Strip* and Lebanese territories,* occupied in 1982. The borders between Israel and its Arab neighbors must be declared inviolable.

2. Ensuring the inalienable right of the Palestinians to self-determination and establishing their own state on Palestinian territories liberated from the Israeli occupation on the West Bank and Gaza Strip. The Palestinian refugees, in accordance with the relevant UN resolutions, should be given real opportunity to return to their homes in Palestine or to obtain proper compensation for their property left behind.

3. The return to the Arabs of East Jerusalem* (occupied by Israel in 1967), an integral part of the Palestinian state. The right of free access to the holy sites of the three religions must be guaranteed in all Jerusalem.

4. The right, reciprocally recognized, of all states of the region to a safe and independent existence and development should be guaranteed.

5. The cessation of the state of war and establishment of peace should be reached between Israel and Arab countries—meaning that all sides concerned, including Israel and the Palestinian state, should make commitments to respect each other's sovereignty, independence, and territorial integrity and settle all problems peacefully by way of negotiations.

6. International guarantees of a Middle East settlement should be worked out and adopted. The role of guarantor should be played by the permanent members of the Security Council of the United Nations or the Security Council as a whole.

Additionally, it was stressed that a just and stable Middle East peace settlement could be worked out and put into practice only by collective means and with participation of all the sides concerned, including the Palestine Liberation Organization* (PLO)—the only legitimate representative of the Arab people of Palestine.

These uncompromising, maximalistic principles of the Brezhnev Plan typically reflected for that period the one-sided, unbalanced approach of the Soviet leadership to the Middle East settlement, which was predetermined by the confrontation of the USSR with the United States and its strategic satellite in the Middle East—Israel.

By virtue of its strict determination, the Brezhnev Plan's potential was weakened as a real basis for starting a Middle East peace process.

Due to these reasons, the new Soviet proposals* concerning the Middle East settlement put forward in July 1984 also failed.

Since the beginning in 1985 of comprehensive reconstruction—*perestroika*—in the USSR, the Soviet attitude toward the Arab–Israeli conflict altered considerably. The new Soviet Middle East policy maintained its adherence to the internationally acknowledged principles of the Middle East settlement based on United Nations Security Council Resolutions 242 and 338. The Soviet position has gradually become less dogmatic and ideological while turning toward actual dialogue and compromise with all the sides involved in the conflict.

For further information see: USSR and Middle East Settlement. 1967–1988 Documents and Materials (in Russian) (Moscow, Politizdat: Ministry of Foreign Affairs of the USSR, 1989).

Galina Emelyanova

BRIT SHALOM. A Jewish organization based in Palestine* and devoted to the promotion of a working arrangement between Zionism* and Arab nationalism. The main goal was to promote a binational state* in Palestine rather than a Jewish state. It was a small and loosely shaped organization composed primarily of intellectuals and other well-known figures and reached its peak in the 1920s and 1930s. In many respects it was more of a debating society and study group than an active political organization. Brit Shalom's membership never exceeded one hundred. Its small size and the fact that its membership was composed of European Jewish intellectuals who were not motivated toward political activism limited the organization's influence. Martin Buber* and Judah Magnes* were among its prominent members.

Joseph E. Goldberg

BRITAIN. See **ENGLAND.**

BRITISH MANDATE FOR PALESTINE. At the end of World War I, the great powers dismantled the Ottoman Empire.* In 1920, prior to being given the Mandate, Great Britain separated the territory east of the Jordan River* from the western portion of Palestine* and created the Emirate of Transjordan.* Abdullah,* the second son of Sherif Hussein,* administered the territory. Great Britain was granted control over Palestine under the League of Nations Mandate System and retained control of the territory from 1922 to 1948. Great Britain's Mandatory obligations were to promote conditions that would enable the indigenous population to assume self-government. During the Mandatory period most of the political, economic, and social institutions of Israel were formed, its political parties were launched, and the careers of its political elite were begun. In the spring of 1947, the British turned the problem of the future of the Mandate over to the United Nations, which established a Special Committee on Palestine* (UNSCOP) to review the situation and offer suggestions for disposition of the territory. UNSCOP's majority report, which called for the partition of Palestine, was adopted by the United Nations General Assembly on November 29, 1947. Britain terminated the Mandate and its presence in Palestine on May 15, 1948.

At the San Remo Conference* in April 1920 the Allies agreed to distribute the Mandates as previously agreed. The French* were given the Mandate for Syria* and Lebanon* and the British for Iraq* and Palestine. The Balfour Declaration* was among the elements of obligation for the Mandatory power for Palestine. The Mandates were ratified by the League of Nations in July.

See also individual entries for the various British royal commissions, White Papers, and government officials.

For further information see: Michael J. Cohen, *Palestine: Retreat from the Mandate: The Making of British Policy, 1936–1945* (New York: Holmes and Meier, 1978); John J. McTague, *British Policy in Palestine, 1917–1922* (Lanham, MD: University Press of America, 1983); John Marlowe, *The Seat of Pilate: An Account of the Palestine Mandate* (London: Cresset Press, 1959); Ylana N. Miller, *Government and Society in Rural Palestine, 1920–1948* (Austin: University of Texas Press, 1985); Norman A. Rose, *The Gentile Zionists: A Study in Anglo-Zionist Diplomacy, 1929–1939* (London: Cass, 1973); Kenneth Stein, *The Land Question in Palestine, 1917–1939* (Chapel Hill: University of North Carolina Press, 1984); Bernard Wasserstein, *The British in Palestine: The Mandatory Government and the Arab–Jewish Conflict, 1917–1929* (London: Royal Historical Society, 1978); Ronald W. Zweig, *Britain and Palestine during the Second World War* (London: Boydell Press [for the Royal Historical Society], 1986).

BROOKINGS REPORT. Shortly after assuming office in 1977, U.S. president Jimmy Carter* assigned a priority to the establishment of peace in the Middle East for his administration, believing that the existing conditions in the Middle East were ripe for resolution. Having concluded that Henry Kissinger's* step-by-step diplomacy* had exhausted its potential, the Carter administration called for a new approach.

The Carter administration based its early foreign policy strategy on a 1975 report entitled, "Towards Peace in the Middle East," issued under the auspices of the Brookings Institution in Washington, D.C. The report was drafted by a panel of Middle East specialists and included Carter's national security adviser, Zbigniew Brzezinski, and National Security Council Middle East specialist, William Quandt.

The report advocated a comprehensive settlement to the Arab–Israeli conflict.

It noted that the United States had moral, political, and economic interests in a stable peace, particularly in the security, independence, and well-being of both Israel and the Arab states. The report feared that the failure to reach a comprehensive settlement would perpetuate the cycle of hostility and violence, further endangering U.S. interests. It also suggested that the resolution of basic elements of the Arab–Israeli dispute would best be achieved through the process of negotiation at either a general conference or in informal meetings. It further recommended that though the United States was best suited to bring about a settlement, cooperation with the Soviet Union* would be beneficial, should it be willing to participate.

The report suggested several integrated elements for a fair and enduring settlement. All parties to the settlement should commit themselves to respect the sovereignty and territorial integrity of the others; withdrawal to agreed boundaries and the establishment of peaceful relations should be carried out in stages over a period of years; peaceful relations required the end of hostile actions against Israel and the resumption of normal international and regional political and economic relations; Israel should withdraw to the June 5, 1967, lines with only mutually accepted modifications; subject to Palestinian acceptance of the sovereignty and integrity of Israel, provisions for Palestinian self-determination must be made, in the form of an independent Palestine state or of a Palestinian entity voluntarily federated with Jordan*; the report suggested no specific solution for the problem of Jerusalem* but recommended that there should be unimpeded access to all of the holy places and no barriers dividing the city; the United Nations Security Council should endorse the peace agreements and provide any necessary support.

The Brookings Report helped to guide the Carter administration in its first year toward attempting to achieve a comprehensive settlement of the Arab–Israeli dispute within the context of a revived Geneva Conference.*

For further information see: The Brookings Middle East Study Group, *Toward Peace in the Middle East: Report of a Study Group* (Washington, DC: Brookings Institution, 1975); Zbigniew K. Brzezinski, *Power and Principle: Memoirs of the National Security Advisor, 1977–81* (New York: Farrar, Straus, and Giroux, 1983); Jimmy Carter, *Keeping Faith: Memoirs of the President* (Toronto: Bantam Books, 1982); William B. Quandt, *Camp David: Peacemaking and Politics* (Washington, DC: Brookings Institution, 1986); William B. Quandt, *Peace Process: American Diplomacy and the Arab–Israeli Conflict since 1967* (Washington, DC: Brookings Institution, 1993); Cyrus R. Vance, *Hard Choices: Critical Years in America's Foreign Policy* (New York: Simon and Schuster, 1983).

Anamika Krishna

BRUSSELS DECLARATION ON THE MIDDLE EAST. On February 23, 1987, the European Community foreign ministers meeting in Brussels issued a declaration on the Middle East in which they backed a proposal for an international peace conference on the Middle East under the auspices of the United Nations and said they were prepared to play an active role in it. The declaration on the Middle East read, in part:

The member states of the European Community have particularly important political, historical, geographical, economic, religious, cultural and human links with the countries and peoples of the Middle East. They cannot therefore adopt a passive attitude towards a region which is so close to them nor remain indifferent to the grave problems besetting it. The repercussions of these problems affect the Twelve in many ways.

At the present time, tension and conflict in the Near and Middle East are continuing and worsening, the civilian population is suffering more and more without any prospect of peace. The Twelve would like to reiterate their profound conviction that the search for peace in the Near and Middle East remains a fundamental objective. They are profoundly concerned at the absence of progress in finding a solution to the Israeli–Arab conflict.

Consequently, they have a direct interest in the search for negotiated solutions to bring just global and lasting peace to the region and good relations between neighbors, and to allow the economic, social and cultural development which has been too long neglected. They have stated the principles on which solutions would be based on several occasions, in particular in their Venice Declaration.*

Accordingly, the Twelve would like to state that they are in favor of an international peace conference to be held under the auspices of the United Nations with the participation of the parties concerned and of any party able to make a direct and positive contribution to the restoration and maintenance of peace and to the region's economic and social development. The Twelve believe this conference should provide a suitable framework for the necessary negotiations between the parties directly concerned.

For their part, the Twelve are prepared to play their role with respect to such a conference and will endeavor to make an active contribution.

BUBER, MARTIN (b. Vienna, 1878; d. Jerusalem,* 1965). A prominent Jewish religious philosopher and intellectual in Palestine* who advocated the concept of a binational state* as a solution to competing Arab and Jewish claims to Palestine.

Buber was the author of many books on Jewish philosophy, general philosophy, Hasidism, theology, Zionist* theory, and the Bible. His fame, which was greater in the non-Jewish world than in Israel itself, was based primarily on his philosophy of a dialogue between God and man, as expressed in his books *Between Man and Man* (1947) and *I and Thou* (1958). He joined Judah Magnes* and the Ihud* movement and advocated Arab–Jewish rapprochement as well as an Arab–Jewish binational state in Palestine.

For further information see: Martin Buber, *On Zion: The History of an Idea* (New York: Schocken, 1973); Martin Buber, *A Land of Two Peoples: Martin Buber on Jews and Arabs* (New York: Oxford University Press, 1983); Maurice Friedman, *Martin Buber's Life and Work: The Early Years 1878–1923* (London: Search Press, 1982); Maurice Friedman, *Martin Buber's Life and Work: The Later Years, 1945–1965* (New York: E. P. Dutton, 1983); Aubrey Hodes, *Martin Buber: An Intimate Portrait* (New York: Viking Press, 1973).

BUILDERS FOR PEACE. After the signing of the Declaration of Principles* by Israel and the Palestine Liberation Organization* (PLO) in September 1993, a group of American Jews and Arab Americans formed a partnership, Builders for Peace, to channel new investment into the Gaza Strip* and West Bank.* Mel Levine and Jim Zogby were the copresidents.

BULL, ODD (b. Oslo, Norway, June 28, 1907). He received his education at Oslo University and at the Norwegian Army Academy. From 1928 to 1931, he served in the Norwegian army, and in 1931 he joined the Norwegian air force. During World War II (1940–45), Bull served in the Norwegian air force in Norway, Great Britain, and Canada. Bull was appointed deputy chief of air staff for the Royal Norwegian Air Force in 1948 and served in this position until 1951, when he became the deputy chief of staff for operations for the Allied Air Forces in Northern Europe. In 1953, Bull was appointed air commander for northern Norway and served in this position until 1956, when he became the commander of Tactical Air Forces in Norway.

General Bull became an executive member of the United Nations Observation Group in Lebanon (UNOGIL) in 1958. During the 1958 Jordanian* crisis, General Bull was appointed as the special representative of the United Nations secretary-general for British air evacuation and flight control from Jordan. In this position General Bull oversaw the evacuation of British troops that had been invited into Jordan by King Hussein* in response to perceived threats from Egyptian* president Nasser* and the United Arab Republic* (UAR).

On April 2, 1963, General Bull became the head of the United Nations Truce Supervision Organization (UNTSO)* in the Middle East with the rank of undersecretary general. He served in that position until July 31, 1970, when he retired. In this position General Bull's main task was to deal with conflicts that arose along the armistice lines between Israel and Jordan, and Israel and Syria.* After the June 1967 war,* however, the main tasks of the United Nations (UN) were to reestablish and supervise a cease-fire line between Israel and Syria, to get the UN observer team working again, and to arrange for a new observer network in the Suez Canal* area, which became the cease-fire line between Israel and Egypt.

For further information see: Odd Bull, *War and Peace in the Middle East: The Experiences and Views of a U.N. Observer* (London: Leo Cooper, 1976).

Donald A. Vogus

BUNCHE, RALPH JOHNSON (b. Detroit, August 7, 1904; d. New York, December 9, 1971). Bunche attended the University of California at Los Angeles and received a B.A. in 1927. He received an M.A. in 1928 and a Ph.D. in 1934 from Harvard. Bunche began his career with the U.S. government in 1940 by working as an analyst of African and Far Eastern affairs for the War Department. In 1944, he moved to the Department of State and became head of the Division of Dependent Area Affairs, dealing with colonial affairs.

In 1947, Bunche joined the permanent Secretariat of the United Nations. At the United Nations Bunche was assigned to the Special Committee on Palestine* (UNSCOP) and assisted in drafting both the majority and minority reports on Palestine partition. After the assassination of Count Folke Bernadotte* in September 1948, Bunche became the chief mediator in the armistice talks between Israel and the Arab states on the island of Rhodes in 1949. These negotiations led to the armistice lines,* which lasted until the 1967 war.* For his efforts as the chief mediator, Bunche received the Nobel Peace Prize in 1950.

In 1956, Bunche, as the United Nations (UN) undersecretary-general, directed the deployment of the United Nations Emergency Force* between Israel and Egypt after the Suez crisis.* These troops were his special responsibility until 1967, when they were removed at the request of Egyptian* president Nasser.*

Bunche became undersecretary-general for special political affairs with the prime responsibility for UN peacekeeping activities in 1957. In this position he organized and directed UN peacekeeping operations in both the Congo (1960) and Cyprus (1962). Bunche also organized the UN Observation Mission in Yemen in 1963 after the war between North Yemen and South Yemen. He retired from the United Nations in 1971.

For further information see: Souad Halila, ''The Intellectual Development and Diplomatic Career of Ralph J. Bunche: The Afro-American, Africanist and Internationalist'' (Ph.D diss., University of Southern California, 1988); Peggy Mann, *Ralph Bunche: UN Peacemaker* (New York: Coward, McCann, and Geoghegan, 1975); Benjamin Rivlin, ed., *Ralph Bunche, The Man and His Times* (New York: Holmes and Meier, 1990); Brian Urquhart, *Ralph Bunche: An American Life* (New York: Norton, 1993).

Donald A. Vogus

BURMA ROAD. A secret road constructed by the Israelis in April 1948, just one month before the start of the War of Independence.* The road was created because the existing road to Jerusalem* had been cut off by the Arab Legion.* This inability to ensure the safety of Jews by Jews, inside Jerusalem, initially caused the Haganah* to take offensive action in March–April 1948, in order to reopen the road.

The operation was known as Operation Nachshon, named after the first man with Moses to leap into the Red Sea to test the waters, and at the end of March 1948, before the ''pipeline of security'' (the Burma Road) was built, David Ben-Gurion* ordered the Haganah's High Command to mobilize their forces in order to open the road. The High Command did approve an initial force of 400 men, which was certainly the largest force ever assembled by the Yishuv* for a single offensive action. However, Ben-Gurion, drawing attention to Jerusalem's ''special conditions,'' argued that there should be at least 1,500 men. He argued for the symbolism and the strategic importance of Jerusalem, but, more important, he argued for the 100,000 or so Jews inhabiting the city at that time. He also knew that the Arabs were acutely aware of this situation and that if they were able to ''liquidate'' these Jews, either ''by hunger or by bullet,'' it would strike a potentially fatal blow to the Yishuv. The High Command's leaders argued that all fronts were in such danger, but on March 31, 1948, all commanders met in Tel Aviv, and all agreed to allocate half their forces to the operation. The sole exception to this was the commanders of the forces in the Galilee, who were under extremely difficult pressure to defend their lands. They were allowed to keep their forces intact.

That same night, the Haganah received their first shipment of weapons from Czechoslovakia, which were sent directly to the men who bore the responsibility for securing the use of the road from Tel Aviv to Jerusalem. The Palmach* unit formed to open the ''Bab El Wad'' (which was the roughly eight-mile strip blocked by Arab arms) was commanded by Shimon Avidan, who led this Har El (God's Hills) Brigade in this mission with the objective to get three large convoys of supplies into the besieged city of Jerusalem. The first three large convoys reached Jerusalem by April 30. Though several dozen trucks were lost in the voyage, the western sectors of Jerusalem were temporarily saved.

The road was blocked by heavily defended Arab positions along the road, at places such as ''Latrun,'' the ''Bab el Wad,'' and the old Crusader castle, ''Kastel.'' Even when it was opened, it was a short-lived experience. Soon the road was too heavily guarded by Arabs and was unusable to the members of the Yishuv. Opening the safe conduit from Rosh Ha'ayin to Jerusalem, running just south along the Bab El Wad corridor, was now the goal. By May 5, 1948, the Arabs held the well-defended area at the foot of the Jerusalem hills known as Latrun. Although the Haganah succeeded in opening an emergency pipeline ''hidden'' from the Arab forces, Israel's competent adversary, the Transjordanian*-trained Arab Legion, was able to hold on to this area until the Six Day War.*

For safety reasons, it was decided that the road would be built only at night, so that the Arabs could not see and fire shells at those building the secret pipeline. Volunteering for this task was the American colonel Mickey Marcus, who had come to the British Mandate* of Palestine as a volunteer charged with organizing the supply and transport sections of the Haganah. Marcus was shot and killed by one of his own sentries during the construction of the road. Nevertheless, the road was built. Within three weeks, both ends of the road met close to the middle, and with extra water pipelines laid by the side of the road, the Jews saved their brothers in Jerusalem from dying of thirst. Moreover, this achievement showed that a committed Yishuv was able to overcome even the greatest of odds, namely, the Arab Legion and the British forces.

For further information see: David Ben-Gurion, *Israel, a Personal History* (New York: Funk and Wagnalls, 1971); David Eshel, *Mid-East Wars: The Israeli Army* (Hod Hasharon, Israel: Eshel-Dramit, 1978).

Yasha Manuel Harari

BURNS, LIEUTENANT GENERAL E.L.M. From August 1954 until November 1956, General Burns served as chief of staff of the United Nations Truce Supervision Organization* (UNTSO), and later he commanded the United Nations Emergency Force* (UNEF) until 1957. Before that he had commanded the fifth Canadian Armored Division in Italy in 1944, and he was active in the United Nations organization following the war.

During his time at UNTSO, he watched the General Armistice Agreement* between Israel and Egypt disintegrate into war. General Burns actively discouraged retaliatory policies and tried to get both sides to settle their disputes at the negotiating table. UNTSO was primarily a neutral oversight agency that had the job of reporting on violations of the armistice. Furthermore, UNTSO was not meant to be a long-term agency; it was assumed that the Armistice Agreement would be the first step in the negotiation of a peace treaty, not merely a cease-fire. After retiring, Burns wrote *Between Arab and Israeli,* in which he examines in detail the failure of the armistice and the return of war.

For further information see: E.L.M. Burns, *Between Arab and Israeli* (New York: Ivan Obolsnsky, 1963).

John Fontaine

BUSH, GEORGE HERBERT WALKER (b. Milton, Massachusetts, June 12, 1924). He served in the U.S. Navy during World War II. After graduating from Yale University in 1948, he settled in Texas. He was elected to Congress in 1966 and 1968. He served as U.S. ambassador to the United Nations, 1971–73, headed the U.S. Liaison Office in Beijing, 1974–75, and was director of the Central Intelligence Agency in 1976–1977. He served as vice president of the United States under President Ronald Reagan,* from 1981 to 1989. He was president of the United States from 1989 to 1993.

President George Bush took office in January 1989 with no long-range strategic plan or specific policies for the Arab-Israeli sector of the Middle East. The end of the cold war and attendant developments preoccupied the administration and the U.S. Congress and entranced the media and the public. In the Arab–Israeli sector, a dialogue with the Palestine Liberation Organization* (PLO), established in the last days of the Reagan administration, continued, but, within the context of a changing international system, the Middle East was not a matter of high national priority.

Bush and Secretary of State James Baker* began their tenures with no master plan or grand design for a comprehensive approach to the Arab–Israeli conflict but instead launched a more modest effort to achieve direct negotiations between the parties. In the spring of 1989, Baker moved incrementally, using a step-by-step process the purpose of which was to reduce tensions, to promote dialogue between Israelis and Palestinians,* and to build an environment that could sustain negotiations.

The initial, low-key efforts focused on establishing an Israel–Palestinian dialogue as a prelude to broader peace negotiations. Proposals by Israel and later by Egyptian* president Hosni Mubarak* and Baker (five-point plan*) sought to invigorate the process. Nevertheless, by the spring of 1990, little had been

achieved beyond wrangling over the fine points of the procedure. The formation
of Yitzhak Shamir's* new government in Israel in June 1990 suggested continued tensions with the United States on the peace process. Also, Arafat's* unwillingness to condemn a terrorist attack on Israel by a PLO faction at the end
of May 1990 led to suspension of the United States–PLO dialogue.

The Iraqi* invasion of Kuwait in August 1990 put the Arab–Israeli peace
process into a form of suspended animation.

The end of hostilities inaugurated a period in which Bush and Baker sought
to reconstruct the world order based on the success against Saddam Hussein*
and Iraq. The general approach was articulated by Bush in an address to a joint
session of Congress on March 6, 1991 (and earlier by Baker in congressional
testimony). They described a new world order* that helped to create new opportunities for peace and stability in the Middle East by closing "the gap between Israel and the Arab states and between Israelis and Palestinians." He
argued, "The time has come to put an end to the Arab–Israeli conflict." In
testimony before the House Foreign Affairs Committee on February 6, 1991,
Baker had noted that the search for a "just peace and real reconciliation for
Israel, the Arab states, and Palestinians" must be resumed.

The perception that the region had undergone sufficient change to make peace
possible provided the impetus for Baker's efforts to achieve progress in the
Arab–Israeli sector.

U.S. determination was stressed by Bush in his speech on March 6, 1991:
"A comprehensive peace must be grounded in United Nations Security Council
Resolutions 242 and 338 and the principle of territory for peace. This must
provide for Israel's security and recognition, and at the same time for legitimate
Palestinian political rights."

Baker's visits to the Middle East in the spring and early summer of 1991
made it clear that there was no agreement to convene a conference that would
lead to bilateral negotiations. The issues in contention included the venue of a
conference (whether in the region or elsewhere), what powers and authority it
would have (whether it would be primarily ceremonial in nature), under whose
auspices it should be conducted (whether the United Nations would be a factor),
which Palestinians and other Arabs could and would attend, and what prior
commitments must be made by the participants.

Eventually, Baker convened the Madrid Peace Conference* at the end of
October 1991.

The Madrid conference did not achieve a substantive breakthrough, although
it eliminated the procedural barriers to direct bilateral negotiations between Israel and its immediate neighbors when Israel and Syrian,* Egyptian, Lebanese,*
and Jordanian*–Palestinian delegations met at an opening public and official
plenary session and delivered speeches and responses. Bilateral negotiations between Israel and each of the Arab delegations followed.

The Madrid meetings were followed by bilateral talks in Washington. The
United States adhered to its role as a facilitator and sought not to intervene on

substantive matters. It was not a party to the bilateral talks, and its representatives were not in the room or at the negotiating table, although it did meet separately with the parties and heard their views and perspectives.

The Madrid-inaugurated process included multilateral discussions* on several regional issues, and an initial organizing conference convened in Moscow in January 1992. The goal was to achieve progress on important regional issues that would reinforce the bilateral negotiations.

The administration sought to ensure continuation of the bilateral and multilateral discussions and helped to ensure the continuation of the process but believed that the time was not yet ready for its involvement—the substantive differences between the parties were too broad and the United States couldn't bridge the gap.

Although the Bush administration was pleased with the inauguration of an essentially irreversible process to create peace in the Arab–Israeli conflict, the situation had not yet reached a point of substantive breakthrough. Nevertheless, the Baker team seemed optimistic that the wide differences between the parties would eventually narrow, and then it would be possible to bridge the gaps.

The Soviet Union became increasingly irrelevant during the Bush administration, and, after its collapse, the successor states focused more on domestic economic and social needs and their political ramifications than on promoting their prestige in the Middle East or elsewhere. Russia played a minor, albeit highly visible, ceremonial role in the Arab–Israeli peace process and in regard to the Gulf crisis. The United States became the sole superpower and emerged as the dominant, essentially hegemonic, force in the Middle East. It was the central external power seeking to direct and facilitate the Arab–Israeli peace process.

In the spring of 1992, the Bush administration became increasingly involved in the quadrennial election process and focused on the reelection of the president. This coincided with Israel's Knesset* election campaign. The Arab–Israeli peace process continued but clearly slowed.

For further information see: Sanford R. Silverburg, ''The Bush Administration and the Middle East,'' *JIME,* no. 9 (Spring 1990):60–71.

C

CAIRO AGREEMENT (1970). Following the Palestinian*–Jordanian* confrontations in September 1970 (Black September*), as many as 235,000 Palestinians relocated in Lebanon.* Yasser Arafat* established his headquarters in Beirut while large numbers of dislocated Palestinians settled in southern Lebanon as well as in the coastal cities of Tyre and Sidon. Various Palestinian groups sought to establish a new front for attacks against Israel in southern Lebanon. The presence of the Palestinians and their attacks against Israel prompted Israeli retaliation raids into Lebanon. In addition to the dangers of making portions of Lebanon a war zone, some segments of the Lebanese population feared that the Palestinians would disrupt the fragile communal balance between the Christian and Muslim sects in Lebanon. The Christian Phalange feared that the creation of a Palestinian state within Lebanon would endanger Lebanese sovereignty. The weak Lebanese government and its army attempted to restrain Palestinian terrorist activity. On November 2, 1969, President Gamal Abdul Nasser* of Egypt* brokered the Cairo Agreement, which was signed by the Lebanese commander in chief and Yasser Arafat. The Cairo Agreement attempted to protect Lebanese sovereignty and security while granting the Palestine Liberation Organization* (PLO) autonomy of action in southern Lebanon. Although the PLO was allowed to carry out attacks against Israel from Lebanese soil, it agreed to fire upon Israel only from inside the Jewish state. Furthermore, PLO camps were required to be some distance from Lebanese towns, and the PLO would refrain from conducting military training in refugee camps. The Cairo Agreement resulted in the PLO's establishing in Lebanon an area under its control with institutional autonomy. Newspapers as well as a news agency were established. Hospitals and clinics under the direction of the Palestinian Red Crescent Society were established. Arafat was successful in gaining diplomatic recognition from a number of states, and the PLO, in turn, established missions in more than 100 countries.

Joseph E. Goldberg

CAIRO AGREEMENT (1994). An agreement signed in Cairo on May 4, 1994, by Yasser Arafat* and Yitzhak Rabin* that contained accord reached on elements of the Declaration of Principles* signed between Israel and the Palestine Liberation Organization* (PLO) in September 1993 and designed to begin its implementation. The agreement formally began Israel's withdrawal from the Gaza Strip* and the Jericho* area and granted Palestinians a measure of self-rule. Its Preamble reaffirmed the desire of both parties to achieve a "just, lasting, and comprehensive peace settlement through the agreed political process . . . which will lead to the implementation of United Nations Security Council Resolutions 242* and 338.*''

The Cairo Agreement consists of twenty-three articles that define the Gaza Strip and the Jericho area, discuss Israeli military withdrawal, specify the transfer of authority, define the structure and composition of the twenty-four-member Palestinian Authority,* and define the Palestinian Authority's jurisdiction and its powers and responsibilities, including its legislative and police powers. In addition, the agreement arranges for passage between Gaza–Egypt* and Jericho–Jordan* and for safe passage* between the Gaza Strip and the Jericho area. It discusses relations between Israel and the Palestinian Authority. In addition, Israeli–Palestinian economic relations and human rights for all are discussed, including provisions for implementation of the agreement as well as resolving differences and preventing hostile action. Confidence-building measures between the parties are specified as well as a temporary international foreign presence in the Gaza Strip and the Jericho area.

The agreement noted that

Israel shall implement an accelerated and scheduled withdrawal of Israeli military forces from the Gaza Strip and from the Jericho Area to begin immediately with the signing of this agreement. Israel shall complete such withdrawal within three weeks from this date.

Israel shall transfer authority as specified in this agreement from the Israeli military government and its civil administration to the Palestinian authority, hereby established. . . .

The Palestinian authority will consist of one body of 24 members which shall carry out and be responsible for all the legislative and executive powers and responsibilities transferred to it under this agreement . . . and shall be responsible for the exercise of judicial functions.

The document was signed by Israel and the PLO and was witnessed by the United States, the Russian Federation, and the Arab Republic of Egypt.

CAIRO CONFERENCE. Winston Churchill,* as British* colonial secretary, organized the Cairo Conference of March 1921 in an attempt to stabilize and clarify the British position in the Middle East and to establish guidelines for future British policy in the region. The Cairo Conference was attended by Britain's leading civilian and military experts on Arab affairs.

The conference determined, in part, that Hashemite dynasties would be established—Feisal ibn Hussein* would be placed on the throne in Baghdad, Iraq,* and his brother Abdullah ibn Hussein* would be given the eastern portion of Palestine* that became Transjordan.*

The Cairo Conference had specific ramifications for the Arab–Israeli conflict in that, while Churchill reiterated British support of the Jewish National Home,* he also issued a "reclarification" of the Balfour Declaration* by separating Transjordan from the Mandate* and restricting Palestine to the area west of the Jordan River.*

For further information see: Aaron S. Klieman, *Foundations of British Policy in the Arab World: The Cairo Conference of 1921* (Baltimore, MD: Johns Hopkins University Press, 1970); Howard Sachar, *The Emergence of the Middle East: 1914–1924* (New York: Alfred A. Knopf, 1969); Howard Sachar, *A History of Israel: From the Rise of Zionism to Our Time* (New York: Alfred A. Knopf, 1991).

Mark Daryl Erickson

CAMP DAVID. The retreat of the president of the United States in Maryland, outside Washington. The negotiations between Israel and Egypt* that followed Anwar Sadat's* visit to Jerusalem* in 1977 were often tense and led to a series of stalemates on a wide number of issues. In the summer of 1978, the deadlock threatened to halt the negotiations and alarmed the United States that the renewed tensions might lead to a situation in which the danger of war would be increased. President Jimmy Carter* sought to break the deadlock through a new and dramatic initiative. U.S. secretary of state Cyrus Vance* made a scheduled trip to the Middle East to persuade Egypt and Israel to resume the talks. On August 8, 1978, the White House announced that both Sadat and Menachem Begin* had accepted Carter's invitation to come to Camp David "for a meeting with the President to seek a framework for peace in the Middle East."

The meetings at Camp David were long (September 5–17, 1978), difficult, and complex and were held in virtual secrecy. Eventually, the parties emerged to announce that agreement had been reached on two documents known subsequently as the Camp David Accords.*

For further information see: Zbigniew Brzezinski, *Power and Principle: Memoirs of the National Security Adviser, 1977–1981* (New York: Farrar, Straus, and Giroux, 1983); Jimmy Carter, *Keeping Faith: Memoirs of a President* (New York: Bantam Books, 1982); Moshe Dayan, *Breakthrough: A Personal Account of the Egypt–Israel Peace Negotiations* (New York: Alfred A. Knopf, 1981); Cyrus Vance, *Hard Choices: Critical Years in America's Foreign Policy* (New York: Simon and Schuster, 1983); Ezer Weizman, *The Battle for Peace* (Toronto: Bantam Books, 1981).

CAMP DAVID ACCORDS. Egyptian* president Anwar Sadat's* historic visit to Jerusalem* in November 1977 was followed by negotiations in which the United States—and President Jimmy Carter* personally—played an active and often crucial role. In September 1978, President Carter, President Anwar Sadat of Egypt, Prime Minister Menachem Begin* of Israel, and their senior aides held an extraordinary series of meetings for thirteen days at Camp David, Maryland, during which they discussed the Arab–Israeli conflict. On September 17, 1978, they announced, at the White House, the conclusion of two accords that provided the basis for continuing negotiations for peace: a ''Framework for Peace in the Middle East'' and a ''Framework for the Conclusion of a Peace Treaty between Egypt and Israel.''

The Middle East framework set forth general principles and some specifics to govern a comprehensive peace settlement, focusing on the future of the West Bank* and the Gaza Strip.* It called for a transitional period of no more than five years during which Israel's military government would be withdrawn (although Israeli forces could remain in specified areas to ensure Israel's security), and a self-governing authority would be elected by the inhabitants of these areas. It also provided that ''Egypt, Israel, Jordan and the representatives of the Palestinian* people'' should participate in negotiations to resolve the final status of the West Bank and Gaza, Israel's relations with Jordan* based on United Nations Security Council Resolution 242,* and Israel's right to live within secure and recognized borders. The Egypt–Israel framework called for Israel's withdrawal from the Sinai Peninsula* and the establishment of normal, peaceful relations between the two states. In addition to the two frameworks there was a series of accompanying letters clarifying the parties' positions on certain issues. The Egyptian Cabinet approved the accords on September 19, and on September 28 the Israeli Knesset* voted eighty-four to nineteen (with seventeen abstentions) to endorse them. The Camp David Accords led to negotiations and to the Egypt–Israel Peace Treaty.*

The ''Framework for Peace in the Middle East agreed at Camp David'' noted that ''the search for peace in the Middle East must be guided by'' a number of elements, including that ''the agreed basis for a peaceful settlement of the conflict between Israel and its neighbors is United Nations Security Council Resolution 242, in all it parts.'' Also:

To achieve a relationship of peace, in the spirit of Article 2 of the United Nations Charter, future negotiations between Israel and any neighbor prepared to negotiate peace and security with it, are necessary for the purpose of carrying out all the provisions and principles of Resolutions 242 and 338.* . . . Peace requires respect for the sovereignty, territorial integrity and political independence of every state in the area and their right to live in peace within secure and recognized boundaries free from threats or acts of force. . . . Security is enhanced by a relationship of peace and by cooperation between nations which enjoy normal relations. . . . Taking these factors into account, the parties are determined to reach a just, comprehensive, and durable settlement of the Middle East conflict through the conclusion of peace treaties based on Security Council Resolution 242 and 338 in all their parts. Their purpose is to achieve peace and good neighborly relations.

To achieve these ends, Egypt and Israel also noted that they should proceed as follows: "Egypt, Israel, Jordan and the representatives of the Palestinian people should participate in negotiations on the resolution of the Palestinian problem in all its aspects." They also provided for "transitional arrangements for the West Bank and Gaza for a period not exceeding five years. In order to provide full autonomy to the inhabitants, under these arrangements the Israeli military government and its civilian administration will be withdrawn as soon as a self-governing authority has been freely elected by the inhabitants of these areas to replace the existing military government." No significant progress was made toward implementation of this framework.

In the second framework concerning a peace treaty between Egypt and Israel, it was agreed: "In order to achieve peace between them, Israel and Egypt agree to negotiate in good faith with a goal of concluding within three months of the signing of this framework a peace treaty between them." Additional concepts included in the framework helped to guide the negotiating process that led to the signing of a peace treaty in the spring of 1979. See also BAGHDAD ARAB SUMMIT (1978).

For further information see: William B. Quandt, *Camp David: Peacemaking and Politics* (Washington, DC: Brookings Institution, 1986).

CANAAN, LAND OF. The biblical name for the area known as Palestine,* later, Israel. Prior to its conquest by the Hebrews under Joshua, the Judges, King Saul, and King David, the area of Palestine was known as the Land of Canaan, the name inherited from the Canaanites, who inhabited parts of the area.

CANADA. Canada's involvement in the Arab–Israeli conflict has often exceeded its actual ability to independently influence regional affairs.

In the late 1940s, a senior Canadian jurist participated in the deliberations of the United Nations Special Committee on Palestine* and helped formulate the plan to partition Mandatory Palestine. As chairman of the United Nations General Assembly's First Committee, the respected Canadian diplomat Lester Pearson was instrumental in mediating competing U.S. and British interests over Palestine's* fate. Canada voted in favor of General Assembly Resolution 181 (II),* which approved the partition plan.

Respecting the interests of Great Britain,* Canada (along with other members of the British Commonwealth) withheld de facto recognition of Israel until December 1948; de jure recognition was extended in May 1949, at the same time that Ottawa supported Israel's application for admission to the United Nations.

Canada began to participate in diplomatic and peacekeeping efforts in the Middle East immediately after the first Arab–Israeli War.* Canadians partici-

pated in the first United Nations Truce Supervision Organization* in Jerusalem,*
and a Canadian officer was appointed the first commissioner-general of the
United Nations Relief and Works Agency* (UNRWA).

Canadian diplomats attempted to facilitate a peaceful resolution to the 1956
Suez conflict,* principally because of the divisions within the Western alliance
caused by U.S. opposition to British and French involvement in the hostilities.
Foreign Minister Lester Pearson was awarded the 1957 Nobel Peace Prize for
his mediatory efforts during the Suez conflict and for organizing the first United
Nations Emergency Force* (UNEF) in Sinai. A Canadian officer was appointed
UNEF's first chief of staff. Ironically, Canada's involvement in UNEF was
initially opposed by Egyptian* president Gamal Abdul Nasser,* who objected
to the display of the British Union Jack insignia on the Canadian uniform.
Nasser ultimately relented, and a contingent of 1,000 Canadians remained with
UNEF until the force was withdrawn, at Egypt's insistence, in the weeks leading
up to the Six Day War.*

In the spring of 1967, Canadian diplomats participated in unsuccessful efforts
at the United Nations (UN) to reestablish calm along the Egyptian–Israeli and
Israeli–Syrian* armistice lines and to organize a multinational flotilla to break
Egypt's blockade of the Strait of Tiran* to Israeli commercial shipping. As a
nonpermanent member of the Security Council in the summer and fall of 1967,
Canada participated in the delicate negotiations leading up to the formulation
and approval of United Nations Security Council Resolution 242.*

Canada contributed troops to UNEF II,* which supervised the Israeli–Egyptian cease-fire and Disengagement Agreements* following the October 1973
Yom Kippur War* and the UN force that monitored the 1974 Israeli–Syrian
disengagement on the Golan Heights.* Canada contributed troops for the first
six months of the UN peacekeeping force in southern Lebanon that was established in 1978 to monitor conditions along the Israel–Lebanon* border. Canada
participated in the Multinational Force and Observers* (MFO), the non-UN international force established in the Sinai Peninsula* in 1982 to monitor the
Egypt–Israel Peace Treaty.*

Over the years there have been some subtle shifts and adjustments in Canada's
approach to the Arab–Israeli conflict. In the 1940s and 1950s, Canadian policy
reflected the continuing influence of Great Britain—hence, Ottawa's early policy
of ''noncommitment'' toward Israel and Pearson's role in mediating the Suez
conflict (thereby extricating London from an embarrassing situation). However,
with Britain's decline in the 1960s, Canada's position on the Middle East was
increasingly tied to that of the United States. This was reflected both in the
readiness of Canadian governments to represent Western interests in regional
peacekeeping efforts and in Ottawa's opposition (often along with only the
United States and Israel) to UN resolutions considered excessively critical of
Israel and supportive of Arab and Palestinian interests.

By the mid-1970s, yet another adjustment in Canada's Middle East policy
occurred. As a net exporter of oil, Canada was basically unaffected by the

Organization of Petroleum Exporting Countries (OPEC)* oil shocks of 1973–
74. Nevertheless, as part of Liberal prime minister Pierre Trudeau's strategy of
diversifying and making more "cost-effective" Canada's international interests
and obligations, Ottawa actively pursued enhanced commercial relations with
the emerging petroleum-based economies of the Middle East.

This new commercial interest in the region precipitated a subtle shift of emphasis in Canada's approach to the Arab–Israeli conflict, away from the generally pro-Israel U.S. position and toward that of the European Community
(which was more sympathetic to Arab political demands). Canadian embassies
and commercial legations were opened for the first time in Arab countries and
in Iran. At the UN, Trudeau only reluctantly agreed to commit Canadian troops
to peacekeeping forces in the Sinai and on the Golan Heights, despite strong
urging from Washington, and Canada increasingly joined its European allies in
abstaining on controversial resolutions relating to Israel and the "question of
Palestine" rather than continuing to oppose such resolutions. Trudeau grudg-
ingly bowed to domestic political pressure to introduce federal legislation prohibiting compliance with the Arab economic boycott of Israel, but he then
permitted extraordinary parliamentary procedures to kill passage of the bill. Under Trudeau, Canadian diplomats were permitted to initiate middle-level contacts
with Palestine Liberation Organization* (PLO) representatives and, in the late
1970s, Canadian officials for the first time declared the country's support for
the concept of a Palestinian "homeland" within identifiable boundaries (i.e.,
the West Bank* and Gaza Strip*). During a brief tenure in power in 1979–80,
Conservative prime minister Joe Clark sought to make further adjustments to
Ottawa's policy in the Middle East, principally by pledging to transfer Canada's
embassy in Israel to West Jerusalem* from Tel Aviv. However, Clark was ultimately compelled to retract this pledge under intense domestic pressure from
Canadian Arabs, as well as bureaucratic and corporate forces concerned about
commercial opportunities in the Arab world. Clark's initiative was also reportedly opposed by U.S. president Jimmy Carter,* who feared that a transfer of
Canada's embassy to Jerusalem would compromise the delicate course of Arab–
Israeli negotiations initiated by Carter, Sadat,* and Begin* at Camp David.*
The domestic political controversy created by the so-called Jerusalem Embassy
affair preempted efforts to reintroduce federal legislation prohibiting compliance
with the Arab boycott of Israel.

In the 1980s, during the tenure of Conservative prime minister Brian Mulroney, attempts were made to balance Canadian interests in the Middle East.
On one hand, Canada joined the international chorus of criticism of Israel's
actions in response to the Palestinian *intifada,** and Canada lifted all restrictions
on diplomatic contacts with the PLO in March 1989. At the same time, Prime
Minister Mulroney drew some critical fire for suggesting that Israeli soldiers
had demonstrated restraint in the early days of the *intifada;* Chaim Herzog made
the first state visit to Canada of an Israeli president in the summer of 1989; and
Canada participated in the multilateral coalition confronting Iraqi* military ad-

venturism in the Persian Gulf. However, throughout the 1980s, Canada's interest in the Middle East (and in foreign affairs in general) declined precipitously as the country confronted a series of domestic economic and constitutional crises.

Canada endorsed the process of direct Arab–Israeli negotiations initiated at the Madrid Peace Conference* (October 1991) and became actively involved in the process's "multilateral track."* At the Moscow Peace Conference (January 1992), Canada agreed to head the working group on the highly sensitive regional refugee issue. As "gavel-holder" for the Refugee Working Group (RWG), Canada sits on the Steering Committee overseeing the activities of the five multilateral working groups. (A meeting of the Steering Committee took place in Canada in February 1994.) The first two meetings of the Refugee Working Group were convened in Ottawa (in May 1992 and November 1992), and Canada continued to coordinate efforts to develop practical ways of improving the living conditions of Palestinian refugees, pending the completion of final-status negotiations involving Israel, the PLO, Jordan, and Egypt (as outlined in the September 1993 Declaration of Principles*). In addition to its leadership role in the refugee talks, Canada progressively broadened its level of active involvement in some of the other multilateral working groups, including those dealing with water resources and arms control and disarmament.

In October 1993, Canada pledged about $55 million over five years in support of the Israel–PLO accord on interim autonomy, over and above Ottawa's continuing support of bilateral and multilateral development programs in the Middle East. In addition, there was speculation that Canadian officials will help implement and/or monitor Palestinian elections in the Gaza Strip and West Bank (as they had in Namibia, South Africa, El Salvador, and elsewhere) and participate in a multinational force to observe possible territorial adjustments on the Golan Heights.*

The current Canadian position on key issues affecting the Arab–Israeli peace process reflects Ottawa's desire to solidify Canada's status as an honest broker and fair-minded arbiter of regional disputes. Canada continues to support "the security, well-being and rights of Israel as a legitimate, independent state in the Middle East." At the same time, Canada recognizes that "for there to be a just peace, the legitimate rights of the Palestinians [represented principally by the Palestine Liberation Organization] must be recognized, including their right of self-determination to be exercised through peace negotiations." Canada does not view the establishment of an independent Palestinian state as a necessary outcome of the interim autonomy agreement achieved between Israel and the PLO; but Canada "would not exclude the creation of a Palestinian state as part of a comprehensive settlement if that were decided by the parties through negotiations." Canada, along with most of its Western allies, does not recognize the permanence of Israeli control over the territories occupied in 1967, including East Jerusalem,* and is opposed to "unilateral actions intended to predetermine the outcome of negotiations." At the same time, Canada has consistently opposed "all attempts to prejudge the outcome of negotiations by one-sided resolutions in international fora,'' such as moves to suspend or expel Israel from the United Nations or its specialized agencies. In this vein, Ottawa advocated the revoking of the infamous "Zionism is racism" resolution* and supported recent Group of Seven (G-7) statements calling on the Arab countries to end their economic boycott of Israel.

Despite its continuing efforts to maintain a "balanced" and "evenhanded" approach toward the region, specific aspects of Canada's Middle East policy have occasionally been criticized by elements of the Canadian–Jewish and –Arab communities (representing populations of about 300,000 and 250,000, respectively). However, on the whole, Israel and key Arab peace partners continue to view Canada as a credible, if not crucial, facilitator of conflict resolution in the Middle East.

For further information see: Baha Abu-Laban, "Arab-Canadians and the Arab–Israeli Conflict," *Arab Studies Quarterly* 10 (Winter 1988):104–26; David J. Bercuson, *Canada and the Birth of Israel* (Toronto: University of Toronto Press, 1985); Canada, Department of External Affairs and International Trade, *The Arab–Israeli Dispute and Canadian Support for Peace in the Middle East: A Chronology* (September 1993); Canada, Department of External Affairs and International Trade, *Canadian Development Assistance in the Middle East* (September 1993); Canada, Department of External Affairs and International Trade, *Canada's Position on Key Issues* (November 1993); Canada, Department of External Affairs and International Trade, *The Multilaterals: A Canadian Perspective*. A Discussion Paper Prepared for the Intersessional Meeting of the Multilateral Steering Committee, Montebello, Quebec (February 8–10, 1994); David H. Goldberg, *Foreign Policy and Ethnic Interest Groups: American and Canadian Jews Lobby for Israel* (New York: Greenwood Press, 1990); Zachariah Kay, *Canada and Palestine: The Politics of Non-Commitment* (Jerusalem: Israel Universities Press, 1978); Paul C. Noble, "Canada and the Palestinian Question," *International Perspectives* (September–October 1983): 3–7; David Taras and David Goldberg, eds., *The Domestic Battleground: Canada and the Arab–Israeli Conflict* (Montreal: McGill-Queen's University Press, 1989).

David H. Goldberg

CANADA CAMP. Canada Camp refers to a Palestinian* refugee camp located in the Sinai Peninsula* bordering the town of Rafa in the Gaza Strip.* Since Israel's withdrawal from Sinai, the fate of its inhabitants hinged on the resolution of outstanding issues between Egypt* and Israel.

Named after the Canadian United Nations forces that occupied the area in the 1960s, the camp was established during the Israeli occupation of the Sinai when they built a road through Rafa. Approximately 5,000 Palestinians were moved into new housing, which, after the Israeli withdrawal, was on the Egyptian side of the border.

When Egypt and Israel signed the accords, they agreed that the separation of families on either side of the border would be temporary. However, when the Taba* dispute developed, their repatriation was blocked. When the dispute was resolved in 1989, Egypt and Israel returned to the refugee problem, with Egypt agreeing to pay each family to build a new home in the Gaza Strip. The Israeli military government set aside a tract of land at Tel Sultan near some of the 3,000 Jewish settlers who had moved to the Gaza Strip. When the first five fathers returned in December 1989 to establish homes for their families, the settlers protested the establishment of what they called a ''terrorist neighborhood.'' In all, some 5,800 people were scheduled to be repatriated over five years.

Canada Camp became a symbol of hardship where fathers and mothers were separated from their children by barbed wire called ''the shouting fence.'' In the afternoon, divided family members would gather at either side and shout back and forth, presenting new brides and relaying news of members who had died.

When the *intifada** began in the occupied territories,* residents of the camp also staged protests, which ended with Egyptian military intervention and several deaths. In 1989, an attack on an Israeli tourist bus in Egypt was thought by Egyptian authorities to have been carried out by individuals from the camp.

David J. Abram

CARTER, JIMMY (James Earl) (b. Plains, Georgia, October 1, 1924). He attended Georgia Tech and graduated from the U.S. Naval Academy. He entered the navy's nuclear submarine program. After his father died in 1953, Carter left the navy to take over the family businesses. He was elected governor of Georgia in 1970. Carter defeated Gerald Ford* in the 1976 election and became president of the United States in 1977. He was defeated by Ronald Reagan* in 1980 when he ran for reelection.

He played an active role in negotiations between Israel and Egypt* that led to the Camp David Accords* and the Egypt–Israel Peace Treaty.* From the beginning of his administration, Carter attempted to ease U.S.–Soviet tensions and believed that the Soviet Union had to participate in the effort to achieve a settlement of the Arab–Israeli conflict. Unlike the Nixon* and Ford* administrations, which promoted step-by-step diplomacy* in the Middle East, Carter believed that a comprehensive approach was required.

The Carter administration inaugurated its Middle East policy with a strong focus on the Arab–Israeli conflict. Carter sought a comprehensive settlement and attempted to reconvene the Geneva Middle East Peace Conference,* which had first met in December 1973 under the cochairmanship of the United States and the Soviet Union, as an appropriate mechanism to achieve that goal. This continued the extensive concern and involvement with resolution of the Arab–Israeli conflict begun by Secretary of State Henry Kissinger* after the Yom Kippur War* of 1973. At the same time, it contrasted with Kissinger's preference for step-by-step diplomacy and a U.S. monopoly on the peace process. Within a matter of weeks of the outset of the administration, Secretary of State Cyrus Vance* had already been sent to the Middle East—his first overseas trip.

The administration's concept of a lasting peace emerged during the spring and summer of 1977. Carter articulated his views on three elements that he saw as central and indispensable: the definition and assurance of permanent peace, the delineation of territory and borders, and the Palestinian* issue.

The definition of peace involved a comprehensive approach that went beyond the end of war.

The United States did not identify precise lines for the future borders between Israel and the neighboring Arab states, but substantial Israeli withdrawal from occupied territories* and negotiated minor adjustments or modifications in the pre-1967 lines were the main elements.

The Palestinian factor increasingly emerged as significant and the most controversial. The traditional U.S. approach, which concentrated on the refugee* and humanitarian aspects of the problem and, after the June war* of 1967, also on terrorism, was given a political component by the Carter administration. Terrorism receded, and while refugees were still a concern, the issue was seen as broader in scope. The administration sought to include provisions for the legitimate interests of the Palestinian people in any settlement. Later, in the U.S.–USSR joint communique* of October 1, 1977, this formulation became "the legitimate rights of the Palestinian people." The idea of a homeland appeared publicly for the first time on March 16, 1977, in Clinton, Massachusetts, when Carter said that the solution required some form of homeland for the Palestinians. "The third ultimate requirement for peace is to deal with the Palestinian problem. The Palestinians claim up 'til this moment that Israel has no right to be there, that the land belongs to the Palestinians, and they've never yet given up their publicly professed commitment to destroy Israel. That has to be overcome. There has to be a homeland provided for the Palestinian refugees who have suffered for many, many years." Carter believed that the boundaries, nature, and political status of the homeland would have to be negotiated, and his preference was that the Palestinian entity (not an independent Palestinian country) be linked with Jordan.*

The Carter administration sought to move in the directions outlined by the president and believed that cooperation with the Soviet Union would help to achieve those goals.

Carter saw the Soviet Union as a benign power, interested in promoting development in the region, not one interested in taking advantage of its difficulties. Cooperation with the Soviet Union reached its zenith on October 1, 1977, when the Carter administration and the Soviet Union issued a joint communique stressing the need for "achieving as soon as possible, a just and lasting settlement of the Arab–Israeli conflict." The statement was designed to accelerate the efforts toward reconvening the Geneva Conference* by eliciting Soviet cooperation. But that communique, which the Soviet Union subsequently tried to have restored as the central factor in the Arab–Israeli peace process, was soon abandoned by the United States because of domestic U.S. protest, opposition from Israel and its supporters, and opposition from Egypt.

The Sadat initiative,* which soon followed and was, in part, a reaction to the joint communique, reflected the desire of President Anwar Sadat* of Egypt to move things forward in his own particular way. The Sadat visit to Jerusalem,* his speech to the Knesset* on November 20, 1977, and the negotiations that followed led the United States to focus its policies somewhat differently. As the post-Sadat visit negotiations began, the United States sought to ensure their progress and took an active role in the deliberations. Finally, in the summer of 1978, Carter invited Sadat and Israeli prime minister Menachem Begin* to Camp David,* Maryland, for a Summit meeting to consider various suggestions for resolution of the Arab–Israeli conflict. After thirteen days at the Summit (September 5–17, 1978), the United States, Egypt, and Israel reached agreement on two accords. On September 17, 1978, Carter announced that a "Framework for Peace in the Middle East" and a "Framework for the Conclusion of a Peace Treaty between Egypt and Israel" would be signed.

Subsequently, the goal of the Carter administration was to implement the Camp David Accords* and to ensure that Egypt and Israel would achieve peace and that they would begin to deal with the question of autonomy* for the Palestinians and, ultimately, a comprehensive peace for the Middle East. Following the signing, Carter appointed presidential envoys to attempt to negotiate the provisions for Palestinian autonomy contained in the "Framework for Peace." Initially, Robert S. Strauss* and, later, Sol M. Linowitz* served in this capacity.

Progress was made—an Egypt–Israel Peace Treaty* was signed in March 1979, and the autonomy talks involving Egypt, Israel, and the United States and focusing on resolution of other aspects of the Arab–Israeli conflict were begun soon thereafter. Nevertheless, Carter's approach was altered by developments in the Middle East. The sector that he had all but ignored, the Persian Gulf and the Arabian Peninsula, soon became the main focal point of U.S. policy. The crisis in Iran and the Soviet Union's invasion of Afghanistan preoccupied the Carter administration during its last months in office even as Egypt and Israel implemented the terms of their peace treaty.

For further information see: Zbigniew Brzezinski, *Power and Principle: Memoirs of the National Security Adviser, 1977–1981* (New York: Farrar, Straus, and Giroux, 1983); Jimmy Carter, *Keeping Faith: Memoirs of a President* (New York: Bantam Books, 1982); Jimmy Carter, *The Blood of Abraham: Insights into the Middle East* (Boston: Houghton Mifflin, 1985).

Joseph E. Goldberg

CASABLANCA CONFERENCE. See **CASABLANCA DECLARATION.**

CASABLANCA DECLARATION. At the invitation of King Hassan II* of Morocco and with the support of the U.S. and Russian governments and hundreds of Arabs and Israelis, corporate executives and government officials met in Casablanca, Morocco, from October 30 to November 1, 1994, at the Middle East/ North Africa Economic Summit, where they explored the idea of creating new economic cooperation in the Middle East and North Africa. At the conclusion of the conference there was agreement on a document called the Casablanca

Declaration, which outlined a plan to link Arab–Israeli peace with regional economic growth. The document also included an endorsement of the Middle East peace process. The delegates recognized that business can provide ''the economic scaffolding for a durable peace'' and that a regional effort was necessary, with help from the international community as well. Therefore, the participants ''explored how best to accelerate the development of the Region and overcome . . . obstacles, including boycotts and all barriers to trade and investment.'' There was a recognized need for free movement of goods, capital, and labor across borders in accordance with market forces as well as technical cooperation among the parties. Experts were called upon to examine different options for funding mechanisms and to report within six months of the conference. A Steering Committee to coordinate the various multilateral structures was established, as was an executive Secretariat to be located in Morocco. The participants indicated they would meet again in Amman, Jordan, in the first half of 1995 for a second Summit.

CAVE OF MACHPELA. Located in Hebron,* the Cave of Machpela is one of the holiest sites in the West Bank.*

The Bible says the tomb was purchased by Abraham from the sons of Heth as a burial place for his wife, Sarah. The patriarchs Isaac and Jacob and the matriarchs Rebecca and Leah were also buried there, according to the Book of Genesis.

The area is known as the Cave of Machpela by Jews. To Muslims it is known as al-Haram al-Ibrahimi.

Over the ages the Jewish community of Hebron has regarded itself as the guardian of the cave, which has been a site of Jewish pilgrimage.

Islamic tradition has sanctified the memories of the prophets Abraham, Isaac, and Jacob, and thus the cave has also been important to Muslims. In the Byzantine and Crusader period, Christian churches were built over it.

In the early days, the site served as a place of worship for believers of all three religions. In 1266, Sultan Rukan al-Din Baibars decreed that Jews and Christians were forbidden to enter the cave. This prohibition was maintained for centuries. Jewish pilgrims and others testify that Jews were permitted to ascend the south stairway only as far as the seventh step, to an opening in the wall of the building over the cave. This situation persisted until the Six Day War.* Thereafter, the cave was again opened to worshipers of all religions.

Nevertheless, there were complications as a consequence of the fact that a mosque had been built over the site of the tombs in the Middle Ages, and thus access to the tombs required passing through the mosque. Various compromises were worked out, but none seemed to satisfy both the Jews and the Muslims, leading to periodic controversies and clashes. See also TOMB OF THE PATRIARCHS; HEBRON MASSACRE.

CAVE OF THE PATRIARCHS. See **CAVE OF MACHPELA.**

CEASE-FIRE (1970). Conflict was sporadically waged between Egypt* and Israel along the Suez Canal* after the Six Day War.* An intensification of Egyptian hostilities in the spring of 1969 and the beginning of the War of Attrition* led to an Israeli response that included deep-penetration* bombing raids into Egyptian territory. These raids prompted Egyptian president Gamal Abdul Nasser* to solicit and acquire direct Soviet assistance, including surface-to-air missiles and military advisers. The acceleration of events and the growing Soviet presence and involvement prompted the Nixon* administration to seek an end to the fighting. Early attempts by Secretary of State William Rogers* proved unsuccessful after their rejection by both Israel and Egypt.

At 2200 GMT on Friday, August 7, 1970, Israel and Egypt began observing a cease-fire that brought an end to the War of Attrition. The cease-fire was proposed in two similar letters from U.S. secretary of state Rogers to United Arab Republic* foreign minister Mahmoud Riad* and Jordanian* foreign minister Zaid Rifai,* dated June 19, 1970. It was intended to last at least ninety days. Egypt agreed to the cease-fire on July 22, 1970, and Israel, after U.S. assurances that the cease-fire would not jeopardize the military balance between Israel and Egypt, accepted the plan on July 31 and communicated this intention on August 4, 1970.

On July 31, the spokesman for the Israeli Cabinet announced: "After consideration of the requests of the U.S. president, and in adherence to the government's basic policy program and authoritative statements, the government resolves to reply affirmatively to the latest peace proposal of the United States."

Among other provisions, the cease-fire agreement noted: "Israel and the UAR will observe ceasefire effective at 2200 GMT Friday, August 7. Both sides will stop all incursions and all firing, on the ground and in the air, across the ceasefire line. Both sides will refrain from changing the military status quo within zones extending 50 kilometers to the east and the west of the ceasefire line. Neither side will introduce or construct any new military installations in these zones."

Each side was to rely on its own means to verify the observance of the cease-fire and allowed for the use of reconnaissance aircraft up to ten kilometers on each side's respective cease-fire line. Violation complaints could be lodged through the United Nations. Each side reaffirmed its adherence to the 1949 Geneva Convention regarding the treatment of prisoners of war and the role of the International Red Cross.

Almost immediately, Israel reported Egyptian violations of the cease-fire. The United States originally claimed that it lacked conclusive evidence to support Israel's allegations, as it did not wish to endanger the commencement of peace talks scheduled to begin on August 25, 1970. On September 3, 1970, after Israel refused to enter into a second round of talks, the United States acknowledged that there had been cease-fire violations. The cease-fire held until the Yom Kippur War.*

For further information see: Yaacov Bar-Siman-Tov, *The Israeli–Egyptian War of Attrition, 1969–1970* (New York: Columbia University Press, 1980); Michael Brecher,

"Israel and the Rogers Peace Initiatives," *Orbis* 18 (1974):402–26; Muhammad Hasanyn Haykal, *The Road to Ramadan* (New York: Quadrangle/New York Times, 1975); David Korn, *Stalemate: The War of Attrition and Great Power Diplomacy in the Middle East, 1967–1970* (Boulder, CO: Westview Press, 1992); Bernard Reich, *Quest for Peace: United States–Israeli Relations and the Arab–Israeli Conflict* (New Brunswick, NJ: Transaction Books, 1977); Lawrence W. Whetten, *The Canal War: Four-Power Conflict in the Middle East* (Cambridge: MIT Press, 1974).

Robert Crangle, Jr., and Noah L. Dropkin

CENTURION TANK. The Centurion was designed and produced in the United Kingdom beginning in 1945. The tank saw its first combat in Korea with the British army. The tank weighs approximately fifty-seven tons and has a maximum road speed of 22 mph and a range of 120 miles. The Centurion has undergone at least thirteen product improvements.

The Centurion entered service with the Israeli Armored Corps in 1959. The Centurion has seen service in the wars of 1967 and 1973 as well as in Lebanon* in 1982. Israel has made significant improvements to their Centurions, which resulted in twice the cruising range, increasing road speed to 27 mph, and increased ammunition storage to seventy-two rounds. The Centurion was also fitted with reactive armor that contains an explosive charge that detonates when hit by high-explosive antitank projectiles to deflect their blast effects and protect the vehicle's crew.

For further information see: Christopher F. Foss, ed., *Jane's Main Battle Tanks,* 2d ed. (London: Jane's, 1986).

Stephen H. Gotowicki

CHAMOUN, CAMILLE (b. Dayr al-Qamr, Lebanon,* 1900; d. August 7, 1987). An integral actor in Lebanese politics, he served in virtually every Parliament from 1934 until his death. Having held several key ministerial posts throughout his career, Chamoun was also involved with the development of the National Pact, served as Lebanon's minister to Great Britain,* and represented Lebanon at the Alexandria Conference* in 1944, where the foundations for the League of Arab States* were laid.

Chamoun's early political alignment was with Bishara al-Khoury's party, the Constitutional Bloc. Elected to power in 1943, Chamoun broke with the party in 1948, when Khoury attempted to amend the constitution to allow himself a second term in office. Under Chamoun's leadership, a diverse group of Khoury opponents coalesced to form the National Socialist Front. In 1952, amid a Cabinet crisis, the front called for a general strike and demanded Khoury's resignation. When the army failed to intervene on his behalf, Khoury resigned, paving the way for Chamoun to succeed him.

Though Chamoun was a popular replacement for Khoury, he lacked a large parliamentary following. Thus, having no firm basis of support, Chamoun instead relied on popular support and reform to strengthen his presidency. Domestically, he worked toward greater economic and political liberalization. However, in the regional and international arenas Chamoun faced his greatest obstacles. Throughout his six years as president, Chamoun adopted pro-Western positions that pitted him against the growing anti-Western and pro-Nasser* sentiment among Lebanon's Muslim population. At the height of the cold war and the burgeoning superpower rivalry in the region, Chamoun's refusal to condemn or condone the Baghdad Pact exacerbated domestic and regional tension. These events, coupled with his refusal to break diplomatic relations with Britain and France* following the Suez crisis* and, later, his acceptance of the Eisenhower Doctrine,* had, by 1957, thrust him into direct conflict with not only Egypt* and Syria* but also Lebanon's Muslims.

The watershed event came in 1957, when Chamoun's electoral victory provoked charges of fraud and heightened fears among the opposition that Chamoun, like Khoury before him, would attempt to amend the constitution. Acts of violent protest occurred throughout the country and peaked on February 22, 1958, when the political union between Egypt and Syria was announced. Massive demonstrations ensued by those who favored Lebanon's incorporation into the United Arab Republic* (UAR). Following the murder of a prominent anti-Chamoun journalist, the opposition demanded the president's resignation and declared a general strike. Within days the general strike turned into an insurrection as Chamoun continued to resist calls to resign. The final blow came on July 14, 1958, when a coup d'état overthrew the pro-Western monarchy in Iraq.* Horrified by these events, Chamoun, under the Eisenhower Doctrine, called upon the United States to intervene militarily on his behalf. Following extensive American mediation, Chamoun was allowed to complete the remainder of his term, provided he not seek to extend his presidency.

Chamoun's term as president left an indelible mark on Lebanon's domestic, regional, and international politics, and his influence continued after his presidency. In 1959, he founded the National Liberal Party and later participated in the Triple Alliance. Chamoun was considered the real power behind Suleiman Franjieh's presidency, under whom he held several key Cabinet positions. Chamoun began building his own private militia to ensure his own, as well as the greater Maronite, interest. Commanded by his son Dany, Chamoun's militia, the Tigers, was instrumental in keeping him in the forefront of Lebanon's political system, as well as safeguarding his power base southeast of Beirut.

Following the outbreak of civil war, a loose coalition of hard-line Maronite groups known as the Lebanese Front came into existence. Whereas Chamoun served as figurehead, Bashir Gemayel* headed the Lebanese Forces, the military command of the front designed to coordinate the activities of the various Maronite militias. The two men maintained a close relationship in which they openly called for a total Syrian withdrawal from Lebanon and advanced the idea of a separate Christian state. As the rivalry between Syria and Israel increasingly manifested itself within Lebanon, Chamoun advocated an Israeli–Maronite alliance as the means of balancing the various forces working within the state. In

1980, however, Bashir Gemayel's Lebanese Forces turned on Chamoun's militia, subsequently eliminating them as an effective fighting force. Despite such actions, the relationship between the two hard-line Maronites endured, with Chamoun remaining president of the Lebanese Front. Following Israel's invasion of Lebanon in 1982* and Bashir Gemayal's assassination in September, the United States was drawn into Lebanon's internationalized conflict. Chamoun was in his mid-eighties when he participated in the 1984 government of National Unity, where he served as minister of finance and housing.

For further information see: Camille Chamoun, *Crise au Liban* (Beirut: al-Fikr al-Hurr Press, 1977); Helena Cobban, *The Making of Modern Lebanon* (London: Hutchinson, 1985); Itamar Rabinovich, *The War for Lebanon 1970–1985* (Ithaca: Cornell University Press, 1985); Kamal Salibi, *Crossroads to Civil War* (London: Ithaca Press, 1976).

Anamika Krishna

CHERBOURG GUNBOAT INCIDENT. An episode involving the escape of five navy missile patrol boats purchased by Israel from France* in the winter of 1969. Five French-built unmarked gunboats attempted to clandestinely depart the Cherbourg, France, shipyard for Israel during the early morning hours of December 25, 1969. The five 40-knot, 270-ton boats were what remained of an Israeli twelve-ship procurement order from 1965. Each 147-foot ship had a range of 1,600 miles and was designed to be equipped with Israel-made Gabriel sea-to-sea missiles.*

In the late 1960s, Israel purchased a large amount of arms from France, including twelve Vendettas built in the Cherbourg shipyards, which were to be used as the core of Israel's missile boat navy. Seven of the ships had been turned over to the Israeli navy by the spring of 1968. Following the raid on Beirut Airport by Israeli forces in December 1968, French president Charles de Gaulle, who opposed the attack on Lebanon,* ordered an arms embargo on Israel that included the five remaining ships. The embargo applied only to the boats' shipment to Israel, not to their manufacture, and thus their production continued without interruption. Israel, which had already provided the design and paid a large down payment on the boats, was concerned about the possibility of an immediate attack by Arab craft equipped with Soviet missiles and was, therefore, looking for ways to circumvent this embargo. Israel's use of French-made helicopters during its Beirut Airport raid* in December 1968 prompted France to tighten the embargo. Israel's expectation of an imminent lifting of the embargo was diminished. With the assistance of sympathetic French officials, Israel acquired the remaining boats under the artificial third-party auspices of Norway.

The design of the Israeli boats was a product of Israel rear admiral Errel's concept of an organic navy that was to include a small force of potent missile boats and small submarines, which would project Israeli naval power without requiring the larger hulls that naval guns demanded. Furthermore, the Soviet development of small-hulled missile boats, such as the Komar- and Osa-class ships, and their export to the Arab world fueled Israel's concern over its ability to defend its shipping and coastline. When, in October 1967, the Israeli destroyer *Eilat** was sunk by such boats, the need for a counterforce of fast-attack missile boats became more pressing as the specter was raised of a larger, more menacing Arab naval attack on Israeli shipping and perhaps even coastline. As such, the boats, already in production in Cherbourg, became a matter of great importance to the Israel Defense Forces,* and their embargo presented Israel with a serious problem in its attempts to overcome its vulnerability.

Three months after the embargo was placed on the five Israeli ships, President de Gaulle resigned, and his successor, Georges Pompidou, did not lift the embargo. As a result, Israel believed that it had no choice left but to immediately extract the five boats from the Cherbourg shipyards in France. The Israelis thought this was of high-enough priority that the boats should be removed even without Paris's permission. In order to assure the legality of such a move, the Israeli government decided to sell the boats to a foreign shipping company, which then, in turn, would be in a position to sell them back to Israel.

The shipping company that agreed to cooperate with Israel was the Starboat Oil and Shipping Company in Panama, which was headed by a Norwegian national named Martin Siemm. The Starboat Company purchased the boats from Israel and signed an agreement stating its willingness to lease them to the Jewish state with the possibility of their full purchase by Israel after three months of leasing. The deal, which was legal, was approved on November 18, 1969, by both the French Foreign and Defense Ministries. Both ministries, however, were unaware of the plans the Norwegian had and that the boats were about to return to Israeli hands.

In late December 1969, eighty Israeli sailors dressed in civilian clothing were sent to Cherbourg and once there were smuggled onto the boats. The Israeli crews had brought food and other supplies and prepared for their journey to Israel. It was decided that the boats would sail on Christmas Eve 1969, when the people of Cherbourg would be least likely to detect the disappearance of the boats. Due to severe weather conditions, the ships could not set out until 2:00 A.M. Their disappearance was not noticed until the following day, and then for the next five days the ships stood at the center of international attention. The boats refueled at sea for fear that a stop at a Mediterranean port could risk their seizure by international authorities.

The news about the escape of the Cherbourg-built boats to Israel caused a governmental crisis in Norway, which was blamed for assisting Israel. In fact, the Norwegian government did not even know about the deal that was privately signed by Martin Siemm. In Paris, too, the government met in emergency session to discuss the escape and decided to declare as persona non grata and expel Admiral (res.) Mordechai Limon, head of Israel's Defense Ministry purchasing mission in France and the mastermind behind the operation. Additionally, General Cazalles, secretary-general of France's Defense Ministry, and General

Louis Bonte, director of international affairs for the Ministerial Delegation for Armament, were removed from their posts.

The Cherbourg boats that arrived in Israel under the pretense that they were to be used during oil excavations were soon repurchased by the Israeli navy and refitted for their original military use. Renamed the Saar-class, or Storm-class, boats, these five were named *Gaash, Soufah, Herev, Hanit,* and *Hetz.*

For further information see: Michael Brecher, *Decisions in Crisis: Israel, 1967 and 1973* (Berkeley: University of California Press, 1980); Elaine Davenport, *The Plumbatt Affair* (London: Andre Deutsch, 1978); Walter Eytan, "The Cherbourg Boats, Memoir," *Midstream* (December 1981): 34–38; Edward Luttwak and Dan Horowitz, *The Israeli Army* (New York: Harper and Row, 1975); Abraham Rabinovich, *The Boats of Cherbourg: The Secret Israeli Operation That Revolutionized Naval Warfare* (New York: Henry Holt, 1988).

Robert Crangle, Jr., and David Wurmser

CHINESE FARM. The Chinese Farm was the site of an important battle in the October War of 1973,* during which both Egypt* and Israel suffered heavy losses.

The farm is located near the southern end of the Suez Canal* on the Sinai Peninsula* and occupies a rise that commands the Tirtur and Akavish Roads, which run southwest to the canal at a point near the Deversoir airfield. Originally a Japanese agricultural farm, the area was nicknamed the Chinese Farm by Israeli soldiers. During the Israeli occupation of the Sinai Peninsula, the area near the Deversoir airfield was identified as one of several potential crossing points along the Suez Canal and accessed by the Tirtur and Akavish Roads.

During the October War, an Israeli probe located a gap* between the Second and Third Egyptian Armies near the Deversoir crossing point. Before a full-scale crossing could be launched, the Egyptian positions at the Chinese Farm, only 1,000 yards north of the roads, had to be captured. Then bridges would be moved down the Akavish Road to the canal.

When the Israeli First Brigade attacked, the Egyptian infantry was unprepared and failed to engage them. The brigade reached the canal and reported that Akavish was clear. General Sharon's* forces advanced along the road and were engaged by artillery and antitank-guided missiles (ATGMs) from Egyptian infantry positions at the farm. One of the bridges to be used in the crossing was damaged, and the road was closed.

The First Brigade attacked the farm on October 14 and, by the morning of the fifteenth, withdrew with heavy casualties in order to regroup. General Gonen refused Sharon's request to continue with the canal crossing unless the roads could be cleared and the bridging equipment moved into place, opening a secure supply line.

A second Israeli armored assault against the Chinese Farm on October 16 was halted for lack of infantry to protect the tanks. That evening an infantry battalion was flown in to lead the attack. By morning they had been halted seventy-five yards in front of the Egyptian positions. For fourteen hours they suffered heavy casualties, while the bridging equipment was moved to the canal.

Alerted to the crossing on October 16, the Egyptians sent three brigades from the north and south to close the Israeli corridor. The brigades were held off with heavy losses. That night the bulk of the Egyptian forces at the Chinese Farm were withdrawn. On October 18, the Israelis took the position, discovering a vast network of trenches, tank firing positions, obstacles, and mines. The ground was covered with ATGM wires and destroyed vehicles.

For further information see: Peter Allen, *The Yom Kippur War* (New York: Charles Scribner's Sons, 1982); Edgar O'Ballance, *No Victor, No Vanquished: The Yom Kippur War* (San Rafael, CA: Presidio Press, 1978); Chaim Herzog, *The War of Atonement October, 1973* (Boston: Little, Brown, 1975).

David J. Abram

CHRISTOPHER, WARREN (b. Scranton, North Dakota, October 27, 1925). He received an undergraduate degree from the University of Southern California in 1945 and later went to Stanford Law School. Christopher entered the practice of law at O'Melvery and Myers, a firm to which he returned between his periods of government service. He served as deputy attorney general of the United States from June 1967 to January 1969. Christopher became deputy secretary of state in February 1977 and remained in that position until January 1981. He helped to negotiate the release of fifty-two American hostages in Iran.

Christopher became the sixty-third secretary of state on January 20, 1993. In this position, he was primarily responsible for the formulation and execution of U.S. Middle East policy, especially that dealing with the Arab–Israeli conflict, during the Clinton* administration. He was an active player, making numerous visits to the region and participating in the Madrid peace process* negotiations in the United States and abroad. He was also involved in the Israel–Palestine Liberation Organization* (PLO) Declaration of Principles* (DOP) and the agreements to implement it, as well as the Israel–Jordan Peace Treaty.* He played an important role in seeking to achieve an agreement between Israel and Syria,* engaging in numerous shuttle diplomacy* efforts between Damascus and Jerusalem.*

Pamela Rivers

CHURCHILL, SIR WINSTON LEONARD SPENCER (b. 1874; d. 1965). Winston Churchill's involvement in Middle Eastern affairs began during his term as colonial secretary, from February 1921 to October 1922. As colonial secretary, Churchill and the newly established Middle East Department were entrusted with the task of devising a new comprehensive and unified British policy toward the areas that had recently come under British control. On the basis of this mandate, Churchill convened the Cairo Conference* in March 1921, where the following decisions were made: Feisal,* the deposed king of Syria,* was to be offered the kingship of Iraq,* and Abdullah,* Feisal's elder brother, was to receive the emirate of Transjordan.* Churchill's efforts were invaluable in securing Hashemite support for the decisions made in Cairo.

In an attempt to quell the rising tide of violence between Arabs and Jews and calm increasing Arab apprehension over Zionist* activities, Churchill, on behalf of the British government, issued the first official White Paper on Palestine on July 1, 1922.* This statement of policy, also known as the Churchill Memorandum, contained the following essential points: it reaffirmed the Balfour Declaration* and declared it unsusceptible to change; a Jewish National Home* was to be founded in Palestine* as of right, but Palestine as a whole was not to be converted into a Jewish National Home; no disappearance or subordination of the Arab population, language, or culture was ever contemplated by the British government; the Zionist Executive may assist only in the general development of Palestine but not in its government; all citizens were to be Palestinians; Jewish immigration to Palestine was to be regulated by the legislative assembly and not exceed economic capacity; and, finally, the British government intended to foster self-government in Palestine in gradual stages. The Churchill White Paper was ultimately rejected by the Arabs but accepted, despite some reservations, by the Zionists.

During and immediately following World War II, the British government was absorbed in non-Middle East matters, maintaining policies in Palestine consistent with those outlined in a new White Paper issued in 1939.* Having become prime minister in 1940, Churchill and his government began, by 1943, contemplating a shift in British policy. In December that year, a Cabinet committee on Palestine proposed a partition plan similar to the one issued by the Peel Commission* in 1937. Churchill, who had supported the Peel Commission and opposed the 1939 White Paper, backed the new proposals. In 1944, Churchill personally informed Chaim Weizmann* of the government's intention to partition Palestine. The recommendations of the Cabinet committee, however, failed to become official policy due to the assassination in Cairo of Churchill's close friend Lord Moyne* by members of the Stern gang* on November 6, 1944. Three years later the United Nations General Assembly approved the partition of Palestine.

Throughout his tenure as British prime minister, from 1940 to 1945, Churchill maintained a great deal of influence over events in the Middle East. He participated in Summit meetings held in Teheran and in Cairo in 1943. In May 1945, his threat to intervene was essential in forcing de Gaulle's decision to desist from further military activity in Syria. He advocated staunch opposition to increasing Soviet aspirations in the region, forcing their retreat from the Turkish Straits in 1945 and from Iran in 1946. During his second term as prime minister, from 1951 to 1955, Churchill saw the increasing radicalism of certain Arab regimes, particularly in Egypt,* as detrimental to British interests. Relations between Britain and Egypt gradually worsened, culminating in the 1956 Suez War,* launched by Churchill's protégé, Prime Minister Anthony Eden.* Following his final years in office, Churchill was not formally connected to events in the Middle East.

For further information see: Reader Bullard, *Britain and the Middle East* (London: Hutchinson University Library, 1964); Winston S. Churchill, *The World Crisis, 1918–1928: The Aftermath* (New York: Charles Scribner's Sons, 1929); Winston S. Churchill, *The World Crisis: 1911–1918,* 3 vols. (New York: Charles Scribner's Sons, 1931); Paul L. Hanna, *British Policy in Palestine* (Washington, DC: American Council on Public Affairs, 1942); Albert H. Hourani, *Great Britain and the Arab World* (London: John Murray, 1945); Aaron S. Klieman, *Foundations of British Policy in the Arab World: The Cairo Conference of 1921* (Baltimore: Johns Hopkins University Press, 1970); Elizabeth Monroe, *Britain's Moment in the Middle East, 1914–1956* (London: Chatto and Windus, 1963; Oscar K. Rabinowicz, *Winston Churchill on Jewish Problems* (New York: Thomas Yoseloff, 1960).

Anamika Krishna

CHURCHILL MEMORANDUM. See **WHITE PAPER OF 1922.**

CITY OF PEACE. See **JERUSALEM.**

CLINTON, BILL (b. Hope, Arkansas, August 19, 1946). William Jefferson Blythe Clinton earned a degree in international affairs from Georgetown University in Washington, D.C., in 1968 and then attended Oxford University for two years as a Rhodes Scholar. He graduated from Yale Law School in 1973. He became active in politics as director of George McGovern's presidential campaign in Texas in 1972 and continued to be involved in political life at various levels thereafter. He was elected to five terms as governor of Arkansas, the first time in 1978. Clinton defeated George Bush* in the 1992 election and became president of the United States in January 1993.

The Clinton administration entered office with no coherent view of the post–cold war world and no overall conception of the foreign and national security policy essential for the post–Gulf War* and post–Madrid Conference* Middle East. There was no specific approach to the Arab–Israeli conflict and its resolution. Some potential elements were foreshadowed by the election campaign, but these were more general than specific and provided little significant insight into the prospective Middle East policies of the administration. The dominant focus was on domestic issues, while foreign policy, in general, and the Middle East, in particular, were given little attention. Nevertheless, Clinton made clear that he wanted to keep the peace process on track and to take those actions necessary to prevent a break in continuity. Clinton made clear his view that the United States should serve as an honest broker and, at times, as a catalyst, and therefore there would be a degree of activism. Secretary of State Warren Christopher* later described the U.S. role as one of a full partner.*

Clinton seemed to believe that Israel would make meaningful concessions only when it is reassured of U.S. support. Consultation and coordination with Israel became an important feature of the process. From the outset the administration sought to facilitate the post–Madrid Conference process inherited from the Bush administration. Christopher and his aides made numerous trips to the region and worked with the parties to facilitate their efforts. Clinton became the host for the signing of the Israel–Palestine Liberation Organization* (PLO) Declaration of Principles* and the Israel–Jordan Washington Declaration.* He also was a witness to the signing of the Israel–Jordan* Treaty of Peace* signed in the region.

CLOSE PROXIMITY TALKS. A framework for Arab–Israeli negotiation that was first recommended by the United States in October 1971 and patterned after the Rhodes talks* of 1949. The talks were so named by the Israeli Cabinet because the parties would meet in close proximity to one another, as they did in 1949 at the Hotel des Roses on the island of Rhodes in pursuit of the Armistice Agreements.* On February 2, 1972, the Israeli Cabinet consented to begin the close proximity talks in pursuit of an interim Suez Canal* agreement. More generally known as proximity talks,* it was envisaged that Israeli and Egyptian* representatives would convene for indirect negotiations in a New York hotel to be mediated by Joseph Sisco,* then U.S. assistant secretary of state. After initially refusing to consent to such talks, Israel eventually agreed. In February 1973, after over a year of diplomatic efforts, Egypt refused to accept the United States as mediator and declined to enter into talks. Further attempts to bring the two sides to talk failed. See also PROXIMITY TALKS.

For further information see: Michael Brecher, *Decisions in Israel's Foreign Policy* (New Haven, CT: Yale University Press, 1975); Henry A. Kissinger, *White House Years* (Boston: Little, Brown, 1979); Bernard Reich, *Quest for Peace: United States–Israel Relations and the Arab–Israeli Conflict* (New Brunswick, NJ: Transaction Books, 1977).
Noah L. Dropkin

CLOSURE OF OCCUPIED TERRITORIES. An Israeli government policy closing the occupied territories* and not permitting the transit by Palestinians* to Israel at the checkpoints between the Gaza Strip* and West Bank* and Israel.

COLD PEACE. A term widely used by Israelis to describe and refer to the nature of the peace established between Egypt* and Israel by the Egypt–Israel Peace Treaty of 1979.* In essence it referred to the lack of "warmth" in the arrangement that Israelis had sought and hoped for; all of the formal provisions were adhered to, but there was a lack of enthusiasm for the normalization of relations, especially by Egypt, as perceived by Israel. Although the relationship has withstood several severe tests, Israelis see it as less than what they had hoped for.

COMMITTEE FOR SECURITY ON THE ROADS. A faction of Kahane Chai,* this is a group of militant Jewish settlers in the occupied territories* who wish to fight Arab terror groups with their own version of terror. The group was branded as an "illegal, terrorist organization" by the government of Israel on March 13, 1994, in response to the Hebron Massacre.* Claiming to be a revenge organization, the committee declared that its main objective would be achieved once terrorism against Jews stops. To achieve this, unidentified members have claimed that "the moment the Arabs see that they are dealing with people who will murder them back, they will be afraid and terrorism will stop."

The Committee for Security on the Roads (CSR) has maintained that its best method for ensuring the safety of Jews in the settlement areas is for the settlers themselves to provide for the safety of Jews who travel through towns inhabited primarily by Arabs.

Generally, the CSR members remain hidden behind masks out of concern that they may be identified by Israel's General Security Services (SHABAK), which, in turn, will treat the CSR just as it treats any terrorists, that is, as members of a violent cell. Israel Defense Forces* (IDF) chief of staff Ehud Barak* has stated that wherever terror exists and by whomever it takes place, the IDF will do all it can to stop it.

Yasha Manuel Harari

COMMITTEE ON THE EXERCISE OF THE INALIENABLE RIGHTS OF THE PA-LESTINIAN PEOPLE. On November 10, 1975, concerned that no progress had been made toward self-determination, national independence, and sovereignty for the Palestinians,* the United Nations General Assembly, by Resolution 3376 (XXX),* established this committee to make recommendations toward achieving those objectives. The committee is more commonly known as the Palestinian Rights Committee. It has maintained the question of Palestine in the forefront of the concerns of the United Nations, especially the General Assembly. The committee's activities are designed to heighten international awareness about the issues relating to the problem of Palestine so as to facilitate a negotiated political solution. The committee has brought matters to the attention of the General Assembly and the Security Council, held commemorative events, dispatched visiting missions to world capitals, and organized seminars and symposia.

COMMON AGENDA. On September 14, 1993, Israel and Jordan* signed a substantive common agenda providing their map for their approach to achieving peace between them. The common agenda:

A. Goal: The achievement of a just, lasting and comprehensive peace between the Arab States, the Palestinians and Israel as per the Madrid invitation.

B. Components of Israel–Jordan Peace Negotiations: 1. Searching for steps to arrive at a state of peace based on Security Council Resolution 242* and 338* in all their aspects; 2. Security: a) Refraining from actions or activities by either side that may adversely affect the security of the other or may prejudge the final outcome of negotiations; b) Threats to security resulting from all kinds of terrorism; c) i. Mutual commitment not to threaten each other by any use of force and not to use weapons by one side against the other including conventional and non-conventional mass destruction weapons; ii. Mutual commitment, as a matter of priority and as soon as possible, to work towards a Middle East free from weapons of mass destruction, conventional and nonconventional weapons; this goal is to be achieved in the context of a comprehensive, lasting and stable peace characterized by the renunciation of the use of force, reconciliation and openness [Note: Item c-ii may be revised in accordance with relevant agreements to be reached in the Multilateral Working Group on Arms Control and Regional Security.]; d) Mutually agreed upon security arrangements and security confidence-building measures; 3. a) Securing the rightful water shares of the two sides; b) Searching for ways to alleviate water shortage; 4. Refugees and Displaced Persons: Achieving an agreed just solution to the bilateral aspects of the problem of refugees and displaced persons in accordance with international law; 5. Borders and Territorial Matters: Settlement of territorial matters and agreed definitive delimitation and demarcation of the international boundary between Israel and Jordan with reference to the boundary definition under the Mandate, without prejudice to the status of any territories that came under Israeli Military Government control in 1967. Both parties will respect and comply with the above international boundary; 6. Exploring the potentials of future bilateral cooperation, within a regional context where appropriate, in the following: a) Natural resources—Water, energy and environment—Rift Valley development; b) Human resources—Demography—Labor—Health—Education—Drug control; c) Infrastructure—Transportation: land and air—Communication; d) Economic areas including tourism; 7. Phasing the discussion, agreement, and implementation of the items above including appropriate mechanisms for negotiations in specific fields; 8. Discussion on matters related to both tracks to be decided upon in common by the two tracks.

C. It is anticipated that the above endeavor will ultimately, following the attainment of mutually satisfactory solutions to the elements of this agenda, culminate in a peace treaty.

On October 1, 1993, Jordanian crown prince Hassan* and Israeli foreign minister Shimon Peres* met at the White House with President Bill Clinton.* They agreed to set up two groups: a bilateral economic committee and a U.S.–Israeli–Jordanian trilateral economic committee. The first meeting of the trilateral committee was held on November 4, 1993, in Paris, and a second was held in Washington on November 30, 1993.

CONCILIATION COMMISSION FOR PALESTINE. See **PALESTINE CONCILIATION COMMISSION.**

CONFERENCE TO SUPPORT MIDDLE EAST PEACE. (Also and popularly known as the DONORS CONFERENCE). A conference convened in Washington on October 1, 1993, at the call of Secretary of State Warren Christopher* to generate funding for the Gaza–Jericho first plan* and the Israel–Palestine Liberation Organization* (PLO) Declaration of Principles* (DOP) resulting from the Israel–PLO negotiations earlier in 1993. At the conference a number of parties pledged to provide funds to help facilitate the process of implementing the agreement.

The United States and Russia cosponsored the international donors conference. Its purpose was to mobilize international resources to produce tangible improvements in the daily lives of Palestinians in the Gaza Strip* and the West

Bank.* More than forty-six countries and international institutions participated. They pledged more than $2 billion in aid to the Palestinians in Gaza and the West Bank over the next five years.

COORDINATING COMMITTEE. A committee established by Israel and the Palestine Liberation Organization* (PLO) to implement the Declaration of Principles.* Its first meeting was on October 13, 1993.

CORAL SEA TANKER. A 68,000-ton cargo ship flying the Liberian flag was transporting oil from the Persian Gulf to Israel on June 11, 1971. As the ship passed through the Bab el Mandeb* on its way to Israel with a crew of thirty-eight Israelis and ten other nationals, it was overtaken by a craft carrying Popular Front for the Liberation of Palestine* (PFLP) terrorists. The craft, which had been lowered from a fishing boat in the vicinity of Perim Island, approached the cargo ship on the starboard side, firing ten bazooka rounds, of which seven struck the ship. Two fires broke out on the ship but were quickly extinguished. The PFLP claimed responsibility for the attack.

David Wurmser

CORPUS SEPARATUM. On November 29, 1947, the United Nations (UN) General Assembly adopted Resolution 181 (II)* partitioning Palestine* along the lines suggested in the United Nations Special Committee on Palestine* (UN-SCOP) majority report. Part III of that resolution provided that the city of Jerusalem* be established as a *corpus separatum* under a special international regime to be administered by the UN. The Trusteeship Council was designated to discharge the responsibility of the administering authority on behalf of the UN. The boundaries of the city were to be essentially the same as recommended in the UNSCOP majority report. The city was to be demilitarized, and paramilitary or military formations were not permitted within its confines. Free access to the holy places and the free exercise of worship were to be assured, subject only to the requirements for public order and decorum. The Mandate* for Palestine was to terminate as soon as possible but not later than August 1, 1948. The independent Arab and Jewish states and the *corpus separatum* for the city of Jerusalem were to come into existence within two months of the evacuation of the armed forces of the Mandatory Power but not later than October 1, 1948. Finally, the resolution created a Palestine Commission and charged it with implementing the partition. The first Arab–Israeli War* precluded implementation of the partition plan, and sovereignty over Jerusalem thus became a legal and political question that remains unresolved.

UN General Assembly Resolution 194 (III)* of December 11, 1948, repeated the main points outlined in the partition plan and established the Palestine Conciliation Commission* (PCC) to promote a peaceful settlement to the dispute.

UN General Assembly Resolution 303 (IV) of December 9, 1949, also reiterated the intention of the General Assembly to create a *corpus separatum* and requested the Trusteeship Council to prepare a statute for Jerusalem—a consti-tution for an international city. The Trusteeship Council's statute for Jerusalem was presented to the assembly on June 14, 1950. During the debate in the Political Committee, draft resolutions were submitted that, in effect, dropped the idea of internationalization for the city. Many of the members and the parties concerned objected to the principle of territorial internationalization, and at this point functional internationalization (i.e., international control over only the holy places) gained wider acceptance.

General Assembly Resolutions 194 (III) and 303 (IV) restated the intention of the General Assembly to create that *corpus separatum*. In response to Res-olution 194, the Palestine Conciliation Commission was established to develop a plan for Jerusalem, and in response to Resolution 303 the UN Trusteeship Council was called upon to draft a statute for the city of Jerusalem. The Trus-teeship Council approved a draft statute for the city of Jerusalem on April 4, 1950, but in light of Israeli and Jordanian* opposition, the Trusteeship Council declined to take further steps without instructions from the General Assembly. The assembly never issued any instructions. From 1952 until 1967, the question of the status of the city of Jerusalem was conspicuous only by its absence from discussion with the UN.

The United Nations General Assembly passed three resolutions (Resolutions 181 [II], November 29, 1947; 194 [III], December 11, 1948; and 303 [IV], December 9, 1949) providing for, and relating to, full territorial internationali-zation of Jerusalem.

Resolution 303 (IV) restated "its intention that Jerusalem should be placed under a permanent international regime, which should envisage appropriate guarantees for the protection of the Holy Places, both within and outside Jeru-salem" and confirmed specifically that "(1) the City of Jerusalem shall be es-tablished as a *corpus separatum* under a special international regime and shall be administered by the United Nations."

In accordance with the request of the General Assembly in Resolution 303 (IV) of December 9, 1949, the Trusteeship Council approved a statute for the city of Jerusalem on April 4, 1950, which was submitted to the governments of Israel and the Hashemite Kingdom of Jordan with a request for their full co-operation. In view of its conclusion that neither government appeared prepared to collaborate in the implementation of the statute, the Trusteeship Council de-cided in a resolution of June 14, 1950, to submit the statute to the General Assembly.

THE CROSSING. A reference to the crossing of the Suez Canal* by the Egyp-tian* army at the outset of the Yom Kippur War* from the western side to the eastern shore, where it attacked Israeli positions in the Bar-Lev Line.*

For further information see: Avraham (Bren) Adan, *On the Banks of the Suez* (San Rafael, CA: Presidio Press, 1980); Saad El Shazly, *The Crossing of the Suez* (San Francisco: American Mideast Research, 1980).

CSS2 MISSILE. The CSS2 is a single-stage, surface-to-surface, liquid-propellant, intermediate-range ballistic missile produced by the People's Republic of China. The Chinese designation for the CSS2 is DF3/3A or "East Wind." The U.S./ North Atlantic Treaty Organization (NATO) designation is CSS2. The CSS2 is based primarily on Soviet technology. It was developed by the Chinese in the late 1960s and entered service in 1971. The CSS2 ballistic missile is sixty-seven feet in length and eight feet in diameter and is capable of carrying either a high-explosive warhead or a nuclear warhead. The missile has a range of approximately 1,800 miles and relies on internal inertial navigational guidance. It is inaccurate and, therefore, of limited military utility. The system is trans-portable but not fully mobile.

In March 1988, it became public knowledge that Saudi Arabia had purchased a quantity of CSS2 missiles from China. It is estimated that Saudi Arabia may have purchased between 30 and 100 CSS2 missiles. The CSS2 that the Saudis purchased is believed to be a modified version of the original missile with a payload of approximately 3,400 pounds and a slightly reduced range of 1,675 miles. The Saudi CSS2 missiles are reported to be armed with a single, high-explosive, conventional warhead. It is believed that these missiles became op-erational in the early 1990s.

Saudi Arabia's acquisition of the CSS2 reflected its desire to supplement its military power but must be considered in the context of its regional concerns after watching the war of cities (extensive use of ballistic missiles) between Iraq* and Iran. Saudi Arabia assured the international community that these missiles were acquired for defensive purposes only, but Iran and Israel did not see them strictly for their deterrent value. Israel perceived the CSS2 as an of-fensive weapon that, if armed with a warhead of mass destruction or even a large, high-explosive warhead, could cause extraordinary destruction. Saudi Ara-bia is reported to have sent discrete messages to Israel through both the United States and Egypt* that the CSS2s would not be directed against Israel.

China's CSS2 sale to Saudi Arabia represented the first sale of an interme-diate-range ballistic missile to a Third World country. This sale helped solidify China's position as a major arms supplier in the Middle East and has raised concerns over its interest in selling its new ballistic missiles, the M-9 and M-11, to regional states such as Iran, Libya, and Pakistan. Thus, the acquisition of CSS2 missiles by Saudi Arabia may be viewed as a destabilizing factor in the Middle East's military balance.

For further information see: W. Seth Carus, *Ballistic Missiles in the Third World: Threat and Response* (New York: Praeger, 1990); Martin S. Navias, *Going Ballistic: The Build-Up of Missiles in the Middle East* (London: Brassey's, 1993); Bernard Reich and

Alexander Huang, "China's Arms Sales to the Middle East: The Case of Saudi Arabia," *Research Report* (London: Institute of Jewish Affairs, 1989); Yitzhak Shichor, *East Wind over Arabia: Origins and Implications of the Sino-Saudi Missile Deal* (Berkeley: University of California at Berkeley, Institute of East Asian Studies, Center for Chinese Studies, 1989).

Jon J. Peterson and Stephen H. Gotowicki

CUNNINGHAM, ALAN GORDON (b. Dublin, 1887). He was a soldier who served as the last British high commissioner for Palestine.* He had a distinguished military career and achieved the rank of general in 1945 and, in that year, was appointed high commissioner for Palestine. He left Palestine on May 14, 1948, when the state of Israel declared its independence.

CZECH–EGYPTIAN ARMS DEAL (Czechoslovakian–Egyptian arms deal). The Czechoslovakian–Egyptian* arms deal reshaped the Arab–Israeli conflict, converting it, in part, into another facet of the cold war and making large quantities of Soviet bloc arms available to the Arab states.

On September 27, 1955, President Gamal Abdul Nasser* of Egypt announced the purchase of a large quantity of arms from Czechoslovakia, which was acting for the Soviet Union. Egypt was to secure arms in exchange for such Egyptian products as cotton and rice. The deal was viewed as the beginning of an arms race in the region not subject to Western influence and control, as had been the case since the Tripartite Declaration of 1950.* The arms included MiG-15 fighters, Ilyushin Il-28* twin-engine jet bombers, Ilyushin-24 troop transport aircraft, vehicles, armored personnel carriers, radar installations, antitank guns, self-propelled guns, recoilless rifles, naval destroyers, submarines, minesweepers, Stalin III heavy tanks, and T-34 medium tanks.

Czechoslovakia had been one of the suppliers of arms and equipment to Israel. During Israel's War of Independence,* Czechoslovakia served as a way station for Israeli arms purchases and a training ground for their pilots. After the war, the eastern bloc was not at all receptive to Israeli requests for arms.

The deal created problems for Israel. Before, Israel figured a ten-year lead over its military opponents, but afterward it required more weapons to maintain that edge. Israel struck deals with France* (primarily) and Britain.* Furthermore, some of their planners began to call for a preemptive war against the Egyptians. Thus, it was also a factor in the 1956 war.*

It marked the beginning of a Soviet effort to increase its presence in the region through arms supplies, trade programs, aid and technical assistance efforts, cultural exchange, and various other techniques. The emergence of the Soviet bloc as a major and virtually uninhibited arms supplier to the Arab states unwilling to enter into Western-conceived control processes (such as the Tripartite Declaration of 1950) changed the conditions and assumptions underlying the arms balance and arms control in the Arab–Israeli sector of the Middle East.

For further information see: Faiz S. Abu-Jaber, ''The Origins of Soviet-Arab Coop-eration,'' *Middle East Forum* 45 (1969):13–44; Uri Bialer, *Between East and West: Israel's Foreign Policy Orientation 1948–1956* (Cambridge: Cambridge University Press, 1990); Michael Brecher, *The Foreign Policy System of Israel: Settings, Images, Process* (New Haven, CT: Yale University Press, 1972); Uri Ra'anan, *The USSR Arms the Third World: Case Studies in Soviet Foreign Policy* (Cambridge: MIT Press, 1969); Zeev Schiff, *A History of the Israeli Army: 1874 to the Present* (New York: Macmillan, 1985).

John Fontaine

D

DAMASCUS PROTOCOL. The Damascus Protocol was issued in December 1915 by the Arab nationalist secret societies of Al-Fatat and Al-Ahd. It expressed Arab demands for an independent Arab state as a primary condition upon which an alliance with the British and revolt against the Ottomans* would be based. The Damascus Protocol was transmitted to Sherif Hussein* of Mecca, who accepted its terms, thereby formalizing an alliance between himself and Arab nationalists. Thus, Arab nationalists accepted Hussein as their spokesman, and he, in turn, presented their demands in future negotiations with the British. The Damascus Protocol provides a foundation for the territorial demands made by Sherif Hussein in the Hussein–McMahon correspondence.* On the basis of the Hussein–McMahon correspondence the Arab Revolt* was launched on June 5, 1916.

For further information see: George Antonius, *The Arab Awakening* (Philadelphia: Lippincott, 1939).

Anamika Krishna

DAYAN, MOSHE (b. Kibbutz Degania, May 20, 1915; d. Tel Aviv, October 16, 1981). He grew up in Nahalal. Dayan was one of the first to join the Palmach* when it was established, on May 18, 1941, and served under Orde Wingate* in his special night squads. From 1939 to 1941, Dayan was detained by the British in Acre* but was released in order to take part in an Allied venture against the Vichy French in Syria* in 1941. On June 7, 1941, Dayan headed a squad of Haganah* members who joined the British in an operation intended to destroy bridges in Syria. During an assault on a police station he was wounded, which resulted in the loss of his left eye. In July 1948, he was made the commanding officer of Jerusalem* while it was under siege. In that capacity he took part in informal negotiations with King Abdullah* of Jordan* and later served as a member of the Israeli delegation to the armistice negotiations on Rhodes.

Between 1950 and 1953, Dayan served as commander of the Southern and Northern Commands of the Israel Defense Forces* (IDF) and later head of the General Branch of Operations in the General Staff. Dayan's appointment as chief of staff in December 1953 followed a stormy Cabinet defense committee meeting in which he was supported by David Ben-Gurion.* Dayan led the IDF during the Sinai War of 1956* and was discharged from the IDF in January 1958. In November 1959, he was elected as a member of the Knesset* on the MAPAI* list and became minister of agriculture in Prime Minister David Ben-Gurion's government. In 1963, Ben-Gurion left his party over the Lavon affair* and established a new political party, RAFI. After much hesitation Dayan joined Ben-Gurion and Shimon Peres.* Nevertheless, he continued to serve as minister of agriculture under Prime Minister Levi Eshkol.* Dayan brought to Israeli agriculture, methods of long-range planning and national allocation of resources such as water. He resigned from the Cabinet on November 4, 1964, when Eshkol tried to prevent him from participating in the formation of defense policy. In 1965, he was elected to the Sixth Knesset on the RAFI ticket. Dayan went briefly to Vietnam to observe and write about the Vietnam War. Just prior to the Six Day War,* by popular demand, Prime Minister Levi Eshkol was forced to appoint Dayan to the post of minister of defense. Although Dayan did not have time to change the IDF's operational plans, his position as minister of defense inspired the country with confidence and helped Eshkol to decide on a preemptive strike. After the war Dayan supported the research and development functions of the Ministry of Defense as a means of replenishing the equipment and ammunition of the IDF, in light of the French* arms embargo. He also initiated the open bridges* policy, providing an infrastructure for coexistence between Israel and the Arabs. When Eshkol died suddenly in February 1969 and was succeeded by Golda Meir,* Dayan remained minister of defense. He was among those blamed by the public for the delay in the mobilization of Israel's reserve forces at the time of the Yom Kippur War.* Nevertheless, exonerated by the Agranat Commission,* Dayan continued to serve under Golda Meir's leadership after the elections of December 31, 1973. When Golda Meir resigned in April 1974, Prime Minister Yitzhak Rabin* did not include Dayan in the Cabinet. Between 1974 and 1977, Dayan served as a member of the Knesset and was active in archaeological excavations. When Menachem Begin* became prime minister after the May 1977 elections, Dayan joined the government as foreign minister and in that capacity played a crucial role in the negotiations that led to the Camp David Accords* and the Egypt–Israel Peace Treaty.* Dayan resigned in 1979 over differences of viewpoint and policy with Begin in regard to the autonomy* negotiations. On April 4, 1981, Dayan established a new political party, Telem, which had as one of its primary goals to support Dayan's proposals concerning the occupied territories.* The party secured two mandates in the 1981 Knesset elections.

Among Dayan's works are "Israel's Border and Security Problems," *Foreign Affairs* 33 (January 1955):250–67; *Diary of the Sinai Campaign* (New York: Harper and Row, 1966); *Story of My Life: An Autobiography* (New York: William Morrow, 1976); *Breakthrough: A Personal Account of the Egypt–Israel Peace Negotiations* (New York: Alfred A. Knopf, 1981).

For further information see: Yael Dayan, *My Father, His Daughter* (New York: Farrar, Straus, and Giroux, 1985); Gabriella Heichal, "Moshe Dayan," in Bernard Reich, ed., *Political Leaders of the Contemporary Middle East and North Africa: A Biographical Dictionary* (Westport, CT: Greenwood Press, 1990), pp. 142–50; Naphtali Lau-Lavie, *Moshe Dayan: A Biography* (London: Vallentine, Mitchell, 1968); Shabtai Teveth, *Moshe Dayan: The Soldier, the Man, the Legend* (Boston: Houghton Mifflin, 1973).

DEAD SEA. The lowest point on earth. Located about thirty miles east of Jerusalem* and shared by Jordan* and Israel, it is forty-nine miles long and eleven miles wide, has a 1,309-foot maximum depth, and is 1,299 feet below sea level. The salty water of the lake has a high content of minerals and other chemical elements, including magnesium chloride, sodium chloride, calcium chloride, potassium chloride, and magnesium bromide. One of Israel's major industries is the extraction of these minerals from the Dead Sea.

DECLARATION OF PRINCIPLES (DOP). Israel and the Palestine Liberation Organization* (PLO) conducted secret negotiations in Oslo,* Norway, that culminated in the signing of the Israel–PLO Declaration of Principles on the White House lawn in Washington, D.C., on September 13, 1993. Israeli foreign minister Shimon Peres* and PLO Executive Committee member Mahmud Abbas (Abu Mazen*) signed the Declaration of Principles. The signing was witnessed by U.S. secretary of state Warren Christopher* and Russian foreign minister Kozyrev* in the presence of President Bill Clinton,* Israeli prime minister Yitzhak Rabin,* and PLO chairman Yasser Arafat.*

As part of the arrangement, Israel recognized the PLO as the representative of the Palestinian people. For its part, the PLO recognized Israel's right to exist in peace and security, accepted United Nations Security Council Resolutions 242* and 338,* and renounced the use of terrorism and violence.

They agreed to the creation of a Palestinian Interim Self-Government Authority* to represent the Palestinian people in the West Bank* and the Gaza Strip* for a five-year transitional period to lead to a permanent settlement. Elections to the council would be held among the Palestinian people in the West Bank and Gaza no later than nine months after the declaration went into force. The jurisdiction of the council covered the West Bank and Gaza Strip territory, except for issues that would be negotiated in the permanent status negotiations. A five-year transitional period would begin upon the withdrawal from the Gaza Strip and Jericho area, and permanent status negotiations were to commence as soon as possible, but not later than the beginning of the third year of the interim period. These negotiations will cover remaining issues, including Jerusalem, refugees, settlements, security arrangements, borders, relations and cooperation with other neighbors, and other issues of common interest.

On October 13, 1993, the agreement entered into force, and negotiations on implementation began. At a ceremony in Cairo on May 4, 1994, Rabin and Arafat signed an agreement on the Gaza Strip and the Jericho area. The agreement set out the terms for implementation of the DOP.

See also CAIRO AGREEMENT (1994); EARLY EMPOWERMENT; ISRAEL–PLO ECONOMIC AGREEMENT.

DECLARATION TO THE SEVEN. In the spring of 1918, a group of seven Arab notables living in Cairo presented a memorandum to the British government that requested a definition and clarification of British policy in the Middle East. The Arabs were perplexed and disturbed over the conflicting agreements and statements made by the British government during 1916–18, specifically, the Hussein–McMahon correspondence,* the Balfour Declaration,* the Sykes–Picot Agreement,* and public statements made by British leaders.

The British replied in June 1918, widely publicizing the response that has become known as the "Declaration to the Seven."

The British government maintained that it recognized the "complete and sovereign independence" of the Arabs inhabiting the areas that were free and independent before the outbreak of the war and in the lands the Arabs themselves emancipated from Turkish control during the war. As for the former Ottoman* territories currently occupied by the Allied forces, reference was made to the Baghdad proclamation of March 1917 and Allenby's Jerusalem declaration of December: "It is the wish and desire of His Majesty's Government that the future government of these regions should be based upon the principle of the consent of the governed, and this policy has and will continue to have the support of His Majesty's Government."

As for the areas still under Turkish control, the British government stated that it was the wish of the government that "the oppressed people of these areas should obtain their freedom and independence, and towards the achievement of this object His Majesty's Government continue to labor."

The British reply to the Arabs was short, but one phrase held particular significance: "the consent of the governed." This was once again reiterated in a final pledge of freedom to the Arabs after the Armistice of Mudros signed in October 1918. The Anglo–French Declaration of November 1918 promised to support national governments in Syria* and Iraq* "elected by their free will." This response was made to pacify the inhabitants and facilitate occupation of the region.

For further information see: Ibrahim Al-Abid, *A Handbook to the Palestine Question—Questions and Answers* (Beirut: PLO Research Center, 1971); Great Britain, Parliamentary Papers, *Miscellaneous No. 4, Statements Made on Behalf of His Majesty's Government during the Year 1918 in Regard to the Future Status of Certain Parts of the Ottoman Empire* (London: His Majesty's Stationery Office, 1939); Peter Mansfield, *The Arabs* (Middlesex, England: Penguin Books, reprint 1987).

Nancy Hasanian

DEEP-PENETRATION RAIDS. After the Six Day War* confirmed Israel's military prowess, Egyptian* president Gamal Abdul Nasser* decided that a War of Attrition* would be the most effective manner by which to dislodge Israel from its positions along the Suez Canal.* In April 1969, Egypt launched artillery strikes and guerrilla attacks against Israeli targets along the Suez Canal, and Israel suffered high levels of casualties. In response, Israel built the Bar-Lev Line* along the canal and utilized its air force. However, instead of simply attacking targets along the canal and in the canal zone, Israel expanded the war into the Egyptian heartland.

On January 7, 1970, Israel launched deep-penetration raids against Egypt. Effective deep-penetration raids were made possible by the acquisition by Israel in the fall of 1969 of the Phantom F-4 aircraft,* which possessed the speed, range, maneuverability, versatility, and load capability essential for such operations. These were attacks against the heartland—targets in the Nile Delta, upper Egypt, and the environs of Cairo—and included military installations and air defense sites. The first targets were Egyptian army and air force supply depots in Inchas and Helwan. In February, Israel attacked surface-to-air missile sites and destroyed a factory used for making antiaircraft missile components. In one incident, however, a school was hit, resulting in significant casualties. Israel had notable military successes in the deep-penetration raids. It was able virtually to employ the Phantoms at will, under difficult circumstances, and to attack targets deep within Egyptian territory, which was heavily defended. The Egyptians responded by requesting further military assistance from the Soviet Union, and the situation began to change in April 1970. In a statement on April 29, 1970, Israel charged that Soviet pilots were flying operational missions for Egypt. "In recent days it has become clear beyond any doubt to the Government of Israel that for the first time Soviet pilots are flying operational missions from military installations under their control in Egypt." While the Soviet pilots were not reported in the canal zone, they had apparently assumed the air defense (missiles and the air cover for them) of much of central Egypt against Israel's deep-penetration raids.

Israel began to restrict its aerial penetration raids to where Israeli pilots were sure to encounter Soviet pilots. It was clear that Soviet pilots were participating in the air defense of Egypt, although how much territory this meant was unclear. Certainly, they offered a cover for the Nile Delta and Aswan areas, but it was unclear if they were to include the canal zone in their operational area. Ultimately, this Soviet involvement led to Israeli–Soviet encounters and to U.S. efforts to effect a cease-fire.* The latter was achieved in August 1970, ending the deep-penetration raids and the War of Attrition.

For further information see: Yaacov Bar-Siman-Tov, *The Israeli–Egyptian War of Attrition, 1969–1970: A Case Study of Limited Local War* (New York: Columbia University Press, 1980); T. N. Dupuy, *Elusive Victory* (Dubuque: Hunt, 1992); Chaim Herzog, *The Arab–Israeli Wars* (London: Arms and Armour Press, 1984); Lawrence L. Whetten, *The Canal War: Four Power Conflict in the Middle East* (Cambridge: MIT Press, 1974).

Simeon Manickavasagam

DEFCON III. DEFCON is a U.S. military acronym for defense readiness condition and is a system of progressive alert postures for use between the U.S. Joint Chiefs of Staff and the commanders of unified and specified commands. Defense readiness conditions are graduated to match situations of varying military threat and range from condition 1 to 5. DEFCON 1 is the highest level of alert and corresponds to a condition of war. DEFCON 2 is a condition in which attack is imminent. DEFCON 3 increases readiness in preparation for a possible outbreak of war. During peacetime, DEFCON 3 is the highest stage of alert. In 1973, most U.S. forces were usually at DEFCON 4 or 5. The exception was in the Pacific, where, as a result of the Vietnam War, they were permanently at DEFCON 3. The Strategic Air Command was usually at DEFCON 4.

On October 24, 1973, the Egyptian Third Army* was cut off and surrounded in the Sinai Peninsula* by Israeli forces. Egypt* then requested that American and Soviet forces deploy to enforce the Security Council's cease-fire resolution, so as to save the Third Army. The United States opposed sending either American or Soviet troops to the Sinai and informed the Soviets they would veto any United Nations (UN) Security Council resolution that would do so. The Soviets proposed what was, in effect, an ultimatum that called for U.S. and Soviet forces to be sent to the Sinai not just to impose a cease-fire but also to impose a final settlement on essentially Soviet terms. The Soviets threatened to act unilaterally if the United States did not agree to the Soviet plan.

Concurrently, Soviet airborne divisions were placed at an increased alert state and readied for deployment. At the same time, Soviet naval strength in the Mediterranean Sea was at an all-time high. The administration formed the view that there was a possibility of a unilateral Soviet move in the Middle East. This was based on a plethora of indicators, including "certain ambiguous developments." The Nixon* administration decided that these Soviet actions could not stand; the United States would not tolerate Soviet intervention in the Middle East. The decision was made that the seriousness of U.S. diplomacy could be shown by an increase in U.S. military readiness to DEFCON 3. At 11:41 P.M., all U.S. military forces were ordered to increase readiness to DEFCON 3. Concerned that the message implied by an increase in alert status would not be received by the Soviets quickly enough, the administration ordered other military actions, which included alerting the eighty-second Airborne Division and ordering the deployment of the aircraft carriers *Franklin Delano Roosevelt* and *America* into the eastern Mediterranean to join the aircraft carrier *Independence* south of Crete.

On October 25, at 5:40 A.M., the United States delivered a reply to the Soviets rejecting their demands but agreeing to send a UN supervision force to the Sinai. At 1:10 P.M., Sadat* formally accepted an international force composed of non-permanent members of the Security Council. At 2:40 P.M., the Soviets informed the United States they would send seventy nonmilitary Soviet representatives to observe the implementation of the cease-fire. Reference to the previous night's threat of unilateral intervention was omitted. U.S. military forces were directed to stand down from DEFCON 3 at midnight, October 25.

For further information see: Walter Issacson, *Kissinger* (New York: Simon and Schuster, 1992); Henry A. Kissinger, *Years Of Upheaval* (Boston: Little, Brown, 1982); Richard Nixon, *Leaders* (New York: Warner Books, 1982); William B. Quandt, *Peace Process* (Washington, DC: Brookings Institution, 1993).

Nolan Wohl and Stephen H. Gotowicki

DEIR YASSIN. Deir Yassin is a small village on the outskirts of Jerusalem,* eighteen miles outside the boundaries of the Jewish state outlined in the United Nations partition plan.* However, it was not far from the highway connecting Tel Aviv and Jerusalem. There also were several large Jewish settlements in the area. Due to Deir Yassin's vulnerability to Zionist* forces, the village leaders had arranged a "mutual agreement of nonaggression" between the village and the neighboring Jewish settlements. When Arab forces requested a base in Deir Yassin, they were refused because the exposed location of the village put the safety of the women and children at stake.

In early April 1948, the Haganah* commenced Operation Nachson (part of Plan D*), which was designed to open up a corridor between Tel Aviv and Jerusalem. When the local commanders of the Irgun* and the Stern gang* approached the Haganah commander, Daniel Shaltiel, with a proposal to attack Deir Yassin, he suggested that other objectives would be more helpful. But the two men insisted on targeting Deir Yassin.

The use of a loudspeaker to warn the villagers of the imminent attack was debated. The idea was abandoned because the loudspeaker van got stuck in a ditch.

On April 9, 1948, the Irgun and the Stern gang attacked Deir Yassin. A debate still rages as to whether the residents of Deir Yassin were warned before the ensuing attack. The Arabs of Deir Yassin put up enough resistance that a Haganah (Palmach)* platoon was called in to assist. Shortly thereafter, the village was captured, and the Palmach withdrew.

Meir Pa'il, a Haganah officer assigned to accompany the two groups, believed that the Irgun and Stern gang wanted vengeance for the casualties they had suffered. Two hundred and fifty-four inhabitants of Deir Yassin, men, women, and children, were slaughtered. Many of the bodies were thrown down the cisterns. More than fifteen homes were blown up.

When the British were advised of the massacre, there was discussion of intervention by British troops, but this did not occur.

Initial newspaper reports describe the capture of Deir Yassin as marking the first cooperative effort since 1942 between the Irgun and Stern groups. This engagement marked the first entry of the Irgunists and Sternists into the battle against the Arabs. A spokesperson claimed that the village had become a concentration point for Arabs, including Syrians* and Iraqis,* planning to attack the western suburbs of Jerusalem. The casualties among the women and children were regretted but inevitable. No mention is made of any massacre.

On April 10, 1948, the Red Cross representative in Jerusalem, Jacques de Reynier, "was alerted of a major outrage." When he contacted the Jewish Agency* and the Haganah, both denied any knowledge of the atrocity and urged that de Reynier not make an investigation. "Not only did they refuse to help me but they also refused to be responsible for what they were sure would happen to me." He drove to Deir Yassin and discovered 244 corpses, mostly women and children.

For further information see: Menachem Begin, *The Revolt* (New York: Nash, n.d.); Nicholas Bethell, *The Palestinian Triangle—The Struggle of the Holy Land, 1935–48* (New York: G. P. Putnam's Sons, 1979); James Cameron, *The Making of Israel* (New York: Taplinger, 1976); Larry Collins and Dominique Lapierre, *O Jerusalem* (New York: Simon and Schuster, 1972); Edgar O'Ballance, *The Arab–Israeli War—1948* (New York: Praeger, 1957); Michael Palumbo, *The Palestinian Catastrophe—The 1948 Expulsion of a People from Their Homeland* (London: Faber and Faber, 1987); Desmond Stewart, *Palestinians: Victims of Expediency* (London: Quartet Books, 1982).

Nancy Hasanian

DEMOCRATIC FRONT FOR THE LIBERATION OF PALESTINE (DFLP). One of the main organizations of the Palestinian* national movement, the DFLP emerged in February 1969 as a left-wing splinter of the Popular Front for the Liberation of Palestine,* headed by Nayef Hawatmeh.* The new group initially assumed the name of People's Democratic Front for the Liberation of Palestine. The DFLP considered it essential for the Palestinian movement to resolutely give up the nationalistic ideology and go over to a Marxist platform. It believed the Palestinian national goals could be achieved only through revolution of the masses.

The radical character of the Democratic Front ideology influenced its political course. The front harshly criticized the so-called progressive Arab regimes because the petty bourgeoisie that formed the social basis of those regimes was neither able to lead the national liberation struggle of Arabs nor able to positively contribute to it. In the front leaders' opinion, the necessary prerequisite for successfully continuing such a struggle was a revolutionary change in the ruling regimes and the accession to power in Arab countries of the working and peasant classes. The Palestinian movement should act as the catalyst in this process. The Democratic Front, consequently, rejected the Fatah* principle of "noninterference by Palestinians in the internal affairs of the Arab states." This aspect of the front policy was dramatically manifested in the conflict between Palestinians and Jordan* in 1970.

Internationally, the DFLP allied itself with such socialist countries as China, Cuba, Vietnam, and North Korea. At the same time, leaders of the front were not inclined toward a close relationship with the Soviet Union,* which they accused of "right revisionism" and strongly condemned for recognizing Israel. This relationship later changed after the 1970 Black September* crisis in Jordan and the increasing involvement of the Soviet government in movements for national liberation.

These events prompted the DFLP to reevaluate critically former guidelines and accelerate the transition of the organization to a more moderate and realistic position. Signs of such a transition could be traced back as far as 1969, when, shortly after its formation, the movement's leadership gave up its irreconcilable attitude to Fatah as representing the "right bourgeois forces" within the Palestinian movement and expressed its readiness to take part in the activities of all the Palestine Liberation Organization* (PLO) agencies.

After the October War of 1973,* the Democratic Front became one of the initiators and the most active advocates of the holistic approach of the PLO to the settlement of the Middle East problem. Acting jointly with Fatah and the pro-Syrian organization Saiqa,* an agreement was worked out at the June 1974 session of the Palestine National Council* (PNC). The PNC "transitional programme" envisaged the creation of a Palestinian ministate on the West Bank* and Gaza Strip.*

In 1977, the DFLP began to deviate from its former union with Fatah, criticizing its leaders for not being resolute and consistent enough to counteract the plans of the "Arab reaction." The Democratic Front flatly rejected the Fahd Plan* (1982) and condemned rapprochement with moderate Arab regimes, chosen by Fatah after Israel's invasion of Lebanon.*

Despite its agreement with Arafat's* policy and its persistent demands to carry out democratic reforms in the PLO, the DFLP always tried to stay in "legal" opposition and emphasized the necessity of maintaining the organizational unity of the Palestine movement. Having boycotted, with most Palestinian groups, the seventeenth session of the PNC in Amman (November 1984) and having condemned the decisions adopted at this session, the DFLP, nevertheless, admitted the lawfulness of the session. Though viewing the Amman accord negatively, the DFLP, unlike the PFLP, remained within the PLO and did not join the alternative Palestine National Salvation Front, organized under the aegis of Syria* in March 1985. Subsequently, the DFLP was one of the architects of the process of Palestine national reconciliation, which resulted in restoring the unity of the PLO at the eighteenth session of the PNC (April 1987).

The Democratic Front played an active part during the initial stage of the intifada* and contributed to setting up the united national leadership of the uprising. By mid-1988, there appeared serious divisions within the DFLP. A small but rather influential group arose within the leadership of the front calling for democratization of the inner party and bringing the policy of the DFLP in line with new Palestinian, regional, and international realities. The representative of the DFLP within the Executive Committee of the PLO, Deputy General Secretary of the Front Yasser Abed-Rabbo,* became the leader of this group, which called itself the Movement of Democratic Renewal. In the opinion of the movement's advocates, the bureaucratic interests of the "conservative" leadership were an obstacle to the pursuit of realistic national interests.

In the early 1980s, it sought a middle position between Yasser Arafat* and the more radical rejectionist groups. It split into two factions in 1991, one essentially pro-Arafat and another, more hard-line faction headed by Nayef Hawatmeh.

In the 1970s, it carried out numerous small bombings and some more spectacular operations in Israel and the occupied territories,* concentrating on Israeli targets such as the 1974 massacre in Maalot.* It continues to concentrate its efforts in Israel and the occupied territories.

DER JUDENSTAAT. Theodor Herzl* was the driving force for the creation of the political ideology and worldwide movement of modern political Zionism.* Herzl wrote *Der Judenstaat* (*The Jewish State*), published in Vienna on February 14, 1896, in which he assessed the situation and problems of the Jews and proposed a practical plan for resolution of the Jewish question. It contains an examination of the status of the Jewish people and a detailed plan for creating a state in which Jews would reconstitute their national life in a territory of their own. Herzl set forth his concept of a Jewish homeland, believing this was the only solution to the Jewish problem. Herzl's pamphlet was the catalyst for a campaign to influence European statemen on behalf of the Zionist cause. As a result of this initiative, the first World Zionist Congress was convened in Basle in 1897, at which the World Zionist Organization* was established. Subsequently, Herzl traveled widely to publicize and gain support for his ideas.

DESERT STORM. See **GULF WAR.**

DFLP. See **DEMOCRATIC FRONT FOR THE LIBERATION OF PALESTINE.**

DIASPORA. A Greek word meaning "scattering," which has been used since the Babylonian exile of 586 B.C. to refer to the dispersion of the Jews and the Jewish communities outside Israel. It is interchangeable with the Hebrew term *galut*. In recent years the term has been applied to the Palestinians. See also PALESTINIAN DIASPORA.

DIRANI, MUSTAFA. Leader of a pro-Iranian group based in Lebanon,* called the Faithful Resistance, who was abducted from Lebanon by Israel on May 21, 1994. He was taken to Israel for questioning about the fate of an Israeli airman, Ron Arad. Dirani was in charge of security for the Lebanese Shiite Muslim militia Amal* when they captured Ron Arad in 1986.

DIRECTOR OF MILITARY INTELLIGENCE (DMI). The director of military intelligence heads the Intelligence Branch (AMAN, acronym for Agaf Modiin) of the Israel Defense Forces* (IDF) General Staff. Its function is to provide intelligence for the planning of Israel's defense policy and for war and to provide intelligence to the IDF and other government bodies, especially the Cabinet. Its dominant focus has been the Arab–Israeli conflict and particularly the neighboring Arab states and the Palestinians. The first head of AMAN was Isar Beeri (1948–49). He was followed by Haim Herzog (1949–50 and 1959–62). Benjamin Gibli served from 1950 to 1955. Yehoshafat Harkabi held the post from 1955 to 1959. Subsequent incumbents included Meir Amit, 1962 to 1964; Aharon Yariv, 1964 to 1972; Eliahu Zeira, 1972 to 1974; Shlomo Gazit, 1974 to 1978; Yehoshua Saguy, 1978 to 1983; Ehud Barak,* 1983 to 1985; Amnon Reshef beginning in 1985; Amnon Shahak,* February 1986 to 1991; Uri Saguy, 1992 to the present.

DISENGAGEMENT OF FORCES. See **ISRAEL–EGYPT DISENGAGEMENT OF FORCES AGREEMENT (1974); ISRAEL–SYRIA DISENGAGEMENT OF FORCES AGREEMENT (1974).**

DJEREJIAN, EDWARD P. (b. 1939). A career U.S. Department of State foreign service officer, he has served as assistant secretary for Near Eastern and South Asian affairs and assistant secretary for Near Eastern affairs. Appointed ambassador to Israel in the Clinton* administration, he presented his credentials to Israel's president in January 1994. He resigned from that post in August 1994 to become head of the James A. Baker III Institute for Public Policy at Rice University.

His foreign service career has spanned over thirty years. Djerejian has represented the United States as ambassador to the Syrian Arab Republic (1988–91); deputy chief of mission, Amman, Jordan* (1981–84); deputy director of northern Arabian affairs in the Near Eastern Bureau of the State Department (1972–74); political/labor officer, Casablanca, Morocco; and political officer, Beirut, Lebanon* (1968–69). From 1985 to 1986, he was detailed to the White House as special assistant to the president and deputy press secretary for foreign affairs.

Ambassador Djerejian has been the recipient of many awards, including a Distinguished Honor Award (1993) in recognition of his contributions to the Madrid Peace Conference.*

He received his bachelor of science degree in foreign service at Georgetown University in 1960. He speaks French, Russian, Arabic, and Armenian.

Pamela Rivers

DOME OF THE ROCK. In 638, Jerusalem* was captured by the Caliph Omar. Construction of the Dome of the Rock began in 685 and was completed in 691.

The building of the octagonal structure was ordered by the Umayyad Caliph 'Abd al-Malik ibn Marwan, who succeeded to the caliphate in 684.

The shrine is known as the Dome of the Rock for the outcropping of rock under the dome, believed by some to be where Abraham offered to sacrifice his son, Isaac, and where the Prophet Mohammed ascended to heaven. Jewish tradition maintains that the rock provided the foundation stone for the building of the First Temple and was the location where the Holy Ark was located during the First Temple period. Because of its religious significance to both Muslims and Jews, the area on which the dome is built is revered by both religions.

Because of the historical and religious significance of the shrine, Jerusalem is considered by Muslims to be the third holiest city of Islam. It is regarded by Jews as the holiest city. Conflict has arisen as a result of both groups' attachment to the area and over which group will control the city and its holy sites. From 1948 to 1967, Jerusalem and the holy sites were controlled by Jordan.* After the Six Day War,* Jerusalem, including the Dome of the Rock, came under Israeli control.

Currently, the Dome of the Rock, as well as all of the religious sites in Israel, is protected by the Israeli government and army. Arguments have continued over the Dome of the Rock and have often led to the outbreak of violence between extremist Jewish groups who want to dismantle the shrine in order to excavate the site or to prepare for the future rebuilding of the Holy Temple there. During periods of unrest, Arab Muslims have tried to disrupt Jewish settlers worshiping at the Western Wall (Wailing Wall),* which is located below the Dome of the Rock.

When the Arab League's* Jerusalem Committee met in Marrakesh, Morocco, on January 23, 1992, to discuss the status of Jerusalem, it asserted that Israel was trying to ''annex, Judaize, and obliterate Jerusalem, insisting on the groundless claim which states that Jerusalem is the eternal capital of the Zionist* entity.'' The committee, headed by King Hassan II* of Morocco, states that Jerusalem is rightfully Arab-Islamic on the basis of Islam's rights to the Dome of the Rock and the Temple Mount. By proclaiming that God has willed the Dome of the Rock and al-Aksa Mosque* to be linked with the holy Ka'ba in Mecca, the committee turned a political question of sovereignty into an inalienable right of ownership based on religious faith.

For some Arabs, the Dome of the Rock exemplifies their claim to the city of Jerusalem. The dome dominates the Jerusalem skyline, and Muslims encourage its depiction on books, artwork, posters, and postage stamps to enforce its prominence as a Muslim symbol of Jerusalem. Religious Jews may not walk on the Temple Mount for fear of committing the sin of stepping on the location of the inner sanctum of earlier Temples, called the Holy of Holies.

All parties involved in the conflict view the Dome of the Rock as a political issue, around which explosive and emotional opinions and occasional violence have centered.

For further information see: Albert Hourani, *A History of the Arab Peoples* (Cambridge: Harvard University Press, 1992); F. E. Peters, *Jerusalem, The Holy City in the Eyes of Chroniclers, Visitors, Pilgrims, and Prophets from the Days of Abraham to the Beginnings of Modern Times* (Princeton, NJ: Princeton University Press, 1985).

Erin Z. Ferguson and Susan L. Rosenstein

DONORS CONFERENCE. See **CONFERENCE TO SUPPORT MIDDLE EAST PEACE.**

DOP. See **DECLARATION OF PRINCIPLES.**

DREYFUS AFFAIR. Alfred Dreyfus, a French Jew and artillery captain attached to the general staff of the French army, was accused in 1894 of selling military secrets to Germany and placed on trial for espionage and treason. He was tried by a military court and sentenced to life in prison. His sentence was contested by a minority group consisting mainly of intellectuals, called Dreyfusards, who claimed the evidence was based on forged documents. Among other developments, it led Émile Zola to write his famous *J'accuse* in 1898. Public opinion became so aroused that the military was forced to reopen the case. Dreyfus was again found guilty, but the sentence was reduced to ten years in prison. Dissatisfaction with the verdict persisted, and in 1906 Dreyfus was exonerated. The sharp controversy that the case triggered caused a wave of anti-Semitic demonstrations and riots throughout France.* The Dreyfus trial was considered an important indicator of growing anti-Jewish nationalistic feeling. Theodor Herzl* covered the first Dreyfus trial as a newspaper correspondent and later said that this convinced him that assimilation was not the solution to the problem of anti-Semitism.

For further information see: Jean-Denis Bredin, *The Affair: The Case of Alfred Dreyfus* (New York: Braziller, 1986); Michael R. Marrus, *The Politics of Assimilation: A Study of the French Jewish Community at the Time of the Dreyfus Affair* (Oxford: Clarendon Press, 1971); Louis L. Snyder, *The Dreyfus Case: A Documentary History* (New Brunswick, NJ: Rutgers University Press, 1973).

DULLES, JOHN FOSTER (b. Washington, D.C., February 25, 1888; d. Washington, D.C., May 24, 1959). He was a graduate of Princeton University (1908), attended the Sorbonne (1908–9), and received his L.L.B. from George Washington University Law School (1911).

Dulles began his career in government in 1917 as a special agent for the Department of State in Central America. He served as an adviser to President Woodrow Wilson* at the Paris Peace Conference (1919)* and was a member of the Reparations Commission.

In 1945, Dulles served as a member of the U.S. delegation to the United Nations Conference in San Francisco and was a delegate to the General Assembly until 1950. From 1950 to 1951, he was a consultant for the State Department during the negotiations of the U.S.–Japanese peace treaty ending World War II in the Pacific.

Dulles initially viewed the world through the prism of his legal training. However, with the rise of the Soviet Union and the advent of the cold war, he saw the Soviets' ascent in the world community as a threat to democracy and felt the best response was to liberate those countries already under the Communist yoke. This required offensive action on the part of the free world, in particular, the United States.

To this end, Dulles saw the Middle East as one of the strategically important arenas for competition. He advocated the establishment of anti-Communist alliances, pro-Western governments, and military alliances to hold back the threat. He was the first U.S. secretary of state to visit the Middle East.

Dulles's anti-Communist biases helped to generate the 1956 Suez War.* In 1955, President Gamal Abdul Nasser* requested arms from the United States to help respond to Israeli attacks. Dulles denied this request, fearing that an arms race would ensue, but offered assistance for the construction of the Aswan Dam. At this point, Nasser turned to the Soviets for arms and, in response, Dulles terminated the Aswan negotiations in July.

As part of his nationalization program, Nasser seized the Suez Canal* in order to use the funds to build the Aswan Dam. Britain* and France* were outraged. Dulles sought to mediate the crisis at the London Conference (August 1956). He proposed United Nations supervision of canal operations and at a second London Conference put forth a plan for an association to collect fees and direct traffic on the canal. In turn, the association would give Egypt* a fair share of the funds. The proposals were rejected by both sides.

On October 29, 1956, the Israelis launched an incursion into Sinai,* and Nasser launched a full-scale response. Britain announced that it was invoking its rights under the October 1954 agreement to intervene if Egypt was attacked by a third party. British and French troops landed at Port Said on November 5, 1956, with the declared declaration of securing unimpeded travel through the Suez Canal. Dulles considered this a breach of peace and persuaded President Dwight Eisenhower* to join with the Soviets at the United Nations and pass a resolution calling for the withdrawal of the invading forces. In the face of world opinion, the aggressors backed down.

As secretary of state, Dulles was instrumental in crafting the Eisenhower Doctrine of 1957,* under which the United States would send troops to the Middle East if a pro-Western government required assistance in turning back a Communist threat. During Dulles's tenure, this policy was activated during the 1958 Lebanon crisis.

For further information see: Isaac Alteras, *Eisenhower and Israel: U.S.–Israeli Relations, 1953–1960* (Gainesville: University Press of Florida, 1993); Herman Finer, *Dulles over Suez: The Theory and Practice of His Diplomacy* (Chicago: Quadrangle, 1964).

Pamela Rivers

E

EARLY EMPOWERMENT. A term used to refer to the transfer to the Palestinians* by the Israelis of certain civil responsibilities in the West Bank.* The transfer of powers was a provision of the Israel–Palestinian Declaration of Principles* signed in September 1993. On August 24, 1994, an agreement on the early transfer of power in the West Bank to the Palestinian National Authority* was initialed in Cairo. The agreement was signed by Israel Defense Forces* (IDF) major general Danny Rothschild* and Palestinian Authority member Nabil Shaath* in a ceremony at the Erez crossing between Israel and the Gaza Strip* on August 29, 1994.

The Agreement on Preparatory Transfer of Powers and Responsibilities provides for the transfer of powers to the Palestinian Authority within five specified spheres: (1) education and culture: responsibility over higher education, special education, cultural and educational training activities, institutions and programs, and private, public nongovernmental, or other educational or cultural activities or institutions; (2) health: authority over all health institutions; (3) social welfare: authority over governmental and nongovernmental organizations and institutions, including charitable societies and institutions and voluntary and nonprofit organizations; (4) tourism: regulating, licensing, grading, supervising, and developing the tourist industry; (5) direct taxation and indirect taxation: authority for the income tax and for value-added tax. The educational system was transferred to the Palestinian Authority on August 28, 1994. On November 15, 1994, Israel transferred authority in the fields of welfare and tourism to the Palestinians. On December 1, 1994, Israel transferred responsibility for health and taxation to the Palestinian Authority. This completed the implementation of the early empowerment agreement.

EAST BANK. A reference to the territory of Jordan* east of the Jordan River,* to distinguish that area from the land west of the Jordan River that Jordan annexed after Israel's War of Independence,* commonly referred to as the West Bank.* Between 1949 and 1967, Jordan identified itself as composed of two territories, the East Bank and the West Bank.

EAST FOR PEACE (Hamizrach Leshalom). An Oriental-Jewish-based peace group organized by a group of intellectuals in Israel after the War in Lebanon,* in part to counter the hard-line image of Oriental Jews. It argued that peace is essential for Israel and that Oriental Jews should play a role in the effort to achieve it.

EAST JERUSALEM. See **JERUSALEM.**

EBAN, ABBA (Formerly Aubrey) (b. Cape Town, South Africa, 1915). Eban grew up in England.* While a student of Oriental languages and classics at Cambridge University, he founded the University Labor Society, was president of the Students' Union, and was active in debating and Zionist* circles. During World War II, he served as a major to the British minister of state in Cairo and then as an intelligence officer in Jerusalem.* In 1946, Eban became the political information officer in London for the Jewish Agency* and, the following year, the liaison officer for the Jewish Agency with the United Nations Special Committee on Palestine.* In May 1948, he became Israel's permanent delegate to the United Nations. From 1950 to 1959, Eban served as Israel's ambassador both to the United States and to the United Nations. In 1959, he was elected to the Knesset* on the MAPAI* list. He served as minister of education and culture from 1960 to 1963 and was deputy prime minister from 1964 to 1965. He also served as president of the Weizmann Institute of Science at Rehovot from 1959 to 1966. In 1966, he became minister of foreign affairs. In this position, which he held until 1974, he sought to strengthen Israel's relations with the United States and with the European Economic Community. During the Six Day War,* Eban presented Israel's position at the United Nations. He served as chairman of the Knesset Committee for Security and Foreign Affairs from 1984 to 1988. In 1988, the Labor Party* dropped him from its list of candidates for the Knesset election.

   For further information see: Abba Eban, *Autobiography* (New York: Random House, 1977); Robert St. John, *Eban* (Garden City, NY: Doubleday, 1972).

ECONOMIC COOPERATION COMMITTEE. A committee established by Israel and the Palestine Liberation Organization* (PLO) under the terms of the Declaration of Principles* to develop and implement projects dealing with water, electricity, finance, transport and communications, trade, industry, labor, social welfare, and other areas.

ECONOMIC DEVELOPMENT. One of the five multilateral negotiations* working groups established as a part of the Madrid Conference peace process.*

EDEN, ROBERT ANTHONY (b. June 12, 1897; d. January 14, 1977). Eden served in the British army during World War I. He became foreign secretary in 1935 and served in that capacity for three years before resigning. When Winston Churchill* formed a government in 1951, Eden was named foreign secretary. In April 1955, he became prime minister.

In early 1955, Eden attempted to secure support for the Baghdad Pact from various Middle Eastern countries. He referred to it as a North Atlantic Treaty Organization (NATO) for the Middle East that would include Iraq,* Turkey, Pakistan, Iran, and Jordan.* Its purpose was to curb Soviet influence as well as to maintain the flow of oil and guarantee access to the Suez Canal.* Owing primarily to the opposition of Egyptian leader Gamal Abdul Nasser,* Iraq became the only Arab state to accept the pact.

In the mid-1950s, Egypt and Israel conducted raids and reprisals against each other along the frontier between Israel and the Egyptian-controlled Gaza Strip.* Nasser sought military assistance from the Soviet Union, which also agreed to finance construction of the Aswan High Dam. This Egyptian move into the Soviet sphere, coupled with Nasser's constant denunciations of the West, concerned Eden,* who believed that the most effective way to check Soviet influence in Egypt was for the United States and Britain to help finance the Aswan High Dam project through the World Bank. Eden felt that Soviet financing of the Aswan project would eventually lead to a decline of Western influence in Africa.

As Nasser intensified his public denunciations of the West, he also attempted to cause tensions in Anglo-Jordanian relations. In March 1956, King Hussein* of Jordan dismissed the head of his Arab Legion,* General Sir John Bagot Glubb.* Jordan had long been a dependent of Britain, and the sudden dismissal angered Eden. Moreover, at the time, Eden felt that Nasser had played a role in the dismissal. Nasser's propaganda against the West and promotion of Arab nationalism had, in Eden's view, made it difficult for King Hussein to maintain close links with Britain.

Eden came to the conclusion that Nasser sought the removal of Western influence in the Middle East. Thus, Nasser's success in courting the Soviets and stirring up Arab nationalism would lead to a strategic defeat for the West in the Middle East. Eden decided to inform Nasser that due to severe economic conditions, Britain would be unable to finance the Aswan High Dam. On July 26, Nasser nationalized the Suez Canal and declared martial law in the canal zone. Eden saw this as an act of aggression against Britain and was determined to respond in a decisive manner. Moreover, he believed that a resolution to the crisis would have to involve the removal of Nasser. Yet, while he preferred to accomplish this peacefully, he had no illusions about the possible need to use force. In this respect Eden found support in France.* French companies had shares in the canal. Also, the French believed that Nasser was aiding Algerian rebels and others against the French in North Africa. The French believed in the use of force at the outset. Both Britain and France were able to enlist the support of Israel. Israel was interested in reducing the threat from a militarized Egypt and in creating the circumstances for negotiations for a peace settlement.

On October 22, 1956, representatives of the three states met in Sevres, outside Paris. Under the terms of what became known as the Protocol of Sevres, Israel would attack Egyptian forces on October 29 and seize control of the Strait of Tiran.* On October 30, both Britain and France would issue ultimatums to both sides calling for a cease-fire and a withdrawal of ten miles from the canal by both sides. If the ultimatums were rejected, the Anglo-French forces would intervene on October 31. Israel agreed not to attack Jordan so long as Jordan remained nonbelligerent.

Once the hostilities began at the end of October, the international condemnation of Britain (especially from the Soviet Union and the United States) became unbearable. The prospect of oil sanctions, a widening of the war, and a dangerous rift with the Americans was too difficult for Eden to ignore. Furthermore, Eden faced pressure from within Parliament. On November 15, Eden agreed to a phased withdrawal of British forces from the canal zone. Eden later lied to Parliament about colluding with Israel and France. The international and domestic outcry arising from this fiasco forced him from office.

For further information see: David Carlton, *Anthony Eden: A Biography* (London: A. Lane, 1981); David Carlton, *Britain and the Suez Crisis* (New York: Basil Blackwell, 1989); Anthony Eden, *Full Circle: The Memoirs of Anthony Eden* (Boston: Houghton Mifflin, 1960); Anthony Eden, *The Reckoning* (London: Cassel, 1965); Anthony Eden, *The Suez Crisis of 1956* (Boston: Beacon Press, 1968); Robert Rhodes James, *Anthony Eden* (London: Weidenfeld and Nicolson, 1986).

Simeon Manickavasagam

EGYPT. Israel's neighbor to the west and the southwest with which it fought in the War of Independence,* the Sinai War,* the Six Day War,* the War of Attrition,* and the Yom Kippur War.* During the War of Independence, Egyptian forces succeeded in retaining a portion of the territory that was to have been a part of the Arab state in Palestine* and known since as the Gaza Strip.* Egypt administered the territory under military control until 1967, except for a brief period in 1956–57, when Israel held the territory during and immediately after the Sinai War. Following the Egyptian Revolution and the accession of Gamal Abdul Nasser* to power in the 1950s, the stage was set for a second round of Arab–Israeli warfare. The 1956 Sinai War was caused by many factors: cross-border raids from Gaza* into Israel, substantial increase in the armaments of the Egyptian army; and the increased activism of the Nasser regime. The withdrawal of British, French, and Israeli forces from Egypt came under pressure from the United Nations and the United States. The conclusion of that conflict was followed by a decade of relative calm along the Egypt–Israel frontier, which was broken by the Six Day War, in which Israel took the Gaza Strip and the Sinai Peninsula.* A War of Attrition initiated by Nasser in the spring of 1969 was terminated by a cease-fire in the summer of 1970. The Egyptian- and Syrian-initiated Yom Kippur War of October 1973 was followed by movement in the direction of a settlement. U.S. secretary of state Henry Kissinger* helped to arrange a Disengagement Agreement,* which was signed in January 1974, and the Sinai II* agreement of September 1975. Following the 1977 initiative of President Anwar Sadat,* Israel and Egypt began negotiations for peace that led to the Camp David Accords* in September 1978 and the Egypt–Israel Peace Treaty* of March 1979. Peace and the normalization of relations followed— ambassadors were exchanged, trade and tourism developed, and continued contacts were sustained between the two states.

EGYPT–ISRAEL DISENGAGEMENT OF FORCES AGREEMENT (1974). See **IS-RAEL–EGYPT DISENGAGEMENT FORCES AGREEMENT.**

EGYPT–ISRAEL PEACE TREATY (1979). A peace treaty signed in Washington, D.C., on March 26, 1979, between the Arab Republic of Egypt* and the state of Israel, under the auspices of the United States, that ended the state of war between the two countries. It was based on the Camp David Accords,* in accordance with United Nations (UN) Security Council Resolutions 242* and 338,* and was signed by Menachem Begin* and Anwar Sadat.* The peace treaty was signed through the efforts of U.S. president Jimmy Carter.*

The treaty contains nine articles, a military annex, an annex dealing with the relations between the parties, and agreed minutes interpreting the main articles of the treaty. To further amplify the agreement, letters exchanged among Begin, Carter, and Sadat were included.

The treaty provided that the state of war between Egypt and Israel was to be ended. Israel agreed to withdraw to the British Mandate* lines between itself and Egypt. This withdrawal would not, however, affect negotiations over the future of the Gaza Strip.* Both parties committed themselves to respecting each other's national sovereignty, agreeing to live in peace and to refrain from acts or threats of violence, belligerency, or hostility. Relations would be fully normalized in all areas.

The Israeli withdrawal would be accomplished in three phrases over a three-year period. The second phase put Israeli troops behind a line stretching from El Arish to Ras Muhammed; the third withdrawal would be to the international boundary. During this three-year period a UN presence would be maintained, and a joint commission would supervise the withdrawal. Limited force zones in Egyptian and Israeli territory were established, and the two countries agreed to station United Nations forces in specified areas that could be removed only through a UN Security Council vote, including the approval of all five permanent members.

Israel was granted free passage through the Suez Canal* and the Strait of

Tiran.* Both parties were enjoined from signing treaties that would in any way conflict with the peace treaty; further, obligations under the peace treaty would have preference over all existing commitments. Disputes between the two parties would be resolved by negotiation or arbitration, and a Claims Commission was to be established to ensure settlement of financial claims to each other's mutual agreement.

Negotiations on Palestinian autonomy* were to begin in April 1979, with the invited participation of Jordan*; failing Jordan's attendance, the two signatories would negotiate alone. A target date of one year later was set for completion of the autonomy talks, to be followed by elections in the West Bank* and Gaza* for a self-governing authority. The five-year transition period mentioned in the Camp David Accords would follow the elections.

EGYPT–SYRIA DEFENSE PACT. On November 4, 1966, Egypt* and Syria* signed, in Cairo, a five-year mutual defense agreement in which the parties were required to come to each other's assistance if either was threatened. It officially entered into force on March 9, 1967, with the exchange of ratification agreements in Cairo. The agreement was established for an initial five-year period, subject to renewal, and set up a joint defense council, including the foreign and defense ministers of each state, as well as a joint command headed by the chiefs of staff of the military forces of the two states. In the event of military operations, the chief of staff of the United Arab Republic* (UAR) armed forces would assume overall command. Under the terms of the agreement, each state would regard armed aggression against the other as an attack against itself and would come to the aid of its defense partner by taking all necessary measures, including the use of armed force, to defeat the aggressor. The parties indicated that the pact was directed not only against Israel but also against reactionary forces in the Arab world (such as Saudi Arabia and Jordan*) that were allies of Zionism* and imperialism.

During the months following the conclusion of the pact, tensions rose markedly between the Arab states and Israel. A massive retaliatory raid into Jordan by Israel in 1966 had been followed by further clashes early in 1967. On April 7, Israel shot down six Syrian aircraft in an aerial encounter. In May 1967, Syria charged that Israel was mobilizing its troops for an attack on the Golan Heights* and requested Egypt to meet its obligations in accordance with the terms of the defense pact. This was to culminate in the closing of the Strait of Tiran* by Egypt. In early June, the Six Day War* began between Egypt and Israel and soon expanded to include Syria and Jordan, joined by other Arab states. The defense pact lapsed in 1971, but Syria and Egypt continued to coordinate defensive and offensive strategy in some areas until the Yom Kippur War,* when they launched a coordinated offensive against Israeli positions.

EILAT (Elat, Elath). Israel's southernmost city is a deepwater port on the Gulf of Aqaba* connecting Israel with the Red Sea and the Indian Ocean. It is named for the ancient city of Eilat, which is mentioned in the Bible as a city through which the Israelites passed during their desert wanderings. The biblical Eilat later served as a port city for numerous empires and conquerers of the area. Prior to the opening of the Suez Canal* to Israeli shipping, Eilat was Israel's major gateway for goods from the Far East, the Indian Ocean, Asia, and East Africa. Eilat's natural beauty and seaside location make it a year-round resort. Modern Eilat was founded in 1948. Its importance increased after 1950, when Egypt* banned Israeli ships from the Suez Canal. Without the canal, the Gulf of Aqaba became Israel's only outlet to the Red Sea. But Egypt also blocked the entrance to the gulf at the Strait of Tiran.* The gulf was opened as a result of the Sinai War of 1956.* Eilat then grew rapidly in both size and importance. Egypt's blockade of the gulf in 1967 was a major cause of the Six Day War.* Eilat also serves as an important center for oil. A pipeline carries oil from the city to Israel's Mediterranean coast. From there it is either exported or sent to a refinery in Haifa.

For further information see: Eliahu Elath, *Israel and Elath: The Political Struggle for the Inclusion of Elath in the Jewish State* (London: Weidenfeld and Nicolson [for the Jewish Historical Society of England], 1966).

EILAT. An Israeli naval destroyer, sunk in 1967. The *Eilat* was originally built in Great Britain* at the outbreak of World War II and served under the name of HMS *Zealous* when it escorted naval convoys carrying war matériel to the Soviet Union. The destroyer was purchased by the Israel Defense Forces* (IDF) in 1955 and entered service in the Israeli navy on July 15, 1956. In the Sinai campaign,* the *Eilat* took part in capturing the Egyptian destroyer, the *Ibrahim al-Awal,* later renamed the *Haifa.*

Following the 1956 war, it became the flagship of the Israeli fleet. It took part in the Six Day War.* In the immediate aftermath of the war, in the war of attrition which lasted from July 2 to 14, 1967, around the northern Sinai Peninsula,* the *Eilat* sank two Egyptian torpedo boats operating off the Roumani coast.

On October 20, 1967, the *Eilat,* carrying 199 crew members, sailed on a routine patrol on a course that brought the ship within 14.5 miles of the shores of Egypt* near Port Said. A day later, still opposite Port Said but farther out to sea, Komar-class Egyptian missile boats moored to the dock fired ship-to-ship missiles at the Israeli ship. The Egyptian ships had remained undetected by the *Eilat,* since they remained stationary. Consequently, the *Eilat* took no special evasive actions until after the missiles were visually sighted.

When the missiles were detected, the *Eilat*'s commander, Yitzhak Ben-Shoshan, ordered the crew to open fire on the missiles, but without effect. The first missile hit the boiler room, causing heavy damage and casualties. A fire broke out on board, and the ship began to list, having been almost broken in half. A second missile struck the ship, causing further casualties and damage. Using a reserve communication link, the ship was able to establish contact with an Israeli unit on shore in the northern Sinai. A rescue mission was rapidly organized, using both ships and helicopters. However, a third missile, also shot from stationary Komar-class boats moored in Port Said, hit the *Eilat,* causing the ammunition to explode. At that point, Ben Shoshan ordered the crew to abandon ship, which was sinking rapidly. A few minutes later, a fourth missile hit the area in which the ship had just sunk and detonated under water. The underwater repercussions of the blast caused additional Israeli casualties, most of whom were still in the water awaiting rescue. Overall, forty-seven of the *Eilat*'s crew died in the attack, and ninety-one were wounded.

After the rescue mission was complete, the chief of staff, Yitzhak Rabin,* appointed his deputy, Haim Bar-Lev,* to head an investigation of the incident. The Bar-Lev investigation concluded that the presence of missiles on Egyptian boats and their ability to fire from stationary positions should have been accounted for and that it had been a mistake to define such patrols as routine. The mishap could have been avoided if the *Eilat* had been operating under battle conditions. Bar-Lev, however, did not find cause to press charges against any of the officers aboard the ship. Regarding the Egyptian missile attack as a premeditated escalation, Israel launched a large-scale artillery bombardment of the Suez oil refineries, gasoline depots, and petrochemical installations four days later. The resulting benzine and asphalt fires burned for days and destroyed neighboring plants, factories, and buildings, causing over $100 million in damage. After the Israeli retaliation, a year of relative quiet settled in along the Egyptian–Israeli Front.

For further information see: Zeev Schiff and Eytan Haber, *Israel, Army and Defense: A Dictionary* (in Hebrew) (Tel Aviv: Zmora, Bitan, Modan, 1976); Chaim Herzog, *The Arab–Israeli Wars* (New York: Random House, 1982).

David Wurmser

EISENHOWER, DWIGHT D. (b. Denison, Texas, October 14, 1890; d. Washington, D.C., March 28, 1969). Following his graduation from the U.S. Military Academy at West Point, he embarked on an illustrious career in the U.S. Army. During his thirty-five years of military service, he rose from the rank of second lieutenant to five-star general. From 1948 to 1950, he served as president of Columbia University. In December 1950, President Harry S Truman* appointed him supreme commander of the North Atlantic Treaty Organization (NATO). He served in that position for one year from April 1951. He was elected the thirty-fourth president of the United States in 1952 and was reelected in 1956.

Eisenhower faced a number of important international issues. The Middle East particularly captured the attention of the Eisenhower administration in the mid-1950s. During the Eisenhower presidency, five serious crises broke out in the Middle East: the oil crisis in Iran, the Egyptian*–Israeli conflict over the Suez Canal,* civil unrest in Syria,* the Lebanese* Civil War, and the revolution in Iraq.* With respect to the Arab–Israeli conflict, the two most serious issues facing the Eisenhower administration were the dispute over the Jordan River* and the Suez crisis of 1956.*

President Eisenhower attempted to look at the Arab–Israeli conflict with greater objectivity and treat the parties to the conflict with greater impartiality than Truman. He looked upon the Tripartite Declaration of 1950* as a valid, fundamental instrument to ensure the neutrality of the United States and the West in the Arab–Israeli conflict. In the early 1950s, Charles T. Main, Inc., an American engineering firm commissioned by the United Nations to study the Jordan River problem, recommended a regional and unified development program for the entire Jordan River system. Prior to the 1956 Suez crisis, President Eisenhower sent a special envoy to the Middle East, Eric Johnston, who promoted a modified version of the Main Plan. Despite obtaining concessions from the Arabs and Israelis on this issue and taking positive steps forward in reconciling Arab–Israeli differences, the Jordan River dispute carried on throughout this administration, the Kennedy* administration, and the Johnson* administration.

The establishment of the United States-sponsored Baghdad Pact in 1955 and the withdrawal of U.S. aid for Egypt's Aswan Dam project helped contribute to greatly strained relations between Egypt and the major governments of the West. In addition to the strained relations between Egypt and the governments of France,* Great Britain,* and the United States, conflict between Israel and Egypt intensified with attacks on Israel from the Egyptian-administered Gaza Strip* and the Egyptian denial of Israeli use of the Suez Canal. Hostilities between Israel (backed by France and Great Britain) and Egypt broke out over the Suez Canal in October 1956. The Eisenhower administration, opposed to the forceful actions of Israel, Great Britain, and France, took two fundamental actions. On November 1, 1956, President Eisenhower ordered U.S. military and some economic aid to Israel to be suspended; and the United States sponsored the United Nations resolution calling for an immediate cease-fire and withdrawal of troops to the 1949 armistice lines.*

Under the Eisenhower administration, U.S. foreign policy was guided, in part, by the Eisenhower Doctrine,* which was introduced in a presidential address delivered before the U.S. Congress on January 5, 1957. Following the Suez crisis of 1956, with the threat of the Soviet Union and Communism very much in the mind of the Eisenhower administration, President Eisenhower declared that the United States would provide assistance to any country in the Middle East threatened by aggression or subversion from Communist forces. Though the U.S. Congress eventually accepted the Eisenhower Doctrine, acceptance of this doctrine by many states in the Middle East was much more tenuous.

For further information see: Isaac Alteras, *Eisenhower and Israel: U.S.–Israeli Relations, 1953–1960* (Gainesville: University Press of Florida, 1993); Dwight D. Eisenhower, *The White House Years: Waging Peace, 1956–1961* (New York: Doubleday, 1965); George Lenczowski, *American Presidents and the Middle East* (Durham, NC:

Duke University Press, 1990). See also the public papers of President Eisenhower published by the U.S. government.

Jon J. Peterson

EISENHOWER DOCTRINE. Following the 1956 Suez campaign,* British* and
French* influence in the Middle East had been greatly reduced. U.S. capabilities
in the region had not filled what was now an apparent Western power vacuum
in the region. President Dwight D. Eisenhower* called for a congressional joint
resolution in an address before Congress on January 5, 1957, that would provide
military and economic assistance for states in the Middle East and would authorize the use of force ''to protect the territorial integrity and political independence of any Middle Eastern state facing overt armed aggression from a
country controlled by international Communism.'' Congress enacted the doctrine
into law in March 1957. On March 28, 1957, though not a full member, the
United States joined the Baghdad Pact military committee. Egypt* and Syria*
did not look with favor on the doctrine and saw it as a new Western policy of
imperialism.

EITAN, RAPHAEL (Formerly Kaminsky; nicknamed Raful) (b. Tel Adashim,
1929). He was educated at Tel Aviv University and Haifa University. He joined
the Palmach* at the age of seventeen. He served as chief of staff of the Israel
Defense Forces* from 1978 to 1983. He first joined the Knesset* in 1984 on
the Tehiya-Tsomet* list and was reelected in the 1988 and 1992 Knesset elections.

ELAZAR, DAVID (Nicknamed Dado) (b. Zaghreb, Yugoslavia, 1925; d. April
1976). He was brought to Palestine* as part of Youth Aliya in 1940. In 1946,
he joined the Palmach.* In the War of Independence,* he participated in the
fighting for Jerusalem* and later in the Sinai Peninsula.* After a period as a
training officer and as an operations officer in the Central Command, he took a
leave of absence in 1953 to study economics and Middle Eastern studies at
Hebrew University. In the Sinai War of 1956,* he fought in the Gaza Strip.*
Elazar was promoted to the rank of major general in 1961, and in November
1964 he was appointed commander of the Northern Command, which, during
the 1967 war, captured the Golan Heights.* Appointed head of the Staff Branch
in 1969, Elazar served as the chief of staff of the Israel Defense Forces* (IDF)
from January 1972 until April 1974. He resigned in April 1974 after the release
of the findings of the Agranat Commission of Inquiry,* which blamed him for
the initial setbacks at the beginning of the Yom Kippur War,* for excessive
confidence in the ability of the army to contain the Egyptian* and Syrian*
attacks without calling up the reserves, for incorrect assessments, and for a lack
of preparedness of the IDF at the outbreak of the war. The commission rec-

ommended the termination of his role as chief of staff. He later joined the Zim Shipping Company as managing director.

For further information see: Generals of Israel (Tel Aviv: Hadar Publishing House, 1968).

ENCLAVE. See **SECURITY ZONE.**

ENGLAND. Israel's relationship with England (the United Kingdom, Great Britain*) antedates Israel's independence and can be traced to the period of World War I, when, among other arrangements concerning Palestine,* the British government issued the Balfour Declaration,* which endorsed the concept of a National Home for the Jewish people in Palestine. The declaration was seen as support for the Zionist* claim to a Jewish state in Palestine. The British were granted the Mandate* over Palestine after the end of the war and retained their control until the establishment of Israel's independence in May 1948. Britain did not support, however, the establishment of the Jewish state and supplied arms to the Arab states during the War of Independence,* in addition to supporting the Arab position in the United Nations. Britain recognized Israel in 1949.

In May 1950, Britain joined with France* and the United States in a Tripartite Declaration* to limit arms sales to the region in an effort to ensure regional stability. The ensuing years were marked by a coolness in relations with Israel, while Britain retained close links with many of Israel's Arab neighbors. Nevertheless, in the fall of 1956, England joined with France and Israel in a tripartite plan to deal with the policies and activities of President Gamal Abdul Nasser* of Egypt.* Nasser sought to accelerate the British withdrawal from Egypt and the Suez Canal* zone and to undermine British influence elsewhere in the Arab world. In July 1956, Nasser nationalized the Suez Canal, which the British regarded as having economic value and strategic significance. Israel invaded Egypt at the end of October 1956 in the Sinai War,* and England and France soon joined in after issuing an ultimatum to both Egypt and Israel. The convergence of interests and the marriage of convenience that resulted soon came apart under the pressure of the international community, especially the United States. In the ensuing decade there was small growth and improvement in relations between Israel and England, which included the sale of some military equipment to Israel. At the same time, England was in the process of reordering its relationship with the Arab states of the Middle East, especially its former colonial territories. Sympathy for Israel was widespread in England at the outbreak of the Six Day War.* Britain's United Nations representative was instrumental in the drafting of United Nations Security Council Resolution 242,* but Britain did not play a major role in trying to achieve peace in the years immediately following the 1967 war. The succeeding years saw a variation in the relationship, with links alternately improving and declining based on changes in personality in decision-making positions in both Britain and Israel. Britain's role in the European Community and its advocacy of the Venice Declaration* of 1980 remained an irritant in the relationship. Nevertheless, other factors, such as a common opposition to terrorism of Middle East origin, proved to be positive factors in the relationship.

For further information see: Doreen Ingrams, *Palestine Papers, 1917–1922: Seeds of Conflict* (London: J. Murray, 1972); Elizabeth Monroe, *Britain's Moment in the Middle East, 1914–1971,* rev. ed. (London: Chatto and Windus, 1981); Bernard Wasserstein, *The British in Palestine: The Mandatory Government and the Arab–Jewish Conflict 1917–1929* (London: Royal Historical Society, 1978); Ronald W. Zweig, *Britain and Palestine during the Second World War* (London: Boydell Press [for the Royal Historical Society], 1986).

ENTEBBE AIRPORT RAID. See **ENTEBBE OPERATION.**

ENTEBBE OPERATION. On July 4, 1976, an Israeli commando operation, code-named Thunderbolt, freed 103 hostages taken from a hijacked jetliner and held at Entebbe Airport, Uganda. The jetliner, Air France flight 139 originating in Tel Aviv, was hijacked on June 27, 1976, by Arab and German terrorists on a flight between Athens and Paris. The plane was flown to Uganda, then under the control of Idi Amin. Israel refused to give in to the hijackers' demands for release of numerous terrorists held in Israel. After a week of negotiations, Israeli commandos, under the command of Brigadier General Dan Shomron, staged a dramatic and successful raid that later was renamed Operation Jonathan in memory of Jonathan (Yoni) Netanyahu, an Israeli officer who was killed during the rescue.

For further information see: Yeshayahu Ben-Porat, Eitan Haber, and Zeev Schiff, *Entebbe Rescue* (New York: Dell Books, 1976); Max Hastings, *Yoni: Hero of Entebbe* (New York: Dial Press, 1979); Yehuda Ofer, *Operation Thunder: The Entebbe Raid* (Harmondsworth, England: Penguin, 1976); William Stevenson, *90 Minutes at Entebbe* (New York: Bantam Books, 1976); Tony Williamson, *Counter Strike Entebbe* (London: Collins, 1976).

ENVIRONMENT. One of the five multilateral negotiations* working groups established as a part of the Madrid Conference peace process.*

ERAKAT, SAEB MOHAMMED (b. Jerusalem, April 28, 1955). He was a student activist in the General Union of Palestinian Students while he studied in the United States. Erakat received a Ph.D. from Bradford University in Britain in 1983 and taught political science at A-Najah University in Nablus. He served as vice chairman of the Palestinian* delegation to the Madrid Peace Conference* beginning in 1991. Subsequently, he has been involved in the peace process, serving as a member of the Palestinian Authority* and as an adviser to Yasser Arafat* and working on the process of establishing elections in Gaza* and Jericho* under the terms of the Declaration of Principles* (DOP).

ERETZ YISRAEL (or Eretz Israel). Eretz Israel or Eretz Yisrael is a Hebrew term meaning "Land of Israel,"* used to refer to Palestine.* The term is found in the Bible, Talmud, and later literature and refers to the land of ancient Israel: all of Palestine, including Judea* and Samaria.*

ESHKOL, LEVI (Formerly Shkolnik) (b. Oratovo, Kiev district of the Ukraine, October 25, 1895; d. February 26, 1969). In January 1914, he set out as part of a contingent representing the youth organization Hapoel Hatzair (the Young Laborer) to the port of Trieste, where he sailed for Jaffa. At first he served as a common farm laborer and watchman but soon became involved in the building of a pumping station and was elected to the Workers' Agricultural Council of Petah Tikva. Eshkol entered military service in the Jewish Legion, and upon demobilization in 1920 he helped to create Degania Bet. When the Histadrut* was created in 1920, Eshkol joined the executive board. He was elected to the Central Council of MAPAI* at its founding in 1929. David Ben-Gurion* became a powerful figure in the party, and, with him, Eshkol was drawn into the party leadership. Eshkol increasingly was seen as a political appendage to Ben-Gurion because of the parallels in their careers and their friendship. After Israel's independence, Eshkol was appointed director general of the Ministry of Defense. Eshkol was appointed head of the Land Settlement Department of the Jewish Agency* in 1949. In 1951, he became minister of agriculture and development and, the following year, minister of finance. Eshkol replaced Ben-Gurion as prime minister in June 1963 and served in that position until his death. He and Ben-Gurion split over the Lavon affair,* which led to the defection of Ben-Gurion from MAPAI and the creation of RAFI. Eshkol was known for his contributions to Israel's economic development in a crucial period and for his skills as a compromiser. He led Israel through the Six Day War* and the crisis that preceded it. He was considered one of the more dovish of Israel's leaders and did not wish to formally annex areas inhabited by large numbers of Arabs. Nevertheless, on June 27, 1967, he issued an administrative order to apply Israeli law and administration to East Jerusalem.*

For further information see: Henry M. Christman, ed., *The State Papers of Levi Eshkol* (New York: Funk and Wagnalls, 1969); Shimon Peres, *From These Men: Seven Founders of the State of Israel* (New York: Wyndham Books, 1980); Terence Prittie, *Eshkol: The Man and the Nation* (New York: Pitman, 1969); Sanford R. Silverburg, "Levi Eshkol," in Bernard Reich, ed., *Political Leaders of the Contemporary Middle East and North Africa: A Biographical Dictionary* (Westport, CT: Greenwood Press, 1990), pp. 166–74.

ES-SAMU. See **SAMU.**

ETZEL. See **IRGUN.**

ETZION BLOC. The Etzion Bloc is a cluster of four Jewish settlements—Kfar Etzion, Masuoth Yitzhak, Ein Tzurim, and Revadim—in the Hebron* mountains

in Judea,* astride the Jerusalem*–Bethlehem*–Hebron Road, twenty-four kilometers to the south of Jerusalem.

Contact with the bloc from Jerusalem became tenuous in early 1948, when,
on January 15, a convoy of Israelis, including a Haganah* platoon, was ambushed by Arab irregulars and was destroyed, leaving no survivors. The link
between the Etzion cluster and Jerusalem was severed completely on March 27,
1948, when the Nabi Samuel Convoy, which had provided supplies to the Etzion
Bloc, was cut off on its way back to Jerusalem and forced to return to the Kfar
Etzion area. From that point on, the Etzion Bloc had no more physical contact
with the emerging Jewish state except for occasional supplies dropped from
aircraft.

Once the Etzion Bloc was severed from Israel, and as the prospect of an
armored attack by the Jordanian Arab Legion* loomed, the settlement group
was forced to consider evacuation and the abandonment of the territory. The
commander of Jewish forces in Jerusalem favored evacuation, yet others in the
emerging Israeli defense establishment opposed it. Similar divisions were revealed among the defenders of the Etzion Bloc, although they eventually decided
to remain and fight. On the eve of the final Arab attack, on May 12, the commander of Israeli forces in Kfar Etzion asked the Central Command in Jerusalem
whether he and his forces should evacuate the kibbutz. Later in the day, the
Russian Monastery, which was used as a perimeter fortress for the Kfar Etzion
area by the Haganah, fell with all but eight of its thirty-two defenders killed.
Despite the fall of the monastery, the reply was negative. On May 13, 1948,
Jordanian Arab Legion armored and infantry forces, as well as numerous Arab
irregular forces, launched the final attack from four different directions. By the
following day, the resistance was broken, the kibbutz fell, and the entire population, soldiers and civilians alike, were massacred. As Kfar Etzion fell, the
other three kibbutzim received orders to surrender as well. Overall, 250 of the
bloc's defenders and residents were killed in the final assault and following
massacre. Only three men and one girl managed to escape from Kfar Etzion
itself.

The two-month stand by the Israeli forces in the Etzion Bloc had diverted
enough Arab forces and attention to keep besieged Jerusalem from falling. As
long as the bloc's forces faced irregular Arab armies, it managed to offer effective resistance. At times, even, the forces in Etzion went on the offensive and
ambushed Arab forces' supply convoys on the road between Jerusalem and
Hebron. Only when Arab regular forces, especially armored elements of the
Jordanian Arab Legion, were diverted to attack the settlement cluster did the
Arabs manage to capture the Etzion Bloc. Some analysts note, however, that
the troops and supplies dedicated to the effort in the Etzion Bloc could have
been better used in the defense of Jerusalem.

The Etzion Bloc's fall and resulting massacre influenced the Haganah and the
successor Israel Defense Forces* (IDF) in the doctrine of evacuating all civilian
settlements that have little or no chance of withstanding attack, rather than con-

sidering the option of resistance and possible surrender. This doctrine was immediately applied, and the Etzion Bloc experience was directly related to the Haganah's decision to evacuate, a few days later, settlements north and west of Jerusalem, specifically Hartuv, Neve Yaakov, and Atarot, which was the location of Jerusalem's airport.

The Etzion Bloc remained in Arab Legion hands until June 7, 1967, when, in the third day of the Six Day War,* it was captured by elements of the Jerusalem Brigade, on their way south to Hebron. Following the 1967 war, when control of the Etzion Bloc was reestablished, Jewish resettlement of the area commenced, mostly aligned with the same Labor-controlled kibbutz movement that settled the area before Israel's independence. These areas have been categorized, following the June 1992 Israeli election, as "security settlements."*

For further information see: Chaim Herzog, The Arab–Israeli Wars (New York: Random House, 1982); Zeev Schiff and Eytan Haber, Israel, Army and Defense: A Dictionary (Tel Aviv: Zmora, Bitan, Modan, 1976).

David Wurmser

EUROPEAN COMMUNITY. See **VENICE DECLARATION; MADRID DECLARATION; BRUSSELS DECLARATION.**

EVENHANDED APPROACH. A reference to U.S. policy concerning the Arab–Israeli conflict and the fact that it was not "evenhanded" but rather was seen as pro-Israel in content and approach. Arab leaders and their supporters were convinced that U.S. policy was interested only in Israel and its security and did not take Arab perspectives into account. Following the Nixon* election victory of 1968, his personal envoy to the Middle East, William Scranton,* suggested that the United States was interested in Israel's security but also was interested in other states in the region and elsewhere and had friends in the Arab world. Thus, the United States "would do well to have a more evenhanded policy." See also SCRANTON MISSION.

***EXODUS* (1947).** A ship bringing illegal immigrants to Palestine* under the auspices of the Haganah* in 1947. The ship, originally named the *President Warfield,* was purchased by the Haganah to transport immigrants to Palestine. It departed from Sete, France,* in July 1947 with a shipload of approximately 4,500 immigrants, but the British escorted the ship to Haifa and boarded it. The refugees were refused permission to enter Palestine and were forced to return in British ships to Europe, mostly to Germany. The *Exodus* incident coincided with the United Nations Special Committee on Palestine's* visit to Palestine. British prime minister Ernest Bevin's* decision not to allow the Jewish refugees to land enabled the Haganah to publicize the event and nurture what has been described as "uncritical sympathy" for Zionism* at a crucial historical point in deliberations over the future of Palestine. The *Exodus* became a symbol of Jewish homelessness and the promise that the creation of a Jewish state could provide a solution to the Jewish question. See also BRITISH MANDATE.

Joseph E. Goldberg

F

F-4 PHANTOM JET. The F-4 Phantom is a twin-engined, two-seat, long-range, all-weather, multirole jet fighter aircraft manufactured by the McDonnell Douglas Corporation. The aircraft is capable of speeds in excess of 1,600 mph and can operate in air-superiority, close-support, interdiction, reconnaissance, or electronic-combat modes. Depending on its mission, the F-4 can carry between six and eight air-to-air missiles (Sparrow III or Sidewinder) or 16,000 pounds of conventional bombs and surface attack missiles. As an air-superiority interceptor, the F-4 Phantom has a combat radius of 900 miles. In a ground-attack mode, the combat radius is extended to 1,000 miles. The aircraft is air-refuelable.

Israel initially ordered fifty Phantom aircraft, and delivery of the first thirty-six began in 1969. Israel utilized Phantom jets (along with A-4 Skyhawk aircraft*) in deep-penetration raids* into Egypt* during the War of Attrition.* By the Yom Kippur War,* Israel is reported to have had 127 F-4Es, which included six RF-4E reconnaissance models.

During the Yom Kippur War, the Israeli air force used the F-4E as its primary strike force. While the F-4E shared the air-superiority role with other Israeli aircraft, it was used primarily as a strike aircraft against hardened targets, such as airfields, and strategic targets where a longer-range aircraft was required. During the Yom Kippur War, the F-4E helped play a fundamental role in destroying a significant portion of Syria's* war economy (destroying oil refineries, oil storage facilities, seaports, airports, power-generating facilities, and so on), quelling the advancing Syrian armor through the Golan Heights,* and defeating many of the Syrian and Egyptian mobile surface-to-air missile sites.

During the Yom Kippur War the Phantom provided Israel with a significant qualitative edge over its adversaries, whose most sophisticated aircraft was the Soviet-supplied MiG-21.* The F-4 was equipped with state-of-the-art radar and automatic fire control computers. The MiG-21 was no match for the F-4 in speed, weapons load, accuracy, combat radius, sortie rate, or range. Thirty-five F-4s were reported lost during the Yom Kippur War, primarily to ground-based air defense missiles.

Since the late 1960s, the McDonnell Douglas F-4E Phantom has been a significant part of the Israeli Air Force. Of the 488 combat aircraft that the Israeli air force maintained between 1972 and 1973, 95 were the McDonnell Douglas F-4E Phantom. During this period, Israel also maintained six reconnaissance RF-4E Phantom IIs. Of the 662 active combat aircraft that the Israeli air force maintained between 1993 and 1994, 112 were the F-4E. During this period, Israel also maintained fourteen reconnaissance RF-4E jet aircraft.

In 1987, Israel initiated a program to extend the service life of its Phantom aircraft well into the next century. Called Phantom 2000, the program includes structural modifications and avionics upgrades.

For further information see: Alvin J. Cottrell, ''The Role of Air Power in the Military Balance of the Middle East—the Function of the Phantom,'' *New Middle East* (April 1970):12–16; Lon Nordeen, *Fighters over Israel* (New York: Orion Books, 1990); Dale R. Tahtinen, *The Arab–Israeli Military Balance since 1973* (Washington, DC: American Enterprise Institute for Public Policy Research, 1974); Michael J. H. Taylor, *NATO Major Combat Aircraft* (London: Tri-Service Press, 1989); Michael J. H. Taylor, ed., *Jane's American Fighting Aircraft of the 20th Century* (New York: Mallard Press, 1991).

Stephen H. Gotowicki and Jon J. Peterson

F-15 EAGLE. The F-15 Eagle is a single-seat, all-weather, supersonic, jet fighter-bomber, built by McDonnell Douglas. The Eagle flies at a top speed of more than Mach 2.5 (over 1,650 mph) and has the ability to climb virtually straight up. The F-15 has an unrefueled combat radius of approximately 320 miles. The F-15's armaments usually consist of four Sidewinder (heat-seeking) and four Sparrow (radar-guided) air-to-air missiles or eight AMRAAMs (advanced, medium-ranged, air-to-air missiles), in addition to its 20mm six-barrel gun. Alternative payloads consist of a wide variety of guided and unguided air-to-ground weapons. Maximum weapon payload is 23,600 pounds. The F-15 is the mainstay of the Israeli Air Force (IAF). By the 1990s, Israel was operating more than fifty F-15s in two squadrons.

The ground-attack variant of the F-15 is known as the F-15E or Strike Eagle. It is a two-seat, dual-role version of the Eagle, capable of conducting long-range, deep-interdiction, air-to-ground missions in day, night, or inclement weather. The F-15E is also capable of flying in the air-interceptor role with little to no modification. The F-15E has a maximum weapon payload of 24,500 pounds. In April 1994, Israel announced it would buy twenty-one F-15Is, the export model of the F-15E, at a cost of over $2 billion. The F-15I will give Israel the ability to strike targets as distant as Iran.

The F-15 has made significant contributions to Israeli security. On June 7, 1981, six F-15s flew defensive air cover for the Israeli F-16 Falcons* used to bomb the Iraqi* Osirak nuclear reactor* near Baghdad. The planes were able to fly over 635 miles during the height of the Iran–Iraq War, without detection. On October 1, 1985, ten F-15s flew 3,000 miles, with midair refueling, to Tunisia and bombed the Palestine Liberation Organization* (PLO) headquarters. The F-15 has also seen extensive use in Lebanon* in both the interceptor and ground-to-ground roles.

For further information see: Victor Flintham, *Air Wars and Aircraft* (New York: Facts on File, 1990); *Jane's All The World's Aircraft 1993–1994;* Bryce Walker, *Fighting Jets* (Alexandria, VA: Time-Life Books, 1984); Ehud Yonay, *No Margin for Error* (New York: Pantheon Books, 1993).

Nolan Wohl and Stephen H. Gotowicki

F-16 FIGHTER AIRCRAFT. The F-16 fighter is a single-seat, single-engine, supersonic, multirole fighter aircraft manufactured by the Lockheed Fort Worth Company. The F-16 became operational with the U.S. Air Force in 1979. It is capable of speeds in excess of Mach 2 (1,300 mph) and operating at altitudes up to 50,000 feet. The F-16 can operate in air-superiority, close-support, interdiction, or reconnaissance-combat modes. In the interdiction mode with two 2,000-pound bombs, two Sidewinder missiles, and external fuel tanks, the F-16C has an unrefueled combat radius of 852 miles. In the air-superiority role with two Sparrow missiles, two Sidewinder missiles, and external fuel tanks, the F-16C can maintain a combat air patrol for slightly over two hours or conduct a point intercept out to 818 miles. The F-16 is controlled by digital electrical signals rather than mechanical control linkages. The F-16A and F-16C are single-seat variants of the F-16. The F-16B and F-16D are two-seat variants.

Israel received its first F-16 in January 1980. Israel purchased 210 F-16s in all variants, F-16A, B, C, and D. In 1993, the United States pledged to provide Israel with an additional fifty F-16As under drawdown legislation. Israel used its F-16s to bomb Iraq's Osirak reactor* in Baghdad in 1981.

Stephen H. Gotowicki

FAHD BIN ABD AL-AZIZ AL SAUD (b. Riyadh, 1921). King of Saudi Arabia since June 1982. Previously, he served as minister of education (1953–60), minister of the interior (from 1962), and second deputy prime minister (from 1968). When Khalid became king after King Feisal's assassination in March 1975, Fahd became crown prince and first deputy prime minister.

King Fahd bin Abd al-Aziz al Saud is both the head of state and prime minister of Saudi Arabia. He is also the highest legal official, serves as the "commander of the faithful," and has given himself the title of the guardian of the holy mosques.

He was born the eleventh son of King Abd al-Aziz ibn Saud (generally known as Ibn Saud). King Fahd's mother, Hassa bint al-Sudairi, is from the powerful Sudairi of the Nejd region in central Arabia, which is closely aligned with the al-Saud. King Fahd was privately educated and quickly demonstrated an aptitude for the subtleties of family and national and international politics. On June 13, 1982, Prince Fahd became the fifth king of Saudi Arabia at the death of his half-brother, King Khalid.

Saudi Arabia, under the leadership of King Fahd, has maintained its traditionally conservative foreign policy. Its stance on Communism and radicalism, combined with its vast oil resources, has made it a political and economic ally of the United States and the West, tempered, however, by U.S. support for Israel.

On August 6, 1981, then Crown Prince Fahd offered an eight-point peace plan, based on United Nations resolutions, designed to create movement in the stalled peace process and present the Saudi view of a just settlement to the Arab–Israeli conflict. The Fahd Plan* was the first major official Saudi pronouncement on the resolution of the conflict and offered an alternative to the rejectionist Arabs who called for war and rejected the Camp David* model for peace. It was rejected by Israel and originally had a cool reception in the United States. Over time, U.S. interest in the Fahd Plan grew. The Fahd Plan was the basis for the plan officially accepted by the Arab League* at the Fez Arab Summit* in September 1982.

Saudi Arabia, under King Fahd, has been supportive of the United States-sponsored Arab–Israeli peace initiative that began with the Madrid Conference* in 1991 in the wake of the Persian Gulf War.*

For further information see: Alexander Bligh, *From Prince to King: Royal Succession in the House of Saud* (New York: New York University Press, 1984); David E. Long, *The United States and Saudi Arabia: Ambivalent Allies* (Boulder, CO: Westview Press, 1985); David E. Long, "Fahd Bin Abd Al-Aziz Al Saud," in Bernard Reich, ed., *Political Leaders of the Contemporary Middle East and North Africa: A Biographical Dictionary* (Westport, CT: Greenwood Press, 1990), pp. 175–80.

Mark Daryl Erickson

FAHD PLAN. In an interview with the Saudi Press Agency on August 7, 1981, Crown Prince Fahd* of Saudi Arabia outlined the principles for a peaceful settlement of the Arab–Israeli conflict. When asked if the government of Saudi Arabia has a practical framework for implementing a just and comprehensive settlement of the Palestinian* problem, he replied:

Naturally, we cannot indulge ourselves in details here, yet there is a set of principles that can be used as guidelines in our search for a just settlement. They are principles that already have been adopted and reiterated many times by the United Nations during the past few years. These principles are: (1) Israeli withdrawal from all the Arab territories occupied in 1967, including Arab Jerusalem*; (2) Removal of the settlements established by Israel in the Arab territories after 1967; (3) Guaranteeing the freedom of worship and religious practices for all religions in the holy places; (4) Asserting the rights of the Palestinian people to return to their homes and compensating those who do not wish to return; (5) Placing the West Bank* and Gaza Strip* under the auspices of the United Nations for a transitional period not exceeding several months; (6) Establishing an independent Palestinian state with Jerusalem as its capital; (7) Affirming the right of all the states in the region to live in peace; (8) Guaranteeing the implementation of these principles by the United Nations or some of its member states.

International reaction to the Fahd Plan was mixed. The United States reacted cautiously, while Prime Minister Menachem Begin* described it as a recipe for Israel's destruction. The Arab League,* excepting Libya, initially gave the plan support. The European Community embraced the plan and pointed out that it was similar to its own Venice Declaration* of 1980.

For further information see: Nadav Safran, *Saudi Arabia: The Ceaseless Quest for Security* (Cambridge: Belknap Press of Harvard University Press, 1985).

Simeon Manickavasagam

FAHMY, ISMAIL (b. Cairo, October 2, 1922). Egyptian career diplomat and politician. Joined the Egyptian Foreign Service in 1946 and served in various posts. He became minister of foreign affairs in 1973 and remained in that post until he resigned in protest over President Anwar Sadat's* visit to Jerusalem* in 1977.

In late October 1973, he was sent by Sadat to confer with President Richard Nixon* and Secretary of State Henry Kissinger* for a crucial meeting in the aftermath of the war to facilitate the disengagement of the Egyptian and Israeli armies. While en route to Washington, he was appointed by Sadat to head the Foreign Ministry.

His meetings with the Nixon administration were important in opening the way to a better relationship with the Americans.

He was involved in formalizing the six-point agreement between Egypt and Israel that solved the first urgent problem on the ground. By ensuring a steady flow of supplies for the besieged Egyptian Third Army* and the town of Suez, it removed the risk of an immediate resumption of warfare.

In his memoirs, Fahmy makes it clear that he tried to be cautious with Kissinger, and thus he tried to meet directly with President Nixon after every talk with Kissinger, to ensure that Kissinger accurately reflected Nixon's position.

According to Kissinger, Fahmy told him in Cairo in October 1973 that Egypt* neither wanted nor needed any American–Soviet observers in the Sinai Peninsula,* which was a Soviet idea. Fahmy was no more eager for a Soviet supervisory role than the American administration.

In light of the upcoming first military Disengagement Agreement,* he advised Sadat to maintain a balanced relationship with both superpowers, arguing that Egypt could play this game and benefit from it because of its political and strategic position. Any submission to any of the superpowers would not be in Egypt's interest.

Fahmy was careful to make the Disengagement Agreement clearly a military document and, as such, not different in any way from the Armistice Agreement signed by the same parties in 1948.

Fahmy was adamant in making it clear to Sadat that the Disengagement

Agreements should not be signed by the minister of war or by him personally but, instead, by the chiefs of staff of the Egyptian and the Israeli armies, underlining its military character.

In February 1974, President Sadat sent Fahmy to Washington to meet with Nixon. Fahmy asked Nixon to instruct Kissinger to go to Damascus to arrange a Disengagement Agreement between Syria* and Israel and an exchange of prisoners. He also informed him that the Arab heads of state agreed to lift the oil embargo* imposed by the oil-producing Arab states as punishment of the United States for assisting Israel during the war.

Fahmy fought hard against any idea of Egypt attending a Middle East peace conference without the presence of the United Nations (UN) Security Council in order to fully internationalize the peace process. He also sought a more active European role in the process.

By the end of 1974, his main objective was to secure adequate supplies of weapons for the Egyptian armed forces from the Soviets. Fahmy advised Sadat that he should make it clear that the Soviets could not take Egypt for granted. Thus, he advised Sadat to continue knocking on the door of the American arsenal.

Although diplomatic ties had been restored with Washington during that year, Fahmy remained somewhat skeptical despite the enormous improvement in American–Egyptian relations. Fahmy saw that the United States was still committed, first and foremost, to Israel.

To Fahmy, as long as Kissinger remained at the helm of American foreign policy, there could be nothing but step-by-step diplomacy.* Kissinger, in his judgment, was too pro-Israel and overconfident in his ability to manipulate people. Fahmy believed that Kissinger simply wanted to hypnotize the Egyptians and sabotage their attempts to strengthen relations with Moscow.

The Egyptian foreign minister welcomed the Joint Declaration issued on October 1, 1977, between the United States and the USSR, in which the superpowers outlined the conditions for peace. Egypt needed the Soviets to counterbalance Israeli influence on the United States.

Fahmy admitted that Sadat's decision to go to Jerusalem was an extraordinary one. But he told Sadat that the visit would achieve success only in terms of publicity in the news media. Fahmy's opposition to Sadat's trip stemmed from his belief that it would harm Egypt's national security, damage its relations with other Arab countries, and destroy Egypt's leading role in the Arab world. He was convinced that Sadat could not convince the Israelis to respond with reciprocal goodwill. On November 17, 1977, Ismail Fahmy resigned in protest.

Fahmy believed that neither the trip to Jerusalem, the speech in the Knesset,* nor the peace treaty would produce any miracles. He did not see the treaty as the embodiment of a just and lasting peace that the Geneva Conference* could have achieved. Thus, he believed that an international conference ought to be convened to deal exclusively with the Palestinian problem. Israel and the Palestine Liberation Organization* (PLO) should be invited to attend, together with the five permanent members of the UN Security Council and Lebanon* and Syria. The creation of an independent Palestinian state with secure boundaries and security guarantees for both Israel and the new state should be the goals of the conclave.

For further information see: Ismail Fahmy, *Negotiating for Peace in the Middle East* (Baltimore, MD: Johns Hopkins University Press, 1983).

Ahmed Elbashari

FAISAL. See **FEISAL.**

FAROUK (King of Egypt, 1920–65). King of Egypt* from his coronation in July 1937 until the 1952 revolution, which put an end to Mohammed Ali's Albanian dynasty, which had been ruling Egypt since 1805. He succeeded his father, King Fuad I. Although initially popular, he soon assumed an autocratic manner of ruling and was regarded by many Egyptians as an uncaring, pleasure-seeking, and ineffectual ruler who was unable or unwilling to deal with the country's problems.

The outbreak of World War II deepened the cleavages in Egyptian politics. The young king early showed his independence by refusing to accede to the Wafd Party demands for dismissal of Ali Maher as chief of the royal Cabinet. The critical issue between King Farouk and Nahhas Pasha of the Wafd became the attitude toward the war. Relations between the king and the British ambassador were getting worse. The king came to symbolize what was suspected to be a pro-Axis attitude, whereas Nahhas Pasha and the Wafd took a pro-Allied stand. The king was forced by an ultimatum from the British ambassador and by a show of British military might surrounding the Abdeen Royal Palace on February 2, 1942, to ask Nahhas Pasha to form the government. Such an incident publicly humiliated the king.

Farouk was overthrown on July 23, 1952, by a group of army officers known as the Free Officers, led by the young lieutenant colonel Gamal Abdul Nasser.* They were disaffected by the king's indifference toward the armed forces' aspirations and the subsequent disastrous performance of the Egyptian army during the first Arab–Israeli War of 1948–49.* Following a considerable debate among the Free Officers, King Farouk and his family were allowed to leave the country on July 26, 1952, after he formally abdicated the throne in favor of his infant son Ahmed Fuad II, who never assumed the duties of the throne due to the abolishment of the monarchy on June 18, 1953. Farouk sailed into exile on the same yacht on which his grandfather Ismail had left for exile some seventy years earlier. He left Egypt for Europe and obscurity. He died in Italy in 1965 and was buried in Al-Refaey Mosque in Cairo.

For further information see: Arthur Goldschmidt, Jr., "Farouk," in Bernard Reich, ed., *Political Leaders of the Contemporary Middle East and North Africa* (Westport, CT: Greenwood Press, 1990), pp. 188–93; Barrie St. Clair McBride, *Farouk of Egypt* (London: Robert Hale, 1967); Mohamed Neguib, *Egypt's Destiny* (New York: Doubleday,

1955); Adel M. Sabit, *A King Betrayed: The Ill-Fated Reign of Farouk of Egypt* (New York: Quartet, 1989); William Stadiem, *Too Rich: The High Life and Tragic Death of King Farouk* (New York: Carroll and Graf, 1991); P. J. Vatikiotis, *The History of Modern Egypt from Muhammad Ali to Mubarak* (Baltimore: Johns Hopkins University Press, 1991).

Ahmed Elbashari

FATAH (Al-Fatah [CONQUEST]). An acronym that, when reversed, stands for Harakat al-Tahrir al-Falistin (Movement for the Liberation of Palestine). Founded in the late 1950s by a group of Palestinian students, including Yasser Arafat,* in Cairo, this is the oldest of the Palestinian organizations. The idea of creating it came from Yasser Arafat and his friends. In 1959 (some say 1962), when Arafat, Salah Khalaf,* Farouk Kaddoumi,* Khalil al-Wazir,* and Khalid al-Hassan* were in Kuwait, Fatah was formed. From the outset it saw the liberation of Palestine* as the primary task, and the victory of the Algerian revolution spurred them. The first armed action against Israel took place on January 1, 1965. However, only after the Six Day War* did Fatah became prominent. The battle at Karameh* in March 1968 between the Israeli army and Fatah forces based in Jordan* enhanced Arafat's prestige.

Headed by Yasser Arafat, it joined the Palestine Liberation Organization* (PLO) in 1968 and won the leadership role in 1969. Its leaders were expelled from Jordan in 1970 and 1971, following the Jordan Civil War.* It then consolidated its position in Lebanon.* Israel's invasion of Lebanon in 1982* led to the group's dispersal to several Arab states, including Tunisia, Yemen, Algeria, and Iraq.* It has several components that have been involved in terrorist attacks, including Force 17* and the Hawari Special Operations Group.* Two of its senior leaders, Abu Jihad* and Abu Iyad,* were assassinated. It is headquartered in Tunis but has bases in various Arab countries.

Fatah's armed wing is known as Al-Asifa.*

For further information see: Ehud Yaari, *Strike Terror: The Story of Fatah* (New York: Sabra Books, 1970).

FATAH HAWKS. Abu Jihad* was coordinator of Fatah's* activities in the occupied territories* and controlled most of their lines of communication, especially before and during the early stages of the *intifada,** until his assassination in April 1988. In this capacity, Abu Jihad was able to rouse many groups to act in support of the Palestine Liberation Organization* (PLO) by defacing buildings in the territories with graffiti, fires, and other actions. One of these groups became known as the Fatah Hawks. They were an armed and paramilitary unit of the PLO within the occupied territories.

This small group of Palestinian youths, which, according to most sources, numbered no more than sixty activists, was founded by the young teenagers who lived through the *intifada* years, known as the al-Shabiba youth movement, and later formed the Black Panthers (in 1990), graduating from rock throwing to petrol bombs and knives. Eventually, these Panthers moved to organized crime, guns, and counterintelligence and to "purifying" their society by shooting "chronic" thieves in the leg and flogging or even killing "loose" women. Their victims included Israeli soldiers, border police, undercover unit operatives, Jews (Israeli and foreign visitors), and Palestinian* collaborators. That changed from rock-throwing children to gun-toting zealots who believe that Israelis can be vanquished and Palestine can be created only with more guns. Their symbol is a submachine gun raised over an olive branch.

Loyal to Yasser Arafat's* branch of Fatah, the Hawks had made enemies of those who opposed his views and often swore to exact revenge upon those other Fatah factions for their ignoble acts of killing other Palestinians.

Since the Declaration of Principles* (DOP) was signed on September 13, 1993, Arafat has called upon his loyal armed guerrillas to put an end to the *intifada* and to begin a transitory phase of policing the Gaza Strip* by themselves. After some understandings were reached between PLO headquarters in Tunis and the small cells in the territories, the Fatah Hawks agreed to support Arafat's decision to seek peace with the Israelis, laying down their guns in a symbolic act. They have since been included in the Palestinian police force. Once the Fatah Hawks officially supported Arafat's views on the DOP, the Israel Defense Forces* (IDF) officially ceased its ongoing searches for known Hawks. In November 1993, Hawk squads were formed all over Gaza* and in Hebron.*

On January 2, 1994, the Hawks paraded in Gaza to celebrate the twenty-ninth anniversary of the foundation of Fatah. That same day, a recorded message from Arafat was broadcast to the people on parade, praising the Hawks and calling them the "leaders of the *intifada;* the leaders of the state."

On February 5, 1994, an undercover Israeli unit spotted and shot three Palestinian fugitives, killing one who happened to be the current leader of the Fatah Hawks. Salim Muwafi, leader of the Rafah Refugee Camp Hawks, was seen with another two wanted men in a house in Rafah, and when the Israeli unit tried to arrest the three, the fugitives opened fire upon the soldiers, and the soldiers returned fire. The Hawks took this action as an indication that, even though the IDF had officially canceled all searches for Fatah Hawk members, it was not serious about its verbal or written commitments. They claimed that Muwafi was hunted down. They called for joint Hawk–HAMAS* protests in the streets after mourning for the loss of the 1,173d martyr of the *intifada* (Muwafi), and the Hawks stated that they were "committed to the cease-fire, but ready to defend themselves if cornered," regardless of what policies were coming out of Tunis.

Then word came that the Hawks had not actually ceased their terrorist acts since the signing of the DOP and that they had no intent to do so, since they viewed Tunis as an allied-but-alien body that had no real understanding of the situation in the territories. The Hawks intended to use the Israelis' soft approach to Arafat's loyalists as a way to continue their activities, in order to show their continued strength and resistance to the Israelis.

FATAHLAND 161

The Hebron Massacre* convinced the Hawks that coexistence, let alone peace with the Israelis, is impossible. They issued a statement calling on Arafat to end the negotiations, which implied that the Palestinian people would never be able to reach their national rights unless they used force.

For further information see: Ze'ev Schiff and Ehud Ya'ari, *Intifada* (New York: Simon and Schuster, 1990).

Yasha Manuel Harari

FATAH REVOLUTIONARY COUNCIL. See **ABU NIDAL ORGANIZATION.**

FATAHLAND. Alternative spellings: Fatah-land, Fatehland, (Al) Arkoub, (Al-) Arqub, (Al-) Urqoub. Fatahland is the Western name given to the Arqub area of Lebanon* controlled by the fedayeen* as early as 1968. It was used as a staging ground for fedayeen attacks against Israeli targets. Fatahland was located in the foothills of Mount Hermon,* bordered by the Hasbani River to the west and Syria* to the east. At different times this area encompassed twenty to fifty square miles. The term *Fatahland* was derived from *Fatah,* one of the major fedayeen movements that occupied the area. Other, smaller fedayeen movements and, at times, Syrian and Libyan volunteer forces were also deployed in the region.

Much of the importance of Fatahland for the fedayeen was its proximity to Syria. Through the Arafat Trail, which traversed Fatahland, the Syrian government provided logistical and military support to the fedayeen. Without bases in Lebanon, the fedayeen would have had difficulties in striking at targets in northern Israel, because the Syrian government controlled raids originating in its territory.

Fatahland became a point of contention between the Israeli and Lebanese governments because fedayeen attacks were originating from the area. The Israelis accused the Lebanese government of not doing enough to curb fedayeen actions against Israel. For their part, the Lebanese attempted to control the fedayeen in Fatahland through the Lebanese army, resulting in open warfare between the two forces. The Israelis, too, took action against bases in Fatahland both in the form of air strikes as well as ground assaults.

Initially, Yasser Arafat* was determined to establish fedayeen forces in the region through military might, but the resolve of the Lebanese army was unyielding. Several Arab states, especially Syria and Iraq, pressed the Lebanese government to allow the fedayeen greater mobility and autonomy. On November 3, 1969, the Palestine Liberation Organization* (PLO) and the Lebanese government signed the Cairo Agreement,* in which, according to the text published in *Al-Nahar* on April 20, 1970, the PLO was to recognize the sovereignty of Lebanon and the authority of its government. In return, the Lebanese were to allow fedayeen raids to be staged against targets deep into Israeli territory from the Arqub region.

For further information see: Frederick C. Hof, *Galilee Divide: The Israel–Lebanon Frontier, 1916–1984* (Boulder, CO: Westview Press, 1985); Edgar O'Ballance, *Arab Guerrilla Power 1967–1972* (London: Faber and Faber, 1974).

Donald A. Pearson

FAWZI, MAHMOUD (b. 1900; d. 1980). A veteran Egyptian* lawyer, diplomat, and statesman, he graduated from the University of Cairo with a law degree and later received his doctorate in law from the University of Rome in 1929. After practicing law, he joined the Egyptian diplomatic service. After serving in numerous posts in New York, New Orleans, Kobe, and Athens, he became the director of nationalities in the Ministry of Foreign Affairs in 1940. He served in Jerusalem* as Egypt's consul general in 1941. In 1946, he joined the Egyptian delegation to the United Nations. In 1952, the new regime in Egypt made him foreign minister. He served from 1958 to 1961 as foreign minister of the United Arab Republic* of Syria* and Egypt. From 1964 to 1967, he served as deputy prime minister. From 1967 until Nasser's* death in 1979, Fawzi served as the president's special adviser on foreign affairs.

Upon assuming power in 1970, President Anwar Sadat* named him prime minister, and he served in that position until 1972, when he became vice president. He remained vice president and a presidential adviser on political affairs until his retirement in September 1974.

Ahmed Elbashari

FEDAYEEN (those who sacrifice themselves). The name *fedayeen* is derived from the Arabic word *feda,* meaning "sacrifice," with fedayeen thus being "men of sacrifice." The original fedayeen were the twelfth-century Hashashins, organized by Ben Subbah, who was known as the Old Man of the Mountains. Within the context of the Arab–Israeli conflict, the fedayeen were formed in the Palestinian* refugee camps following the first Arab–Israeli War.* The term has been widely applied to Palestinian groups and individuals engaged in sabotage and guerrilla or terrorist activity.

Since the fedayeen were not strong enough to battle Israeli forces directly, it was believed among both Arab and Palestinian leaders that the fedayeen could be used to provoke Israel into military conflict with neighboring Arab states through attacks on both military and civilian targets. Gamal Abdul Nasser* of Egypt* began supplying and paying the fedayeen in 1955 and ultimately controlled some of them through his regular army. Syrian* president Hafez Assad* has also used his influence to manage fedayeen activity.

The term began to be used publicly to refer to Palestinians trained and equipped by Egypt who launched raids from the Gaza Strip* into Israel, beginning in the summer of 1955, to spy, commit sabotage, or kill Israelis. The low-intensity conflict between Israel and Egypt that had continued after the Armistice Agreements of 1949* intensified during 1955. Groups of Palestinians in the Gaza Strip were trained by Egyptian Military Intelligence for raids into Israel.

Their first attack was launched late in August 1955 and penetrated some twenty-seven miles into Israel, attacking both civilian and military targets. Israel responded to these attacks, and they were a factor in the 1956 Suez War.*

In July 1968, the Palestine National Council* amended its National Covenant* to include the endorsement of fedayeen action as "the nucleus of the Palestinian popular liberation war" (Article 10). It was hoped that fedayeen forces could be united and that their activities against Israel could be coordinated; however, the diverse movements held such conflicting opinions and beliefs that differences were irreconcilable. This led to infighting between movements and brought about splinter organizations.

Over the years, fedayeen units have been organized in the occupied territories,* Egypt, Jordan,* Syria, and Lebanon.* The most prominent organizations include the Action Group for the Liberation of Palestine (AGLP), Arab Liberation Front* (ALF), Arab Nationalist Movement (ANM), Front for the Popular Struggle (FPS), Palestinian Liberation Front* (PLF), Palestinian National Front (PNF), Palestinian National Liberation Movement (Fatah*), Palestinian Salvation Front (PSF), Popular Democratic Front for the Liberation of Palestine (PDFLP), Popular Front for the Liberation of Palestine* (PFLP), Popular Front for the Liberation of Palestine—General Command* (PFLP–GC), Popular Liberation Force (formerly, the Palestinian Liberation Army*), Vanguard of the Popular Liberation War (Saiqa*).

For further information see: Jillian Becker, *The PLO: The Rise and Fall of the Palestinian Liberation Organization* (London: Weidenfeld and Nicolson, 1984); Eliezer Ben-Rafael, *Israel-Palestine: A Guerrilla Conflict in International Politics* (Westport, CT: Greenwood Press, 1987); Joseph Churba, *Fedayeen and the Middle East Crisis* (Maxwell Air Force Base, AL: Documentary Research Division, Aerospace Studies Institute, 1969); Yehoshafat Harkabi, *Fedayeen Action and Arab Strategy* (London: Institute for Strategic Studies, 1968) [Adelphi Papers No. 53]; Edgar O'Ballance, *Arab Guerrilla Power 1967–1972* (London: Faber and Faber, 1974); Bard E. O'Neill, *Revolutionary Warfare in the Middle East: The Israelis vs the Fedayeen* (Boulder, CO: Paladin Press, 1974); Zeev Schiff and Raphael Rothstein, *Fedayeen: Guerrillas against Israel* (New York: David McKay, 1972).

Donald A. Pearson and John Fontaine

FEISAL IBN HUSSEIN (b. Taif, Hejaz, 1885; d. September 1933). A son of Sherif Hussein* of Mecca, he was among the leaders of the Arab forces in the Arab Revolt.* Feisal and his followers entered Damascus in October 1918, where he set up an Arab administration. At the Paris Peace Conference,* Feisal presented the Hashemite and Arab case for an independent Arab kingdom. By 1918, Feisal believed that the French* were not sympathetic to Arab aspirations and met with Chaim Weizmann,* in part because he saw the Jews as potential allies in their quest. He signed an agreement* with Chaim Weizmann on Arab–Jewish cooperation. In March 1920, he was proclaimed king of Syria* (an undefined area that included Lebanon,* Transjordan,* and Palestine*), but the San Remo Conference* confirmed the French Mandate, and Feisal eventually was forced to leave Syria. He was proclaimed king of Iraq* in August 1921. See also FEISAL–WEIZMANN AGREEMENT; CAIRO CONFERENCE.

For further information see: Neil Caplan, ''Faisal Ibn Husain and the Zionists: A Reexamination with Documents,'' *The International History Review* 5 (November 1983): 516–614.

FEISAL–WEIZMANN AGREEMENT. Chaim Weizmann* went to Aqaba in May 1918 to meet Feisal ibn Hussein* and to seek closer cooperation between the Zionists* and the Arabs under the leadership of Sherif Hussein* and his son Feisal. Feisal assured Weizmann of his goodwill toward Zionist aspirations and attributed past misunderstandings between the Arabs and the Jews to the machinations of the Ottoman Turks.* On a number of subsequent occasions Feisal claimed that he shared Weizmann's objectives and, during a meeting in London in December 1918, noted that ''no true Arab can be suspicious or afraid of Jewish nationalism.'' These exchanges of sentiment and perspective were formalized in a document signed on January 3, 1919, in which Feisal and Weizmann pledged to work with each other to achieve the goals of both the Zionists and the Arabs. Feisal renounced any claim to Palestine,* which would become the territory of the Jews and would be separate from the new Arab state. He appended a statement that this agreement would be valid only if the Arabs obtained their independence as formulated by him in an earlier memorandum for the British.

In the agreement Weizmann gained Feisal's recognition of Zionist aims in Palestine, in exchange for which Weizmann supported Feisal's claims against the French in Syria.* The preamble recognized the close racial and historical bonds between the Arab and Jewish people and acknowledged that the nationalist aspirations of both could be facilitated by collaborating in the development of the Arab state and Palestine. The first article provided for the establishment of duly accredited agents of both Arabs and Jews within their respective territories. Article 2 provided for the establishment of ''definite boundaries between the Arab State and Palestine'' to be determined by a commission convened after the peace conference. The third article called for the establishment of a constitution and administration in Palestine that would fulfill all of the guarantees of the Balfour Declaration.* Article 4 called for the implementation of necessary measures to ''encourage and stimulate immigration of Jews into Palestine on a large scale, and as quickly as possible.'' The article also called for creating measures that would protect the rights of the Arab peasant and tenant farmer and advance their economic development. The fifth article called for the protection of the free exercise of religion and the prohibition of religious tests as a basis for civil and political rights. Article 6 provided that Muslim holy places should be under Muslim control. The seventh article called upon the Zionist Organization to establish a commission to assess the economic possibilities of the country and propose the best means for its development. The Zionist Organization would place the commission, as well, at the disposal of the Arab states to make the same assessments and proposals for the Arab state. Further, the Zionists were expected to assist in "providing the means for developing the natural resources and economic possibilities." Article 8 called upon both parties to act in accord and harmony on all matters, and the ninth article provided for British arbitration of any disputes that may arise.

In later statements before the King–Crane Commission,* Feisal repudiated Zionist aspirations. Later in 1919, in discussions with Sir Herbert Samuel,* Feisal confirmed his desire to cooperate with the Zionists in the development of the area. However, Feisal also made clear his position that he would not support Zionist immigration into Palestine unless he secured an independent Arab state in Syria. Later, Feisal noted that the Arabs could not yield Palestine and could not accept Jewish supremacy there. By the end of 1919, cooperation between Feisal and the Zionists had ended. Various explanations have been offered by one side or the other for the change in Feisal's position. Clearly, he altered his view from one of sympathy for Zionist aspirations to one in which a clash between Arab and Jewish demands became inevitable. It is probable that at one point Feisal saw the Zionists as valuable allies in the postwar negotiations, particularly with the French, for a future Arab state and that later, in part because of opposition from the Arabs in Palestine and questions from other Arab sources, he believed that this was not the path to be followed.

For further information see: G. Stern, "The Weizmann–Feisal Agreement," *New Outlook* 12 (March–April 1969):20–25.

Joseph E. Goldberg

FEZ ARAB SUMMIT (SEPTEMBER 1982). The twelfth Arab Summit conference convened at Fez, Morocco, on November 25, 1981. It adjourned and later resumed in Fez in September 1982, under the chairmanship of King Hassan II* of Morocco. The 1982 meeting was in response to the War in Lebanon.* It occurred in the wake of the forced evacuation of the Palestine Liberation Organization* (PLO) from Beirut and the issuance of U.S. president Ronald Reagan's* fresh-start initiative* on September 1, 1982, and during the continued Israeli military action in Lebanon.*

On September 8, 1982, the members of the Arab League* met for the twelfth Summit meeting of the heads of state. The outcome of the 1982 Fez Arab Summit was a plan for peace between Israel and the Arab states that included the call for establishing a Palestinian* state. The peace plan was based on the proposals suggested by King Fahd* of Saudi Arabia on August 6, 1981, and was signed by all Arab heads of state in attendance. Libya, rejecting negotiation with Israel, did not attend the meeting, and Egypt* had not yet been readmitted to membership in the league following its peace with Israel. While differing in content, the Fez Plan and the Reagan proposal were not deemed by the Americans to be incompatible. However, Israel's government of Prime Minister Menachem Begin* rejected the idea of a peace that called for the dismantling of settlements and the establishment of a Palestinian state.

Mark Daryl Erickson and Simeon Manickavasagam

FEZ PEACE PLAN. The Arab Summit in Fez, Morocco, in September 1982, adopted the following resolution concerning the Arab–Israeli conflict, which, in effect, constituted a peace plan:

The conference greeted the steadfastness of the Palestine* revolutionary forces, the Lebanese* and Palestinian peoples and the Syrian* Arab Armed Forces and declared its support of the Palestinian people in their struggle for the retrieval of their established national rights.

Out of the conference's belief in the ability of the Arab nation to achieve its legitimate objectives and eliminate the aggression, and out of the principles and basis laid down by the Arab summit conferences, and out of the Arab countries' determination to continue to work by all means for the establishment of peace based on justice in the Middle East and using the plan of President Habib Bourguiba,* which is based on international legitimacy, as the foundation for solving the Palestinian question and the plan of His Majesty King Fahd ibn 'Abd al-'Aziz* which deals with peace in the Middle East, and in the light of the discussions and notes made by their majesties, excellencies and highnesses the kings, presidents and emirs, the conference has decided to adopt the following principles: 1. Israel's withdrawal from all Arab territories occupied in 1967, including Arab Jerusalem.* 2. The removal of settlements set up by Israel in the Arab territories after 1967. 3. Guarantees of the freedom of worship and the performance of religious rites for all religions at the holy places. 4. Confirmation of the right of the Palestinian people to self-determination and to exercise their firm and inalienable national rights, under the leadership of the PLO [Palestine Liberation Organization*], its sole legitimate representative, and compensation for those who do not wish to return. 5. The placing of the West Bank* and Gaza Strip* under UN [United Nations] supervision for a transitional period, not longer than several months. 6. The creation of an independent Palestinian state with Jerusalem as its capital. 7. The drawing up by the Security Council of guarantees for peace for all the states of the region, including the independent Palestinian state. 8. Security Council guarantees for the implementation of these principles.

FIDAYUN. See **FEDAYEEN.**

15 MAY ORGANIZATION. Formed in 1979 from the remnants of Wadi Haddad's* Popular Front for the Liberation of Palestine—Special Operations Group (PFLP-SOG). Led by Muhammad al-Umari, who is known as Abu Ibrahim or the "bomb man." In the early 1980s, it claimed responsibility for bomb attacks against Israeli and American targets. This organization was never a part of the Palestine Liberation Organization* (PLO) and reportedly was disbanded in the mid-1980s.

FIVE-POINT PLAN. In October 1989 (although formally released on December 6, 1989), Secretary of State James Baker* announced a five-point plan to clarify

Egyptian president Hosni Mubarak's* ten-point proposal* and thereby to advance the prospects for movement in the peace process. The five points were:

1. The United States understands that because Egypt* and Israel have been working hard on the peace process, there is agreement that an Israeli delegation should conduct a dialogue with a Palestinian delegation in Cairo. 2. The United States understands that Egypt cannot substitute itself for the Palestinians and Egypt will consult with Palestinians on all aspects of that dialogue. Egypt will also consult with Israel and the United States. 3. The United States understands that Israel will attend the dialogue only after a satisfactory list of Palestinians has been worked out. 4. The United States understands that the Government of Israel will come to the dialogue on the basis of the Israeli Government's May 14 initiative. The United States further understands that Palestinians will come to the dialogue prepared to discuss elections and the negotiating process in accordance with Israel's initiative. The U.S. understands, therefore, that Palestinians would be free to raise issues that relate to their opinion on how to make elections and the negotiating process succeed. 5. In order to facilitate this process, the U.S. proposes that the Foreign Minister of Israel, Egypt, and the U.S. meet in Washington within two weeks.

The proposal ultimately failed to achieve the intended negotiations.

FIVE PRINCIPLES OF PEACE. See **JOHNSON'S FIVE PRINCIPLES OF PEACE.**

FLYING ARTILLERY. A term used to describe Israel's use of its air force in response to Egyptian* shelling strikes and commando raids in 1969 and 1970 during the War of Attrition* along the Suez Canal.* Because of Israel's inferior artillery capabilities, the Israeli air force was used against the superior Egyptian artillery emplacements. The Israel Defense Forces* were structured to rely on their air force and armored units. They were not designed to act against artillery capabilities equal to that which Egyptian president Gamal Abdul Nasser* employed against the Bar-Lev Line.*

Nasser's War of Attrition was initiated in an attempt to debilitate Israeli defense fortifications through continuous and heavy artillery bombardments. For the three-month period between May and July 1969, the Israel Defense Forces sustained a large number of casualties. This was significant for their size and history. Serious consideration for the use of Israel's air force was first suggested by General Ezer Weizman,* chief of operations, in early July 1969. Weizman requested that the air force be used to counter the artillery bombardments.

Defense Minister Moshe Dayan* and Prime Minister Golda Meir* sought to avoid using the air force, even for limited purposes. Both believed it would lead to an escalation that might result in a Soviet intervention. Because the Israel Defense Forces were spread along the Suez Canal, the Golan Heights,* and the Jordan River,* the Meir government feared that an absence of action could lead to a situation that might call for more costly maneuvers in the future.

The use of the air force as flying artillery was attractive for two reasons:

Israel had clear pilot superiority over Egypt, and, because the air force consisted almost entirely of regular troops, additional reserves would not be needed. For these reasons the decision was made to use the air force rather than increase Israeli artillery positions and ground troops.

The Israeli air strikes that followed were aimed at artillery units, radar installations, and Soviet-supplied surface-to-air missiles. The short-term effects gained by the Israeli air force resulted in Egyptian artillery bombardments dropping from a high of 311 incidents in June, to 207 in July, to 72 in August. Nasser reacted to the Israeli air force by shifting Egypt's use of artillery fire to mortar shelling and small-arms fire.

Israel's flying artillery was challenged by Egyptian air units. Egypt sustained heavy material losses in the air battles that followed. From the initiation of Israel's flying artillery strategy to the war's conclusion, Egypt lost forty-eight aircraft, compared to Israel's loss of five. In the first two months of the offensive, Israel completed over 1,000 sorties, compared to Egypt's 100. Much of Israel's success was attributed to its 1969 acquisition of American-made McDonnell Douglas A-4 Skyhawk* fighter jets procured under a Johnson* administration order for forty-eight planes. The first four A-4s arrived in Israel on September 5, 1969. The A-4s were maneuverable, long-range bombers that provided Israel with a technological advantage over existing Egyptian aircraft.

Israel's use of its air force as flying artillery is often perceived as a watershed moment during the War of Attrition. Although the introduction of its air force was significant on its own, the Israelis heightened its role to include air strikes far into Egyptian territory. These deep-penetration raids* were used by Israel as a method of counterattrition, aimed at drawing the attention of the Egyptian populace to the consequences of Nasser's Suez hostilities.

For further information see: Yaacov Bar-Siman-Tov, *The Israeli–Egyptian War of Attrition, 1968–1970* (New York: Columbia University, 1980); Mohamed Heikal, *The Road to Ramadan* (New York: Quadrangle, 1975); Chaim Herzog, *The Arab–Israeli Wars, from the War of Independence to Lebanon* (London: Arms and Armour, 1984); David Korn, *Stalemate: The War of Attrition and Great Power Diplomacy in the Middle East, 1967–1970* (Boulder, CO: Westview Press, 1992); Bernard Reich, *Quest for Peace* (New Brunswick, NJ: Transaction Books, 1977); Lawrence Whetten, *The Canal War* (Cambridge: MIT Press, 1974).

Robert Crangle, Jr.

FORCE 17. Force 17 was established in the early 1970s by Ali Hassan Salameh as a small bodyguard unit and personal security force whose function was to protect Yasser Arafat* and other Palestine Liberation Organization* (PLO) leaders. It grew in size and, in addition to its security functions, carried out assassinations and attacks on Arafat's instructions against Palestinian rivals. In 1985, it reportedly expanded its operations to include terrorist attacks against Israeli targets. It claimed responsibility for killing three Israelis in Cyprus in 1985 and has been active in Israel and the occupied territories.*

FORD, GERALD RUDOLPH (b. Omaha, Nebraska, July 14, 1913). Gerald Rudolph Ford was educated at the University of Michigan and Yale University. After serving in the U.S. Navy during World War II, he was elected to the U.S. House of Representatives in 1949, where he served until Richard Nixon* selected him to serve as vice president after the resignation of Spiro Agnew in 1973. He became president after Richard Nixon's resignation in August 1974 and served until January 1977.

Ford's policy objectives in the Arab–Israeli conflict centered on Secretary of State Henry Kissinger's* concept of step-by-step* and shuttle diplomacy.* Ford allowed Kissinger to continue to pursue foreign policy objectives similar to those in the Nixon administration. Before becoming president, Ford's exposure to foreign affairs had been minimal, and his views remained unformed beyond a general stand against Communism. This allowed Kissinger a great deal of leeway, and Ford's decisions on foreign policy questions often were ultimately based on Kissinger's views.

Ford found that his outspoken support of Israel as minority leader of the House did not translate well into necessary presidential caution. Most indicative of his shift in views is a statement he made in April 1971, before an annual American Israel Public Affairs Committee* (AIPAC) policy conference. He claimed that Washington should not force Israel to ''negotiate with the U.S. rather than Egypt on the territorial question,'' but four years later, President Ford allowed such a circumstance to replace peace negotiations with Egypt.*

After brokering Disengagement Agreements* between Israel and Egypt and Syria* in early 1974, Kissinger was unable to secure additional agreements in the fall of 1974 and early 1975. An attempt to secure an agreement between Israel and Jordan* became impossible when the Arab League* at the Rabat Summit* endorsed the Palestine Liberation Organization* (PLO) as the sole legitimate representative* of the Palestinians in October 1974. Kissinger then turned his attention to Egypt, but differing positions concerning the extent of Israeli withdrawal and the level of Egypt's nonbelligerency, including disputes over the valuable Sinai Peninsula* oil fields (including Abu Rudeis*) and a communications center, led these talks nowhere after numerous shuttles between the two parties. The process was suspended in the spring of 1975, and Ford announced a reassessment of U.S. Middle East policy. Military and economic agreements with Israel were suspended during the process, which lasted from March 22 until early June.

The reassessment was attacked by pro-Israeli forces. The result was a letter to President Ford signed by seventy-six senators that stressed the necessity for Israel to ''obtain a level of military and economic support adequate to deter a renewal of war.'' With an overwhelming number of senators supporting a strong relationship with Israel, Ford eventually returned to pursuing step-by-step diplomacy after meeting with both Anwar Sadat* and Yitzhak Rabin* in June. The negotiations were restarted, and on September 1, 1975, the Sinai II Accords* were signed.

This was the only substantial agreement concerning the Arab–Israeli conflict reached during the Ford administration.

For further information see: Gerald R. Ford, *A Time to Heal: The Autobiography of Gerald R. Ford* (New York: Harper and Row and the Reader's Digest Association, 1979); Steven L. Speigel, *The Other Arab-Israeli Conflict: Making America's Middle East Policy, from Truman to Reagan* (Chicago: University of Chicago Press, 1985).

Erin Z. Ferguson

FOUR-POWER TALKS. The permanent representatives to the United Nations of France,* the USSR,* the United Kingdom,* and the United States met on April 3, 1969, in New York to begin consideration of how they could contribute to a peaceful settlement in the Middle East. They based their approach on United Nations Security Council Resolution 242* and reaffirmed their support for the Jarring mission.* These consultations continued over the months that followed but had no significant success in achieving movement toward solution of the Arab–Israeli conflict.

FRAMEWORK FOR PEACE IN THE MIDDLE EAST. One of the two Camp David Accords* announced at the White House on September 17, 1978, which were to provide the basis for continuing negotiations for an Arab–Israeli peace. The accords were a result of the negotiations among U.S., Egyptian,* and Israeli delegations at the Summit meeting at Camp David* in September 1978. This framework set forth general principles and some specifics to govern a comprehensive peace settlement, focusing on the future of the West Bank* and the Gaza Strip.*

FRAMEWORK FOR THE CONCLUSION OF A PEACE TREATY BETWEEN EGYPT AND ISRAEL. One of the two Camp David Accords* announced at the White House in Washington, D.C., on September 17, 1978, which were to provide the basis for continuing negotiations for an Arab–Israeli peace. The accords were a result of the negotiations among U.S., Egyptian,* and Israeli delegations at the Summit meeting at Camp David* in September 1978. This framework called for Israel's withdrawal from the Sinai Peninsula* and the establishment of normal, peaceful relations between the two states. Negotiations followed between Egypt and Israel, and these led to the Egypt–Israel Peace Treaty in March 1979.*

FRANCE. France has been actively involved throughout the Arab–Israeli conflict, though changes within the global and regional context have imposed constraints on the range of options available to France in pursuit of its objectives.

French interest in the Near East was initially a religious one. During the Crusades, it sent forces to the Near East as part of its *mission civilisatrice* to defend Christendom. Over time, economic and political interests complemented that religious interest. In the nineteenth century, close ties were developed with the Maronites and other Christian groups in what is now Lebanon,* based on shared religious values and Maronite control of important sectors of the economy in Mount Lebanon. Traditional French interests in the holy places of Jerusalem* led to a bloody confrontation with Tsar Nicholas I of Russia in the 1850s. The Russian defeat in the Crimean War (1854–56) resulted in French, British, and Austrian agreement to protect the Ottoman Empire* from further Russian expansion and to preserve its territorial integrity. When violence broke out between Christian and Druze communities in 1860–61, the French intervened on behalf of the Christians. The French established *lycées* in Lebanon and Egypt* for the children of its citizens, bringing with it French culture and language. French missionaries established St. Joseph's University in Beirut in 1875. The Levant became so important for French trade with the Far East that the French explorer and engineer Ferdinand de Lesseps obtained a contract from the Egyptian viceroy, Ismail Pasha, in 1856 for the construction of a canal over the Isthmus of Suez. Opened in 1869, the Suez Canal* guaranteed a faster and less expensive voyage for French and British ships on their way to the Orient.

The outbreak of World War I had a profound effect on French policy in the Middle East. The Sykes–Picot Agreement,* signed between Britain and France on May 16, 1916, noted that ''France and Great Britain* are prepared to recognize and protect an independent Arab state or Confederation of Arab states'' and laid the groundwork for the French Mandate in the Levant. Sir Mark Sykes of Great Britain and Francois Georges Picot* of France exchanged notes that envisaged French control of the Levant coast in what is now Syria* and Lebanon.* The French delineated a ''Greater Lebanon,'' which included Mount Lebanon, Beirut, Sidon, Tyre, southern Lebanon, the Beka Valley,* and the Akkar Plain in the north.

Between World War I and World War II, France ruled the areas of Syria and Lebanon under a League of Nations Mandate that authorized France to assist the native population and offer ''services'' that would ''expedite'' the development of these areas as independent states. Revolts broke out in 1920 and 1926 as France dealt with the growth of Arab nationalism. Realizing that its control over the Mandated areas was waning, France began to transfer power gradually to the Syrians. The new Syrian Parliament ratified a Franco–Syrian treaty in September 1936 in the hope that an eventual reunification with Lebanon would occur, but the Popular Front government of Leon Blum refused to ratify the treaty. French troops were eventually pulled out of Syria at the end of 1946.

The fall of Vichy France and the establishment of the Fourth Republic (1946–58), with its weak executive and strong Parliament, ushered in a new era in foreign policy. This era was marked by closer cooperation with Israel. France also became the principal supplier of the Israeli military. That close military alliance, as well as the revolt against French rule in Algeria, led to the 1956 Suez crisis.* Believing Nasser* to be the key supporter of the Algerian Front de Liberation Nationale (FLN), France, along with Britain and Israel, attacked Egypt. Eventually, those three parties withdrew from the canal zone in 1957.

The debacle in Egypt and the war against Algeria led ultimately to the downfall of the Fourth Republic and the rise of the Fifth Republic, led by Charles de Gaulle. De Gaulle believed that France's unequivocal support of Israel during the Fourth Republic was an obstacle to his policy of attempting to reestablish the "grandeur" of France as a world power. He believed that the developing countries of the Third World would view a new France with no colonial ties as an alternative to superpower dependence. In the Middle East, this became known as de Gaulle's *politique arabe,* where closer ties were sought with the Arab world.

The 1967 Arab–Israeli War* marked the beginning of a new period in French Middle East policy. De Gaulle believed that a solution to the tensions between Israel and the Arab states lay with the regional states as well as the "Big Four Powers"—the United States, USSR, Britain, and France. The French supported United Nations (UN) Security Council Resolution 242,* and official French policy deemed Israeli withdrawal from the occupied territories* a prerequisite to any lasting peace in the area.

As a result, Franco–Israeli relations deteriorated further. De Gaulle's "global solution" specified three conditions to end hostilities: (1) evacuation of the territories seized by force, (2) an end to the state of war, and (3) mutual recognition of each of the states involved. The four-power talks* began in March 1969, but, by June 1970, the talks became deadlocked.

The resignation of de Gaulle and the election of Georges Pompidou did not alter the Gaullist doctrine of grandeur or the French tilt toward the Arab world. The Arab oil embargo* prompted France to choose a policy of close involvement with the Arab oil-exporting states, for it underscored French vulnerability to the oil weapon.* Oil accounted for approximately 70 percent of French energy consumption. France was receiving 73 percent of its oil from the Persian Gulf. France agreed in 1975 to open a Palestine Liberation Organization* (PLO) liaison and information office in Paris, but the French did not regard the PLO as the sole representative of the Palestinian people. Under Valéry Giscard d'Estaing, France became the first European Community* member to link the Palestinian question to the overall peace process. On several occasions during Giscard's presidency, the French voted in the United Nations to criticize Israeli settlement policies on the West Bank.* In 1975, it asserted that the Palestinians had a right to a *patrie independente,* or independent homeland. On June 13, 1980, the French government joined in the Venice Declaration,* which called for all of the states to live in secure, recognized, and guaranteed borders; Israel to withdraw from the territories it occupied in 1967; members of the PLO to be included in any future negotiations; and sustained diplomatic action to reach a just solution to the Palestinian issue, which was not simply a matter of refugees.

François Mitterrand's interest in the Arab–Israeli conflict reflected the Gaullist desire to play a more active role in the peace process. However, Mitterrand believed that France had lost its way as an honest broker. He was critical of the *politique arabe* practiced by de Gaulle, Pompidou, and Giscard and believed that a step-by-step approach to the Arab–Israeli conflict along the lines of Henry Kissinger's* strategy would secure a place for France in future negotiations. Rejecting a multilateral approach, Mitterrand sought a new posture on the Arab–Israeli conflict based on a more conciliatory approach toward Israel. This policy ushered in a precarious French balancing act between Israel and the Arab states.

Mitterrand supported the Camp David Accords* and was also the first French head of state since de Gaulle to visit Israel, in March 1982. However, the Israeli bombing of a French-built nuclear reactor at Osiraq* in Iraq and the Israeli invasion of Lebanon stalled the Franco–Israeli rapprochement. Although France embraced United Nations Security Council Resolutions 242 and 338,* which referred only to the Palestinian ''refugee'' component of the Arab–Israeli conflict, France subsequently took the position that the Palestinians were the key to any overall settlement of the conflict. Its first major initiative into that arena was the Franco–Egyptian draft resolution presented to the United Nations Security Council (UNSC) in July 1982, which called for all of the states in the region to live within secure and recognized borders in accordance with UNSC Resolution 242, mutual and simultaneous recognition between all of the interested parties, and representation of the Palestinian people, including the PLO, at peace negotiations. Yet, the Reagan* fresh-start initiative* of 1982 undercut this initiative.

During the 1980s, France walked a fine line between distancing itself from the United States and its policies while trying to curry favor with the Palestinians and the Arab states. France committed over 700 troops to the United Nations Interim Force in Lebanon* (UNIFIL) and was also part of the multinational forces sent to Beirut to monitor the withdrawal of Palestinian forces from that city and later to protect the Palestinian refugee camps in Beirut. In July 1984, Mitterrand visited King Hussein* in Jordan,* and, in November of that same year, he visited Hafez al-Assad* in Syria. With the 1984 election of Shimon Peres's* Labor government, France believed that Israel would be more amenable to some sort of accommodation with the Palestinians and the Arab states. On February 23, 1987, the foreign ministers of the European Community, with French backing, proposed an international conference to address the Arab–Israeli conflict under United Nations auspices.

After Yasser Arafat* renounced the use of terrorism, accepted Israel's right to exist, and embraced UN Security Council Resolutions 242 and 338 in 1988, President Mitterrand received him in Paris on May 2, 1989. France attempted to play a further role within the area by announcing two peace plans. The first, on September 24, 1990, called for Lebanese, Palestinians, and Israelis to begin peace talks, though it did not mention the use of an international conference. The second occurred before the onset of the Gulf War* on January 14, 1991. This latter plan had two distinct phases in order to avoid formally linking the crisis in the Persian Gulf with the Arab–Israeli conflict. Both of them were placed before the UN General Assembly, but no movement was made on them.

The movement toward a United States-sponsored international peace conference in Madrid* after the Gulf War impelled France either to support the U.S. initiative or risk being completely marginalized. France generally supported the ten rounds of negotiations between Israel and the Arab states and, like most of the external powers, was caught off-guard by the PLO–Israel Declaration of Principles.*

France has endorsed the moves made by Israel and the PLO in the Declaration of Principles, as well as the recent signing of the peace treaty between Israel and Jordan,* though it still seeks a stronger participatory role in resolving the Arab–Israeli conflict, although it is limited by its midlevel economic, political, and military capabilities.

For further information see: David Allen and Alfred Pijpers, eds., *European Foreign Policy Making and the Arab-Israeli Conflict* (The Hague: Martinus Nijhoff, 1984); Sylvia K. Crosbie, *A Tacit Alliance: France and Israel from Suez to the Six Day War* (Princeton, NJ: Princeton University Press, 1974); Stanley Hoffman, "Gaullism by Any Other Name," *Foreign Policy,* no. 57 (Winter 1984–85): 38–57; Edward A. Kolodziej, *French International Policy under De Gaulle and Pompidou: The Politics of Grandeur* (Ithaca, NY: Cornell University Press, 1974); Timothy J. Piro, "France," in Bernard Reich, ed., *The Powers in the Middle East: The Ultimate Strategic Arena* (New York: Praeger, 1987), pp. 226–66; Ghassan Salamé, "Torn between the Atlantic and Mediterranean: Europe and the Middle East in the Post-Cold War Era," *Middle East Journal* 48, no. 1 (Spring 1994): 226–49; Pia Christina Wood, "France and the Israeli-Palestinian Conflict: The Mitterrand Policies, 1981–1992," *Middle East Journal* 47, no. 1 (Winter 1993): 21–40.

Timothy J. Piro

FREE LEBANON. A term used by Saad Haddad* to refer to southern Lebanon,* in which Israel had established its security zone* and in which the Free Lebanon Militia* or the South Lebanese Army* operated.

FREE LEBANON MILITIA (FLM). See **SOUTH LEBANESE ARMY.**

FREIJ, ELIAS (b. Bethlehem,* 1921). The Christian mayor of Bethlehem, beginning in 1972. He is the chairman of the Association of West Bank Chambers of Commerce. Freij has been considered by the Israelis as a moderate with a pro-Jordanian* leaning in his positions toward resolving the Arab–Israeli conflict. In February 1986, King Hussein* of Jordan* announced that he could no longer work with the Palestine Liberation Organization* (PLO) in a search for Middle East peace "until their word is their bond." The king called upon West Bank* Palestinian leaders to join him in abandoning the PLO. Freij was one of the few West Bank mayors to publicly support the king. This was not the only time that he has defied the PLO. In December 1988, he gave an interview to an Israeli newspaper in which he expressed a desire for a United Nations-supervised truce in the West Bank and Gaza Strip.* It was reported that Yasser Arafat* said before a group of Palestinians meeting in Riyadh, Saudi Arabia, on January 1, 1989, that "anyone trying to stop the revolt exposes himself to the bullets of his own people." Freij later denied that the threats were intended for him, although he retracted his suggestion on January 3, 1989, saying that "it is the PLO, our sole and legitimate representative, which makes the decision, and the decision of the PLO does not support my proposal." Freij has been a delegate to the peace negotiations with Israel. In 1994, he was sworn in as a member of the Palestinian Authority.*

Joseph E. Goldberg

FRESH-START INITIATIVE. On September 1, 1982, U.S. president Ronald Reagan* enunciated the fresh-start initiative, also known as the Reagan plan, to settle the Israeli–Palestinian* conflict. Secretary of State George P. Shultz* was the architect of this plan, which was based on Camp David* and the principle of the exchange of land for peace* set forth in United Nations (UN) Security Council Resolution 242.* The initiative called on the Palestinians to recognize that their own political aspirations are inextricably bound to recognition of Israel's right to a secure future. Reagan asked the Arab states to accept the reality of Israel and the reality that peace and justice are to be gained only through hard, fair, direct negotiations. Other than Jordan,* no other Arab state was included in this initiative. Jordan was to be empowered to negotiate on behalf of the Palestinians. What appeared to be a positive resolution of the Lebanon* crisis seemed to provide a conducive atmosphere for a new peace initiative to restart the stalled Arab–Israeli peace process.

Regarding the West Bank* and Gaza Strip,* Reagan said "that peace cannot be achieved by the formation of an independent Palestinian state in those territories, nor is it achievable on the basis of Israeli sovereignty or permanent control over the West Bank and Gaza." Instead it called for a confederation among the West Bank, Gaza, and Jordan. The United States called for a five-year transitional period, during which the Palestinians of the West Bank and Gaza would have full autonomy over their own affairs. The Palestinians would have a self-governing authority arrived at by free elections. They would have control over land and resources. Jews would continue to have the right to live in the West Bank and Gaza, but there would be a freeze on additional settlements. Palestinians in East Jerusalem* would be able to have elections, allowing for local self-rule. Jerusalem,* though, would remain an undivided city. Its final status would be decided through negotiation.

The purpose of the five-year transitional period would be to prove to the Israelis that Palestinian autonomy would not threaten their security and prove to the Palestinians that they would be able to run their own affairs. The extent of the Israeli withdrawal from the territories would be equal to the security and nature of peace Israel got in exchange. A successful five-year transitional period would hopefully create the confidence needed for a final resolution and wider participation among other Arab states in these talks. It was the U.S. view that self-government by the Palestinians of the West Bank and Gaza in association with Jordan offered the best chance for peace. Israel reacted negatively to the initiative, while the Arab world's response was generally positive. Jordan's King

Hussein* at first gave discreet support and tried to convince Yasser Arafat* and the Palestine Liberation Organization* (PLO) to support the plan. Hussein was not able to get the PLO to agree to allow Jordan to negotiate on behalf of the Palestinians. The crisis in Lebanon at the time put the Lebanon issue at the forefront of U.S. diplomacy, and the fresh-start initiative was given a lowered priority. By April 1983, Jordan's King Hussein had distanced himself from any further involvement with the plan.

For further information see: Alan J. Kreczko, "Support Reagan's Initiative," *Foreign Policy,* no. 49 (Winter 1982–83): 140–53; Juliana Peck, *The Reagan Administration & the Palestinian Question: The First Thousand Days* (Washington, DC: Institute for Palestine Studies, 1984); William B. Quandt, *Peace Process* (Washington, DC: Brookings Institution, 1993); George P. Shultz, *Turmoil and Triumph* (New York: Charles Scribner's Sons, 1993).

Nolan Wohl

FROG MISSILE. *FROG* is an acronym that stands for "free range over ground" and describes a family of heavy, unguided battlefield missiles developed and produced by the Soviet Union beginning in the mid-1950s. The FROG is a spin-stabilized, unguided, surface-to-surface missile with a range of approximately forty miles. The FROG is almost thirty feet long and twenty-one inches in diameter and weighs about two tons. The FROG can be launched with either a high-explosive or a nuclear warhead. Seven variants of the FROG have been developed—referred to as FROG-1 through FROG-7. FROG-7 missiles were provided by the former Soviet Union to Egypt,* Syria,* Iraq,* and Libya. Syria reportedly fired FROG missiles against Israel in the Yom Kippur War,* but with little effect.

Stephen H. Gotowicki

FROZEN PEACE. A term used to refer to the nature of the peace established between Egypt* and Israel after the Egypt–Israel Peace Treaty of March 1979.* See also COLD PEACE.

FULL PARTNER. A term used to refer to the nature of the U.S. role in the efforts to achieve an Arab–Israeli peace. After Anwar Sadat's* visit to Jerusalem* in 1977, negotiations between Israel and Egypt* continued but were often interrupted by discord between the two parties. The United States generally sought to ensure the progress of the discussions. As open disputes between Egypt and Israel developed, the United States often sought to persuade the parties to reduce public recriminations and continue private negotiations. As part of this process, Sadat conferred with Jimmy Carter* at Camp David* in early February 1978 and later announced that the United States was no longer a "go-between" but a "full partner in the establishment of peace." On August 8, 1978, when the White House announced that Sadat and Menachem Begin* had accepted Carter's invitation for the Summit meeting at Camp David, Secretary of State Cyrus

Vance* and Sadat held a news conference in Egypt at which Vance noted that the United States would be a ''full partner'' in the negotiations. Begin reacted by stating, ''I don't know what it means to be a full partner.'' The phrase was later applied in other situations when the United States sought to emphasize that it would be more intensely involved in the peace process.

G

GABRIEL SHIP-TO-SHIP MISSILE. The Gabriel is a ship-to-ship missile developed and produced by Israel. It was introduced into service in 1970 and deployed on Israeli *Saar*-class gunboats. The Gabriel has a length of eleven feet and a diameter of 12.8 inches and weighs 882 pounds. It has a guided seeker head and a 330-pound high-explosive warhead. Two versions have been produced—the Gabriel I and the extended-range Gabriel II. The Gabriel I has a reported range of twelve to fourteen miles. The Gabriel II has a range of twenty-five miles.

For further information see: Ronald Pretty, ed., *Jane's Pocket Book of Missiles* (New York: Collier Books, 1975); *The World's Missile Systems,* 2d ed. (Pomona, CA: General Dynamics, 1975).

Stephen H. Gotowicki

GALILI DOCUMENT (Galili plan). Israeli Prime Minister Golda Meir* asked Yisrael Galili to head a special Cabinet committee, the Inter-Ministerial Settlement Committee, to establish a government policy on Jewish settlements* in the occupied territories.* Galili, a member of Ahdut Haavoda, was a minister without portfolio. The Meir government was under political pressure to establish a policy because of the submission of a proposal by Defense Minister Moshe Dayan* in July 1973 to build a port city at Yamit* in the Sinai Peninsula* and to allow Jews to privately purchase land in the occupied territories. The Dayan proposal was favored by only one faction of the Labor Party,* RAFI, and viewed with disfavor by most members of the MAPAI* and Ahdut Haavoda factions of Labor. The Galili Document (Mismakh Galili) was approved by Labor's leadership on August 17, 1973. The preamble to the document states that the four-year working program for the territories "does not involve any change in their political standing, nor in the status of their inhabitants and refugees. UNRWA* [United Nations Relief and Works Agency] will continue with its operations.'' The document called for the rehabilitation and economic development of the Gaza Strip,* Judea,* and Samaria.* For the Gaza Strip, vocational training schemes, improved educational and health services, jobs for artisans, and new housing projects were called for. In Judea and Samaria, the Galili Document proposed raising funds for the development of the area's economic infrastructure, as well as improving its basic services. Financial support from international sources would be sought for these projects, as well as encouraging Israeli businessmen to establish industrial plants in the territories. Senior civilian posts within the local administration would be filled by local inhabitants, and the open bridges* policy would continue. The most controversial aspect of the proposal concerned its policy on outposts and settlements. In the next four years, additional settlements would be created in the Rafiah approach and the Jordan rift and on the Golan Heights.* The Israel Lands Authority was authorized to acquire land in the territories for settlement and for leasing to private persons and companies. But private land acquisitions would be approved only when the Lands Authority was not interested in such a purchase and when the acquisition came ''within the framework of Government policy.'' The proposal also called for the continued population and industrial development of Jerusalem* and its environs and the settlement of Nebi Samuel. The government would study the feasibility of establishing a deep-sea port to the south of Gaza—which meant that the decision had been effectively postponed. This was the first time that the Labor Party had articulated a long-range settlements policy in print.

Joseph E. Goldberg

GALUT. See **DIASPORA.**

GAMASSY, ABDUL GHANI (b. 1921). He graduated from the Military Academy in 1939 and later acquired Command and Staff College Certificates. He had further military studies in the United States and the Soviet Union. He attended the General Staff College, where he graduated in 1951. From 1959, he was the commander of the armoured battalion and corps college. In 1966, he became the chief of military operations of land forces. In 1967, he was named chief of staff of the Second Army. In 1968, he became the deputy director of military intelligence. He then served as chief of operations (planning for the 1973 war*) and deputy chief of staff.

In November 1973, President Anwar Sadat* appointed him as chief of staff, replacing Lieutenant General Shazli.* He played an important role in the subsequent negotiations with General Aharon Yariv of the Israel Defense Forces*—where Egyptian* and Israeli officers met face-to-face for the first time—concerning the Disengagement Agreements* of the Egyptian and Israeli forces. In December 1974, Sadat named him minister of war. He retained the position after it was renamed minister of defense. He held that position until October

1978, when he retired from active service and was named the president's adviser on military affairs. He supported Sadat's peace initiative* with Israel and headed the Egyptian delegation to the Egyptian–Israeli Military Committee negotiations in 1978. He was active in the negotiations for the Camp David Accords* and the Egypt–Israel Peace Treaty.* He was promoted to field marshal rank in 1979.

For further information see: Mohamed Abdel Ghani El-Gamasy, *The October War: Memoirs of Field Marshal El-Gamasy of Egypt* (New York: Columbia University Press, 1993).

Ahmed Elbashari

THE GAP. The turning point of the Yom Kippur War* in the Sinai Peninsula* came after Israel discovered a gap between the Second and Third Egyptian Armies at the Deversoir air base, north of the Great Bitter Lakes of the Suez Canal.* By exploiting this gap, the Israelis were able to threaten the Egyptian Third Army,* prompting Egypt* to call for a cease-fire.

From the start of the war, Israeli forces sought to cross the Suez Canal, taking the war to the enemy's territory as called for in their military doctrine. While some preparations for a crossing had been made prior to the war, the Egyptian attack caught the Israelis off-guard, and they were not prepared to make a crossing until after the Egyptian advance toward the Gidi* and Mitla* Passes had been stopped on October 14.

The line of responsibility between the two armies passed through the Great Bitter Lakes. Israeli prewar plans for a crossing north of Deversoir had been obtained by the Egyptians, prompting them to concentrate forces just north on a rise called the Chinese Farm.*

The operation began with Ariel Sharon's* division, led by an armored brigade, clearing a corridor to the crossing point at Deversoir. Despite Israeli losses to the Egyptian forces entrenched at the Chinese Farm, they pushed on to the canal.

Alerted to the crossing on October 16, the Egyptians believed at first that it had been a small reconnaissance unit. When they did react, two brigades from the Second Army and one brigade from the Third closed in on the Israeli corridor from the north and south in an attempt to close the gap. The Israelis detected the approaching brigades and ambushed them.

After several days of fighting to clear the corridor, the Israelis managed to position two bridges, crossing first one and then another armored division over to the west bank of the canal. On the other side they fanned out, enlarging the gap and attacking the surface-to-air missiles (SAMs) that had protected the Egyptians from the Israeli air force.

By exploiting the gap between the two armies and clearing the area of SAMs, the Israelis were able to press their attack with tanks supported by ground-support aircraft. On October 19, Israeli tanks reached the Suez–Cairo Road. Effectively, this blocked supplies from reaching the Third Army. Despite their tenuous supply line, the Israeli threat to the besieged Egyptians prompted the intervention of the Soviet Union* and the United States in calling for a cease-fire that went into effect on October 24, 1973. See also CHINESE FARM.

For further information see: Hassan el Badri, Taha el Magdoub, and Mohammed Dia el Din Zohdy, *The Ramadan War, 1973* (Dunn Loring, VA: T. N. Dupuy Associates, 1978); Chaim Herzog, *The War of Atonement, October 1973* (Boston: Little, Brown, 1975).

David J. Abram

GAZA. A city located in, and capital of, the Gaza Strip.* Often the term is used synonymously with the Gaza Strip, and thus references to Gaza may refer to the city or the entire area. It was one of the major cities of the Philistines.

Gaza, along with Jericho,* was turned over by Israel to the Palestine Liberation Organization* (PLO) after their negotiations in Oslo* and the signing of the Declaration of Principles* in Washington in September 1993. After the creation of the Palestinian autonomy,* Yasser Arafat* established its headquarters in the city.

GAZA AND JERICHO FIRST. See **CAIRO AGREEMENT (1994); DECLARATION OF PRINCIPLES; EARLY EMPOWERMENT; ISRAEL–PLO ECONOMIC AGREEMENT (1994); SAFE PASSAGE ROUTE.**

GAZA DISTRICT. See **GAZA STRIP.**

GAZA RAID OF 1955. After the 1952 Egyptian Revolution, the regime was preoccupied with domestic issues. The Lavon incident* in 1954 did not cause an especially sharp reaction from the Egyptian government; the agents and personnel involved were tried and sentenced. Israel did not launch major retaliatory raids against Egypt* for attacks along their mutual frontier until February 1955, when Israel launched a major attack against an Egyptian military post in Gaza.* Egyptian president Gamal Abdul Nasser* later claimed that this raid led him to begin training Palestinian refugees* as fedayeen* for attacks against Israel later in 1955.

Israel claimed its actions in Gaza were triggered by concern about threats from Palestinian fighters operating from the Gaza Strip,* which was then in Egyptian hands. This concern became a decision to act with the reentry of David Ben-Gurion* into the Israeli Cabinet. On February 28, 1955, Israeli forces attacked a series of targets in the Gaza Strip, including Egyptian army headquarters in Gaza, ambushing a relief convoy. There was a loss of thirty-eight Egyptian lives, with thirty military and civilian personnel injured. This was the largest military engagement since the Armistice Agreement.*

The Gaza raid conformed to the Israeli doctrine of retaliation. Israel's motives for the raid were outlined in a statement by Ambassador Abba Eban* on March 23, 1955, before the United Nations (UN) Security Council. He explained that the government of Israel would not allow Egyptian belligerency to go unpunished. Rather than reduce attacks on Israel, Egypt organized the fedayeen and increased its infiltration into Israel. The end result was an increase in tension in the area, culminating in the 1956 Suez War.* The attack led Nasser to give the Palestinian fighters his full support. The UN Security Council condemned Israel for the attack, and both sides were instructed to refrain from further provocative acts. No evidence was subsequently found by General E.L.M. Burns,* the UN Emergency Force (UNEF) commander, to support Israeli claims that Gaza was being used as a base against them.

The Gaza incident raised fears in Egypt about Israeli intentions; border incidents between the two countries in March 1955, along with the difficulties in negotiations, led to further military clashes. Serious fighting in August–November 1955 resulted in 109 Egyptian deaths; indirect negotiations brought active hostilities to a halt, and the status quo was maintained until the outbreak of the Suez War in the following year.

For further information see: Lieutenant General E.L.M. Burns, *Between Arab and Israeli* (New York: I. Obolensky, 1963); Fred J. Khouri, "The Policy of Retaliation in Arab–Israeli Relations," *Middle East Journal* 20, no. 4 (Autumn 1966): 435–55; Meron Medzini, ed., *Israel's Foreign Relations: Selected Documents, 1947–1974* (Jerusalem: Ministry for Foreign Affairs, 1976).

John Fontaine

GAZA STRIP. The southernmost section of the coastal plain of Mandatory Palestine.* It is some twenty-five miles long and between four and eight miles wide. The territory was held by the Egyptian army at the end of Israel's War of Independence.* Its major city is Gaza,* and there is substantial citrus agriculture. It lies between Israel and Egypt* but belongs to neither. The territory, heavily populated by Palestinians, was to have been part of a Palestinian Arab state under the terms of the 1947 United Nations partition plan* for Palestine. However, it was taken by the Egyptian army during the 1948–49 war and placed under Egyptian military administration. Held briefly by Israel in 1956–57, the Gaza Strip then returned to Egyptian control, where it remained until 1967, when Israel occupied the area during the Six Day War.* Egypt did not claim sovereignty over the Gaza Strip as a part of the Egypt–Israel Peace Treaty,* and negotiations concerning its status made little progress until 1993. Violence and protests directed at Israel and the Israeli administration in the area increased considerably beginning in late 1987, and both Jews and Arabs have been killed during the course of the *intifada.* In the Oslo talks,* the Gaza Strip was the main territory to be turned over to the Palestinian authority.* A transitional period of no more than five years would exist, with an elected Palestinian council exercising limited controls. Israeli troops would control the external borders and continue to maintain the security of existing Israeli settlers in the area. During the third year of the interim period, negotiations over the permanent status of Gaza and Jericho* would take place. See also OCCUPIED TERRITORIES.

For further information see: Meron Benvenisti and Shlomo Khayat, *The West Bank and Gaza Atlas* (Jerusalem: West Bank Data Base Project, 1988); Mordechai Gichon,

"The History of the Gaza Strip: A Geo-Political and Geo-Strategic Perspective," in Lee I. Levine, ed., *The Jerusalem Cathedra* (Jerusalem: Yad Itzhak Ben-Zvi Institute, 1982), pp. 282–317; Marianne Heiberg and Geir Ovensen, *Palestinian Society in Gaza, West Bank and Arab Jerusalem: A Survey of Living Conditions* (Oslo: Fagbevegelsens senter for forskning, utredning og documentasjon [FAFO], 1993); Ann Lesch, "Gaza: Forgotten Corner of Palestine," *Journal of Palestine Studies* 15 (Autumn 1985): 43–61; Nimrod Raphaeli, "Gaza under Four Administrations," *Public Administration in Israel and Abroad* 9 (1968): 40–51; Arlette Tessier, *Gaza* (Beirut: Palestine Liberation Organization Research Center, August 1971).

Joseph E. Goldberg

GAZA-JERICHO AGREEMENT. See **CAIRO AGREEMENT (1994); EARLY EMPOWERMENT; ISRAEL–PLO ECONOMIC AGREEMENT (1994); SAFE PASSAGE ROUTE.**

GEMAYEL, AMIN (b. Bikfayya, Lebanon,* November 10, 1942). He received a master's degree in law from St. Joseph's in 1966. Amin rose through the political, not the military, ranks of the Phalange. After a brief career managing his own law practice, he entered the Lebanese Chamber of Deputies by inheriting his uncle Maurice Gemayal's seat.

He became president of Lebanon after his brother, Bashir,* was assassinated in 1982. In 1982, Amin Gemayel called on the international community to launch a "Marshall Plan" to help rebuild Lebanon. Several conferences were held with various aid organizations, and projects were introduced with the support of the United States, France,* and the World Bank. He also turned to the United States for political, military, and economic aid. The United States worked to rebuild the Lebanese army. Lebanon and Israel negotiated an agreement, signed on May 17, 1983,* that was strongly opposed by Syria* and that was eventually abrogated by Lebanon under Syrian pressure.

At the beginning of his presidency, Gemayal appeared as a man who could create a national consensus, but his term ended in 1988 with no end to either international instability or the conflict with Israel.

For further information see: Amin Gemayel, "Lebanon: The Price and the Promise," *Foreign Affairs* 63 (Spring 1985): 759–77; Theodor Hanf, *Coexistence in Wartime Lebanon* (London: Center for Lebanese Studies, 1993); Samir Khalaf, *Lebanon's Predicament* (New York: Columbia University Press, 1987).

Simeon Manickavasagam

GEMAYEL, BASHIR (b. Beirut, Lebanon*; d. Beirut, September 14, 1982). He was the youngest son of Pierre Gemayal. Bashir Gemayal graduated from St. Joseph's University in 1971 with degrees in law and political science. In 1970, he was kidnapped and held at Camp Tal al-Zaater during a period of heavy fighting. His release was arranged by Kemal Jumblatt and Yasser Arafat.* Later, he became the political director of the Phalange (Kataeb) office in the stronghold of Ashrafiyah. His accomplishments were chiefly military, not political. At twenty-three, he commanded militia units in various encounters with the Palestinians. He was the deputy commander of the Phalangist militia during the successful siege of the Palestinian Camp Tal al-Zaater and became chief of the Kataeb Military Council in 1976. His military victories helped spur the unification of the various Lebanese militias into the Lebanese Forces in 1976, and he became head of the Joint Command Council.

He resorted to military engagements to enhance his authority. In 1978, he eliminated the Franjieh militia. He followed that victory with another over the militia controlled by Camille Chamoun's National Liberal Party. However, while his father, Pierre, depended on the Syrians for political and military aid, Bashir turned to the Israelis. The Israelis had intervened in Lebanon on several occasions. He attempted to use these as a pretext to try to oust the Syrians from Lebanon. To this extent he would provoke the Syrians with direct attacks. On one occasion, the Syrians responded by shelling Ashrafiyah and East Beirut. The Israel Defense Forces* responded by threatening Syria and by overflying Syrian positions along the Golan Heights.* The Syrians were forced to back down.

His political views prior to becoming president were hard-line, and he made no effort at compromise. He opposed the National Pact and believed in the creation of a new republic. Nonetheless, upon his election as president, he attempted to pursue more centrist policies. He condemned the Israeli invasion of Lebanon in 1982 and refused to recognize Israel. His open dissociation from Israel improved his standing with the Muslims. However, before officially assuming office, he was killed in an explosion at his party's headquarters. His military victories had made him a hero to many, and in death he has been seen by some as a martyr.

For further information see: Theodor Hanf, *Coexistence in Wartime Lebanon* (London: Center for Lebanese Studies, 1993); Samir Khalaf, *Lebanon's Predicament* (New York: Columbia University Press, 1987).

Simeon Manickavasagam and Joseph E. Goldberg

GENERAL UNION OF PALESTINIAN STUDENTS. Many young Palestinians pursued their university education in Egypt.* In the early 1950s, Palestinian students' associations existed in various Egyptian universities, where they were viewed as cultural associations, since Palestinian students studying in Egypt were not allowed to be involved in politics. In 1951, while studying at Cairo University, Yasser Arafat* saw that the associations presented opportunities for the Palestinians to unify and mobilize their forces. ''Because the infrastructure of the Palestinians had been destroyed, we had nothing. So the students' organization actually was not a union of students: it was one of the establishments for unity, identity, and support.''

Arafat ran for the presidency of the Union of Palestinian Students in 1951 and was successful in the election of 1952. He was able to gain the support of the Muslim Brotherhood.* Arafat was successful in changing the title of the organization to the General Union of Palestinian Students. In Arafat's mind, this transformed the association from a cultural organization into a political one. It was given permission to publish a magazine, *The Voice of Palestine,* which was distributed throughout the Arab world and was used to mobilize the Palestinians. Arafat is also credited with obtaining financial aid for Palestinian students from other Arab states as well as Egypt. In 1955, the General Union of Palestinian Students was invited to participate in an international conference of Communist youth organizations. Arafat attended the conference in Warsaw.

The General Union of Palestinian Students was an incubator for nurturing Palestinian nationalism and organizing a generation of young Palestinians.

For further information see: Alan Hart, *Arafat: A Political Biography* (Bloomington: Indiana University Press, 1984); Janet Wallach and John Wallach, *Arafat: In the Eyes of the Beholder* (New York: A. Lyle Stuart Books, 1990).

Joseph E. Goldberg

GENEVA CONFERENCE (1973). In an effort to resolve the Arab–Israeli conflict after the Yom Kippur War,* a Geneva Conference, attended by Egypt,* Israel, and Jordan,* met briefly in December 1973. The conference was jointly chaired by the United States and the Soviet Union.* The potential use of the conference in Geneva to resolve the Arab–Israeli dispute was stalled by Syria's* boycott of it and by the Israeli refusal to negotiate in any form with the Palestine Liberation Organization* (PLO), whose participation was demanded by the Arab parties to the conflict. An Egyptian–Israeli military committee was established.

Reconvening the conference became a central element of Soviet policy, but this demand and the Soviet Union's role in the settlement of the Arab–Israeli conflict were largely obscured by the shuttle diplomacy* of Henry Kissinger.* Momentum for a reconvening of the Geneva Conference, with superpower involvement, increased briefly in the early months of the Carter* administration and reached a zenith in October 1977 with the issuance of a joint U.S.-Soviet communique on the Middle East.* The peace initiative by President Anwar Sadat* of Egypt all but ended the Geneva Conference as a potential negotiating forum, although it was retained as an element of Soviet policy.

GIDI PASS. A mountain pass in the Sinai Peninsula* that runs parallel to the Mitla Pass* and was cut through the mountain range that runs parallel to the Suez Canal.* This pass provided additional flexibility in the movement, on an east–west axis, of Egyptian (and later, Israeli) military forces in the Sinai Peninsula. The pass was a major focal point of activity in the Six Day War.*

For further information see: Chaim Herzog, *The Arab–Israeli Wars: War and Peace in the Middle East* (London: Arms and Armour Press, 1982).

GLASSBORO, NEW JERSEY, SUMMIT MEETING (1967). In June 1967, President Lyndon Johnson* invited Soviet premier Alexei Kosygin, who planned to attend the United Nations General Assembly session in New York, to meet with him. Arrangements were made to confer in Glassboro, New Jersey, a college town located about midway between Washington and New York.

Johnson and Kosygin discussed the Middle East and other issues in the relations of the two states. Kosygin emphasized the necessity for Israeli withdrawal from all of the occupied territories* and accused the United States of protecting aggression. Johnson, in turn, presented a comprehensive plan for a Middle East settlement, emphasizing that the issues were greater than Israeli withdrawal from territory. No tangible and specific progress was anticipated, given the wide gap between the United States and the Soviet Union, and no agreements emerged from the Glassboro Summit. Although the Summit did not achieve any significant breakthrough on the Middle East, there were the benefits of improving their understanding of each other.

In essence, Kosygin's efforts at both Glassboro and the United Nations were to avenge the Arab defeat in the Six Day War* and to salvage the Soviet Union's position and investment in the area. At the United Nations he orchestrated a diplomatic effort to have Israel condemned for aggression and ordered to withdraw from territories occupied in the conflict. He also argued that Israel should be punished and forced to pay reparations.

GLUBB, JOHN BAGOT (b. Preston, Lancashire, April 16, 1897; d. 1983). Lieutenant General Sir John Bagot Glubb, known in the Arab world as Glubb Pasha, played an instrumental role in the formation of the Hashemite Kingdom of Jordan's* Arab Legion* as a disciplined and effective fighting force that was to play an instrumental role in Jordan's* capture of the West Bank* in 1948 and provide crucial internal security during volatile periods in the kingdom.

Glubb was the son of a British general. He attended the Royal Military Academy and served with the British forces in France* during World War I. After the war he served with the British forces in Iraq,* attaining the rank of captain, while helping the Iraqi government to quell bedouin uprisings and raids. These experiences helped Glubb to gain an understanding of, and respect for, the bedouin lifestyle and knowledge of strategy and tactics required for desert operations.

Major Glubb was transferred to Jordan in 1930 to organize a special bedouin unit within the Arab Legion. Under his command, the elite camel-mounted Desert Mobile Force was created, which incorporated Glubb's concepts of a military unit functioning in a desert environment. Glubb's force attracted bedouins to its ranks and helped to create a strong and enduring identification of the bedouin with the monarchy that has persisted through King Hussein's* reign.

In 1939, Lieutenant General Glubb was appointed commander of the entire Arab Legion. In Israel's War of Independence,* the Arab Legion, commanded by Glubb and about forty British officers, occupied most of the West Bank and assumed control of the strategic Jerusalem–Tel Aviv Highway. The Arab Legion fought better and held its positions longer than any other Arab force in the conflict. The fighting left the legion occupying the Old City of Jerusalem* and much of the Arab areas of the West Bank.

In 1956, King Hussein, seeking to Arabize the army's officer corps, nationalized the command of the Arab Legion and dismissed Glubb and other British officers. Glubb was knighted for his service to the crown of the United Kingdom of Great Britain* and Northern Ireland. Glubb authored a number of books on Jordan and the Arab Legion.

For further information see: John Bagot Glubb, *The Story of the Arab Legion* (London: Hodder and Stoughton, 1948); John Bagot Glubb, ''Violence on the Jordanian–Israeli Border,'' *Foreign Affairs,* 32 (July 1954): 552–62; John Bagot Glubb, *A Soldier with the Arabs* (London: Hodder and Stoughton, 1957); John Bagot Glubb, *The Changing Scenes of Life: An Autobiography* (London: John Murray, 1983); James D. Lunt, *Glubb Pasha, A Biography: Lieutenant-General Sir John Bagot Glubb, Commander of the Arab Legion, 1939–1956* (London: Harvill Press, 1984).

Joseph E. Goldberg and Mark Daryl Erickson

GOLAN HEIGHTS. A zone east of the Huleh Valley and the Sea of Galilee* that abuts Mount Hermon.* It is a sparse territory some forty-one miles long and fifteen miles wide. The border between Israel and Syria* has been in dispute since Israel's independence in 1948. In 1949, the Israel–Syria Armistice Agreement* designated small areas on the western side of the border as demilitarized zones. Many of the clashes between Syria and Israel from 1949 to 1967 developed from Israel's efforts to assert control over these parcels of land. Between 1949 and 1967, Syria often shelled Israeli settlements in the north from positions on the Golan Heights. In the Six Day War,* Israel occupied the territory and began to establish settlements there. It was placed under military administration. During the Yom Kippur War,* Syria briefly recaptured a portion of the Golan Heights, but Israel took additional Syrian territory. The Israel–Syria Disengagement of Forces Agreement* of 1974 resulted in Syria's regaining some of the land lost in 1967. No major incidents and only a few minor ones have occurred since 1974, when the United Nations Disengagement Observer Force* (UNDOF) was established between Israel and Syria on the Heights. Since the late 1970s, the focus of Israeli–Syrian tension has been in Lebanon* because of the use by the Palestine Liberation Organization* (PLO) of Syrian-controlled Lebanese territory for strikes against Israel.

On Monday, December 14, 1981, the government of Israel presented a bill to the Knesset* that applied the law, jurisdiction, and administration of the state to the Golan Heights. The Golan Heights Law provided:

1. The Law, jurisdiction and administration of the state shall apply to the Golan Heights, as described in the Appendix. 2. This Law shall become valid on the day of its passage in the Knesset. 3. The Minister of the Interior shall be charged with the implementation of this Law, and he is entitled, in consultation with the Minister of Justice, to enact regulations for its implementation and to formulate in regulations transitional provisions

concerning the continued application of regulations, orders, administrative orders, rights and duties which were in force on the Golan Heights prior to the application of this Law.

The bill passed all three readings required in the Knesset and was adopted by a vote of sixty-three in favor and twenty-one against. Explaining this action, Prime Minister Menachem Begin* declared, "[I]n this matter of the Golan Heights there is a universal, or nearly universal, national consensus in Israel." Begin also stated that the law did not alter Israel's readiness to negotiate all outstanding issues with Syria, including the issue of final borders. The government cited several reasons for proposing the bill to the Knesset. After fourteen years of administration, the Syrians had rejected all efforts to bring them into a peace process. The Syrians had refused to accept the Camp David* peace process, had installed missiles in Lebanon that were a direct threat to Israel, and, in their occupation of Lebanon, had directly aided the PLO in its border attacks against Israel. The action by the Knesset changed the status of the Golan Heights from military to civil jurisdiction. The Druze farmers who lived there had the option of receiving Israeli citizenship.

The United States condemned the act, stating that the swift nature of the Israeli action surprised the United States, was harmful to the peace process, and violated the Camp David Accords.* In a prepared statement, the State Department spokesman said, "We have stated that we do not recognize Israel's action, which we consider to be without legal effect. In our view, their action is inconsistent with both the letter and the spirit of UN Security Council Resolution 242* and 338.* We continue to believe that the final status of the Golan Heights can only be determined through negotiations between Syria and Israel based upon Resolutions 242 and 338." On December 17, 1981, the United Nations Security Council adopted unanimously a resolution that "[d]ecides that the Israeli decision to impose its laws, jurisdiction and administration in the occupied Syrian Golan Heights is null and void and without international legal effect; Demands that Israel, the occupying power, should rescind forthwith its decision." The United States voted in favor of a Syrian-sponsored United Nations Security Council resolution condemning the Israeli action and demanding that Israel rescind the legislation. The United States also announced that it was suspending the United States–Israel Strategic Memorandum of Understanding. In addition, the U.S. administration canceled several bilateral economic agreements that would have provided Israel with opportunities to sell Israeli-made arms to nations friendly to the United States, using U.S. credit dollars. The administration also canceled several planned purchases of Israeli-made arms.

Israel's view of the importance of the Heights grew after 1967. In military terms it was not accepted that missiles and airpower eliminated the value of defensive topography and buffer space. Israel has generally argued that wars are won on the ground, by the army. Thus, the geography of the Heights had value as a buffer. Israel had also established a civilian infrastructure on the Heights that had some value and included settlement and investment in agriculture, industry, and recreation. There was also the Druze population.

For Syria, the return to the Golan Heights was a matter of great significance and national pride. Syria wanted a return to its sovereignty.

In the negotiations following the Madrid Peace Conference,* the Golan Heights was central to Syria's demands. The debate eventually settled on the question of Israeli withdrawal for peace. Syria sought a return to a situation of full sovereignty over the Heights in exchange for less than full peace with Israel, and Israel sought full peace in exchange for withdrawal from the territory. The nuances were especially critical. Syria sought an Israeli commitment to full withdrawal from the Golan before it would define its conception of peace. Israel sought a Syrian commitment to full peace (clearly defined) before it would commit itself to withdrawal.

For further information see: Jerry Asher, *Duel for the Golan* (New York: William Morrow, 1987); Muhammad Muslih, "The Golan: Israel, Syria, and Strategic Calculations," *Middle East Journal* 47 (Autum 1993):611–32; Jac Weller, "The Golan Heights: Capture and Defense," *Army Quarterly* 101 (January 1971):215–25.

GOLDMANN, NAHUM (b. Visznevo, Lithuania, 1894; d. 1982). He was raised in Frankfurt and studied at the University of Heidelberg, where he received his doctorate of law degree in 1920. He was actively engaged in Zionist* activities as a youth, and his first visit to Palestine* took place in 1913. During World War I, Goldmann was responsible for Jewish affairs at the German Foreign Ministry, where he attempted to gain support for the establishment of a Jewish homeland in Palestine. After the war, he founded, with Jacob Klatzkin, an independent Zionist magazine. This was also when he attended his first Zionist Congress, and he attended every congress after that.

From 1935 to 1939, Goldmann served as the Jewish Agency* representative at the League of Nations. He organized the World Jewish Congress, together with Stephen Wise, and it held its first conference in 1936. In 1940, Goldmann moved to the United States. During the Mandate,* he voiced support for the partition plan because he felt that the achievement of Jewish sovereignty over some part of Palestine was more significant than acquisition of territory. During World War II, Goldmann represented the Jewish Agency in Washington, D.C. He attended the Biltmore Conference* in 1942 and helped formulate its program. After the war, Goldmann served as representative of the World Jewish Congress to the League of Nations in Geneva, where he worked on the refugee program. After Israel's establishment, Goldmann remained active in Jewish and Israeli affairs and emphasized the importance of the World Zionist Organization* to the Jewish state. His positions often placed him at odds with Israel's leadership.

In 1949, he served as the joint chairman of the Jewish Agency. In 1951, he participated in the framing of the Jerusalem Program.* He served as president of the World Jewish Congress from 1953 to 1977 and as president of the World

Zionist Organization from 1955 to 1968. Goldmann was involved in the negotiations with the Federal Republic of Germany, under Konrad Adenauer, for reparations payments to Israel and to Holocaust* survivors. In 1962, Goldmann settled in Israel but did not actively take part in the country's political system. In 1968, he moved to Switzerland and remained active in the Jewish world until his death.

In the April 1970 issue of *Foreign Affairs* he proposed that, as a solution to the Arab–Israeli conflict, Israel should be made a permanently neutralized state along the lines of Switzerland. This would be based on a cease-fire between Israel and the Arab states and a solution to the refugee problem that would be supported by the superpowers. The proposal created a storm of controversy.

For further information see: Nahum Goldmann, *The Autobiography of Nahum Goldmann: Sixty Years of Jewish Life,* trans. Helen Sebba (New York: Holt, Rinehart and Winston, 1969); Nahum Goldmann, "The Future of Israel," *Foreign Affairs* 48 (April 1970):443–59.

Joseph E. Goldberg and David Salzberg

GOOD FENCE. A reference to the programs of cooperation along the frontier between Israel and Lebanon.* On July 19, 1976, Israeli defense minister Shimon Peres* announced the "good fence" program along the Lebanese–Israeli frontier. The program provided the mostly Christian Lebanese villages along the border with both humanitarian and military assistance by the Israel Defense Forces* (IDF). The humanitarian efforts provided such services as delivery of water and medicine, employment, and access to Israeli markets to sell and purchase goods. Technical agricultural advice on planting and growing crops has been provided by Israel to the residents of South Lebanon. Military assistance was established to help the Lebanese protect themselves from fedayeen* activity in the area: Lebanese army units, commanded by Major Saad Haddad,* were supplied with arms and ammunition; concurrently, the Israelis began training the area militias for operations against fedayeen forces. Eventually, IDF forces supplied logistic support for operations conducted by Haddad's forces.

The good fence program was an attempt by the Israeli government to establish a security zone* along the Lebanese–Israeli border without creating an extensive, overt IDF presence in southern Lebanon. It was hoped that the security zone would function as an early-warning system in the event of fedayeen incursions into the region, which might have otherwise been directed more easily against targets within Israel proper. However, Palestinian attacks against Israeli villages, mostly by means of indirect rocket and artillery fire, continued. By March 1978, the good fence program had been successful only in creating a security perimeter near the Christian enclaves, leaving the easternmost section of the Lebanese–Israeli border less secure. As a result, Israel's March 15, 1978, Operation Litani* endeavored to push Palestinian forces away from the border region and establish a more direct presence on the Lebanese side of the border.

For further information see: Beate Hamizrachi, *The Emergence of the South Lebanon Security Belt: Major Saad Haddad and the Ties with Israel, 1975–1978* (New York:

Praeger, 1988); Frederick C. Hof, *Galilee Divide: The Israel–Lebanon Frontier, 1916–1984* (Boulder, CO: Westview Press, 1985); Gertrude Samuels, "Israel's New Experiment in Peace," *New Leader* (September 27, 1976): 9–11.

Donald A. Pearson

GOREN, SHLOMO (b. Poland; d. Tel Aviv, October 29, 1994). He immigrated to Palestine* in 1925 and studied at Hebrew University in Jerusalem.* He served in the Haganah* before Israel's independence and later joined the Israel Defense Forces* (IDF). He became a paratrooper and was appointed an army chaplain. During the Six Day War* he served as Israel's chief military chaplain, held the rank of brigadier general, and accompanied the troops that captured Arab East Jerusalem.* When the IDF troops took the Western Wall* in the Old City,* he blew a shofar (a ram's horn) in celebration. He served as Israel's Ashkenazi chief rabbi from 1972 to 1983.

In his later years he was an outspoken critic of Israel's reconciliation with the Palestine Liberation Organization* (PLO) and the evacuation of Jewish settlements* in the West Bank.* Shortly after the signing of the Declaration of Principles* (DOP), Rabbi Goren said that every Jew was obliged to kill Yasser Arafat* because he threatened Jewish lives. He had also suggested that soldiers could refuse to obey orders to dismantle Jewish settlements in the West Bank. He argued that the Law of Moses requiring the settling of the land of Israel overrode government policies and that soldiers should therefore disobey orders to evacuate Jewish settlements in the West Bank and Gaza Strip.*

GOVERNMENT HOUSE. Government House is a building located on the Hill of Evil Counsel south of the Old City* of Jerusalem* on the road from Jerusalem to Bethlehem. It served as the residence of the British high commissioner of Palestine during the British Mandatory* period. During the Israeli War of Independence,* Government House was located in an area that the United Nations (UN) Central Truce Supervision Board declared, on August 27, 1948, as a "neutral zone" to be supervised by UN observers to ensure that the area was free of all military personnel. The building served as the United Nations headquarters in Jerusalem. During the Six Day War,* Jordanian troops invaded the demilitarized area and occupied the UN observers' headquarters until it was captured by Israeli forces.

Joseph E. Goldberg

GOVERNMENT HOUSE OF SIDON. A term for most local buildings of political importance inside Lebanon.* The most direct example of the Arab–Israeli conflict involving such an institution occurred at the Government House in the city of Sidon. This building has historically been the center of southern Lebanese political and legislative affairs. During the War in Lebanon,* the Israel Defense Forces* (IDF) entered and occupied this structure on the morning of December 16, 1982, ousting all of the local authorities and employees from the facilities.

The building then became the IDF's headquarters in southern Lebanon until the 1985 withdrawal from Lebanon, except for the security zone,* when it was handed over to local authorities.

The handing-over ceremony actually took place on April 20, 1984, when the IDF gave command of the installation to the southern Lebanese forces. Colonel Edward Tu'mah, commander of the gendarmerie company and governor of South Lebanon, replaced the Israelis and emphasized that the internal security forces would take charge of security at the Government House and also promised to replace as many of the employees previously working there as possible.

After Government House was returned to the control of the local authorities, it regained its importance in southern Lebanese political affairs as the center for political events and was the direct link for communications between Christian general Michel Aoun and the Christian-led militias of the south, who supported Israel. It readjusted to a fully functioning arm of the Lebanese government in the post-Lebanese Civil War.

Yasha Manuel Harari

GOVERNMENT OF NATIONAL UNITY. An Israeli coalition government of Labor* and Likud* formed following the 1984 Knesset* election that lasted until the 1988 Knesset election, at which time a variant was formed. During the first twenty-five months of the government, Shimon Peres* served as prime minister, and Yitzhak Shamir* as foreign minister. They "rotated" their positions in October 1986, and Shamir served as prime minister, and Peres as foreign minister until the end of the government's tenure.

For further information see: Bernard Reich and Gershon R. Kieval, *Israel: Land of Tradition and Conflict,* 2d ed. (Boulder, CO: Westview Press, 1993).

GREAT ARAB REVOLT. See **ARAB REVOLT.**

GREAT BRITAIN. See **ENGLAND.**

GREEN LINE. The frontier lines between Israel and the neighboring Arab states (Egypt,* Jordan,* Lebanon,* Syria*) established by the Armistice Agreements* of 1949 and lasting until the Six Day War.* After the conflict it was replaced by the purple line.*

For further information see: David J. Schnall, *Beyond the Green Line: Israeli Settlements West of the Jordan* (New York: Praeger, 1984).

GROMYKO, ANDREI ANDREYEVICH (b. Old Bromyki, Belorussia, July 6, 1909, or July 18, 1909; d. Moscow, USSR, July 2, 1989). He attended a professional technical school and a graduate-level agricultural school in Minsk and did graduate study at the Research Institute of Agricultural Economics. Gromyko entered the Soviet Foreign Service in 1939 and served as counselor at the embassy in the United States from 1939 to 1943, ambassador to the United States and minister to Cuba from 1943 to 1946, Soviet representative to the United Nations Security Council from 1946 to 1949, and deputy foreign minister from 1949 to 1952, first deputy minister of foreign affairs 1949 to 1952 and 1953 to 1957. Gromyko was the Soviet ambassador to Great Britain from 1952 to 1953. He became a full member of the Soviet Politburo in April 1983. He served as the foreign minister of the Union of Soviet Socialist Republics from 1957 to 1985. From 1985 to 1988, he was president of the Soviet Union.

Gromyko's lengthy career involved him in many aspects of Middle Eastern affairs—especially the Arab–Israeli conflict. As deputy foreign minister, he gave a speech in the United Nations General Assembly on May 14, 1947, in which he stated that the Soviet Union did not favor a solution to the Palestinian question that would result in the creation of either a wholly Jewish or a wholly Arab Palestine. According to the Soviet Union, both Arab and Jew had historic rights to the country. The Soviet Union favored a federal state. If such a solution proved unworkable, Gromyko indicated that the USSR would work for the creation of two independent states—one Arab and one Jewish. He emphasized that the Soviet Union's policy was not intended to be at the expense of the Arabs, but the policy reflected the Soviet foreign policy principle of the right of every people to self-determination.

In 1948, after Israel had declared its independence and was attempting to acquire arms for the Israel Defense Forces* (IDF), Gromyko helped arrange an Israeli arms purchase from Czechoslovakia, circumventing an arms embargo imposed on the combatants.

In 1967, Foreign Minister Gromyko officially visited Egypt* in late March and early April for talks with President Gamal Abdul Nasser.* At the end of that visit, the two countries issued a communique of friendship and mutual confidence. As Nasser's confidence grew in the spring of 1967, and his actions against Israel became bolder, Gromyko sent a letter to Nasser informing him that the USSR would not allow Israel to defeat Egypt. After fighting broke out, Gromyko led the Soviet delegation in an emergency session of the United Nations General Assembly that had been called to discuss the war. He then met with U.S. ambassador Arthur Goldberg to compose a U.S.–Soviet compromise agreement for the withdrawal of forces. The agreement was rejected by the combatants, and the matter was sent back to the United Nations Security Council.

On June 13, 1969, Gromyko ended a visit to Egypt by publishing a communique that pledged full Soviet support for Egypt's struggle to liquidate the consequences of aggression. Throughout 1971 and 1972, he met with U.S. officials and pushed for an interim agreement that would be linked in detail to a final settlement. Once the basis of a final settlement was accepted, the interim period should be no longer than one year. The Soviet proposals were unacceptable to Israel. In private conversations with Israeli foreign minister Abba Eban,* Gromyko emphasized that the Soviet Union supported Israel's right to exist. After a settlement of the Arab–Israeli conflict, there would be no reason diplomatic relations between the two countries could not be reestablished.

Both the Soviet Union and the United States recognized that Moscow's support for the Arabs and U.S. support for Israel could possibly bring the two powers into conflict against each other. At the May 1972 Moscow Summit, U.S. secretary of state Henry Kissinger* and Gromyko agreed to contact each other when regional instabilities arose.

Gromyko was also foreign secretary during the Yom Kippur War,* when the dangers of a direct conflict between the two powers became a matter of serious concern. Gromyko met at the United Nations on September 24, 1975, with then Israeli foreign minister Yigal Allon.* He informed Israel that the Soviet Union favored the creation of a Palestinian state. In April and October 1976, the Soviet Union proposed plans for reconvening the Geneva Peace Conference,* with the Palestinian Liberation Organization* (PLO) as a full participant. Neither the United States nor Israel would accept participation by the PLO.

In January 1980, after the Egypt–Israel Peace Treaty,* the Soviet Union gave attention to its relationships with Syria and the Palestinian Steadfastness Front. In a joint communique with the Syrian government, Gromyko criticized the United States and Israel for attempting to "split . . . the ranks of the Arab and Moslem countries, drive a wedge between them and their friends—the USSR— and subvert the unity and principles of the nonaligned movement." Gromyko promised Syria continued military aid.

For further information see: Robert O. Freedman, *Soviet Policy toward the Middle East since 1970,* 3d ed. (New York: Praeger, 1982); Robert O. Freedman, *Moscow and the Middle East: Soviet Policy since the Invasion of Afghanistan* (Cambridge: Cambridge University Press, 1991); Andrei Andreevich Gromyko, *Only for Peace: Selected Speeches and Writings* (Oxford: Pergamon Press, 1979); Andrei Andreevich Gromyko, *Memoirs* (New York: Doubleday, 1989); Henry Kissinger, *White House Years* (Boston: Little, Brown, 1979).

Joseph E. Goldberg

GUINNESS, WALTER EDWARD. See **LORD MOYNE.**

GULF OF AQABA. Israel also refers to it as the Gulf of Eilat, derived from the port city of Eilat* at its head. The Gulf of Aqaba lies between the Sinai* and Arabian Peninsulas and connects to the Red Sea from the Israeli port of Eilat and Jordanian port at Aqaba* at its northern end. The Gulf of Aqaba is about 100 miles long with a coastline shared by Israel, Egypt,* Jordan,* and Saudi Arabia. It is between twelve and eighteen miles wide. At the southern end, where the gulf meets the Red Sea, there are two islands: Tiran and Sanafir. The navigable channel is the Strait of Tiran* between Tiran and the coast of the Sinai Peninsula and is three nautical miles wide. The point on the Sinai coast directly facing Tiran is Ras Nasrani, near Sharm el-Sheikh.* Egypt set up gun emplacements there to prevent shipping through the Strait of Tiran. Israel silenced the guns on November 3, 1956. Israel's use of the Strait of Tiran and the Gulf of Aqaba has been a factor in the relations between Egypt and Israel and in the Sinai* and Six Day* Wars. Since the Israeli occupation of the Sinai Peninsula in 1956 and later withdrawal in 1957, Israeli ships have used the strait and the gulf, except for a brief interruption in 1967.

On February 11, 1957, U.S. secretary of state John Foster Dulles* stated in an aide-mémoire,* "The United States believes that the Gulf comprehends international waters and that no nation has the right to prevent free and innocent passage in the Gulf through the Straits giving access thereto." This was among the factors that helped to convince Israel to withdraw from Sinai after the 1956 war.

Nasser's* announced blockade of the strait in 1967 was considered by Israel as a war provocation (causus belli) and by the United States as a major act leading to the conflict. To avoid a repetition of the blockade, the United Nations Security Council Resolution 242* of November 1967, the basic document in the quest for an Arab–Israeli peace settlement, called for freedom of navigation in international waterways.

The narrowness of the Gulf of Aqaba and the disparate claims by the coastal states have the potential to cause problems of maritime boundary delimitations. Both Egypt and Saudi Arabia have claimed twelve-mile territorial seas and additional six-mile contiguous zones. Israel has claimed six-mile territorial seas, and Jordan has claimed three miles without any contiguous zones.

Since the Gulf of Aqaba is deep, and no natural resources have been discovered in it, no disputes over exploitation rights have arisen, but disputes over navigation, mostly concerning shipping to and from Eilat, have occurred.

After the Israeli occupation of the western shore of the Strait of Tiran in 1967, ships of all states again enjoyed the right of passage through the strait and the gulf. The 1979 Egypt–Israel Peace Treaty* provided that after Israel withdrew from the shores and entrances of the Gulf of Aqaba in 1982, to ensure freedom of navigation, the area would be controlled by a multinational force established by the concerned parties and stationed in the area of Sharm el-Sheikh.

For further information see: Lincoln M. Bloomfield, *Egypt, Israel and the Gulf of Aqaba in International Law* (Toronto: Carswell, 1957); Eliahu Elath, *Israel and Elath: The Political Struggle for the Inclusion of Elath in the Jewish State* (London: Weidenfeld and Nicholson [for the Jewish Historical Society of England], 1966); Ali A. El-Hakim, *The Middle Eastern States and the Law of the Sea* (Syracuse, NY: Syracuse University Press, 1979); *Egypt's Unlawful Blockade of the Gulf of Aqaba* (Jerusalem: Ministry for Foreign Affairs, Information Division, [1967]); Paul A. Porter, *The Gulf of Aqaba: An International Waterway. Its Significance to International Trade* (Washington, DC: Public Affairs Press, 1957).

GULF OF EILAT. See **GULF OF AQABA.**

GULF WAR. The invasion of Kuwait by Iraq* in August 1990 and the subsequent Gulf War (Desert Storm) that began in January 1991 and terminated in March of that year affected the Arab–Israeli conflict in a number of ways. Although the peace process was moribund by the time Saddam Hussein* invaded Kuwait, the Arab–Israeli conflict became a tool in his efforts to split the United States-led coalition and to gain Arab world support.

Yasser Arafat* and other Palestinians championed Saddam Hussein, whose antipathy to Israel was well known, arguing that his actions supported the Palestinian position, and Saddam Hussein sought to use the Palestinian cause to help rally support for his efforts against Iran and Kuwait. After the invasion of Kuwait, he sought to link his control of that territory acquired through aggression with Israel's occupation of the West Bank* and the Gaza Strip,* despite the obvious dissimilarities between the two situations. His argument that the Scud missile* attacks on civilian targets in Israel were in support of the Palestinian cause was a cover for the real motive: to break the coalition united against him. The image of Palestinians "cheering the Scuds from the rooftops" further confirmed Israeli doubts about the chances for real peace negotiations. In allying the Palestine Liberation Organization* (PLO) with an agressor against whom much of the international community was aligned, Arafat raised doubts about his and the PLO's credibility. However justified the support for Saddam Hussein may have been within the Palestinian and Arab worlds, to many Israelis it reinforced the argument that Palestinians posed a threat to the existence of the Jewish state. Later, this view was modified, but not eliminated, by the Oslo talks* outcome.

On the other hand, the serious damage done to Iraq's offensive capability during the Gulf War postponed the threat and clearly improved Israel's security position in the short term. The war also highlighted the significant division in the Arab world.

Virtually from the outset, Saddam Hussein sought to divert attention from his aggression by calling attention to the Arab–Israeli conflict. The United States resisted Saddam Hussein's attempts to create a linkage between the Gulf and the Arab–Israeli issues. Nevertheless, a series of matters made clear that there would be a sustained postcrisis effort to deal anew with Arab–Israeli issues, even if there was no formal linkage between the two questions. During and immediately after the hostilities, the Bush* administration (in the persons of the president and Secretary of State James Baker*) spelled out a concept of a New World Order* in which efforts to resolve the Arab–Israeli conflict figured prominently.

For further information see: Bernard Reich, "Israel and the Iran-Iraq War," in Christopher C. Joyner, ed., *The Persian Gulf War: Lessons, for Strategy, Law, and Diplomacy* (New York: Greenwood Press, 1990), pp. 75–90; Bernard Reich, "Israel and the Persian Gulf Crisis," in Ibrahim Ibrahim, ed., *The Gulf Crisis: Background and Consequences* (Washington, DC: Center for Contemporary Arab Studies, Georgetown University, 1992), pp. 228–46.

GUR, MORDECHAI (Nicknamed Motta) (b. Jerusalem,* May 5, 1930). At the age of seventeen, he joined the youth battalion of the Haganah* during the Mandate* period and later served in the Palmach.* After Israel's War of Independence,* he attended Hebrew University and studied politics and Oriental studies while still in the military. Gur became a paratrooper and helped to develop the Israeli style of commando raids on Arab targets across the lines before the Sinai War.* He commanded the Golani Brigade from 1961 to 1963. During the Six Day War* he commanded the paratroop brigade that captured East Jerusalem* and the old walled city. In August 1967, he became commander of the Gaza Strip* and northern Sinai.* Gur is a graduate of École de Guerre, Paris. He served as military attaché in Washington from August 1972 until December 1973. He become chief of staff of the Israel Defense Forces* (IDF) from 1974 to 1978, taking over following the resignation of David Elazar.* After leaving the IDF in 1978, he became director general of a division of Koor industries. In 1981, Gur ran for the Knesset* on the Labor Party list and won a seat. He served as minister of health in the National Unity government* established in 1984 and became minister without portfolio in the government established in December 1988. Gur is known in Israel for his children's books about a commando unit and its fighting mascot, a dog named Azit. He became deputy minister of defense in the Rabin*-led government established in 1992.

GUSH EMUNIM (Bloc of the faithful). A movement founded after the Six Day War* that promotes the establishment of Jewish settlements in Judea,* Samaria,* and Gaza* as a means of retaining these areas, especially the West Bank.* It is an aggressive settlement movement that combines religious fundamentalism and secular Zionism* to create a new political force. Its leaders assert a biblically based Jewish claim to Judea and Samaria but profess a belief that peaceful and productive coexistence with the Arabs is both possible and desirable. But it was not until after the Yom Kippur War* that it organized politically in order to oppose further territorial concessions and to promote the extension of Israeli sovereignty over the occupied territories.* The founding meeting of Gush Emunim took place in March 1974 at Kfar Etzion, a West Bank kibbutz that had been seized by the Arabs in Israel's War of Independence* and recovered by Israel in the Six Day War. Among those playing leading roles were Rabbi Moshe Levinger* (the leader of the Kiryat Arba* settlers), Hanan Porat (one of the revivers of Jewish settlement in Gush Etzion*), Rabbi Haim Druckman (educator and one of the leaders of the Bnai Akiva religious youth movement and subsequently a member of the Knesset), Rabbi Eliezer Waldman, and Rabbi Yohanan Fried.

Gush Emunim began as a faction within the National Religious Party (NRP), but, because of distrust of the NRP's position concerning the future of Judea and Samaria, the Gush left the party and declared their independence. The Gush Emunim people—mostly yeshiva graduates, rabbis, and teachers—launched an information campaign to explain their position. Gush Emunim has since refused to identify with any political party and has gained a unique political status. During the tenure of the government of Yitzhak Rabin* from 1974 to 1977, Gush Emunim protested the Disengagement Agreements with Egypt* and Syria,* staged demonstrations in Judea and Samaria to emphasize the Jewish attachment to those parts of the Land of Israel, and engaged in settlement operations in the occupied territories. Included in these activities was a mass rally, which was held in Tel Aviv's Malkhei Yisrael Square to urge recognition of Judea and Samaria as an inseparable part of the country. Gush Emunim's primary commitment is to settlement beyond the 1949 Armistice Agreement* demarcation lines, which had served as the de facto borders between Israel and the Jordanian*-annexed West Bank and between Israel and the Egyptian-administered Gaza Strip* and Sinai Peninsula* from 1949 to 1967. Gush Emunim continued to push for settlements in all parts of Eretz Israel.*

Gush Emunim's spiritual authorities and political leaders were educated in Yeshivat Merkaz Harav, whose founder was Avraham Yitzhak Hacohen Kook,* the first Ashkenazi chief rabbi of Eretz Yisrael. Kook believed that the era of redemption for the Jewish people had already begun with the rise of modern Zionism and the growing Zionist enterprise in Palestine.* Israel's victory in the Six Day War transformed the status of Kook's theology. It seemed clear to his students that they were living in the messianic age and believed that redemption might be at hand. Kook's views were expounded by his son, Rabbi Zvi Yehuda Kook,* who succeeded him as the head of Yeshivat Merkaz Harav. Gush Emunim has become a highly complex social and institutional system, including a settlement organization, regional and municipal councils, and independent economic corporations. In addition, it possesses a spiritual leadership composed of distinguished rabbis and scholars.

For further information see: Moshe Kohn, *Who's Afraid of Gush Emunim?* (Jerusalem: Jerusalem Post, [1976]); David Newman, ed., *The Impact of Gush Emunim: Politics and Settlement in the West Bank* (New York: St. Martin's Press, 1985); Ehud Sprinzak, "Gush Emunim: The Tip of the Iceberg," *Jerusalem Quarterly,* no. 21 (Fall 1981): 28–47; Ehud Sprinzak, *The Ascendance of Israel's Radical Right* (New York: Oxford University Press, 1991).

GUSH ETZION. See **ETZION BLOC.**

H

HABASH, GEORGE (b. Lydda, Israel, 1925 or 1926). A founding member of the Arab Nationalist Movement (ANM), George Habash is the leader of the Popular Front for the Liberation of Palestine (PFLP).*

The son of a Greek Orthodox middle-class grain merchant, George Habash left Lydda in 1944 and entered the American University in Beirut, where he studied medicine and received his M.D. degree in 1951. As a student, Habash was influenced by Marxism and became active in the founding of the Arab Nationalist Movement, which espoused the cause of Palestinian* and Arab unity, and was strongly influenced by Gamal Abdul Nasser's* appeal for Arab unity. Habash shared Nasser's view that Arab unity was the surest means by which to destroy the Jewish state.

Habash led one of the first Palestinian paramilitary groups. He disagreed, however, with Palestine Liberation Organization* (PLO) leader Yasser Arafat.* On December 7, 1967, Habash founded the PFLP. The establishment of the PFLP followed the defeat of the Arab states in the Six Day War.*

Following the Six Day War, Habash and others became disillusioned with Nasserism and more convinced of the necessity of social revolution and the validity of the application of Marxist–Leninist principles to Palestinian circumstances. Habash and the PFLP advocated a revolutionary transformation of Arab countries simultaneously with their armed struggle against Israel. The PFLP position, which endangered existing Arab regimes, made cooperation with Habash difficult.

In 1968, Habash left Jordan* and went to Syria* to request permission to allow the PFLP to conduct terrorist operations against Israel from Syrian territory. The Syrians were suspicious of Habash because of his involvement with the Arab Nationalist Movement, which was a rival of Syria's dominant Baath

Party. Habash was arrested and held in a Syrian prison for seven and a half months before escaping in November 1968 to the Al Wadia refugee camp.

In 1970, Habash and the PFLP led Palestinian opposition to the Rogers Plan* as a solution to the Arab–Israeli conflict. This same year the PFLP and other PLO groups advocated the overthrow of the Jordanian regime and engaged in armed conflict with it. On September 6, 1970, the PFLP hijacked three international airliners and forced two of them to land in Jordan. Arafat condemned the action and demanded the release of the hostages. The PFLP later blew up the two airliners, along with the third airliner, which they had forced to land in Cairo. Because of this action, the PFLP was suspended by the PLO Central Committee. Nevertheless, Habash and his organization continued to play a central role in the 1970 Jordanian Civil War.*

Under Habash's guidance, the PFLP conducted numerous terrorist acts. In July 1968, it hijacked an Israeli El Al airliner en route to Israel from Rome. In another act, the PFLP joined with the Japanese Red Army and murdered twenty-seven civilians in the Lod Airport terminal in Tel Aviv. In July 1973, the PFLP hijacked a Japanese airliner en route to Libya, where it was destroyed. In addition, the PFLP made numerous attacks on buses and other civilian targets in Israel.

There has also been dissension within the PFLP. A number of splinter groups held that Habash had departed from his original ideas. In 1969, Nayef Hawatmeh* left to form the Popular Democratic Front for the Liberation of Palestine* (PDFLP), and later that year Ahmed Jibril* left with Syrian support to form the Popular Front for the Liberation of Palestine—General Command* (PFLP—GC). A third split came in 1972, when the Popular Revolutionary Front for the Liberation of Palestine (PRFLP) was formed.

Habash challenged Arafat's leadership of the PLO and formed the Rejection Front, in which the PFLP joined with the Arab Liberation Front* (ALF), the PFLP—GC, and the Front for the Popular Palestinian Struggle (FPPS) in a unified power base to challenge Arafat's leadership of the PLO. Many believed that if Habash was not Christian, he might have been successful in unseating Arafat.

In 1983, after the PLO was forced to leave Lebanon* as a consequence of the War in Lebanon,* Habash took the PFLP out of the PLO, though he cooperated with mainstream PLO action in 1987 in support of the *intifada*￼* arising in December of that year in the Gaza Strip* and areas of Judea* and Samaria.* Habash continued his attacks on Israel and the South Lebanese Army* (SLA) from bases in southern Lebanon.

In January 1992, while living in Tunis, Habash suffered a number of strokes and was flown to Paris to receive medical treatment. When his presence in France* became publicly known, controversy followed. The French wanted to question Habash about a series of bombings in Paris that took place in 1986. Claiming that there were no French or international warrants for his arrest, the French allowed Habash to return to Tunis.

For further information see: Jillian Becker, *The PLO: The Rise and Fall of the Palestine Liberation Organization* (London: Weidenfeld and Nicholson, 1984); Helena Cobban, *The Palestinian Liberation Organization* (Cambridge: Cambridge University Press, 1984); John K. Cooley, *Green March, Black September: The Story of the Palestinian Arabs* (London: Frank Cass, 1973); Alain Gresh, *The P.L.O., The Struggle Within: Towards an Independent Palestinian State,* trans. A. M. Barrett (London: Zed Books, 1985); Emile F. Sahliyeh, *The PLO after the Lebanon War* (Boulder, CO: Westview Press, 1986); Emile Sahliyeh, "George Habash," in Bernard Reich, ed., *Political Leaders of the Contemporary Middle East and North Africa: A Biographical Dictionary* (Westport, CT: Greenwood Press, 1990), pp. 213–21.

Yasha Manuel Harari and Karin J. England

HABIB, PHILIP CHARLES (b. Brooklyn, New York, February 25, 1920; d. France, May 25, 1992). He was educated at the University of Idaho and the University of California (Berkeley), where he received a B.S. and Ph.D., respectively. Habib served in the U.S. Army from 1942 to 1946 and reached the rank of captain. In 1949, he entered the U.S. Foreign Service and served as third secretary of the embassy in Canada from 1949 to 1951. From 1952 to 1954, he served as the second secretary in the embassy in New Zealand, and from 1955 to 1957 he was a research specialist in the State Department in Washington, D.C. Habib was the U.S. consulate general in Trinidad from 1958 to 1960, and from 1960 to 1961 he served as a foreign affairs officer at the Department of State in Washington, D.C. After this position, Habib served as the counselor for political affairs at the U.S. Embassy in the Republic of Korea from 1962 to 1965. He served in the same position in the Republic of Vietnam from 1965 to 1967. Habib served with the rank of minister from 1966 to 1967 and with the rank of ambassador from 1969 to 1971. During the years 1968 to 1971, Habib was the highest-ranking career diplomat in the American delegation to the Vietnam peace talks in Paris. He was ambassador to South Korea from 1971 to 1974, assistant secretary of state for East Asian and Pacific affairs from 1974 to 1976, and undersecretary of state for political affairs from 1974 until his retirement in 1978.

Habib was recalled from retirement in 1981 by President Ronald Reagan* to be a special envoy to the Middle East to negotiate a cease-fire between Israel and the Palestine Liberation Organization* (PLO) and to defuse the crisis between Syria* and Israel over the placement of Syrian missiles in Lebanon.* The cease-fire was agreed to and went into effect on July 24, 1981.

Habib was recalled again by President Reagan in 1982 following Israel's invasion of Lebanon. At this time Habib practiced shuttle diplomacy* and achieved a cease-fire and the evacuation of the PLO from Lebanon. Habib also succeeded in negotiating the Lebanese–Israeli Agreement of May 17, 1983,* which stated that "the state of war between Israel and Lebanon has been terminated and no longer exists" and that both nations would "respect the sovereignty, political independence and territorial integrity of each other"; he did not succeed, however, in removing all foreign forces from Lebanon. Lebanon abrogated the agreement under pressure from Syria.

Habib was a special presidential envoy to Central America (1986–87) and then a senior research fellow at the Hoover Institute.

For further information see: Alexander M. Haig, Jr., *Caveat: Realism, Reagan, and Foreign Policy* (New York: Macmillan, 1984); Steve Posner, *Israel Undercover: Secret Warfare and Hidden Diplomacy in the Middle East* (Syracuse, NY: Syracuse University Press, 1987); Bernard Reich, *The United States and Israel: Influence in the Special Relationship* (New York: Praeger, 1984).

Donald A. Vogus

HADDAD, SAAD GEORGES (b. Marj Ayoun, Lebanon,* December 11, 1937; d. January 14, 1984). Major Saad Georges Haddad was the first commander of the Free Lebanon Militia* (FLM), which was later to become the South Lebanese Army* (SLA). Saad Georges Haddad was the son of a Maronite mother and a Catholic father. He was raised a Catholic. His father was a well-to-do farmer who had served as a corporal in the Troupes Special du Levant under the French. He was named Saad, meaning "luck," because, on the day of his birth, his family received money from relatives in the United States.

Haddad began his officer training in the United States at Fort Benning, Georgia, in advanced infantry. He was first noticed by the Israelis when he aided a unit of Israeli commandos who got lost in southern Lebanon while chasing Palestinian* terrorists. Haddad was stripped of his command and commission in the Lebanese army when he refused to let the Lebanese army take control of southern Lebanon in 1976.

When the Free Lebanon Militia was established in 1978, Major Haddad became its first commander. The FLM was a militia commanded by Christian officers, but its troops came from the poor, local Shiites in southern Lebanon who sought to fight the Palestinian terror gangs. They operated within Israel's self-pronounced security zone,* or, as Haddad said, "Free Lebanon." FLM troops were financed by Israel.

Under Haddad's guidance, the FLM attempted to deny the use of southern Lebanon to the Palestinian terrorists. Their methods were controversial. They kidnapped, extorted, and shelled local Shiite towns to prevent them from supporting the Palestinians. In 1980, he ordered the kidnapping and murder of two Irish United Nations (UN) peacekeepers, which caused great tension between Ireland and Israel. The FLM penetrated towns as far north as the Awali River north of Sidon. Under his leadership from 1978 to 1984, the level of Palestinian attacks was kept to a minimum, but he could not stop them completely. The FLM won major battles at Taibe and El Khiam, Shuba and El Meri, Operation Cooperative, and the Litani Operation.* Because he openly battled Shiites who supported the Palestinians, he was condemned by Saudi Arabia and the United Arab Emirates for "splitting the forces of his country."

In October 1983, Haddad turned his command over temporarily to a fellow

Maronite Christian, Sharbal Barakat, because of illness. His battle with cancer was kept secret in order to maintain the morale of his forces. He was treated at the Rambam Hospital in Haifa. In the first week of 1984, his family admitted, on Israeli television, that he had incurable cancer. He died one week later.

At his funeral in Marj Ayoun, representatives of the Israeli government and the Israel Defense Forces (IDF)* praised him as a patriot to his people and a true friend of Israel. In the Israeli Cabinet meeting that day, Prime Minister Yitzhak Shamir* opened the session with a minute of ''standing in silence'' in memory of Saad Haddad.

Haddad was succeeded as commander of the Free Lebanese Militia by Major General Antoine Lahad,* who renamed it the South Lebanese Army.

For further information see: Beate Hamizrachi, *The Emergence of the South Lebanon Security Belt: Major Saad Haddad and the Ties with Israel, 1975–1978* (New York: Praeger, 1988).

Yasha Manuel Harari and Joseph E. Goldberg

HADDAD, WADI (b. Haifa, 1929; d. East Germany, April 1978). He came from a Greek Orthodox family. His father was a teacher. The family left Haifa after the establishment of Israel in 1948. He studied at the American University Medical School in Beirut. Upon graduation, Haddad worked in refugee camps. He and Dr. George Habash,* a classmate, formed the Arab Nationalist Movement, which later became the Popular Front for the Liberation of Palestine* (PFLP).

Haddad has been identified as the strategist who was responsible for the hijacking of airliners and other terrorist acts. The first of those hijackings was an El Al Israeli airliner seized in July 1968 and diverted to Algeria. Four airliners were hijacked in September 1970; three of them were blown up in the Jordanian desert, and the fourth was destroyed at the Cairo Airport. He is reputed to have planned the attack on the Tel Aviv Airport by the Japanese Red Army in May 1972, during which nearly thirty people were killed, and many more were wounded. In October 1977, Haddad was said to have been the strategist who directed the seizure of a Lufthansa airliner that was diverted to Somalia. Later, West German commandos stormed the plane and secured the release of the hostages.

Dr. George Habash and other leaders of the PFLP came to the view that hijackings were more damaging to their cause than beneficial. On this issue, Haddad was forced out of the organization in 1976. He later commanded a splinter branch of the PFLP, the Foreign Operations Branch.

Joseph E. Goldberg

HADERA. City in Israel. Site of a major terrorist attack on April 13, 1994, after the Hebron Massacre* in 1994. It was a HAMAS*-sponsored terrorist bombing of a passenger bus in Hadera on Yom Hazikaron, Israel's Memorial Day, a week after a similar attack in Afula.* United Nations secretary-general Boutros-Ghali* issued a statement:

The Secretary-General was outraged to learn of the bomb attack on a passenger bus in the Israeli town of Hadera today, in which six Israeli civilians were killed and more than two dozen injured. He condemns in the strongest possible terms this latest act of violence, as well as the recent escalation of violent incidents which have resulted in Israeli and Palestinian casualties. The Secretary-General urges the Government of Israel and the Palestine Liberation Organization* (PLO) to continue their negotiations and to implement the Declaration of Principles without delay.

HAGANAH (Defense). In April 1909, the Yishuv* (the Jewish community in Palestine*) established a defense organization, Hashomer (the watchmen) to replace an earlier defense group, the Shomrim (watchman). Hashomer was unable to defend adequately the Jewish community during the riots in the early decades of the twentieth century. It was disbanded in May 1920, and in June of that year the Haganah was established under the control of Ahdut Haavoda, later under the authority of the Histadrut.* Community control was later established by the creation of a national command that represented all segments of the Yishuv's political groupings.

The Yishuv recognized the dangers it faced by the growing Arab violence and the difficulty that the Jewish community faced by the British refusal to allow the Jews to bear arms. For this reason the Haganah was a clandestine defense organization. Representatives from the Yishuv were sent abroad to seek aid from other countries as well as from Jews living outside Palestine.

To compensate for their lack of personnel and funds, the Jewish community was organized into defense blocs across the country. Jewish settlements were created for both settlement and defense. By 1937, Haganah began to prepare plans for the defense of Palestine in the event of an eventual British withdrawal. Plan Avner called for the reorganization of Haganah into divisions as well as the growth of its numbers.

Orde Charles Wingate,* a captain in the British army, arrived in Palestine in 1936. He had a profound influence on the military thinking and development of the Haganah. The British recognized the need to secure the petroleum pipeline in Palestine and allowed Wingate to train Haganah night squads to fight Arab terrorists. Through Wingate the Haganah began to develop their expertise in guerrilla tactics, in improvisation, and in resourcefulness.

The British also created a legal Jewish police force in 1937, which was enlarged by a Supernumerary Police. By 1939, it numbered around 22,000. Their training and the facilities established for them were taken over by the Haganah.

In 1938, Yohanan Rathner, a professor at the Haifa Technion, was made chief of staff. The attempt was to make the Haganah more professional with military guidance. During the Arab Revolt,* Yitzhak Sadeh* proposed the establishment of a mobile force to patrol areas rather than waiting to be attacked. The ''nomad'' patrol units were created in 1936. Later, in 1941, the Haganah decided to establish the Palmach,* companies of commando troops that, as shock troops, could help defend the Yishuv against Arab attack and possibly against Axis forces. Sadeh was appointed the first commander of the Palmach. He was also to be appointed chief of staff when the Haganah began its revolt against the British.

With the outbreak of World War II, the Yishuv cooperated with the British. Many members of the Haganah joined the British forces, and some units of Haganah were incorporated into their forces as well. In late 1942, Haganah cooperation with the British ended. It once again began to emphasize aiding illegal Jewish immigration into Palestine.

A new constitution for the Haganah was written in 1943, in which the Yishuv defined it as a popular defense force and no longer a militia. Women, as well as men, seventeen years of age and upward would be accepted. Six months of basic training were established, with a year and a half of active military service. Following active service, Haganah members served in the reserves.

Officially Haganah ceased to exist on May 31, 1948, when the Israel Defense Forces* were constituted. In the early months of Israel's provisional government, David Ben-Gurion* was concerned that Israel's defense forces remain depoliticized and under civilian control. To ensure this, Ben-Gurion abolished the position of chief of the Haganah National Command held by Yisrael Galili, a member of MAPAM,* a left-wing socialist party. A number of his General Staff threatened to resign over Ben-Gurion's action, and the prime minister allowed him to serve for a few additional months. Ben-Gurion dissolved the Palmach on the same grounds—that its loyalty might be to a political party and not to the state of Israel. He wanted the Israel Defense Forces to be a source of consensus and help render insignificant the numerous differences among the Jewish state's population.

For further information see: Efraim Dekel, *SHAI: The Exploits of Hagana Intelligence* (New York: Thomas Yoseloff, 1959); Meir Mardor, *Haganah* (New York: New American Library, 1966); Munya M. Mardor, *Strictly Illegal* (London: Robert Hale, 1957); Amos Perlmutter, *Military and Politics in Israel: Nation-Building and Role Expansion* (London: Frank Cass, 1969); Ze'ev Schiff, *A History of the Israeli Army (1870–1974)* (New York: Simon and Schuster, 1974).

Joseph E. Goldberg

HAGANAH BET. See **IRGUN.**

HAIG, ALEXANDER (b. Philadelphia, December 2, 1924). Alexander Meigs Haig, Jr., graduated from West Point in 1947 and later received advanced degrees from the Naval War College and Georgetown University. While in the military, he served as deputy special assistant to the secretary and deputy secretary of defense from 1964 to 1965. His only combat experience was between 1966 and 1967 in Vietnam. Haig served as the senior military adviser to the assistant to the president for national security affairs from 1969 to 1970. He then became the deputy assistant to the president for national security affairs and served from 1970 to 1973. Haig left the army in August 1973 to become the White House chief of staff and stayed in this position until October 1974. Upon leaving as White House chief of staff, Haig returned to military duty as the commander in chief, U.S. European Command. He retired from the U.S. Army and as North Atlantic Treaty Organization (NATO) commander in 1979. In 1980, President Ronald Reagan* appointed him secretary of state, and he served until June 26, 1982, when he resigned.

As secretary of state, Haig attempted to create a "strategic consensus" in which moderate Arab states would align with Israel in an anti-Soviet military defense system. This led to the United States selling five AWACS aircraft to Saudi Arabia in the spring of 1981. During his tenure as secretary of state, Haig was also faced with the problems of the Israeli raid on Osirak,* Iraq, in June 1981, the attempts to revive the Fahd Peace Plan* in October 1981, and the Israeli invasion of Lebanon* on June 6, 1982. The Israeli invasion of Lebanon and disagreements within the Reagan administration over a U.S. response to the invasion led to Haig's resignation on June 26, 1982. In the Reagan administration, Haig was seen as an ally of Israel, and he argued against Secretary of Defense Weinberger's efforts to invoke sanctions and other measures against Israel for the invasion of Lebanon.

For further information see: Alexander M. Haig, Jr., *Caveat: Realism, Reagan, and Foreign Policy* (New York: Macmillan, 1984); Roger Morris, *Haig: The General's Progress* (New York: Playboy Press, 1982).

Donald A. Vogus

HAMAS. The Islamic Resistance Movement (IRM), HAMAS (Harakat al-Muqawama al-Islamiyya) literally means "enthusiasm" or "zeal" in Arabic. The Palestinian Islamist organization was founded, according to its own official history, on December 14, 1987. The ultimate goal of this movement is to establish an Islamic state in lands with Muslim populations, including Israel. This movement is an offshoot of the Muslim Brotherhood,* whose presence in the Gaza Strip* can be traced to 1928. As a component of the Muslim Brotherhood, HAMAS considers itself the most recent link in the long chain of the jihad against Zionist* occupation.

During Israel's War of Independence,* the brotherhood sent volunteer units from Cairo to train and fight with local Palestinian* forces to prevent the establishment of Israel. After the Arab defeat, the Brotherhood began to set up cells among the populace.

The Brotherhood's program for the liberation of Palestine was gradualist; activism was delayed until after the growth of a generation prepared to launch a holy war against Israel. It circulated publications that stressed that all of Palestine, including the area in which Israel was established, remained Islamic land. Not one inch could be negotiated with the Jews. The Brotherhood envisioned the battle against Zionism as religious rather than nationalistic and sought to foster that awareness in the Palestinians.

In the late 1980s, other Islamic groups began responding to the Israeli oc-

cupation by initiating a series of military operations against Israeli targets. Unlike the activist Islamic Jihad* factions, the Muslim Brotherhood remained on
the fringe in the opening days of the *intifada.* In February 1988, the secular
nationalists established the Unified National Command, which would direct and
coordinate the *intifada.* The Muslim Brotherhood broke a long-standing tradition
of abstention from armed resistance.

HAMAS was formed by a circle of Gazans led by the Muslim cleric Sheikh
Ahmed Ismail Yassin,* an Islamist activist, former chairman of the Islamic
Congress, and the most powerful Brotherhood leader in Gaza.* This initial group
also included Dr. Abd al Aziz Rantisi, who took over the leadership of HAMAS
when Sheikh Yassin began serving a life sentence in prison. He structured the
new organization, designating commanders for political affairs, military matters,
and propaganda, and established contact with Brotherhood activists in the West
Bank.* Their members were recruited from mosques and charitable institutions.

Israel did not begin a forceful crackdown on the Islamic movements until
Israel had allowed Muslim fundamentalists to achieve positions of power in the
religious establishment. Once ensconced in those positions, they also became a
political force. Israel chose to overlook the doctrine of the fundamentalist movements that called for the destruction of Israel and the creation of an Islamic
Palestine, seeking to exploit the rise of fundamentalism, thereby weakening the
support and popularity of the nationalists. Not long after the beginning of the
intifada, Israel concluded that the fundamentalists were more of a threat than
the Palestine Liberation Organization* (PLO). It was obvious that religious fervor was helping to fuel the revolt. In May 1989, Yassin was arrested and charged
with having caused the death of two Israeli soldiers. Israeli authorities declared
HAMAS a terrorist organization.

Despite a change in tactics and the resort to armed resistance as opposed to
its historical passive resistance and new name (HAMAS), the goals and ideological tenets of the Muslim Brotherhood have remained consistent: the Islamic
people have a consciousness of their duties before God in the defense of Palestine, God's blessed country and that of the prophets, an Islamic *waqf* (trust)
upon the Muslim generations until the day of Resurrection.

The Covenant of the Islamic Resistance Movement—Palestine states that HA-
MAS derives its ideological origin, fundamental precepts, and worldview from
Islam. Both HAMAS and the Brotherhood believe that the Palestinian problem
is an Islamic problem and can be solved only from the Islamic perspective. Its
goal is to "conquer evil, break its will and annihilate it so that truth may prevail,
so that the country may return to its rightful place, and so that the call may be
broadcast over the Minarets proclaiming the Islamic state."

Jihad for the liberation of Palestine is obligatory for all Muslims. The struggle
against the Jewish occupation requires that Islamic education guide the *umma*
(Muslim community), scholars, journalists, and teachers in order to eliminate
"the effects of the Ideological Invasion that was brought about at the hands of
the Orientalist and Missionaries." Nationalism is approached from an Islamic

perspective; it is considered part of the religious ideology. There is no greater glory in nationalism or "depth in devotion" than jihad. The motto of the movement is "Allah is its goal, the Messenger is its leader, the Qur'an as its constitution, Jihad as its methodology, and death for the sake of Allah is its most coveted desire."

HAMAS is opposed to peace initiatives or solutions and international peace conferences. It considers relinquishing any part of Palestine as giving up part of its religion, and it sees no solution to the Palestinian problem "except by Jihad." "The initiatives, options and international conferences are a waste of time." Since the signing of the Declaration of Principles* (DOP), HAMAS's goal has been to undermine the peace process and to replace the PLO as the leadership of the Palestinians. HAMAS has been viewed as the Islamic alternative to the secular and leftist PLO.

After the signing of the DOP, HAMAS has been responsible for a number of significant and violent anti-Israel attacks, including a bus incident in Afula* (April 6, 1994), a bus incident in Hadera* (April 13, 1994), a street attack in Jerusalem* (October 9, 1994), the kidnapping of an Israeli soldier (Nahshon Waxman*) (October 1994), and the bombing of a bus in Tel Aviv (October 19, 1994), among others.

HAMAS opposes any compromise that would permit a continuation of what it views as non-Muslim occupation of Muslim lands. Thus, HAMAS is against the U.S.-backed Middle East peace process begun at Madrid.*

The nature of HAMAS affiliations and relations with the Islamic Republic of Iran is a matter of controversy. HAMAS admits to ties with Sunni Islamist movements in Jordan,* Algeria, the Sudan, and Tunisia and to receiving financial aid from "the international Islamic movement" but denies that it has received aid from any government.

For further information see: Ziad Abu-Amr, "Hamas: A Historical and Political Background," *Journal of Palestine Studies* 22 (Summer 1993): 5–19; Helena Cobban, "The PLO and the Intifada," *Middle East Journal* 44, no. 2 (Spring 1990): 207–33; "Charter of the Islamic Resistance Movement (Hamas) of Palestine," *Journal of Palestine Studies* 22 (Summer 1993):122–34; Islamic Association for Palestine, *Charter of the Islamic Resistance Movement (HAMAS) of Palestine* (Dallas, TX: IAP Information Office, 1990); Jean-Francois Legrain, "The Islamic Movement and the Intifada," in Roger Heacock and Jamal R. Nasser, eds., *Intifada—Palestine at the Crossroads* (New York: Praeger, 1990); Ze'ev Schiff and Ehud Ya'ari, eds., *Intifada. The Palestinian Uprising—Israel's Third Front,* trans. I. Friedman (New York: Simon and Schuster, 1989).

Nancy Hasanian

HAMAS CHARTER. The charter of the Islamic Resistance Movement (HAMAS*) credits Islam with providing the movement's "thinking, interpretations and views about existence, life and humanity." HAMAS, as part of the Muslim Brothers in Palestine,* is one of the links in "the Chain of Jihad in the confrontation" with the Zionist invasion, with Israel, which began in 1936 with

Izzed Din al-Qassim.* Palestine, according to Article 11 of the charter, is an Islamic *waqf* (religious trust) that cannot be renounced or abandoned by any Arab country or countries or by any leader or organization. It is an individual duty on all Muslims to wage jihad against the enemy on the land of the Muslims. Peaceful resolutions and international conferences are viewed as contrary to the beliefs of HAMAS. ''There is no solution to the Palestinian problem except by Jihad.''

The Palestine Liberation Organization* (PLO) is viewed as a relative of HAMAS in the fight against Israel, but HAMAS believes the PLO view of Palestine as a secular state cannot be substituted for the Islamic nature of Palestine. Arab states must support the jihad and must be prevented from entering into agreements with Israel.

HAMMARSKJOLD, DAG (b. Sweden, 1905; d. Northern Rhodesia, September 18, 1961). He was born to a prominent Swedish political and noble family; his father was prime minister of Sweden during World War I. Hammarskjold was educated in the law at Uppsala University in the mid-1920s. In 1930, he received a master's degree in political economy and in 1934 a Ph.D. in economics from the University of Stockholm. Hammarskjold began his international career in the late 1940s as head of the Swedish delegation to the Organization of European Economic Cooperation. In 1951, he was appointed vice minister of foreign affairs for Sweden. He became United Nations (UN) secretary-general on March 31, 1953, where he served until his death. His overriding belief was that the UN must be given an increased presence in the world to affect political reality. He considered the UN more as a preventive measure than a corrective force.

Hammarskjold's significant involvement in the Arab–Israeli conflict began with the passing of a UN resolution on April 4, 1956, that stipulated that Hammarskjold would conduct a fact-finding mission to survey the various aspects of enforcement and compliance with the Armistice Agreements of 1949* and that he would make recommendations he believed would reduce border tensions. One of Hammarskjold's most important achievements on this trip in April 1956 was to persuade Israel and Egypt* to agree in principle to publicize that they agreed to adhere to Article II, paragraph 2 of the general Armistice Agreement, which said that they would not fire upon each other or attempt to cross the armistice line. Not specified in this agreement was whether the Suez Canal* would be opened to international and, in particular, Israeli shipping.

In the fall of 1956, tensions over the Suez Canal were reaching a critical point. Hammarskjold was continuously trying to negotiate an agreement to avert a war among France,* Britain,* Israel, and Egypt. Unknown to Hammarskjold, the British, French, and Israelis had already decided to seize the canal by force. Shortly before war broke out, Hammarskjold received concessions from the Egyptians that led him to consider a proposal to run the canal as a partnership between Egypt and the primary users. After helping construct the November 3 cease-fire agreement between Israel and Egypt, Hammarskjold was able to convince France and Britain to agree that as soon as Israel and Egypt signed the cease-fire agreement, and as soon as the UN endorsed a peacekeeping presence in the Sinai,* they would cease all military action. Hammarskjold knew that the establishment of the United Nations Emergency Force* (UNEF) was essential to stop further military escalation in the Middle East. On November 5, he began writing the blueprint for deploying the first United Nations Emergency Force. This document both laid out the foundations for a new kind of international activity and set out principles for future peacekeeping operations.

At midday on Tuesday, November 6, the report was sent to the French and British. They approved it and informed Hammarskjold that they would cease fire by midnight. On November 7, the General Assembly approved the peace-keeping mission as outlined by Hammarskjold.

After the Suez crisis, Hammarskjold remained active in alleviating tensions in the Middle East, with varying results. During the years 1957–59, Hammar-skjold became involved several times with Israel and its Arab neighbors. On one occasion, when a conflict seemed possible between Israel and Jordan* over the status of Mount Scopus,* Hammarskjold was successful in helping the par-ties settle their differences. On two other occasions he was not so successful. These both occurred in 1959, when he tried to promote a settlement of the Israeli–Egyptian dispute over Israel's right to use the Suez Canal. Another fail-ure was an attempt at a general peace treaty between Israel and the Arab states.

His most lasting effect on the Arab–Israeli conflict was the creation of the UNEF. Hammarskjold's efforts to achieve peace in the Middle East continued until his death. He was posthumously awarded the Nobel Peace Prize for 1961.

For further information see: Brian Urquhart, *Hammarskjold* (New York: Harper and Row, 1972); Mark W. Zacher, *Dag Hammarskjold of the United Nations* (New York: Columbia University Press, 1970).

Erin Z. Ferguson

HAMMAS. See **HAMAS.**

HARAM AL-SHARIF. The Haram al-Sharif encompasses the Temple Mount,* on which are the al-Aksa Mosque* and the Dome of the Rock.* The area is the third holiest site in Islam after Mecca and Medina. The Dome of the Rock marks the spot from which it is believed Mohammed ascended to heaven. The wall forming the perimeter of this area includes what is more commonly known as the Western (or Wailing) Wall,* a holy place for the Jews as the wall of the Temple* compound. To the Arabs this was the wall to which Mohammed teth-ered his horse al-Buraq, after which the wall is named.

HASBANI RIVER (Hebrew name, Senir). The northwestern source of the Jordan River* that originates in southeastern Lebanon,* near Hasbayya, about twelve miles north of the Israel–Lebanon border. The springs produce about 120 million cubic meters of water per annum, with the rains adding flash floods. The potential denial of the Jordan River waters has been a matter of concern in the Arab–Israeli conflict.

Joseph E. Goldberg

HASSAN, HANI (b. Haifa, 1937). He received a degree in construction engineering from the University of Darmstadt in Germany. In the early 1960s, Hani Hassan was the leader of the Union of Palestinian Students in Europe and then the president of the General Union of Palestinian Students.* He led an underground commando group in Germany and joined Fatah* in 1963, when he became an adviser to Yasser Arafat.* In 1976, he was accused by Arafat of being an agent for Israel's Mossad* and was said to have poisoned Arafat's food.

Joseph E. Goldberg

AL-HASSAN, KHALID (ABU SAID) (b. Haifa, 1928; d. Rabat, Morocco, October 7, 1994). Following the 1948 war,* he went to Lebanon.* From Lebanon he went to Syria,* where he taught English and mathematics at the Arab Institute in Damascus. In Syria he became involved with the Muslim Brotherhood* and attempted to get its support to establish a commando group. Hassan was arrested in Syria for his association with the Brotherhood but was later released. Upon his release he accepted a position with an import company in Kuwait, where he met and became actively involved with Yasser Arafat* in the late 1960s and became a member of Fatah's* first Central Committee. Although he had strong reservations on the degree to which the Palestinian* cause could depend on Arab support, Hassan advocated that coordination with Arab governments was a necessity. He was concerned with persuading Arab governments to support the Palestinian cause. To this end, Hassan promoted using the Palestinian cause as a means to nurture Arab unity itself—thus requiring Arab governments to support the Palestinians. Hassan had viewed his position as one of realism—a recognition that Palestinian military force could not be effective until Arab states were prepared to fight alongside the Palestinians.

Abu Said was a member of the Palestine Liberation Organization* (PLO) Executive Committee and the Political Department and the Palestinian Parliament. He served as chairman of the Palestine National Congress Foreign Relations Committee and as a PLO roving ambassador and troubleshooter.

For further information see: Alan Hart, *Arafat: Terrorist or Peacemaker?* (London: Sedgwick and Jackson, 1984); Moshe Shemesh, *The Palestinian Entity, 1959–1974: Arab Politics and the PLO* (London: Frank Cass, 1988).

Joseph E. Goldberg

HASSAN IBN TALAL, H.R.H. CROWN PRINCE (b. 1948). Hassan is the youngest brother of King Hussein* and the son of King Talal.* He was educated at Oxford University in Great Britain.* In 1965, he was named crown prince rather than his older brother, Muhammad, who was passed over because he suffers from schizophrenia, as did King Talal. Hassan has played a strong role in Jordan's* social and economic development. He also was extensively involved in the peace negotiations with Israel, especially the 1993 discussions in Washington that led to the Common Agenda* and the subsequent Israel–Jordan Peace Treaty.*

For further information see: Prince Hassan, *Search for Peace* (New York: St. Martin's Press, 1984); El Hassan Bin Talal, "Jordan and the Peace Process," *Middle East Policy* 3 (1994):31–40.

HASSAN II. King of Morocco (b. 1929). He is a direct descendant of the Prophet Mohammed, with the title of cherif (sherif), and serves as commander of the faithful, leading the Muslims in Morocco. Hassan received an Arab–Muslim and French education. He studied law at Bordeaux University. He was appointed crown prince by his father in July 1957 and also became chief of staff of the armed forces. Hassan became king of Morocco in February 1961 after the death of his father, Mohammed V. He survived two major military coup attempts, in July 1971 and August 1972. He has pursued a strongly nationalist policy over the issue of the Spanish (Western) Sahara, claiming the area for Morocco, since the 1970s.

King Hassan facilitated the connection between President Anwar Sadat* of Egypt* and Israel in the 1970s by allowing for initial contacts between Israel (represented by Moshe Dayan*) and Egypt (represented by Hassan Tuhami) to take place, under his auspices, in Morocco.

Over the years he also allowed for some contacts between the Jews of Morocco and Israel, including the visits of Israelis to Morocco.

In 1986, Israeli prime minister Shimon Peres* was invited to Morocco, where he met with King Hassan at Ifrane. Although the Hassan–Peres Summit* did not yield any substantive outcomes, the fact that the meeting took place and was publicly acknowledged was an important milestone.

The day after the signing of the Israel–Palestine Liberation Organization* (PLO) Declaration of Principles* in Washington in September 1993, Israeli prime minister Yitzhak Rabin* and his entourage flew to Morocco on the return trip to Israel for an official visit. The establishment of formal diplomatic relations soon followed.

In late October and early November 1994, he hosted an economic Summit meeting in Casablanca. Its purpose was to foster economic cooperation and development in the Middle East and North Africa and thereby to foster and promote the Arab–Israeli peace process. See also CASABLANCA DECLARATION.

For further information see: Moshe Dayan, *Breakthrough: A Personal Account of the Egypt–Israel Peace Negotiations* (New York: Alfred A. Knopf, 1981); James Andrew Miller, "Hassan II," in Bernard Reich, ed., *Political Leaders of the Contemporary Middle East and North Africa: A Biographical Dictionary* (Westport, CT: Greenwood Press, 1990), pp. 221–33; John Waterbury, *The Commander of the Faithful: The Moroccan Political Elite—A Study in Segmented Politics* (New York: Columbia University Press,

1970); I. William Zartman, *Destiny of a Dynasty: The Search for Institutions in Morocco's Developing Society* (Columbia: University of South Carolina Press, 1964).

HASSAN–PERES SUMMIT (1986). Then Israeli prime minister Shimon Peres* visited King Hassan II* in Morocco on July 22 and 23, 1986. Peres arrived in Fez, Morocco, on July 21 in an Israeli military plane from Tel Aviv. Peres was accompanied by three personal advisers, as well as Rafi Edri, a member of Israel's Knesset* of Moroccan origin, who played an important role in organizing the meeting. On their arrival the Israelis were met by an official delegation and were taken to the King in Ifrane, near Fez. Hassan and Peres met a number of times, both with and without advisers, during the visit. The meetings were not the first between Hassan and Israeli leaders, but all the previous sessions were kept secret.

Neither party substantially changed its positions. But the meetings were important, for Hassan was now the second Arab leader to come forward and publicly, officially, and openly meet with senior Israeli officials. Although there had been numerous private and secret meetings, not only with Hassan but with other Arab leaders by Israeli officials, this was open and official.

At the end of their meetings on July 23, they issued a joint statement:

On July 22 and 23 1986, His Majesty King Hassan II received Mr. Shimon Peres, Prime Minister of Israel, in his Ifrane Palace. During these talks, which were accomplished with frankness and devoted essentially to the study of the Fez Plan,* the Moroccan King and the Israeli Prime Minister made an in-depth examination of the situation in the Middle East as well as of the conditions of form and substance capable of establishing an effective peace in that part of the world.

His Majesty King Hassan II presented and explained the value of each element of the Fez Plan which is two-folded: On one hand: because it is the only document objectively valid since it could be the basis of a just and durable peace and, on the other hand, to form the object of an Arab consensus, excluding any other plan or project of peace.

As for Mr. Peres, he presented his observations on this Fez Plan, and he put forward propositions as concerns the conditions which he deems necessary to the establishment of peace.

Since this meeting had a purely exploratory meaning and never for a moment aimed at the start of negotiations, His Majesty King Hassan II will inform the Arab leaders and Mr. Peres will inform his Government of the points of view which developed during the course of the discussions.

HATIKVA (THE HOPE). Anthem of the Zionist* movement and the national anthem of the state of Israel, which expresses the hope and yearning of the Jew for the return to Zion.* It was written by Naftali Herz Imber and first published in Jerusalem* in 1886.

HAWARI GROUP. Also known as Fatah Special Operations Group, Martyrs of Tal Al Za'atar, Amn Araissi. A part of Yasser Arafat's* Fatah* apparatus, it is named after its leader, Colonel Hawari, who was killed in a car crash in May 1991. It includes some former members of the 15 May Organization.* It has been tied to Iraq* and in 1985 and 1986 carried out attacks against Syrian* targets but also against American targets.

HAWATMEH, NAYEF (b. Salt, Jordan,* 1935). Born to Christian parents, he was educated in Amman, Cairo, and Beirut. He later worked in the export-import trade. Hawatmeh joined the Arab Nationalist Movement in 1954. Because of his political activities, he was imprisoned in Jordan in 1957 and later in Iraq.* He served the Arab Nationalist Movement in Beirut and as its adviser to South Yemen. Hawatmeh later wrote a book entitled, *The Crisis of the South Yemen Revolution.* Around 1965, together with a number of other Arab nationalists, he formed the Vengeance Youth movement, which then later combined with a number of other organizations to form the Popular Front for the Liberation of Palestine* (PFLP), which began operations in October 1967. Because of his ideological and personal disputes with PFLP leader George Habash,* Hawatmeh took a leftist segment out of the organization and formed the Popular Democratic Front for the Liberation of Palestine* (PDFLP). It had links to other Marxist groups and proclaimed itself opposed to all reactionary movements within the Arab world. Hawatmeh argued that the liberation of Palestine* from the Israelis depended on a combined military and political effort of all Arab states after there had been a successful class struggle within the Arab world. The PDFLP viewed its responsibility as destroying reactionary Arab states as well as liberating Palestine. It also identified the United States as an enemy of progressive Arab forces. In 1973, Hawatmeh traveled to Moscow, where he organized Arab students studying within the USSR. The Soviets supplied him with arms. Despite appeals to Israel to form a "single democratic state" for Arabs and Jews, Hawatmeh has been responsible for numerous terrorist raids. On May 15, 1974, Hawatmeh's terrorists occupied a school at Maalot* in the western Galilee of Israel. Twenty-five Israeli teenagers were killed, and seventy were wounded. Following the attack, Hawatmeh said in a Beirut news conference that the raid was aimed against U.S. secretary of state Henry Kissinger's* peace mission to the Middle East.

Joseph E. Goldberg

HAWK MISSILE. The HAWK surface-to-air missile system is an American-designed and -produced, low-to-medium-altitude, mobile air-defense missile that became operational in 1959. The missile has a two-stage, solid-propellent rocket motor and radar homing guidance and travels at supersonic speeds. The HAWK missile is approximately seventeen feet long and weighs 1,383 pounds. It has a range of up to twenty-five miles and operates from altitudes of 10 feet to 53,000 feet. Over the years, the HAWK has had three major improvements to maintain its effectiveness. The standard firing battery has two firing platoons, each with a tracking radar, and three triple-missile launchers.

Israel received its first HAWK missile systems in 1964. Its first effective engagement was in May 1969, when the Israel Defense Forces* shot down an Egyptian MiG-21* during the War of Attrition.*

Other countries in the Middle East that have the HAWK missile in their inventories include Egypt,* Iran, Jordan,* Kuwait, and Saudi Arabia.

For further information see: Bernard Blake, ed., *Jane's Weapon Systems,* 19th ed. (London: Jane's Information Group, 1988).

Stephen H. Gotowicki

HAYCRAFT COMMISSION. Sir Thomas Haycraft, then chief justice of Palestine,* headed a Commission of Inquiry into the anti-Jewish riots in Jerusalem* and other locations that took place in 1920 and 1921. Among other conclusions he determined that the Arabs had been responsible for the violence but also that they had legitimate concerns about Jewish economic and political power, especially perceived influence on the Mandatory* government.

The Haycraft Commission of October 1921 was an attempt by the British government to assess the 1920 Arab attacks on Tel Chai* and other Jewish settlements in the Galilee, as well as anti-Jewish riots in Jerusalem. After riots in Jaffa, chief justice of Palestine Sir Thomas Haycraft was appointed by the high commissioner for Palestine, Herbert Samuel,* to head a Commission of Inquiry to report on the situation and offer recommendations. This commission also included Harry Luke, deputy governor of Jerusalem, and J. N. Stubbs of the Land Department (with Jewish and Arab assessors to help them). They were "to enquire into the recent disturbances in the town and neighborhood of Jaffa and to report thereon."

During this time in Palestine, Jewish socialists were seeking to organize both Jewish and Arab workers. The socialists were divided, however, and, on May Day 1921, Ahdu Haavoda and MAPAI* held counterprocessions. This demonstration, which the Zionist Commission insisted began as peaceful, sparked Arab violence, which spread to Jewish communities. The Arabs saw this as an invasion of Bolsheviks encouraged by the Zionists* to attack their mosques. The Arab mob went to the Zionist Commission's hostel and murdered thirteen members. The next day martial law was declared, and the police and British soldiers forcefully suppressed disorder. In the end 47 Jews were killed, and 146 wounded, and 48 Arabs were killed, and 73 wounded.

The Haycraft Commission members had firsthand knowledge of the conditions in the area and also wished to uphold the traditional impartiality of British law. Their report criticized both British policies and the head of the Zionist Commission. The criticism of Dr. Eder, the head of the Zionist Commission, concerned comments he made to Palestinians. His removal was discussed.

The Haycraft Commission acknowledged Arab responsibility for the violence but also acknowledged their legitimate grounds for discontent. The hostility was connected to the increasing Jewish immigration. The Arabs felt that the political and economic changes in their community were due to Jewish immigration and

Zionist policy. The Arabs believed that the Zionist Commission was completely ignoring them as a serious factor in the politics of Palestine. On the other hand, members of the Jewish community suggested that the Arab riots were sparked by those who had lost privileges they once enjoyed under the Ottomans. In addition, they suggested the riots were instigated by people who wished to discredit the British government. The commission rejected the contention that the riots were primarily anti-British and not anti-Zionist. The commission declared that "the feeling against the Jews was too genuine, too widespread, and too intense to be accounted for in this superficial manner." The Arabs felt that the immigration was not only a means of political and economic subjugation but also a direct cause of unemployment. This hostility was felt by all classes of Arabs, both Muslim and Christian Arabs. The commission went so far as to say that the Arab discontent with British rule was founded on the widely held Arab assumption that the British government was not simply pro-Zionist but under the influence of Zionists.

The Haycraft Commission brought to the forefront the necessity of the British government to solve the three biggest issues facing Palestine: immigration, land settlement, and development. Immigration had been temporarily suspended because of the disturbances, and Britain saw the need to clarify its policies on Palestine. Winston Churchill,* then colonial secretary, wrote the White Paper of 1922,* which took into consideration Haycraft's findings. He reaffirmed British support of the Balfour Declaration* and the right of the Jewish people to a home in Palestine.

Monica M. Boudjouk

HEBRON (Hevron). Sometimes referred to as Kiryat Arba.* A town southwest of Jerusalem* in the hills of Judea.* It is one of the oldest cities in the world and played an important part in the ancient history of the Jewish people. It was the residence of the Jewish patriarchs and served as King David's capital before he conquered Jerusalem.* According to Jewish tradition, the Jewish patriarchs (Abraham, Isaac, and Jacob) and the matriarchs (Sarah, Rebecca, and Leah) are buried in the Cave of Machpela* in Hebron. The traditional site of the cave, over which a mosque was erected, is one of the most sacred of Jewish shrines. Between Israel's War of Independence* and the Six Day War,* when Israel captured the city, Israelis had no access to the city or the cave. The Arabs call it Al Khalil. Al Khalil means "friend," the designation given to Abraham, considered a holy man in Islam and father of the Arab people through his son Ishmael, who lived and was buried in Hebron. Abraham's full nickname, Al Khalil Al Rahman, means "the friend of God." Jewish legend explains the name Hebron as a combination of two words: Haver-Naeh, meaning a "nice friend," which alludes to Abraham, since the Bible says, "a nice friend—that is Abraham" (Genesis, 4:13). Hebron was the scene of riots during the Arab Revolt of 1929.*

It was a town of uninterrupted Jewish residence from ancient times until

August 1929, when some Jews were killed during an Arab demonstration, and the remainder of the Jewish community fled the area. Jews did not return to Hebron until it came under Israeli control during the Six Day War. At that time the Jewish community returned not to the city itself but nearby. The government of Israel decided that the Arab inhabitants of the city could develop the city as they wished and that Jews could establish, next to Hebron, a Jewish settlement using the ancient name of the city—Kiryat Arba.

After the Six Day War, Rabbi Moshe Levinger* led some of his followers on a return to Hebron to resettle Jews in the city from which they had been driven following the 1929 massacre. They moved into the Park Hotel in Hebron and refused to leave. Later, the Israeli government created the settlement of Kiryat Arba nearby. However, in the 1970s, the settlers returned to the center of Hebron, reclaiming some of the buildings owned by Jews in 1929. They formed new settlements and religious schools. The schools are in the middle of Hebron. Levinger and his followers also sought to reestablish a Jewish presence at the Cave of the Patriarchs.*

HEBRON MASSACRE. On February 25, 1994, a Jewish settler, Dr. Baruch Goldstein, opened fire with an assault rifle on Arab Muslim worshipers in the crowded mosque of the Tomb of the Patriarchs* in Hebron,* killing at least 29 people and wounding more than 100. He was killed by some of the surviving Arabs. Palestinians rioted and clashed with Israeli soldiers throughout the occupied territories.* It was the bloodiest single day in the occupied territories since the Six Day War.*

A major concern was the effect of the event on the peace process that had been initiated by the Israel–Palestine Liberation Organization* (PLO) Declaration of Principles* (DOP) signed in September 1993. Although the talks halted, subsequently they resumed.

On March 18, 1994, the United Nations Security Council adopted Resolution 904,* condemning the February 25, 1994, attack on Palestinians* in Hebron, commonly referred to as the Hebron Massacre. The resolution was adopted after weeks of intensive negotiations. The resolution condemned the attack, but not Israel, and called for an acceleration of the peace process. The resolution also called for a "temporary international or foreign presence."*

An Israeli commission under Supreme Court president Meir Shamgar* investigated the incident. The impact of the massacre on the peace process was immediate. Israeli–Palestinian talks on implementing the Declaration of Principles stopped. Bilateral talks in Washington involving Israelis, Jordanians,* Lebanese,* Palestinians, and Syrians* came to a halt a couple of days before the scheduled recess. Although formal negotiations stopped, contacts between the parties did not. Israelis and Palestinians quickly resumed contact to address the security concerns that became apparent with the massacre. The Israelis and Palestinians reached agreement on security arrangements that put international observers in Hebron. They later resumed negotiations to implement the DOP. The cave was declared off-limits to worshipers on February 25, 1994, and was not reopened for Muslim or Jewish prayer until November 7, 1994, when increased security and new regulations were put into place. See also TIPH.

HERUT PARTY (Tenuat Haherut—Freedom Movement). A political party founded by the Irgun* in 1948 after the independence of Israel and the dissolution of the Irgun. Herut is descended from the Revisionist Movement* of Vladimir Zeev Jabotinsky.* The party was based largely on the members and supporters of the Irgun, which grew out of the Revisionist (New Zionist) Organization.* The Revisionists advocated militant, ultranationalistic action as the means to achieve Jewish statehood. Revisionism called for the creation of a Jewish state in "Greater Israel" (all of Palestine* and Jordan*), rapid mass immigration of Jews into Palestine, formation of a free-enterprise economy, rapid industrialization—as opposed to agricultural settlements—to increase employment opportunities, a ban on strikes, and a strong army. In order to effect these policies and because they were outnumbered by leftist and moderate elements in the World Zionist Organization,* the Revisionists formed the New Zionist Organization in 1935. Their rejection of the socialist and liberal Zionist leadership and its conciliatory policy toward the Mandatory* power led Revisionists to form two paramilitary groups: Irgun Zvai Leumi (Etzel),* founded in 1937, and the even more radical LEHI* (Stern gang*), founded in 1939–40. The Irgun was commanded by Menachem Begin* after 1943. Betar,* the Revisionist youth movement, was founded by Jabotinsky in 1920 and continues as the Herut youth wing. Begin founded Herut in June 1948 to advocate the Revisionist program within the new political context of the state of Israel. Herut's political orientation has changed little over the years. It advocates the "inalienable" right of Jews to settle anywhere in Israel, in its historic entirety, including Judea* and Samaria* (the West Bank).* Herut advocates the unification of Eretz Israel* within its historic boundaries and favors a national economy based on private initiative and free competition. Other policies include a minimum of economic controls, a restructured free enterprise system to attract capital investment, and the right to strike. Within Herut and Likud,* Menachem Begin was the primary force from Israel's independence until his retirement in 1983. He was regarded by many as a heroic figure because of his role as a leader of the underground in the Israeli struggle for independence. He was also a skillful politician and a charismatic figure. Upon Begin's retirement, Yitzhak Shamir* became prime minister and party leader, although he was challenged within Herut, especially by David Levy* and Ariel Sharon.* In 1965, Herut combined with the Liberal Party to form GAHAL. In 1973, GAHAL and several small parties combined to form Likud.

HERZL, THEODOR (b. Pest, Hungary, May 2, 1860; d. Edlach, Austria, July 3, 1904). The founder of modern political Zionism,* he was the driving force for the creation of the political ideology and the worldwide movement that led to the establishment of Israel. Herzl was an assimilated Jew who later moved from Hungary to Vienna. He studied law but became involved in literature and wrote short stories and plays. He worked as the Paris correspondent of the Viennese daily newspaper *Neue Freie Presse* from 1891 to 1895. Growing anti-Semitism in France* contributed to Herzl's interest in the Jewish problem. As a journalist, he observed the trial of Alfred Dreyfus* and was affected by the false accusations leveled against the French-Jewish army officer and by the episodes of anti-Semitism that accompanied the trial and the disgrace of Dreyfus. Herzl wrote *Der Judenstaat** (*The Jewish State*), published in Vienna in 1896, in which he assessed the situation and problems of the Jews and proposed a practical plan— the establishment of a Jewish state—for resolution of the Jewish Question.* Herzl argued, ''Let the sovereignty be granted us over a portion of the globe large enough to satisfy the rightful requirements of a nation; the rest we shall manage for ourselves.'' Subsequently, Herzl traveled widely to publicize and gain support for his ideas. He found backing among the masses of East European Jewry and opposition among the leadership and wealthier segments of the Western Jewish communities. On August 23, 1897, in Basel, Switzerland, Herzl convened the first World Zionist Congress representing Jewish communities and organizations throughout the world. The congress established the World Zionist Organization* (WZO) and founded an effective, modern, political Jewish national movement with the goal, enunciated in the Basle Program,* the original official program of the WZO: ''Zionism seeks to establish a home for the Jewish people in Palestine* secured under public law.'' Zionism rejected other solutions to the ''Jewish Question'' and was the response to centuries of discrimination, persecution, and oppression. It sought redemption through self-determination. When Herzl died, he was buried in Vienna; in August 1949, his remains were reinterred on Mount Herzl in Jerusalem.*

For further information see: Alex Bein, *Theodor Herzl: A Biography* (Philadelphia: Jewish Publication Society of America, 1942); Theodor Herzl, *The Complete Diaries of Theodor Herzl,* 5 vol., ed. Raphael Patai (New York: Herzl Press, 1960); Theodor Herzl, *The Jewish State: A Modern Solution to the Jewish Question* (New York: Herzl Press, 1970); Ernst Pawel, *The Labyrinth of Exile: A Life of Theodor Herzl* (New York: Farrar, Straus, and Giroux, 1989).

HEZBOLLAH (Alternative spellings: Hizbal(l)ah, Hezbal(l)ah, Hizbol(l)ah, Hezbol(l)ah, Hizbul(l)ah, Hezbul(l)ah). Also known as Islamic Jihad,* Revolutionary Justice Organization, Organization of the Oppressed on Earth, Islamic Jihad for the Liberation of Palestine. Founded in Lebanon* in 1982 as a result of a merger between Hussain Mussawi's Islamic Amal and the Lebanese branch of the Dawa Party, the Party of God is a Shiite guerrilla organization bent on the destruction of Israel and the Great Satan (the West in general and the United States particularly) and on undermining the Arab–Israeli peace process. It is dedicated to the creation of an Iranian-style Islamic republic in Lebanon and removal of non-Islamic influences. It is an anti-Western and anti-

Israeli organization, closely allied with Iran, but there have been rogue operations as well. Hezbollah has been involved in numerous anti-United States terrorist attacks, including the truck bombing of the U.S. Marine barracks in Beirut in October 1983 and the U.S. Embassy in September 1984. Various elements of the group were responsible for kidnapping and detaining most of the U.S. and other Western hostages in Lebanon. Islamic Jihad claimed credit for the car bombing of Israel's Embassy in Buenos Aires, Argentina, in March 1992.

Hezbollah was formed in Baalbek, Lebanon, during the early 1980s by a group of Shiite clerics united by radical and activist Shiism. As clerics or theology students, they had been affiliated with the academy of religious learning in Najaf, Iraq.* At Najaf they studied with the prominent Iraqi Shiite cleric Muhammad Baqir al-Sadr, an associate of Ayatollah Khomeini; al-Sadr was executed by Saddam Hussein* in 1980.

A number of Hezbollah's original members came from Amal, then the largest Shiite organization, in a protest over Amal's secular leanings and its policies of accommodation with the 1983 Lebanese government of Bashir Gemayel.* Others came from smaller indigenous Lebanese Shiite organizations.

Now a mass organization, Hezbollah began as a relatively informal group of clerics with a common background. Radical Shiites from Amal joined, as did the entire memberships of several smaller Shiite organizations, who appear to have retained their own structure and freedom of independent action, turning Hezbollah into something of an Islamist umbrella organization.

Hezbollah activities include violent opposition to Israel's military control of a security zone* in southern Lebanon, anti-American and anti-Western operations, and social welfare, health care, and antipoverty activities among Shiites.

The ideology of Hezbollah is Islamist and Shiite, activist, internationalist, and anti-Western. It incorporates Shiite traditions of hierarchical charismatic leadership, messianic expectations, and the constant struggle to attain a Shiite vision of justice. Hezbollah's ultimate goal is an Islamic state throughout the Middle East. Hezbollah believes in a global struggle between Islam and the West (including Israel).

Their theorists recognize that local Islamization is relatively unimportant due to Lebanon's small size and factionalized religious composition. Hezbollah acts tactically to use Lebanon as a secure base to combat what it views as Western incursions.

Hezbollah's leading intellectual figure and spiritual father is Sheikh Muhammad Hussein Fadlallah, a prominent Beirut Shiite cleric. He is Hezbollah's guide, mentor, and occasional spokesman, while actual operations are directed by other individuals, such as Abbas Mussawi.* In his many writings, interviews, and public statements, Fadlallah has outlined the basic ideology and strategy of Hezbollah. Hezbollah has implemented this program with both political and violent activities.

The Lebanese organization has strong ideological, theological, and organizational ties to the Islamic Republic of Iran, which provides financial assistance and arms. Iran sent revolutionary guard contingents to Baalbek, Hezbollah's headquarters. Hezbollah's leading figures cooperate closely with the several hundred Iranians who appear to be permanently stationed in Baalbek.

Iran has, at times, employed Hezbollah to act as its surrogate within Lebanon's volatile environment. Syria,* an ally of Iran, has given Hezbollah relative freedom of action and unfettered dominance over Shiite regions of Lebanon, such as the Baalbek area and the southern slums of Beirut. In many of these districts, Iranian-style controls over public conduct have been instituted. Iranian funds also support Shiite religious schools, Islamic law courts, reconstruction of public religious institutions, and social welfare programs. Numerous Iranian institutions have been transplanted to Lebanon's Shiite-dominated areas, including the Martyrs' Foundation (a charitable fund), the Ministry of Islamic Guidance (a government office that polices the Islamic character of government activities), and the Ministry of Intelligence and Internal Security.

The Party of God tends to operate in small units. Its forces in southern Lebanon are widely dispersed in small groups that rely on information and support from the local Shi'a populations. Major operations believed to have been carried out by the Party of God include, but are not limited to, the taking of most, if not all, of the Western hostages in the 1980s; the 1983 suicide bombing of the U.S. Marine and French Foreign Legion barracks in Beirut; the 1984 attack on the U.S. Embassy complex in Beirut; and the bombing of the Israeli Embassy in Buenos Aires in 1992. See also SHEIKH ABBAS MUSSAWI.

For further information see: Ayla Hammond Schbley, ''Resurgent Religious Terrorism: A Study of Some of the Lebanese Shi'a Contemporary Terrorism,'' *Terrorism,* 12 (1989):213–48; ''TVI Report Profiles: Hizbollah (Party of God),'' *TVI Report* 9 (1990): 1–6; W. Andrew Terrill, ''Low Intensity Conflict in Southern Lebanon: Lessons and Dynamics of the Israeli-Shi'ite War,'' *Conflict Quarterly* (Winter 1984): 14–15.

Anamika Krishna and Donald A. Pearson

HIBBAT ZION. See **HOVEVEI ZION.**

HIGHER ARAB COMMITTEE. See **ARAB HIGHER COMMITTEE.**

HISTADRUT (General Federation of Labor in Israel). The General Federation of Labor in Israel was founded in Haifa, Palestine,* in December 1920 as a federation of Jewish labor. It later admitted Arabs to full membership. The purpose was to unite and organize all workers, to raise their standard of living, and to defend their economic interests, as well as to represent their interests in other areas. It is the country's biggest employer, controlling some 60 percent of the country's industry. It controls the Hapoel sports organization, the Naamat women's organizations, and the biggest health insurance fund—Kupat Holim. The Histadrut provides a wide range of services to its members. It cooperates with the government in numerous areas related to foreign and domestic policy and carries out many functions that are normally government activities in other modern states. Many of its leaders have served in major government posts (including that of prime minister) before and after working in Histadrut. Its decision-making bodies are organized along partisan political lines, and the organization as a whole has long been closely aligned with the leaders and policies of the Israel Labor Party.*

The Histadrut's constitution stated: "The General Federation unites all workers in the land, as long as they live by their own toil without exploitation of another's labor, for the arrangement of all settlement and economic matters as well as cultural affairs of workers in the land, for the upbuilding of a Jewish workers' commonwealth in Eretz Israel."* The convention also established a workers' bank (now known as Bank Hapoalim), Israel's biggest bank. The Histadrut evolved into a major institution in the Yishuv* and in the state of Israel.

The Histadrut has a number of elements. The General Convention is the supreme authority of the Histadrut and is its legislature. Its decisions bind all members and all units of the organization. It is elected once every four years in general, direct, secret, and proportional elections. The convention chooses the Council (Moetzet Hahistadrut), whose composition is based on, and reflects, the political makeup of the convention. The Histadrut Council is the supreme institution of the Histadrut between conventions. The Histadrut Executive is the governing executive body. It is chosen by the Council in keeping with the party makeup of the Histadrut Convention. It chooses the Central Committee and the secretary-general. The Histadrut Central Committee is its Cabinet. It is chosen by the Executive and formally serves as its secretariat, conducting the day-to-day operations of the Labor Federation. It is composed only of members of the ruling coalition. The Histadrut secretary-general is chair of the Executive and of the Council and is extremely powerful. Among the more prominent early secretaries-general of the Histadrut were David Ben-Gurion* (1921–35); David Remez (1935–45); Yosef Sprinzak (1945–49); Pinhas Lavon* (1945–50, 1955–61); Mordechai Namir (1951–55); Aharon Becker (1961–69); Yitzhak Ben-Aharon (1969–73); Yeruham Meshel (1973–84); Israel Kessar (1984–93); Chaim Haberfeld (1993–94); Chaim Ramon (1994–   ).

HIZBALLAH (PARTY OF GOD). See **HEZBOLLAH.**

HOLOCAUST (The Shoah). Its origins were in Germany in January 1933, when the Nazis took power. It ended with the surrender of Nazi Germany at the end of World War II in May 1945. The period of Nazi control of Germany saw increasingly negative actions against Jews in the territories under Nazi Germany's control—an ever-increasing area as Adolph Hitler's military successes conquered more and more countries and their populations. Under Nazi Germany millions of European Jews lived in agony and fear, and millions were tortured and murdered. These were part of the systematic attempt to exterminate the

Jewish people. After World War II, large portions of the remaining Jewish population migrated to Israel.

Israel remembers the Holocaust each year on the twenty-seventh day of Nisan of the Jewish calendar—known as Yom Hashoah.

For further information see: Yehuda Bauer, *A History of the Holocaust* (New York: F. Watts, 1982); Lucy S. Dawidowicz, *The War against the Jews, 1933–1945* (London: Weidenfeld and Nicolson, 1975); Lucy S. Dawidowicz, *The Holocaust and the Historians* (Cambridge: Harvard University Press, 1981); Evyatar Friesel, "The Holocaust and the Birth of Israel," *Wiener Library Bulletin* 32 (1979):51–60; Martin Gilbert, *Atlas of the Holocaust* (London: Michael Joseph [in association with the Board of Deputies of British Jews], 1982); Yisrael Gutman and Chaim Schatzker, *The Holocaust and Its Significance* (Jerusalem: Zalman Shazar Center, 1984); Joseph P. Schultz and Carla L. Klausner, *From Destruction to Rebirth: The Holocaust and the State of Israel* (Washington, DC: University Press of America, 1978); David M. Szonyi, ed., *The Holocaust: An Annotated Bibliography and Resource Guide* (New York: Ktav Publishing House, 1985).

HOLST, JOHAN JORGEN (b. Oslo, Norway, November 29, 1937; d. Oslo, Norway, January 13, 1994). Foreign minister of Norway who facilitated the Israel–Palestine Liberation Organization* (PLO) negotiations in Oslo,* Norway, in the spring and summer of 1993 that led to the signing of the Declaration of Principles* in Washington in September 1993. Holst was a former defense minister and was appointed foreign minister in April 1993. He studied political science at Columbia University and at the University of Oslo, from which he received his degree in 1965. He later was a visiting professor at Carleton University in Ottawa, Canada. Holst served as head of the Norwegian Institute for International Affairs.

HOLY LAND. The Holy Land is a name for historic Palestine* that carries a deep religious significance for the three major monotheistic world religions. Jews, Christians, and Muslims all have a deep religious connection to the towns, cities, mountains, and rivers of Palestine, with the holy city of Jerusalem* at its heart. Despite, and perhaps because of, a shared sacred affinity to the Holy Land, Palestine has been the site of ancient and bitter intercommunal conflict.

The biblical stories of the Israelite prophets and kings have played a historically important role in the theology and philosophy of both Judaism and Christianity. Jews of the Diaspora* made the Holy Land a spiritual focal point of their religion and prayed "next year in Jerusalem" in hopes of being able to return. Both Jews and Christians believe that Palestine is the Promised Land* pledged to the Patriarch Abraham and his children and that Jews will return to the Holy Land before the eschatological end of days. For this reason, according to Jewish theology, immigrating or "going up" (aliyah) to the Holy Land has a special significance to Jews of the Diaspora.

The Holy Land is also sacred to Christians as the place of the birth, ministry, and death and the Resurrection of Jesus Christ. The places that Jesus visited in the course of his life have become important pilgrimage shrines. During the Middle Ages the Holy Land was the site of intense European efforts, or Crusades, to secure access to the Christian shrines. Christians believe that Jesus Christ will return to Jerusalem and establish a millennial kingdom after the Temple* is rebuilt.

Muslims, who acknowledge most of the Hebrew patriarchs and Jesus Christ as prophets of Allah, also have deep religious ties to the Holy Land. Most important of religious sites in the Holy Land to Muslims is the city of Jerusalem, where, according to their doctrine, the prophet Mohammed, after praying on the Temple Mount,* accompanied by the angel Gabriel, made a nocturnal journey to Jerusalem, where he ascended through the heavens into the presence of Allah. The Dome of the Rock mosque,* completed in A.D. 691, is built on the site where Mohammed is supposed to have made his ascent and is considered the third holiest place in the world after Mecca and Medina. The Dome of the Rock mosque is built on the Temple Mount, where the Jewish Temple was located, a remnant of which, the Western Wall,* is an important pilgrimage shrine for Jews.

For further information see: David B. Burrell et al., *Voices from Jerusalem: Jews and Christians Reflect on the Holy Land* (New York: Paulist Press, 1992); Richard I. Cohen, *Vision and Conflict in the Holy Land* (New York: St. Martin's Press, 1985); Robert L. Wilken, *The Land Called Holy: Palestine in Christian History and Thought* (New Haven, CT: Yale University Press, 1992).

Mark Daryl Erickson

HOPE-SIMPSON REPORT (MAY 1930). The Hope-Simpson Report was submitted to the British government in August 1930 and was published at the same time as the Passfield White Paper* in October 1930. Concerned with the economic and social plight of the Palestinian Arabs mentioned in the Shaw Report,* Sir John Hope-Simpson, a retired British civil servant who had served in India, was asked "to examine the questions of immigration, land settlement and development." He went to Palestine in May 1930. His report, as characterized in the Passfield White Paper, stated "that at the present time and with the present methods of Arab cultivation there remains no margin of land available for agricultural settlement by new immigrants, with the exception of such undeveloped land as the various Jewish agencies hold in reserve." The condition of the Arab peasant farmer, Hope-Simpson contended, "leaves much to be desired." The Arab population has not had the advantages of capital, science, and organization that the Jewish settlers have enjoyed. Further, the report contended that the constitution of the Enlarged Jewish Agency* signed in Zurich on August 14, 1929, called for the employment of Jewish labor in land cultivation. Although such policies make sense for the promotion of the Jewish national movement, the report held that they violated Article 6 of the Mandate,* which "must ensure that the rights and position of other sections of the population are not prejudiced.'' Because immigration is closely related to employment issues and land development policy, the Hope-Simpson Report called for the coordination of Jewish immigration with unemployment figures in Palestine.* ''The economic capacity of the country to absorb new immigrants must therefore be judged with reference to the position of Palestine as a whole in regard to unemployment.'' As a result, the report called for the suspension of Jewish Immigration Certificates to Palestine. The Jewish community in Palestine strongly contested the methodology used by the Hope-Simpson committee to measure land use and available land for settlement, as well as the findings of the report.

For further information see: Great Britain, Colonial Office, *Palestine: Report on Immigration, Land Settlement and Development by John Hope Simpson* (London: H.M.S.O., 1938) [Cmd. 3686].

Joseph E. Goldberg

HOTEL TALKS. The popular name for the proximity* or close-proximity* talks. So named because, under the framework envisaged by the United States, Israeli and Egyptian* representatives would meet for indirect talks in a New York hotel to be mediated by U.S. assistant secretary of state Joseph Sisco.*

For further information see: Michael Brecher, *Decisions in Israel's Foreign Policy* (New Haven, CT: Yale University Press, 1975); *New York Times,* October 23, 1971; February 3, 1972; February 18, 1972; February 23, 1973; William B. Quandt, *Decade of Decisions: American Policy toward the Arab–Israeli Conflict, 1967–1976* (Berkeley: University of California Press, 1977); Bernard Reich, *Quest for Peace: United States–Israel Relations and the Arab–Israeli Conflict* (New Brunswick, NJ: Transaction Books, 1977).

Noah Dropkin

HOVEVEI ZION (Lovers of Zion). A movement that was established in 1882 as a reaction to the widespread pogroms in Russia (especially Odessa) in 1881, for the purpose of encouraging Jewish settlement in Palestine* and achieving a Jewish national revival there. The founders concluded that the way to save the Jewish people was to return to Zion* and rebuild the land. They generally favored practical Zionism*—settlement in Israel. The members of the Hovevei Zion movement joined farm villages or established new ones (such as Rishon Le-Zion, Zichron Yaakov, and Rosh Pina) in conformity with their view that immigration and settlement in Palestine would alleviate the problems of the Jewish communities in Europe.

For further information see: Ehud Luz, *Parallels Meet: Religion and Nationalism in the Early Zionist Movement (1882–1904)* (Philadelphia: Jewish Publication Society, 1988); Michael Stanislawski, *For Whom Do I Toil? Judah Leib Gordon and the Crisis of Russian Jewry* (New York: Oxford University Press, 1988).

HUSSEIN IBN ALI (Sherif of Mecca) (b. 1852/53/54?; d. Amman, 1931). Sherif Hussein ibn Ali was born to the Banu Hashem clan of the Qureish tribe, to which the Prophet Muhammad belonged. A descendant of the prophet, Hussein bore the hereditary title of Sherif of Mecca. For many years he was in forced exile and under surveillance in Constantinople by the Ottoman sultan Abdul Hamid. Following the Young Turks' revolution in 1908, he was allowed to return to Mecca, where he was appointed emir.

Hussein was initially unsuccessful in February 1914 in his efforts to obtain British support for his plans to conduct a revolt against Turkey. By November of that year, Lord Kitchner conveyed a message to Sherif Hussein indicating British support for Arab assistance in their conflict against Turkey. Correspondence between Sherif Hussein and the British high commissioner in Cairo, Sir Henry McMahon, subsequently began in July 1915. Through an exchange of letters, known as the Hussein–McMahon correspondence,* the two parties set out their respective demands and concessions. For Hussein, an Arab Revolt* not only required military and financial assistance but ultimately would be contingent upon a British promise for an independent Arabia. Hussein, on the strength of McMahon's word and the integrity of the British government, declared war against Turkey on June 5, 1916, thus officially launching the Arab revolt.

On October 29, 1916, Hussein unilaterally proclaimed himself "King of the Arab countries," a move that not only embarrassed the British but raised the ire of other rivals in Arabia. In a compromise solution, Hussein was proclaimed King of the Hejaz. In the years that followed, Hussein learned of the other agreements made by the British, which he believed contradicted the pledges that had been made to him. At the end of World War I, he sent his son Feisal to represent him at the Paris Peace Conference.* Hussein refused to endorse the final peace settlement as it, in effect, implemented the terms of the Sykes–Picot Agreement* and established mandates in the region, instead of complete Arab independence.

From 1920 onward, relations between Hussein and the British became tense. In 1920, the British suspended Hussein's subsidy, plunging him into both financial and military difficulties. Then, in 1921, he refused to agree to an Anglo-Hejazi treaty that would have formally provided him with British assistance and defense against external aggression. He also rejected the agreements reached at the Cairo Conference.*

Hussein's greatest regional rival and threat came from Abdul Aziz ibn Saud.* The long-standing animosity between the two erupted in several violent clashes. In May 1919, Nejdi and Wahhabi tribesmen inflicted a serious defeat on King Hussein's warriors, forcing the British to intervene on his behalf. Following the decision of the Turkish National Assembly to abolish the caliphate, Hussein declared himself caliph on March 7, 1924. Hussein's insolence sparked protest throughout the Muslim community. Incensed by his latest move, ibn Saud and the Wahhabis launched a massive offensive in the Hejaz, capturing Ta'if in September 1924. Unable to withstand the attack, Hussein abdicated his throne on October 3, in favor of his oldest son, Ali. However, ibn Saud's warriors continued their attack and seized Mecca eleven days later. The former king escaped to Aqaba, leaving Ali in control of Jedda. Ali was forced to abdicate over a year later, as ibn Saud was subsequently proclaimed King of the Hejaz. Hussein spent the remainder of his life in exile in either Cyprus or Transjordan.

For further information see: George Antonius, *The Arab Awakening* (Philadelphia: Lippincott, 1939); Philip P. Graves, *Memoirs of King Abdullah* (London: Jonathan Cape, 1951); Aaron S. Klieman, *Foundations of British Policy in the Arab World: The Cairo Conference of 1921* (Baltimore: Johns Hopkins University Press, 1970); Zeine N. Zeine, *The Struggle for Arab Independence: Western Diplomacy and the Rise and Fall of Faisal's Kingdom in Syria* (Beirut: Khayat, 1958).

Anamika Krishna

HUSSEIN (KING HUSSEIN I) (b. Amman, Jordan,* November 14, 1935). King Hussein bin Talal* of the Hashemite Kingdom of Jordan claims to be the forty-second-generation direct descendant of the Prophet Muhammed through the male line of the prophet's grandson Al-Hassan. His parents were Prince Talal bin Abdullah* and Princess Zein Al-Sharaf bint Jamil.

The king has two brothers—Prince Muhammad and Crown Prince Hassan*—and one sister, Princess Basma.

King Hussein's branch of the Hashemite family ruled in Mecca from 1201 until 1925. His great-grandfather, Sherif Hussein* ibn Ali, was emir of Mecca and later king of the Hejaz and led the Arab Revolt* of 1916 against the Ottoman Empire. Sherif Hussein's second son, King Abdullah, founded the emirate of Transjordan* on April 11, 1921. The emirate assumed the name of the Hashemite Kingdom of Jordan on formal independence from Great Britain* on March 22, 1946.

King Hussein completed his elementary education in Amman and received his secondary education at Victoria College in Alexandria, Egypt,* and at Harrow School in England. King Abdullah was assassinated at the al-Aksa* Mosque in Jerusalem* on July 21, 1951, while attending prayers there with his grandson Hussein. King Talal ruled for only a brief period because of mental health problems, and Hussein was proclaimed king of the Hashemite Kingdom of Jordan on August 11, 1952. A Regency Council was appointed until Hussein's formal accession to the throne on May 2, 1953, when he came of age. During that interim period he attended the Royal Military Academy at Sandhurst, England.

King Hussein married Queen Noor Al-Hussein on June 15, 1978. They have four children, and he has an additional seven children from three previous marriages. He also has an adopted daughter.

King Hussein has written three books: *Uneasy Lies the Head: The Autobiography of His Majesty King Hussein I of the Hashemite Kingdom of Jordan* (New York: Bernard Geis Associates, 1962), *My War with Israel* (New York: William Morrow, 1969), and *Mon Metier de Roi* (1975).

For further information see: Peter Gubser, *Jordan: Crossroads of Middle Eastern Events* (Boulder, CO: Westview Press, 1983); Peter Gubser, ''Hussein Ibn Talal,'' in

Bernard Reich, ed., *Political Leaders of the Contemporary Middle East and North Africa: A Biographical Dictionary* (Westport, CT: Greenwood Press, 1990), pp. 233–40; James Lunt, *Hussein of Jordan: Searching for a Just and Lasting Peace* (New York: William Morrow, 1989); James Morris, *The Hashemite Kings* (New York: Pantheon, 1959); Peter Snow, *Hussein: A Biography* (Washington, DC: Robert B. Luce, 1972); Gerald Sparrow, *Hussein of Jordan* (London: George C. Harrap, 1960).

HUSSEIN, SADDAM (b. Tikrit, Iraq,* April 27, 1937). Saddam was born after his father's death and lived with his mother and her brother, Khairallah Talfah. Talfah was a nationalist army officer who participated in an earlier rebellion against British troops and would become the main influence in Saddam's early years. Saddam attempted to follow in his uncle's military career but failed the entrance exams to the Baghdad Military Academy and received no formal military training.

He became active in the Baath Party at an early age. It is believed he chose this party because his uncle's cousin was Ahmad Hassan al-Bakr, who was a high-ranking member in the party and who was also from Tikrit. In 1958, General Abdul Qassim and Colonel Arif overthrew the monarchy and brutally murdered its members. The Baathists participated in the ensuing government. When Qassim jailed Arif, the Baathists, including Saddam Hussein, attempted to assassinate Qassim. The attempt failed, and Saddam was forced to flee to Syria.* In 1963, Qassim was overthrown, and Saddam returned to Iraq. Arif became president, and Bakr, prime minister. The Baathists proceeded to expand their power and influence in the government and some sectors of the military. Hussein helped engineer another coup against Arif, but this, too failed. Saddam was forced to escape to Syria again. However, he tried to return secretly to Iraq, only to be discovered and jailed for two years. In 1966, Arif was killed in a plane crash and was succeeded by his brother. Finally, in a coup in 1968, the Baathists overthrew the government. Bakr became president, and Saddam became secretary-general of the Baath Party. Over the next six years Saddam moved to eliminate his rivals and to isolate Bakr. By 1974, Hussein was in actual command of Iraq. However, he remained cautious and never removed Bakr from the presidency officially. He forced Bakr to appoint him to the rank of general in order to improve his standing with the military. Saddam forced Bakr to resign and became president of Iraq in 1979.

In 1980, convinced that he could defeat Iran quickly, he launched an invasion to recapture the Shatt-al-Arab waterway. The war was lengthy and eventually became a stalemate and even took a series of negative turns for the Iraqi military. In 1988, Saddam agreed to a cease-fire that left the boundaries unchanged. However, he faced a massive debt and an oversized military that was costly to the Iraqi budget. This contributed to his decision to launch an invasion of Kuwait in August 1990, but he failed to anticipate the strong reaction this would bring from other nations. He attempted to legitimate his belligerence by claiming to represent the Palestinian* cause.

Israel's concerns about Saddam Hussein were not inaugurated by the invasion of Kuwait. They had been long-standing. Israel remained technically at war with Iraq since the War of Independence* and Iraq's subsequent refusal to sign an Armistice Agreement. Iraq also fought against Israel in the Six Day* and Yom Kippur* Wars. Saddam was among those who opposed Egyptian president Anwar Sadat's* initiative* to make peace with Israel. Baghdad also gave sanctuary to anti-Israel Palestinian terrorist groups.

Saddam Hussein's growing ambitions in the region and beyond were of increasing concern to Israel. In the spring of 1990, Saddam Hussein threatened to "burn half of Israel," and he sought to develop an atomic-biological-chemical capability. Israel opposed the invasion from the outset but was kept from joining the allied coalition by a U.S. government concern that its joining would split the coalition with the withdrawal of the Arab participants. Israel also opposed the concept of linkage between Saddam Hussein's invasion and occupation of Kuwait and Israel's occupation of Arab territory in the Six Day War. During the hostilities Iraq launched Scud missiles against Israeli cities and civilian populations. There were concrete damage and psychological effects on a country that was, to an extent, paralyzed by the uncertainty of the attacks.

After the end of the hostilities, the war created an opportunity for the Bush* administration to pursue an Arab–Israeli peace as part of its New World Order.* This ultimately led to the Madrid Peace Conference.* Failing to heed warnings from the United Nations and the United States, the Iraqi military was ejected from Kuwait in a decisive military campaign that left the Iraqi military and economy in shambles.

Saddam continued to wield power in Iraq despite predictions that he would be overthrown. However, Iraq has been shackled by international sanctions by a global community that sees Saddam Hussein as a tyrant bent on regional hegemony.

For further information see: Amazia Baram, "Saddam Hussein, a Politial Profile," Jerusalem Quarterly, no. 17 (Fall 1980): 115–44; Amazia Baram, "Saddam Hussein," in Bernard Reich, ed., Political Leaders of the Contemporary Middle East and North Africa: A Biographical Dictionary (Westport, CT: Greenwood Press, 1990), pp. 240–49; John Devlin, The Baath Party: A History from Its Origins to 1966 (Stanford, CA: Hoover Institution Press, 1976); Amir Iskabdar, Saddam Hussein, the Fighter, the Thinker and the Man (Paris: Hachette Realities, 1980); Efraim Karsh, Saddam Hussein (New York: Free Press, 1991); David Kimche, The Last Option (New York: Charles Scribner and Sons, 1991); Phebe Marr, The Modern History of Iraq (Boulder, CO: Westview Press, 1985).

HUSSEIN BRIDGE (Sheikh Hussein Bridge). In the wake of the Israel–Jordan Peace Treaty* on November 10, 1994, the bridge was opened to create a second northern border crossing between Jordan and Israel to supplement the existing Allenby Bridge.*

HUSSEIN'S UNITED ARAB KINGDOM PLAN. In a March 15, 1972, speech in Amman, King Hussein* of Jordan* proposed a union of the East Bank* and the West Bank* to be named the United Arab Kingdom. Characterized as a regaining of the Palestinians'* legitimate rights and "based in its essence on liberation," the plan envisioned two peoples in one country, sharing a similar outlook and with autonomy for each party. Proponents could emphasize a compromise to the difficult question of Palestinian self-determination while opponents regarded Hussein's plan as an attempt to expand Hashemite rule and enlarge Jordan at the expense of Palestinian rights.

The structure of the proposed kingdom as outlined in the plan envisioned two autonomous regions possessing identical institutions within a federal framework. The West Bank plus "further Palestinian territories to be liberated and whose inhabitants opt to join," to be named Palestine, and the East Bank, or Jordan, would have a separate Supreme Court, National Assembly, and governor; Jerusalem* (presumably East Jerusalem) and Amman would be the capital of Palestine and Jordan, respectively. The federal institutions would be similar in the two regions: there would be the Supreme Court and National Assembly in Amman, the federal capital. The king would head the executive branch, and the government would be responsible for national "matters relating to the Kingdom as a sovereign international entity ensuring" the safety, stability, and development of the union.

The proposal was made during a period of hostility between Jordan and the Palestine Liberation Organization* (PLO) and on the eve of West Bank municipal elections. Hussein's statements were an attempt to preempt both pro-PLO candidates and the PLO leadership on the Palestinian issue. Jordanian–Palestinian relations had been tainted with suspicion since King Abdullah's* 1950 annexation of the West Bank with Transjordan,* and they worsened after 1967, when Israel occupied the area and Palestinian guerrillas, or fedayeen,* attacked Israeli targets from Jordanian territory. In September 1970, Hussein used his army to crush the fedayeen along the Syrian border. The following July, after Hussein had expelled PLO leaders and guerrillas from Jordan, the Eighth Palestine National Council* (PNC) went on the offensive against the king, resolving that Jordan east of the river was part of Palestine and must be liberated.

The reaction within the region was unambiguously negative. The Arab countries and their sponsored organizations completely rejected Hussein's plan, and the next day, after "careful study," the PLO's Executive Committee declared that only Palestinians can determine their future, that the Jordanian government was not working for Palestinians' rights or addressing the key issue of Palestinian liberation and was, in fact, collaborating with Zionists.* The committee emphasized that their dispute was with the Jordanian regime and not the people. One month later the PNC's adopted political program again attacked the monarchy by calling for a "democratic national regime" in Jordan.

The day after Hussein's speech, Israeli prime minister Golda Meir* spoke before the Knesset* and called the plan a one-sided statement to "spur extremist elements against Israel.'' She noted that the king had not used the term *peace* or *Israel* at all, highlighting Hussein's definition of Palestine, and faulted him for assuming that a Palestinian solution could be achieved without a Jordanian–Israeli peace agreement. Meir stated that the status of the West Bank was not an internal Jordanian matter, since Jordan no longer controlled that area, and insisted that peace could be achieved only through bilateral negotiations, not unilateral declarations. The same day, the Knesset approved a resolution essentially reaffirming Meir's speech and adding that without a peace treaty, Israel would maintain the post-cease-fire status quo.

The union proposal did not gain any support over time, nor did Jordanian–PLO relations improve. In June 1974, the Twelfth PNC conference issued a statement renewing its call for a regime change in Jordan, labeling it a "reactionary monarchical regime." It also contended that Jordan was hostile to the Palestinian cause, noted its inaction during the 1973 war,* and accused the government of cooperating with "Zionist and imperialist forces." The Arab states, still upset over Hussein's unilateral declaration, declared the PLO the "sole legitimate representative of the Palestinian people" at its Rabat Summit* on October 28, 1974.

For further information see: Clinton Bailey, "Changing Attitudes toward Jordan in the West Bank," *Middle East Journal* 32 (Spring 1978):155–66.

Paul S. Robinson, Jr.

HUSSEIN–ARAFAT AGREEMENT OF FEBRUARY 11, 1985. The 1985 agreement between Jordan's* King Hussein* and the Palestine Liberation Organizations's* (PLO) leader Yasser Arafat* was another attempt to create momentum in resolving the Palestinian* issue. On February 11, 1985, in Amman, Hussein and Arafat agreed to five main points as a framework for a comprehensive peace plan in the spirit of the 1982 Fez Plan* and United Nations (UN) resolutions. It called for Israeli withdrawal from the occupied territories*; Palestinian self-determination within the context of a confederated Arab state of Jordan and Palestine; a resolution of the Palestinian refugee problem according to UN resolutions; a "resolution of the Palestinian question in all its aspects''; and the convening of an international conference sponsored by the UN Security Council's permanent members, including all parties to the conflict, and with PLO participation within a Jordanian delegation.

The text read, in part:

The Government of the Hashemite Kingdom of Jordan and the Palestine Liberation Organization have agreed to march together towards the realization of a just and peaceful settlement of the Middle East problem and to put an end to the Israeli occupation of the Arab occupied territories, including Jerusalem,* in accordance with the following principles: 1. Land in exchange for peace. . . . 2. The right of the Palestinian people to self-determination. The Palestinians will exercise their inalienable right to self-determination . . . within the framework of an Arab confederal union . . . between the two states of

Jordan and Palestine. . . . 3. The solution of the Palestinian refugee problem in accordance
with the resolutions of the UN. 4. The solution of the Palestinian problem in all its
aspects. 5. . . . the peace negotiations will be held within the framework of an international conference.

The agreement was another episode in Jordanian–Palestinian relations stretching back to the annexation of the West Bank* by King Abdullah* of Transjordan,* its loss by Jordan in 1967, through the various Arab League* declarations
concerning the PLO, to armed conflict in 1970 and subsequent tensions. The
significance of the agreement lay in its implication: negotiations with Israel.
Hussein thought that an international conference with PLO representation within
a Jordanian delegation—ideas previously rejected by Israel—could set the foundations for a "responsible" role for the PLO. The agreement also reintroduced
the idea of confederation, which aroused memories of the 1950 annexation and
King Hussein's 1972 United Arab Kingdom proposal.*

The 1985 agreement occurred during a time of ambiguous relations between
Jordan and the PLO. The Palestine National Council's* February 2, 1983, political resolution had mentioned a future relationship with Jordan developing on
the basis of confederation between two independent states, but this occurred in
the context of the PLO's defeat during Israel's 1982 invasion of Lebanon.* Ties
did not improve, and, three months later, Jordan ended negotiations with the
PLO, attributing its actions to divisions within the PLO Executive Committee.
Jordan's statement reaffirmed the PLO's role as the sole legitimate representative* of the Palestinian people; declared that confederal relations would resolve
the Palestinian question in accordance with the 1982 Reagan Plan* and the Fez
Plan;* and proclaimed continued support for the Palestinians in the occupied
territories.*

During the next two years, a Jordanian–Palestinian rapprochement and PLO
actions, statements, and hints encouraged King Hussein's belief that the PLO
might be more amenable to enter some sort of dialogue with Israel. The PLO
had reestablished relations with Egypt in December 1983, and it appeared that
the PLO might alter long-standing objections to United Nations Security Council
(UNSC) Resolutions 242* and 338* and its adherence to the "three noes" of
the 1967 Arab League Khartoum Summit.* In September 1984, Jordan resumed
relations with Egypt,* and King Hussein stated a framework for talks: an international conference including the PLO, rather than bilateral negotiations with
Israel, based on land for peace* and Resolution 242. Although King Hussein's
statements received an indifferent response in November at the Seventeenth
Palestine National Council meeting in Amman, three months later he had
reached an agreement with Arafat.

Events over the next year were not encouraging as King Hussein worked to
soften Arafat's stance and gain the endorsement of the United States and other
Arab states. Nine days later, the PLO Executive Committee qualified its acceptance, stating the right to Palestinian self-determination and a fully independent

state. At the Arab Summit at Casablanca in August, the Arab League* reaffirmed the Fez Plan with no consideration of the Hussein–Arafat Agreement. The next month a radical PLO faction attacked Israeli citizens in Cyprus, and in October the Palestine Liberation Front hijacked the *Achille Lauro** cruise ship and killed an American passenger. By the first anniversary of the agreement, King Hussein had grown weary trying to persuade Arafat and the PLO to renounce the use of violence and to accept UNSC Resolution 242. Hussein also had become frustrated over the lack of Arab support and the unenthusiastic response from the United States. To Hussein, the United States seemed quite uncooperative: U.S. officials had refused to meet with a Jordanian–Palestinian delegation in August; the Reagan* administration was opposed to an international peace conference; and a proposed arms sale to Jordan was withdrawn due to U.S. congressional opposition over Jordan's refusal to have direct negotiations with Israel.

On February 19, 1986, the king suspended his ties with the PLO, citing a lack of progress toward peace talks and the PLO's refusal to accept Resolutions 242 and 338. In July, Hussein ordered all PLO offices closed and ordered Arafat's deputy, Khalil Wazir (Abu Jihad*), to leave Jordan. The PLO formally renounced the 1985 agreement in April 1987.

For further information see: Emile Sahliyeh, "Jordan and the Palestinians," in William B. Quandt, ed., *The Middle East: Ten Years after Camp David* (Washington, DC: Brookings Institution, 1988).

Paul S. Robinson, Jr.

HUSSEIN–McMAHON CORRESPONDENCE. The Hussein–McMahon correspondence was a series of letters written between Sherif Hussein* of Mecca, the Turkish-appointed emir of Mecca, and Sir Henry McMahon, Great Britain's* high commissioner in Egypt.* The letters were exchanged between July 14, 1915, and March 10, 1916. The correspondence contains His Majesty's government's pledges to support postwar Arab independence and the creation of an Arab state in exchange for Arab military support against Turkey. In the context of Britain's conflicting pledges to different parties, the Hussein–McMahon correspondence preceded the Sykes–Picot Agreement* and the Balfour Declaration.*

In his letters, Hussein pledged to proclaim an Arab Revolt* against the Turkish Ottoman Empire* in support of the British war efforts in return for Great Britain's pledge to support postwar Arab independence and provide arms, equipment, and gold to support the Arab forces. Hussein was not motivated by personal ambitions alone but was guided by the Damascus Protocol,* a document drafted by members of the clandestine Arab movement in Damascus. This protocol called for an Arab Revolt against Turkey in exchange for British acknowledgment of the independence of Arab countries bounded on the north by the districts of Mersina, Alexandretta, and Aleppo along the 37-degree north latitude to the border of Persia; on the east by the Persian frontier and the Persian Gulf;

on the south by the Indian Ocean; and on the west by the Red Sea and the Mediterranean back to Mersina.

Although initially evasive on the issue of boundaries, in his second letter to Hussein, dated October 24, 1915, McMahon pledges to "recognize and support the independence of the Arabs in all the regions within the limits demanded by the Sherif of Mecca," subject to certain modifications. These modifications were the exclusion of the two districts of Mersina and Alexandretta and portions of Syria* "lying to the west of the districts of Damascus, Homs, Hama, and Aleppo." McMahon cited Britain's desire not to act to the detriment of its ally, France,* on this issue. Hussein agreed to the exclusion of Mersina and Alexandretta but did not accept the exclusion of the portions of Syria. In deference to the alliance, Hussein postponed the issue of Syria until the "first opportunity" at the end of the war. Palestine* was never directly mentioned or addressed in the correspondence. This letter, in particular, contained the pledges that became the basis for the Arab view of British betrayal after World War I.

In constructing the postwar peace arrangements, Britain, in concert with France, reneged on its wartime pledges to support Arab independence. Both Britain and France sought mandates in Palestine and Syria at the expense of Arab independence. The Arabs cited the Hussein–McMahon correspondence as evidence of Britain's pledges for Arab independence and the boundaries of the Arab state. His Majesty's government claimed that the whole of Palestine west of the Jordan River* had been excluded from Arab rule as part of the portions of Syria lying west of Damascus excluded by Sir McMahon's pledge.

For further information see: George Antonius, *The Arab Awakening* (New York: Capricorn Books, 1965); Isaiah Friedman, *The Question of Palestine 1914–1918: British–Jewish–Arab Relations* (New York: Schocken Books, 1973); Great Britain, Colonial Office, *Correspondence between Sir Henry McMahon and the Sharif of Mecca, July 1915–March 1916,* Command 5957 (London: His Majesty's Stationery Office, 1939); Great Britain, Colonial Office, *Report of a Committee Set Up to Consider Certain Correspondence between Sir Henry McMahon and the Sharif of Mecca in 1915 and 1916,* Command 5974 (London: His Majesty's Stationery Office, 1939); Elie Kedourie, *In the Anglo-Arab Labyrinth: The McMahon–Husayn Correspondence and Its Interpretation, 1914–1939* (New York: Cambridge University Press, 1976); Rashid Ismail Khalidi, *British Policy towards Syria and Palestine 1906–1914: A Study of Antecedents of the Hussein–McMahon Correspondence, the Sykes–Picot Agreement and the Balfour Declaration* (London: Ithaca Press [for the Middle East Centre, St. Antony's College], 1980).

Stephen H. Gotowicki

HUSSEIN'S RENUNCIATION OF THE CLAIM TO THE WEST BANK. On Sunday, July 31, 1988, in a nationally televised speech to his subjects, King Hussein* of Jordan* declared that he was renouncing Jordan's thirty-eight-year-old claim of sovereignty to the West Bank* territory that was annexed by his grandfather King Abdullah.* "We respect the wish of the PLO [Palestine Liberation Organization*], the sole legitimate representative of the Palestinian people, to secede from us in an independent Palestinian state.'' Among other observations, Hussein noted: ''Jordan is not Palestine,* and the independent Palestinian state will be established on the occupied Palestinian land after its liberation, God willing. There the Palestinian identity will be embodied, and there the Palestinian struggle shall come to fruition, as confirmed by the glorious uprising of the Palestinian people under occupation.''

In his speech, Hussein stated that Jordanian disengagement measures were meant ''to enhance Palestinian national orientation and highlight Palestinian identity.'' He stated that in the past, Jordan's administrative relationship with the West Bank was viewed by some as a deterrent to the achievement of an independent Palestinian state in the West Bank. These statements were taken by some observers as a means to circumvent criticism from the PLO and others in the Arab world of the king's past financial and political efforts as a bid to usurp the PLO as the official representative of the Palestinians.

The king also warned Palestinians residing in Jordan that he would not tolerate any challenge to his rule from within and that he would safeguard national unity. Some attributed this statement to the king's realization that his influence and popularity among Palestinians had waned because of the *intifada,** as well as the ability of the PLO to successfully orchestrate the uprising. Added to this was the reaffirmation at the Algiers Summit of the PLO as the legitimate representative of the Palestinian people.

The king reaffirmed Jordan's commitment to being part of the peace process and mentioned its contributions toward an international peace conference, the purpose of which was to achieve a just and comprehensive peace settlement to the Arab–Israeli conflict ''and the settlement of the Palestinian problem in all its aspects.''

Perhaps the most crucial part of the speech came when the king declared that Jordan is not Palestine and that an independent Palestinian state would be established on the occupied territory after its liberation. This dealt a serious blow to both Israel as well as the United States. For a number of years, some in Israel, including elements of Likud* and Labor,* had advocated the policy that Jordan was Palestine, so there was no point in discussing self-determination for the Palestinians, as their homeland existed in Jordan. Hussein made clear that this was no longer an option.

Reaction from Israel was disbelief. The Labor Party's proposed ''Jordan Option''* was now not possible. Israel was left in a position from which there was no one to negotiate the fate of the West Bank but Yasser Arafat* and the PLO. The Israeli concern was somewhat alleviated in the weeks that followed with King Hussein's clarification that Jordan would not necessarily reject a Jordanian confederation with a future Palestinian state.

For Israel's Labor Party, the effect of the king's words was even more dramatic. As part of its platform, Labor had adopted the Jordan Option for peace. This called for the return of the West Bank and Gaza Strip* to Jordan in exchange for full peace. The king's statement forced the party to reassess its policy and to be more open to the possibility that a Palestinian state may be the only option available for the occupied territories.* The United States had long considered Jordan to be the means by which the Palestinians could be part of negotiations without having to directly deal with the PLO. This expectation was in accordance with the September 1975 Memorandum of Agreement* between the United States and Israel, in which the latter promised that it would not recognize or negotiate with the PLO until certain conditions were met. With Hussein's speech, if Israel and the United States wished to bring the Palestinians into the negotiations, they could no longer ignore the PLO, as the king no longer wished to provide the facade of legitimacy he had in the past. Hussein did not want the occupied territories under Jordanian control to serve as an appeasement of Israel and U.S. reluctance to deal with the PLO. The same held true with the PLO: if they wished to be part of negotiations, they could no longer hide behind the rationale that if they worked through Hussein, they were not really negotiating with Israel.

Debate followed concerning the king's intent. The general consensus revolved around two options. The first was that Hussein had grown increasingly frustrated with the stalemate in the peace process and wished to provide the impetus to get the negotiations moving again.

In response to Jordan's disengagement, the PLO declared the independence of the Israeli-occupied territories. The Palestinian Declaration of Independence* was later read by Yasser Arafat at a special Palestine National Council meeting at Algiers on November 15, 1988.

A more likely scenario was that this was a direct challenge to the PLO. For thirty-eight years, Jordan had provided administrative links with the West Bank, employing several thousand civil servants to provide for human services at the cost of almost $5 million a month. Growing tired of criticism from the PLO that he exercised undue influence over the territory via the support he provided, Hussein's disassociation would force the PLO to take actions to prove it was capable of administering the territories more effectively than Hussein could. Perhaps the king wished to set up the PLO for failure in hopes that the West Bankers would see that association with Jordan is their best alternative.

Since Israel's occupation of the West Bank in 1967, Jordan continued to provide administrative and legal services initiated after Jordan annexed the West Bank in 1950. After 1967, most West Bank schools were Jordanian-financed and -managed, residents were issued Jordanian passports, Jordanian dinars were accepted as currency, births and deaths were Jordanian-registered, and West Bank Palestinian representatives consisted of half of Jordan's sixty-member lower house of Parliament. Jordan allocated nearly $50 million every year to the West Bank, which included the paying of partial or full salaries of 21,000 teachers, health workers, and civil servants.

As the *intifada* continued, King Hussein and his advisers feared that Jordan, whose Palestinian population in 1988 was estimated to be as high as 70 percent, might experience problems similar to those in the Israeli-occupied territories.

While King Hussein gave official support to the *intifada,* he took measures prohibiting public demonstrations and the dissemination of *intifada* propaganda.

Many believe the king's preemptive disengagement was done to demonstrate the extent of Palestinian dependence on Jordan and how ill prepared the PLO was to replace Jordan's financial and administrative roles, and, possibly, to expect a Palestinian call for a return of Jordan's presence. In these ways Hussein's disengagement was both defensive and retaliatory.

The speech marked the end of Jordan's administrative support of the West Bank, severing a thirty-eight-year-old claim by the Hashemites to the territory it ruled until 1967. Thus, Jordan was to force the PLO into the role it always claimed, the sole legitimate representative of the Palestinians; suggest to the United States and Israel that they could no longer avoid negotiating with the PLO; and help Jordan's failing economy by eliminating the outflow of millions of dollars a month to support the West Bank.

For further information see: "A King Bows Out. Maybe." *Economist,* August 6, 1988, pp. 29–30; Arthur Hertzberg, "The Turning Point," *New York Review of Books,* October 13, 1988, pp. 56–60; James Hunt, *Hussein of Jordan* (New York: William Morrow, 1989); Raphael Israeli, *Palestinians between Israel and Jordan: Squaring the Triangle* (New York: Praeger, 1991); John Kifner, "Hussein Surrenders Claims on West Bank to the PLO; U.S. Peace Plan in Jeopardy: King Warns Palestinians Residing in Jordan to Maintain Stability," *New York Times,* August 1, 1988, p. 4(A); Daniel Pipes and Adam M. Garfinkle, "Is Jordan Palestine?" *Commentary* 86 (October 1988):35–42; Ze'ev Schiff and Ehud Ya'ari, *Intifada. The Palestinian Uprising—Israel's Third Front,* trans. I. Friedman (New York: Simon and Schuster, 1989); Janet Wallach, *Arafat, in the Eyes of the Beholder* (New York: Carol, 1990).

Pamela Rivers, Nancy Hasanian, and Robert Crangle, Jr.

HUSSEINI, FAISAL (b. Baghdad, Iraq,* July 1940). He holds a B.A. degree from Damascus Military College in Syria.* He is the son of legendary Palestinian fighter Abdel Qader Husseini, who died in the battle for Jerusalem* in 1948. He studied in Cairo and Baghdad. He moved up in Palestine Liberation Organization* (PLO) ranks in Beirut and Damascus and returned to the West Bank* in 1967. He was a leading figure in the Palestinian–PLO negotiations with Israel begun at the Madrid Peace Conference.*

For further information see: " 'A Castle with Forty Doors': An Interview with Faisal Husseini, Head of the Palestinian Delegation," *Middle East Insight* 9 (May–June 1993): 20–23.

Nancy Hasanian

AL-HUSSEINI, HAJJ AMIN (b. Jerusalem,* 1893; d. Beirut, July 4, 1974). Born to the prominent Palestinian* al-Husseini family, Hajj Amin Al-Husseini studied in Jerusalem, Cairo, and Istanbul. In 1910, he accepted a commission in the Turkish artillery. The al-Husseini family often held the post of mufti of Jerusalem as well as other administrative positions in Palestine.

Hajj Amin participated in the violence at the Nebi Musa celebrations on April 20, 1921, and fled to Transjordan,* where he took refuge among the bedouin. The first British high commissioner of Palestine, Sir Herbert Samuel,* pardoned Hajj Amin and appointed him the mufti of Jerusalem in 1921. Though Samuel was aware of Hajj Amin's extremism and anti-Jewish sentiments, the appointment was a conciliatory gesture in an attempt to strengthen the role of the Islamic community within Palestine and obtain their cooperation.

In January 1922, Hajj Amin was appointed president of the Supreme Moslem Council. The combined responsibilities gave him great influence throughout the Muslim community. He was responsible for making appointments as well as providing money. By 1936, Hajj Amin dominated the Muslim Arab community.

British intelligence largely held him responsible for leading the 1936 strike and rebellion that resulted in Muslim attacks against Jewish and British targets as well as members of the rival Arab Palestinian family, the Nashashibis.* The British administration debated his deportation—fearful that deportation or arrest would result in increased Arab violence and not address the Arab demands for ending Jewish immigration and land purchases in Palestine.

In 1939, after the Arab rejection of the British White Paper, the Mandatory government decided not to allow Hajj Amin to participate in the St. James Conference* because of his participation in terrorism during the 1939 protests. Before the British could act, he fled Palestine by boat and was intercepted by a French patrol boat off the Lebanese* coast. He was taken to Beirut, where he established a network in Lebanon that enabled him to continue his anti-British and anti-Jewish activities in Palestine. He was able to engage in propaganda, raise funds, purchase arms, and send infiltrators into Palestine from Beirut. Sir Harold MacMichael,* British high commissioner, failed in his efforts to persuade the French to deport him from the area. In October, 1939, Hajj Amin escaped into Iraq.

During World War II, he supported the Axis powers. He helped organize pro-Axis forces in Iraq. In 1941, Hajj Amin went to Berlin, where he became a propagandist for the Nazis. He broadcast over Radio Berlin encouragement to Muslims throughout the Middle East to conduct a jihad against the British. In 1948, after the state of Israel was created, King Abdullah* of Jordan* took control of a significant portion of what had been designated the Arab Palestinian state. The king ignored the Arab Higher Committee,* where the mufti had the greatest influence. Hajj Amin helped establish the all-Palestine government in Gaza* in 1948, but it was of little significance.

For further information see: Daniel Carpi, ''The Mufti of Jerusalem: Amin el-Husseini and His Diplomatic Activity during World War II (October 1941–July 1943),'' *Studies in Zionism,* no. 7, (Spring 1983): 101–31; Philip Mattar, *The Mufti of Jerusalem: Al-Hajj Amin al-Husayni and the Palestinian National Movement,* rev. ed. (New York: Columbia University Press, 1992); Joseph B. Schechtman, *The Mufti and the Fuhrer— The Rise and Fall of Hajj Amin El-Husseini* (New York: Thomas Yoseloff, 1965); Taysir

Jbara, *Palestinian Leader Hajj Amin Al-Husayni, Mufti of Jerusalem* (Princeton, NJ: Kingston Press, 1985).

Joseph E. Goldberg

HUSSEINI, HATEM I. He served as the Palestine Liberation Organization* (PLO) representative in Washington and as a member of the Palestine National Council.* He is native of Jerusalem.* In 1948, his family left Jerusalem for Aleppo, Syria.* He grew up in Beirut and was later educated at the American University in Cairo. Husseini came to the United States, where he earned his Ph.D. in political science at the University of Massachusetts. He taught at Smith College. He worked for the League of Arab States* and then opened the Palestine Liberation Office in 1978.

Joseph E. Goldberg

IBN SAUD (b. 1881; d. November 8, 1953). Born Abdul Aziz ibn Abdul Rahman Al-Saud, his exact date of birth has never been clearly established; but historians generally accept the year 1881. At the age of ten, Ibn Saud fled with his family to exile in Kuwait after the collapse of the second Saudi state. In 1902, he left Kuwait to reestablish the Saudi kingdom and, with a band of forty followers, retook Riyadh (the former capital). He added to his conquests, and the kingdom of Saudi Arabia was formally declared on September 16, 1932, after many years of fighting and negotiation to unite the various tribes of the Nejd. He was thus the founder and first king of Saudi Arabia.

Ibn Saud based his rule on two principles: Wahhabism and tribal alliances. The Wahhabist movement was a purist movement, formed to rid Islam of secular and modernist trends. Under the banner of this movement, Ibn Saud was able to recapture the spirit of the first and second Saudi states. Tribal alliances were achieved in one of two ways: either through subsidies paid to leaders or through blood ties secured by marriage. Ibn Saud married several times (keeping within the Koranic limit of four wives) to integrate the bloodlines of the Al-Saud with other leading tribes in the Nejd, thus securing loyalty.

Early in the creation of the kingdom, Ibn Saud chose to ally his state with the British Empire. Ibn Saud recognized the ascendancy of the empire in the early twentieth century. This relationship would change in the interwar years. The British failed to settle the Palestine* question in favor of the Arabs, which was the desire of Ibn Saud. Additionally, the British did not negotiate a military alliance and refused to sell arms to the kingdom. Perceptive to the changes taking place in the international community, Ibn Saud recognized the growing power of the United States. In February 1945, he met with President Franklin Roosevelt, and both leaders pledged future cooperation. Even though there were fundamental differences on such issues as U.S. policy in Palestine, the relationship grew into one where each viewed the other as an important element in its foreign and security policies.

For further information see: David A. Howarth, *The Desert King: Ibn Saud and His Arabia* (London: Collins, 1964); Joseph Kostiner, ''Abd al-Aziz ibn Sauda,'' in Bernard Reich, ed., *Political Leaders of the Contemporary Middle East and North Africa: A Biographical Dictionary* (Westport, CT: Greenwood Press, 1990), pp. 14–24.

Pamela Rivers

IBRAHIM MOSQUE. During Byzantine rule in the first half of the fourth century, Emperor Constantine ordered a church built in Hebron.* The church was situated at the southeastern corner of the compound where the marble tombs of Abraham, Isaac, Jacob, Sarah, Rebecca, and Leah are believed to be located. The finished basilica, with four porticoes with an unroofed central atrium, enclosed only Isaac and Rebecca's tomb and left the others outside. The building was converted into a mosque by Muslims in the seventh century, but Jews were allowed to maintain and operate their synagogue in the building. The Crusaders converted the building into the Church of St. Abraham in the eleventh century, and they may have installed the six ornamental tombs present today. The real tombs are sealed below, in the Cave of the Patriarchs.*

In 1267, the Mamluk sultan al-Zahir Baybars converted the building into the Ibrahim Mosque and refused admittance to Christians and Jews, although Jews could mount first five, then seven, steps on the side of the eastern wall and insert petitions into a hole, where they would fall into the cave.

In the Six Day War,* Israel took the site from Jordan,* and they allowed the Muslims to maintain and operate the mosque. Following the war, the mosque at the Cave of the Patriarchs became a popular center of pilgrimage, particularly among Jews with strong religious and nationalist feelings who touted Israel's victory in the war as an act of God. Jews began to settle in and around Hebron.

The mosque has been the site of several twentieth-century violent encounters between Muslims and Jews, dating back to the British Mandate.* In 1929, a group of Muslims murdered fifty-nine Jews whose families were citizens of Hebron's ancient Jewish community. In May 1980, six Jews from Kiryat Arba* were ambushed and killed on their way home from the shrine.

The most notable recent incident occurred on February 25, 1994, when Dr. Baruch Goldstein opened fire into the mosque during Muslim prayer, killing Arab worshipers—the Hebron Massacre.*

For further information see: Albert Hourani, *A History of the Arab Peoples* (Cambridge: Belknap Press of Harvard University Press, 1991); F. E. Peters, *Jerusalem, the Holy City in the Eyes of Chroniclers, Visitors, Pilgrims, and Prophets from the Days of Abraham to the Beginnings of Modern Times* (Princeton, NJ: Princeton University Press, 1985).

Erin Z. Ferguson

IDF. See **ISRAEL DEFENSE FORCES.**

IFRANE SUMMIT. See **HASSAN–PERES SUMMIT.**

IHUD. A Jewish group in Palestine* during the British Mandate* that advocated an Arab–Jewish binational state* in Palestine. Judah Magnes* believed that a determined effort should be made to avert a direct clash between Arabs and Jews. Along with others such as Martin Buber,* he helped to form, in 1942, a group called Ihud (Unity). It advocated a binational solution to the problem of Palestine and argued for that view before the United Nations Special Committee on Palestine.* After the establishment of Israel, Ihud (and Magnes) argued for the establishment of a confederation in the Middle East that would include Israel and Arab states.

For further information see: Martin Buber, et al., eds., *Towards Union in Palestine: Essays on Zionism and Jewish–Arab Cooperation* (Jerusalem: Ihud (Union) Association, 1947); Judah L. Magnes, *Like All Nations?* (Jerusalem: Weiss Press, 1930); Judah L. Magnes, *Palestine—Divided or United? The Case for a Bi-National Palestine before the United Nations* (Jerusalem: Ihud (Union) Association, 1947); Judah L. Magnes and Martin Buber, *Arab-Jewish Unity: Testimony before the Anglo-American Inquiry Committee for the Ihud (Union) Association* (London: Gollancz, 1947).

ILYUSHIN IL-28 BOMBER. A twin-engined, subsonic, tactical light bomber designed and produced by the Soviet Union beginning about 1950. The Il-28 has a maximum speed of 560 mph and a maximum altitude of 40,000 feet. It is armed with up to four 23mm guns and can carry a bomb load of up to 6,614 pounds. It has a maximum range of approximately 1,490 miles. The Il-28 has a crew of three.

In the Middle East, Il-28s were acquired by Egypt,* Syria,* Algeria, and North and South Yemen. It played only a minor role in the Arab–Israeli Wars. In the Six Day War,* twenty-seven of Egypt's Il-28 bombers were destroyed on the ground during Israel's preemptive air strike. Syria unsuccessfully attempted to bomb the oil refineries in Haifa with its Il-28 bombers and had two of them shot down by the Israeli air force.

For further information see: Chaim Herzog, *The Arab–Israeli Wars* (Tel Aviv: Steimatzky, 1984); Michael J. H. Taylor, ed., *Jane's World Combat Aircraft* (Surrey, Jane's Information Group, 1988).

Stephen H. Gotowicki

INSUBSTANTIAL ALTERATIONS. A phrase in American secretary of state William P. Rogers's* December 9, 1969, speech before the Galaxy Conference on Adult Education entitled, "A Lasting Peace in the Middle East: An American View," which later became known as the Rogers Plan.* This phrase referred to the United States' policy regarding adjustments in the 1949 armistice lines* in order to provide secure political borders for both Israel and its Arab neighbors in light of the June 1967 war,* in which Israel gained control of the West Bank,* the Gaza Strip,* the Sinai Peninsula,* and the Golan Heights.* This is the first specific American qualification of United Nations Security Council Resolution 242* regarding the amount of territory to be returned to the Arab countries as part of a peace settlement. With this pronouncement, Rogers accepted that not all of the territory captured by Israel in 1967 need necessarily be returned. Resolution 242 called for "[w]ithdrawal of Israeli armed forces from territories occupied in the recent conflict." Pending negotiation, though, "any changes in the preexisting lines . . . should be confined to insubstantial alterations required for mutual security."

   For further information see: Michael Brecher, "Israel and the Rogers Peace Initiatives," *Orbis* 18 (1974): 402–26; Michael Brecher, *Decisions in Israel's Foreign Policy* (New Haven, CT: Yale University Press, 1975); David Korn, "U.S.–Soviet Negotiations of 1969 and the Rogers Plan," *Middle East Journal* 44 (1990): 37–50; Robert J. Pranger, *American Policy for Peace in the Middle East, 1969–1971: Problems of Principle, Maneuver, and Time* (Washington, DC: American Enterprise Institute for Public Policy Research, 1971); William B. Quandt, *Decade of Decisions: American Policy Toward the Arab–Israeli Conflict, 1967–1976* (Berkeley: University of California Press, 1977); Bernard Reich, *Quest for Peace: United States–Israel Relations and the Arab–Israeli Conflict* (New Brunswick, NJ: Transaction Books, 1977); Saadia Touval, *The Peace Brokers: Mediators in the Arab–Israeli Conflict, 1948–1979* (Princeton, NJ: Princeton University Press, 1982); U.S. Department of State, "A Lasting Peace in the Middle East: An American View," *Department of State Bulletin* (January 5, 1970): 7–11.

Noah Dropkin

INTERIM SELF-GOVERNMENT ARRANGEMENTS (ISGA). Under the terms of the Camp David Accords,* autonomy* is a transitional five-year period during which Palestinians* will assume day-to-day responsibility for civil and administrative affairs, with final status negotiations to begin in the third year. In the invitation to the Madrid peace talks,* the cochairs (the United States and the Soviet Union) set a goal of reaching agreement within one year on interim self-governing arrangements that would last for five years, with negotiations on permanent status to commence at the beginning of the third year.

   Following the Madrid Peace Conference,* bilateral negotiations began between Israel and Syria,* Lebanon,* Jordan,* and the Palestinians. Under the terms of the arrangements agreed to, the subject of negotiations between Israel and the Palestinians was to be interim self-government arrangements. This was reaffirmed at the bilateral round held in Madrid between the Israeli delegation and the joint Jordanian–Palestinian delegation. The two-track process* was to see Israel negotiate bilaterally with the Palestinians, and these negotiations would be limited to the subject of interim self-government arrangements (ISGA). Proposals were exchanged for an interim self-governing authority. On January 14, 1992, the Palestinian delegation presented an outline of the model for Palestinian Interim Self-Governing Authority (PISGA), as part of the interim arrangements for self-government.

   Eventually, the negotiations were subsumed in the Oslo talks* and the Declaration of Principles* (DOP) negotiations.

INTERNATIONAL CONFERENCE. A concept, strongly and often endorsed by the Soviet Union, that the resolution of the Arab–Israeli conflict should be achieved at an international conference involving the parties and the superpowers. The Soviet Union sought a reconvening of a variant of the Geneva Conference* of 1973 as a means to that end. The United States generally opposed the idea, preferring bilateral negotiations between the parties in the region. Thus, for example, in congressional testimony on March 17, 1988, Secretary of State Shultz* explained the U.S. proposals for achieving comprehensive peace through bilateral, face-to-face negotiations, launched by a properly structured international conference. He argued that

the United States has been a consistent and firm supporter of direct, bilateral negotiations between Israel and all of its neighbors as the means to achieve a comprehensive peace. The United States has always been willing to consider any approach which could lead to direct negotiations, including an international conference. The United States opposes, and will not participate in, an international conference designed to replace bilateral negotiations.

INTIFADA. Arab uprising in the West Bank* and Gaza Strip* that began in December 1987 in strong and violent opposition to continued Israeli occupation of those territories. The Palestinian* uprising became a test of wills and policy between Palestinians in the territories occupied* by Israel in the Six Day War* and Israel. Israel sought to end the uprising and to restore law and order. The Palestinians saw the uprising as a means to end Israeli occupation and to promote an independent Palestinian state. Palestinians sought to accelerate the political process and, in particular, to gain a representative role for the Palestine Liberation Organization* (PLO) in negotiations with Israel and the United States. Confrontation and violence marked the evolution of the *intifada,* with a growing toll of casualties on both sides. For the Palestinians, the *intifada* seemed to provide a catharsis but also a high cost in casualties, imprisonment, loss of education and employment, and growing divisions within the Palestinian population. For Israel, the *intifada* posed a major challenge on a number of counts, including damage to its international image, divisions within the body politic on how to respond, the monetary costs of increased military reserve duty, and the costs of other disruptions of the economy.

The *intifada* began with a series of incidents, including the stabbing to death of an Israeli by a Palestinian in Gaza City, a traffic accident in which four Palestinians were killed, and subsequent riots in the Jabaliya refugee camp in early December 1987. Over the ensuing period the violence grew and gained increasing international attention for the status of the Palestinians in the West Bank and Gaza Strip. Eventually, Israeli defense minister Yitzhak Rabin* argued that this was not classical terrorism but civilian violence carried out by a considerable portion of the Palestinian population by means available to every individual, such as stones, Molotov cocktails, barricades, and burning tires. The difficulty was to devise a means to defuse the violence. For both sides the *intifada* became a test of political wills portending continuation over time.

Most Israelis believed that Israel's occupation of the territories had provided the Palestinians with important economic and social opportunities. Though there had been incidents of violence in the occupied areas, the standard of living of Palestinian Arabs had greatly improved. Many had hoped that the improved economic conditions would provide a bridge for eventual acceptance and peace between Israel and the Arab community.

In the initial stages of the *intifada,* there was public disagreement whether the government's tougher policy was necessary. Most Israelis did not experience the *intifada* firsthand but knew it only through its press and television accounts. Israelis were aware, of course, that their reserve duty in the Israel Defense Forces* (IDF) had been extended and experienced the protests when posted in the territories.

The impact was direct on the Israel Defense Forces. Many soldiers experienced "moral stress." The soldiers were not trained for such duty, even though they knew that such responsibilities were necessary. The IDF was accused by Yehoshua Saguy, a Likud* member of the Knesset* and a former director of military intelligence, of providing no military guidance to the government on how to stop the revolt. In addition, the military costs of the *intifada* strained the defense budget. Extended reserve time and the additional arms and ammunition that were required left the IDF with reduced funds for training and maintenance. Questions were raised within Israel as to whether the IDF reports of incidents were accurate and whether all of the incidents were being reported. A number of Israelis refused to serve in the IDF or in the territories because of moral objections.

The Likud Party criticized Labor* for its moderation in dealing with the uprising while members of the Labor Party indicted Likud for its policy of attempting to establish a greater Israel through territorial expansion. Nevertheless, Labor minister Yitzhak Rabin, as minister of defense, was responsible for policy that further divided Labor over those who would trade land for peace and those who would accept the PLO as a negotiating partner.

By April 1988, more than forty Israeli peace groups could be identified. Many retired military officers were involved in the peace movement and called for negotiation with some representative body of Palestinians who were willing to recognize Israel and enter into peace talks. Peace Now,* one of the oldest peace groups, was viewed as cautious, and it was outflanked by groups that were willing to gamble far more on negotiations.

Israel recognized its difficulties. The problems of who could be counted on to be an acceptable negotiating partner with Israel, of how to balance security concerns with withdrawal from territory, and how to resolve the issue among Israel's citizens as to whether it could withdraw from biblical territory were all intertwined with the moral issues raised by the *intifada.*

Eventually, the *intifada* gave way to the Madrid Peace Conference,* which followed the Persian Gulf War,* and the concerns of the Palestinians were addressed in the bilateral and multilateral talks that followed the initial plenary session. The signing of the Declaration of Principles* (DOP) seemed to put an end to the *intifada* in the formal sense of that event but did not end the violence and tension in the occupied territories, which now took on a new form.

For further information see: F. Robert Hunter, *The Palestinian Uprising: A War by Other Means,* rev. ed. (Berkeley: University of California Press, 1993); Zachary Lockman and Joel Beinin, eds., *Intifada: The Palestinian Uprising against Israeli Occupation* (Boston: South End Press, 1989); Yossi Melman and Daniel Raviv, *Behind the Uprising: Israelis, Jordanians, and Palestinians* (Westport, CT: Greenwood Press, 1989); Don Peretz, *Intifada: The Palestinian Uprising* (Boulder, CO: Westview Press, 1990); Ze'ev Schiff and Ehud Ya'ari, *Intifada: The Palestinian Uprising—Israel's Third Front* (New York: Simon and Schuster, 1990).

Joseph E. Goldberg

IRAQ. An Arab state in the Middle East situated in the northeastern portion of the Arabian Peninsula on the Persian Gulf. Although Iraq does not border Israel, it has been an active participant in the Arab–Israeli conflict for much of the period since 1947 and has fought against Israel in Israel's War of Independence,* the Six Day War,* and the Yom Kippur War.* It remains in a state of war with Israel and has been associated with the Arab confrontation states. Iraq was among those Arab states that took the lead against Egyptian* president Anwar Sadat's* overtures to Israel in 1977 and 1978, it opposed the Egypt–Israel Peace Treaty of 1979,* and it harbored and supported anti-Israel Palestinian* terrorist groups. In 1981, Israel destroyed Iraq's Osirak nuclear reactor,* arguing it was developing nuclear weapons. At the same time, during the course of the Iran–Iraq War (from 1980 to the cease-fire of 1988), it was preoccupied with developments in the Gulf area, and the cause against Israel became of much lesser consequence. With the end of Gulf hostilities, Israel became increasingly concerned about Iraqi intentions, particularly with the large size, capability, and battle experience of Iraq's military, its ability and willingness to use missiles and chemical-biological warfare in its war with Iran, and its support of the Palestinian cause against Israel. The Iraqi attack against, and occupation of, Kuwait in August 1990 and the crisis that followed confirmed many Israeli fears. During the Persian Gulf War* between Iraq and the international coalition, Iraq launched thirty-nine Scud missiles* against Israel, which killed and wounded Israelis and caused substantial property damage. This unprovoked attack occasioned substantial concern and debate in Israel about an appropriate response. The government decided that it would accede to requests by the United States that it not respond militarily to the aggressive acts by Iraq. Israel was not permitted to join the anti-Iraqi coalition out of concern that this would lead to withdrawal of the Arab members and thereby crack the coalition.

IRGUN (Irgun Tzvai Leumi—Etzel). Also called Haganah Bet.* A Jewish military organization in Palestine* formed in 1931 and headed by Abraham Tehomi (formerly Silber), organized on a military basis. It stressed military training and discipline. In its early years, civilian backing was provided by a broadly based board consisting of representatives of all nonsocialist parties in the Yishuv.* The rank and file of the organization consisted overwhelmingly of members of Betar* and young Revisionists,* but the Revisionist Movement* had, at that stage, no decisive influence over the body. In 1937, Tehomi reached an agreement with the Haganah* for the merger of the two defense bodies. This led to a split in Etzel in April 1937. Etzel asserted that only active retaliation would deter the Arabs. Its ideology, based on the teachings of Vladimir Zeev Jabotinsky,* was built on the principle that armed Jewish force was the prerequisite for the Jewish state and that every Jew had a natural right to enter Palestine. Irgun's first commander was Robert Bitker, who was succeeded by Moshe Rosenberg and then by David Raziel. Its symbol was a hand holding a rifle over the map of Palestine, including Transjordan,* with the motto *rak kach* ("only thus"). The Jewish Agency* strongly denounced Irgun's "dissident activities," which the British administration countered by suppression and mass arrests. Until May 1939, Irgun's activities were limited to retaliation against Arab attacks. After the publication of the British White Paper of 1939,* the British Mandatory* authorities became Irgun's main target. Another major field of activity was the organization of Aliya Bet* (illegal immigration) and helping "illegal" immigrants land safely.

With the outbreak of World War II, Irgun announced the cessation of anti-British action and offered its cooperation in the common struggle against Nazi Germany. Its commander in chief, David Raziel, was killed in Iraq* in May 1941, while leading Irgun volunteers on a special mission for the British. Raziel's successor was Yaakov Meridor, who, in turn, was replaced by Menachem Begin* in December 1943, and he remained in command until 1948.

In January 1944, Irgun declared that the truce was over and that a renewed state of war existed with the British. Irgun demanded the liberation of Palestine from British occupation. Irgun's attacks were directed against government institutions such as immigration, land registry and income tax offices, and police and radio stations. Limited cooperation was established in the late fall of 1945 among Irgun, LEHI,* and Haganah with the formation of the Hebrew resistance movement. Cooperation among the three forces lasted, with occasional setbacks, until August 1946. On July 22, Etzel blew up the British army headquarters and the Secretariat of the Palestine government in the King David Hotel* in Jerusalem.*

When, after the United Nations adopted the Palestine partition plan* on November 29, 1947, organized Arab bands launched anti-Jewish attacks, Irgun vigorously counterattacked. Among these attacks was the capture, on April 10, 1948, of the village of Deir Yassin* by Irgun-LEHI forces, which resulted in 240 Arab civilian casualties.

When the state of Israel was proclaimed on May 14, Irgun announced that it would disband and transfer its men to the Israel Defense Forces.* For several weeks, however, until full integration was completed, Irgun formations continued to function as separate units.

On June 20, 1948, a cargo ship, the *Altalena*,* purchased and equipped in Europe by the Irgun and its sympathizers and carrying 800 volunteers and large quantities of arms and ammunition, reached Israel's shores. Irgun demanded that 20 percent of the arms be allocated to its still-independent units in Jerusalem, but the Israeli government ordered the surrender of all arms and the ship. When the order was not complied with, government troops opened fire on the ship, which consequently went up in flames off Tel Aviv. On September 1, 1948, the remaining units disbanded and joined the Israel Defense Forces.

For further information see: J. Bowyer Bell, *Terror out of Zion: Irgun Zvai Leumi, LEHI and the Palestinian Underground, 1919–1949* (New York: St. Martin's Press, 1977); Yitzhaq Ben-Ami, *Years of Wrath, Days of Glory: Memoirs from the Irgun* (New York: Robert Speller, 1982); Giora Goldberg, ''Haganah, Irgun and 'Stern'; Who Did What?'' *Jerusalem Quarterly,* no. 25 (Fall 1982): 116–20; Samuel Katz, *Days of Fire: The Secret History of the Irgun Zvai Leumi and the Making of Israel* (Garden City, NY: Doubleday, 1968); Moshe Pearlman, *The Army of Israel* (New York: Philosophical Library, 1950); Joseph B. Schechtman, *Fighter and Prophet: The Vladimir Jabotinsky Story, The Last Years* (New York: Thomas Yoseloff, 1961); Ze'ev Schiff, *A History of the Israeli Army* (New York: Macmillan, 1985).

IRGUN TZVAI LEUMI (NATIONAL MILITARY ORGANIZATION, ETZEL). See **IRGUN.**

ISGA. See **INTERIM SELF-GOVERNMENT ARRANGEMENTS.**

ISLAMIC JIHAD. Some observers identify Islamic Jihad as part of Hezbollah.* Hezbollah has denied this. One reason for connecting the two groups is the influence that the Lebanese Shiite cleric, Sheik Muhammad Hussein Fadlallah, has had on both movements. The Islamic Jihad views itself as conducting a holy war in the name of Islam against the West for the eroding of Islamic culture as a consequence of Western influence. Islamic Jihad literature emphasizes the importance of Islamic cooperation and views itself as a small elite force. The movement believes that an Islamic society cannot be established through peaceful means. Violence, patterned after the Iranian Revolution, was a necessity and could be achieved only through martyrdom. Whether it is independent of Hezbollah or not, Islamic Jihad also is based in Lebanon* and receives strong Iranian support, including advisers from the Iranian Revolutionary Guards. In an interview with the Jordanian* newspaper, *Shihan,* in October 1993, Fathi al-Shaqaqi, identified as the leader of the Islamic Jihad movement, claimed that his organization is ''an independent Islamic movement and its decisions, actions, and policies are based on its own convictions. We define our positions vis-à-vis forces and regimes on the basis of their stand toward Palestine* and Islam.'' He also indicated that Syria* provides support.

The group claimed responsibility for the bombing of the American Embassy in Beirut and the suicide attacks on the U.S. Marine and French military head-quarters in 1983. On April 14, 1985, the Islamic Jihad claimed responsibility for an attack on a restaurant near Madrid, Spain, in which eighteen people were killed and eighty-two wounded. In March and April 1985, the Islamic Jihad attacked a Jewish film festival and an Israeli-owned bank. On May 19, 1980, Islamic Jihad assumed responsibility for street bombings in Riyadh, Saudi Arabia, that killed one person and injured three others. One of the blasts was across the street from a housing complex where U.S. advisers to the Saudi National Guard were staying. The caller, claiming to speak for Islamic Jihad, said that the attacks were in order to shake the reactionary Saudi dynasty. Twenty-seven persons were injured in attacks on a Copenhagen, Denmark, synagogue and a nearby Jewish home for the aged and on the Northwest Orient Airlines offices in the Danish capital on July 22, 1985. These attacks were claimed by Islamic Jihad as well.

Islamic Jihad opposed the Palestine Liberation Organization* (PLO)–Israel Declaration of Principles* (DOP) as well as the Israel–Jordan Peace Treaty.* The movement, unlike many of the fundamentalist groups, cooperated with other Palestinian factions in the early stages of the *intifada** but later abandoned their cooperation.

Joseph E. Goldberg

ISLAMIC RESISTANCE MOVEMENT. See HAMAS.

ISMAIL, HAFEZ (b. 1919). He graduated from the Military Academy in 1937 and from the Royal Military Academy in Great Britain* in 1939. He was an active infantry officer in the Egyptian army. He served as the military attaché at the Egyptian Embassy in Washington in 1950. In 1953, he was appointed the director of the chief commandant of the Egyptian army forces office. In 1955, he was elected as a member of the Inter-Allied Command of Egypt,* Syria,* Jordan,* and Saudi Arabia.

Ismail held a number of political and diplomatic positions. He served as ambassador to Great Britain, Italy, and France* between 1967 and 1970. In 1970, he was named the director of the General Intelligence Services.

In 1971, he was chosen by President Anwar Sadat* to be his national security adviser, a position he held until 1974. In that capacity, Ismail served as a secret channel between Cairo and Washington when Sadat decided to engage in a dialogue with the Nixon* administration in search of a peaceful settlement to the Arab–Israeli conflict before going to war in 1973. At that time Egypt did not have formal diplomatic relations with the United States. He met with President Richard Nixon and his national security adviser Henry Kissinger.* Ismail emphasized to the American administration that Egypt wanted to make substantial progress in peace negotiations.

He served later as Egypt's ambassador to the Soviet Union from 1974 to 1977 and to France in 1977.

For further information see: Henry Kissinger, *White House Years* (Boston: Little, Brown, 1979).

Ahmed Elbashari

ISRAEL DEFENSE FORCES (ZAHAL) (IDF). Israel's military is under a unified command of land, air, and sea forces. It is subject to the authority of the government and carries out its policy. The minister of defense is in charge of the IDF and is a civilian, although he may have had a previous career as a professional military man (e.g., Moshe Dayan,* Ezer Weizman,* and Yitzhak Rabin*). A special ministerial committee generally headed by the prime minister deals with security matters on behalf of the government.

Military service in the armed forces is compulsory, and eligible men and women are drafted at eighteen. Men serve for three years, women for two. Men remain eligible for reserve duty until fifty-five, while women remain eligible until they reach twenty-four. Israel's Arab citizens are not required to serve, but they can, and some do, volunteer. Druze men have been drafted into the IDF since 1957 at the request of their communities. The IDF is composed of a small standing force consisting of career officers, noncommissioned officers, and draftees, as well as reserve officers. The reserve forces are regularly called to active status for training and service, and they constitute the bulk of the defense forces. The IDF is responsible for the security of the country, and its primary task is to defend the state from the enemy. Nevertheless, it performs other tasks that serve the public good. It helps in the absorption of new immigrants, the enhancement of education for recruits, and the provision of teachers to some developing areas.

For further information see: Yigal Allon, *Shield of David: The Story of Israel's Armed Forces* (London: Weidenfeld and Nicolson, 1970); Edward Luttwak and Dan Horowitz, *The Israeli Army* (New York: Holt, Rinehart, and Winston, 1975); Ze'ev Schiff, *A History of the Israeli Army (1870–1974)* (New York: Simon and Schuster, 1974); Jehuda L. Wallach, *Israeli Military History: A Guide to the Sources* (New York: Garland, 1984).

ISRAEL–EGYPT DISENGAGEMENT OF FORCES AGREEMENT (1974). In late October 1973, the United Nations Security Council adopted Resolution 338,* which called for an immediate cease-fire and the implementation of United Nations Security Council Resolution 242* and explicitly required negotiations "between the parties." Subsequently, U.S. secretary of state Henry Kissinger* negotiated the Israel–Egypt Disengagement of Forces Agreement* of 1974. It brought about the reaffirmation of the cease-fire achieved at the end of the Yom Kippur War,* the disengagement and separation of Israeli and Egyptian* military forces, and the creation of disengagement zones between the opposing forces.

In the agreement, they noted: "Egypt and Israel will scrupulously observe the cease-fire on the land, sea and air called for by the U.N. Security Council and will refrain from the time of the signing of this document from all military or paramilitary actions against each other.'' They also provided the details of the principles for the separation of their military forces. The final paragraph noted: ''This agreement is not regarded by Egypt and Israel as a final peace agreement. It constitutes a first step toward a final, just and durable peace according to the provisions of Security Council Resolution 338 and within the framework of the Geneva Conference.''*

The agreement was signed at Kilometer 101* by ''military representatives of Egypt and Israel.''

ISRAEL–EGYPT PEACE TREATY. See **EGYPT–ISRAEL PEACE TREATY.**

ISRAEL–JORDAN DIPLOMATIC RELATIONS. On November 27, 1994, Israel and Jordan* issued a Joint Declaration concerning the Establishment of Diplomatic Relations between the State of Israel and the Hashemite Kingdom of Jordan. The declaration noted: ''The Government of the State of Israel and the Government of the Hashemite Kingdom of Jordan, in accordance with the Peace Treaty* that was signed on 26 October 1994, and desirous to build and develop relations of friendship and cooperation, hereby declare, as of today, the establishment of diplomatic relations at ambassadorial level. . . . The two countries will exchange ambassadors very soon.''

ISRAEL–JORDAN PEACE TREATY. On October 17, 1994, Israel and Jordan* initialed a peace agreement in Amman, Jordan. The signing ceremony took place on October 26, 1994, in the Jordan Valley, with a large group of international guests watching the ceremony. Prime Minister Abdul-Salam Majali of Jordan and Prime Minister Yitzhak Rabin* of Israel signed the treaty while U.S. President Bill Clinton* served as a witness.

The peace treaty comprised thirty articles and includes five annexes, which address boundary demarcations, water issues, police cooperation, environmental issues, refugees, and mutual border crossings. It resolved the major outstanding issues between the two parties in the areas of security, border demarcation, water, and the establishment of normalized relations. The border was to be based on maps drawn up by the British Mandate.* Jordan agreed to lease back (for twenty-five years, with an option to renew) to Israel cultivated agricultural lands that Israel agreed to return to Jordan. Both countries agreed to ''recognize the rightful allocations of both of them in Jordan River* and Yarmuk River* waters and Araba/Arava ground water'' and operate jointly new water purification plants. Israel also agreed to transfer water to Jordan from existing sources. Jordan and Israel agreed not to join, aid, or cooperate with a party whose goal was to attack the other side, and neither would allow any military force or equipment that may harm the other to enter their territory. They would cooperate in combating terrorism and seek to solve the refugee problem. They would establish peace and full diplomatic and normalized relations. Israel would also recognize Jordan's special role with respect to the Muslim holy places in Jerusalem.* Economic cooperation, especially tourism, would be sought as a pillar of peace.

ISRAEL LABOR PARTY (Mifleget Haavoda Haisraelit). On January 21, 1968, MAPAI* merged with two other Labor parties, Ahdut Haavoda and RAFI, to form the Israel Labor Party. The merger of the Labor parties did not eliminate the differences between the coalition's components but instead shifted the quarrels to the intraparty sphere. Within the confines of the Labor Party the problems of political leadership and succession for the government of Israel were resolved. Beginning with the 1969 Knesset* election, the Labor Party was joined in an election alliance (the Alignment) with MAPAM,* although both parties retained their own organizational structures and ideological positions. The new party retained Labor's dominant position until 1977, when lackluster leadership, corruption scandals, and the founding of the Democratic Movement for Change made way for the Likud* victory. Likud was also successful in 1981. In 1984, Shimon Peres* was given the mandate to form the new government. He formed a government of National Unity,* with himself as prime minister for an initial period of two years.

Labor's policies are Zionist* and socialist. They include support for the immigration of Jews to Israel, establishment of a social welfare state, a state-planned and publicly regulated economy with room for the participation of private capital, full employment, minimum wages, and the right to strike. Labor stands for the separation of religion and the state, although it has historically made major concessions to the religious parties in this area. It supports equality for minorities, including the Arabs of Israel, and believes in a negotiated settlement with the Arab states without prior conditions; that is, it has not rejected the possibility of returning some of the occupied territories* to Arab sovereignty. It has pursued the "Jordan Option*" as the preferred means of achieving peace. Shimon Peres served as the party's head until 1992. Peres, once an ally of Moshe Dayan* and David Ben-Gurion* in RAFI, served as defense minister in Rabin's* government (1974–77). In 1984, he became prime minister in the National Unity government. Yitzhak Rabin, Peres's chief rival for the leadership of the Labor Party and the Alignment, assumed leadership following Labor's first primary election to select its head. A former prime minister, chief of staff during the Six Day War,* and former ambassador to the United States, Rabin served as minister of defense in the government of National Unity formed in 1984 and continued in that position in the government formed in December 1988. Peres became minister of finance in December 1988, when Labor again joined with Likud to form the government. Rabin was later selected as party leader. Labor, with Rabin at the head of the election list, emerged from the June 1992 Knesset election as the largest party in Israel's Parliament. In July, a Rabin-led government received Knesset approval, and it began to function with Rabin as prime minister and Shimon Peres as foreign minister. The new government became especially active in the peace process that led to the Declaration of Principles* (DOP) as well as various implementing agreements between Israel and the Palestine Liberation Organization* (PLO). Israel and Jordan* negotiated a peace treaty* that was signed in October 1994. Rabin's Labor-led government was also successful in expanding Israel's diplomatic relations with a wide range of states (including China and India), as well as establishing growing links with Arab states in North Africa and the Persian Gulf.

For further information see: Myron J. Aronoff, *Power and Ritual in the Israeli Labour Party: A Study in Political Anthropology* (Assen/Amsterdam: Van Gorcum, 1977); Gershon R. Kieval, *Party Politics in Israel and the Occupied Territories* (Westport, CT: Greenwood Press, 1983); Peter Y. Medding, *Mapai in Israel: Political Organization and Government in a New Society* (New York: Cambridge University Press, 1972); Yonathan Shapiro, *The Formative Years of the Israeli Labour Party* (London: Sager, 1976).

ISRAEL–LEBANON AGREEMENT, MAY 17, 1983. Following the War in Lebanon* in 1982, Israel and Lebanon* engaged in negotiations under the auspices of the United States concerning the withdrawal of foreign forces from Lebanon and related arrangements. After months of discussion starting on December 28, 1992, and more than thirty-five sessions alternately held in Khalde, Kiryat Shmona, and Netanya, with the support of U.S. secretary of state George Shultz's* shuttle diplomacy,* an agreement was signed on May 17 in the Israeli town of Kiryat Shmona and the Lebanese town of Khalde in four languages: English and French (the binding versions), Hebrew, and Arabic.

President Ronald Reagan* had sent Shultz to the region to break an impasse that had developed. He focused on the withdrawal of foreign forces from Lebanon but also consulted on the status of the broader initiative. Shultz began by holding exploratory meetings with Menachem Begin* and Amin Gemayel* in an effort to achieve better understanding of their positions. His shuttle diplomacy sought to reconcile their perspectives.

The Israel–Lebanon Agreement did not constitute a "peace treaty," but the countries agreed "to respect the sovereignty, political independence and territorial integrity of each other" and to "confirm that the state of war between Israel and Lebanon has been terminated and no longer exists." The "existing international boundary between Israel and Lebanon" was accepted as the border between the two states. Israel undertook "to withdraw all its armed forces from Lebanon," and both states agreed to refrain from hostile actions, including propaganda, against each other.

A Joint Liaison Committee, in which the United States would participate, was established to supervise the implementation of the agreement. Each party could, if desired, "maintain a liaison office on the territory of the other party." An annex concerning security arrangements provided for the establishment of a specifically delineated "security region" in which the Lebanese authorities "aimed at detecting and preventing hostile activities as well as the introduction into or movement through the Security Region of unauthorized armed men or military equipment.'' Joint supervisory teams (Israel and Lebanon) would verify the provisions. The annex provided that ''within 8 to 12 weeks of the entry into force of the present agreement, all Israeli forces will have been withdrawn from Lebanon. This is consistent with the objective of Lebanon that all external forces withdraw from Lebanon.'' The United States assured Israel that it was not obliged to begin a pullout until Syria and the Palestine Liberation Organization* (PLO) withdrew.

U.S. Ambassador Morris Draper noted: ''The goal of the United States in the future will be to assure that this agreement is carried out efficiently in the spirit of full cooperation as attested by the recent visit to the area by Secretary of State Shultz, as well as by the consistent view of President Reagan. The United States will not take its responsibility lightly.'' The Lebanese representative, Antoine Fattal, said: ''If we today are signing this agreement . . . it is because Lebanon is in need of urgent tranquility and order. Lebanon wants to survive.'' The Israeli negotiator, David Kimche, said that the accord marked ''a beginning of a new chapter in our histories'' and called on Syrian* president Assad* to withdraw his forces from Lebanon. Reagan hailed the agreement as ''a significant step forward'' and said ''we have crossed an important threshold in the path to peace. . . . It can lead to the restoration of Lebanon's sovereignty throughout its territory while also insuring that southern Lebanon will not again become a base for hostile actions against Israel.''

Subsequently, Shultz met with Syrian president Assad and Saudi Arabian officials. He told reporters that Syria had a legitimate point in questioning whether the establishment of an Israeli security zone* in southern Lebanon threatened Syrian security, but he remained optimistic and pledged that the United States would continue to do ''everything we can'' to settle the crisis. Israeli foreign minister Yitzhak Shamir* said that Shultz's shuttle diplomacy had succeeded in bridging some of the differences that prevail between Lebanon and Israel.

Syria rejected the agreement, and Palestinian leaders, meeting in Damascus, also opposed it. Syria objected to the Israeli security presence in southern Lebanon, claiming that it infringed on Lebanese sovereignty and Syrian security. Despite the professed concern for the future of Lebanon, Assad's motives seemed more Syria-oriented. Syria sought to regain the Golan Heights,* and if this was not possible through a process such as that proposed by the Reagan initiative, then it would play the spoiler by preventing negotiations. Assad wanted to ensure that any negotiations would take Syria's concerns into account and that Syria's leadership of the negotiating team and control of its positions would be assured. Syria also sought to maintain (and enhance) its role and influence in Lebanon, a historical aspect of the Syria–Lebanon relationship that harks back to the period when Lebanon was a part of Greater Syria. There was concern that Israeli or pro-Israeli control of the Beka Valley* and the contiguous areas would provide relatively easy military access to Damascus in the event of conflict. Despite his opposition to the agreement, Assad sought to avoid a direct conflict with Israel, if Syria could not be assured of additional Arab support, thereby avoiding a repeat of the losses suffered during the 1982 war.

The Soviet Union's negative reaction was multifaceted. On May 9, Tass issued a statement in which it charged that the United States and Israel were "grossly violating" Lebanese territory, and it demanded the "unconditional withdrawal" of Israeli troops from Lebanon as the "first and foremost" condition for bringing peace to that country. It insisted that U.S. and other foreign troops should be withdrawn so that Lebanon would be free of all foreign troops and could be united and independent. The Soviets also charged that Israel was preparing another Middle Eastern war. Soviet support for the Syrian position took the form of statements as well as continued military supply (and military advisers) and economic assistance.

Although signed and ratified by both states, Lebanon abrogated the agreement in March 1984 under heavy pressure from Syria.

ISRAEL–MOROCCO DIPLOMATIC RELATIONS. On September 1, 1994, Israel and Morocco announced that they would establish low-level diplomatic relations. Initially, they would establish liaison offices in Tel Aviv, Israel, and Rabat, Morocco, to deal with such matters as business and cultural exchanges. Morocco thus became the second Arab state, after Egypt,* to establish diplomatic relations with Israel. This followed earlier contacts, both public and private, between the two states. Immediately after the signing of the Israel–Palestine Liberation Organization* (PLO) Declaration of Principles* (DOP) in September 1993, Israeli prime minister Yitzhak Rabin* and his entourage, on their flight back to Israel, stopped for an unexpected official and public visit in Morocco on September 14, 1993. See also CASABLANCA DECLARATION; HASSAN II, KING OF MOROCCO; HASSAN–PERES SUMMIT.

ISRAEL–PLO AGREEMENTS. See **CAIRO AGREEMENT (1994); DECLARATION OF PRINCIPLES; EARLY EMPOWERMENT; ISRAEL–PLO ECONOMIC AGREEMENT (1994); SAFE PASSAGE ROUTE.**

ISRAEL–PLO ECONOMIC AGREEMENT (1994). On April 29, 1994, in Paris, Israel and the Palestine Liberation Organization* (PLO) signed an economic agreement. Abu Alla* (Ahmed Karia)* signed for the PLO, and Avraham Shohat, finance minister, signed for Israel. The agreement lays out the relationship between the economies of Israel and the Palestinians. It takes into consideration the economic needs of the Palestinians for growth and development and their special ties with the Arab world; it also safeguards the economic interests of Israel.

The agreement is long (thirty pages, plus annexes and lists) and deals with a variety of subjects, including imports and import taxes, labor, monetary and fiscal policy, direct taxation, indirect taxation, agriculture, industry, energy, tourism, and insurance. The Palestinian Authority* will establish a monetary authority, not a central bank, whose main function will be to regulate and supervise banks operating in the autonomy areas, to manage foreign exchange reserves, and to supervise foreign exchange transactions. A Palestinian Tax Administration will conduct its own direct tax policy, including income tax on individuals and corporations. A value-added tax (VAT) system similar to that operating in Israel will be instituted by the Palestinian Authority. Palestinians will continue to work in Israel. Agricultural and manufactured goods will be allowed to enter Israel freely, with some quotas on some agricultural products. A Palestinian Tourist Administration will be established to control matters relating to tourism in the areas under control of the Palestinian Authority. Israeli businesses will be able to invest in Jericho* and Gaza,* and Palestinians in the autonomous regions will be able to invest in Israel.

Article 1 (in paragraphs 1 and 2) of the "Protocol on Economic Relations between the Government of the State of Israel and the P.L.O., Representing the Palestinian People" notes:

1. This protocol established the contractual agreement that will govern the economic relations between the two sides and will cover the West Bank* and the Gaza Strip* during the interim period. The implementation will be according to the stages envisaged in the Declaration of Principles* on Interim Self Government Arrangements signed in Washington, D.C. on September 13, 1993 and the Agreed Minutes thereto. It will therefore begin in the Gaza Strip and the Jericho Area and at a later stage will also apply to the rest of the West Bank, according to the provisions of the Interim Agreement and to any other agreed arrangements between the two sides. 2. The Protocol, including its Appendices, will be incorporated into the Agreement on the Gaza Strip and the Jericho Area (in this Protocol—the Agreement), will be an integral part thereof and interpreted accordingly. This paragraph refers solely to the Gaza Strip and the Jericho Area.

ISRAEL–SYRIA DISENGAGEMENT OF FORCES AGREEMENT (1974). An agreement between Syria* and Israel achieved in May 1974 through the shuttle diplomacy* of U.S. secretary of state Henry Kissinger.* It brought about the reaffirmation of the cease-fire achieved at the end of the Yom Kippur War,* the disengagement and separation of Israeli and Syrian military forces on the Golan Heights,* and the creation of disengagement zones between the opposing armies.

ISTIQLAL PARTY. In December 1931, an Islamic conference composed mainly of Palestinians* and Syrians* was convened in Jerusalem* for the purpose of establishing a Pan-Arab National Covenant, which would serve as a basis for calling a General Arab Congress. "The Manifesto to the Arab World" was published in December 1931 and stressed the indivisibility of the Arab countries while condemning local and regional policies, as well as imperialism. It noted that "Palestine is an Arab country and natural part of Syria."

Because of differences between the king of Saudi Arabia and Amir Abdullah* of Transjordan,* the Palestinian group decided to establish a political party within Palestine. The mufti of Jerusalem, Hajj Amin al-Husseini,* talked with them but later withdrew his support.

On August 4, 1932, eleven Palestinians established the Istiqlal (Independence) Party. The founders were young Palestinians who had attained professional standing and were from throughout the country. Because earlier Palestinian Arab national movements had failed as a consequence of competition and rivalry between the leading Jerusalem families, the Husseinis and the Nashashibis,* Istiqlal attempted to rise above local and personal conflicts. Its platform incorporated the "Manifesto to the Arab World" and demanded "complete independence for the Arab countries." It sought parliamentary Arab rule in Palestine, the denial of the Balfour Declaration,* and an end to the British Mandate.* It organized public meetings, published a newspaper, issued manifestos, and, at one point, encouraged noncooperation and nonpayment of taxes. To defeat Zionism,* Istiqlal contended, the British Mandate had to end.

The party's peak strength and greatest influence came in 1933. The mufti effectively worked against the party, and, by 1935, he had succeeded in discrediting its leadership. By 1941, it was an organization in name only.

For further information see: Issa Khalaf, *Politics in Palestine: Arab Factionalism and Social Disintegration, 1939–1948* (Albany: State University of New York Press, 1991); Baruch Kimmerling and Joel S. Migdal, *Palestinians: The Making of a People* (New York: Free Press, 1993); Yehoshua Porath, *The Emergence of the Palestinian–Arab National Movement, 1918–1929* (London: Frank Cass, 1974).

Joseph E. Goldberg

J

JABOTINSKY, VLADIMIR ZEEV (b. Odessa, Russia, 1880; d. New York, 1940). He was the founder of the World Union of Zionist Revisionists* in 1925, which later branched off into the New Zionist Organization.* The union advocated the establishment of a Jewish state, increased Jewish immigration, and militant opposition to the British Mandatory* authorities in Palestine.* His philosophy provided the ideological basis for the Herut Party.* He studied law in Berne and Rome but became interested in the Zionist cause with the growth of pogroms in Russia and became an active figure in the Zionist movement. After the beginning of World War I, he promoted the idea of a Jewish Legion as a component of the British army, and he later joined it. In March 1921, he joined the Zionist Executive but resigned in January 1923 because of dissatisfaction with British policy and with lack of resistance to the British anti-Zionist policy. In 1923, he founded Brit Trumpeldor (Betar),* and in 1925 the World Union of Zionist Revisionists was formed in Paris, and he became president. Jabotinsky later seceded from the World Zionist Organization* and founded (in Vienna in 1935) the New Zionist Organization, of which he became president. He campaigned against the British plans for partition of Palestine and advocated and promoted illegal Jewish immigration to Palestine. His remains were transferred to Israel and reburied on Mount Herzl in Jerusalem* in July 1964.

For further information see: Vladimir Jabotinsky, *The Jewish War Front* (London: Allen and Unwin, 1940); Vladimir Jabotinsky, *The Story of the Jewish Legion* (New York: Ackerman, 1945); Joseph B. Schechtman, *The Vladimir Jabotinsky Story,* 2 vols., vol. 1: *Rebel and Statesman: The Early Years,* vol. 2: *Fighter and Prophet: The Last Years* (New York: T. Yoseloff, 1956–61); Yaacov Shavit, *Jabotinsky and the Revisionist Movement, 1925–1948* (London: Frank Cass, 1988).

JAPAN. Oil is, and has been, Japan's foremost important source of energy and has been called "the blood of the Japanese economy." Ever since oil replaced coal as the principal source of energy in the early 1960s, a stable and consistent supply of oil has been the base of Japanese economic development. Hence, Japan's relations with the Middle East have naturally been centered around economic issues. Before the 1973 oil shock, Japan was able to be somewhat indifferent to political developments in the region so long as there was a cheap and consistent supply of oil. The outbreak of the Arab–Israeli conflict in 1948 did not attract much Japanese attention, as Japan was busy reconstructing its war-devastated land and economy.

When Japan reopened its diplomatic activities in 1952, it was a latecomer to the Arab–Israeli question. Japan carefully established balanced relations with both Arabs and Israel. Japan established diplomatic relations with Israel in 1952. In the following year, Japan began its first involvement in Palestinian* issues by financially supporting activities of the United Nations Relief and Works Agency for Palestine Refugees in the Near East* (UNRWA), even though Japan was not even a member of the United Nations (UN).

Balanced relations with the Arabs and Israel continued for about a decade, but their character changed in 1967. Foreign Minister Takeo Miki, at the United Nations General Assembly, expressed concern about the situation in the Middle East and called for an immediate withdrawal of Israeli forces from the occupied areas.* There, he explained, the government's position that no aggrandizement of territory by means of a fait accompli of occupation was admissible. Being a member of the United Nation's Security Council at that time, the ambassador to the UN, Senjin Tsuruoka, attempted to coordinate the arranging of United Nations Resolution 242,* which came into effect on November 22, 1967. Ambiguity in the English text of the resolution centered over the lack of the definite article before the word "territory" and whether Resolution 242 referred to withdrawal from all territory. Japan's position was stated in Foreign Minister Miki's speech at the UN General Assembly in the following year: any territorial expansion by force is unacceptable, and Israeli armed forces should be withdrawn from all the occupied territories.*

While this marked a change in Japan's Middle East policy, Japan was not yet ready to make a clear commitment to either side. On one hand, Japan had to approach the Arab–Israeli issue in a way that did not harm its relationship with the United States. The existence of the U.S.–Japan Security Treaty since 1960 prevented Japan from openly supporting the Palestinians at the expense of United States–Japan relations. On the other hand, Japan had to show to the oil-producing Arab states that Japan was seriously concerned about the Palestinian problem. This has been a long-standing diplomatic dilemma for Japan. Its voting behavior at the United Nations General Assembly between 1969 and 1971 reveals the difficult situation Japan has had to face. While Japan abstained from voting on General Assembly resolution 2525B in December 1969, it voted for resolution 2628 in November 1970. In the same year, Japan again abstained from voting for resolution 2672C (XXV),* which recognized the right of the Palestinian people to self-determination. Before 1970, Japan was ready to accuse Israel of being an aggressor but reluctant to fully endorse Palestinian self-determination. Again, this reflects Japan's careful attitude not to be too committed to the Arab–Israeli problem.

Japan's attitude toward the Arab–Israeli question was so sensitive that any single pressure could change its policy. For example, in May 1971, King Feisal of Saudi Arabia visited Japan. In a joint communique, King Feisal and Prime Minister Eisaku Sato declared that force should not be used for the settlement of international disputes and that the problem of Palestine should be solved on the basis of rightfulness and justice in conformity with the UN Security Council Resolution 242, that is, the total withdrawal of Israeli forces from the occupied territory. Due to Saudi Arabia's strong insistence, the following indirect reference to the Palestinian right to self-determination was included in the communique: "[T]he people concerned should be entitled to their lawful rights." This joint communique opened the way for Japan to vote for General Assembly Resolution 2792D in December 1971, which was Japan's first public recognition of the right of the Palestinian people to national self-determination.

At this time there was growing pro-Arab sentiment among Japan's political left. To the leftists who opposed the United States–Japan Security Treaty, the Arab–Israeli conflict was taken to be the best example of "American imperialism." The left made use of public sympathy toward the Palestinians for the purpose of getting rid of American influence in Japan. From this segment came the anti-imperialism squad—the so-called United Red Army, known as the Japanese Red Army—which initiated an indiscriminate attack at Lod International Airport in 1972.

For a majority of the Japanese population, the Arab–Israeli conflict began with the first oil shock of 1973, when they suddenly realized that Middle East politics directly affected their economic life. As is clear from a statement by Chief Cabinet Secretary Susumu Nikaido, 1973 was "the turning point in Japan's Middle East policy." Japan was prompt in reaffirming its position to support rights of the Palestinian people for self-determination and stressed the demand for the withdrawal of Israeli forces from all territories occupied in the 1967 war. Moreover, Japan took an unusually severe stance toward Israel by stating, "[T]he government of Japan will continue to observe the situation in the Middle East with grave concern, and depending on further developments, may have to reconsider its policy toward Israel."

It is clear from this statement that the government of Japan had departed from balanced diplomacy at Israel's expense. The departure was an incumbent choice for Japan, whose principal Middle East policy objective was a stable supply of oil. By 1972, 81.6 percent of Japan's oil came from the Middle East. Japan's survival was dependent on the Middle East. The dialogue between Prime Minister Tanaka and U.S. secretary of state Henry Kissinger* prior to Nikaido's statement failed because the United States could not assure an alternative stable supply of oil to Japan if it was deprived of oil from the Middle East.

The basic Japanese position toward the Arab–Israeli problem formulated at this time is still valid today: (1) Peace in the Middle East should be established through negotiations based on Security Council Resolutions 242 and 338,* which call for (a) Israeli withdrawal from all territories occupied since 1967; (b) recognition of the right of national self-determination for the Palestinian people, including the right to establish an independent state; and (c) recognition of the right of Israel to exist; (2) the Palestine Liberation Organization* (PLO) is the representative of the Palestinian people; and (3) Japan will work vigorously to assist the peace efforts of the relevant parties.

In 1973, Japan sent two special envoys to the Middle East and North Africa for the purpose of constructing new relations with Middle Eastern countries. The following year, Japan also voted for the UN resolution to invite the PLO to the General Assembly. Japan's relations with the PLO were established in 1976 by the visit of PLO political bureau chief Farouq Kaddoumi.* This visit led to the opening of the PLO's Tokyo office the following year. Japan's relation with the PLO reached its highest point when PLO chairman Yasser Arafat* visited Japan in 1981. Even though that visit was not an official invitation, Arafat met Prime Minister Suzuki and other top-level government officials, making Japan's relations with the Middle East unique among other Organization for Economic Cooperation and Development (OECD) countries.

In the field of economic assistance, growth in the amount of Japan's Official Development Assistance (ODA) to the Middle East was remarkable. During the period 1970–78, ODA to the Middle East grew twenty-seven times to $339.8 million. In addition, Japan's aid to Palestinian refugees through the United Nations Relief and Works Agency (UNRWA) grew nine times between 1970 and 1980. Due to these efforts, Japan could survive bad years following the oil shock. But in terms of Arab–Israeli peace, almost nothing has been done.

This Arab-oriented Middle East policy continued for about a decade. But as both the price and supply of oil became stable and constant, Japan shifted its Middle East policy back to its original "all direction" diplomacy. Beginning from the mid-1980s, Japan moved to restore relations with Israel. The 1984 visit of Kimche, the director general of the Israeli Ministry of Foreign Affairs, resulted in the formation of an Israeli–Japan Parliamentary Friendship League. The visit of a group of Japanese members of Parliament to Israel and the visit of Israeli prime minister Shamir* to Japan in 1985 opened a new age in Japan–Israel relations. Foreign Minister Uno's visit to Israel in 1988 marked the first official visit by a member of the Japanese government. Following the visit of a research group organized by the Japan Federation of Economic Organizations (Keidanren), the amount of trade between the two countries grew by 3.6 times to $1.1 billion during the 1980s.

At the same time, Japan began to expand its relations with the Palestinians by providing new forms of aid. Apart from continuing to financially support

UNRWA's activities, Japan began to provide technical assistance to the Palestinian refugees through the Japanese International Cooperation Agency (JICA). Besides, Japan took a new approach to the Palestinian issue by establishing a Japan–Palestinian Development Fund within the United Nations Development Program (UNDP) for the purpose of providing aid to the people living in the West Bank* and Gaza Strip.*

In an effort to expand Japan's diplomatic presence in the Middle East, Take Shita's Cabinet in the mid-1980s recognized the need to return to a policy of balanced diplomacy. This sharply contrasted with the period before 1973. In the 1980s, the "policy of balance" was meant to support Japan's active participation in diplomatic efforts to solve disputes. As the Japanese government sought to adopt an independent approach to the Arab–Israeli dispute, there was a growing perception within the government that the same level of commitment to both Israel and Arab states was the necessary step toward achieving general peace in the region. Japan applied the same diplomatic concept during the Iran–Iraq* War by keeping both diplomatic channels open, despite the fact that the United States and other Western nations openly sided with Iraq. Japan's financial aid to Syria,* which amounted to 12 percent of the total ODA contribution to the entire Middle East during 1986 and 1989, shows, again, Japan's desire to have strong relations with all of the parties in the Middle East.

Soon after the end of the 1991 Gulf War,* Foreign Minister Nakayama paid a second official visit to Israel. There, he spent some time visiting the West Bank and East Jerusalem* and discussing with Palestinian representatives possible Japanese aid to the region. Following this visit, the Japanese government for the first time decided to provide funding to Japanese nongovernmental-organizations (NGOs) to help the Palestinians in Lebanon* and the West Bank.

Meanwhile, as a part of its efforts to establish confidence among parties to the peace process, Japan made efforts during the London Summit meeting in 1991 to remove obstacles to Middle East peace by calling for suspension of the Arab boycott* as well as the suspension of the Israeli policy of building settlements* in the occupied territories. Japan strongly supported the 1991 UN General Assembly resolution to revoke the 1975 resolution equating Zionism with racism.* This "balanced commitment" has been Japan's new approach to the Middle East question from the mid-1980s onward.

Japan's active participation in the multilateral peace talks initiated by the United States at the Madrid Peace Conference in 1991* marks a new era of Japan's commitment to Middle East peace. Among the five groups of multilateral talks,* Japan now chairs the section on environment and is the co-organizer of the sections on regional economic development, water resources, and refugees with the United States and the European Community (EC). After Israel and the PLO officially recognized each other, Japan wasted little time in announcing financial support for the Gaza–Jericho First* scheme, contributing $200 million for the first two years. In addition, Japan is planning to actively support regional economic development. Japan's commitment to the Arab–Israeli peace process, in a real sense, is a continuing process.

For further information see: Kunio Katakura and Motoko Katakura, *Japan and the Middle East* (Tokyo: Middle East Institute of Japan, 1991); Ronald A. Morse, ed., *Japan and the Middle East in Alliance Politics* (Washington, DC: Wilson Center, 1985); Eisuke Naramoto, ''Japanese Perceptions on the Arab–Israeli Conflict,'' *Journal of Palestine Studies* 20 (Spring 1991):79–88; Sanford R. Silverburg and Bernard Reich, *Asian States' Relations with the Middle East and North Africa: A Bibliography, 1950–1993* (Metuchen, NJ: Scarecrow Press, 1994); Michael M. Yoshitsu, *Caught in the Middle East: Japan's Diplomacy in Transition* (Lexington, MA: Lexington Books, 1984).

Kohei Hashimoto

JARRING MISSION. On November 22, 1967, the United Nations (UN) Security Council unanimously adopted Resolution 242,* submitted by the United Kingdom, containing the principles for a just and lasting peace in the Middle East and providing for the appointment of a United Nations special representative to work toward that end. This established the framework for the Jarring mission in its effort to achieve peace in the Arab–Israeli conflict following the Six Day War* of 1967.

On November 23, 1967, UN secretary-general U Thant* informed the Security Council that Ambassador Gunnar V. Jarring of Sweden has been invited and had agreed to accept the appointment as special representative and would be ''proceeding to the Middle East very soon.''

At the time of his appointment, Jarring was serving as ambassador of Sweden to the Soviet Union. Prior to that post, Ambassador Jarring served at various times as Swedish minister to India, Ceylon, Iran, Iraq,* and Pakistan. He was director of the Political Division of the Swedish Ministry of Foreign Affairs from 1953 to 1956 and permanent representative of Sweden to the United Nations from 1956 to 1958, during which time he served on the Security Council from 1957 to 1958. After leaving the United Nations, Ambassador Jarring served for a period as Swedish ambassador to the United States.

Following his appointment and after consultation with the parties concerned and with the concurrence of the government of Cyprus, Jarring established the headquarters of the United Nations Middle East Mission (as his effort was officially called) in Cyprus. From there he began a round of visits in the Middle East. From the outset there was no consultation with the Syrian* government, which refused to accept Resolution 242 and the Jarring mission.

From this beginning, Jarring continued to develop and maintain contacts with Lebanon,* Israel, Jordan,* and Egypt* (the United Arab Republic* [UAR])— the four governments concerned—although discussions with Israel, Egypt, and Jordan predominated. During the year following the inauguration of his mission, Jarring held numerous meetings with the parties to the dispute in an effort to achieve some progress.

Mahmoud Riad,* Egypt's foreign minister, told Jarring on March 7, 1968, during the envoy's visit to Cairo that Egypt would refuse to meet with the Israelis in Cyprus then and in the future to discuss possible peace. Israel had accepted a Jarring proposal to meet, and Jordan had not formally responded by the time of Egypt's rejection. Despite the Egyptian rejection, Jarring pursued his efforts through the first four months of 1968. In April 1968, Jarring proposed to the Middle Eastern states that the talks be moved to New York rather than Cyprus as originally proposed.

Egypt, Israel, and Jordan accepted the proposal to mediate based on United Nations Security Council Resolution 242. Israel insisted on direct talks with the Arab states while Egypt would accept only indirect negotiations. U.S. president Lyndon Johnson* sent Egyptian president Gamal Abdul Nasser* a message on May 13, 1968, urging him to take advantage of the opportunity for peace. By the time the Jarring mission had reached this point, the United Nations envoy had held forty-one meetings with Israeli and Arab leaders in Amman, Cairo, and Jerusalem.*

On January 29, 1969, Jarring returned to United Nations headquarters in New York and, following a series of meetings with the permanent representatives of the disputants and the representatives of other member states, concluded that his best contribution to breaking the deadlock would be to submit a series of questions to the parties, designed to elicit their attitude toward Resolution 242.

Jarring had hoped that their responses might show some encouraging features enabling him to invite the parties for a series of meetings. But they generally restated past positions and showed serious divergences between the Arab states and Israel. Jarring concluded that he had exhausted the moves he could usefully make at that time and returned to his post in Moscow. The War of Attrition* intervened to preclude effective progress, and the Jarring mission was stalled.

The mission was reactivated on January 5, 1971. Jarring renewed discussions with the parties at United Nations headquarters in New York.

Exchanges of views and meetings with the parties led Ambassador Jarring to launch his February 1971 initiative. Jarring sought to break the imminent deadlock by seeking parallel and simultaneous prior commitments from Israel and Egypt on the major issues in dispute and the prerequisites of a settlement between them. With this in mind, on February 8, 1971, he handed identical aide-mémoires to the representatives of Egypt (UAR) and Israel requesting that they should make commitments to him.

The replies of February 1971 reflected the wide gaps between the positions of the parties. With these apparent divergences on the question of Israeli withdrawal, the Jarring mission had reached an impasse.

Although Jarring resumed discussions with the parties in New York and on later visits to Cairo, Amman, and Jerusalem in January 1972, no progress was made, and the mission remained deadlocked and in suspended animation.

For further information see: Bernard Reich, "The Jarring Mission and the Search for Peace in the Middle East," *Wiener Library Bulletin* 26 (1972):13–20.

Joseph E. Goldberg

JERICHO. Located northwest of the northern end of the Dead Sea.* Ancient Jericho is considered by some to be the oldest city in the world—dating back to 7,000 B.C. It is mentioned in the Bible and was conquered by the Israelites led by Joshua when they entered the Land of Canaan.* The city was built and rebuilt throughout the centuries.

Jericho, along with the Gaza Strip,* was turned over by Israel to the Palestine Liberation Organization* (PLO) after their negotiations in Oslo* and the signing of the Declaration of Principles* in Washington in September 1993.

JERICHO MISSILE. The Jericho I and II missiles are Israeli-produced short- and intermediate-range, surface-to-surface ballistic missiles. Israeli development of the Jericho missile was originally conducted in cooperation with the French Dassault Company beginning in 1963. The basic design of these missiles was based on Dassault's MD-600 missile.

The Jericho I is believed to have a range of over 300 miles and to be armed with a conventional, high-explosive warhead. The Jericho I had its first flight test in 1967 and is believed to have entered service in 1973.

The Jericho II is Israel's most advanced ballistic missile. It is a two-stage missile capable of ranges of over 940 miles. Reportedly, the Jericho II can carry a 1,430-pound payload with either a conventional, high-explosive warhead, a chemical warhead, or a nuclear warhead. It is believed that the Jericho II has an internal inertial navigational guidance system with an additional terminal guidance system. Development of the Jericho II ballistic missile began in the mid-1970s with Israel Aircraft Industries as the prime contractor. First test flights for the Jericho II started in 1986.

Both the Jericho I and Jericho II are said to be road-mobile, though a number of reports also indicate that the missiles are located in caves in the Negev Desert and are launched from railroad flatcars.

Israel views its Jericho missile systems and the devastating warheads that they may carry as a deterrent and a guarantee for its survival. As of 1995, the Jericho missile systems had not been tested in combat, although there are reports that Israel's nuclear forces, of which the Jericho missile systems are believed to be a part, were on alert during the Yom Kippur War* and the Persian Gulf War* of 1991. During the latter war, it was reported that an American reconnaissance satellite spotted the deployment of Jericho II launchers at a military base in the Negev Desert near Dimona, Israel's atomic research facility, and at a test facility south of Tel Aviv.

With the knowledge gained with its Shavit II space launch system, Israel may now have the technology to extend the range of its Jericho missiles, or a follow-on system, to intercontinental ranges.

For further information see: W. Seth Carus, *Ballistic Missiles in the Third World: Threat and Response* (New York: Praeger, 1990); Seymour M. Hersh, *The Samson Option: Israel's Nuclear Arsenal and American Foreign Policy* (New York: Random House,

1991); Martin S. Navias, *Going Ballistic: The Build-Up of Missiles in the Middle East* (London: Brassey's, 1993).

Jon J. Peterson and Stephen H. Gotowicki

JERUSALEM. According to Jewish tradition, the name Jerusalem (Yerushalayim) was derived from two Hebrew words: *ir* (city) and *shalom* (peace). Over the ages it has been referred to by other names, including God's city, the city of justice, the faithful city, and the Holy City. For Muslims, Jerusalem is al-Quds (the Holy One).

Jerusalem is Israel's largest city and its declared capital. It is a city holy to Jews, Christians, and Muslims. Part III of the United Nations partition plan* for Palestine* adopted on November 29, 1947, dealt with the status of Jerusalem and recommended that the city be established as a *corpus separatum,** an international city to be governed by a distinct international regime administered by the United Nations Trusteeship Council. Jerusalem's city limits included Bethlehem* to the south, Ein Kerem to the west, Abu Dis to the east, and Shu'fat to the north. A governor was to be appointed by the Trusteeship Council, but the administration of the city and local powers were to be granted to autonomous segments of the existing population. Jerusalem was to be a demilitarized area, and its security was to be entrusted to a specially created police force composed of members recruited from outside Palestine. The United Nations Trusteeship Council was to review the governance of Jerusalem after ten years.

Jerusalem is not specifically mentioned in Israel's Declaration of the Establishment of the State. The document does state, however, that Israel will "safeguard the Holy Places of all religions." After the independence of Israel and the ensuing War of Independence,* Jordanian* forces controlled the eastern sections of the city, and Israel controlled the western sections. An Armistice Agreement* signed in 1949 between Israel and Jordan agreed that there would be free access to the holy places of Jerusalem by all people and that the Jewish institutions located on Mount Scopus* (Hebrew University and the Hadassah Hospital) could reopen. These obligations were not fulfilled by the Jordanian government. Jordan controlled East Jerusalem,* including the walled Old City,* and Israel controlled West Jerusalem,* the New City, after the war.

West Jerusalem is the modern part of the city. The 1948 Israeli Areas of Jurisdiction and Powers Ordinance provided that any part of Palestine designated by the minister of defense under the occupation of the Israel Defense Forces would come under Israeli law. East Jerusalem includes the walled Old City, the site of many ancient holy places.

Jews consider Jerusalem a Holy City because it was their political and religious center in biblical times. About 1000 B.C. King David made Jerusalem the capital of the united Israelite tribes. David's son, King Solomon, built the first Temple of the Jews in the city. The Western Wall* or Wailing Wall is all that remains of the Temple area and remains a holy site for Jews. Jerusalem served as the capital city of the Jewish people for 1,065 years.

Christians consider Jerusalem holy because Jesus was crucified there, and many events in his life took place in the city. Among the sacred sites for the Christians is the Church of the Holy Sepulcher, believed to stand on the hill of Calvary, or Golgotha, where Jesus was crucified and buried. The church there is shared by several Christian sects. During the Ottoman period, a "status quo" arrangement was accepted that allows Christians authority over their holy places. It is still in force.

For Muslims, the Prophet Mohammed's revelation "perfected" the teachings of both Judaism and Christianity. As such, the holiness of Jerusalem to the other faiths was introduced to Islam as well. The city is not mentioned by name in the Koran. In the Koran it states: "Praise be to Allah who brought his servant at night from the Holy Mosque to the Remote Mosque, the precincts of which we have blessed" (Sura 17:1). This has been interpreted to mean that the Prophet Mohammed was transported from Mecca to Jerusalem, although there is also an interpretation that the Remote Mosque refers to heaven. Jerusalem is now held to be Islam's third holiest city, after Mecca and Medina, located in Saudi Arabia. Muslims believe that the Prophet Mohammed, the last prophet of Islam, ascended to heaven from Jerusalem. He came to the Temple Mount,* where the Temple* of Solomon was built, and placed his foot on a rock. This is the site where the Dome of the Rock* (mosque of Omar) was completed in 691 and is near the Western Wall. The rock is believed in Jewish tradition to be where Abraham prepared to sacrifice his son Isaac as God commanded. The al-Aksa Mosque,* the Dome of the Rock, and the Wall of al-Buraq (the Temple Wall) are enclosed in an area known as Haram al-Sharif* (the Noble Enclosure).

Jerusalem was a focus of the Christian Crusaders, who captured the city in 1099 and ruled it until Saladin (Salah a-Din) recaptured it in 1187, restoring it to Muslim control.

From 1952 to 1967, the question of Jerusalem was conspicuous only by its absence from discussion in the United Nations. During those fifteen years, the matter was never referred to in the General Assembly. Moreover, on only three occasions has the subject been mentioned in the Security Council: in 1957, when there was some discussion of the status of certain areas lying between the Israeli- and Jordanian-held parts of Jerusalem; in 1958, when there was a brief reference to the question of Mount Scopus; and in 1965, when Jordan filed a complaint about a proposed Israeli Independence Day Parade to be held in Jerusalem but did not request a meeting of the Security Council. There was no discussion of internationalizing Jerusalem or protecting the holy places.

Israel captured the Jordanian-controlled area of Jerusalem in the Six Day War* of 1967. The Israeli Knesset* passed the Law and Administration Ordinance (Amendment No. 11) Law, 1967, which extended its law, jurisdiction, and administration to areas that were previously part of the British Mandate.* Administrative and municipal integration of Jerusalem was the consequence. Prime Minister Menachem Begin* stated in 1978 that "Jerusalem is one city, indivisible, the Capital of the State of Israel," whereas Egyptian president Anwar Sadat* stated at the same time that "Arab Jerusalem is an integral part of the West Bank*" and "should be under Arab sovereignty." President Sadat did agree that the municipal functions of the city should not be separated.

On July 30, 1980, the Knesset passed the Basic Law: Jerusalem, Capital of Israel, 5740-1980. It declared:

Jerusalem united in its entirety is the capital of Israel. Jerusalem is the seat of the President of the State, the Knesset, the Government and the Supreme Court. The Holy Places shall be protected from desecration and any other violation and from anything likely to violate the freedom of access of the members of the different religions to the places sacred to them or their feelings with regard to those places.

It also provided that the government would work for the development and prosperity of the city and the welfare of its inhabitants and would give special priority to this activity.

In the Madrid Peace Conference* convened in October 1991, Israel insisted that Jerusalem should not be discussed, nor should any of Jerusalem's Palestinian inhabitants participate in the joint Jordanian–Palestinian delegation. The formal invitation from the United States and the Soviet Union to Madrid did not mention Jerusalem. The United States later declared in a letter of assurances to the Palestinians that in its view Jerusalem should never again be divided, that its final status should be determined through negotiations, and that the lack of Jerusalemites from the delegation would not endanger the claims of the Palestinians to Jerusalem. The United States also stated that it did not recognize the annexation of East Jerusalem by Israel. Israel did allow Faisal al-Husseini,* a resident of Jerusalem, to participate in the Palestinian delegation.

The Declaration of Principles* (DOP) signed by Israel and the Palestine Liberation Organization* on September 13, 1993, had two provisions concerning Jerusalem: Palestinians living in Jerusalem will have a right to participate in the election process (Annex 1), and the status of Jerusalem is a subject not for interim arrangements but is to be left for later discussions on a permanent settlement (Article V, 3). In the subsequent negotiations to implement the DOP and in the actions of the parties, Jerusalem remained a major issue of controversy and difficulty, suggesting that its historical status as the focal point of regional and international attention would continue to force it to the center of the negotiations to achieve a comprehensive Arab–Israeli peace.

For further information see: M. A. Aamiry, *Jerusalem: Arab Origins and Heritage* (London: Longman, 1978); H. Eugene Bovis, *The Jerusalem Question, 1917–1968* (Stanford, CA: Hoover Institution Press, 1971); Henry Cattan, *Jerusalem* (London: Croom Helm, 1981); Hassan bin Talal, *A Study on Jerusalem* (London: Longman, 1979); Elihu Lauterpacht, *Jerusalem and the Holy Places* (London: Geerings of Ashford, 1968); Adnan Abu Odeh, "Two Capitals in an Undivided Jerusalem," *Foreign Affairs* 71 (Spring 1992):183–88; Richard H. Pfaff, *Jerusalem: Keystone of an Arab–Israeli Settlement* (Washington, DC: American Enterprise Institute for Public Policy Research, 1969); A. L. Tibawi, *Jerusalem: Its Place in Islam and Arab History* (Beirut: Institute for Palestine

Studies, 1969); U.S. House of Representatives, Committee on Foreign Affairs, *Hearings: Jerusalem: The Future of the Holy City for Three Monotheisms,* 92nd Congress, 1st Session, July 1971; Evan M. Wilson, *Jerusalem: Key to Peace* (Washington, DC: Middle East Institute, 1970).

JERUSALEM (Jewish Quarter of the Old City). During the three and a half centuries of Roman conquest and domination of Jerusalem, Jews were not permitted to enter the city. However, under Byzantine rule, Jews began to trickle back, and a more general revival of the Jewish community in the city began in earnest upon the arrival of the Arabs.

The revival of the Jewish community, however, once again was terminated with the invasion of the Crusaders. Within a short period, the Jewish community in Palestine was reduced to a few thousand, largely by slaughter. When the Crusaders were expelled by Saladin, and, later, when Ottoman control of the city was established under Sultan Suleiman, the Jewish community of Jerusalem again briefly revived. However, the overwhelming poverty of the scholars and the rise of Safed as a religious and spiritual center, limited the size of the Jewish community.

In the century that followed Sultan Suleiman, local Turkish rulers began to actively hinder the consolidation of the city's Jewish population. By 1553, the number of Jews in the city had dropped to about 1,000.

After Safed's decline at the end of the sixteenth century, the Jewish community of Jerusalem again began a shallow revival, mostly due to the efforts of Bezalel Ashkenazi, who had come to Jerusalem from Egypt.* A stream of immigrants, mostly from Italy, the Maghreb, and Arabized Jews, wandered to Jerusalem in the early 1600s. This revival encountered a setback under the repressive regime of Governor Muhammad ibn Faoruk, which began in 1625, but the shortness of his tenure allowed the community to recover quickly. Toward the end of the seventeenth century, Jerusalem had replaced Safed as the spiritual center of the Kabbalist movement of mystics. By the end of the seventeenth century, there were as many as 1,200 Jews, one-sixth of whom were Ashkenazi, in Jerusalem. This exceeded the number allowed to live there under the Turkish quota and, therefore, required a system of bribery to stave off limited expulsion.

In 1700, an immigration of 500 Sabbatean Jews from Poland settled in Jerusalem and began to establish a community around a courtyard that was later the site of the Hurvah Synagogue, but their abrasive behavior and growing financial indebtedness to the Arabs led to friction with older Jewish residents in the city and the Arabs. In 1720, Arabs broke into the Hurvah Synagogue and burned the Torah scrolls. They also seized the site and barred Jews from reestablishing the synagogue for nearly 100 years.

In the mid-1700s, Constantinople began to encourage a revival of the city as a whole, which benefited the Jewish community. Economic improvements attracted more immigrants from Europe, and a number of prominent yeshivas were established. Wealthy Jews from all parts of the Diaspora* began to take an active interest in these religious seats of learning and began to contribute to the establishment of more yeshivot and the maintenance of those already existing. Much of the work of Jerusalem scholars began also to be published across the Mediterranean. By the later part of the century, about 10,000 Jews may have been living in Jerusalem.

At the end of the eighteenth century, there was another decline in Jerusalem's Jewish population, largely as a result of the general decline of Jerusalem's status, the decay of the Ottoman Empire,* and the stagnation that befell the more distant provinces of the empire. A series of severe plagues and natural disasters also contributed to the decline. Within years, the Jewish community was again reduced to perhaps as few as 2,000, according to a visiting Dutch Jew, and the entire Jewish population of Palestine as a whole had declined to 6,000.

The modern revival of Jerusalem's Jewish community began in the early part of the 1800s and is linked to the intrusion of outside European powers. In 1840, the Europeans imposed on the Turks a reasserting of the European Capitulations throughout the empire. The Capitulations agreement stipulated that resident European nationals held a legal and financial immunity under the protection of their respective consuls. Also in 1840, Moses Montefiore, Cremieux, and Munk, after the blood libel pogroms in Damascus, negotiated an understanding with the sultan to protect the Jews and appoint a chief rabbi (Hakham Bakshi) of Palestine* to reside in Jerusalem. In the 1840s, new clinics were established in the Jewish Quarter, and the first printing presses were established. By 1854, the Rothschild Hospital was opened, to be followed within a year by the Bikkur Holim Hospital. The series of agreements stimulated Jewish immigration, and, by 1856, the Jewish population of Palestine as a whole had jumped to 9,000 from only 5,000 in 1840. In 1864, an Anglo-Turkish understanding, driven, in part, by the growing romantic-nationalist sympathy for the plight of the Jews by many in the British elite, such as Lord Byron and George Eliot, extended the legal rights to all Jewish residents as well. By 1865, more than half of the Old City's 18,000 residents were Jews, according to British consul reporting.

Also by 1860, Moses Montefiore had established the first settlement of Jews outside the walls, in the area that came to be known as Yemin Moshe. Ironically, the growth of the Jewish city beyond the walls led to a slowing, but not stopping, of the growth of the Jewish community within the walls, where conditions remained unsanitary and cramped. In fact, these conditions, widespread throughout the walled city, led to a severe plague in 1864, claiming hundreds of victims.

Still, Jerusalem as a whole (new and walled cities) prospered in the latter half of the century, and by 1900, 45,000 people lived in Jerusalem, of whom more than 28,000 were Jews, and by 1912, 70,000 people lived in the city, of whom more than 45,000 were Jews. During World War I, the city again suffered major economic setbacks, and the population as a whole declined to 55,000 on the eve of General Allenby's entry. In 1922, the population had rebounded to 62,000, of whom 33,000 were Jews.

Increasing political tensions between Jews and Arabs led to riots, some of them severe, by 1920. While the Jewish population of the New City expanded during the following period, the Old City,* especially after the even more severe riots in 1926, began to decline. In late August 1929, another severe riot erupted against the Jews, this time spreading over all Palestine. Jewish merchants, feeling unprotected in the close confines of the Old City, began to move their shops to the New City. This process accelerated after the outbreak of the Arab uprising in 1936, especially because the Old City had become one of the focal points for organizing Arab resistance to the British government.

After partition,* as the British began disengaging from the country, the Jews of Jerusalem as a whole and the Jewish Quarter in particular came under siege. The British continued to provide safe transport of supplies to the Old City from the New City, but as they continued the gradual withdrawal, they pressed the Jewish community within the Old City to evacuate. The Haganah,* in response, ordered that no Jew be allowed to leave the Old City, at the same time that the British instigated a series of provocations against Jews, some of which resulted in fatalities, to try to frighten the Jewish population to leave. By the time the British left Jerusalem on May 13, 1948, 150 Jewish fighters and about 1,700 Jewish inhabitants remained in the Old City. The siege of the Old City tightened as a result of Britain's complete withdrawal from Palestine, the declaration of the state of Israel, and the invasion of Palestine by Arab armies on May 14–15. After a series of Arab offensives that, by May 16, led to Israel's withdrawal from several New City neighborhoods, such as Neve Yaakov and Atarot, the battle concentrated on the Old City, the Jewish population of which faced dehydration and starvation. Sanitary services had been cut off, and stores were shut down. The city had been reduced in size to about eleven fortifications.

The declaration of independence of Israel also marked the beginning of continuous artillery barrages of the Jewish Quarter of the Old City. By May 17, Etzel* and Haganah forces inside the walled city reported that the territory had begun to fall, meter by meter. Attempts to penetrate the Old City to send reinforcements were only partially successful. On May 28, the Jewish Quarter of Jerusalem finally surrendered to the Jordanian Arab Legion,* and its defenders were taken captive. After the new Israel Defense Forces* (IDF) began to accumulate strength in the last moments before the second cease-fire on July 17, 1948, they tried one last time to recapture the Jewish Quarter of the Old City in Operation Kedem. It failed, and the city remained divided, leaving the Old City without Jews for the first time in 1,500 years. The Jordanian Legion also razed all buildings in the Jewish Quarter.

This division lasted until June 7, 1967, when, after repeated attempts on June 5 and 6, the IDF entered the Lion's Gate near the Temple Mount* and captured the Old City as part of its overall capture of the entire West Bank.* The city was officially reunited on June 28, 1967, and the reconstruction of the Jewish Quarter began. The Jewish Quarter of the Old City now hosts a vibrant community.

David Wurmser

JERUSALEM PROGRAM. The central issue debated at the twenty-third Zionist Congress,* which met in Jerusalem* from August 14 to 30, 1951, was the status of the Zionist movement after the establishment of Israel. The Basle Program* no longer corresponded with the reality of the post-1948 situation and was replaced by the Jerusalem Program. Its central clause stated, "The task of Zionism is the consolidation of the State of Israel, the ingathering of the exiles in Eretz Israel and the fostering of the unity of the Jewish people." In the twenty-seventh congress, held in Jerusalem June 9 to 19, 1968, the Jerusalem Program was modified, and additional paragraphs, focusing on the goals of Zionism, were added to it. Among these were references to the unity of the Jewish people, the centrality of Israel in the life of the Jewish people, and the ingathering of the Jewish people in its historic homeland through aliyah from all lands. The principles of the Jerusalem Program reconfirmed the relationship among Israel, Zionism, and the Jewish people. It read:

The aims of Zionism are: The Unity of the Jewish People and the centrality of Israel in its life; the ingathering of the Jewish People in its historic homeland, Eretz Yisrael, through aliya from all lands; the strengthening of the State of Israel, founded on the Prophetic ideals of justice and peace; the preservation of the identity of the Jewish People through the fostering of Jewish and Hebrew education and of Jewish spiritual and cultural values; the protection of Jewish rights everywhere.

Joseph E. Goldberg

JEWISH AGENCY (Jewish Agency for Palestine, Jewish Agency for Israel). Established in the 1920s under the terms of the Palestine Mandate* to advise and cooperate with the British authorities in the task of establishing the Jewish National Home* in Palestine.* Article 4 of the Mandate for Palestine provided for the recognition of an appropriate "Jewish Agency" as a "public body for the purpose of advising and cooperating with the Administration of Palestine in such economic, social and other matters as may affect the establishment of the Jewish National Home and the interests of the Jewish population in Palestine, and subject always to the control of the Administration, to assist and take part in the development of the country." Article 6 of the Mandate stipulated that the British administration of Palestine should, "in cooperation with the Jewish Agency," encourage settlement by Jews on the land. Article 11 provided that the administration might arrange with the Jewish Agency "to construct or operate, upon fair and equitable terms, any public works, services and utilities, and to develop any of the natural resources of the country, insofar as these matters are not directly undertaken by the Administration." The Mandate itself recognized the World Zionist Organization* (WZO) as such Jewish Agency (Article 4) and directed the WZO to "take steps in consultation with His Britannic Majesty's Government to secure the cooperation of all Jews who are willing to assist in the establishment of the Jewish National Home.'' The WZO, on its part, undertook to take steps to secure such cooperation.

The Zionist Organization performed its functions until a Jewish Agency for Palestine (which included non-Zionist and Zionist Jews) was formally constituted in 1929. It provided the apparatus for worldwide Jewish participation in the building of the Jewish home in Palestine. The Jewish Agency worked with the government of the Yishuv* and particularly with the Vaad Leumi. Generally, the agency promoted immigration, settlement, and economic development and mobilized support for Jewish efforts in Palestine. Its political department acted as the ''foreign ministry'' of the quasi government in Palestine. It negotiated with the Palestine government and Great Britain,* and it represented the cause of the Jewish National Home before appropriate organs of the League of Nations and the United Nations. The Jewish Agency's officials, along with those of the Vaad Leumi and other organs of the Yishuv, provided Israel's ministries with a trained core of civil servants and political leaders. David Ben-Gurion,* who served as Israel's first prime minister and minister of defense, was chairman of the Executive of the Jewish Agency, and Moshe Shertok (later Sharett),* was a director of the agency's political department. One of the main tasks of the Jewish Agency during the period of the British administration of Palestine was to represent the Zionist movement and world Jewry at large before the Mandatory government, the League of Nations, and the British government in London. It also served as part of the governing structure of the Yishuv. It promoted Zionism,* encouraged and facilitated immigration, raised funds, engaged in social-welfare activities, promoted Jewish culture, developed economic enterprises, and formulated domestic and external policies for the Jewish community.

It was realized long before May 15, 1948, that the future independent and sovereign Jewish state would be fully responsible for the conduct of its domestic and foreign affairs and that some functions hitherto exercised by the Jewish Agency would have to be transferred to the state. On the other hand, it was obvious that the state would not, and could not, deal with all matters that had been in the purview of the Jewish Agency (in particular, immigration, absorption of immigrants, and settlement), not only for financial reasons but also because they were a global Jewish responsibility and not an internal affair of Israel. It was believed that the Jewish Agency would be needed to express the partnership of the Jewish people all over the world with Israel in the historic enterprise of building the state and to channel and utilize properly the aid that was expected and forthcoming from Diaspora* Jewry.

The Jewish Agency/World Zionist Organization, even though nongovernmental, performs functions instrumental to Zionism and important to the government's activities; its personnel often move to and from positions of responsibility within the government. Upon independence, the government of Israel began to assume many of the functions previously performed by this institution and formalized its relationship with it through legislation and administrative decisions. The Jewish Agency today is responsible for the organization of Jewish immigration to Israel; the reception, assistance, and settlement of immigrants; care of children; and aid to cultural projects and institutions of higher learning. It fosters Hebrew education and culture in the Diaspora, guides and assists Zionist youth movements, and organizes the work of the Jewish people in support of Israel.

The mutual relations of the state and the Jewish Agency were put on a firm legal basis by the law on the Status of the World Zionist Organization—Jewish Agency of 5713 (1952), Article 4 of which declares: "The State of Israel recognized the WZO as the authorized agency that will continue to operate in the State of Israel for the development and settlement of the country, the absorption of immigrants from the diaspora and the coordination of the activities in Israel of Jewish institutions and organizations active in those fields." After the Six Day War* of 1967, it was suggested that while the WZO–Jewish Agency should remain in charge of immigration, the absorption and integration of immigrants should become largely a responsibility of the government. A new Ministry for the Absorption of Immigrants was established.

For further information see: Ernest Stock, *Beyond Partnership: The Jewish Agency and the Diaspora, 1959–1971* (New York: Herzl Press, 1992).

JEWISH NATIONAL FUND (Keren Kayemet le Israel). Various organizations and units were created to carry on the work of the World Zionist Organization,* including the Jewish National Fund (JNF), founded in 1901 at the Fifth Zionist Congress and charged with land purchase and development in Palestine.* It now focuses on afforestation and reclamation of land in Israel. In 1960, the Knesset* passed the Israel Land Administration Act, which transferred ownership of the land owned by the Keren Kayemet to the state of Israel.

For further information see: Henriette Hannah Bodenheimer, "The Status of the Keren Kayemeth: A Study of Their Origin, Based on the Known as well as Hitherto Unpublished Sources," in *Herzl Year Book* (New York: Herzl Press, 1964–65), pp. 153–81; Ira Hirschmann, *The Awakening: The Story of the Jewish National Fund* (New York: Shengold, 1981).

JEWISH NATIONAL HOME. The phrase was first used by participants at the first World Zionist Congress, in Basle, Switzerland, in August 1897, which created the World Zionist Organization* (WZO). The official Basle Program* stated that the underlying goal of Zionism was the establishment of "a home for the Jewish people in Palestine* secured under public law." It was understood in this context that a "national home" entailed a sovereign political entity, as Theodor Herzl* had argued in *Der Judenstaat**: "Let sovereignty be granted us over a portion of the globe large enough to satisfy the rightful requirements of a nation."

The phrase *national home* as used in the Balfour Declaration* to describe a political entity did not have any precedent in international law. The British declaration used the ambiguous term *national home* partly in an attempt to assuage the fears of prominent Jews in England as well as those of the non-Jewish inhabitants of Palestine. See also WHITE PAPER OF 1922.

Mark Daryl Erickson

JEWISH QUARTER OF JERUSALEM. See **JERUSALEM, JEWISH QUARTER OF THE OLD CITY.**

JEWISH QUESTION. The establishment of liberal democratic regimes in Europe in the nineteenth century gave hope to the Jews that they could live as a minority, securely and with dignity as full citizens in their respective countries while still being faithful to their religious traditions. However, by the end of the nineteenth century, many European Jews were convinced that the promises of equality and dignity for Jews would not be fulfilled. Writing in 1882, Leon Pinsker, an early political Zionist, published a pamphlet in Berlin, *Autoemancipation: A Warning of a Russian Jew to His Brethren,* which addressed the Jewish question. For Pinsker and later political Zionists,* the Jewish Question concerned the fact that Jews who constitute a distinct element in the midst of various nations cannot be assimilated. Because equality for Jews does not exist, Pinsker argued, neither can harmony, because a harmonious relationship between the Jew and the non-Jew requires full equality. Only when such equality exists can the Jewish Question be solved. Despite their distinctiveness, he wrote, the Jews fail to possess the attributes of a nation: a common language, customs, and land. The attributes of Jewish national character have not been formed because the Jews have not lived in one country. It is the Jewish misfortune that they do not desire their independence.

Theodor Herzl's* *Der Judenstaat** (*The Jewish State**) articulates the nature of the Jewish Question in terms similar to those of Pinsker. Jews who have lived in lands for over a century, he emphasized, are still viewed as aliens. ''Who belongs and who does not belong is decided by the majority; it is a question of power.'' Whether the Jew wishes to be a distinct nation or not is beside the question. ''We are a nation—the enemy makes us a nation whether we like it or not.'' The solution to the Jewish Question for Herzl was the establishment of a Jewish state.

From the formulation of the Jewish Question as an unbearable consequence of being dispersed from their land and the failure of the most tolerant states to provide a solution to the Jewish Question arose the idea and justification for political Zionism: the creation of a political movement by the Jews to reestablish a state of their own.

Joseph E. Goldberg

THE JEWISH STATE. See **DER JUDENSTAAT.**

JIBRIL, AHMED (b. Yazur, 1936/37?). He left his home area with his family in 1948 and moved to Jordan* and later Syria.* In Damascus, he attended the military college, and, in 1956, he became an officer in the Syrian army engineering corps. In 1958, Jibril was ousted from the Syrian army for having alleged Communist sympathies and for engaging in political activities, and he resettled in Cairo. During the 1960s, Jibril founded the National Front for the Liberation of Palestine* with the goal of destroying Israel. In 1967, Jibril joined with George Habash's* Popular Front for the Liberation of Palestine.* However, in 1968, he split with Habash and formed the Popular Front for the Liberation of Palestine—General Command* (PFLP—GC).

The PFLP—GC conducted numerous bomb attacks, guerrilla assaults, and suicide operations against Israel and Jewish targets worldwide. Jibril emphasized the use of high technology in terrorist operations and has sought to give the PFLP—GC a conventional military capability as a complement to its terror activities. He opposes those in the Palestinian camp who seek moderation with Israel and is against the peace process. His goal remains the destruction of Israel.

Jibril's group was linked to the bombing of Swiss Air flight 330 on February 21, 1970, which killed all forty-seven passengers and crew. Also on that day, a similar bomb exploded on an Austrian airline flight from Frankfurt to Vienna, but the plane was able to land safely. In 1972, an El Al flight from Rome to Tel Aviv was able to land after a bomb detonated on board. In 1982, Jibril captured three Israel Defense Force* reservists and traded them for 1,150 detainees held in Israel. In 1983, Jibril took part in a Syrian-sponsored rebellion of dissident Palestinian guerrillas against Arafat.* From 1984 to 1985 he joined the National Alliance and National Salvation Front of anti-Arafat groups in the Palestine Liberation Organization* (PLO), as well as non-PLO opponents of Arafat. In 1987, he and his group were suspended from the PLO. One of Jibril's most significant acts was the November 1987 hang glider attack on an Israeli army base in northern Israel, which killed six and wounded seven.

For further information see: Samuel M. Katz, *Israel versus Jibril: The Thirty-Year War against a Master Terrorist* (New York: Paragon House, 1993).

Joseph E. Goldberg and David Salzberg

JOHNSON, LYNDON BAINES (b. between Stonewall and Johnson City, Texas, August 27, 1908; d. San Antonio, Texas, January 22, 1973). In August 1930, Lyndon Baines Johnson graduated from the Southwest Texas State Teachers College. Before starting a career in politics, he was a teacher, a secretary to U.S. Congressman Richard M. Kleberg of Texas from 1932 to 1935, and director of the National Youth Administration in Texas.

From 1937 to 1949, he represented Texas's Tenth Congressional District in the U.S. House of Representatives. While a congressman, he also served with distinction as a lieutenant commander in the U.S. Navy from December 1941 to July 1942. During his brief service in the navy, he was awarded the Silver Star. After his twelve-year career in the U.S. House of Representatives, he represented Texas for twelve years in the U.S. Senate, where he became majority leader. In 1960, he lost the Democratic Party's presidential nomination. However, John F. Kennedy,* the Democratic presidential nominee, chose him as his vice presidential running mate. In the Kennedy administration, Lyndon Baines Johnson was an active vice president.

Following the assassination of Kennedy, Vice President Johnson assumed the office of president of the United States. After finishing Kennedy's term in office, President Johnson ran for reelection against the Republican presidential nominee, Senator Barry M. Goldwater, and won reelection. As the president of the United States, Johnson's foreign policy focused largely on the conflict in Southeast Asia, but it also focused on the Arab–Israeli conflict, which escalated into armed hostilities in June 1967.*

President Johnson, in a May 23, 1967, public statement, noted that his position with respect to the Middle East was no different from that of past U.S. administrations. He declared that ''the United States is firmly committed to the support of the political independence and territorial integrity of all the nations of the area. The United States strongly opposes aggression by anyone in the area, in any form, overt or clandestine.'' He also said that the United States ''has consistently sought to have good relations with all the states of the Near East.''

After the hostilities ended, Johnson articulated his position on the future of the Arab–Israeli conflict in an address at the State Department's Foreign Policy Conference for Educators on June 19, 1967. He declared that the United States was committed to a peace in the Middle East that is based on five principles.* The Johnson administration would later support the British-sponsored United Nations (UN) Security Council Resolution 242,* based on the premise of land for peace and incorporating most of Johnson's five principles of peace.

The Johnson administration's policy modifications in its dealings with Israel and the Arab states and in its approach to the Arab–Israeli conflict were perceived by the Arab world as biased in favor of Israel. Egypt* (the United Arab Republic* [UAR]), Syria,* Iraq,* Yemen, Algeria, and Sudan broke diplomatic relations with the United States at the time of the Six Day War.*

For further information see: Vaughn Davis Bornet, *The Presidency of Lyndon B. Johnson* (Lawrence: University Press of Kansas, 1983); Lyndon Baines Johnson, *The Vantage Point: Perspectives of the Presidency, 1963–1969* (New York: Holt, Rinehart, and Winston, 1971); Fred J. Khouri, *The Arab–Israeli Dilemma,* 3d ed. (Syracuse, NY: Syracuse University Press, 1985); George Lenczowski, *American Presidents and the Middle East* (Durham, NC: Duke University Press, 1990).

Jon J. Peterson and Erin Z. Ferguson

JOHNSON MISSION. In the Kennedy* administration the Arab refugee* question was given increased attention by the United States through the Palestine Conciliation Commission* (PCC), of which it was a member. On August 21, 1961, the PCC appointed Joseph E. Johnson, the president of the Carnegie Endowment for International Peace in New York City, ''to be its Special Representative to undertake a visit to the Middle East to explore with the host Governments and with Israel practical means of seeking progress on the Palestine Arab refugee problem.'' He visited the region, met with Israeli and Arab leaders, investigated the problem, and submitted a report to the PCC in which he suggested that the possibility of progress exists but ''as matters now stand there is no prospect of an early resolution of the Palestine question as a whole and . . . there are many indications that no progress can be made on the Palestine Arab refugee question apart from, or in advance of, an overall settlement.'' Johnson remained in his post until January 31, 1963, but, despite some optimism, he achieved no tangible results.

For further information see: Joseph E. Johnson, ''Arab vs. Israeli: A Persistent Challenge to Americans,'' *Middle East Journal* 18 (Winter 1964):1–13.

JOHNSON'S FIVE PRINCIPLES OF PEACE. Following the end of the Six Day War,* strong diplomatic efforts were made by the Arab states and the Soviet bloc to force the Israel Defense Forces* to withdraw from the territory they had occupied during the hostilities. A United Nations General Assembly Emergency Session had been called by the Soviet Union, and it was convened on June 19, 1967, with Soviet premier Aleksei Kosygin in attendance. On the same day, U.S. president Lyndon Johnson* addressed the State Department's Foreign Policy Conference for Educators to express the U.S. position. Johnson stated, ''Certainly, troops must be withdrawn; but there must also be recognized rights of national life, progress in solving the refugee problem, freedom of innocent maritime passage, limitation of the arms race, and respect for political independence and territorial integrity.'' Johnson committed the United States to an Arab–Israeli peace based on five fundamental principles: (1) ''every nation in the area has a fundamental right to live and to have this right respected by its neighbors,'' (2) ''justice for the refugees,'' (3) ''the right of innocent maritime passage must be preserved for all nations,'' (4) ''limits on the wasteful and destructive arms race,'' and (5) ''respect for political independence and territorial integrity of all the states of the area.''

No specific U.S. program of negotiation incorporating the five principles was put forward, and Johnson noted that ''we are ready . . . to see any method tried, and we believe that none should be excluded altogether. Perhaps all of them will be useful and all will be needed.''

For further information see: Lyndon B. Johnson, ''Principles for Peace in the Middle East,'' *Department of State Bulletin* (July 10, 1967):31–34.

JOHNSTON PLAN. In October 1953, President Dwight D. Eisenhower* announced that Eric Johnston was being sent to the Middle East as a personal representative with the rank of ambassador to explore with the governments of the region steps that could be taken to contribute to a general improvement of the situation. He sought to bring about a resolution of the water* issues plaguing the region. Johnston was a hydraulic engineering expert and head of the International Advisory Board of the Technical Cooperation Administration, a former president of the U.S. Chamber of Commerce, and head of the Motion

Picture Association of America. Johnston sought to find an economic approach to the refugee* problem, utilizing a scheme for the equitable division of the waters of the Jordan River* and its tributaries among its riparian states for irrigation and the supply of electric power to develop the region and to provide employment for the local population. Many of the workers would be drawn from the refugees who would be resettled in the region. It was believed that a comprehensive plan for the development of the Jordan Valley would contribute to the stability of the Middle East. It would provide irrigated land to some of the refugees as well as a livelihood, and this would be a step toward resolution of the refugee issue.

Johnston presented his proposals, urging the governments of the region to consider the concept of coordinated development of the Jordan River watershed. Israel, Jordan,* Syria,* and Lebanon* agreed to study his plan. Johnston visited the Middle East four times, the last time in 1955. After his mission Johnston concluded that the ''one-inch line had been reached'' but realized that it could, indeed, be a very long inch. The politics of the area prevented the realization of the concept of the full and equitable utilization of the Jordan River system. Although approved at a technical level by the Arab League,* the plan was strongly opposed within the Arab world, essentially on political grounds, and eventually was rejected. In the negotiations leading to, and in the implementation of, the Israel–Jordan Peace Treaty* this again emerged as a central issue.

For further information see: The Jordan Water Problem: An Analysis and Summary of Available Documents (Washington, DC: American Friends of the Middle East, 1964); U.S. Department of State, *Bulletin* (December 28, 1953).

Anamika Krishna

JOINT COMMUNIQUE BY THE GOVERNMENTS OF THE UNITED STATES AND THE UNION OF SOVIET SOCIALIST REPUBLICS, OCTOBER 1, 1977.

Having exchanged views regarding the unsafe situation which remains in the Middle East, US Secretary of State Cyrus Vance* and Member of the Politbureau of the Central Committee of the Communist Party of the Soviet Union (CPSU) and minister for Foreign Affairs of the USSR A. A. Gromyko* have the following statement to make on behalf of their countries, which are cochairmen of the Geneva Peace Conference* on the Middle East:

1. Both governments are convinced that vital interests of the peoples of this area, as well as the interests of strengthening peace and international security in general, urgently dictate the necessity of achieving, as soon as possible, a just and lasting settlement of the Arab–Israeli conflict. This settlement should be comprehensive, incorporating all parties concerned and all questions.

The United States and the Soviet Union believe that, within the framework of a comprehensive settlement of the Middle East problem, all specific questions of the settlement should be resolved, including such key issues as withdrawal of Israeli Armed Forces from territories occupied in the 1967 conflict; the resolution of the Palestinian question, including insuring the legitimate rights of the Palestinian people; termination of the state of war and establishment of normal peaceful relations on the basis of mutual recognition of the principles of sovereignty, territorial integrity, and political independence.

The two governments believe that, in addition to such measures for insuring the security of the borders between Israel and the neighboring Arab states as the establishment of demilitarized zones and the agreed stationing in them of UN troops or observers, international guarantees of such borders as well as of the observance of the terms of the settlement can also be established should the contracting parties so desire. The United States and the Soviet Union are ready to participate in these guarantees, subject to their constitutional processes.

2. The United States and the Soviet Union believe that the only right and effective way for achieving a fundamental solution to all aspects of the Middle East problem in its entirety is negotiations within the framework of the Geneva peace conference, specially convened for these purposes, with participation in its work of the representatives of all the parties involved in the conflict including those of the Palestinian people, and legal and contractual formalization of the decisions reached at the conference.

In their capacity as cochairmen of the Geneva conference, the United States and the USSR affirm their intention, through joint efforts and in their contacts with the parties concerned, to facilitate in every way the resumption of the work of the conference not later than December 1977. The cochairmen note that there still exist several questions of a procedural and organizational nature which remain to be agreed upon by the participants to the conference.

3. Guided by the goal of achieving a just political settlement in the Middle East and of eliminating the explosive situation in this area of the world, the United States and the USSR appeal to all the parties in the conflict to understand the necessity for careful consideration of each other's legitimate rights and interests and to demonstrate mutual readiness to act accordingly.

JOINT EMERGENCY COMMITTEE. A Joint Emergency Committee, composed of members of the Executive of the Jewish Agency* and the Vaad Leumi (National Council) of the Jewish community in Palestine,* was formed in the autumn of 1947, at which time the United Nations was considering the future of the Palestine Mandate,* and it had become obvious that the British were intent on withdrawal. The committee was formed to make appropriate arrangements for the transfer of power from the Mandatory administration to the government of the proposed Jewish state, and it sought to fill the void created by the disintegration of the British role. The Joint Emergency Committee drafted a legal code and a proposed constitution; it developed a roster of experienced civil servants willing to serve the future government; and it instituted vigorous recruitment for the Haganah* to preserve the security of the Jewish community of Palestine. It disbanded in March 1948 and was succeeded by the Peoples Council, which became the de facto government of Israel on independence.

JORDAN (Formerly Transjordan). The Hashemite Kingdom of Jordan is Israel's neighbor to the east, with which it has fought in several wars and with which it signed a peace treaty* in 1994. Following the War of Independence,* Jordan and Israel signed an Armistice Agreement,* which established the frontiers between the two states during the period from 1949 to 1967. During the 1948 war, Jordan occupied a portion of the territory of the Palestine Mandate* that had been allocated to the Arab state of Palestine and retained control of that area, which became known as the West Bank.* It later annexed that territory, an act recognized only by Great Britain* and Pakistan. The frontier between the two states varied from peaceful to one across which raids and reprisals took place. Jordan joined in the Arab fighting against Israel in the Six Day War,* during which time Israel took control of the West Bank and East Jerusalem* from Jordan but abstained during both the Sinai War* and the War of Attrition.* During the Yom Kippur War,* King Hussein* committed only token forces to the battle against Israel, and these fought alongside Syrian troops in the Golan Heights.*

Negotiations between senior Israeli officials and King Abdullah* took place prior to the creation of Israel, and substantial high-level contacts between the two states have continued over the years since. The open bridges policy* of Moshe Dayan* increased the flow of people and goods across the Jordan River* between Jordan and Israel. Numerous other contacts of various kinds at various levels and on numerous themes have taken place. The concept of a Jordan Option* had assumed that Jordan could represent the Palestinians in resolving the Arab–Israeli conflict. The secret Israel–Palestine Liberation Organization* (PLO) talks in Oslo* followed by the signing of the Declaration of Principles* (DOP) ended that option. Israel and Jordan accelerated their negotiations, which culminated in the 1994 peace treaty.

JORDAN ARAB ARMY. Under the British Mandate,* the Transjordanian* military forces were under the command of British officers. Britain financed the Jordanian forces, and their officers filled the top positions within the Arab Legion.* Anglo-Jordanian training and planning were coordinated through a Joint Defense Board. Until 1956, the Jordan Arab Legion also included police forces. By 1956, the forces, composed of infantry, artillery, armored corps, and a small air force, numbered approximately 23,000 men. Most of the soldiers were bedouin and were considered politically reliable and loyal to the monarchy. Palestinians,* recruited into the force from 1951 to 1956, served in border defense positions. The Arab Legion was renamed the Jordan Arab Army in 1956. John Bagot Glubb,* a career British officer who had been hired by the Jordanian monarchy, was discharged on March 1, 1956. King Hussein* replaced him with Lieutenant Colonel Ali abu Nuwwar as chief of staff. The newly appointed major general created a Fourth Infantry Brigade, whose officers and soldiers were largely Palestinian. Nuwwar formed a group of Free Officers and, together with Sulayman al-Nabulsi, leader of the Jordanian National Socialist Party, attempted to stage a coup against the monarch in April 1957. The revolt failed, and both were dismissed, as well as Nuwwar's successor as chief of staff, General Ali al-Hayyari, who refused to purge the officers corps. Fifty to 70 officers were arrested for conspiring to overthrow the monarchy, the Fourth Infantry

Brigade was disbanded, and military personnel were reorganized. In 1965, the Jordanian army expanded in size to meet the objectives of a Unified Arab Command established in principle at the Arab Summit meeting at Cairo in June 1964. Egypt,* Saudi Arabia, and Syria* contributed funds to the Jordanian forces. At the same time, the United Arab Republic* attempted to persuade Jordan to standardize its military equipment and replace its dominantly British weapons systems with Soviet equipment. King Hussein rejected this. Because of the composition of the Jordanian population, political reliability has been a major concern of the Jordanian forces. The king refused to allow the formation of Palestinian units. Jordan's dependence on outside financial support has also proven to be a liability for the king, making it difficult to modernize their weapons as well as limiting their strategic alternatives. Despite these difficulties, the Jordanian Arab Army has been considered one of the best Arab fighting forces in the Middle East.

Joseph E. Goldberg

JORDAN CIVIL WAR. In the wake of the Six Day War* and in the midst of the War of Attrition,* Palestinian guerrillas began to operate against Israel from their refugee centers in Jordan* and Lebanon.* The Palestinian forces, known as fedayeen* or commandos, also established a de facto state within a state in Jordan and grew in power until they began to threaten the control of the Hashemite monarchy.

On September 6, 1970, members of the Popular Front for the Liberation of Palestine* (PFLP) hijacked and destroyed four planes belonging to Swissair, Pan Am, TWA, and BOAC. These planes were taken to remote airstrips in Jordan, where the Palestinians,* using civilian hostages, negotiated for the release of Palestinians interned in several European states who had been convicted in previous terrorist attacks against Israelis. Following an assassination attempt and sporadic violence, King Hussein* attempted to regain sovereignty in his country; by mid-September the situation had devolved into a virtual civil war between the Jordanian army and the Palestinian forces. The Jordanian forces had the advantage of a mechanized army, which they effectively used to crush Palestinian resistance in the refugee camps. The destruction of the Palestinian organization in Jordan became known by the Palestinians as their Black September.* The Jordanian Civil War helped to further the deep schism between Jordan and the Palestine Liberation Organization* (PLO) and ended effective Palestinian political or military activity on the east bank of the Jordan. The Palestinian leadership moved to refugee camps in Lebanon, setting the stage for the later Lebanese Civil War.

The Jordanian Civil War almost developed into a broader conflict. On September 18, with the Palestinians on the defensive, Syria* sent armored units across the border into Jordan—ostensibly to aid the Palestinians but also to gain control of its southern neighbor. Jordan reacted by moving its army to the Syrian Front, though the Syrians held the advantage in both armor and airpower. Although 300 Syrian tanks were able to penetrate into northern Jordan, the Jordanians were able to repel the first attack and maintain control of strategic roads.

Both Israel and the United States were concerned with the Syrian threat to broaden the conflict and its ramifications for the region. The United States reacted with a highly visible response by moving ships of the Sixth and Atlantic Fleets into the eastern Mediterranean and placing forces in the United States and Germany on alert. Israel responded by reinforcing its positions in the Golan Heights.*

Facing a renewed Syrian attack and using Washington as a communication conduit, King Hussein asked Israel to use its airpower to attack the Syrian forces inside Jordan. The mobilization in Israel and its threats to use its air force against the Syrians, combined with the obvious military preparations of the U.S. forces, obviously registered with both the Soviets and their Syrian clients. Ultimately, the Syrians refrained from using their superior airpower against the Jordanian armor, and the Syrian tanks turned back into Syria.

For further information see: Clinton Bailey, *Jordan's Palestinian Challenge, 1948–1983: A Political History* (Boulder, CO: Westview Press, 1984).

Mark Daryl Erickson

"JORDAN IS PALESTINE." The basic concept of this slogan is that Jordan* was part of historic Palestine,* and, therefore, Palestine includes territory on both banks of the Jordan River.* Jordan is thus a Palestinian state, even if it is under Jordanian control. This suggests that the solution to the Arab–Israeli conflict already exists, since there is a Palestinian state east of the Jordan River, and thus there is no need for another one west of the Jordan River, where Israel is located. It also strengthens Israel's claim to all of the territory west of the Jordan River. The phrase gained some currency in Israel and elsewhere among Israel's supporters by suggesting that the solution to the Arab–Israeli conflict could be found by identifying Jordan as Palestine and thereby reducing the threat to Israel by reducing the claims to the West Bank* and Gaza Strip* and parts of Israel. The proponents of this view base their statement on two assertions. First, the original British Mandate* for Palestine included East Jordan*; second, the majority of East Jordan's population is Palestinian. Opponents argue that neither assertion is accurate.

This view was not accepted by either the Palestinian leadership or the king of Jordan. When he discussed the relationship of Jordan to Palestine in his address of July 31, 1988, renouncing Jordan's claim to the West Bank, King Hussein* specifically noted, "Jordan is not Palestine."

For further information see: Daniel Pipes and Adam Garfinkle, "Is Jordan Palestine?" *Commentary* 86 (October 1988):35–42.

JORDAN OPTION. An approach to a peaceful resolution of the Arab–Israeli conflict in which Israel and Jordan* would negotiate to determine the future of the West Bank* and Gaza Strip* because Jordan had been the power controlling the West Bank and appeared amenable to possible participation in a peace process. This approach sought to bypass the Palestine Liberation Organization* (PLO) as the representative of the Palestinians and the appropriate negotiating partners with Israel. It was a major element of the policy of the Israel Labor Party.*

JORDAN RIVER. The Jordan, some 205 miles long, flows north to south through the Sea of Galilee* and ends in the Dead Sea* and forms the boundary between Palestine* and Transjordan.* The Jordan originates in the snows and rains of Mount Hermon,* and its sources are the Hasbani River* in Lebanon,* the Banias River in Syria,* and the Dan in Israel. Because of the scarcity of water* in the region, the river has been the subject of substantial negotiations designed to share the waters among the riparian states. It has also been a source of tension that has contributed to the conflicts in the region. It was among the more sensitive and problematic issues in the negotiations between Israel and Jordan that led to, and derived from, the Israel–Jordan Peace Treaty* of 1994.

For further information see: Kathryn B. Doherty, "Jordan Waters Conflict," *International Conciliation,* no. 553 (Carnegie Endowment for International Peace, 1965); Miriam R. Lowi, *Water and Power: Politics of a Scarce Resource in the Jordan River Basin* (Cambridge: Cambridge University Press, 1993); Edward Rizk, *The Jordan River* (New York: Arab Information Center, 1964); Samir N. Saliba, *The Jordan River Dispute* (The Hague: Martinus Nijhoff, 1968); Georgiana G. Stevens, *Jordan River Partition* (Stanford, CA: Hoover Institution on War, Revolution and Peace, 1965).

JORDAN RIVER BORDER CROSSING. On November 10, 1994, Israel and Jordan* inaugurated the new crossing near the Israeli town of Beit Shean that provided additional links between the two countries.

JORDANIAN OPTION. See **JORDAN OPTION.**

JORDAN–ISRAEL DIPLOMATIC RELATIONS. See **ISRAEL–JORDAN DIPLOMATIC RELATIONS.**

JORDAN–ISRAEL PEACE TREATY. See **ISRAEL–JORDAN PEACE TREATY (1994).**

JORDAN–PLO ACCORD OF FEBRUARY 11, 1985. See **HUSSEIN–ARAFAT AGREEMENT OF FEBRUARY 11, 1985.**

JUDAH. See **JUDEA.**

JUDEA. Latin for "Judah," the southern province of the land of Israel. In 933 B.C., after the death of King Solomon, the Land of Israel was divided into two kingdoms, the kingdom of Judah and the kingdom of Israel. The kingdom of

Judah bordered on Ayanot in the north, the frontier with Arabia in the south, Jordan* in the west, and Jaffa in the east. The kingdom was one-third the size of the northern kingdom of Israel, had no normal access to the sea, and had no important trade routes. The kingdom of Judah (Judea) maintained its capital at Jerusalem* until 586 B.C., when the Babylonians destroyed the Temple,* ended the kingdom, and took the leadership and much of the Jewish population in exile to Babylon. Under Cyrus of Persia, the Jews were allowed to return to Jerusalem, and the rebuilding of the Temple began. Judah came under Roman rule in 63 B.C. and was renamed Judea, thereby becoming the third province of Roman-occupied Palestine.* In the north was the Galilee province, in the center was Samaria, and in the south was Judea.

David Salzberg

JUDEA AND SAMARIA. Terms used in Israel to refer to the West Bank.* The West Bank of the Jordan River,* constituting approximately 5,590 kilometers, is composed of two dominant areas: the highland area and the Jordan Rift. Judea* and Samaria* constitute the highlands. The highland area north of Jerusalem* is known by its biblical name, Samaria. The dominant population center within Samaria is Nablus. In addition to Nablus, Jenin to the north and Kalkilye to the southwest are population centers, though none of the Samarian towns are large in size. South of Jerusalem is the area known as Judea, with its dominant population center being Hebron.* In addition to Hebron, among Judea's towns are Bethlehem,* Beit Jala, Ramallah, and El-Bire. Jerusalem is at the center of both Judea and Samaria. Judea and Samaria lie along the main watershed between the Mediterranean Sea and the Jordan River. Judea and Samaria are considered the biblical Land of Israel, and for the Greater Israel Movement there is a religious responsibility to resettle Eretz Yisrael.* The obligation, according to the Greater Israel Movement, is to maintain those territories in which the Jewish people had a historic right to live. On the eve of the Jewish Passover in 1968, a group from the Greater Israel Movement, led by Rabbi Moshe Levinger,* arrived in Hebron and reestablished a Jewish settlement at Kiryat Arba* next to the old city of Hebron. The Cave of the Machpela,* which Abraham bought as a burial cave, is located at Hebron. The settlement of Eli, north of Jerusalem, overlooks the archaeological site of Shilo, which was both a political and religious center of the biblical period and lies between Ramallah and Nablus. Because of the biblical connection of Judea and Samaria and the conquest of the land by the Israel Defense Forces* in the Six Day War,* those segments of the Israeli population who believe they have an obligation to maintain this biblical territory have been against returning this territory in any overall peace settlement.

Joseph E. Goldberg

JUNE WAR (1967). See **SIX DAY WAR.**

K

KACH (Thus). A political party on the extreme right of Israel's political spectrum founded and led by Rabbi Meir Kahane* until his death. It is essentially a secular nationalist movement that focuses on the Arab challenges to Israel and its Jewish character. KACH's symbol is a Yellow Star of David with a clenched fist thrust through it, and its name is an acronym for "this is the way."

Like the Jewish Defense League that Kahane had established in the United States, members of KACH held that violence may succeed where diplomacy fails and that violence expresses the frustration of the truly loyal Jew. Jews are defined by those who observe all of the commandments of God in the Torah, selflessly and without exception. They claim that to do otherwise is to impede the redemption of Israel and cause only needless death and violence.

In the 1984 Israeli Knesset* election, after failure in previous attempts, KACH succeeded in gaining nearly 26,000 votes and a seat in Parliament. Kahane had campaigned on a theme of "making Israel Jewish again" by seeking the expulsion of the Arabs from Israel, as well as from the West Bank* and Gaza.* KACH introduced a bill into the Knesset in July 1984 that called for the transfer of Arabs to beyond Israel's borders. Initially, the party was banned from participation in the election by the Central Elections Committee, but the ruling was reversed by the Supreme Court—a move that gained the party additional publicity and probably facilitated its efforts to secure a Knesset seat. Despite Kahane's success in the 1984 elections, he was considered an extremist, even by many on the right, and his political ideology and programs remained marginal in Israel. He was ruled out as a political ally and coalition partner by all the major factions in the Knesset, including Tehiya.* Kach was banned from participation in the 1988 Knesset election by the Central Elections Committee on the grounds that it was racist. Israel's High Court upheld the Elections Committee's decision on October 16, 1988, claiming that KACH was racist and antidemocratic. Part of the reason for this decision was the fear that KACH would receive the third largest segment of votes in the upcoming elections (anywhere from three to twelve seats) and that the Likud* Party would then have to appoint Kahane as a Cabinet minister if they intended to form a government. Kahane had stated that if he received this block of seats, he would want the position of defense minister. This idea spurred Likud members to seek the early end of Kahane's political career.

After the murder of Rabbi Kahane, Rabbi Avraham Toledano was chosen as his successor in March 1991. Members of KACH carried out violent acts in the streets of Jerusalem* after the funeral.

After the Hebron Massacre* of February 25, 1994, Israel's president Ezer Weizman* and Prime Minister Yitzhak Rabin* denounced the Kahane groups as foreign implants and an errant weed that relied on non-Israeli-born Jews, who do not perceive the conflict between Arabs and Jews in the same way as the majority of Israelis, to do their unethical work. The Knesset outlawed racist groups.

On March 13, 1994, the Israeli Cabinet issued a statement:

[T]he Government declares that the groups designated hereunder are terrorist organizations: a. the Kach Movement, whose central activists are today Baruch Marzel, No'am Federman and Tiran Pollak; b. the Kahane Chai* Movement, whose central activists are Binyamin Kahane, David Axelrod and Yekutiel Ben-Yaakov. This announcement applies to the terrorist organizations detailed above as well as to any group of people acting to achieve the aims of that nature, which the above-mentioned groups have been working to achieve, through means similar to those which the above-mentioned groups have used, even if they bear different names or designations, whether permanently or from time to time. In addition, this announcement will apply to factions or groups attached to the above-mentioned organizations.

KACH and Kahane Chai were formally banned, and their members (especially those living in the West Bank settlements of Kiryat Arba* and Kfar Tapuach) had their firearms permits revoked. The Jerusalem police closed and sealed the offices of both organizations in the city for six months.

For further information see: S. Daniel Breslauer, *Meir Kahane: Ideologue, Hero, Thinker* (Lewiston, NY: Edwin Mellen Press, 1986); Yair Kolter, *Heil Kahane* (New York: M. Rachlin Printing, 1986); Jay Shapiro, *Meir Kahane: The Litmus Test of Democracy in Israel* (Dollard des Ormeaux, Quebec: Dawn Publications, 1988); Ehud Sprinzak, *The Ascendance of Israel's Radical Right* (New York: Oxford University Press, 1991).

Joseph E. Goldberg

KADDOUMI, FAROUQ (ABU LUTUF, sometimes: Faruq al-Qaddumi) (b. Nablus, 1931). His family moved from Nablus to Haifa when he was very young, and he was educated there. After Israel's War of Independence,* the family returned to Nablus. He joined the Baath Party in 1948 and remained a member for a decade. He worked for ARAMCO in Saudi Arabia in the early 1950s, where he became politically active. In 1954, he went to Cairo to study economics at American University in Cairo. Kaddoumi was one of many young Palestinians studying at Egyptian universities who belonged to the General Union of Palestinian Students.* He met Yasser Arafat* in Kuwait after the 1956 war* when Arafat went to Kuwait to establish a contracting company and was employed by the Department of Public Works. He was attracted to Arafat because of the promise of the liberation movement. In June 1970, he was placed on the newly formed, twenty-seven-member Palestine Liberation Organization* (PLO) Central Committee and then became a member of the thirteen-member PLO Executive Committee.

Kaddoumi has been the PLO's foreign minister since 1973 and head of the Political Department of the PLO. After the Six Day War,* he was Fatah's* liaison with Egypt. In October 1974, at the Arab Summit meeting in Rabat, Morocco, he was instrumental in the wording of the resolution declaring the PLO as the "sole legitimate representative of the Palestinian people." Kaddoumi developed contacts with many European diplomats and successfully negotiated the opening of PLO offices in a number of countries.

Kaddoumi opposed the Declaration of Principles* (DOP) and the accord with Israel in 1993–94.

Joseph E. Goldberg

KAHAN COMMISSION OF INQUIRY. After the War in Lebanon,* Christian Phalangist forces massacred Palestinians* at the Sabra and Shatila* refugee camps in the Beirut area. The resultant anguish within Israel and consequent public pressure led to the decision of the Cabinet on September 28, 1982, to establish a Commission of Inquiry. "The matter which will be subjected to inquiry is: all the facts and factors connected with the atrocity carried out by a unit of the Lebanese Forces against the civilian population in the Shatila and Sabra camps." The Commission of Inquiry consisted of Yitzhak Kahan, president of the Supreme Court, who served as commission chairman; Aharon Barak, justice of the Supreme Court; and Yona Efrat, a reserve major general in the Israel Defense Forces.* After several months of testimony, the commission released its findings on February 8, 1983.

The commission found that while the Phalangist militia bore direct responsibility for the killings, the government of Israel and some of its top officials had to bear indirect responsibility due to their actions, or lack thereof. Of particular concern was the lack of consideration or indifference on the part of Israeli government officials to the danger that the Phalangists would carry out atrocities against the civilian population in the camps, given their desire for revenge over the killing of their leader, Bashir Gemayel,* and their known antipathy to the Palestinians.

Of Prime Minister Menachem Begin,* the commission found that having not been informed of the Phalangists' entry into the camps until some thirty-six hours after the fact; and given the glowing reports he had received from the defense minister, Ariel Sharon,* and the chief of staff, he was led to believe that all operations were nearing completion in a normal manner and therefore had no direct knowledge of the massacres. However, the prime minister was chastised for his lack of interest in Phalangist actions while inside the camps. Equally chastised for their seeming indifference were the foreign minister, Yitzhak Shamir,* and the director of military intelligence,* Major General Yehoshua Saguy. Among other recommendations it suggested that Saguy not continue as director of military intelligence and that Division Commander Brigadier General Amos Yaron not serve in the capacity of a field commander in the Israel Defense Forces. Among other results of the report and recommendations was the resignation of Ariel Sharon as minister of defense.

The harshest criticism was reserved for Defense Minister Ariel Sharon and Chief of Staff Rafael Eitan,* on whom the commission laid responsibility for the decision to send the Phalangists into the camps. As such, it was their responsibility for both the adoption and implementation of the decision.

The commission questioned Eitan's failure to take into consideration the possibility of the Phalangists' taking vengeance against the civilians in the camps, as well as his failure to order measures to avoid such a danger. This was considered a breach of duty by Eitan, but, given the fact that he was scheduled to complete his term of office the following month, no punitive action was recommended by the commission.

The commission charged Defense Minister Sharon with personal responsibility for the decision to allow the Phalangists to enter Sabra and Shatilla. During his testimony to the commission, Sharon stated that no one could have possibly imagined the atrocities carried out by the Phalangists at the time the decision was made. This was not accepted by the commission, which found that Sharon "disregarded any apprehensions about what was to be expected because the advantages to be gained from the Phalangists' entry into the camps distracted him from the proper consideration." Sharon was charged with nonfulfillment of duty and failure to meet his humanitarian obligation to the occupants of the camps. The commission recommended that Sharon be removed from office.

On February 10, 1983, the Israeli Cabinet voted sixteen to one to oust Ariel Sharon from his position as minister of defense. Sharon submitted his resignation but eventually was reinstated as minister without portfolio. Critics of the report said that it did not go far enough.

For further information see: Weston D. Burnett, "Command Responsibility and a Case Study of the Criminal Responsibility of Israeli Military Commanders for the Pogrom at Shatilla and Sabra," *Military Law Review* 107 (Winter 1985):71–189; Martin Edelman, "The Kahan Commission of Inquiry," *Midstream* 29 (June–July 1983):11–14; "Judgement in Jerusalem," *New Republic* (March 7, 1983):9–12; R. T. Naylor, "From Bloodbath to Whitewash," *Arab Studies Quarterly* 5 (Fall 1983):337–61; *The Beirut Massacre: The Complete Kahan Commission Report* (Princeton, NJ: Karz-Cohl, 1983).

Pamela Rivers

KAHANE, MEIR (b. Brooklyn, New York, August 1, 1932; d. Manhattan, New York, November 5, 1990). Meir Kahane was born to an Orthodox Jewish family. During his youth he joined Betar,* a right-wing Jewish youth movement. He went on to study law and religion and become an Orthodox rabbi.

Kahane was first arrested in 1947, at age fifteen, for pelting Ernest Bevin,* the then British foreign secretary, on an official visit to New York, with eggs and tomatoes and smashing his car window. In later years, Kahane became an active and militant supporter of Jewish interests, as he saw them. He founded the Jewish Defense League (JDL) in 1968 as an organization to protect elderly Jews from street hoodlums in New York. The JDL, under Kahane's leadership, evolved into a militant organization adopting violent tactics. The first attacks were against Soviet targets in the United States in an attempt to promote better Soviet policy toward Jewish emigration. Two of the best-known attacks were the 1971 bombing of the Soviet cultural building in Washington, D.C., and the 1971 bombing of Amtorg, the Soviet trade center in Manhattan. Although the violent methods of Kahane and the JDL were highly controversial, many credit Kahane and his group for the increase in Jewish emigration from the Soviet Union in 1973.

In 1971, Kahane emigrated to Israel and became an Israeli citizen. He became involved in Israeli politics and called for the expulsion of Arabs from Israel, as well as attempting to have sexual relations between Arabs and Jewish women declared illegal. As the leader of KACH,* a right-wing political party both in the Israeli Knesset* and in Judea* and Samaria,* he briefly served in the Knesset after the 1984 elections. KACH was declared by Israel's High Court on October 16, 1988, to be a racist and undemocratic organization and was not allowed to present a list for election to the Knesset.

On November 5, 1990, Meir Kahane was murdered in New York City following a lecture he had given. Kahane's accused assassin (Egyptian*-born El Sayed Noseir, an Islamic fundamentalist with alleged ties to Middle Eastern Arab terror cells) was himself shot while fleeing the scene after the attack, by an on-site policeman. Noseir was jailed, tried, defended by attorney William Kuntsler, and acquitted in December 1991 by a Manhattan jury, when Kuntsler convinced the jury that Noseir had been framed by Kahane's disciples, who he claimed had killed the rabbi in a money dispute. However, Noseir was convicted on lesser charges, such as criminal possession of the weapon that killed Kahane. This verdict was so outrageous that many mainstream and usually anti-Kahane Jewish groups demanded that U.S. attorney Rudolph Giuliani reopen the case. He recommended that the Federal Bureau of Investigation (FBI) reopen the investigation.

Rabbi Kahane wrote a number of books, including *The Story of the Jewish*

Defense League (Radnor, PA: Chilton Books, 1975); *Uncomfortable Questions for Comfortable Jews* (Secaucus, NJ: Lyle Stuart, 1987); and *They Must Go* (New York: Grosset and Dunlap, 1981).

For further information see: S. Daniel Breslauer, *Meir Kahane, Ideologue, Hero, Thinker* (Lewiston, NY: Mellen Press, 1986); Robert I. Friedmann, *The False Prophet: Rabbi Meir Kahane—from FBI Informant to Knesset Member* (Brooklyn, NY: Lawrence Hill Books, 1990).

Yasha Manuel Harari

KAHANE CHAI (Kahane Lives). A political movement named after Rabbi Meir Kahane,* who emigrated to Israel in 1971 and established a political movement that the Israel High Court declared on October 16, 1988, to be racist and undemocratic and, consequently, not eligible to present a list for elections to the Knesset.* The political party, KACH,* was successful in the 1984 elections and sent Rabbi Kahane to the Knesset. Kahane Chai follows the same basic ideological positions of KACH and has been used both within and outside Israel to raise money for KACH as well as to recruit new members.

Kahane Chai and KACH were denounced by the Israeli government following the Hebron Massacre* of February 25, 1994, committed by Dr. Baruch Goldstein, a member of Kahane Chai. Both organizations were formally banned in February 1994, and members of their groups living in West Bank* settlements had their firearms permits revoked.

The decision banning extremist Jewish groups inside Israel spurred vehement resistance from the groups' members, and their U.S. counterparts also felt the impact as they no longer had support from their Israeli link to lobby for their cause in Washington. See also KACH.

Yasha Manuel Harari

KAIS, ABDELKARIM HAMAD (ABU ADNAN) (b. 1927; d. August 14, 1992). A founding member of the Palestine Liberation Organization,* he was also a founder of the Democratic Front for the Liberation of Palestine.* He was a member of the Palestine National Council.* The Palestinian news agency reported that he died of natural causes but did not say when or where the death occurred, only that he would be buried in Tunis.

Joseph E. Goldberg

KAMEL, MOHAMED IBRAHIM (b. 1927). He graduated from the University of Cairo with a degree in law in 1947. In 1953, he was asked to serve in the Revolutionary Command Council. After serving in foreign posts in Mexico, Canada,* Zaire, Sweden, and West Germany, he became President Anwar Sadat's* minister of foreign affairs in 1977. He participated in the Camp David* negotiations but resigned the day before the signing of the accords.* He claimed that President Sadat—without prior consultations with the Egyptian* negotiating team—had made unacceptable, significant concessions to the Israelis.

For further information see: Muhammad Ibrahim Kamil, *The Camp David Accords: A Testimony* (Boston: KPI, 1986).

Ahmed Elbashari

KARAMEH. On March 21, 1968, a 15,000-man unit of the Israel Defense Forces* (IDF) crossed the Jordan River* and launched an assault against the villages of Karameh (northeast of the Allenby Bridge*) and Shune (on the Dead Sea plain). In a speech before the Knesset* on the same day, Israeli prime minister Levi Eshkol* claimed that the assault was in response to repeated terrorist attacks launched from bases in Jordan.* He further stated that despite denials of direct participation in the attacks, the Jordanian army had indeed been involved in the fighting, and the government was unable to control the activities of the fedayeen* operating in its territory. Therefore, Israel had no choice but to defend itself.

Each side claimed victory. Before their withdrawal from Karameh, the Israelis searched homes and destroyed several installations. They claimed to have killed 150 terrorists and captured some 138 more. The Jordanians claimed that 100 Israelis had been killed and forty-five Israeli tanks had been destroyed. Civilian casualties were quite low, given an operation of this size, as the Israelis had dropped leaflets on Karameh warning its Jordanian inhabitants to put away their arms and stay inside during the assault.

The raid was over in less than twenty-four hours. A week later the world community expressed its outrage by its condemnation of the raid. Even the United States voted in the affirmative, arguing that the Israeli response was not proportional to the provocation.

On a psychological level, the clear winner at Karameh was Fatah.* With help from the Jordanian army, they were able to hold their ground and inflict substantial losses on the IDF. As word of their accomplishment spread, membership requests climbed. The condemnation by the United Nations added to the fedayeen legend.

For their part, the Israelis were able to score a small victory when they were able to launch the attack at Karameh and not evoke a military response from other Arab states in the region. However, even though they managed to destroy several fedayeen installations and capture a cache of weapons, the Israelis did not succeed in stemming terrorist attacks on Israeli territory and citizens.

The incident at Karameh is important for the psychological boost it provided to the budding Palestine Liberation Organization* (PLO). Their ability to hold off the Israelis while sustaining heavy losses made them folk heroes in the eyes of their fellow Arabs. However, Karameh may have also marked the beginning of the end for the PLO in Jordan, as the fedayeen began to expect further political concessions from King Hussein,* which he was unwilling to accept. The PLO's use of Jordan as a base of operations for raids into Israel invited the kind of Israeli reprisals like Karameh that King Hussein was unwilling to risk.

Barely two years later, the Jordan Civil War* erupted, ending with the expulsion of the PLO from Jordan.

For further information see: Jillian Becker, *The PLO: The Rise and Fall of the Palestine Liberation Organization* (New York: St. Martin's Press, 1984); Levi Eshkol, "Why Israel Struck," *Jewish Frontier* 35 (April 1968):4–5; James Feron, "Israelis Cross the Jordan to Raid 'Terrorist Bases': Land Forces Move over Cease-Fire Line for the First Time—Amman Reports Destruction of Four Tanks," *New York Times,* March 21, 1968; James Feron, "Israelis Withdraw after Raid in Jordan; Attack Denounced in Security Council: Troops Strike Villages on East Bank Described as Bases for Terrorists," *New York Times,* March 22, 1968; Drew Middleton, "Malik Says Soviets Would Back Any Sanctions—U.S. Deplores Assault," *New York Times,* March 22, 1968; Bard E. O'Neil, *Armed Struggle in Palestine: A Political-Military Analysis* (Boulder, CO: Westview Press, 1978); Anne Sinai and Allen Pollack, *The Hashemite Kingdom of Jordan and the West Bank: A Handbook* (New York: American Academic Association for Peace in the Middle East, 1977).

Pamela Rivers

KARAMI, RASHID (b. 1921; d. 1987). A Lebanese Sunni Muslim from Tripoli. In 1953, he became Lebanon's* minister of economy. The following year he became minister of economic and social affairs and served in that post until September 1955, when he became Lebanon's prime minister. He served until 1956. Karami also served as prime minister from 1958 to 1960, from 1961 to 1964, from 1965 to 1966, from 1966 to 1968, from 1969 to 1970, from 1975 to 1976, and from 1984 to 1987. In 1984, Karami attempted to bring the sectarian parties together in an effort to achieve national reconciliation in a unity government. When Lebanon was being drawn into the Arab–Israeli conflict, Karami was an eloquent spokesman for the Palestinian* cause.

Joseph E. Goldberg

KARIA, AHMED SULEIMAN (Sometimes spelled Korei or Qurai or Qeria. Also known as Abu Alaa or Abu Alla). Palestine Liberation Organization* (PLO) official who served as director of finances for Yasser Arafat.* He began the unofficial discussions with Israeli academics Yair Hirschfeld and Ron Pundik that led to the Oslo talks,* and he continued to lead the delegation that negotiated the Declaration of Principles* between Israel and the PLO in 1993. He continued to negotiate with Israel on economic issues. He headed the Palestinian Economic Council for Development and Reconstruction.* In September 1994, he resigned from his position as trade and economics minister in the Palestinian Authority,* reportedly because of dissatisfaction and frustration with the way Yasser Arafat was governing. Arafat did not accept the resignation.

KATYUSHA ROCKET. Katyusha rockets are small-caliber, unguided, Soviet ground-to-ground rockets fired from the early versions of Soviet-made multiple rocket launchers (MRLs). MRLs were first developed by the Soviet Union and heavily used during World War II as cheap, simple substitutes for conventional artillery. They were used for their shock value and saturation effects. Technically, Katyusha rocket units are the 82mm rocket fired from the BM-8 MRL and the 132mm rocket fired from the BM-13 MRL; however, the name Katyusha has been applied to a broad range of Soviet artillery rockets. Since the development of these two rocket systems in the 1930s, the Soviet Union has produced several rockets and MRLs: the 300mm rocket fired from the BM-30 and BM-31 MRLs, the 310mm rocket fired from the BM-31 MRL, the 250mm rocket fired from the BM-25 MRL, the 240mm rocket fired from the BM-24 MRL, the 220mm rocket fired from the BM-27 MRL, the 200mm rocket fired from the BMD-20 MRL, the 140mm rocket fired from the BM-14 MRL, and the 122mm rocket fired from the BM-11 and BM-21 MRLs.

The BM-21, 122mm multiple-rocket launcher, which was introduced by the Soviet Union in 1964, is considered the most widely employed artillery rocket system in the world. There are a number of versions of the BM-21, 122mm MRL: the M1972 (developed by Czechoslovakia), the M1975, the M1976, the BM-21/Bucegi (developed by Romania), and the BM-21/Isuzu (developed by the Palestine Liberation Organization* [PLO]). China and India also have a version of this particular rocket system. North Vietnam employs a single-tube version of the BM-21, 122mm MRL. The rocket in this system is fired from an eight-foot tube mounted on a sixty-two-pound tripod.

The standard BM-21 MRL is mounted on the back end of the Soviet-made URAL 375 truck and can carry forty short-range or long-range 122mm rockets. The short-range version of this rocket has a range of over 12,000 yards while the long-range version can reach distances of nearly 22,300 yards. Both versions can be armed with a 42.8-pound, high-explosive chemical, smoke, or biological warhead. These Soviet rocket systems are said to have eight times the destructive capacity of the BM-13, 132mm Katyusha MRL. Eighteen Soviet BM-21, 122mm MRLs can rain down more than sixteen tons of high explosives onto a target in a period of twenty seconds. Between 1993 and 1994, armies of the Middle East and North Africa fielded well over 2,100 multiple-rocket launchers. The primary Soviet MRLs fielded by these armies were the BM-11 and BM-21, 122mm MRLs (although a few armies also fielded the BM-24, BM-14, and BM-13 MRLs).

Despite their inaccuracy and inconsistency, relatively poor range coverage, and difficulty in maintaining a sustained rate of fire compared with other forms of artillery, rocket artillery used during the Arab–Israeli military engagements has displayed a devastating ability to saturate an area with a large number of high-explosive warheads in a short period of time. During the June War of 1967,* Egyptian* armed forces operated Soviet MRLs (possibly BM-24 or BM-31 MRLs), which were mounted on trucks and could fire twelve rockets singly or in a salvo. While the Egyptian armed forces operated MRLs at the Sinai front, Syrian* artillery, at that time considered to be the most efficient part of the Syrian army, deployed Soviet MRLs at the Syrian front. During the October War of 1973,* BM-21 MRLs were used by both the Arabs and Israelis as ground support for their advancing military forces. Israeli forces captured Arab MRLs during the June war of 1967 and used them against the Arab armed forces in the October War of 1973. One notable instance of extensive rocket artillery employment during the October War is the Egyptian attack on Israeli positions at the Suez Canal* on October 17–24, 1973. At this juncture of the war, Israeli forces, which were establishing bridgeheads on the east and west banks of the Suez Canal and which were moving portable bridges into place across the canal, came under a heavy barrage of Egyptian rocket artillery fire. During the Lebanese* conflict of the 1980s, Palestinian forces extensively used their version of the BM-21 MRL (a MRL carrying thirty 122mm rockets and mounted on the back of a 2.5-ton, 6 × 6 Japanese Isuzu truck) against Israeli forces operating in southern Lebanon.

The political and psychological impact of rocket artillery employment during the Arab–Israeli conflict is even more significant. The frequent Palestinian bombardment of northern Israel with 122mm rockets in the early 1980s was a significant factor that helped trigger Israel's decision to send forces into southern Lebanon. Following its intervention in southern Lebanon, Israeli citizens in northern Israel and military forces operating in the ''security zone''* across southern Lebanon have been terrorized by 122mm rocket attacks from the pro-Iranian Islamic forces known as Hezbollah,* or the Party of God. Attacks from these forces frequently stem from their opposition to an Israeli presence in southern Lebanon and progressive movement in the Middle East peace process.

For further information see: Frank Aker, *October 1973: The Arab–Israeli War* (Hamden, CT: Shoestring Press, 1985); Chris Bellamy, *Red God of War: Soviet Artillery and Rocket Forces* (London: Brassey's Defence Publishers, 1986); Shelford Bidwell, *Brassey's Artillery of the World* (Oxford: Brassey's, 1981); Christopher Chant, *A Compendium of Armaments and Military Hardware* (London: Routledge and Kegan Paul, 1987); Richard A. Gabriel, *Operation Peace for Galilee: The Israeli–PLO War in Lebanon* (New York: Hill and Wang, 1984); Edgar O'Ballance, *The Third Arab–Israeli War* (Hamden, CT: Shoestring Press, 1972); Edgar O'Ballance, *No Victor, No Vanquished: The Yom Kippur War* (San Rafael, CA: Presidio Press, 1978); J. W. Ryan, *Guns, Mortars & Rockets* (London: Brassey's, 1986).

Jon J. Peterson

KAWASMEH, FAHD. He was elected mayor of Hebron,* his hometown, in 1976. Kawasmeh was deported from the West Bank* in 1980 following the murder of six Jewish students who were trying to live in Hebron. He was assassinated in Amman, Jordan,* on December 29, 1984, shot on the doorstep of his home by gunmen who used pistols equipped with silencers. Black September* claimed responsibility for the murder. That same month, Kawasmeh had been elected to the Palestine Liberation Organization* (PLO) Executive Committee.

Joseph E. Goldberg

KENNEDY, JOHN FITZGERALD (b. Brookline, Massachusetts, May 29, 1917; d. Dallas, Texas, November 22, 1963). In 1941, following his educational career at Harvard University (1936–40) and Stanford Business School (1940–41), John F. Kennedy entered the U.S. Navy. During World War II, the PT boat that he commanded, PT 109, was struck by a Japanese* destroyer. Lieutenant Kennedy won a Purple Heart and the Navy and Marine Corps Medal for his acts of courage during this incident. Lieutenant Kennedy served in the U.S. Navy until April 1945.

In 1946, he began a career in politics that spanned seventeen years. He represented Massachusetts's Eleventh Congressional District in the U.S. House of Representatives from 1947 to 1953. From 1953 to 1961, Kennedy served the state of Massachusetts in the U.S. Senate.

John F. Kennedy became the Democratic Party's nominee for the presidency of the United States in 1960. In the presidential election on November 8, 1960, he narrowly defeated Republican vice president Richard M. Nixon* to become the thirty-fifth president of the United States. During his few years of service as president before his untimely death, John F. Kennedy and his administration faced a number of international crises that were linked to the Soviet Union and the threat of Communism. Some of the more important crises that occurred during the Kennedy administration were the Communist threat to Southeast Asia during the early 1960s, the Bay of Pigs invasion of 1961, the Berlin crisis of 1961, and the Cuban missile crisis of 1962. The Nuclear Test Ban Treaty of 1963 and the emerging U.S. space program were two other major subjects that captivated the attention of the Kennedy administration in the area of foreign affairs.

During his short tenure as president of the United States, John F. Kennedy did not face the same level of conflict in Arab–Israeli affairs that his predecessor, Dwight D. Eisenhower,* and his successor, Lyndon Baines Johnson,* had to face. Nonetheless, President Kennedy and the United States were still involved in issues pertaining to the Arab–Israeli conflict. President Kennedy was particularly warm to the Middle Eastern state of Israel. During his term in office, President Kennedy pledged nineteen times that the United States would support Israel's security in the event of an Arab attack on the Jewish state. In one instance, Meyer Feldman, an assistant to the president, was secretly dispatched to Israel to inform the Israelis that the United States would commit the U.S. Sixth Fleet to the Jewish state's protection. In addition to the Kennedy administration's commitments to Israel's survival, President Kennedy was also relatively noncritical of Arab nationalism. Prior to the crisis in United States–Arab relations caused, in large part, by the conflict and intervention in Yemen, he attempted, through personal correspondence with Egyptian president Gamal Abdul Nasser* and the extension to Egypt* of the PL-480 Food Program, to foster warmer relations with Egypt than what had been fostered under the Eisenhower administration. Though unsuccessful, Kennedy also attempted to address the refugee* situation in the Middle East. In a letter dated May 11, 1961, to President Nasser, Kennedy declared: "Underlying tensions do, however, remain, not the least of which is the unresolved Arab–Israeli controversy. . . . We are willing to help resolve the tragic Palestine refugee problem on the basis of the principle of repatriation or compensation of properties . . . and to be helpful in making progress on other aspects of this complex problem.''

For further information see: John Fitzgerald Kennedy, *John F. Kennedy on Israel, Zionism and Jewish Issues* (New York: Herzl Press, 1965); Theodore C. Sorensen, *Kennedy* (New York: Harper & Row, 1965); George Lenczowski, *American Presidents and the Middle East* (Durham, NC: Duke University Press, 1990).

Jon J. Peterson

KEREN HAYESOD (Palestine Foundation Fund). The major fund-raising and financial institution of the World Zionist Organization* that financed its activities in Palestine.* The 1920 Zionist* conference created the fund to finance immigration to Palestine and rural settlement there, and, in March 1921, it was registered as a British company. In subsequent years it funded the building of the Jewish state in Palestine and Israel. Its funds came from contributions and financed activities in the areas of immigration, absorption, settlement, water* resource development, and economic investment. Keren Hayesod was incorporated as an Israeli company by a special act of the Knesset,* the Keren Hayesod Law of January 18, 1956.

KEREN KAYEMET LE ISRAEL. See **JEWISH NATIONAL FUND.**

KFIR FIGHTER AIRCRAFT. The Kfir is an Israeli-designed and -produced single-seat, multirole, supersonic fighter aircraft with a design similar to the French Dassault Mirage III/5. The Kfir was developed in the early 1970s. It was first introduced to the public in April 1975 and flew its first combat mission in 1977. The Kfir has a maximum speed of Mach 2.3 (1,515 mph) and an operational altitude of 58,000 feet. The Kfir was designed to be employed in either an air-defense or ground-attack role. The Kfir is armed with two 30mm cannons and, depending on its mission, can be armed with air-to-air missiles (Sidewinder, Python, or Shafrir), air-to-surface missiles (Shrike, Maverick, or GBU-15), conventional bombs, cluster munitions, napalm, air-to-ground rockets, electronic countermeasure pods, and other specialized weapons pods. Unrefueled combat radius for the Kfir in the air-defense role with fuel drop tanks and two air-to-air missiles is 548 miles. In the ground-attack role with drop tanks, 2,600 pounds of bombs, and two air-to-air missiles, the Kfir has a combat radius of 737 miles. The Kfir is air-refuelable.

Israel produced more than 200 of the Kfir fighters, and, over the years, the aircraft has been improved. The Kfir has seen combat service in Lebanon.* In 1985, the U.S. Navy leased twelve Kfir aircraft for three years to use for U.S. Navy training. In 1986, the U.S. Marine Corps leased an additional thirteen Kfirs for a similar role.

For further information see: Michael J. H. Taylor, ed., *Jane's World Combat Aircraft* (Surrey: Jane's Information Group, 1988).

Stephen H. Gotowicki

KHADDAM, ABDUL HALIM. A Sunni Muslim from the Syrian coastal town of Banyas, Abdul Halim Khaddam was educated at Damascus University, where he received his bachelor of law degree. A lawyer who joined the Syrian Baath Party, he became friends with Syrian* president Hafez al-Assad* in school. Khaddam was appointed provincial governor of Hamma and was in charge during the 1964 insurrection. He was also the governor in Kuneitra* when the city was captured by Israel in the Six Day War.* In 1975, Khaddam was one of three Syrian Sunni Muslims to guide Syrian policy during the Lebanese Civil War, and he made frequent trips to Lebanon* in an attempt to end the fighting. Khaddam was Syrian foreign minister, and, in 1984, he became vice president. Abu Nidal's* organization attempted to assassinate him in December 1976 in Syria and again at the Abu Dhabi Airport on October 25, 1977. In November 1983, when Assad became ill, Khaddam was one of six men selected to carry out the day-to-day affairs of Syria.

Joseph E. Goldberg

KHALAF, SALAH (Abu Iyad) (b. Jaffa, Palestine,* 1933; d. January 1991). A Fatah* leader. He lived in Gaza* from 1948 to 1951, when he left to pursue his studies in Cairo. He returned to Gaza as a teacher in 1957. Abu Iyad is one of Yasser Arafat's* oldest friends. He has been a member of Fatah since 1963, a spiritual godfather to the Black September* group, and the executive responsible for Palestine Liberation Organization* (PLO) security and counterintelligence. In his early years he was a member of the Muslim Brotherhood* and met Arafat in 1951 while on a mission for the brotherhood. Salah Khalaf became Arafat's assistant when the latter was elected president of the Union of Palestinian Students* in Egypt* in 1952.

In the early 1970s, Khalaf was one of Fatah's most outspoken critics of Jordan* and King Hussein.* He had called for the assassination of the king in order to establish a Palestinian base of operations in Jordan and later advocated that the Hashemite regime be replaced by a Palestinian state. Jordanian authorities arrested him in September 1970 and sentenced him to death, though he was allowed to leave Jordan. In October 1974, Khalaf was implicated in an aborted assassination plot directed at King Hussein at the Rabat Arab Summit.

Khalaf was the second-in-command of the Palestinian Liberation Organization and one of Yasser Arafat's closest confidants. When he was fifteen years old, in what he termed the worst day of his life, he and his family were forced into exile to the Gaza Strip.* The Jewish state of Israel was born, and Khalaf's lifelong involvement with the Palestinian struggle was about to begin. After completing high school in Gaza, he attended Cairo University, where he became dedicated to Palestinian politics. In Cairo he met Yasser Arafat. In 1956, Arafat, Khalaf, and Abu Jihad* formed the Palestinian National Liberation Movement.

Abu Iyad is the coauthor, along with Yasser Arafat, of the strategy of the Palestinian struggle. Abu Iyad authored a book titled, *My Home, My Land,* in which he outlined the tenets of this struggle. He claimed the Palestinians needed an independent organization in order for them to mount a credible campaign for a separate homeland. They would have to rely on themselves and not on the Arab countries to achieve their goals. The campaign for a Palestinian entity was more important than the goal of Arab unity. Palestinians would have to rely on revolutionary violence as the main weapon of this struggle. The cause of Arab unity would be better served if Arabs and Palestinians worked together to ensure the creation of a separate homeland.

Abu Iyad was the head of the Intelligence and Security Apparatus of Fatah and the PLO. He also oversaw the PLO's clandestine units, including the Special Operations Group and Force 17.* However, his notoriety stems from his founding of the Black September terrorist organization. He has been held responsible for some of the bloodiest terrorist incidents, including the slaughter of Israeli athletes at the 1972 Munich Olympics.* The 1973 seizure of the Saudi Embassy in Khartoum and the murders of the American ambassador and other diplomats as well as the 1976 assassination of the American ambassador to Lebanon* were carried out at his behest.

He personified the PLO's penchant for violence. He asserted the right of the Palestinian resistance to resort to revolutionary violence as a means of achieving the PLO's goals. However, he drew a curious distinction between revolutionary violence and terrorism. Terrorism, he maintained, was undertaken outside the framework of an organization and lacked strategic goals. Its motives were subjective and did not represent the people's goals. Revolutionary violence, however, was an organized movement. This type of violence was used to maintain international focus on a particular cause. The use of revolutionary violence became insignificant through success on the political front.

This violent tendency was tempered by a pragmatic approach to the Palestinian struggle. In October 1968, Khalaf affirmed the PLO's strategic objective that called for the creation of a democratic state where all Jews, Christians, and Muslims could live together equally. He also became the first PLO official in 1974 to call for the creation of a Palestinian "ministate" next to Israel as an alternative to a separate homeland. He had even spoken openly about the possibility of mutual recognition but affirmed the need to make concessions only from a position of strength. Thus, Abu Iyad was a realist who understood years ago that an Israel that feels secure about its safety might be more accommodating toward some type of Palestinian homeland. When Saddam Hussein invaded Kuwait in 1990 and subsequently linked the Palestinian issue with an Iraqi* withdrawal, Khalaf was quoted as rejecting such an association, despite Arafat's support. It was widely believed that Abu Iyad's assassination was carried out at the behest of Saddam Hussein because of Abu Iyad's opposition to this linkage. He was assassinated in January 1991 by Palestinians identified as Abu Nidal's* men.

For further information see: Abu Iyad, with Eric Rouleau, *My Home, My Land: A Narrative of the Palestinian Struggle* (New York: Times Books, 1981).

Nancy Hasanian and Joseph E. Goldberg

KHALIL, MUSTAFA (b. 1920). Prime minister of Egypt* from October 1978 to May 1980 and foreign minister from February 1979 until May 1980, Khalil was a leading negotiator for the Egyptian side at Camp David* and throughout the peace treaty discussions.

He graduated in engineering from the University of Cairo and received a doctorate from the University of Illinois.

Trained as a civil engineer, Khalil first came to political prominence as one of the few civilian members of the Supreme Executive of the Arab Socialist Union in 1962–64, having served from 1956 as minister of communications and transport and on the board of the Permanent Council for National Production from 1955.

Khalil served as deputy prime minister for broadcasting and television in 1964–65 and as deputy prime minister for industry, mineral resources, and electrification in 1965–66. Khalil's technological background provided a basis for his rapid advancement under a regime that constantly stressed the role of the technocrat in national development, though policy disputes led him to resign from the Cabinet in September 1966. He became head of the Broadcasting Corporation in 1970 and, from 1970 to 1976, was secretary-general of the Arab Socialist Union. Since November 1977, Khalil has been a member of Egypt's National Security Council. Following the Cabinet reshuffle of May 1980, he assumed the post of deputy chairman for foreign affairs in the National Democratic Party.

He accompanied Sadat* on his visit to Israel in November 1977 and took part in the negotiations at Camp David and the Egypt–Israel Peace Treaty.* He served from October 1978 to May 1980 (when Sadat became his own prime minister) as prime minister and from June 1979 also as foreign minister.

KHARTOUM ARAB SUMMIT. At the Khartoum Arab Summit on September 1, 1967, the Arab states agreed to unite their efforts "to eliminate the effects of the [Israeli] aggression" in the Six Day War* and to secure Israeli withdrawal from the occupied territories* within the framework of "the main principles" to which they adhere: "no peace with Israel, no recognition of Israel, no negotiation with it, and adherence to the rights of the Palestinian people in their country." See also THREE NOES.

KIBYA (QIBYA). The first major retaliatory raid by Israel to acts of provocation and murder along its borders with the neighboring Arab states took place against Kibya. Differences on how to respond to Arab infiltration attacks on Israel had

existed within the Israeli government since the early 1950s. The dominant position, advanced by Israel's first prime minister and defense minister, David Ben-
Gurion,* Pinhas Lavon,* and Moshe Dayan,* called for strong reprisals. In their
judgment, Arab attacks threatened the very existence of the Jewish state. Force,
they contended, was understood by the Arabs. Furthermore, neighboring Arab
countries would be forced to keep their borders free from infiltrators if they
wished to avoid Israeli retaliation raids. The reprisal response was identified as
a position supported by the Israel Defense Forces.* A second position, associated with Moshe Sharett,* who was prime minister from December 1953 to
November 1955 and foreign minister from 1948 to June 1956, called for restraint
in response. Sharett contended that force alone could not resolve Israel's security
concerns and that diplomacy must also be used if retaliation from all sides was
to end.

On October 13, 1953, infiltrators from Jordan* murdered a thirty-two-year-
old mother and two of her children and wounded another of her children in the
settlement of Yehud. This attack was one among a number that had taken place
in recent months. Jordan, fearful of an Israeli raid, allowed Israeli soldiers to
enter its territory in an attempt to locate the attackers. The effort failed, but
Jordan promised that it would continue to hunt for the murderers. Israeli intelligence had identified Kibya, a Jordanian village, as one of the major bases used
by the infiltrators. In response, the Israeli General Staff proposed that the village
be occupied and fifty of its houses destroyed in an act of revenge and deterrence.
Sharett opposed the operation. He emphasized the willingness of the Jordanian
government to aid in bringing the murderers to justice. Nevertheless, on the
evening of October 14 into the early morning of October 15, a combined Israeli
force of paratroopers and members of a special antiterrorist group, Unit 101,*
led by Ariel Sharon,* attacked Kibya. Approximately twelve Jordanian soldiers
were killed in the initial attack. An Israeli mortar unit diverted attention from
the main thrust by attacking an outlying area. Forty-five Kibya houses were
blown up. Despite orders to check the houses for occupants, approximately sixty
residents hiding in the houses were killed. Sharon understated the Jordanian
losses. Israel claimed that the civilians were killed by mistake, but the Jordanian
government insisted that they had been systematically murdered. Diplomatic
reaction from around the world was swift. Britain condemned the attack and
threatened to send military support to Jordan. The United States also condemned
the attack and withheld a promised aid package. A United Nations Security
Council Resolution of November 24, 1953, condemned the attack.

Though the attack did result in a temporary decrease in infiltration in the area,
the diplomatic costs to Israel were substantial. Furthermore, the killing of civilians produced an ethical debate about Israeli policy within the Jewish state
as well as intensifying the differences within the government over the policy of
retaliation.

For further information see: Hal Lehrman, "Kibya, Jerusalem and the River Jordan:
Exploring the Sources of U.S.–Israel Misunderstanding," *Commentary* 17 (April 1954):

317–29; Benny Morris, *Israel's Border Wars: 1949–1956* (Oxford: Oxford University Press, 1993).

Joseph E. Goldberg

KILOMETER 101. On October 28, 1973, following the Yom Kippur War* and United Nations (UN) Security Council Resolution 338,* negotiations between senior Egyptian* and Israeli military officials began at Kilometer 101 along the Cairo-Suez Road. The talks, mediated by Henry Kissinger,* resulted in a six-point agreement, signed by Egyptian general Abdul Ghani Gamassy* and Israeli general Aharon Yariv on November 11, 1973. The six-point agreement was the first bilateral accord signed by the two parties since 1949 and represented a promising start to the future of direct negotiations. The agreement stipulated the following: (1) Egypt and Israel agreed to observe scrupulously the cease-fire called for by the United Nations Security Council; (2) both sides agreed that discussions between them would begin immediately to settle the question of the return to the October 22 positions in the framework of agreement on the disengagement and separation of forces under the auspices of the UN; (3) the town of Suez would receive daily supplies of food, water, and medicine, and all wounded civilians in the town of Suez would be evacuated; (4) there would be no impediment to the movement of nonmilitary supplies to the East Bank; (5) the Israeli checkpoints on the Cairo–Suez Road would be replaced by UN checkpoints, and, at the Suez end of the road, Israeli officers could participate with the UN to supervise the nonmilitary nature of the cargo at the bank of the canal; and (6) as soon as the UN checkpoints were established on the Cairo-Suez Road, there would be an exchange of prisoners of war, including wounded.

On November 16, Generals Gamassy and Yariv met at Kilometer 101 to discuss the implementation of the six-point agreement. Point one of the agreement was not officially observed until the final Disengagement Agreement was signed on January 18, 1974. In accordance with point three, Israel allowed UN-driven vehicles to bring nonmilitary assistance into the town of Suez, and all wounded were subsequently evacuated. Point four permitted the nonmilitary resupply of the besieged Egyptian Third Army Corps.* Israeli checkpoints along the Cairo–Suez Road were replaced by UN checkpoints, with Israel maintaining supervision over the nature of the supplies as called for by point five of the agreement. The exchange of prisoners stipulated in point six began on November 5, under the auspices of the International Red Cross, and ended on November 22, 1973.

Point two of the agreement remained the most contentious and ultimately led to the breakdown of the Kilometer 101 talks. Kissinger feared that an early agreement on disengagement would either derail or delay the Geneva Peace Conference,* where he planned for the issue of disengagement to be the first stage of the conference. Thus, he reportedly encouraged the Israelis to withhold their position until Geneva, consequently contributing to the termination of Gamassy and Yariv's seminal talks. Discussions on disengagement and the separation of forces were resumed in Geneva, but without resolution. Kissinger was able to mediate talks to a successful conclusion when the chiefs of staff of Egypt and Israel signed a Disengagement Agreement* on January 18, 1974.

For further information see: Ismail Fahmy, *Negotiating for Peace in the Middle East* (Baltimore: Johns Hopkins University Press, 1983); Matti Golan, *The Secret Conversations of Henry Kissinger: Step-by-Step Diplomacy in the Middle East* (New York: Quadrangle Books, 1976); Henry Kissinger, *Years of Upheaval* (Boston: Little, Brown, 1979); William B. Quandt, ''Kissinger and the Arab–Israeli Disengagement Negotiations,'' *Journal of International Affairs* (Spring 1975):33–48; William B. Quandt, *Decades of Decision: American Policy toward the Arab–Israeli Conflict, 1967–1976* (Berkeley: University of California Press, 1977); William B. Quandt, *Peace Process: American Diplomacy and the Arab–Israeli Conflict since 1967* (Washington, DC: Brookings Institution, 1993).

Anamika Krishna

KING ABDULLAH. See ABDULLAH, KING OF JORDAN.

KING–CRANE COMMISSION. The initial suggestion to create a Commission of Inquiry regarding the future of the Near Eastern territories of the Ottoman Empire* was made by Amir Feisal ibn Hussein.* He had attended the Paris Peace Conference* in January 1919 as a representative of his father, seeking to further the Arab case for independence. Citing President Woodrow Wilson's* principles of self-determination, he proposed that a Commission of Inquiry be sent to Syria* and Palestine* to survey the inhabitants and find out what they desired. At a meeting of the Big Four in March 1919, Wilson proposed that a commission visit Syria to elucidate the state of opinion in the region and report on its findings to the peace conference.

When it came time to designate who would represent the powers, France,* Great Britain,* and Italy withdrew. Wilson appointed two men: Henry C. King, the president of Oberlin College, and Charles R. Crane, an industrialist. The King–Crane Commission was the first significant American involvement in the political affairs of the area, although, in the final analysis, the inquiry had no real effect as neither the Allies nor the United States gave it serious consideration.

King and Crane arrived in Palestine in June 1919, conducted interviews, and studied reports and documents. In August, the commission submitted its report to the American delegation for use at the peace conference. Generally, it argued against Zionist* objectives and sought to include Palestine within a larger Syrian Mandate that would also include Lebanon.*

By the time the peace treaty was signed on July 21, they had visited thirty-six of the more important towns and had spoken to delegations from throughout Syria and Palestine. The final report was given to Wilson but never formally presented to the peace conference due to the hostility toward the French claims in Syria. Copies were given to both the French and the British.

The King–Crane Commission Report consisted of three sections: data, general considerations, and recommendations. It emphasized that whatever foreign administration went into Syria, it should not go in as a colonizing power but as a Mandatory.* It would maintain the Mandate with the definite understanding that the "well-being and development" of the Syrian people constituted a "sacred trust." Therefore, the Mandate should have a limited term, the date of expiration to be determined by the League of Nations. Since the goal was to assist in the creation of an independent and self-sufficient state, capable of standing on its own at the end of the Mandatory period, the commission stressed that the Mandatory administration should create educational and economic programs, the training of citizens for independent self-government, and the ensurance of religious liberty. It further recommended that Syria be placed under one Mandatory power, which would result in a real and efficient unity. The territory should be kept intact—not split into smaller areas—and given precise boundaries.

The fourth recommendation of the commission, based on the consensus of the Syrian people, was that Amir Feisal should be made head of the "new united Syrian state." This new state would best be governed by a "constitutional monarchy along democratic lines."

In the matter of Palestine, the commission recommended severe modification of the Zionist program of unlimited immigration of Jews into Palestine.

The commission stated that "a national home* for the Jewish people is not equivalent to making Palestine into a Jewish state" and cautioned that the establishment of a Jewish state cannot be accomplished without interfering with the civil and religious rights of the existing non-Jewish communities in Palestine. The Zionists had made it known, in discussions with the commissioners, that "they looked forward to the complete dispossession of the present non-Jewish inhabitants of Palestine, by various forms of purchase."

The commission also warned of the intense anti-Zionist sentiment that existed in Syria, as well as in Palestine. It did not give serious consideration to the Zionists' claim of a "right" to Palestine based on an occupation of 2,000 years prior and recommended that a "greatly reduced" Zionist program be initiated by the conference and only on a gradual basis.

The commission also concluded, in light of its study, that the Mandate should go to America, the preference of the peoples of Syria and Palestine. In lieu of that arrangement, Great Britain would be satisfactory. However, 60 percent of the petitions presented to the commission strongly protested against a French Mandate.

For further information see: Harry N. Howard, *The King–Crane Commission: An American Inquiry in the Middle East* (Beirut: Khayats, 1963).

Nancy Hasanian

KING DAVID HOTEL. The preeminent luxury hotel in Jerusalem* since its construction in 1930, it was designed by Swiss architect Emile Vogt. After World War II, in addition to functioning as a hotel, it housed the headquarters for the British military and civilian command in Palestine.*

On July 22, 1946, the Irgun Zvai Leumi,* led by Menachem Begin,* bombed the hotel. The bombing reduced twenty-eight rooms on six floors in the southwest corner of the building to a pile of rubble and killed a total of ninety-one people: forty-one Arabs, twenty-eight British, seventeen Jews, and five others. The bombing occurred at 12:37 P.M. on a Monday, one of the busiest hours of the busiest day of the week.

One purported reason for the operation was to destroy documents that the British had taken from the Jewish Agency* on June 29. According to the operation's commander, Amihai Paglin, this goal resulted in pressure to increase the quantity of explosives and to minimize the warning period. Others deny that the operation was designed to destroy specific documents and argue that the operation was a political act, a demonstration that the Irgun* could strike at the very heart of the British governance of Palestine.

The explosives were packed into seven milk churns, which were loaded onto a stolen pickup truck. The truck and a stolen taxi were then driven to the hotel by the assault party, who were dressed as Arabs. The Irgun gained entrance to the hotel at 11:45 A.M. through the service entrance, which was not guarded. Three armed men held up the doorman, rounded up the rest of the basement staff, and held them under guard while others unloaded the milk churns. The milk churns were placed in the café, directly under the Secretariat's office. Israel Levi, the leader of the party, connected detonators and timing devices, together with a booby trap to prevent any attempt to disarm the bombs, and placed notices on the churns reading "mines—do not touch" in three languages.

At some point during the operation, the Irgun men were challenged by a British officer who came down to the basement. The Irgun struggled to get him into the kitchen where the other prisoners were held, but he escaped despite being shot in the stomach. The officer managed to report to the hotel manager that some Arabs in the basement had shot him. British security officers investigated and came across the assault party as it attempted to withdraw. Alarms were sounded, and shots were fired. The assault team abandoned the truck and escaped by foot through the hotel garden to their taxi. Although two of the team were hit, the entire team escaped, six in the taxi and others by foot into the Jewish Quarter of the Old City.*

Considerable controversy has surrounded the fact that when the milk churns exploded at 12:37 P.M., the British authorities had received no warning. The Irgun has maintained that it did not intend to cause ninety-one deaths and that the British were to be given thirty minutes' warning. It appears, however, that the woman charged with telephoning the British authorities failed to complete the call until two minutes before the explosion. At that time, the British authorities' attentions were diverted away from the hotel by the escaping assault team and the bombs on the Arab barrows. This was just as well because any attempt to evacuate the building just before the explosion would have resulted in the entire staff of the Secretariat rushing to the stairs in the southwest corner of the building.

The bombing was the bloodiest operation undertaken by the Irgun and violated its self-imposed limitation against unnecessary killing. The Irgun's reputation was tarnished by the event, but the bombing demonstrated the intensity of the Jews' opposition to British rule, the willingness of at least some to resort to violence, and the cost to Britain of attempting to continue to govern Palestine. The following year, Britain decided to relinquish control over Palestine and referred the matter to the United Nations.

The King David Hotel was rebuilt in 1948, and two floors were added. Since then it has been the preeminent luxury hotel in Jerusalem and the host to numerous dignitaries and conferences.

For further information see: Thurston Clarke, *By Blood and Fire: The Attack on the King David Hotel* (New York: G. P. Putnam's Sons, 1981).

Richard G. R. Schickele

KIRYAT ARBA. A Jewish settlement established at Hebron* after the Six Day War.* The name Kiryat Arba or Kiryat Haarbah is mentioned in the Bible: "Kiryat Arba, that is Hebron" (Joshua, 15:54); "Hebron, formally called Kiryat Arba" (Judges, 1:10); "Kiryat Arba, that is Hebron" (Genesis, 35:27); and "some of the men of Judah* lived in Kiryat Arba and its villages" (Nehemiah, 11:25). According to Jewish tradition, Kiryat Arba (the Town of Four) was given this name in memory of the four couples of patriarchs and matriarchs who were the founders of the Israelite nation: Adam and Eve, Abraham and Sarah, Isaac and Rebecca, and Jacob and Leah. All these forefathers, with the exception of Adam and Eve, are thought to be buried in the nearby Cave of Machpela.*

KIRYAT SHMONA MASSACRE. (Alternate spellings: Qiryat Shmonah, Kiryat Shimona, Kiryat Shemona.) On April 11, 1974, three members of the Popular Front for the Liberation of Palestine—General Command* (PFLP—GC), also known as the Jibril Front, entered the town of Kiryat Shmona, killing eighteen Israelis (eight civilian adults, eight children, and two soldiers) and wounding sixteen others. The attack was one of the first fedayeen* suicide missions against Israel and ushered in a new strategy of entering Israeli settlements and killing everyone in sight. The Israeli government responded to the raid by attacking villages in southern Lebanon* believed to harbor fedayeen forces; it also began the policy of responding to fedayeen raids emanating from Lebanon with increasing harshness.

Kiryat Shmona is located between the Golan Heights* and the hills of Upper Galilee at the northern end of the Hula Valley. At the time of the incident, it was inhabited by approximately 18,000 Israelis, mostly Sephardic and Edot Hamizrach Jews.

The attack on Kiryat Shmona occurred on the one-year anniversary of the Israeli commando attack in Beirut. It also coincided with the peace negotiations being held in Geneva,* which the PFLP—GC opposed.

The three assailants were identified as a Syrian,* a Palestinian,* and an Iraqi.*

Evidently, they had intended to enter the Yanosh Korczak Elementary School and take the children hostage; however, the school was empty because of the Passover holiday. Upon leaving the school, they were discovered and pursued by the Israel Defense Forces.* The three men fled into an apartment building, shooting at everyone they saw with their AK-47 Kalishnikov rifles. After barricading themselves in an upper apartment, a gun battle with Israel Defense Forces ensued. In the end an explosion took place from within the apartment, killing all three; it was never determined whether a stray bullet struck the explosives on the suicide belt of one of the attackers, or whether one of them had set off the explosion himself.

The Israeli government blamed the Lebanese government for having allowed the insurgents to infiltrate Israel from Lebanese territory. The Lebanese government responded by stating that the raid had actually originated in Israel proper.

For further information see: Beate Hamizrachi, *The Emergence of the South Lebanon Security Belt: Major Saad Haddad and the Ties with Israel, 1975–1978* (New York: Praeger, 1988); "Israelis Attack Border Villages in Lebanon," *New York Times,* April 15, 1974; Juan De Onis, "Mideast Talks Called Terrorists' Target," *New York Times,* April 13, 1974; "Palestinian Group Says Suicide Squad Carried Out Worst Raid Since '73," *New York Times,* April 12, 1974; Terence Smith, "Dayan Says Raids against Lebanon Will Be Continued," *New York Times,* April 14, 1974; Terence Smith, "Israel Cautions Lebanese after Raid by Terrorists," *New York Times,* April 12, 1974.

Donald A. Pearson

KISSINGER, HENRY A. (b. Furth, Germany, May 27, 1923). He came from an Orthodox Jewish family but turned away from his Orthodox Jewish roots as an adult. Kissinger and his family emigrated to the United States in 1938, fleeing Nazi persecution. He served with the U.S. Army during World War II in Europe. He earned his B.A. (1950) and his Ph.D. (1956) at Harvard. He remained at Harvard, where he became a professor of government in 1962. He became an adviser on security matters under Presidents Eisenhower,* Kennedy,* and Johnson.* He was also Nelson Rockefeller's 1968 presidential campaign foreign policy adviser. In 1969, President Nixon* named him national security adviser (NSA), and, in 1973, secretary of state. Kissinger was the chief architect of U.S. foreign policy in both the Nixon and Ford* administrations. President Ford replaced him as NSA in 1975, though he remained secretary of state. His diplomacy was marked by realpolitik and by a global balance of power. Kissinger engaged in personal diplomacy, often with secret, behind-the-scenes negotiations. In 1973, together with North Vietnamese representative Le Duc Tho, he won the Nobel Peace Prize for helping to end U.S. military involvement in Vietnam.

During the first year and a half of the Nixon administration, Kissinger was kept from dominating Middle East policy. In 1969, Kissinger advocated strong backing for Israel until the Arabs decided to break their ties with Moscow. Kissinger opposed the Rogers Plan* because it defined a final settlement before a foundation for its implementation could be established. He was against the State Department's launching of initiatives in general, and he successfully helped to undermine State's initiatives. Kissinger believed in a policy that would keep Israel strong. This policy would result in a diplomatic stalemate that would force the Arabs to realize it was pointless to rely on Soviet support. The Arabs, he believed, should be made to think that they could not count on the United States and Soviets to pressure Israel to make concessions unless they were prepared themselves to make concessions. Kissinger viewed the Middle East as an extension of the superpower conflict and was concerned about the global ramifications of the Arab–Israeli conflict. He wanted to reduce Soviet influence in the Arab–Israeli conflict and believed that Soviet involvement made the conflict dangerous. This view led to the Kissinger policy of linkage in the Middle East to get the Soviets to restrain their Arab allies.

During the War of Attrition,* Kissinger moved Nixon away from an even-handed approach to supplying Israel with increased aid to counter Soviet military aid to Egypt.* During the spring of 1970, Kissinger's argument that the growing Soviet presence in Egypt could be handled only by a strong support of Israel was starting to be accepted by Nixon. Kissinger noted that if Nasser* was able to recover the Sinai Peninsula* by arms supplied by the Soviets, Soviet influence would grow throughout the region. During the Jordan crisis (1970),* Kissinger helped to successfully engineer a policy of using Israel as a counter to Syria.* To accomplish this, Kissinger gained control of U.S. Middle East policy from the State Department. The policy toward the Arab–Israeli conflict was now one of standstill diplomacy. There was increased military aid to Israel, which now was treated as a junior partner against Soviet influence in the Middle East. Kissinger squashed any new peace initiatives arising from the State Department. He believed that war would be prevented by maintaining the military balance in Israel's favor. He wanted to frustrate the Arabs so they would break with the Soviets.

Kissinger did not foresee the Yom Kippur War*; he misjudged the Arab reluctance to go to war. During the war he delayed answering Israeli requests for a major U.S. resupply effort because he wanted the war to end in a way that would most likely result in a permanent settlement between the Arabs and Israelis. The task of day-to-day diplomacy during the war was left to Kissinger, but Nixon made the key decisions. When the Soviets, toward the latter part of the conflict, were on the verge of sending Soviet troops, Kissinger made the decision to order a DEFCON III* alert, which put the U.S. military on a worldwide alert. Kissinger exerted U.S. pressure on Israel not to finish off the Egyptian Third Army* and force a debacle on the Egyptians. He engineered the cease-fire between the Arabs and Israelis, ending the Yom Kippur War. After the war, through shuttle diplomacy,* Kissinger helped to negotiate the Egyptian–Israeli Disengagement Agreement* (January 18, 1974), the Israeli–Syrian Disengagement Agreement* (May 31, 1974), and the Israeli–Egyptian Sinai II Accords* (September 4, 1975).

For further information see: Ishaq I. Ghanayem, *The Kissinger Legacy* (New York: Praeger, 1984); Matti Golan, *The Secret Conversations of Henry Kissinger: Step-by-Step Diplomacy in the Middle East* (New York: Quadrangle/New York Times Book Company, 1976); Walter Issacson, *Kissinger* (New York: Simon and Schuster, 1992); Henry A. Kissinger, *White House Years* (Boston: Little, Brown, 1979); Henry A. Kissinger, *Years of Upheaval* (Boston: Little, Brown, 1982); William B. Quandt, *Peace Process* (Washington, DC: Brookings Institution, 1993); Edward R. F. Sheehan, *The Arabs, Israelis, and Kissinger: A Secret History of American Diplomacy in the Middle East* (New York: Reader's Digest Press, 1976).

Nolan Wohl

KLINGHOFFER, LEON (d. October 8, 1985). A sixty-nine-year-old former small appliance manufacturer from New York City, Klinghoffer and his wife, Marilyn, were aboard the cruise ship *Achille Lauro** when it was hijacked on October 7, 1985, off the coast of Alexandria, Egypt.* The hijackers claimed to be from the Palestine Liberation Front* and demanded the release of fifty Palestinian prisoners by Israel. If their demands were not met, they threatened to kill American and British passengers. Eyewitness accounts reported that the hijackers selected passengers based on national origin and shuffled their passports to compose the "death list." Some hostages later reported that the hijackers appeared to single out those passengers with Jewish-sounding names, including the wheelchair-confined Klinghoffer. On October 8, 1985, Klinghoffer was shot, and his body was thrown overboard, off the coast of Syria.*

Pamela Rivers

KNESSET. Israel's Parliament. The Knesset is the supreme authority in the state of Israel, and its laws are theoretically the source of all power and authority. In reality, the decisions are made by the prime minister and the government or Cabinet and ratified in the Parliament. It is based, to a significant degree, on the British model, as adapted to Israel's needs. It is a unicameral body of 120 members elected by the public at large for a term not to exceed four years.

KOLLEK, TEDDY (b. Vienna, 1911). He immigrated to Palestine* in 1934 and in 1936 became a founder of Kibbutz Ein Gev. From 1940 to 1947, he served on the staff of the Political Department of the Jewish Agency.* After Israel's independence he became minister at Israel's Embassy in Washington. Between 1952 and 1964, he served as director general of the prime minister's office and became a close adviser of David Ben-Gurion.* In 1966, he was elected mayor of Jerusalem* at the head of the RAFI Party (a political party founded by Ben-Gurion when he and his followers left MAPAI*) ticket. When Jerusalem was unified as a consequence of the Six Day War,* he was confronted by the challenges of extending city services to East Jerusalem* and serving as mayor of a diverse city composed of Jews and Arabs. In 1978, his One Jerusalem Party, composed of Labor Party members and personal supporters, took control of

Jerusalem's city council. He remained mayor of Jerusalem until he was defeated by Ehud Olmert in the election of November 1993. Earlier, Prime Minister Yitzhak Rabin* had declared that the results of the election would be a test of the Declaration of Principles* (DOP) agreement with the Palestine Liberation Organization* (PLO) that was signed in Washington in September 1993. Subsequently, that was revised, and the defeat was attributed to other factors, including his age and disaffection built up over his extensive period of public service.

Kollek served as mayor of Jerusalem for twenty-eight years. During much of that period he changed the landscape of Jerusalem with substantial building programs. In his tenure the growth of the Jewish population in East Jerusalem was such that, by the time he left office, there was a Jewish majority in the eastern half of the city that had been exclusively Arab under Jordanian control prior to the Six Day War. During his tenure, Kollek stressed that while Israeli sovereignty over the entire city was unassailable, he was a conciliator who sought to reduce tensions in the city between Jew and Arab as well as between the secular and the religious Jewish communities.

KOMAR MISSILE BOAT. The Komar is a fast attack vessel, similar to the OSA, produced in the Soviet Union in the early 1960s. It displaces eighty tons and has a maximum speed of thirty knots and a range of 400 miles. The Komar is armed with twin 25mm guns and two Styx ship-to-ship missile launchers.

In the Middle East, the Komar was procured only by Egypt* (1962–67) and Syria* (1963–66). In October 1967, an Egyptian Komar sank the Israeli destroyer *Eilat.** In 1970, Israeli jets sank an Egyptian Komar. During the Yom Kippur War,* the Israelis sank two Egyptian and three Syrian Komar boats.

For further information see: Richard Sharpe, ed., *Jane's Fighting Ships,* 95th ed. (Surrey: Jane's Information Group, 1992).

Stephen H. Gotowicki

KOOK, RABBI AVRAHAM YITZHAK HACOHEN (b. Griva, Latvia, 1865; d. Jerusalem,* 1935). Chief rabbi of Palestine.* He studied in various Eastern European yeshivot and served as rabbi for a number of communities. In 1904, he settled in Palestine, where he served as rabbi of the Jewish community of Jaffa. Stranded in Switzerland and England during World War I, he returned to Palestine in 1919 and became the rabbi of the Ashkenazi community of Jerusalem. When the chief rabbinate of Palestine was established in 1921, Kook was chosen Ashkenazi chief rabbi of Palestine and held that position until his death. He developed a nationalist-religious philosophy and pursued the Zionist* ideal. He established his own yeshiva in Jerusalem (Merkaz Harav), where he focused on the ideal of a religious-national renaissance for the Jewish people. Rabbi Kook contended that Jewish nationalism and the Jewish religion composed a whole. The separation of the two would ultimately distort both. In an appeal to Orthodox Jewry, Rabbi Kook emphasized that Jewish secularism was also part of the whole of Judaism, though it emphasized only one aspect: nationalism. The Orthodox must not oppose Jewish nationalism, he emphasized, because the spirit of Israel that is manifested in Jewish nationalism also reflects the divine. The responsibility of the Orthodox is to bring forth that divine spirit expressed in the nationalist expression. In this way Rabbi Kook attempted to reconcile the division between the religious and secular communities.

He was outspoken in his criticism of the administration of the British Mandate* in Palestine.

For further information see: S. Zalman Abramov, *Perpetual Dilemma: Jewish Religion in the Jewish State* (Rutherford, NJ: Fairleigh Dickinson University Press, 1976).

Joseph E. Goldberg

KOOK, RABBI ZVI YEHUDA (b. Lithuania, 1891; d. 1982). He was educated at Jewish religious schools as well as at a university in Germany. He immigrated with his parents to Palestine* in 1904, where his father, Rabbi Avraham Yitzhak Hacohen Kook,* later became chief rabbi. He became head of the Merkaz Harav Yeshiva and published numerous religious and other commentaries. He was an ardent Zionist. He participated in Gush Emunim* activities and became the movement's spiritual mentor.

KOREI, AHMED SULEIMAN. See **KARIA, AHMED SULEIMAN.**

KOZYREV, ANDREI (b. Brussels, Belgium, March 27, 1951). He was educated at the Moscow State Institute of International Relations. From 1968 to 1969 he worked at the Kommunar factory in Moscow. He became a member of the staff of the Ministry of Foreign Affairs and was named head of sector in 1974, a position he held until 1986. From 1986 to 1990 he was head of the Department of International Organization. In 1990, Kozyrev became a member of the State Duma. Kozyrev aligned himself with those who foresaw the end of the USSR and aided in the formation of the Commonwealth of Independent States. Kozyrev was cohost, with U.S. secretary of state James Baker,* of the January 1992 Middle East Peace Conference in Moscow. During the conference, Kozyrev stated Russia's commitment to legitimate Palestinian participation in the peace process. However, little progress was made at the meeting, which proceeded without the Palestinian delegation. The Palestinians were barred by the United States and Russia because their delegation was not properly constituted. As foreign minister of the Russian Federation, he witnessed the signing of the Israel–Palestine Liberation Organization* (PLO) Declaration of Principles* in Washington on September 13, 1993.

KUNEITRA. The principal city of the Golan Heights.* Once a city of 37,000 people, most of Kuneitra's inhabitants fled or were driven off after it fell to Israeli forces in the June 1967 war.* At the time, a mistaken report from radio

Damascus that the city had fallen may have precipitated the rout of Syrian* units west of the city who thought that they had been surrounded.

Israeli forces accepted a United Nations-mandated cease-fire on June 10 after securing Kuneitra. The loss of the city was an embarrassment for the ruling Syrian Baathist* regime, especially for then defense minister Hafezal–Assad.*

Because of Kuneitra's importance as a "prestige" objective, Israeli units in the city were surrounded by the Syrians during the October 1973 war* until being relieved on October 11.

During the spring 1974 disengagement talks,* Syria demanded the return of Kuneitra and a symbolic sliver of land to the west of the city. Israel agreed to return the demilitarized city to Syrian control but retained an observation post on the hills overlooking it from the west.

Before withdrawing, Israel leveled the city in a manner reminiscent of the destruction of Israeli settlements in the Sinai Peninsula.* This has perpetuated Syrian mistrust of Israel and contributed to tensions between the two countries.

For further information see: Chaim Herzog, *The War of Atonement, October, 1973* (Boston: Little, Brown, 1975); Patrick Seale, *Assad of Syria: The Struggle for the Middle East* (Berkeley: University of California Press, 1988).

                                                                    David J. Abram

L

LABOR PARTY. See **ISRAEL LABOR PARTY.**

LAHAD, ANTOINE. Major General Antoine Lahad, a Christian Lebanese* soldier formerly of the Lebanese army, became commander of the mostly Christian Free Lebanon Militia* (FLM) on April 4, 1984, after the death of his predecessor, Major Saad Georges Haddad.*

Immediately upon taking command, he changed its name to the South Lebanese Army* (SLA), for he claimed that it was no longer for just Christians but for all the freedom-loving peoples of South Lebanon. In the first two months of his command, he met with several Shiite leaders of southern Lebanon and had already increased his non-Christian contingency to 20 percent. The actual transfer of command occurred in the town of Bint Jubayl, at which time Lahad stated that he supported the relationship with Israel as a positive one, since Israel shared the common interests of the southern Lebanese people, and that this relationship must continue if there was to be a comprehensive peace in the region in the future. He declared that his role was clear: ''[t]o maintain security in [the] region and good relations with the Israelis.'' He also stated that his intentions were to guarantee the security of Israel's northern border, to preserve coexistence between all regional sects, and to lend full support to all institutions of the rightful Lebanese state. Also, Lahad increased the salary of his soldiers. Along with the increase in funds, Lahad managed to secure Israeli delivery of more vehicles to his forces.

Lahad has been criticized by some foreign observers and news sources for implementing punitive measures against people who resist his recruitment processes, and forcing people into serving in the SLA, and for his punitive measure of destroying homes of resisters, especially when SLA officers are killed.

Lahad has been cited for his frank openness about the roles of the Israel Defense Forces (IDF) and the SLA in southern Lebanon and the methods that the SLA uses to fend off terrorist attacks from the Shiite militiamen and other terrorists.

The IDF has found that Lahad's ability to keep the southern Lebanese Shiite terror gangs in check has been effective enough to warrant their continued maintenance of the SLA, to act as a "buffer force" between hostile Muslim forces and the Israeli frontier.

Lahad has led the SLA to continued success in maintaining relative quiet in the security zone* over the last ten years. Also, Lahad represents non-Israeli Arabs who support the Jewish state and are prepared to continue doing so. Beyond that, Israel has recognized the need to keep Lahad strong, until such time as the Syrian*-controlled Lebanese government is ready to sign a peace treaty with them and as soon as it reintegrates without prejudice Lahad and his forces into the regular Lebanese army.

Yasha Manuel Harari and Joseph E. Goldberg

LAND FOR PEACE. An internationally accepted formula for resolution of the Arab–Israeli conflict based on United Nations Security Council Resolutions 242* and 338.* The general concept is that Israel would return land (how much remains in dispute and, thus, to be negotiated) occupied during the Six Day War* in exchange for peace, recognition, and normalization with the Arab world.

LAND OF ISRAEL MOVEMENT. A political movement that began its efforts shortly after the Six Day War* and argued that Israel should retain the territories occupied (West Bank* and Gaza Strip*) in the war and establish settlements there. Much of its program and its supporters were later incorporated into Gush Emunim* and Tehiya.*

LANDAU, HAIM (b. 1916; d. October 6, 1981). Haim Landau was a leader of the Irgun* underground and later served as a minister in Menachem Begin's* government. Prior to the independence of Israel, he served as an engineer in the British Public Works Department in Palestine* and secretly in the Irgun Zvai Leumi. In 1944, after a number of Irgun leaders were captured in a cooperative British and Haganah* effort, known as "the Season," Landau rose to the Irgun's High Command. Prior to British withdrawal from Palestine in 1948, he became chief of staff. He was one of the founders of the Herut Party* following Israel's independence, and he served in the Knesset* until 1977. During the Six Day War,* he was a minister in the Government of National Unity.*

Joseph E. Goldberg

LARSEN, TERJE ROD. Terje Rod Larsen was the director general of the Oslo-based Norwegian Institute for Applied Social Science (FAFO), whose own research focused on the living conditions of the Palestinians* in the West Bank* and Gaza Strip.* His wife, Mona Juul, was a member of Norwegian Foreign Ministry's Secretariat. At that time, the wife of then Norway's defense minister, Johan Jorgen Holst, was Marienne Heiberg, who was a specialist on Palestinian society and had authored a study for FAFO.

Larsen and his wife had long been committed to contributing to the peace efforts between Israel and the Palestinians. Peace, in his judgment, was a necessary condition for alleviating the living conditions of the Palestinians. His hopes for success through the Madrid Conference* process had ended by April 1992.

That month Larsen traveled to Israel, where he made contact with Yossi Beilin, then a Labor Party* member of Israel's Knesset.* Beilen had known Larsen for a number of years and was sympathetic with his appeal for negotiations, but they were unsuccessful. Larsen meanwhile contacted Norway's defense minister. Holst took Larsen's proposal for establishing a back channel for negotiations between the Palestine Liberation Organization* (PLO) and Israel through Norway seriously.

When the Labor Party was returned to power in Israel in 1992, Beilin was named deputy foreign minister. Larsen again contacted him, and, through Beilin's suggestion, he contacted Yair Hirschfeld, a professor of Middle East history at Haifa University. Both Larsen and Hirschfeld agreed that a peace agreement would be encouraged if the antagonists could sign a joint declaration of principles.

The first contact between an Israeli representative, Hirschfeld, and a PLO representative, Ahmed Suleiman Karia* (Abu Alla), who had been responsible for PLO finances, took place on December 4, 1992, at a restaurant in the Forte Crest St. James Hotel in central London. After a number of meetings, both sides agreed to begin secret negotiations in January 1993.

Larsen emphasized informality among the participants. A house in the small town of Sarpsborg, south of Oslo, was the site of the first talks. From these discussions the Sarpsborg Document was produced, which was the first draft of a Declaration of Principles* (DOP). This ultimately was the foundation upon which the Gaza and Jericho First initiative* rested.

In various other settings in Norway, negotiations between Israel diplomats Uri Savir,* director general of the Foreign Ministry (and later Yoel Zinger,* a lawyer) and the PLO representative, Abu Alla, took place. Larsen, present at all of the negotiating sessions, ensured that the talks continued. An accord—the DOP—was signed on September 13, 1993, in Washington, D.C.

On May 26, 1994, United Nations (UN) secretary-general Boutros Boutros-Ghali* asked Terje Rod Larsen to be the UN deputy secretary-general for the

Middle East. He assumed the position in June 1994. Larsen has responsibility for coordinating all UN efforts in the Middle East.

Joseph E. Goldberg

LATRUN. A locality with a monastery at the foot of the Judean* hills on the road from Tel Aviv to Jerusalem.* The monastery was founded in the nineteenth century by French Trappist monks. It is located at a strategic crossroads linking the Mediterranean coast to Jerusalem where the coastal plain meets the Judean hills.

As far back as ancient times, which includes Joshua's conquest of Canaan,* the Maccabean Revolt, and the Bar Kochba Revolt, the Latrun area was a zone of conflict.

Britain controlled the area around Latrun during the Mandatory* period. The British quickly recognized the unique, strategic importance of the location, not only for the region of Palestine* but for the entire coastal Levant, and built a fortified police station in the town near the crossroads in order to protect it. There was a detention camp where Jewish political prisoners were held. Britain also established in Latrun a water-pumping station for the Rosh Haayin–Jerusalem water pipeline.

In the War of Independence,* Latrun was a key strategic point that played a major role in the contest over Jerusalem. A major effort was made by the Jews during the War of Independence to take Latrun to open the road from Tel Aviv to Jerusalem. An alternative Burma Road* was built. The Haganah* and, later, the Israel Defense Forces* (IDF) tried to pass convoys of supplies and weapons through Latrun to Jerusalem, but the Arabs, who controlled the area and the police station following the British evacuation on May 14, 1948, stopped the Israelis. In the days that followed Israel's Declaration of Independence, the Israelis briefly took the town and the police station, held it for two days (May 16 and 17), and successfully passed two convoys to Jerusalem. However, pressures on various other nearby fronts caused the Israelis to evacuate the strategic site, causing it to fall to the Fourth Battalion of the Arab Legion* on the eighteenth.

At that moment, the Israelis had missed one of the greatest opportunities of the War of Independence. On May 15, when Israel's neighbors invaded Palestine, the Arab mercenary who led the attacks on Latrun, Fauzi el-Kaukji, withdrew his forces to the north, believing that his task of putting pressure on Israeli forces in the crossroads area was complete and that his forces would be replaced automatically by Arab Legion commander John Bagot Glubb.* However, Glubb's forces were not due to arrive in the area until May 18, leaving the Israeli Givati Brigade operating in the area three days to consolidate, expand, and fortify their holding of not only Latrun but the entire surrounding area, which was vital for the defense of Jerusalem. However, inexperience of Israeli commanders, almost total absence of effective intelligence, and overall structural disorganization, which afflicted the Israeli forces in the first days of Israel's independence, all contributed to Israel's failure to seize the opportunity, allowing Glubb's forces to retake Latrun on May 18.

The continuing isolation of Israeli forces in Jerusalem caused the IDF to attempt at least five further efforts at capturing Latrun (including Operations Bin Nun Alef, Bin Nun Bet, and Yoram). All failed, inflicting large casualties on numerous key Israeli units, including the Harel, Givati, Alexandroni, Yiftah, and seventh Brigades. The military judgment of investing limited human and military resources to retake Latrun is debated to this day, as is the series of decisions that led Israeli forces to surrender Latrun to Glubb's forces rather than consolidate Israeli control and make it irreversible when it had the chance on May 15–18.

According to the cease-fire agreement signed with Jordan* in 1949, control of Latrun was awarded to the Arab Legion. An Arab fortress remained connected to Jordanian forces in Ramallah in the Samarian area through a single road and was separated from Israel by the creation of a buffer zone, which remained under neither side's control. Despite the stipulations of the cease-fire agreement, Arab Legion forces blew up the water-pumping station in Latrun to cut off Jerusalem from its water supply near Rosh Haayin. The cease-fire also stipulated that the crossroads would remain in an abandoned area controlled by neither side. Israeli convoys to provide basic supplies to Jerusalem would be permitted under United Nations (UN) escort. Resupply convoys were halted, however, when the Arabs attacked the first convoy attempting to reach Jerusalem through Latrun. The abandoned area was also to be divided between the two sides for agricultural use, though attempts at farming were frequently the targets of sniper attacks and raids.

The village of Latrun, the monastery, and the crossroads remained in Jordanian–Arab hands following the War of Independence until the Six Day War of 1967.* When fighting began in the West Bank,* however, the salient fell to the Israelis without any resistance.

David Wurmser

LAUSANNE CONFERENCE (1949). On December 11, 1948, the United Nations (UN) General Assembly adopted Resolution 194 (III),* which established a "Conciliation Commission consisting of three States Members of the United Nations" and which, among other functions, was mandated to "extend the scope of the negotiations provided for in the Security Council Resolution (62) of 16 November 1948 and to seek agreement by negotiations conducted either with the Conciliation Commission or directly, with a view to the final settlement of all questions outstanding between them." Among the issues that the resolution specifically identified was the return of refugees* to their homes as well as compensation for loss of property. France,* Turkey, and the United States were the three states members which provided representatives for the Palestine Conciliation Commission.*

As specified in the resolution, the Palestine Conciliation Commission attempted to mediate among the Arabs and Israel in order to transform the Armistice Agreements* into permanent peace treaties. A conference was held at Lausanne opening on April 27, 1949. Israel and four neighboring Arab states were invited to Lausanne. Israel's delegates were Walter Eytan and Elias Sasson. Jordan's* delegation included Jamal Tuqan, Edmund Rock, Walid Salih, and Musa al-Husseini. Syria* sent Farid al-Sad and Ahmad Shukayri. Egypt's* included Rashid al-Shawwa and Musa Surani. The Arab Higher Committee* also sent a delegation.

Israel was critical of the Palestine Conciliation Commission's decision to treat the four Arab states as one delegation rather than to have Israel meet with four distinct delegations. In their judgment, this helped nurture Arab intransigence. At Lausanne the Arab delegation made it evident that they did not recognize Israel. The Arab delegates were housed at the Lausanne Palace in the upper part of town, and the Israelis at the lakeside. In addition, the Arabs refused to sit in the same room with the Israelis, requiring the mediators to move not only from room to room but from one part of Lausanne to another—thus exaggerating further the negotiating conditions established in January 1949 at Rhodes, where at least the delegations were on separate floors of a single hotel, the Hotel des Roses. Occasional direct meetings did take place, but they were not acknowledged by the Arab delegations.

The Arab delegation insisted that the repatriation and return of the Arab refugees, as well as a return to the 1947 borders, should take place prior to any discussions of peace. Israel insisted that the refugee issue should be discussed in the context of a general peace discussion. Israel sought recognition while at the same time denying its responsibility for having created the refugee problem.

The Lausanne Protocol was signed on May 12, 1949. This document was intended by the Palestine Conciliation Commission to establish the grounds upon which Israel and the Arabs could reach agreement on "territorial adjustments." Because the document had been amended so many times, the intent of its final form became another source of disagreement. A note containing a map of Palestine* as partitioned and the UN partition resolution itself was attached to the protocol. The Israeli delegate explicitly stated Israel's reservations about the attachment of the note because they did not wish this territorial configuration to prejudice future deliberations on territorial adjustment. The Arab copy of the note did not contain the Israeli reservation, and they have insisted that the Lausanne Protocol established the 1947 partition resolution as the basis for future territorial adjustments. The secretary of the Palestine Conciliation Commission, Pablo de Azcarate, later denied that, when the protocol was drafted and signed, anyone gave it the Arab construction.

For further information see: Pablo de Florez Azcarate, *Mission in Palestine, 1948–1952,* trans. Teener Hall (Washington, DC: Middle East Institute, 1966); N. Bar-Yaacov, *The Israel–Syrian Armistice: Problems of Implementation, 1949–1966* (Jerusalem: Magnes Press, 1967); Neil Caplan, *The Lausanne Conference, 1949: A Case Study in Middle East Peacemaking* (Syracuse, NY: Syracuse University Press, 1993); Walter Eytan, *The*

First Ten Years: A Diplomatic History of Israel (London: Weidenfeld and Nicolson, 1958).

Joseph E. Goldberg

LAVON, PINHAS (Formerly Lubianiker) (b. 1904; d. 1976). He was the key figure in the ''affair'' that clouded Israel's political life for almost a decade from the mid-1950s to the mid-1960s, and that affair resulted in the downfall of a government and split the country's ruling Labor Party.*

He was born in Poland and attended Lvov University. Lavon immigrated to Palestine* at twenty-five. He became active in the MAPAI Party* and served as its secretary from 1935 to 1937. After Israel's independence, he was elected to the First Knesset.* Lavon served as minister of agriculture and then of supply and rationing before becoming minister of defense in 1953. He was forced to resign in February 1955. He was elected secretary of the Histadrut* in June 1956 and held that post until 1960. See also LAVON AFFAIR.

LAVON AFFAIR. Pinhas Lavon* was Israel's defense minister in 1954, when Israeli agents were arrested in Egypt,* apparently for trying to bomb U.S. facilities in Cairo and Alexandria and other targets in an effort to turn the United Kingdom and the United States against Egypt. The government of Prime Minister Moshe Sharett* had not been consulted, and Lavon claimed that he had not been aware of the plan. However, Colonel Benjamin Gibli, head of military intelligence, insisted that Lavon had personally instructed him to proceed. An inquiry was ordered, but no conclusion was reached. Lavon resigned from the government and was elected secretary-general of the Histadrut.* As a consequence of later revelations, the Cabinet was convinced that the evidence against Lavon had been fabricated, and the government issued a statement that the 1954 operation had been ordered with Lavon's knowledge. Prime Minister David Ben-Gurion,* who had been outvoted in the Cabinet, called the resolution a miscarriage of justice. In protest against the intrusion of the executive into the sphere of the judiciary, Ben-Gurion resigned and brought down the government. He told his party that he would not accept a mandate to form a new government as long as Lavon represented the party as secretary-general of the Histadrut. The party Central Committee ousted Lavon in 1961.

The 1954 Lavon affair centered around Israeli defense minister Pinhas Lavon's decision to order intelligence chief Benjamin Gibli to activate spy rings in Cairo and Alexandria, Egypt. The rings were composed of Egyptian Jews who were supposed to plant bombs at the American and British Embassies as well as sites frequented by Westerners. Responsibility for the resulting attacks would be blamed on the Muslim Brotherhood,* and it was hoped that this would prove to be an embarrassment to Egyptian president Gamal Abdul Nasser,* by creating the impression that he would not be able to provide adequate protection for foreign nationals in Egypt. Ultimately, it was hoped that the British would refuse to withdraw their troops from the Suez Canal* zone in order to protect their citizens. The plan backfired as the conspirators in Egypt were caught, tried, and executed.

Perhaps the most interesting aspect of the Lavon affair, as it became known, was the length of time it took between the actual event and the revelation of the incident to the Israeli public. The story did not break until 1960 because the government felt that it was necessary to keep the nature of the incident secret for reasons of national security. Until that time, the public believed that Nasser had invented the charges of espionage against those who were executed in order to further persecute the Jews.

An investigatory committee in 1955 under Justice Olshan of the Supreme Court and Major General Yaakov Dori, retired chief of staff of the Israel Defense Forces,* was unable to establish guilt or innocence regarding the central question of who gave the order to activate the agents. However, fearing detrimental testimony about him by Shimon Peres,* then director general of the Defense Ministry (with whom he had a personal feud), Lavon requested of Prime Minister Moshe Sharett to see Peres's testimony. Sharett refused, and Lavon resigned his post in protest.

Upon resuming his position as prime minister, Ben-Gurion appointed a new investigatory committee under Supreme Court Justice Cohn. Lavon mounted an intense public relations campaign to establish the notion that he had been framed. The commission found that too much time had elapsed between the initial investigation and the event and that guilt or innocence was impossible to establish.

For further information see: S. Z. Abramov, "The Lavon Affair," Commentary 31 (February 1961):100–105; Moshe Bar-Natan, "The Lavon Affair," Jewish Frontier 28 (January 1961):4–6; Erwin Frenkel, "The Lavon Affair: Its Political Implications," Midstream 7 (April 1961):60–69; J. L. Talmon, "Lavon Affair—Israeli Democracy at the Crossroads," New Outlook 4 (March–April 1961):23–32+.

Pamela Rivers

LAW OF RETURN (1950). The law was adopted by the Knesset* on July 5, 1950. It assures virtually unlimited and unfettered Jewish immigration to Israel by providing that every Jew has the right to immigrate to Israel to settle there unless the applicant is engaged in an activity "directed against the Jewish people" or one that may "endanger public health or the security of the state." An amendment in 1954 also restricted those likely to endanger public welfare. The 1950 law has provided the formal basis for the substantial immigration (aliyah)* that has taken place since independence. The concept of unlimited immigration, which has been reinforced by the programs and actions of successive governments and has had overwhelming support in Parliament and from Israel's Jewish population, has resulted in hundreds of thousands of Jewish immigrants from more than seventy countries coming to Israel.

LAWRENCE, T. E. (Thomas Edward, b. 1888; d. 1935). He was one of a group of British military liaison officers who encouraged, trained, advised, and supported the Arab forces that revolted against the Ottoman Empire* in 1916. As a British army intelligence officer and Arabist serving in Cairo, Lawrence urged his superiors to support the Arab Revolt* with arms and gold and to use Arab aspirations for independence as a strategic weapon against Turkey. When they agreed, he was assigned as a military liaison officer with the Arab forces of Prince Feisal,* third son of Sherif Hussein* of Mecca, who was the nominal leader of the Arab Revolt.

Under Lawrence's tutelage, Feisal's Arab forces conducted hit-and-run guerrilla attacks against Turkish forces in the Hejaz region and effectively closed the strategic Damascus-to-Medina railway. This occupied Turkish forces that otherwise would have opposed the British. Later, Lawrence led Feisal's forces to major victories in Aqaba,* Dar'a, and finally Damascus. Lawrence motivated the sometimes cynical, self-serving sheikhs with his personal bravery, commitment to the Arab cause, and British promises of postwar Arab independence.

Lawrence appeared to be motivated by conflicting goals. On one hand, he was a genuine supporter of Arab independence. On the other, he was committed to serve the strategic interests of Britain. There are indications that he knew His Majesty's government had made conflicting promises to different groups in the region and had little genuine interest in Arab independence beyond defeating Turkey. This did not seem to dissuade him in his devotion to his duty or the Arab Revolt.

After the war, Lawrence unsuccessfully lobbied for Arab independence at the 1919 Paris Peace Conference.* He strongly argued against the creation of the French Mandate over Lebanon* and Syria* because it divided the Arab peoples.

In 1921, Lawrence was enlisted as an adviser on Arab affairs to Winston Churchill,* then British colonial minister, for the Cairo Conference.* In Cairo, Britain decided to withdraw its Mandate over Iraq,* substituting an alliance with Iraq. This arrangement served as a partial fulfillment of England's* wartime promises of Arab independence, although it was motivated primarily by Britain's desire to reduce its military commitment in the area rather than interest in fulfilling its wartime promises.

In the end, the Arab Revolt was significantly influenced by Lawrence's efforts. In this, his contributions are legendary. Although he wittingly or unwittingly served as an instrument of Britain's wartime manipulation of the Arabs, Lawrence tried to use his postwar notoriety and influence to gain the independence promised the Arabs. In this, he met with only limited success.

For further information see: Richard Aldington, *Lawrence of Arabia: A Biographical Enquiry* (London: Collins, 1969); George Antonius, *The Arab Awakening* (Beirut: Librairie Du Liban, 1969); Phillip Knightly and Colin Simpson, *The Secret Lives of Lawrence of Arabia* (London: Thomas Nelson and Sons, 1969); T. E. Lawrence, *Revolt in the Desert;* John E. Mack, *A Prince of Our Disorder: The Life of T. E. Lawrence* (Boston: Little, Brown, 1976); Jeffrey Meyers, *T. E. Lawrence: A Bibliography* (New York: Garland, 1974); Jeffrey Meyers, ed., *T. E. Lawrence: Soldier, Writer, Legend: New Essays* (New York: St. Martin's Press, 1989); Jeffrey Meyers, *The Wounded Spirit: T.*

E. Lawrence's Seven Pillars of Wisdom (New York: St. Martin's Press, 1989); Suleman Mousa, *T. E. Lawrence: An Arab View* (New York: Oxford University Press, 1966); Stephen E. Tabachnick, ed., *The T. E. Lawrence Puzzle* (Athens, Georgia: University of Georgia Press, 1984); Jeremy Wilson, *Lawrence of Arabia: The Authorized Biography of T. E. Lawrence* (New York: Atheneum, 1990).

                                                                    Stephen H. Gotowicki

LAWRENCE OF ARABIA. See **T. E. LAWRENCE.**

LEAGUE OF ARAB STATES. The League of Arab States was founded March 22, 1945, in Alexandria, Egypt,* to coordinate increased Arab economic, cultural, and political unity. Headquartered in Cairo, its members are Egypt, Iraq,* Lebanon,* Saudi Arabia, Syria,* Jordan,* Yemen, Libya, Sudan, Tunisia, Morocco, Kuwait, Algeria, the United Arab Emirates, Bahrain, Oman, Mauritania, Somalia, Djibouti, and the Palestine Liberation Organization* (PLO). The Arab League Council is the highest decision-making body, composed of the heads of member states and based on equal representation (Article 3). To further the goal of strengthened relations (Article 2), six commissions were established (Article 4) to consider issues of trade, finance, communications, culture, nationality, and social concerns. Other accords were signed to foster cooperation: a joint defense and economic agreement (1950) to coordinate military defense measures; the Arab Economic Unity Agreement (1960); and the Arab Common Market (1965) to reduce regional trade barriers and promote intraregional trade.

The formation of an Arab coordinating body had been encouraged by Britain in line with its policies to gain influence in the Near East and assistance against Germany during World War II. Anthony Eden,* then secretary of state for foreign affairs, in a May 22, 1941, speech at Mansion House and in comments to the House of Commons on February 24, 1943, stated that Britain would view favorably any plan to strengthen Arab ties. Later that year (July 31–August 5), the prime minister of Egypt, Nahhas Pasha, and of Iraq, Nuri al-Said, met to discuss issues of federation and collaboration among Arab states.

A follow-up conference in Alexandria concluded on October 10, 1944, with Egypt, Syria, Transjordan,* Iraq, and Lebanon* signing a protocol to establish a plan for a League of Arab States. The league would be based on equal representation, deal with common issues, strengthen inter-Arab relations, work toward an independent Lebanon within existing frontiers, demand that Britain cease Jewish immigration and land purchases, and propose an Arab National Fund to buy land in Palestine. On March 22, 1945, the charter was signed by Egypt, Iraq, Syria, Lebanon, Saudi Arabia, Transjordan, and North Yemen.

The Arab League considered the Jewish–Arab dilemma shortly after its founding, studied the 1946 report of the Anglo–American Committee of Inquiry* on the Jewish refugee issue, and also decided to boycott ''Zionist* goods''—the start of the Israeli Boycott Office. The Arab League rejected (December 17, 1947) the United Nations' (UN) November 29, 1947, partition plan,* called for an independent Arab state in Palestine,* and resolved (February 9, 1948) to prevent the birth of the Jewish state. However, competing national interests hindered military and political coordination before the 1948 war* and limited the league's effectiveness during the fighting.

As the top policy forum, the council has held regular Summits since January 1964 in Cairo, where the league encouraged the creation of the Palestine Liberation Organization to represent the Palestinians. At the Khartoum Conference* three months after the June 1967 war,* Arab League states issued their "three noes"*—no peace with Israel, no recognition of Israel, and no negotiations with Israel—and the oil-rich states agreed to provide financial aid to the "front-line" states of Jordan, Syria, and Egypt. The October 1974 Rabat conference* one year after the October 1973 war* recognized the PLO* as the sole legitimate representative* of the Palestinians and renewed aid to the front-line states.

The league's solidarity on the Arab–Israeli conflict, in terms of the Khartoum Declaration, ended when Egypt and Israel signed the Camp David Accords* on September 17, 1978. The Arab League expelled Egypt on March 26, 1979, and "temporarily" moved its headquarters to Tunis (Article 10 declares Cairo the permanent seat). Shifting away from the hard-line Khartoum Declaration at their 1982 summit, the league adopted the Fez Plan* as the solution to the Arab–Israeli conflict. The plan essentially reaffirmed existing policy and demanded complete Israeli withdrawal for the territories occupied in 1967, including East Jerusalem,* as well as an independent Palestinian state. Seven years later the league readmitted Egypt (May 1989) after the PLO (December 1983) and Jordan (September 1984) had led the way in renewing relations.

Since the Camp David Accords and the Iraq–Iran War, the Arab League has been politically fragmented. The charter compels members toward consensus (unanimous votes) since majority votes bind only the majority (Article 7), but differing national policies have constrained the league's policymaking. In the 1980s, the league was forced to mediate disputes between members and could not effectively formulate policy (the 1989 Taif Accords on the Lebanese situation are a notable exception, although the league's involvement dates to the crisis's beginning). Postponed (November 1983), semiboycotted (August 1985), and divisive Summits resulted in policy inaction: members separately renewed relations with Egypt; the Fez Plan was reaffirmed unchanged (1985); and no action was taken against Morocco when King Hassan* met with Shimon Peres,* then Israel's foreign minister, in 1987. The 1990–91 war against Iraq and the postwar Arab–Israeli peace talks demonstrate the league's relative unimportance: it was unable to reach a consensus about Iraq's invasion of Kuwait and pushed to the margins of the peace talks where the only practical coordinating is among those in the bilateral negotiations—Jordan, Syria, and Lebanon—and the PLO.

For further information see: Boutros Boutros-Ghali, "The Arab League," *International Conciliation,* no. 498 (May 1954):387–448; Hussein A. Hassouna, *The League of Arab States and Regional Disputes: A Study of Middle East Conflicts* (Dobbs Ferry, NY: Oceana Publications, 1975); Robert W. MacDonald, *The League of Arab States: A Study in the Dynamics of Regional Organization* (Princeton, NJ: Princeton University Press, 1965).

Paul S. Robinson, Jr.

LEBANON. Israel's neighbor to the north. During the War of Independence,* Lebanon joined in the fighting against Israel despite its Christian majority and the control of the body politic by that segment of the population. Lebanon essentially abstained from participation in the Sinai War,* the Six Day War,* and the War of Attrition.* After the Palestine Liberation Organization* (PLO) was ousted from Jordan* in September 1970, the PLO moved into Lebanon via Syria* and established a base of operations. Attacks against targets in Israel by the PLO from Lebanon led to Israeli retaliatory strikes as well as two major military operations: Operation Litani (1978)* and Operation Peace for Galilee (1982)* or the War in Lebanon.* While the PLO was building its base of operations and striking against Israel, these developments were contributing to the disintegration of Lebanon, which had already begun because of disagreements among the various Lebanese factions over the distribution of socioeconomic and political power. A civil war broke out in Lebanon in 1975 and has continued since. Meanwhile, with the absence of effective control from Beirut, the PLO was able to use Lebanese territory for attacks into Israel. After a number of these strikes into Israel, in March 1978, Israel launched Operation Litani. Despite the subsequent establishment of the United Nations Interim Force in Lebanon* (UNIFIL), periodic attacks into Israel continued. In June 1982, Israel launched Operation Peace for Galilee, the War in Lebanon, to rectify the situation. Subsequently, the United States brokered an agreement between Israel and Lebanon—the May 17, 1983 agreement*—which called for the withdrawal of Israeli forces from Lebanon. The agreement was subsequently abrogated by the Lebanese government. Israel completed its withdrawal from Lebanon in 1985 while a security zone* was established in Lebanon along Israel's northern border. Tensions and fighting within Lebanon have continued since. Clashes between Israel and Hezbollah* and Islamic Jihad* forces have occurred with regularity, and Lebanese territory has been a base of operations for various groups seeking to upset the peace process inaugurated at Madrid* and the Israel–PLO Declaration of Principles* (DOP), which was signed in 1993.

LEBANON WAR (1982). See **WAR IN LEBANON.**

LEEDS CASTLE. On July 18 and 19, 1978, talks were held, at the invitation of the United States, in Leeds Castle, England,* between the foreign ministers of Egypt* and Israel. Proposals for a settlement in the West Bank* and the Gaza Strip* were discussed as part of a way to reach agreement in negotiations that could lead to peace treaties between Israel and Egypt and with other states willing to move in that direction. This was an important step in the Egypt–Israel peace process that led to the Camp David Accords* and, later, the signing of the Egypt–Israel Peace Treaty* in 1979.

LEHI (LOHAMEI HERUT YISRAEL—FIGHTERS FOR THE FREEDOM OF ISRAEL, STERN GROUP). See STERN (GANG) GROUP.

LEVINGER, RABBI MOSHE (b. Jerusalem,* 1935). He planned and initiated the Jewish return to Hebron* at Passover in 1968 and continues to live in a settlement there, Kiryat Arba.* Later, Levinger and his followers reconstructed the Jewish Quarter of Hebron and its main synagogue. He was involved in the creation of Gush Emunim* and has been among its leaders and activists. He has been a strong voice and activist for Israel's retention of the West Bank.*

LEVY, DAVID (b. Rabat, Morocco, December 21, 1937). He has lived in the development town of Beit Shean since immigrating to Israel with his family in 1957.

A former construction worker, he began his political career in the Histadrut* and served as chairman of its Likud* faction. He was the Likud candidate for the position of secretary-general of the Histadrut in the 1977 and 1981 elections, but he failed to win. First elected on behalf of the Herut Party faction of GAHAL to the Seventh Knesset* in October 1969, he has been reelected to all subsequent Knessets on behalf of the same faction in the Likud bloc. Levy was appointed minister of immigrant absorption in June 1977 and minister of construction and housing in January 1978. In August 1981, he became deputy prime minister and minister of construction and housing and retained those posts in the National Unity government* established in 1984. In the government established in December 1988, he became deputy prime minister and minister of construction and housing. He became minister of foreign affairs in the Likud-led government established by Prime Minister Yitzhak Shamir* in June 1990, while retaining the position of deputy prime minister. During his tenure he suggested, among other ideas, an Israeli withdrawal from the Gaza Strip.*

For further information see: Aryeh Avnery, *David Levy* [in Hebrew] (Israel: Revivim Publishing House, 1983).

LIAISON COMMITTEE. A committee established by Israel and the Palestine Liberation Organization* (PLO) to provide for the smooth implementation of the Declaration of Principles.* It was to deal with issues requiring coordination and any other matters that may be referred to it by other negotiating committees. Its first meeting was on October 13, 1993.

LIBERTY INCIDENT (1967). An episode between a U.S. communications and intelligence-gathering ship, *Liberty,* and Israel's air force and navy during the third day of the Six Day War.* The American vessel was attacked by Israeli jet fighters and torpedo boats off the coast of the Sinai Peninsula* near the Gaza

Strip.* Thirty-four American crewmen were killed, and seventy-five were injured in the June 8, 1967, attack. Although the Johnson* administration accepted Israel's apology for its actions, the incident is an example of U.S.–Israeli diplomatic tension.

Israeli military sources, following numerous attempts at identification by both visual and verbal means, misidentified the *Liberty* as the Egyptian* supply ship *El Quseir*. Based on this information, an attack consisting of machine-gun and napalm strikes was ordered. This was followed by five torpedo launches, one of which hit the *Liberty*'s right side. The landing of the single torpedo was responsible for a majority of the casualties, killing an estimated twenty-five. As a result of the attack, the *Liberty* was nearly sunk.

Not until one of the three attacking torpedo boats made a closer, follow-up strike did the Israelis realize they were not attacking an Egyptian merchant ship. An immediate cease-fire was then ordered, and some time later there was an undisputed identification of the *Liberty*. After the cease-fire, the crippled *Liberty* sailed to Malta.

Two days later, on June 10, Israel's ambassador to Washington relayed an Israeli apology to Secretary of State Dean Rusk* in which the attack was described as a "tragic accident." The initial U.S. response stated that "at the time of the attack, the *U.S.S. Liberty* was flying the American flag and its identification was clearly indicated in large white letters and numerals on its hull. It was broad daylight and the weather conditions were excellent." There were assertions of negligence: "[T]here is every reason to believe that the *U.S.S. Liberty* was identified, or at least her nationality determined, by Israeli aircraft approximately one hour before the attack."

The Israelis held to their assertion that while the attack on the ship was in error, it was not done in malice or contempt for the United States. Furthermore, however mistaken the initial sightings and information gathered on the day of the attack might have been, the *Liberty*'s unannounced locality in a recognized area of hostility came to be the overriding reason, the Israelis said, for their attack. None of the Israeli military personnel involved in the incident, either directly or indirectly, were held accountable for their actions.

Following initial American questioning over the attack, the Johnson administration eventually reversed itself and officially accepted Israel's position and apology. In the years that followed, Israel paid over $3 million in reparations to the families of the thirty-four killed and over $3.5 million to those wounded. In 1983, Israel paid an additional $6 million to the U.S. government for physical damage to the ship.

Questions concerning the incident remain unanswered. Were the Israelis capable of making not one, but numerous errors? One theory suggests that Israel might have knowingly attacked the *Liberty,* an American intelligence ship known to be operating in the area, as a means of preventing the United States from obtaining sensitive information concerning war operations. Others have added that the Johnson administration, while fully absorbed with its involvement

in Vietnam, quickly accepted the Israeli apology and in so doing played a role
in an alleged Israeli cover-up.

For further information see: James M. Ennes, Jr., *Assault on the "Liberty": The True
Story of the Israeli Attack on an American Intelligence Ship* (New York: Random House,
1979); Hirsch Goodman and Ze'ev Schiff, "The Attack on the Liberty," *Atlantic* 254
(September 1984):78–84; Stephen Green, *Taking Sides: America's Secret Relations with
a Militant Israel* (New York: William Morrow, 1984); Donald Neff, *Warriors for Jerusalem: The Six Days That Changed the Middle East* (New York: Simon and Schuster,
1984); Anthony Pearson, *Conspiracy of Silence: The Attack on the U.S.S. Liberty* (New
York: Quartet Books, 1978).

Robert Crangle, Jr.

LIKUD (Union). Likud was established in 1973, and the alliance crystallized at
the time of the 1977 elections. It consisted of the GAHAL Alliance (Herut and
the Liberals); the La'am Alliance (the State List and the Free Center); Ahdut (a
one-man faction in the Knesset*); and Shlomzion, Ariel Sharon's* former party.
Likud first came to power in Israel in 1977, ousting the Labor Party,* which
had led the government since Israel became independent. Although Likud retained its government position after the 1981 elections, its majority in the Knesset seldom exceeded two or three votes. In 1984, Likud lost its plurality and
joined with the Labor Alignment to form a government of National Unity* in
which it shared power and ministerial positions. In the 1988 Knesset election,
it again emerged as the dominant party, but without a majority. A Likud-
dominated government with Yitzhak Shamir* as prime minister and with Labor
as the junior partner was formed in December 1988. After losing a vote of no
confidence in the spring of 1990, Shamir succeeded in establishing a right-of-
center coalition in June of that year. That government led Israel at the Madrid
Peace Conference* and in the subsequent bilateral Washington rounds* of negotiations and in the multilateral talks* until the 1992 election. Likud, led by
Shamir, lost to Labor Alignment in the elections of 1992.

Likud is right of center, strongly nationalist, and assertive in foreign policy.
It has focused on retaining the territories west of the Jordan River* occupied
by Israel in the Six Day War* and has strongly opposed negotiations with the
Palestine Liberation Organization,* regarding it as a terrorist organization committed to the destruction of Israel. Likud has emphasized the need for economic
and social betterment of Israel's disadvantaged, primarily in the Oriental Jewish
community. Its economic programs regard free enterprise as the preferred mechanism, and it has campaigned on themes of dismantling the socialist mechanisms
established during the Labor Party's control of the Israeli polity and economy.
Since the retirement of Menachem Begin* from political life, Yitzhak Shamir
was the party leader. Among the other major party figures are Moshe Arens,*
Ariel Sharon, David Levy,* and Benny Begin. After the party's loss of power
in the 1992 Knesset election, both Shamir and Arens announced their retirement
from political life, although Shamir remained in the Knesset. In March 1993,

Likud held an internal election to select a new party leader. In that election, Benjamin Netanyahu* was chosen as the party's leader.

LINKAGE. A term used to refer to the "linkage" or connection between the two Camp David Accords*—one that centered on Israel–Egypt* negotiations focusing on the Sinai Peninsula* and the other on the Palestinians* and the future of the West Bank* and Gaza Strip.* Israeli prime minister Menachem Begin* sought to ensure that there was no necessary connection between an Israel–Egypt Agreement and resolution of the Palestinian question. Egyptian president Anwar Sadat* sought to ensure a relationship between the two issue areas and any agreements reached with regard to them in order to avoid the charge that he had made a separate peace* and abandoned the Palestinians. Throughout the period between the Camp David Accords and the Egypt–Israel Peace Treaty,* this was a constant issue in the negotiations. Eventually, the matter was resolved, in the minds of Begin and Sadat, with the specific language contained in the Egypt–Israel Peace Treaty and the accompanying letters.

LINOWITZ, SOL (b. Trenton, New Jersey, December 7, 1913). He received his education from Hamilton College and Cornell University Law School. After receiving his law degree, Linowitz worked for the U.S. government from 1942 to 1946. He then entered private business and became chairman of the board and chief executive officer of Xerox International in 1966. In 1966, Linowitz became U.S. ambassador to the Organization of American States and U.S. representative on the Inter-American Committee of the Alliance for Progress. Linowitz served in this position until 1969, when he returned to private law practice. In 1977, Linowitz served as the U.S. conegotiator for the Panama Canal Treaties. In 1979, President Carter* appointed Linowitz to replace Robert Strauss* as his personal ambassador to the Middle East.

As Carter's personal ambassador to the Middle East, Linowitz was responsible for continuing the peace talks between Egypt* and Israel and implementing the Camp David Accords.* These talks broke down in May 1980. However, in September 1980, Linowitz was able to secure a commitment by Egypt and Israel to resume the autonomy talks* and their statement that they remained committed to the Camp David Accords. Linowitz's approach to the talks emphasized the process as a means of overcoming visceral fears and suspicions, and he used this approach in an attempt to define autonomy for the Palestinians in the West Bank* and Gaza* territories.

Linowitz's publications include *The Making of a Public Man: A Memoir* (Boston: Little, Brown, 1985).

Donald A. Vogus

LIPKIN-SHAHAK, AMNON. See **SHAHAK, AMNON.**

LITANI OPERATION. See **OPERATION LITANI.**

LITANI RIVER. The river rises several kilometers west of Baalbek in the Beka Valley* in Lebanon,* a few kilometers from the headwaters of the Orontes River, which flows into Syria.* The Litani lies entirely within Lebanon. It flows southwest down the axis of the valley and then turns west, emptying into the Mediterranean Sea. The Litani is 145 kilometers (ninety miles) long. It receives its water* from springs, surface runoff in winter months, and subsurface waters. Some of the annual flow from the Litani is diverted to the Awali River for power generation for Beirut and other coastal cities. The Litani–Awali system provides about two-thirds of the hydropower generated in Lebanon.

Given the shortage of fresh water resources in Israel, the early Zionists* thought that Israel should have access to water of the neighboring countries. In 1943, a private Zionist company, the Palestine Water Corporation, studied the Litani River in cooperation with Lebanese engineers and concluded that the Litani could not be fully utilized in Lebanon and that the diversion of its water to Israel for power generation was feasible. Israel, in turn, could supply power to Lebanon in exchange for the water it received from Lebanon. The idea of the utilization of Litani waters was taken seriously in Israel. One of the reasons for Israel's disappointment with the Johnston Plan* was said to be that it did not include Litani diversion.

The Litani River witnessed serious fighting between the Palestine Liberation Organization* (PLO) and Israeli troops in 1978. During that time the Israel Defense Forces,* in Operation Litani,* occupied a ten-kilometer-wide strip north of the Israeli–Lebanese border to the Litani River. In subsequent encounters damage was caused to the pumping equipment and the distribution network. The economic losses resulting to Lebanon have been considerable.

For further information see: Thomas Naff and Ruth C. Matson, *Water in the Middle East: Conflict or Cooperation?* (Boulder, CO: Westview Press, 1984).

Anamika Krishna

LODGE–FISH RESOLUTION. See **PUBLIC RESOLUTION NO. 73, 67TH CONGRESS, SECOND SESSION, SEPTEMBER 21, 1922.**

LOHAMEI HERUT YISRAEL. See **STERN (GANG) GROUP.**

LONDON CONFERENCE (1939). See **ST. JAMES CONFERENCE.**

LORD MOYNE. See **MOYNE, LORD.**

LUBRANI, URI (b. Haifa, 1926). He was a member of the Haganah* and the Palmach* and served in Israel's War of Independence* as a captain. He was educated at University College, London, from 1953 to 1956. He served as private secretary to Prime Minister Moshe Sharett* (1950–53); adviser for foreign affairs to Prime Minister David Ben-Gurion* (1956–59); chief of the prime minister's private bureau (1959–61); assistant director of the prime minister's

Office (1961–64); ambassador to Uganda and Burundi (1964–67); ambassador to Ethiopia (1967–71); director of Koor Industries Management Board; and head of the Israeli mission in Teheran with the rank of ambassador (1973–78). From 1979 to 1983, he was in private business. Since 1983, he has served as Israel government coordinator of Lebanon affairs. He served as the chief Israeli delegate to the talks with Lebanon in the Washington rounds* after the Madrid Peace Conference.*

M

M-48 PATTON TANK. The M-48 Patton tank is a main battle tank that was produced from 1952 to 1956 in the United States by the Fisher Body Division of General Motors Corporation, the Ford Motor Company, and the Chrysler Corporation. The standard M-48 Patton main battle tank is manned by a crew of four. With its gun forward, it is thirty-one feet in length and twelve feet wide. With a combat weight of approximately 108,000 pounds, it can travel up to thirty mph. It has a range of 310 road miles.

During the Six Day War,* the M-48 and the British Centurion* tanks were the best tanks in the Israeli inventory. The Israeli army upgraded their stocks of M-48 Patton tanks to reach a capability that is similar to the M-60 (the M-48's successor). The M-48 Patton tank was one of the main battle tanks used by the Israeli army during the Six Day War and the Yom Kippur War.* During the Yom Kippur War, the advantage that Isreali M-48A2 tanks had over the Soviet tanks manned by the Arab armies was dramatic. A ballistic computer, superior range finder, and a gun that shot twice the range of guns on the Arab tanks helped the M-48A2 main battle tank used by the Israeli armor units to defeat Arab armor units during the war.

For further information see: David Eshel, *Chariots of the Desert: The Story of the Israeli Armoured Corps* (London: Brassey's Defence Publishers, 1989).

Jon J. Peterson

M-60 TANK. The M-60 series tank is an American-designed and -produced main battle tank that entered service in 1960. It is armed with a 105mm cannon and carries sixty-three rounds of ammunition. The M-60 fires a wide variety of explosive projectiles, including APFSDS (armor-piercing, fin-stabilized discarding sabot), HEAT (high-explosive, antitank), HE (high explosive), APERS-T (antipersonnel with tracer), and smoke rounds. The M-60 is also armed with a 7.62mm coaxial machine gun with 6,000 rounds of ammunition and a turret-mounted .50-caliber machine gun with 900 rounds of ammunition. The M-60 has a crew of four. It weighs approximately sixty tons and has a maximum road speed of thirty mph and a range of 315 miles.

Over the years, various improved models of the M-60 have been introduced. The most significant improvements were contained in the M-60A3 and included turret stabilization, an improved engine, and a much improved fire control system. The fire control system included a laser range finder (effective to 5,000 meters), a solid-state ballistic computer, and a passive thermal gunner's night sight.

Israel received its first M-60 tanks in 1968 and has been the largest user of the M-60 outside the United States. Israel has approximately 1,400 M-60, M-60A1, and M-60A3 tanks. Israel has continued to pursue improvement programs to enhance the M-60's armor, ammunition, and fire control systems and extend its service life.

Other countries in the Middle East that have M-60 tanks in their inventories include Bahrain, Egypt,* Iran, Jordan,* Oman, Saudi Arabia, Tunisia, and Yemen.

For further information see: Christopher F. Foss, ed., *Jane's Main Battle Tanks,* 2d ed. (London: Jane's, 1986); Christopher F. Foss, ed., *Jane's Armour and Artillery,* 14th ed. (London: Jane's Information Group, 1994).

Stephen H. Gotowicki

MAALOT. An Israeli settlement in the northern Galilee that lies atop the Ein Ziv Valley.

On the night of May 13, 1974, a terrorist penetration into Israeli territory was discovered, and the Israel Defense Forces* (IDF) began a search. The same day, a group of high school students from Safed were on a field trip approved by the Ministry of Education and the Israeli police. Local area police asked the students and their escorts to move to the Nativ Meir School in Maalot itself rather than spend the night in a nearby grove.

A few minutes earlier, about two kilometers north, unidentified men tried to hail a car driving toward an Israeli settlement. When the driver failed to stop, the unidentified men opened fire, killing two occupants of the car, wounding the driver, and disabling the engine. Even though the car was disabled, it continued to roll down the slope another two kilometers north, stopping at Moshav Elkosh.

Security forces assumed the terrorists would escape to Lebanon* and concentrated their search north toward the border. The three-man Palestine Liberation Organization* (PLO) squad, however, was on a suicide mission and did not intend to escape. They continued south toward Maalot, shooting into a house, killing a mother, father, and son, and then killing a street sweeper. Moving toward the school, they captured a teacher asleep in a car at the school's entrance and forced him to enter the school and ask the teachers inside to open the school doors. Not knowing that the teacher had been coerced by terrorists, the teacher inside opened the door, whereupon the three terrorists quickly entered the building and secured it. In the confusion several students, teachers, and soldiers escaped by jumping out of windows, but eighty-five students, two first-aid specialists, and a teacher remained. The terrorists concentrated all the hostages into one room and wired it with explosives before Israeli officials could arrive. In the negotiations that followed, the terrorists demanded that twenty of their comrades held in Israeli jails be released and that they be flown to Damascus, along with the hostage children. The International Committee of the Red Cross, as well as the Romanian and French* ambassadors in Israel, served as intermediaries to the terrorist groups, and they, too, were to be flown to Damascus along with the hostages. Once these demands were met, the children would be freed. If their demands were not met by 6:00 P.M. the following day, the school building would be dynamited.

The Israeli government allowed the release of the twenty terrorists in jail but refused to accede to the demand to fly the hostages with them to Damascus. As the deadline neared, and no progress was made, the Israeli government decided to storm the school. In the raid, which began a few minutes before the deadline expired, twenty-one children, three terrorists, and a soldier died. In sum, the terrorist attack claimed thirty-five lives (mostly children), and seventy more were injured.

David Wurmser

MAAPILIM. The illegal immigrants who entered Palestine* despite the strict immigration quotas imposed by the British Mandatory* authorities. The beginning of such immigration, called *haapalah,* dates to 1934. It peaked in the post–World War II period, with the aim of providing refuge for Holocaust* survivors. According to some estimates, approximately 120,000 illegal immigrants entered Palestine. See also ALIYAH BET.

MAC. See **MIXED ARMISTICE COMMISSION.**

MACDONALD, (JAMES) RAMSEY (b. Lossiemouth, Moray, Scotland, October 12, 1866; d. at sea, November 9, 1937). The son of an unmarried servant, Ramsey MacDonald ended his elementary study at the age of twelve, although he continued as a tutor and student for an additional six years. A member of the Fabian Society, he joined the Labor Party in 1894. He won election to the House of Commons in 1906 and in 1911 became the parliamentary leader of the Labor Party. MacDonald lost election to Parliament in 1918, following his public statement that the declaration of war against Germany was morally wrong, but he won reelection in 1922. Ramsey MacDonald became the first Labor prime minister on January 22, 1924, when the Liberal Party supported Labor against the Conservatives.

MacDonald visited Palestine* in 1922 and wrote a number of articles in a Zionist* journal, *The New Palestine,* in which he expressed his admiration for the Zionists' pioneer spirit. Although the Labor Party had expressed no views on Zionism, the colonial secretary in MacDonald's government, Sydney Webb, was strongly anti-Zionist. On October 21, 1930, a statement of policy on Palestine from Lord Passfield (Sydney Webb) was issued that reinterpreted the Balfour Declaration* in light of available land for cultivation in Palestine. The Passfield White Paper* suggested that increased Jewish immigration would leave the Arabs landless. Parliament debated the policy on November 18, 1930, and MacDonald's government was subjected to intense criticism. Lloyd George asserted that MacDonald had violated the trust placed in him by the British people by breaking a promise made by a previous British administration. MacDonald and Passfield met with the Zionist leadership, and Chaim Weizmann* converted the prime minister to a position supportive of Zionist aspirations. In a letter sent by MacDonald to Chaim Weizmann and read on the floor of the Commons by MacDonald on February 13, 1931, the prime minister confirmed the British government's desire to encourage Jewish settlement in Palestine and noted that such immigration could take place without endangering the rights of the Arab population.

For further information see: David Marquand, *Ramsay MacDonald* (London: Jonathan Cape, 1977); Christopher Sykes, *Crossroads to Israel: 1917–1948* (Cleveland and New York: World, 1965).

Joseph E. Goldberg

MACHPELA. See **CAVE OF MACHPELA.**

MACMICHAEL, SIR HAROLD ALFRED (b. England,* October 15, 1882; d. Folkestone, England, September 19, 1969). He received a B.A. degree from Cambridge University in 1904. He was a British public servant who joined the Sudan Political Service in 1905 and served successively as inspector in the provinces of Kordofan, Blue Nile, and Khartoum and as a political and intelligence officer with the Expeditionary Force that reoccupied Darfur in 1916. Subsequently, he became subgovernor of Darfur Province and later assistant civil secretary. From 1926 to 1933, MacMichael was civil secretary and, periodically, acting governor general. From 1933 to 1937, he served as high commissioner and commander in chief of Tanganyika Territory. He served as high commissioner and commander in chief for Palestine* (and also as high commissioner for Transjordan*) from 1938 to 1944. MacMichael's appointment was partially designed to reassure the Arab world that the problem of Palestine would be handled sympathetically, because he had a reputation as a renowned Arabic scholar and had prepared several publications on the Sudan. His tenure in Palestine was characterized by increasing Arab–Jewish tension and the intensification of efforts by both communities to secure their goals for the future of

Palestine. It was a period during which the plight of European Jewry became critical, and there was an accelerated deterioration of relations between the Jewish community and the British government over the issue of Jewish immigration. By the time MacMichael left Palestine at the end of August 1944, there was virtually no contact between the high commissioner and the Jewish quasi-government in Palestine.

As high commissioner for Palestine, MacMichael was faced with the problems of restricting Jewish immigration to Palestine, combating terrorism, and assisting with the partition schemes.

Following the issuance of the White Paper* on May 17, 1939, MacMichael implemented its policies rigidly. In dealing with Jewish immigration to Palestine, he enforced the British policy of placing illegal immigrants in internment camps; when this proved to be ineffective, he and the British government attempted to slow the immigration by encouraging other nations to deny Jews transit to Palestine. The illegal refugees who did reach Palestine were sent on to Mauritius in the Indian Ocean.

This policy of restricting Jewish immigration led to the Struma disaster in early 1942, in which over 800 people lost their lives. MacMichael was held personally accountable for this tragedy by many Jews, and it was one of the reasons that there was an attempt on his life in August 1944, shortly before he left Palestine.

MacMichael's publications included *The Tribes of Northern and Central Kordofan, A History of the Arabs in the Sudan and Some Account of the People Who Preceded Them and of the Tribes Inhabiting Darfur, History of the Anglo–Egyptian Sudan, Malta, Report on a Mission to Malaya,* and *The Sudan.*

For further information see: Gavriel Cohen, "Harold MacMichael and Palestine's Future," *Zionism,* no. 3 (April 1981):133–55.

Donald A. Vogus

MADRID DECLARATION (JUNE 27, 1989). The twelve heads of state of the European Community met in Madrid, Spain, at their semiannual European Community Summit on June 26 and 27, 1989. At the end of the summit they issued their first formal statement on the Middle East since the Venice Declaration* of June 1980.

The published text of their Declaration on the Middle East follows:

The European Council has examined the situation in the Middle East conflict in the light of recent events and of contacts undertaken over several months by the Presidency and the Troika (the incumbent Presidency, its immediate predecessor and successor) with the parties concerned, and it has drawn the following conclusions:

1. The policy of the Twelve on the Middle East conflict is defined in the Venice Declaration of 13 June 1980 and other subsequent declarations. It consists in upholding the right to security of all States in the region, including Israel, that is to say, to live

within secure, recognized and guaranteed frontiers, and in upholding justice for all the peoples of the region, which includes recognition of the legitimate rights of the Palestinian* people, including their right to self-determination with all that this implies.

The Twelve consider that these objectives should be achieved by peaceful means in the framework of an international peace conference under the auspices of the United Nations, as the appropriate forum for the direct negotiations between the parties concerned, with a view to a comprehensive, just, and lasting settlement.

The European Council is also of the view that the Palestine Liberation Organization* (PLO) should participate in this process. It expresses its support for every effort by the permanent members of the Security Council of the United Nations to bring the parties closer together, create a climate of confidence between them, and facilitate in this way the convening of the international peace conference.

2. The Community and its Member States have demonstrated their readiness to participate actively in the search for a negotiated solution to the conflict, and to cooperate fully in the economic and social development of the peoples of the region.

The European Council expressed its satisfaction regarding the policy of contacts with all the parties undertaken by the Presidency and the Troika, and has decided to pursue it.

3. The European Council welcomes the support given by the Extraordinary Summit Meeting of the Arab League,* held in Casablanca, to the decisions of the Palestinian National Council in Algiers,* involving acceptance of Security Council Resolutions 242* and 338,* which resulted in the recognition of Israel's right to exist, as well as the renunciation of terrorism.

It also welcomes the efforts undertaken by the United States in its contacts with the parties directly concerned and particularly the dialogue entered into with the PLO.

Advantage should be taken of these favorable circumstances to engender a spirit of tolerance and peace with a view to entering resolutely on the path of negotiations.

4. The European Council deplores the continuing deterioration of the situation in the Occupied Territories* and the constant increase in the number of dead and wounded and the suffering of the population.

It appeals urgently to the Israeli authorities to put an end to repressive measures, to implement Resolutions 605, 607 and 608 of the Security Council and to respect the provisions of the Geneva Convention on the Protection of Civilian Populations in Times of War. They appeal in particular for the reopening of educational facilities in the West Bank.*

5. On the basis of the positions of principle of the Twelve, the European Council welcomes the proposal for elections in the Occupied Territories as a contribution to the peace process, provided that the elections are set in the context of a process towards a comprehensive, just, and lasting settlement of the conflict; the elections take place in the Occupied Territories including East Jerusalem,* under adequate guarantees of freedom; no solution is excluded and the final negotiation takes place on the basis of Resolutions 242 and 338 of the Security Council of the United Nations, based on the principle of "land for peace."

6. The European Council launches a solemn appeal to the parties concerned to seize the opportunity to achieve peace. Respect by each of the parties for the legitimate rights of the other should facilitate the normalizing of relations between all the countries of the region. The European Council calls upon the Arab countries to establish normal relations

of peace and cooperation with Israel and asks that country in turn to recognize the right of the Palestinian people to exercise self-determination.

MADRID PEACE CONFERENCE. The end of the cold war and the Gulf War* suggested new possibilities in the quest for an Arab–Israeli peace. After the Gulf War, President George Bush* and Secretary of State James Baker* suggested that the New World Order* facilitated such an effort. Baker made eight trips to the region in the months after the end of the Gulf War and eventually believed that it would be possible to convene a peace conference. In October, the United States and the Soviet Union issued invitations* to Israel, Jordan,* Lebanon,* Syria* and the Palestinians* to an opening conference in Madrid,* Spain. The invitation provided details on the sessions and the approach to be followed. It reflected compromises by all sides developed in the course of Baker's shuttle diplomacy.*

The Arab–Israeli peace conference convened in Madrid, Spain, beginning October 30, 1991. In an opening plenary session, Israeli and Syrian, Egyptian,* Lebanese, and Jordanian–Palestinian delegations met and delivered speeches and responses. These were followed by bilateral negotiations between Israel and each of the Arab delegations. The conference was an important step on the road to peace in that it involved direct, bilateral, public, and official peace negotiations between Israel and its Arab neighbors.

The cosponsors' letter of invitation laid out the framework for negotiations. These included a just, lasting, and comprehensive peace settlement based on United Nations Security Council Resolutions 242* and 338*; direct bilateral negotiations along two tracks, between Israel and the Arab states and between Israel and the Palestinians; and multilateral negotiations* on regionwide issues, including arms control and regional security, water,* refugees,* environment, and economic development. The bilateral and multilateral negotiations would complement each other.

The Middle East Peace Conference began ceremonially with a three-day session. All parties were represented by official fourteen-member delegations. The Jordanian–Palestinian delegation had fourteen representatives from each area. The Palestinians also sent a six-person advisory team that had no official standing but coordinated policy with the Palestine Liberation Organization* (PLO). The parties sat at a T-shaped table.

Presidents George Bush and Mikhail Gorbachev opened the conference. Bush called for peace based on security for Israel and fairness for the Palestinians. He said that "territorial compromise is essential for peace" and that only direct talks between Israelis and Arabs could bring peace about; the superpowers could not impose it. Israeli prime minister Yitzhak Shamir* recounted the history of the Jews and argued that the cause of conflict is not territory but Arab refusal to recognize the legitimacy of Israel. He did not mention the occupied territories* or Israeli settlements.* Palestinian delegation head Heidar Abdelshafi* asserted that the Palestinians were willing to live side by side with Israelis and accept a transitional stage, provided it led to sovereignty. He called on Israel to give Palestinian refugees displaced since 1967 the right to return and to stop settlements. Abd al-Shafi referred to the unnamed PLO as "our acknowledged leadership." Jordan foreign minister Kamal Abu Jaber, rebutting a common Israeli view, declared that Jordan has never been, and will not be, Palestine. Syrian foreign minister Sharáa* contended that Resolutions 242 and 338, or the "land for peace"* formula, should be implemented.

MADRID PEACE CONFERENCE LETTER OF INVITATION. Following is the text of the invitation jointly issued by the United States and the Soviet Union, dated October 18, 1991, to the Madrid Peace Conference* on October 30, 1991:

After extensive consultations with Arab states, Israel and the Palestinians,* the United States and the Soviet Union believe that an historic opportunity exists to advance the prospects for genuine peace throughout the region. The United States and the Soviet Union are prepared to assist the parties to achieve a just, lasting and comprehensive peace settlement, through direct negotiations along two tracks, between Israel and the Arab states, and between Israel and the Palestinians, based on United Nations Security Council Resolutions 242* and 338.* The objective of this process is real peace.

Toward that end, the president of the U.S. and the president of the USSR invite you to a peace conference, which their countries will co-sponsor, followed immediately by direct negotiations. The conference will be convened in Madrid on October 30, 1991.

President Bush* and President Gorbachev request your acceptance of this invitation no later than 6 P.M. Washington time, October 23, 1991, in order to ensure proper organization and preparation of the conference.

Direct bilateral negotiations will begin four days after the opening of the conference. Those parties who wish to attend multilateral negotiations* will convene two weeks after the opening of the conference to organize those negotiations. The co-sponsors believe that those negotiations should focus on region-wide issues of water,* refugee* issues, environment, economic development, and other subjects of mutual interest.

The co-sponsors will chair the conference which will be held at ministerial level. Governments to be invited include Israel, Syria,* Lebanon* and Jordan.* Palestinians will be invited and attend as part of a joint Jordanian–Palestinian delegation. Egypt* will be invited to the conference as a participant. The European Community will be a participant in the conference, alongside the United States and the Soviet Union, and will be represented by its presidency. The Gulf Cooperation Council [GCC] will be invited to send its Secretary-General to the conference as an observer, and GCC member states will be invited to participate in organizing the negotiations on multilateral issues. The United Nations will be invited to send an observer, representing the secretary-general.

The conference will have no power to impose solutions on the parties or veto agreements reached by them. It will have no authority to make decisions for the parties and no ability to vote on issues of results. The conference can reconvene only with the consent of all the parties.

With respect to negotiations between Israel and Palestinians who are part of the joint Jordanian–Palestinian delegation, negotiations will be conducted in phases, beginning with talks on interim self-government arrangements.* These talks will be conducted with the objective of reaching agreement within one year. Once agreed, the interim self-government arrangements will last for a period of five years; beginning the third year of the period of interim self-government arrangements, negotiations will take place on permanent status. These permanent status negotiations, and the negotiations between Israel and the Arab states, will take place on the basis of Resolutions 242 and 338.

It is understood that the co-sponsors are committed to making this process succeed. It is their intention to convene the conference and negotiations with those parties who agree to attend.

The co-sponsors believe that this process offers the promise of ending decades of confrontation and conflict and the hope of a lasting peace. Thus, the co-sponsors hope that the parties will approach these negotiations in a spirit of good will and mutual respect. In this way, the peace process can begin to break down the mutual suspicions and mistrust that perpetuate the conflict and allow the parties to begin to resolve their differences. Indeed, only through such a process can real peace and reconciliation among the Arab states, Israel and the Palestinians be achieved. And only through this process can the peoples of the Middle East attain the peace and security they richly deserve.

MADRID PEACE PROCESS. After the Madrid Peace Conference,* two tracks of further diplomacy were established—one bilateral and one multilateral. Israel and each of its interlocutors met in a series of bilateral negotiations in Washington. Each of these Washington rounds* represented some new achievement. There were also multilateral negotiations* that convened in various world capitals and focused on a series of functional issues important to the Arab–Israeli conflict.

MAGNES, JUDAH LEON (b. San Francisco, 1877; d. New York, 1948). He was ordained as a rabbi at Hebrew Union College in 1900. An ardent Zionist,* he was active in many of the Zionist organizations prior to his settling in Palestine* in 1922. Magnes helped to found the American Jewish Committee, which sought to speak for the Jewish community in the United States and to act in its defense against anti-Semitism, and served on its Executive Committee from 1906 to 1918. He helped to found Hebrew University and became its chancellor in 1925. After reorganization, he became the president of the university in 1935, a post in which he remained until he died. Magnes became an advocate of a binational state* in Palestine as a means of preventing bloodshed, which he believed would be associated with efforts to establish a Jewish state, and in 1929 he helped to found Brit Shalom.* In 1942, he founded the Ihud* (Union) organization for better understanding between Arabs and Jews. Magnes continued to advocate a binational state until after the establishment of Israel.

For further information see: Norman Bentwich, *For Zion's Sake: A Biography of Judah L. Magnes* (Philadelphia: Jewish Publication Society of America, 1954); Judah L. Magnes, *Like All Nations?* (Jerusalem: Weiss Press, 1930).

MAHAL. Acronym for Mitnadvei Hutz Laeretz (foreign volunteers). MAHAL was a group of some 3,000 Jewish and non-Jewish soldiers who came to Palestine* to fight in Israel's War of Independence.* Most had previous and considerable military experience in World War II serving in the armed forces of the United States, Britain, Canada,* and South Africa, as well as those of the Soviet Union and various East European countries. Their influence was particularly acute in services that required specialized skills and training, particularly the air force, the navy, the artillery corps, and the armored corps. Many of Israel's first pilots were MAHAL volunteers. The first of these volunteers joined the Haganah* even prior to Israel's independence.

For further information see: David J. Bercuson, *The Secret Army* (New York: Stein and Day, 1983); A. Joseph Heckelman, *American Volunteers and Israel's War of Independence* (New York: Ktav Publishing House, 1974); Joseph Hochstein and Murray S. Greenfield, *The Jews' Secret Fleet: The Untold Story of North American Volunteers Who Smashed the British Blockade [of Palestine],* 3d ed. (Jerusalem: Gefen, 1988).

David Wurmser

MAJDAL SHAMS. A Druze village on the Golan Heights.* At an altitude of 1,175 meters, it is located adjacent to the Syrian* border just under the southern slopes of Mount Hermon.* The village was captured by the Israel Defense Forces* (IDF) on June 12, 1967, in the last day of the Six Day War.* During the 1973 Yom Kippur War,* the village remained in Israeli hands, held by Golani infantry forces under the command of Amir Drori, even though Syrian forces of the Seventh and Sixty-eighth Infantry Divisions and of the Moroccan Expeditionary Force were deployed opposite the town. Most of the Syrian forces in the area of Majdal Shams had to be diverted three kilometers south due to the stiff Israeli resistance of Avigdor Ben-Gals' Seventh Armored Division near Massade in the "Valley of Tears." A coordinated Arab attack on Majdal Shams never materialized, except for an ill-planned and equally ill-fated attack by the Moroccan forces. From Majdal Shams two Israeli mechanized infantry and regular infantry companies launched numerous failed attacks to recapture the Mount Hermon fortress on October 8, 1973, and finally a successful attack on October 20.

Majdal Shams's population of 5,000 is considered to be pro-Syrian, in contrast to neighboring Massade, also a Druze village, which is considered mostly pro-Israeli. Most of the residents of the community have refused to accept Israeli citizenship, in the belief that they will eventually be returned to Syrian sovereignty. Just before the 1992 Israeli elections, U.S. president George Bush* and Labor Party chief Yitzhak Rabin* discussed the possible return of Majdal Shams to Syria as part of either an interim settlement between Israel and Syria on the Golan Heights* or as some sort of unilateral goodwill gesture by Israel.

David Wurmser

MANDATE. See **BRITISH MANDATE.**

MANDATE FOR PALESTINE. See **BRITISH MANDATE FOR PALESTINE.**

MANDELBAUM GATE. Named after Rabbi Baruch Mandelbaum. The rabbi immigrated to Palestine* from Poland in 1871 and settled in the Old City of Jerusalem.* In 1927, the family left the walled city and built a series of single-story buildings in the Motzarara neighborhood. These buildings were used as dormitories for gifted students and rabbis and came to be known as the Mandelbaum houses. In the battles of the War of Independence,* the buildings were destroyed, and in the meeting between the commander of the Jerusalem area, Moshe Dayan,* and the chief Jordanian* officer, Colonel Abdallah Tal, it was agreed that resupply convoys to Mount Scopus* would cross the border from the Mandelbaum houses at the edge of Samuel Hanavi Street. The convoys to Mount Scopus left the Mandelbaum gate every two weeks. At each end of the crossing, there were checkpoints established. At first, the United Nations used this crossing, but afterward Christian Arabs who left on holidays to celebrate and tourists requesting to cross into Israel also used it. At that time, an official control and customs station was established. The crossing was operative for nineteen years, with only one interruption, when the Jordanians claimed that two of those going to Mount Scopus had a criminal past. The border point was captured in 1967, and the buildings were dismantled when the city was reunified.

David Wurmser

MAPAI (MIFLEGET POALEI ERETZ ISRAEL) (Israel Workers Party). MAPAI originated with the union of two smaller political parties, Ahdut Haavoda and Hapoel Hatzair, in 1930, but the roots of the movement can be traced to the turn of the century in Europe, especially Russia. Its program focused on the development of the Jewish people in Israel as a free working people rooted in an agricultural and industrial economy and developing its own Hebrew culture. It supported membership in the world movement of the working class and co-operation in the struggle to eliminate class subjugation and social injustice in any form. It endorsed the building of a Jewish commonwealth focusing on labor, equality, and freedom. Its program was a combination of Zionist* and socialist ideologies. MAPAI soon became the dominant party in the Yishuv.* The two parties that formed it had established the Histadrut* in 1920, and under their leadership it became the embodiment of the Jewish community in Palestine.* MAPAI controlled the Histadrut as well as the National Council and the Jewish Agency.* Many of the noted figures in the creation of Israel came from MAPAI, including David Ben-Gurion,* Moshe Sharett* (formerly Shertok), Golda Meir* (formerly Meyerson), Moshe Dayan,* and others. In the elections for the Knesset,* from Israel's independence until 1965, when MAPAI ran in the framework of the Alignment, it won the largest number of seats, and its leader was given the mandate to form the government. All of Israel's prime ministers and Histadrut secretaries-general as well as many other senior members of the Israeli administrations and political elite were MAPAI members in the period from its founding until its merger into the Israel Labor Party.* It was the leading member of all government coalitions and generally held the key portfolios of defense, foreign affairs, and finance as well as the post of prime minister. The party permeated the government, the bureaucracy, the economy, and most of the other institutions of Israel. Political advancement in Israel and party membership were generally coincident. In 1965, MAPAI joined with Ahdut Haavoda to form the Alignment to contest the Knesset election. In 1968, the Alignment joined with RAFI to form the Israel Labor Party.

MAPAM (MIFLEGET POALIM HAMEUHEDET) (United Workers Party). MAPAM was organized in 1948, when Hashomer Hatzair merged with radical elements from Ahdut Haavoda. It is a left-wing socialist–Zionist Jewish–Arab party. From its beginnings, the party was more Marxist than MAPAI.* The former Ahdut Haavoda members left in 1954 because of MAPAM's pro-Soviet orientation and acceptance of Arabs as party members. Although the party's domestic policy was essentially indistinguishable from MAPAI's, MAPAM's share of the vote in national elections declined steadily before it joined the Alignment for the 1969 elections. MAPAM ended its alliance with Labor* in September 1984 over the issue of the formation of a government of National Unity* with Likud.* The veteran leader, Victor Shemtov, retired as party head. It has supported the principle of compromise concerning the trade of territories for peace in the Arab–Israeli conflict. It supports the return of most of the territories, except for minor border changes required for security, in exchange for peace. It has expressed its readiness to negotiate with any authorized Palestinian* element that will declare its willingness to recognize Israel and to cease terrorism. MAPAM joined with Shinui and the Citizens' Rights Movement to form MERETZ to contest the 1992 Knesset election. MERETZ ran on a platform stressing the need for territorial compromise in order to resolve the Arab–Israeli conflict and a freeze on the expansion of existing settlements and building of new settlements in the occupied territories.* It won twelve seats in Parliament.

MASADA. A natural rock fortress built by Herod in the Judean desert on the shore of the Dead Sea,* located south of Ein Gedi. The siege of Masada figured prominently in Josephus's writings. During the Jewish revolt against Rome, a group of about 1,000 Jewish Zealots held out against a Roman siege for seven months in A.D. 72. When the Romans finally entered the fortress, they found that the defenders had committed suicide rather than submit to the Roman forces. This heroic stand, that Jews were prepared to die in freedom rather than submit to slavery, created a symbolic significance for Israel after its independence. It has also led to an Israeli tradition that, as part of the induction into certain units of the Israel Defense Forces,* they ascend to the fortress and pledge that ''Masada shall not fall again.'' Excavations of the site by archaeologist Yigael Yadin* have documented much of the historical writings of Josephus concerning Masada.

David Wurmser

MAY 17 AGREEMENT (1983). See ISRAEL–LEBANON AGREEMENT, MAY 17, 1983.

MCMAHON–HUSSEIN CORRESPONDENCE. See HUSSEIN–MCMAHON CORRESPONDENCE.

MECHDAL. A Hebrew word meaning omission or failure as a consequence of inaction. It was a term widely used in Israel in the aftermath of the Yom Kippur War* of 1973 to refer to the failures of the government and of the military to be fully prepared for the outbreak of this war and to respond to the initial attacks. This was attributed to an intelligence lapse. Israeli intelligence had misinterpreted and misevaluated Egyptian and Syrian* military buildups prior to the Yom Kippur War as basically routine. This, in turn, was related to the conception that Egypt* and Syria were not prepared for conflict with Israel, lacking superior airpower, and therefore would not undertake such an action.

The interim report of the Agranat Commission,* which dealt with some of the matters associated with the Yom Kippur War, led to the resignation of the chief of staff and the replacement of the chief of military intelligence and his deputy, as well as of other senior intelligence officers. Other officers of the Israel Defense Forces* (IDF) were removed from command positions.

MEIR, GOLDA (Formerly Meyerson) (b. Kiev, May 3, 1898; d. December 8, 1978). In 1903, the family moved to Pinsk and, three years later, settled in Milwaukee. She graduated from high school in Milwaukee and attended the Milwaukee Normal School for Teachers. At age seventeen she joined the Poalei Zion (Workers of Zion) Party. She married Morris Meyerson in December 1917, and in 1921 they moved to Palestine.* They settled in Kibbutz Merhaviah but later moved to Tel Aviv and then to Jerusalem.* In 1928, Mrs. Meyerson became secretary of the Women's Labor Council of the Histadrut* in Tel Aviv. When MAPAI* was formed in 1930, by the merger of Ahdut Haavoda and Hapoel Hatzair (Young Workers), she quickly became a major figure in the new party. In 1934, she was invited to join the Executive Committee of the Histadrut and became head of its Political Department. In 1946, when the British Mandatory* authorities arrested virtually all the members of the Jewish Agency* Executive and the Vaad Leumi that they could find in Palestine, Mrs. Meir became acting head of the Political Department of the Jewish Agency, replacing Moshe Shertok (later, Sharett*), who was imprisoned in Latrun. In the months immediately preceding Israel's declaration of independence she met secretly with King Abdullah* of Transjordan* to dissuade him from joining the Arab League* in attacking Jewish Palestine, but her efforts failed. In early June 1948, Mrs. Meir was appointed Israel's first minister to Moscow but returned to Israel in April 1949. She was elected to the First Knesset* in 1949 on the MAPAI list and became minister of labor in the government, a post she held until 1956, when she became foreign minister for a decade under Prime Ministers David

Ben-Gurion* and Levi Eshkol.* As minister of labor her principal function was the absorption of hundreds of thousands of immigrants who arrived in Israel in the first years after independence. Mrs. Meir initiated large-scale housing and road-building programs and strongly supported unlimited immigration, and she helped to provide employment and medical care for the immigrants. When she succeeded Moshe Sharett as foreign minister in 1956, she Hebraized her name and became known as Golda Meir. As foreign minister she concentrated on Israel's aid to African and other developing nations as a means of strengthening Israel's international position. She resigned as foreign minister in January 1966 and was succeeded by Abba Eban.* Because of her enormous popularity in MAPAI, Mrs. Meir was prevailed on to accept appointment as general secretary of MAPAI and, in that position, was prime minister Levi Eshkol's closest adviser. In January 1968, she was instrumental in facilitating the union of MAPAI, RAFI, and Ahdut Haavoda as the Israel Labor Party.* After serving for two years as secretary-general, she retired from public life. Following Eshkol's death in February 1969, party leaders prevailed upon her to succeed Eshkol, and she became Israel's fourth prime minister in March 1969. She retained the National Unity government* that Eshkol had constructed at the time of the Six Day War.* In the Knesset election at the end of October, the Labor Party won fifty-six seats, and she once again became prime minister. She led Israel through the trauma of the Yom Kippur War* and its aftermath. Following the 1973 election, which was postponed until December 31, she had great difficulty in forming a government with Moshe Dayan* continuing in his role as minister of defense. In April 1974 she resigned.

The turmoil in the political process and political life of Israel at the time of the Yom Kippur War set in motion forces that subsequently affected the political process. The effect was not obvious in the December 1973 Knesset election, and the profile of the new Parliament was not substantially different from that of its predecessor. Golda Meir was charged with creating a new government and did so in early 1974, only to resign a month later, primarily because of dissension within the Labor Party that centered on the question of political responsibility for lapses at the outset of the war. Yitzhak Rabin* was chosen prime minister with the support of the MAPAI establishment and of both Golda Meir and Pinhas Sapir, who were leading members of the old guard.

Golda Meir wrote *My Life* (New York: G. P. Putnam's Sons, 1975); *This Is Our Strength* (New York: Macmillan, 1963); and "Israel in Search of Lasting Peace," *Foreign Affairs* 51 (April 1973):447–61.

For further information see: Marver H. Bernstein, "Golda Meir," in Bernard Reich, ed., *Political Leaders of the Contemporary Middle East and North Africa: A Biographical Dictionary* (Westport, CT: Greenwood Press, 1990), pp. 325–32; Marie Syrkin, ed., *A Land of Our Own: An Oral Biography by Golda Meir* (Philadelphia: Jewish Publication Society, 1973); Marie Syrkin, *Golda Meir: Woman with a Cause* (New York: Putnam, 1963).

MEMORANDUM OF UNDERSTANDING (MOU). In November 1981, Israel and the United States negotiated and signed a Memorandum of Understanding on Strategic Cooperation, in which it was agreed that United States–Israel strategic cooperation "is designed against the threat to peace and security of the region caused by the Soviet Union or Soviet-controlled forces from outside the region introduced into the region." The MOU was suspended in December 1981 in the wake of Israel's extension of its law and jurisdiction to the Golan Heights,* but additional memorandums were signed in subsequent years.

MERKAVA TANK. The Merkava (''chariot'' in Hebrew) is Israel's first indigenously produced tank. Israel decided to design and produce its own tank in 1967 in order to reduce its dependence on foreign sources for its tank needs. Detailed design began in earnest in 1970. The first prototype Merkava was produced in 1974, and the first production tanks were delivered to the Israeli army in 1979. Design priorities of the new Merkava emphasized enhanced armored protection, firepower, and mobility. The tank was also designed to maximize repair parts compatibility with Israel's existing M48, M60, and Centurion tanks.*

The turret of the Merkava can accept either a 105mm or 120mm cannon. Initial models (Mark 1 and Mark 2) were armed with the 105mm cannon. Recent models (Mark 3) have been armed with the 120mm gun. The Merkava has a combat crew of four. Its maximum road speed is about twenty-nine mph, with a 250-mile range. The Merkava can carry a basic load of up to ninety-two 105mm rounds on board the tank. Fully loaded for combat, it weighs approximately sixty-nine tons. The Merkava is equipped with both an NBC (nuclear, biological, and chemical) protection system and an explosive suppression system to provide crew fire protection if hit.

The Merkava first saw combat with the Israel Defense Forces* in the War in Lebanon* in 1982.

For further information see: Christopher F. Foss, ed., *Jane's Armour and Artillery, 1991–1992* (Surrey: Jane's Information Group Limited, 1992).

Stephen H. Gotowicki

MIG-17 JET AIRCRAFT. The MiG-17 was the successor to the Soviet MiG-15, both designed by Mikoyan Gurevitch. It was designed to rectify the defects of the MiG-15, especially its aerodynamics, and was equipped with one turbo jet engine. In addition to having a more powerful engine than the MiG-15, the MiG-17 had extensive modifications to its control surfaces and had a new wing design. The plane was tested in the first weeks of January 1950 and was immediately put into production. Units of the Soviet air force received the plane in 1952.

A single-seat interceptor-fighter, the Soviet Union built many versions of the MiG-17 (named Fresco in the North Atlantic Treaty Organization Code). The planes were originally ground-controlled, but the Soviets later equipped the aircraft with airborne radar for interception purposes. The Fresco had a gross weight of 12,500 pounds and a length of 36⅓ feet, with a wing span of thirty-one feet. Its maximum speed was 0.98 Mach, and it had a combat radius of 325 miles. Its armaments could vary, but it was often armed with three 23mm cannons or two 23mm cannons and one 37mm cannon and could carry a load of two 550-pound bombs or thirty-two rockets.

The Soviets produced over 9,000 MiG-17 aircraft before they ended production in 1958. Poland, Czechoslovakia, and the People's Republic of China produced versions of the MiG-17 under license. The plane was used by all Warsaw Pact countries as well as by Egypt,* Iraq,* and Syria.*

Estimates vary as to the number of MiG-17s sold to the Arab countries. Prior to the Six Day War,* it is estimated that Egypt had 100 MiG 15/17s. Seventy-five of the planes were destroyed on the first day of the fighting, and during the entire war it is estimated that Egypt lost 95. In the Yom Kippur War,* Egypt had an estimated 200 MiG-17s, while in 1985 estimates place the number of these aircraft at 70. By 1995, the Egyptian air force retained approximately 30 of the planes in operation. Syria possessed 40 MiG-17s, and it lost 23 of them in the Six Day War. In the Yom Kippur War, Syria was estimated to have had 120 of the aircraft. Iraq, according to Israeli figures, lost 9 MiG-17s in the Six Day War and in 1994 was estimated to have about 30 remaining.

For further information see: Enzo Angelucc, *Rand McNally Encyclopedia of Military Aircraft, 1914–1980* (Chicago: Rand McNally, 1981); Chaim Herzog, *The Arab–Israeli Wars* (New York: Vintage Books, 1982); Mark Lambert, ed., *Jane's All the World's Aircraft, 1994–1995* (Surrey, England: Jane's Information Group, 1994); Nadav Safran, *From War to War: The Arab–Israeli Confrontation, 1948–1967* (New York: Pegasus, 1969).

Joseph E. Goldberg

MIG-19 JET AIRCRAFT. The MiG-19 is a single-seat, supersonic, limited all-weather fighter aircraft designed and produced in the Soviet Union beginning in 1955. The MiG-19 has a maximum speed of Mach 1.45 (957 mph) and a maximum operational altitude of 58,725 feet. The MiG-19 was designed primarily as an interceptor but has a limited ground-attack capability. The MiG-19 is armed with two or three 30mm cannons and can carry air-to-air missiles, air-to-air rockets, and conventional bombs. Combat radius with two external fuel tanks is 426 miles. Some versions of the MiG-19 were day fighters only and were equipped with optical gunsights. China produced more copies of the MiG-19, under the designation J-6, than did the Soviet Union. Egypt* was the primary customer of the MiG-19/J-6 in the Middle East.

Israel faced Egyptian MiG-19s during the Six Day War,* the War of Attrition,* and the Yom Kippur War.* However, with its rudimentary capabilities, the MiG-19 proved no match for Israel's more sophisticated A-4 Skyhawks,* Mirages,* and F-4 Phantoms.*

For further information see: Michael J. H. Taylor, ed., *Jane's World Combat Aircraft* (Surrey: Jane's Information Group, 1988).

Stephen H. Gotowicki

MIG-21 JET AIRCRAFT. The MiG-21 (North Atlantic Treaty Organization [NATO]-codenamed Fishbed and Mongol) is a single-seat, supersonic, Soviet-made jet aircraft that can be employed in interceptor, fighter-bomber, or reconnaissance roles. The MiG-21 has a maximum speed of 1,056 mph and a maximum design altitude of 59,055 feet. It is armed with a 30mm cannon and can carry up to 2,200 pounds in bombs, air-to-air missiles, and air-to-ground rockets. The MiG-21 has a combat radius of 460 miles, depending on its combat load.

The MiG-21 was first flown in June 1956. Since then the Soviet Union has produced eighteen versions of it. The MiG-21 versions that have been most widely used in the Arab–Israeli conflicts are the MiG-21F and the MiG-21PFMA.

The first MiG-21s were deployed in 1957 and 1958 to the Soviet air force. At the beginning of the Six Day War,* Egypt* had approximately 160 MiG-21s, and Syria* had 40 MiG-21s. It was the mainstay of both air forces. They were used to provide a first-line interceptor aircraft capability as part of their air defense against the growing and impressive Israeli air force. Because of the short range of the MiG-21, it could not provide escort capability for Egypt's slow bombers. This limited the strategic capability of an Arab attack. Recognizing this problem, in March 1971, Egyptian president Anwar Sadat* requested that the Soviet Union supply to Egypt the Soviet MiG-23, which was an advanced interceptor. The Soviet condition was that the planes would be supplied only if they were flown by Soviet pilots and remained under Soviet control. Though the Egyptians accepted this, the delivery of the MiG-23 was delayed. Instead, the Soviets provided the Egyptians with additional MiG-21s and agreed to provide air-defense crews. The failure of the Soviets to supply the advanced interceptor remained a point of dissatisfaction with the Egyptians.

The preemptive Israeli air strike in 1967 destroyed large portions of the Egyptian air force. It is estimated that Egypt by mid-1969 had a total of about 100 MiG-21s, during the War of Attrition* they had approximately 100 to 200 MiG-21s, and prior to the Yom Kippur War* they had approximately 210 to 220 MiG-21 aircraft.

The Syrian air force began to acquire Soviet equipment in 1956. Because many of their airplanes were based in Egypt in 1956 and were lost in the Sinai War,* the Russians resupplied them with MiG-17s. During the Six Day War, Syria had a three-squadron regiment flying the MiG-21F. These planes were destroyed by an Israeli attack and were replaced with MiG-21F/PF. A large number of the Syrian aircraft were destroyed in the Yom Kippur War, but they were also replaced by the Soviets. Estimates are that from 1973 to 1976, the

Soviet Union supplied the Syrian air force with at least 140 MiG-21s of various versions.

The MiG-21F was the front-line aircraft used by the Arab air forces in the Yom Kippur War. Even with the MiG-21, Arab air forces did not acquit themselves well in combat with the Israeli air force. A large number of MiG-21s were destroyed on the ground before they could be used against Israel. The MiG-21s used by the Arab states also lacked much of the sophisticated target acquisition and fire control technology used in Israeli fighters. Finally, the lack of effective air combat training of the Arab pilots compared to their Israeli counterparts placed them at a great tactical disadvantage. Despite these shortcomings, the Israeli air force considered the MiG-21 an efficient, high-altitude interceptor.

For further information see: Enzo Angelucci, *Rand McNally Encyclopedia of Military Aircraft, 1914–1980* (Chicago: Rand McNally, 1981); Jon D. Glassman, *Arms for the Arabs: The Soviet Union and War in the Middle East* (Baltimore: Johns Hopkins University Press, 1975); Chaim Herzog, *The Arab–Israeli Wars* (New York: Vintage Books, 1984); Mark Lambert, ed., *Jane's All the World's Aircraft, 1994–1995* (Surrey, England: Jane's Information Group, 1994); Lon C. Nordeen, *Fighters over Israel* (New York: Orion Books, 1990); Michael J. H. Taylor, *Soviet and Eastern European Major Combat Aircraft* (London: Tri-Service Press, 1990).

Stephen H. Gotowicki

MIG-29 JET FIGHTER AIRCRAFT. The MiG-29 fighter aircraft is a two-seat, two-engine, supersonic, multirole fighter aircraft designed and produced in the Soviet Union in the early 1980s. The MiG-29 is capable of attaining speeds of Mach 2.3 (1,520 mph) and a maximum altitude of 55,775 feet. It can operate in the air-superiority, interdiction, and close air-support roles and can be armed with close-range infrared air-to-air missiles, medium-range, radar-guided air-to-air missiles, bombs, explosive submunition dispensers, and 80mm, 130mm, and 240mm air-to-ground rockets. Maximum range for the MiG-29 with internal fuel stores is 932 miles; with external fuel tanks, the range is 1,305 miles.

In the Middle East, the MiG-29 has been procured by Iran, Iraq,* and Syria.*

Stephen H. Gotowicki

MILSON, MENAHEM. Educated at the Hebrew University, Harvard, and Cambridge, Menahem Milson is a professor of Arabic language and literature at the Hebrew University of Jerusalem.* He served as an officer in Israel's Unit 101* and in 1956 fought at the Mitla Pass.* Milson, a reserve colonel in the Israel Defense Forces,* served as an adviser on Arab affairs to the military commander of the West Bank* from 1976 to 1978. Although he advocated strict policies toward the Palestine Liberation Organization* (PLO), Milson also believed that Israel must nurture a moderate Palestinian leadership in the territories if Israel was eventually to live in peace with the Arabs.

Milson's article, "How to Make Peace with the Palestinians," published in the May 1981 issue of *Commentary,* captured the attention of the Israeli government. Critical of Israel's administration of the territories, Milson emphasized that the noninterventionist policy placed the moderate Palestinians at a disadvantage. The moderates had been intimidated into silence by the PLO, while Israel's guarantee of freedom of expression in the territories ensured that the PLO could take advantage of the climate to mobilize the population. Israel had to attempt to counter, if not eliminate, PLO influence in the territories. No mention was made in the article as to the ultimate fate of the territory—whether it was to be federated with Jordan,* independent, or under Israeli control.

Military Order 947 established a civilian administration in the area, and Milson served as head of the civil administration of Judea and Samaria* from November 1981 to September 22, 1982, when he resigned over the Begin* government's administration's initial decision not to establish a commission to investigate the Sabra and Shatila massacre.* Understanding the nature of political and social life in the Arab world, Milson believed that Israel should utilize the rules of Arab life to its own advantage. Cooperation is rewarded whether the patronage is in the form of money, jobs, or housing. Noncooperation, in turn, is costly, whether it is the loss of a job or the failure to acquire housing or a village project. In all cases, Milson emphasized in his administrative procedure, Israel must act in accord with both Israeli and Jordanian Law.

In an attempt to create support for his policies, Milson established village leagues.* Because the PLO had been influential in the population centers but had not increased their influence in the traditionally politically apathetic rural areas of the territories, it was hoped that Israel could influence through patronage the largest percentage of the West Bank population, which was rural. Despite these attempts, Arab participants in the village leagues were identified as quislings and ridiculed.

As violence increased in the territories, Milson became increasingly dissatisfied with how the Begin administration handled the riots. He insisted that Israel must combat the Palestine Liberation Organization but not the Palestinians. The Begin policies, he insisted, made no such distinction and undermined Israel's ability to promote a moderate Palestinian leadership. In September 1982, Milson resigned his position.

For further information see: Menahem Milson, "How to Make Peace with the Palestinians," *Commentary* (May 1981):25–35; Menahem Milson, "How Not to Occupy the West Bank," *Commentary* 81 (April 1986):15–22.

Joseph E. Goldberg

MIRAGE JET AIRCRAFT. A single-seat supersonic fighter aircraft designed and produced in France* in the early 1960s. The Mirage III was designed as a high-altitude, all-weather interceptor but could also perform ground support missions. The Mirage 5 was designed as a ground-attack fighter using the same air frame and engine as the Mirage III. The Mirage III/5 has a maximum speed of Mach 2.2 (1,460 mph) and an maximum operational altitude of 55,775 feet. It is armed with two 30mm cannons and can carry a combination of air-to-air missiles, conventional bombs, air-to-surface rockets, and external fuel tanks, with a total external load of 8,818 pounds. Its combat radius is about 550 miles in the interceptor role and 745 miles in the ground-attack role.

Israel acquired Mirage fighters from France in the early 1960s and used them with great success in the Six Day War,* the War of Attrition,* and the Yom Kippur War.* When France embargoed the delivery of additional Mirage aircraft to Israel at the onset of the Six Day War, Israel designed and produced the Kfir fighter,* based on the Mirage design, in the early 1970s as a replacement.

For further information see: Chaim Herzog, *The Arab–Israeli Wars* (Tel Aviv: Steimatzky, 1984); Michael J. H. Taylor, ed., *Jane's World Combat Aircraft* (Surrey: Jane's Information Group, 1988).

Stephen H. Gotowicki

MITLA PASS. A mountain pass that sits astride the southernmost point of two major east–west movement axes in the central Sinai Peninsula.* The pass lies in the uplifted outer rim of the a-Tih Plateau about twenty-five miles east of Suez City. The relief in this area reaches 1,000 meters above sea level and is dominated by imposing and precipitous rock walls.

The central Sinai is the region most suitable for high-speed, armored military operations. The northern third of the Sinai Peninsula, the coastal zone, is characterized by undulating sand dunes, which greatly restrict off-road movement—undesirable in armored operations. The southern Sinai is dominated by high mountains, which make it unsuitable for rapid military operations.

The hard gravel surface conditions surrounding the Mitla Pass are ideal for tank warfare. East of the pass are the broad plains of the Central Sinai—to the west, the plains leading to the Suez Canal.* The heights surrounding the pass provide cover, concealment, good observation, and long fields of fire, making them suitable for defensive operations as well.

The Mitla Pass has been considered critical strategic terrain in each of the major Arab–Israeli wars. In the 1956 war,* Israeli paratroopers were dropped in the Mitla Pass to secure it. In the 1973 war,* the Egyptians* considered it a major objective, and the area between the Mitla Pass and the Suez Canal was the site of some of the most intense armor battles of the war.

For further information see: S.L.A. Marshall, *Sinai Victory: Command Decisions in History's Shortest War, Israel's Hundred-Hour Conquest of Sinai* (New York: William Morrow, 1958); Efraim Orni and Elisha Efrat, *Geography of Israel* (Jerusalem: Israel Universities Press, 1971); Steven J. Rosen, *Military Geography and the Military Balance in the Arab–Israeli Conflict* (Jerusalem: Hebrew University, 1977).

Stephen H. Gotowicki

MIXED ARMISTICE COMMISSION (MAC). The Mixed Armistice Commission was established by the United Nations General Assembly to resolve disputes and clashes along Israel's borders with its Arab neighbors. There were individual commissions for Israel and each of its Arab neighbors. Each was composed of Israeli and Arab representatives and United Nations officials. It investigated complaints brought by one side or the other and then determined responsibility and reported to the United Nations. They functioned under the supervision of the United Nations Truce Supervision Organization* (UNTSO).

In the spring of 1949, Armistice Agreements* were signed between Israel and each of its neighbors (Egypt,* Lebanon,* Jordan,* Syria*). Each Armistice Agreement set up a Mixed Armistice Commission composed of an equal number (two or three) of members appointed by each of the parties, with a chairman (who had the deciding vote) designated by the chief of staff of UNTSO.

The Mixed Armistice Commissions had a checkered history.

The Egypt–Israel Mixed Armistice Commission (EIMAC) functioned from 1949 to 1956. The Israelis never boycotted its meetings, and the most important violations, cross-border attacks, and retaliations of the armistice took place along this frontier. After the Israeli invasion of Sinai* in 1956 and the withdrawal in 1957, EIMAC was not reconvened. It was replaced by UNEF.*

The Israel–Lebanon MAC (ILMAC) met periodically and rarely had difficult complaints to deal with.

The Israel–Syria MAC, which surveyed the Israel–Syria frontier, was far more complex. There were several places where Syrian troops were occupying territory awarded to Israel under the partition plan* along the relatively short frontier. A number of serious incidents occurred. After 1951, Israel declined to participate in the MAC.

A large number of incidents occurred along the frontier between Israel and Jordan between 1949 and 1967 that the Israel–Hashemite Kingdom of Jordan MAC* (IHKJMAC) dealt with, with varying degrees of effectiveness. In addition, UNTSO, as a result of an agreement between Israel and Jordan in Jerusalem* that predated the Armistice Agreement, was responsible for supervising the Israeli and Jordanian enclaves on Mount Scopus.*

MNF. See **MULTINATIONAL FORCE.**

MOLEDET (HOMELAND) PARTY. An Israeli right-wing nationalist political party created for the 1988 Knesset* election by Israel Defense Forces* reserve general Rehavam (''Gandhi'') Zeevi. It advocated the transfer of the Arab population of the occupied territories* to Arab countries. Moledet won two seats in the Knesset elected in November 1988. It joined the coalition government headed by Prime Minister Shamir* in February 1991. In January 1992, Moledet resigned from the government because of Shamir's willingness to discuss an interim agreement on Palestinian self-rule in the West Bank* and Gaza Strip.* It increased its Knesset representation to three seats in the June 1992 election.

MOROCCO. See **ISRAEL–MOROCCO DIPLOMATIC RELATIONS.**

MORRISON–GRADY COMMITTEE. In the summer of 1946, President Harry S Truman* established a special cabinet committee to discuss the implications of the report of the Anglo–American Committee of Inquiry.* Three members of the special committee, led by Henry F. Grady, met with a British delegation headed by Deputy Prime Minister Herbert Morrison. The Morrison–Grady Committee's report was presented to the House of Commons on July 31, 1946, and called for the division of Palestine* into four areas: a Jewish province, an Arab province, the Negev,* and a district of Jerusalem.* The latter two districts were to be governed by the Central Authority while the Arab and Jewish provinces were to have their own legislatures. The British high commissioner would, in turn, select from these legislatures a prime minister and council of ministers for each of the provinces. Immigration into Palestine was to be based on the economic absorptive capacity of the province and would be determined by the Central Authority. Because immigration levels were dependent on central government approval, the Zionists rejected the Morrison–Grady Plan. In the United States, bipartisan congressional opposition to the report, as well as administration dissatisfaction, led President Truman to formally reject the plan. President Truman informed Prime Minister Clement Attlee on August 12, 1946, of the U.S. rejection and urged Britain to admit refugees* into Palestine.

For further information see: Michael J. Cohen, *Palestine and the Great Powers, 1945–1948* (Princeton, NJ: Princeton University Press, 1982); Great Britain, Colonial Office, *Proposals for the Future of Palestine, July 1946–February 1947* (London: H.M.S.O., 1947).

MORTADA, SAAD (b. El Faiyum, Egypt, July 25, 1923). He studied law and graduated from the University of Cairo (formerly King Fouad University) in 1944. After serving in the Ministry of Interior, he joined the Ministry of Foreign Affairs and worked in the Economic Department in Cairo before being posted as Vice Consul in New Delhi, India, in 1949. He subsequently served in a variety of posts abroad, as well as at the Ministry in Cairo, and completed post-graduate studies at the College of Europe in Bruges, Belgium. Between 1967 and 1972 he served as Chef de Cabinet of the office of the Director of the Egyptian Information Service. In July 1972 he became the first Egyptian Ambassador to the United Arab Emirates, and in 1974 the Ambassador to Senegal. He was Egypt's Ambassador to Morocco when President Anwar Sadat,* en route to Cairo from Washington after signing the Camp David Accords,* stopped in Rabat to explain his policy motives to King Hassan II.* In 1980 he was nominated by Boutros Boutros-Ghali,* then the Egyptian Minister of State for Foreign Affairs, to be Egypt's first Ambassador to Israel, and on February 22, 1980, he assumed his official duties in Tel Aviv. He was recalled to Cairo on September 23, 1982, to protest Israel's involvement in the Sabra and Shatila* refugee camps massacre. He retired from the diplomatic service on July 25, 1983.

Ahmed Elbashari

MOSSAD—HAMOSSAD LEMODIIN VETAFKIDIM MEYUHADIM. The Institute for Intelligence and Special Missions. Created on September 1, 1951, Mossad is Israel's equivalent of the U.S. Central Intelligence Agency. Among its missions is the collection of political, social, economic, and military information in and on foreign countries, especially all aspects of Arab politics, society, and foreign policy. See also SHIN BET.

For further information see: Michael Bar-Zohar, *Spies in the Promised Land: Isar Harel and the Israeli Secret Service* (Boston: Houghton Mifflin, 1972); Stanley Blumberg and Gwinn Owens, *The Survival Factor: Israeli Intelligence from World War I to the Present* (New York: G. P. Putnam's Sons, 1981); Richard Deacon, *The Israeli Secret Service* (New York: Taplinger, 1978); Dennis Eisenberg, Uri Dan, and Eli Landau, *The Mossad Inside Stories: Israel's Secret Intelligence Service* (New York: Paddington, 1978); Stewart Steven, *The Spymasters of Israel* (New York: Macmillan, 1980).

AL-MOUALEM, WALID (b. Damascus, Syria,* July 17, 1941). He received a B.A. degree in economics from Cairo University in 1965 and then entered the Syrian Ministry of Foreign Affairs. He served in various posts and rose through the ranks from an initial posting as attaché in the Syrian Embassy in Dar es Salaam in 1965 to ambassador to Romania from 1975 to 1980. From 1981 to 1985, he was director of the Department of Documentation and from 1985 to 1990 of the Department of Special Offices in the Ministry of Foreign Affairs in Damascus. He became ambassador to the United States in 1990. As Syrian ambassador to Washington, he met with the Israeli ambassador to the United States, Itamar Rabinovich,* in informal talks (the ambassador's talks*) to discuss the peace process between the two states. He is the author of a number of books, published in Arabic, on Syrian and other Middle Eastern topics.

Ahmed Elbashari

MOUNT BA'AL HAZOR. At 1,016 meters' altitude, Ba'al Hazor is the highest point in Samaria* (West Bank,* north of Jerusalem*), considered by some Israeli military analysts of critical strategic importance in terms of early aerial warning and surveillance over the Jordan Valley to the east and the Israeli coastal plane to the west. The peak lies north of the Jericho*–Ramallah Road, about one kilometer west of the Arab town of Taibe and one kilometer east of Ofra, ten kilometers to the northeast of Ramallah, and next to the Israeli settlement of Beth El and the archaeological site of biblical Beth El. Ba'al Hazor also lies three kilometers east of the strategic intersection of the Ramallah–Nablus Road and the Allon Highway, which is the major north–south route from Kfar Adumim northward along the "spine" of the Samarian Mountains.

David Wurmser

MOUNT HERMON. Jebal As-Sheikh in Arabic. A series of east–west-oriented peaks forming the northern border of the Golan Heights.* It contains territory held by Israel, Syria,* and Lebanon.* In biblical times, Mount Hermon was considered the home of the Canaanite goddess Anat. The highest peak of the Hermon (2,814 meters) lies a few meters inside Lebanon along the Syrian–Lebanese border and is part of the demilitarized zone between Syria and Israel. The "Israeli" peak of Mount Hermon, which includes "Snow Outlook" (Mitzpeh Shlagim), is at 2,224 meters.

Israel first captured the lower peak of Mount Hermon on the last day of the Six Day War,* on June 12, 1967, where it established an early-warning and observation post for monitoring Syrian forces operating near Kuneitra.* The Israeli-held Hermon fell to the Syrians in the first hours of the Yom Kippur War* on October 6, 1973, and remained under Syrian control for two weeks despite numerous Israeli attempts to recapture it. By October 22, not only had Israeli forces recaptured the "Israeli" Hermon, but a paratroop company led by Hezi Shelach under Nadel's Paratroop Brigade had proceeded to take the Syrian Hermon peak (2,814 meters) eight kilometers to the north in what became known as "Operation Dessert."

As part of the 1974 Disengagement Agreements* between Syria and Israel, the Israel Defense Forces* (IDF) vacated the Syrian Hermon peak (2,201 meters) half a year after its capture and withdrew to Mitzpeh Shlagim, in exchange for the area's becoming a demilitarized zone under United Nations (UN) monitors.

Mount Hermon is the single most dominating feature of the entire Golan Heights plain, which was originally under the British Mandate* for Palestine* but was ceded to the French Mandate of Syria by Britain in 1921 as agreed upon under the Herdige–Leyques Treaty of December 1920, in which the French* and British agreed among themselves on the precise delineation of territory between the French and British Mandates. Mount Hermon's dominance of the plateau makes it the most critical strategic feature in the northern Golan Heights, making it the "strategic pivot" of the tricountry region. In Israeli hands the peak provides the IDF with an excellent early-warning and aerial surveillance capability of the entire southern Beka Valley* in Lebanon and the Golan plain all the way northeast to Damascus. The Israeli fortress on "Hermon Shoulder" (Ketef Hermon) at 2,072 meters also overlooks the Israeli Hula Valley and Israeli-held positions on the Golan Heights and, when in Syrian hands, could effectively render impossible Israeli surprise maneuvers in the northern Galilee, southern Lebanon, and the Golan Heights.

David Wurmser

MOUNT MEIRON. At 1,208 meters' altitude, it is the highest mountain in the Galilee. It and neighboring Mount Canaan, including the town of Safed (Zefat) on the southeast slopes of Mount Canaan, are the dominant strategic features of the northern Galilee, with aerial and early-warning implications for Israel Defense Forces* (IDF) in southern Lebanon. Mount Meiron is especially important for early warning in the central sector of Israel's security zone.* It also dominates the strategic Bet Kerem Valley, which separates the Lower Galilee from the Upper Galilee.

Mount Meiron was captured as part of Israel's Plan D,* the archtypal overall Israeli defense plan formulated in March 1948 to seize strategic terrain in areas where the major thrust of the Arab invasion on May 15 was anticipated. Mount Meiron fell to Israeli hands on April 28 during "Operation Yiftah," which was the Upper Galilee aspect of Plan D, since Arab forces were focusing their effort on nearby Safed, which finally fell to Israeli forces on May 10.

David Wurmser

MOUNT OF OLIVES. Mountain overlooking Jerusalem* from the east. It has three peaks. The highest peak, also known as Mount Scopus,* is 2,684 feet above sea level and is the site of the Hebrew University of Jerusalem, which was founded in 1925. On the second peak lies the Augusta Victoria Hospital, which was built in 1898. The Arab village of al-Tur lies on the third peak.

In the Bible it is known as the Ascent of the Olives, and it is said that King David used to worship there. At the foot of the mountain, tombs from the First and Second Temple* periods can be found. Since ancient times, the Mount of Olives has been a significant burial place for the Jews of Jerusalem, for it is believed that in the end of days the Messiah will ascend the Mount, and there the Prophet Ezekiel will blow the trumpet for the resurrection of the dead.

During Israel's War of Independence,* the top of the Mount, despite being surrounded by Arab territory, remained in Israeli hands. The Armistice Agreement froze the situation as it was, and this caused many incidents and flare-ups in the area. Israel was allowed to keep police on the Mount. These police contingents were changed every two weeks by a United Nations (UN)-supervised convoy that traveled through Jordanian*-held territory. The Jewish cemeteries and monuments at the base of the Mount were desecrated and vandalized by Arabs, and it was not until after the Six Day War* that the entire Mount came under Israeli control. At this point Hebrew University returned to its original location, which it had left due to the fighting in 1948.

David Salzberg

MOUNT SCOPUS. (Har Hatzofim) A hill in Jerusalem.* Site of the first campus of Hebrew University of Jerusalem, which was cut off from Jewish Jerusalem in the War of Independence* but remained under Israel's control. The enclave was held by a small Israeli presence relieved periodically by convoys escorted by the United Nations (UN). In the Six Day War,* Israel recaptured the surrounding territory, and Hebrew University began to rebuild and expand its facilities on Mount Scopus.

Mount Scopus lies on the northeastern side of Jerusalem's Old City.* It is 2,700 feet (827 meters) high, dividing Jerusalem and Bethlehem* on one side and the wilderness of Judea,* the Jordan Valley, the Dead Sea,* and the Mountains of Moab on the other.

On July 24, 1918, the first foundation stones of the Hebrew University were laid on Mount Scopus. It was formally dedicated in 1925. The Hadassah Hospital and Medical Center were also built on the Mount. The institutions on the Mount flourished until the period between 1945 and 1947, when fighting between Jews and Arabs ensued. After 1947, riots broke out due to the United Nations' adoption of a partition plan* for Palestine.* This caused suspension of all academic work at Hebrew University, evacuation of the Hadassah Hospital and Medical Center, and great damage to many buildings.

In the partition plan of 1947, the city of Jerusalem was to be a *corpus separatum** (a separate body), administered by the United Nations under a special international regime. Israel reluctantly agreed to this scheme, because it was a nonnegotiable part of the partition plan, which Israel accepted in principle. But the Arabs refused to divide Jerusalem. Fighting erupted between Jews and Arabs.

During the first cease-fire of the 1948 war, a UN mediator was able to arrange for the demilitarization of Mount Scopus. The Israel–Jordan* Armistice Agreements* were concluded in April 1949. The demarcation line bisected the city of Jerusalem; on one side the Old City* and eastern neighborhoods were held by Jordan, and on the other the western (new) part of the city was held by Israel. Mount Scopus was to be an Israeli enclave in the midst of Jordanian territory.

Article 8 of the Armistice Agreements allowed Israel access to holy places, normal functioning of the institutions of Mount Scopus, and free movements of traffic on vital roads. An agreement concluded between Israel and Jordan on July 7, 1948, allowed supplies to reach Mount Scopus biweekly through special convoys. The Israeli civilian police garrison on the Mount was also to be replaced biweekly.

Throughout the existence of the Armistice Agreements, Jordan refused to comply with Article 8 of the agreements. Jews were not permitted to go to the Western Wall* in the Old City, and Hebrew University and the Hadassah Hospital went unused (other campuses were built in the New City), because teachers and students were denied access to these institutions. There was constant tension between the Israeli police garrison stationed on Mount Scopus and the inhabitants of the Arab village Issawiya, in the Israeli part of the demilitarized zone, and Jordan occasionally interfered with the convoys to the Mount and with communications with the New City.

In November 1957, Jordan complained that Israel was abusing its rights under the Armistice Agreements by bringing too many supplies into the Mount Scopus enclave. In December 1957, UN secretary-general Dag Hammarskjold* went to Jerusalem and Amman to negotiate an agreement. In January 1958, he sent Francis Urrutia, ambassador of Columbia, to oversee the new agreement. In early 1958, however, the conflict erupted again. In May 1958, after Jordanian soldiers opened fire on Israeli patrols on Mount Scopus, killing four Israeli policemen and Colonel George Flint, a UN officer who had been sent to Mount Scopus in an attempt to arbitrate the dispute, Ralph Bunche,* assistant to Hammarskjold, and then Hammarskjold himself, came to Amman and Jerusalem to attempt to work out a solution. Nevertheless, they managed to achieve only a temporary respite.

During the Six Day War, Israel captured all of Jerusalem and the surrounding areas. Mount Scopus became part of greater Jerusalem, and the university buildings were restored. Studies were resumed in the fall of 1969 at the Mount Scopus campus of Hebrew University.

For further information see: Meron Benvenisti, *Jerusalem, the Torn City* (Minneapolis: University of Minnesota Press, 1976); H. Eugene Bovis, *The Jerusalem Question: 1917–1968* (Stanford: Hoover Institution Press, 1971).

MOUNT ZION. A hill in Jerusalem* located outside Zion gate of the old walled city. An old tradition places the tomb of King David on Mount Zion.

MOUSSA, AMR. See **AMR MUSA.**

MOYNE, LORD (b. Dublin, Ireland, March 29, 1880; d. Cairo, Egypt,* November 6, 1944). Walter Edward Guinness was the third son of Sir Edward Cecil Guinness, first earl of Iveagh, and Adelaide Guinness. He was educated at Eton. He served in the British army in the Boer War in 1901–2, where he was twice wounded and decorated with the Queen's Medal. During World War I, Guinness served at Gallipoli, Egypt, on the Western Front as a major in the Suffolk Imperial Yeomanry. He married Evelyn Erskine in 1903, with whom he had two sons and a daughter. A member of the Conservative Party, Guinness ran unsuccessfully for Parliament in 1906 but was victorious in a parliamentary election in 1907. He served in Parliament until 1931, when he was named first baron Moyne in 1932. Lord Moyne served as undersecretary of state for war from October 1922 to October 1923. He later served as financial secretary of the treasury, minister of agriculture and fisheries, and joint parliamentary secretary to the Ministry of Agriculture. In 1941, Lord Moyne became secretary of state for the colonies. One of the important decisions that Lord Moyne was involved with as the newly appointed colonial secretary was whether or not the British should establish a Jewish army to help the British war effort. Britain recognized the value that such a force would have for its defense efforts in the Middle East, but many British officials, including Lord Moyne, believed that the creation of a Jewish division would have negative repercussions within the Arab world and perhaps encourage them to support the Germans. In addition, there was the fear that a Jewish division would be used after the war to militarily support the creation of a Jewish state in Palestine.* Lord Moyne proposed a ''Greater Syria'' Plan, which would have divided the region into four states: ''Greater Syria,'' which would have consisted of Syria,* Transjordan,* and the Arab portions of Palestine and Lebanon*; a Jewish state; a Christian Lebanon; and Jerusalem* under British protection. Upon the sudden death of Lord Lloyd, Lord Moyne was appointed deputy minister of state for the Middle East in August 1942. In January 1944, he was appointed minister resident in the Middle

East. On Monday, November 6, 1944, Lord Moyne returned to his Cairo residence, and, when he got out of his car, he was shot by two armed gunmen.
Moyne and his chauffer were both killed. Two members of the Stern gang*
(LEHI* or Fighters for the Freedom of Israel), twenty-year-old Eliahu Hakim
and twenty-three-year-old Eliahu Bet-Zouri, were arrested. They were convicted
on January 11, 1945, and condemned to death. Both were hanged on March 23,
1945. The murder of Lord Moyne was condemned by the Yishuv* leadership
as well as by Winston Churchill.* Rather than creating sympathy for the Zionist*
cause, the assassination hardened the British position toward altering their White
Paper of 1939.*

Joseph E. Goldberg

MUALEM, WALID. See **WALID AL-MOUALEM.**

MUBARAK, MOHAMMED HOSNI (b. Kafr-el Musilha, May 4, 1928). Mu-
barak has been president of the Arab Republic of Egypt* since October 1981.
He was born in an Egyptian village in the province of Minufia located in the
Nile delta. His father was a small landowner. Mubarak grew up among peasants.
He graduated with honors from the Military Academy in 1949, served as a
military pilot in the Sinai,* and was an instructor at the Air Force Academy.

Mubarak participated as a pilot in repelling the combined 1956 attack by
Israel, Great Britain,* and France* against Egypt. In 1959, he was appointed
commander of a Tu-16 bomber* squadron, and a few years later, commander
of an air brigade.

During the 1964–65 period, Mubarak studied at the Grunze Military Academy
in the USSR. In 1966–67, Mubarak stayed in Yemen as a member of the Egyptian military contingent rendering assistance to the Republican government in
its struggle against the Saudi-backed monarchists.

During the Six Day War,* Mubarak commanded an air brigade. Following
the defeat of the Arabs in that war, Mubarak was appointed superintendent of
the Air Force College in Bilbeis. The top organizational qualities and high professionalism displayed by him at that post led to his being appointed air vice
marshal chief of staff of the air force in 1969 by then president Gamal Abdul
Nasser.* In 1971, Mubarak became the air force commander in chief. His contribution to the successful operations of Egypt's air force against Israeli airfields
in the early period of the October 1973 war* resulted in his promotion to the
rank of lieutenant general. In 1974, Mubarak became close to President Anwar
Sadat,* who headed Egypt after Nasser's death in 1970. Under President Sadat,
Mubarak became commander in chief of the air force in 1972 and air marshal
in 1974. Mubarak's efficiency, loyalty, and high political professionalism contributed to his being appointed vice president by Sadat in 1975. Mubarak remained in the shadow of Sadat.

When Mubarak became president after President Sadat's assassination* on
October 6, 1981, some Egyptian and international circles did not take him se-

riously, regarding him only as a transitional political figure. Having inherited a country that seemed to be incurably ill both economically and politically and rejected by the entire Arab world, Mubarak, in the course of his presidency, gradually and consistently returned Egypt to the status of a leading Arab state and restored some internal political stability. He was elected secretary-general of the National Democratic Party, becoming its chairman in January 1982. He made clear his commitment to the Camp David* process, though negotiations were soon stalled in consequence of Israeli actions in Lebanon.*

Overcoming confrontation, establishing mutually beneficial ties with Egypt's foreign partners, and continuing a dialogue with various sociopolitical forces within the country became President Mubarak's principal political concerns.

Most impressive are the successes of Mubarak's foreign policy. He has developed and normalized relations simultaneously with the United States and Russia. Mubarak has viewed ties with both powers as an integral factor necessary for stability in the region. Full diplomatic relations were reestablished with the USSR in 1984, when Mubarak officially visited the Soviet Union.

While adhering to the Egyptian–Israeli accord,* Egypt under Mubarak has been able to break out of the complete isolation in the Arab world imposed after the peace treaty with Israel. He has accomplished this by taking various pro-Arab political and propagandistic démarches and displaying restraint in further developing relations with Israel. Egypt has reestablished its relations with Iraq,* Jordan,* and the moderate wing within the Palestine Liberation Organization* (PLO). It has also been reinstated in the Organization of the Islamic Conference. In 1987, the Arab Summit in Amman approved the right of individual Arab countries to establish diplomatic relations with Egypt. During the two years that followed, Egypt restored diplomatic relations with most Arab states.

The finale of Egypt's reintegration in the Arab ranks was the decision of the Arab Summit in Casablanca in 1989 to reinstate Egypt into the Arab League* and relocate its headquarters from Tunisia back to Egypt.

Mubarak served as an instructor in the Air Force Academy until 1959, when he was sent on training missions to the Soviet Union. These missions culminated in a higher studies course there in 1964–65. Returning to Egypt, Mubarak held the post of base commander at a number of different air force installations.

For further information see: Louis J. Cantori, "Egyptian Policy under Mubarak: The Politics of Continuity and Change," in Robert O. Freedman, ed., *The Middle East after the Israeli Invasion of Lebanon* (Syracuse, NY: Syracuse University Press, 1986); Louis J. Cantori, "Hosni Mubarak," in Bernard Reich, ed., *Political Leaders of the Contemporary Middle East and North Africa: A Biographical Dictionary* (Westport, CT: Greenwood Press, 1990), pp. 367–72; Robert Springborg, *The Political Economy of Mubarak's Egypt* (Boulder, CO: Westview Press, 1988).

Galina Emelyanova and Joseph E. Goldberg

MUBARAK TEN-POINT PROPOSAL (1989). See **TEN-POINT PLAN.**

MUFTI OF JERUSALEM. See **HAJJ AMIN AL-HUSSEINI.**

MUHSIN, ZUHAYR. Former leader of al-Saiqa.* Muhsin articulated the view that there were no differences "between Jordanians,* Palestinians,* Syrians,* and Lebanese.* We all constitute a part of one people. We speak about Palestinian identity only for political reasons."

He was a Syrian Baathist who, in July 1971, became a member of the Palestine Liberation Organization* (PLO) Executive Committee. The nominal chief of PLO military operations, he was killed in the French Riviera resort of Cannes while gambling.

Joseph E. Goldberg

MULTILATERAL NEGOTIATIONS. In the wake of the Madrid Peace Conference,* a multilateral diplomatic track was established to focus on salient functional issues of the Arab–Israeli conflict. It was designed to complement the bilateral negotiations (the Washington rounds*) by bringing a larger number of regional and extraregional parties together to develop coordinated approaches to regional problems. It also fostered broader human contact between Arabs and Israelis. Its purpose was also to establish a conducive regional environment for progress in making peace.

The multilateral track consists of five working groups dealing with issues that affect the region as a whole: water,* the environment, economic development, refugees,* and arms control and security. The Steering Group guides the multilateral process, chaired by the United States and Russia, as the Madrid Conference cosponsors.

Thirty-six parties attended the Moscow organizational meeting in January 1992. They established five working groups. The Arms Control and Regional Security Working Group focuses on confidence-building measures as well as arms control issues, including information exchange and maritime procedures. The Economic Development Working Group addresses infrastructure, training, and tourism development. The Environment Working Group enhances the regional parties' abilities to deal with maritime pollution, wastewater treatment, environmental management, and desertification. The Water Resources Working Group focuses on water conservation, water sector training needs, desalination, and enhancing water data availability. The Refugee Working Group addresses family reunification, training and job creation, public health and child welfare, and social and economic infrastructure.

Multilateral Steering Group
(United States/Russia: cochairs)

Round 1   January 28–29, 1992, Moscow, Russia
Round 2   May 27, 1992, Lisbon, Portugal
Round 3   December 3–4, 1992, London, U.K.
Round 4   July 7, 1993, Moscow, Russia
Round 5   December 15, 1993, Tokyo, Japan
Round 6   July 12–13, 1994, Tabarka, Tunisia

Arms Control and Regional Security
(United States/Russia: colead organizers)

Round 1   January 28–29, 1992, Moscow, Russia

Round 2   May 11–14, 1992, Washington, D.C.

Round 3   September 15–17, 1992, Moscow, Russia

Round 4   May 18–20, 1993, Washington, D.C.

Round 5   November 2–4, 1993, Moscow, Russia

Round 6   May 3–5, 1994, Doha, Qatar

Round 7   December 13–15, 1994, Tunis, Tunisia

Economic Development
(European Union: lead organizer; United States/Japan: coleaders)

Round 1   January 28–29, 1992, Moscow, Russia

Round 2   May 11–12, 1992, Brussels, Belgium

Round 3   October 29–30, 1992, Paris, France

Round 4   May 4–5, 1993, Rome, Italy

Round 5   November 8–9, 1993, Copenhagen, Denmark

Round 6   June 15–17, 1994, Rabat, Morocco

Environment
(Japan: permanent gavel holder; EU: co-organizer)

Round 1   January 28–29, 1992, Moscow, Russia

Round 2   May 18–19, 1992, Tokyo, Japan

Round 3   September 26–27, 1992, The Hague, Netherlands

Round 4   May 24–25, 1993, Tokyo, Japan

Round 5   November 15–16, 1993, Egypt

Round 6   April 6–7, 1994, The Hague, Netherlands

Round 7   October 24–26, 1994, Manama, Bahrain

Refugees
(Canada: lead organizer)

Round 1   January 28–29, 1992, Moscow, Russia

Round 2   May 13–15, 1992, Ottawa, Canada

Round 3   November 11–12, 1992, Ottawa, Canada

Round 4   May 11–13, 1993, Oslo, Norway

Round 5   October 12–14, 1993, Tunis, Tunisia

Round 6   May 10–12, 1994, Cairo, Egypt

Water Resources
(United States: lead organizer; Japan/EU: coleaders)

Round 1   January 28–29, 1992, Moscow, Russia

Round 2   May 14–15, 1992, Vienna, Austria

Round 3   September 16–17, 1992, Washington, D.C.

Round 4   April 27–29, 1993, Geneva, Switzerland

Round 5   October 26–28, 1993, Beijing, China

Round 6   April 17–20, 1994, Muscat, Oman

Round 7   November 7–9, 1994, Athens, Greece

MULTINATIONAL FORCE 1. The first of two multinational forces (MNF) arrived in Lebanon* on August 25, 1982, and withdrew on September 10, 1982. It was responsible for the safety of the Palestine Liberation Organization* (PLO) units that were leaving Lebanon and going to Syria* and other Arab states, the safety of the families of those fleeing who chose to remain in Beirut, and the safety of civilian camps from the Israel Defense Forces* and the Phalange.

On June 6, 1982, Israeli troops invaded Lebanon in Operation Peace for Galilee.* The Lebanese government had lost effective control over large portions of its territory, and the PLO had increased its attacks on Israeli settlements in northern Israel with more sophisticated weaponry. On June 3, the Israeli ambassador to Great Britain, Shlomo Argov,* was attacked by members of the Abu Nidal* terrorist group outside a hotel in London. The next afternoon, the Israeli air force launched an attack on the major PLO camps in southern Lebanon, reaching as far north as Beirut's suburbs, commencing the War in Lebanon.* As the Israel Defense Forces advanced into southern Lebanon, beyond the Litani River,* the PLO fled to Beirut's southern suburbs along with some Syrian forces. IDF and Phalangist forces encircled the area, allowing no escape route for the PLO and Syrian troops.

The encirclement of Beirut and the PLO and Syrian forces within the southern suburbs proved to be a dangerous situation. The safe passage for the PLO and Syrian forces from Lebanon had been arranged through a series of diplomatic agreements. Ambassador Philip Habib* succeeded in arranging a cease-fire after weeks of negotiation. Among other requirements, the PLO armed forces were to leave Lebanon.

On August 15, in a letter to the U.S. ambassador, Robert Dillon, the Lebanese government officially requested the presence of a multinational force to oversee the evacuation of PLO forces from Beirut. President Ronald Reagan* agreed to the deployment of U.S. troops several days later and noted that the purpose of the force was to assist the Lebanese armed forces in carrying out their responsibility for the safe and orderly departure of PLO leaders, officers, and combatants in Beirut from Lebanese territory.

The MNF consisted of French, Italian, and American troops.

The withdrawal plan for the PLO to evacuate Lebanon was negotiated separately among Israel, Syria, the PLO, Lebanon, and the members of the MNF.

The safe evacuation of the armed PLO troops began as soon as the MNF arrived. Upon the completion of the evacuation, the MNF left Lebanon, leaving the safety of the remaining Palestinians and their camps in the hands of the Lebanese government. The government, weak both before and after the Israeli invasion, was unable to protect the Palestinians. This facilitated the return of a multinational force to the area September 26 shortly after MNF 1 left (see MNF 2).

For further information see: Robert B. Houghton, *Multinational Peacekeeping in the Middle East* (Washington, DC: Foreign Service Institute, U.S. Department of State, 1984); Anthony McDermott and K. Skjelsbaek, eds., *The Multinational Forces in Beirut, 1982–1984* (Miami: Florida International University Press, 1991); Ramesh Thakur, *International Peacekeeping in Lebanon: United Nations Authority and Multinational Force* (Boulder, CO: Westview Press, 1987).

Matthew Dorf

MULTINATIONAL FORCE 2. After Multinational Force (MNF) 1* withdrew, the protection of the remaining Palestinians* fell to the Lebanese* government. This proved tragic as the Christian militias, especially the Phalange, operated unchecked. The first contingents of the second multinational force (MNF 2) arrived in Lebanon September 26, 1982, only sixteen days after MNF 1 departed. The French and Italians arrived on September 26 with 1,500 troops and 1,400 troops, respectively. The United States landed a force of 1,400 on September 29. All three contingents brought armored vehicles and artillery support weapons in expectation of a worsening situation. The British sent a small armored-car force in February 1983.

The assassination of Bashir Gemayel* sparked the deployment of MNF 2. Gemayel, who had led the Christian factions in West Beirut, was killed on September 14. This led to the Israel Defense Forces* (IDF) entering West Beirut to prevent a complete breakdown of whatever order existed. But by September 17 and 18, reports that local military and militia forces had entered Palestinian camps at Sabra* and Shatila* and massacred civilians began to appear in the Western media. The ineffectiveness of the Lebanese government to provide protection to the Palestinians led to the deployment of MNF 2, with the support of the government through an exchange of notes when the troops first landed.

When MNF 2 landed and took up its positions, some sense of normalcy returned to southern Lebanon, Beirut specifically. An agreement for Israeli withdrawal was reached on May 17, 1983,* but negotiations between Syria* and the United States never materialized. This agreement was later rescinded by the Lebanese government after the MNF 2 forces began evacuating Beirut. In fact, the Palestine Liberation Organization* (PLO) and Syria sought the failure of the May 17 accord and began rearming the Druze in the Shouf Mountains.

When the IDF began to withdraw from their positions, intensive fighting broke out among the Druze, the Palestinians, the Shia supported by Syria, and the Lebanese armed forces and their allies, the Christian militia. The IDF withdrawal began August 28, 1983, when they vacated positions in the south of the city and in the Shouf. When the IDF withdrawal to the Awali River was completed on September 4, the Lebanese armed forces were unable to occupy some areas that the IDF had left. Ultimately, the Lebanese forces withdrew from all but one position in the Shouf.

Without Lebanese control, the MNF 2 forces in Beirut were shelled by Druze and Muslim militias. As fighting intensified, the MNF 2 troops were often in the line of fire or dangerously close to it. Since the MNF 2 had no mandate, they were unable to return fire or take aggressive peacekeeping steps, such as positioning themselves between warring factions.

Although France and the United States used their offshore and air weapon systems to aid the Lebanese, the ground forces did little to thwart the efforts of the factions fighting in Beirut. The militias did not fear the MNF 2 ground troops, and, as the violence escalated, the troops came under sniper attacks and suicide bombings. The most deadly attack occurred on October 23, when 241 U.S. marines and fifty-nine French soldiers were killed. As Syria began to reassert its influence and resupply the antigovernment militia, the MNF 2 forces assumed a self-protection role. By February 1984, the situation had worsened to the point that, on February 7, the Lebanese foreign minister requested the contingents of the MNF 2 to deploy to safer locations. The British left the next day, followed by the Americans and the Italians. The French held out until March 31. The USSR vetoed a French resolution in the United Nations calling for peacekeeping efforts to be assumed by the United Nations (UN). The MNF 2 failed in its mission to uphold peace and order and the Lebanese government.

For further information see: Robert B. Houghton, *Multinational Peacekeeping in the Middle East* (Washington, DC: Foreign Service Institute, U.S. Department of State, 1984); Anthony McDermott and K. Skjelsbaek, eds., *The Multinational Force in Beirut, 1982–1984* (Miami: Florida International University Press, 1991); Ramesh Thakur, *International Peacekeeping in Lebanon: United Nations Authority and Multinational Force* (Boulder, CO: Westview Press, 1987).

Matthew Dorf

MUNICH OLYMPICS MASSACRE (1972). On September 5, 1972, eight members of Black September* killed eleven Israeli athletes who were participants in the 1972 Olympic Games in Munich, Germany. This attack was part of an ongoing international terror campaign by Palestinian groups against Israel and its supporters. It was code-named Ikrit and Baram.

Early in the morning of September 5, 1972, eight members of the Black September organization broke into the Olympic Village and captured thirteen Israeli athletes in their apartments. Two Israeli athletes, Gad Zobari and Tuvia Sokolavsky, were able to escape in the initial confusion, and two Israeli athletes, Yossef Romano and Moshe Weinberger, were killed as they fought back against the terrorists. The remaining nine, Yossef Gutfreund, Amitzur Shapira, Andrei Spitzer, Kehat Shorr, Yacov Springer, Eliezer Halfin, Mark Slavin, David Marc Berger, and Zeev Friedman, were held hostage in hope that the German and Israeli authorities would meet the terrorists' demands. These demands included the release of 234 prisoners held by the Israelis and the West German authorities, including the leaders of the terrorist Baader-Meinhof gang, Ulrike Meinhof and Andreas Baader, who had been captured three months previously. The terrorists also wanted three planes to take them to a safe destination after their demands had been met.

High-ranking German officials, including a federal minister, a Bavarian minister, the mayor of the Olympic Village, a former mayor, and the police commissioner, offered to take the place of the Israeli athlete hostages. The terrorists, however, did not accept the trade. The Israelis refused to negotiate with the Black September terrorists and refused to release the prisoners held in Israel. A stalemate ensued that lasted all day.

In the face of both German and Israeli unwillingness to release any prisoners, the terrorists' demands changed. They reduced their demands to one plane, which was to fly them to Cairo, where they would execute their hostages if the Israelis did not free the 234 Palestinians. The terrorists traveled to the airport with their hostages in two helicopters. When they were about to board the plane to Cairo, they were attacked by a West German antiterrorist team. During the ensuing firefight, the terrorists killed the nine remaining Israeli athletes, and the Germans killed five of the eight terrorists; three were captured.

Despite Israeli protestations that they should be canceled, the Olympic Games were allowed to continue. At the Olympic Village, after all of the national flags were lowered to half-mast, the Arab countries protested, and their flags were raised to full-mast. The West Germans ultimately released the captured three Black September terrorists in exchange for a hijacked Lufthansa plane. The Israelis responded to the Munich attack by forming a special secret antiterrorist group that hunted down and killed the Palestinians* responsible for organizing and planning the Munich attack.

The attack also led to a hardening of Israeli public resolve against dealing with the Palestinians on any level. Israel notified the United States and other Western governments that it would not participate in efforts to achieve a settlement in the Arab–Israeli conflict until Arab terrorism stopped.

For further information see: John Cooley, *Green March, Black September: The Story of the Palestinian Arabs* (London: Cass, 1973); Christopher Dobson, *Black September; Its Short, Violent History* (New York: Macmillan, 1974); Serge Groussard, *The Blood of Israel: The Massacre of the Israeli Athletes, the Olympics, 1972* (New York: Morrow, 1975); George Jonas, *Vengeance: The True Story of an Israeli Counter-Terrorist Team* (New York: Simon and Schuster, 1984); Richard Mandell, *The Olympics of 1972: A Munich Diary* (Chapel Hill: University of North Carolina Press, 1991); Edgar O'Ballance, *Language of Violence: The Blood Politics of Terrorism* (San Rafael, CA: Presidio Press, 1979).

Mark Daryl Erickson and Simeon Manickavasagam

MUSA, AMR (b. Cairo, Egypt,* October 3, 1936). He graduated in 1957 from the Law School of the University of Cairo and joined the Egyptian Foreign Service in 1958. He was posted in several positions. In 1977, he was named director of the International Organizations Department in the Foreign Ministry. He served in the Research Department, at the Egyptian Embassy in Bern, Switzerland, in the Permanent Mission to the United Nations in New York, and in the office of the foreign minister. In 1987, he was named ambassador to India. In 1990, he was named once again director of the International Organizations Department of the Foreign Ministry. Musa was a member of several high-level Egyptian delegations to the Organization of African Unity, to the Arab League,* to Islamic conferences, and to the Nonaligned Movement meetings.

In 1990, Minister Musa was named permanent representative of Egypt to the United Nations, the post he held until he was named minister of foreign affairs. During his tenure at the United Nations, he was very active in articulating Egypt's position regarding regional nuclear nonproliferation issues. He became foreign minister of Egypt in 1991 and, thus, deeply involved in the Madrid Conference* and the negotiations that followed.

Ahmed Elbashari

MUSLIM BROTHERHOOD. See HAMAS.

MUSSAWI, SHEIKH ABBAS (b. Jabihshit, Lebanon*; d. Lebanon, February 16, 1992). He served as director of a religious school in Baalbek and was a protégé of the Iran cleric, Ali Akbar Mohtashemi.

Mussawi was elected secretary-general of the Party of God* in 1990 after having been a leader of the group over the previous decade. The stated goal of the movement was to drive Western political, cultural, and economic influence from Lebanon and the rest of the Middle East and to replace it with Iranian-inspired Islamic fundamentalist doctrine. They have periodically sought to abort Middle East peace negotiations, in part by launching raids against Israel in the security zone* in Lebanon. The Party of God has claimed responsibility for the 1983 bombing of the U.S. Embassy in Beirut and the marine compound in Beirut, as well as similar attacks on the French* and others. Israeli forces killed Mussawi in an attack on February 16, 1992.

N

NAHAL (Derived from the Hebrew words Noar Halutzi Lohaim—Fighting Pioneering Youth). A formation within the Israel Defense Forces* that combines military training and operations with pioneering settlement and agricultural training. After completing basic training, NAHAL groups are assigned to settlements for a period of combined agriculture and military training. The program derives from the security needs of the pioneering agricultural settlements that developed from the immigration to Palestine* starting in the latter part of the nineteenth century. The hostile environment and security situation in Palestine helped to dictate the requirement for self-defense against armed attack. The NAHAL program was formalized in the summer of 1948 by Prime Minister David Ben-Gurion* for the specific purpose of encouraging the flow of people into the agricultural settlements and maintaining the pioneering spirit. Since its establishment, NAHAL has created new settlements and assisted in the establishment of others; it has opened up undeveloped areas and created a presence at sensitive border points. Originally a unit with Gadna (the Israeli Youth Corps), it was separated from it in September 1949.

NAHHALIN. On the evening of March 26, 1954, four Arab infiltrators attacked Kessalon, a moshav in the Jerusalem* corridor, killing a guard and wounding another member. Israel launched a retaliatory raid, named Mivtza Arye (Operation Lion), during the night of March 28, 1954, against Nahhalin, a southern West Bank* village, which the Israelis believed to be a major staging area for terrorist attacks.

During Israel's War of Independence,* Nahhalin was the site of an Arab massacre of a Jewish convoy in which thirty-five Israelis were murdered. The Israeli 890 Paratroop Battalion, led by Ariel Sharon,* had orders to attack only soldiers from the Jordanian Arab Legion* and National Guardsmen. In the attack Sharon's forces killed a number of Jordanian* soldiers, including a relief force, but they also wounded a number of Arab villagers, including the village *mukhtar,* one of the National Guard members. Jordanian reports of the raid claimed that village homes, as well as the mosque, had been damaged, though Israel denied these charges. The reprisal was strongly condemned by England* and the United States, which believed that such attacks did little to reduce the tension. Israelis debated the policy of retaliation but believed that such attacks were necessary to deter terrorism.

Joseph E. Goldberg

AL-NAJJAR, MUHAMMAD (ABU YUSIF, d. Beirut, 1973). Fatah's* first military commander and a leader of the Black September* organization. He was killed in Beirut during an Israeli raid.

Joseph E. Goldberg

AL-NAKBA (The catastrophe, the disaster). A reference to the Arab–Israeli War of 1948–49* and its consequences, especially for the Palestinians,* that is widely used in the Arab world, particularly among Palestinians.

AL-NASHASHIBI FAMILY. Under the Ottoman Empire* in the nineteenth century, influential positions among the Palestinians* shifted from mainly religious ones to those of a political and administrative nature. Turkish Ottoman officials were appointed to the highest levels, but appointments of tax collectors, mail deliverers, and other public functionaries were distributed among Palestinian families. In Jerusalem,* unlike Nablus and Jaffa, notable families did not owe their influence either to commerce or to agriculture, although many of the families were landowners.

One of the Jerusalem families at the end of the nineteenth century rising in social and political importance was the Nashashibi family. At the end of the nineteenth century and into the twentieth century, its conflicts with the Husseini and Khalidi families were bitter. Unlike the other two families, the importance of the Nashashibis was connected to Ottoman rule. With the British Mandate,* the Husseinis and Khalidis had closer associations than the Nashashibis, who ultimately established good relationships with the Mandatory power. Throughout the first half of the twentieth century, the Nashashibis led an organization allied with other conservative segments of Palestinian society, including most Muslim notables in Jerusalem, to contest the dominance of the Husseinis.

During the Arab riots of 1929, which were led by Amin al-Husseini* and the Supreme Muslim Council, which he headed since 1922, the role of the Nashashibi family was slight. Because the Husseinis justified their rioting in the name of nationalism and Arab rights, their prestige increased among the population. Unable to resist the pressure, the Nashashibi newspapers began to print vicious and untrue accounts of the Jews. The family also joined in the Arab economic boycott of the Jews.

On December 11, 1931, a meeting of those opposed to the mufti and the Husseini family was held in Jerusalem. It was called the Congress of the Palestinian Muslim Nation. The Nashashibis were active participants at the meeting, which addressed the internal governance of Muslim affairs. The congress called upon the British to examine the financial records of the Supreme Muslim Council as well as to hold new elections for its membership.

Nashashibi influence suffered again on May 7, 1932, when the Palestinian High Court of Justice dismissed a legal petition presented by citizens in Hebron* opposed to the Husseinis. The challenge concerned how religious donations collected in Hebron were distributed by the Supreme Muslim Council. The Muslims in Hebron did not want their funds distributed in Jerusalem. A successful petition might have reduced the Supreme Muslim Council's influence, one of the foundations of the Husseini family's influence. Many Palestinians viewed the petition as against Jerusalem. For this reason some of the opposition groups in Jerusalem that traditionally supported the Nashashibis did not. It opened a split between the Khalidi family and the Nashashibis in which the former family established a front with the Husseinis to contest the Jerusalem municipal elections of 1936. At a national meeting on March 20, 1933, Fakhri al-Nashashibi supported a resolution calling for noncooperation with the government as well as nonpayment of taxes. His position was supported by Shakib al-Nashashibi.

One of the leading members of the Nashashibi family was Raghib al-Nashashibi, who had served as the mayor of Jerusalem and was unseated in 1927 by the Supreme Muslim Council. He resigned as president of the Congress of the Palestinian Muslim Nation in July 1933 in opposition to the riots. He informed the high commissioner of Palestine that he would oppose demonstrations and attempt to stop them. Raghib al-Nashashibi did, in fact, attempt to persuade villagers around Jerusalem not to participate in the riots.

In 1933, Raghib Nashashibi met with Emir Abdullah* of Transjordan* as part of a Palestinian delegation to discuss the situation of Palestine. He supported Abdullah's proposal to enter into an agreement with the Jewish Agency* to cooperate for a common purpose. Because of strong Arab nationalist positions, the proposal did not succeed. At this time, the Husseinis and their supporters began to denounce Abdullah and his ideas. Raghib and the Nashashibis supported him. The alliance between them became more formal in September 1935, when they cooperated with the British against anti-Italian propaganda. Abdullah and the Nashashibis continued their close alliance until the annexation. The Nashashibis were part of a victorious electoral alliance in the Jaffa and Gaza* elections of June 1934.

The Nashashibis ultimately were not able to compete against the Husseinis. Strikes in 1936 initiated by young radical Muslims associated with the mufti started in Nablus, Jerusalem, and Jaffa and soon spread throughout Palestine and were accompanied by violence. More Arabs were killed than Jews or British.

The Nashashibis especially were targeted. The National Defense Party, organized by the Nashashibis in 1934 to advance a moderate position toward the British and the Zionists,* no longer was a force after 1939.

For further information see: Issa Khalaf, *Politics in Palestine: Arab Factionalism and Social Disintegration, 1938–1948* (Albany: State University of New York Press, 1991); Baruch Kimmerling and Joel S. Migdal, *Palestinians: The Making of a People* (New York: Free Press, 1993); Nasser Eddin Nashashibi, *Jerusalem's Other Voice: Ragheb Nashashibi and Moderation in Palestinian Politics 1920–1948* (London: Ithaca Press, 1991); Taysir N. Nashif, *The Palestine Arab and Jewish Political Leadership: A Comparative Study* (New York: Asia Publishing House, 1979); Yehoshua Porath, *The Emergence of the Palestinian–Arab National Movement, 1918–1929* (London: Frank Cass, 1974); Yehoshua Porath, *The Palestinian Arab National Movement: From Riots to Rebellion, 1929–1939* (London: Frank Cass, 1977).

Joseph E. Goldberg

NASSER, GAMAL ABDUL (b. Bani Mor, Egypt,* 1918; d. Cairo, Egypt, September 1970). He was president of Egypt from 1956 until 1970.

As a leader of the Free Officers he planned and led the revolution that overthrew the monarchy of King Farouk* in Egypt on July 23, 1952, although General Mohammed Naguib was made the titular head of the new government. Nasser was the son of a postmaster. He graduated from the Military Academy in 1938 and served in a number of positions. He was involved in the fighting during the first Arab–Israeli War* and was surrounded with his troops in the Faluja pocket.

Nasser formally became president in 1956. He had a significant impact on regional and international politics. Nasser opposed the Baghdad Pact and at the Bandung Conference joined the ranks of the leadership of the nonaligned world. The British and American decision not to fund the Aswan Dam project or to provide arms led Nasser to turn to the Soviet Union and the Soviet bloc for arms and aid. The Czech–Egyptian arms deal of 1955* inaugurated a Soviet role in the Arab world. Nasser also nationalized the Suez Canal,* an act that led to the Suez War.* He emerged as a strong Arab nationalist leader and a major force in Third World politics. In 1958, Syria* joined with Egypt in the United Arab Republic,* and Nasser became its president. He was involved in virtually all developments in the Arab world.

In May 1967, he took the steps that ultimately led to the Six Day War* when he mobilized Egyptian troops and sent them into Sinai* to replace the United Nations Emergency Force* (UNEF). He announced the blockade of the Strait of Tiran,* and eventually Egypt and Israel went to war, in which Egypt lost control of the Gaza Strip* and the Sinai Peninsula. After the war Nasser sought to recoup his position in Egypt and the Arab world. In 1969, he launched the War of Attrition* in an effort to force Israel to withdraw from the Suez Canal and to reopen that waterway. He was able to secure a significant enhancement in Soviet support in the form of advanced military equipment and some operational military assistance. He died while in the process of resolving disputes between Jordan* and the Palestine Liberation Organization* (PLO), which led to the signing in Cairo in September 1970 of the Cairo Agreement* between Jordan and the PLO.

Nasser wrote *The Philosophy of the Revolution: Egypt's Liberation* (Washington, DC: Public Affairs Press, 1955), in which he saw Egypt as the center of the Arab, Islamic, and African circles, and "Nasser's Memoirs of the First Palestine War," *Journal of Palestine Studies* 2 (Winter 1973):3–32.

For further information see: Raymond Baker, *Egypt's Uncertain Revolution under Nasser and Sadat* (Cambridge: Harvard University Press, 1978); Abdul Magid Faris, *Nasser: The Final Years* (London: Ithaca Press, 1994); Ellis Goldberg, "Gamal Abdul Nasser," in Bernard Reich, ed., *Political Leaders of the Contemporary Middle East and North Africa: A Biographical Dictionary* (Westport, CT: Greenwood Press, 1990), pp. 379–88; Joel Gordon, *Nasser's Blessed Movement: Egypt's Free Officers and the July Revolution* (New York: Oxford University Press, 1992); Jean Lacoutre, *Nasser* (New York: Alfred Knopf, 1973); Faysal Mikdadi, *Gamal Abdul Nasser: A Bibliography* (Westport, CT: Greenwood Press, 1991); P. J. Vatikiotis, ed., *Egypt Since the Revolution* (New York: Praeger, 1968); Peter Woodward, *Nasser* (London: Longman, 1992).

NATHAN, ABIE. Born in Iran and trained in the Indian air force, he came to Israel during the War of Independence* in 1948 and served as an air force captain until 1951. He became a peace activist. In 1966, he flew a private plane to Egypt* and later campaigned around the world for peace. Among his numerous activities to achieve peace, he started a ship-based radio station, the Voice of Peace,* to broadcast to Israel and the Arab world from beyond the territorial waters of the adversaries.

NATIONAL FRONT FOR THE LIBERATION OF PALESTINE (NFLP). See **POPULAR FRONT FOR THE LIBERATION OF PALESTINE (PFLP).**

NATIONAL HOME. See **JEWISH NATIONAL HOME.**

NATIONAL UNITY GOVERNMENT. See **GOVERNMENT OF NATIONAL UNITY.**

NATIONAL WATER CARRIER. Israel has always suffered a scarcity of water.* To overcome regional imbalances in water availability, most of Israel's water sources are linked in a grid of which the National Water Carrier is the central artery. Put into operation in 1964, the carrier brings water from the north and central regions, primarily Lake Tiberias, through a series of pipes, aqueducts, open canals, reservoirs, tunnels, dams, and pumping stations to various other parts of the country, including the semiarid northern Negev.*

NATSHE, MUSTAFA. He served as the acting mayor of the West Bank* town of Hebron.* In July 1983, Major General Uri Orr, commander of the Israel Defense Forces* in the region, issued an order dismissing Natshe from his position as well as dismissing the Hebron City Council. Orr acted in response to the fatal stabbing in Hebron of a resident from Kiryat Arba.* In December 1983, the No. 18 bus in Jerusalem* was bombed. The East Jerusalem* newspaper, *Al Fajr,* carried on its front page a letter condeming the bombing and attacks of any kind against civilian targets. Such acts, the letter emphasized, are "detrimental to any Palestinian–Israeli understanding." Natshe was one of five prominent Palestinians to sign the letter.

Joseph E. Goldberg

NEGEV. The triangular southern portion of Israel. It extends from Beersheva south to the port of Eilat* on the Gulf of Aqaba.* The Negev is a semidesert tableland from 1,000 to 2,000 feet (300 to 610 meters) above sea level. It has limestone mountains and flatlands and is covered by a layer of fertile loam, which must have water to grow crops. The Israelis have farmed part of the Negev by irrigation with water brought through the National Water Carrier* from Lake Kinneret (the Sea of Galilee) through canals and pipelines. They have also mined phosphates and copper.

For further information see: Michael Oren, "The Diplomatic Struggle for the Negev, 1946–1956," *Studies in Zionism* 10 (1989):197–215.

NETANYAHU, BENJAMIN (Bibi) (b. October 21, 1949, Tel Aviv). On March 25, 1993, he was elected leader of the Likud,* following Menachem Begin* and Yitzhak Shamir.* He was the first Israeli-born leader of the party. He lived in the United States as a teenager and graduated from the Massachusetts Institute of Technology.

In November 1991, Benjamin Netanyahu was appointed deputy minister in the prime minister's office. Elected to the Knesset* in 1988, he was appointed Israel's deputy minister of foreign affairs the same year. His previous diplomatic posts were ambassador to the United Nations (1984–88) and deputy chief of mission to the United States (1982–84).

Netanyahu's recommendations for combating terrorism have been widely discussed in both the U.S. and international community. With his colleagues at Israel's Mission to the United Nations (UN), he led the effort that opened the UN Nazi War Crimes Archives (1987).

Before entering public life, Netanyahu served as a soldier and officer in the Israel Defense Forces* from 1967 to 1972.

An M.B.A. graduate of the Massachusetts Institute of Technology, Netanyahu has worked in various consulting and management positions in industry both in the United States and in Israel.

Since 1976, he has been a director of the Jonathan Institute, a Jerusalem* foundation researching terrorism. This institute was established in the name of

Lieutenant Colonel Jonathan Netanyahu, his brother, who was killed leading the
rescue party during the 1976 raid on Entebbe.*

He is the editor of *Terrorism: How the West Can Win* (New York: Farrar,
Straus and Giroux, 1986) and *International Terrorism: Challenge and Response*
(New Brunswick, NJ: Transaction Books, 1981) and the author of *A Place
among the Nations: Israel and the World* (New York: Bantam Books, 1993).

Pamela Rivers

NETUREI KARTA (Aramaic: Guardians of the City). A group of religious extremists who live primarily in the Mea Shearim (Hundred Gates) section of
Jerusalem* and in Bnei Brak. The name is derived from a passage in the Jerusalem Talmud in Aramaic that refers to those who devote themselves to the
study of the Torah as the guardians of the city. The Talmud states that religious
scholars are guardians and defenders of the city of Jerusalem.

The Neturei Karta number a few thousand families. Most of the Neturei Karta
are from the old Yishuv* (settlement), but they have been joined more recently
by some immigrants from Hungary, disciples of Rabbi Joel Teitelbaum of Sat-
mar.

For the Neturei Karta, the establishment of the state of Israel was an act of
rebellion against God. They believe Jews are obligated to wait for God to reestablish a Jewish state through messianic redemption. The reestablishment of the
Jewish state by human action will bring about divine punishment (other Orthodox groups, such as the National Religious Party, view the efforts by the Jews
in the Holy Land as a precursor to the coming of the Messiah). Any display of
loyalty to the state of Israel or recognition of its legitimacy is, in their opinion,
contrary to Jewish law; therefore, they do not recognize the state of Israel and
view the Zionists* and their movement as an enemy of the Jewish people.

The Neturei Karta refuse to have anything to do with a Jewish government
in Israel. They will not vote in any elections or recognize the Israeli courts as
a system of justice. They pay no taxes and refuse to register for military service.
The Israeli government tries to ignore them, except when they create overt
public disturbances.

In 1935, an extreme right-wing group broke away from the Agudat Yisrael
(the organization representing the mainstream of Orthodox Judaism), because
the Agudat Yisrael attempted to restrain their demands for a separate independent ultraorthodox community. This splinter group called itself Hevrat Ha-Haim
(the Organization of Haim), after Rabbi Joseph Haim Sonnenfeld, their leader.
The name Neturei Karta was first used in 1938 by youths, including members
of the Hevrat Ha-Haim, who strongly opposed the Jewish community's levying
of the voluntary defense tax, the Kofer Ha-Yishuv.

The purpose of the Neturei Karta was to create a society free of Zionist
influence. Among other things it advocated education in the traditional Jewish
manner, implying opposition to the Bet Ya'akov (House of Jacob) girls' school
of the Agudat Yisrael, where the language of instruction was Hebrew.

The Agudat Yisrael cooperated with the Jewish community and the Jewish Agency* during World War II. This led Neturei Karta to attack the Agudah in their newspaper *Ha-Homah* (the Wall), which began circulating in 1944. During the Orthodox Community Committee elections in 1945, Neturei Karta managed to gain control. Anyone educating his daughters in the Bet Ya'akov Schools was excluded from membership.

During the 1948 Arab–Israeli War,* Neturei Karta opposed the creation of the state of Israel and fought for the internationalization of Jerusalem. They have been an outspoken voice against the state of Israel since its inception and continue to hold demonstrations against violations of Jewish laws, such as the desecration of the Sabbath.

The group adheres to strict Orthodox views and follows the lifestyles that were brought to Israel from Eastern Europe. Their dress codes are the traditional long coat and black hats of Eastern European origins. They oppose the use of the Hebrew language for everyday communication because it is the holy language, and its use would imply acceptance of Israel as the Jewish state. Instead, they speak Yiddish. Neturei Karta's opposition to Israel has led it to indicate a willingness to work with groups such as the Palestine Liberation Organization* and Arab states that oppose the Zionist enterprise. They have raised the Palestinian flag and have indicated that they wish to be part of a proposed Palestinian state.

For further information see: Charles S. Liebman and Eliezer Don-Yehiya, *Civil Religion in Israel* (Berkeley: University of California Press, 1983); Charles S. Liebman and Eliezer Don-Yehiya, *Religion and Politics in Israel* (Bloomington: Indiana University Press, 1984); Real Jean Isaac, *Israel Divided* (Baltimore: Johns Hopkins University Press, 1976).

Joseph E. Goldberg

NEW WORLD ORDER. The end of hostilities in the Gulf War* inaugurated a period in which U.S. president George Bush* and Secretary of State James Baker* sought to reconstruct the world order based on the success against Saddam Hussein.* Iraq* was vanquished and humiliated, and its ability to wage war was significantly reduced. The general approach was articulated by Bush in an address to a joint session of Congress on March 6, 1991. He argued that aggression was defeated and that the war was over. He called it a victory for every country in the coalition and for the rule of law. Bush also identified four key challenges: (1) create shared security arrangements; (2) control the proliferation of weapons of mass destruction and the missiles used to deliver them; (3) create new opportunities for peace and stability in the Middle East by closing "the gap between Israel and the Arab states and between Israelis and Palestinians*," and he argued that "the time has come to put an end to the Arab–Israeli conflict"; and (4) foster economic development for the sake of peace and progress.

Earlier, in testimony before the House Foreign Affairs Committee on February

6, 1991, Baker outlined the challenges facing the construction of what the administration called the New World Order. There was the need for new and different security arrangements to deter aggression and to prevent conflicts. Regional arms (both conventional and weapons of mass destruction) control must help to reduce arms flow into an area that is already very overmilitarized. Economic reconstruction and recovery must occur. The search for a just peace and real reconciliation for Israel, the Arab states, and Palestinians must be resumed. He noted the goal of reducing U.S. dependence on imported energy resources.

NEW ZIONIST ORGANIZATION. A worldwide Zionist organization created at a constituent congress in September 1935 after members of the Union of Zionists–Revisionists decided to secede from the World Zionist Organization* (WZO). Its goals included a Jewish majority on both sides of the Jordan River* and the establishment of a Jewish state in Palestine.* It rejoined the WZO in 1946.

1948 WAR. See **WAR OF INDEPENDENCE.**

1956 WAR. See **SINAI WAR.**

1967 WAR. See **SIX DAY WAR.**

1969–70 WAR. See **WAR OF ATTRITION.**

1973 WAR. See **YOM KIPPUR WAR.**

1982 WAR. See **WAR IN LEBANON.**

NIXON, RICHARD MILHOUS (b. Yorba Linda, California, January 9, 1913; d. New York, April 22, 1994). He graduated from Whittier College in 1934 and Duke University Law School in 1937. He married Thelma Patricia Ryan on June 21, 1940. He served in the U.S. Navy during World War II. Nixon served in the House of Representatives (1947–50) and in the U.S. Senate (1950–60). He was vice president under President Eisenhower* from 1953 to 1961. Nixon won the Republican presidential nomination in 1960 but lost a close election to John F. Kennedy.* In 1962, he ran for governor of California and lost. Nixon became the thirty-seventh president of the United States in 1969 after defeating the Democratic candidate, Hubert H. Humphrey, and the Independent candidate, Alabama governor George Wallace, in the 1968 presidential election. Ending the Vietnam War was Nixon's central foreign policy preoccupation. He won a landslide reelection against the Democratic candidate, Senator George McGovern, in 1972. Nixon resigned the presidency at noon, August 9, 1974, under the pressure of the Watergate scandal.

The Nixon administration came to office proclaiming an evenhanded Middle

East policy. This meant the administration was less inclined than its predecessors to support the policies of Israel. His administration was chiefly concerned with how the Arab–Israeli conflict would affect the U.S.–Soviet relationship. From early 1969 until August 1970, the administration pursued a political settlement based on United Nations Security Council Resolution 242.* The United States initially engaged in active diplomacy that manifested itself in the four-power talks.* The four-power talks were combined with two-power talks (bilateral talks between the United States and Soviet Union) regarding the Arab–Israeli conflict. Nixon's secretary of state William Rogers initiated the Rogers Plan* to achieve peace between the Arabs and Israelis. The Nixon administration facilitated the negotiation of the cease-fire between Israel and Egypt,* which took effect on August 8, 1970, to end the War of Attrition.* In early 1970, escalation of Soviet involvement in the Middle East led to a change in the Nixon administration's policy. Then National Security Adviser Henry Kissinger* replaced Secretary of State Rogers as the architect of U.S. Middle East policy.

During the Jordan Civil War* (September 1970), the Nixon administration vigorously supported King Hussein* of Jordan against the Palestine Liberation Organization* (PLO) and Syria.* The administration convinced Israel to use its military assets to support King Hussein and put pressure on Syria. After the Jordan crisis, Nixon focused on the superpower rivalry and worked to keep the balance of power in Israel's favor. There were no new major peace initiatives taken. The U.S.–Israeli relationship became closer. Israel was now viewed as a strategic asset, and U.S. aid to Israel increased significantly.

The Egyptian–Syrian attack on Israel, October 6, 1973, initiating the Yom Kippur War,* caught both the U.S. administration and the Israelis by surprise. They both thought that because the Israelis were militarily superior to the Arabs, the Arabs would not engage in a war that would assure them a military defeat. The administration had been holding out a political alternative to the Arabs to recover their former territories. This political initiative made it even more un-likely that the Arabs would initiate hostilities. During the war, the Nixon ad-ministration tried to work out a cease-fire with the Soviet Union on the basis of the status quo ante. Soon after, the administration offered a cease-fire in place, which would have given the Arabs a nominal land gain early in the war. The administration held back on a full-scale military resupply of Israel, to see if the Arabs would accept the cease-fire in place and to judge the full extent of the Soviet resupply of the Arabs. The administration refused to link a cease-fire to the terms of a final settlement. The administration wanted the war to end in a way that would best facilitate a permanent settlement between the Arabs and Israelis. When the Israelis were having difficulties on the battlefield, and the massive Soviet airlift became apparent, Nixon ordered a full-scale U.S. airlift to resupply the Israelis. When the Soviets, toward the latter part of the conflict, were on the verge of sending Soviet troops, the administration ordered a DEF-CON III alert.* This put the U.S. military on a worldwide alert. Through the efforts of Secretary of State Kissinger, a cease-fire was reached between the

Arabs and Israelis. Kissinger was also able to engineer disengagement of military forces accords between the Israelis and the Egyptians and Syrians in the Sinai and Golan Heights,* respectively.

For further information see: Henry A. Kissinger, *White House Years* (Boston: Little, Brown, 1979); Henry A. Kissinger, *Years of Upheaval* (Boston: Little, Brown, 1982); Robert S. Litwak, *Detente and the Nixon Doctrine* (New York: Cambridge University Press, 1984); Richard Nixon, *The Memoirs of Richard Nixon* (New York: Grosset and Dunlap, 1978); William B. Quandt, *Peace Process* (Washington, DC: Brookings Institution, 1993).

Nolan Wohl

NOBEL PEACE PRIZE. Yasser Arafat,* Shimon Peres,* and Yitzhak Rabin* won the 1994 Nobel Peace Prize. The formal announcement in October 1994 noted:

The Norwegian Nobel Committee has decided to award the Nobel Peace Prize for 1994, in alphabetical order, to Yasir Arafat, Shimon Peres and Yitzhak Rabin, for their efforts to create peace in the Middle East. For several decades, the conflict between Israel and its neighbor states, and between Israelis and Palestinians,* has been among the most irreconcilable and menacing in international politics. The parties have caused each other great suffering. By concluding the Oslo Accords, and subsequently following them up, Arafat, Peres and Rabin have made substantial contributions to a historic process through which peace and cooperation can replace war and hate. In his 1895 will, Alfred Nobel wrote that the Peace Prize could be awarded to the person who, in the preceding year, "shall have done the most or the best work for fraternity between nations." The award of the Nobel Peace Prize for 1994 to Arafat, Peres and Rabin is intended by the Norwegian Nobel Committee to honor a political act which called for great courage on both sides, and which has opened up opportunities for a new development towards fraternity in the Middle East. It is the Committee's hope that the award will serve as an encouragement to all the Israelis and Palestinians who are endeavoring to establish lasting peace in the region.

A member of the committee resigned in protest after it was decided to include Arafat in the group to receive the prize.

The prizes were formally awarded in a ceremony in Oslo, Norway, on December 10, 1994.

O

OAPEC. See **ORGANIZATION OF ARAB PETROLEUM EXPORTING COUNTRIES.**

OCCUPIED AREAS. See **OCCUPIED TERRITORIES.**

OCCUPIED TERRITORIES. In the Six Day War* Israel occupied various territories, including the Sinai Peninsula,* the Gaza Strip,* the West Bank,* East Jerusalem,* and the Golan Heights.* Although commonly referred to as occupied territories, they are often referred to in Israel as the administered areas. See WEST BANK; GAZA STRIP; GOLAN HEIGHTS; SINAI PENINSULA; EAST JERUSALEM; JUDEA AND SAMARIA.

For further information see: Mordechai Nisan, *Israel and the Territories: A Study in Control 1967–1977* (Ramat Gan, Israel: Turtledove, 1978).

OCTOBER COMMUNIQUE. See **JOINT COMMUNIQUE BY THE GOVERNMENTS OF THE UNITED STATES AND THE UNION OF SOVIET SOCIALIST REPUBLICS, OCTOBER 1, 1977.**

OCTOBER WAR (1973). See **YOM KIPPUR WAR.**

OIL EMBARGO. See **OIL WEAPON.**

OIL WEAPON (OIL EMBARGO). Since the 1950s, many in the Arab world have favored the idea of using oil as a policy instrument in the Arab–Israeli conflict. The idea is that oil production above certain limits did not make economic sense for Arab oil-producing states. Not producing this additional oil would help to sustain a higher price. Production beyond these levels could be seen as a political favor to Western states that required and consumed the oil. Some of these states, in the judgment of Arab leaders, were not supportive of the Arab position in the conflict and tended to accept or to support Israel's position. Thus, it was appropriate for Arab oil-producing states to act, on the basis of both economic and political considerations, and to cut back on their oil production to meet their economic requirements and not to support the Western states that were not supporting the Arab position in the Arab–Israeli conflict.

Warnings by Arab leaders seemed to be ignored. In 1973, prior to the outbreak of hostilities, Saudi Arabia, in particular, issued a number of statements in which a warning concerning oil was made, if not always clearly and explicitly. With the outbreak of hostilities, pressures for Arab oil production cuts were intensified.

The oil weapon employed during the Yom Kippur War* had a significant impact on Arab political fortunes and was substantially more successful than the comparable effort during the Six Day War.*

A meeting of the six Gulf member states of the Organization of Petroleum Exporting Countries* (OPEC) (five Arab states and Iran) decided on October 16, 1973, to increase the price of crude oil, a move that had been promoted primarily by Iran.

On October 17, ministers of ten members (Saudi Arabia, Kuwait, Iraq,* Libya, Algeria, Egypt,* Syria,* Abu Dhabi, Bahrain, and Qatar) of the Organization of Arab Petroleum Exporting Countries* (OAPEC), meeting in Kuwait, stated in a communique:

Therefore, the Arab Oil Ministers meeting in Kuwait today have decided to reduce their oil production forthwith by not less than five percent of the September (1973) level of output in each Arab oil-exporting country, with a similar reduction to be applied each successive month, computed on the basis of the previous month's production, until such time as total evacuation of Israeli forces from all Arab territory occupied during the June 1967 War is completed, and the legitimate rights of the Palestinian people are restored. The conferees took care to ensure that reductions in output should not affect any friendly state which has extended or may in the future extend effective concrete assistance to the Arabs. Oil supplies to any such state will be maintained in the same quantities as it was receiving before the reduction. The same exceptional treatment will be extended to any state which takes a significant measure against Israel with a viewing to obliging it to end its occupation of usurped Arab territories.

The ostensible purpose was to force a change in U.S. Middle East policy. The decision permitted considerable flexibility for the individual countries— there was no collective decision to embargo oil shipments to the United States (or anyone else), and Iraq did not concur in the cutback decision. Each state could, in effect, determine the timing and extent of the action it wished to pursue, whether with regard to the United States or other powers. Within days production cutbacks were announced, and most OAPEC states proclaimed an embargo on oil shipments to the United States and Holland (because of that country's pro-Israel stand). Initially, Japan* and the West European states were targeted as not supportive of the Arab position, but as their views became "less biased," their oil supplies were increased. The decisions reached in Kuwait in October were subsequently modified at a series of meetings over the following months, and those oil-consuming states pursuing increasingly pro-Arab policies were progressively rewarded by greater oil supplies. Despite the various modifications in Arab policy with regard to many states, the United States and Holland remained the focus of the embargo until March 18, 1974, when, among other decisions, the Arab oil ministers, meeting in Vienna, lifted the embargo on Arab oil shipments to the United States.

The Arabs generally viewed the oil weapon as having been successful, with a number of accomplishments, including changes in U.S. policy, closer identification of Japan and European Community countries with the Arab perspective, severing of relations between the African states and Israel, the support of the Islamic and nonaligned bloc of states for the Arab cause, and the encouragement of Israel's international political isolation.

For further information see: Fuad Itayim, "Arab Oil—The Political Dimension," *Journal of Palestine Studies* 3 (Winter 1974):84–97; Fuad Itayim, "Strengths and Weaknesses of the Oil Weapon," in *The Middle East and the International System, II. Security and the Energy Crisis* (London: International Institute for Strategic Studies, 1975); Jordan J. Paust and Albert P. Blaustein, "The Arab Oil Weapon—A Threat to International Peace," *American Journal of International Law* 68 (July 1974):410–39; Riad N. el-Rayyes and Dunia Nahas, eds., *The October War: Documents, Personalities, Analyses, and Maps* (Beirut: An-Nahar Press Services, 1973); Eugene V. Rostow, "The Illegality of the Arab Attack on Israel of 6 October 1973," *American Journal of International Law* 69 (April 1975):272–89; Ibrahim F. E. Shihata, "Destination Embargo of Arab Oil: Its Legality under International Law," *American Journal of International Law* 68 (October 1974):591–627; U.S. House of Representatives, Committee on Foreign Affairs, *The United States Oil Shortage and the Arab–Israeli Conflict, Report of a Study Mission to the Middle East from 22 October to 3 November 1973* (Washington, DC: Government Printing Office, 1973).

OLD CITY. The historic core of Jerusalem,* within sixteenth-century, Turkish-built walls with its holy places—renowned churches, mosques, and synagogues.

OPEC. See **ORGANIZATION OF PETROLEUM EXPORTING COUNTRIES.**

OPEN BRIDGES POLICY. The term refers to the bridges across the Jordan River* between Jordan* and the West Bank* and Israel as well as to the links between Israel and Jordan developed after the Six Day War.* Moshe Dayan* was Israel's minister of defense and allowed the shipment of goods (mostly agricultural produce) and, later, the crossing of people between the two sides of the river.

During the Six Day War, Israeli sappers blew up all the bridges over the Jordan River. At the end of 1967, the Jordan Engineering Corps put up two Bailey bridges over the river, one each to replace the Allenby Bridge* (on the Jericho–Amman Highway) and the Damya Bridge (on the Nablus–Amman Road). These bridges subsequently provided the links for the movement of people and trade between the West Bank and Jordan. Both Israeli and Jordanian authorities soon accepted the reality of the people's needs and agreed that the bridges would be open. Dayan is credited with conceiving the open bridges policy, which was meant to "normalize" life in the West Bank as much as possible. At the most basic level, the policies were intended to allow West Bank residents restricted contact with Jordan.

One rationale for the open bridges strategy was to discourage West Bank Palestinians from assisting armed fedayeen* attacks. In this context, the open bridges were part of a broader Israeli security policy (the Allon Plan*), which included the creation of border security settlements to deter infiltration. Dayan also anticipated a peace treaty. The open bridges policy sought as well to lay a foundation for "peacetime" relations in the West Bank. He envisioned Palestinian* Arabs living in a confederation with Israel while maintaining links to the rest of the Arab world. In an attempt to lower its visible presence in the West Bank, as well as conform to international law, the Israeli government allowed the continuation of existing administration and personnel, restored essential services, and encouraged local authorities to deal with public welfare projects—essentially trying to leave many aspects of daily life unchanged.

The implementation of the open bridges policy began with the free movement of people and goods across the Jordan River to maintain prewar trade relations and family and personal contacts. The next stage allowed free movement between the West Bank and Israel—the passage of Arabs from outside the West Bank to visit relatives in the occupied areas* during summer months, later expanded to the entire year. In 1968, Arabs in occupied areas could work in Israel. In light of two decades of Arab hostility, the policies were considered quite liberal. Free movement to cross into Jordan or the green line* into Israel from the West Bank still required permission from both Israel and the Arab states.

Jordan also had an interest in the open bridges policy. Whatever future King Hussein* had in mind for the West Bank necessitated maintaining contacts across the Jordan in order to influence official and popular opinion. While Israel implemented its West Bank program, Hussein attempted to preserve his power and authority by continuing to finance the civil administration and adopting security measures related to crossing into Jordan. Both Israel's and Jordan's policies, however, were highly flexible over the years as they restricted and reextended access across the Jordan River. The policies typically received greater attention during times of crisis such as the 1973 war* or during Israeli–Palestinian and/or Jordanian–Palestinian trouble. Access was then usually restricted. In July 1986, for example, Palestinians in the West Bank demonstrated against King Hussein. Hussein had just cut his ties to the Palestine Liberation

Organization* (PLO) and closed its Jordanian offices. After the demonstrations, he called for "firm controls" on crossings but promised continuation of "open bridges."

The open bridges policy also had implications for Israel's attempt to cultivate relations with Jordan and resolve the Palestinian question. Allowing increased and continued contact between the Palestinians and Jordanians, the policy was seen by some as a step toward the "Jordan is Palestine*" solution and by others as a way for Jordan to co-opt Palestinian nationalism. While Israel has maintained its open bridges policies, King Hussein's renunciation* of any claims to the West Bank on July 31, 1988, appeared to nullify a part of the policy's original objective—Jordanian financial and civil support for West Bank institutions.

For further information see: Shabtai Teveth, *Moshe Dayan: The Soldier, the Man, the Legend,* trans. Leah Zinder and David Zinder (Boston: Houghton Mifflin, 1973).

Paul S. Robinson, Jr., and Joseph E. Goldberg

OPERATION ACCOUNTABILITY. In July 1993, Israel sent forces into southern Lebanon in response to the launching of mortar shells and Katyusha rockets* into the towns, kibbutzim, and moshavim of northern Israel. In a speech to the Knesset* on July 28, 1993, Prime Minister Yitzhak Rabin* noted that Israel Defense Forces* (IDF) troops were operating in Lebanon* in order to ensure security and a normal life for the inhabitants of northern Israel. The purpose of the operation in southern Lebanon was described as restoring the security of the inhabitants of Israel's northern settlements. The battle was described as mainly with the terrorists of Hezbollah,* who were supported by Iran, although Palestinian organizations also took part in the terror attacks. Following the attacks by Hezbollah and other terrorist organizations against Israel's northern settlements, the government decided to act to restore the security of the inhabitants of the northern settlements by hitting Hezbollah as severely as possible. The operation began on July 25, 1993. To do that, Israel sought to drive civilian Lebanese populations in South Lebanon northward from their villages from which Hezbollah terrorists operated. This was designed to allow freedom of action to fight the terrorists without harming the civilian populations and, in the wake of this operation, to give to the Lebanese government and its outside supporters an opportunity to rein in Hezbollah's terrorists operating from Lebanon.

OPERATION ARYE. See **NAHHALIN.**

OPERATION BABYLON. See **OSIRAQ/TAMMUZ REACTOR.**

OPERATION BADR. The name given by Egypt to the military operation of crossing the Suez Canal* and launching the Yom Kippur War.* The name is derived from the Battle of Badr during the month of Ramadan in the year 624, in which the Islamic forces of the Prophet Mohammed won their first victory. The crossing of the canal took place on the tenth day of the month of Ramadan in the Islamic year 1393 (October 1973).

For further information see: Hassan el Badri, Taha el Magdoub, and Mohammed Dia el Din Zohdy, *The Ramadan War, 1973* (Dunn Loring, VA: T. N. Dupuy Associates, 1978).

OPERATION ENTEBBE. See **ENTEBBE OPERATION.**

OPERATION JONATHAN. See **ENTEBBE OPERATION.**

OPERATION KISLEV. At the end of May 1948, numerous small and seemingly insignificant military operations were launched by the Israelis. Operation Kislev occurred after the termination of hostilities in 1949. It threatened the stability of the fragile cease-fire as well as raised the specter of British involvement on behalf of the Jordanian Arab Legion.* While the operations were small, and the territories under question were minute, these operations were extremely important to achieve a proper military and geographic position based on a strategy known as Plan Dalet.*

Operation Kislev began on November 29, 1950, when the Arab–Israeli conflict had settled into a rather quiet period marked more by fedayeen*–Israeli commando skirmishes, raids, and reprisals than by organized combat by regular forces. It was a response to an earlier Jordanian action.

In early 1950, the Jordanians* closed the only road between Eilat* and the rest of Israel. A rather tense situation developed when the Arab Legion mobilized and deployed near the closed road. The Israelis affirmed their intention to reopen the road, by force if necessary—a statement that brought a warning from the British, who maintained connections with the Arab Legion. After Great Britain's warning, the Israelis again indicated that they would attack. The deputy commander of the company sent to reopen the road later wrote: "They [the Jordanians] decided to block the road to Eilat at Kilometer 78. This blockade was done with the full knowledge that blocking the road will cause the development of Eilat to cease, and this would cause the construction of a land bridge between Jordan and Egypt.*"

Ironically, though the Israelis felt they must open the road, they openly admitted that they did not know whether it actually crossed Israeli territory at that point. The borders were not clear, and the Jordanians claimed it was in their territory, and thus they had the right to close it. The Israelis did not deny this but still asserted that there was no alternative but to reopen it, by force if necessary. In fact, some high-ranking Israelis at the time openly stated that it was possible, if not likely, that the road actually passed through Jordanian territory.

Operation Kislev was executed by Armored Brigade Number 7 under Colonel Goder. At 4:00 P.M. on November 30, 1950, the units reached the area of the blockade and forced it open. There was complete surprise since Israeli armored units moved without stopping for two days to reach the area well ahead of what the Jordanians expected. Nothing came of the British threat, and the Jordanians did not respond beyond the area, so the tension was diffused. To the Israelis it proved the political, as well as military, effectiveness of surprise and swift, decisive victory.

This was an important operation at the time since it revealed the centrality of the emphasis placed on territorial command. Settlements had to be set up in territories that were deemed strategically necessary without dependence on reinforcements from Israel's geographic core. In early 1950, the establishment of Eilat as a major city was such an indication.

David Wurmser

OPERATION LION. See **NAHHALIN.**

OPERATION LITANI. On March 11, 1978, an Israeli bus was attacked on the Haifa–Tel Aviv Road, and thirty-four people were killed. Israel believed that the infiltrators received their instructions from Abu Jihad,* and responsibility was claimed by Palestine Liberation Organization* (PLO) spokesmen. The Israel Defense Forces* were ordered to enter southern Lebanon to eradicate terrorist bases adjacent to the Israel–Lebanon* border and those special bases from which terrorists had infiltrated deep into Israel to conduct those types of operations. From these bases in southern Lebanon, terrorist groups shelled Israeli settlements and carried out various operations within Israel. This was not considered by Israel as a retaliatory raid, arguing that there could be no retribution for the murder of innocent civilians. The goal of the operation was to prevent further attacks of the PLO and to ensure the safety of Israelis.

Israel completed Operation Litani on June 13, 1978, with the final phase of its withdrawal from South Lebanon. The operation began on the night of March 14, 1978, when Israeli troops crossed the Israeli–Lebanese* frontier and deployed over a wide area. The forces ultimately advanced to the Litani River,* with the exclusion of the port city of Tyre. The Israelis sought to destroy the logistic bases and infrastructure of the Palestinians.* Large quantities of weapons, ammunition, and war matériel were found.

OPERATION MALKHIA B. Operation Malkhia B occurred in the first stages of Israel's War of Independence.*

Operation Malkhia B is evidence of Israel's desire to avoid second "flanking" fronts while engaging another front, not dissimilar to the reasoning behind Operation Peace for Galilee.* Operation Malkhia B was the first example of the evolution of Plan Dalet* to include a process of segmenting, separating, and isolating fronts, holding some fronts in abeyance while concentrating on other fronts. It also reveals that Israel sees the Lebanese* front as more of a flank to the Syrian* Front than a front in its own right. Operation Malkhia B was designed both to close down the Lebanese front as well as to isolate it from the Golan Heights* front.

In May 1948, the Israeli intelligence services discovered that the Lebanese had reinforced positions near the town of Malkhia with armored vehicles. In that region, near Rosh Pina and the Israeli fortress of Yiftach above it, there was no Israeli armored force that could resist. There was considerable fear that the Lebanese force could cut the Hula Valley off from the rest of Israel by proceeding from Rosh Pina to Kibbutz Ayelet Hashachar and the Sea of Galilee.* Israeli forces in the upper Hula Valley, facing the Syrians, were in danger of being cut off. Furthermore, the Israeli forces operating just south of the Sea of Galilee near Beth Shean, deployed to stop Syrian and Iraqi* forces operating near Shaar HaGolan and Hamat Gader (the thin dividing valley between the plains in Jordan* and the Golan Heights above), were in danger of being left without reinforcements from the Central Galilee region since these reinforcements would be needed to stabilize the front along the northern sector of the Sea of Galilee. Without reinforcements and without proper ability to defend Tiberias since the Zefat region in the central part of the Galilee was already under attack, it was not clear that Tiberias would be adequately defended. Thus, Israeli troops were in danger of losing control of eastern Galilee. Therefore, the Israelis launched Operation Malkhia B to eliminate any possibility of intervention from the Lebanese Front, therein allowing all forces to concentrate against the Syrians and Iraqi reinforcements along the two ends of the Sea of Galilee.

The problem in executing the plan was that the Israelis were vastly outnumbered. Therefore, the Lebanese forces would have to be quickly and decisively defeated. Yet, the Israelis had no armored forces in the region and few troops to engage the Lebanese. Furthermore, the Israelis discovered the flanking front opening only on May 20–25, 1948. They had only two or three days to react before major fighting would erupt along the Syrian and Iraqi Fronts. The result was to try to defeat the Lebanese forces through surprise and maneuver. First, only a few vehicles could be "armored" on a temporary basis. The unit to be employed was Palmach* Company 3. It had just captured some Scout and Humber armored patrol vehicles. The Israelis quickly mounted a 20mm gun on these vehicles. Six vehicles, Sandwich-type, were added to this force, but they installed on them 81mm and 52mm guns. A Fiat and another Sandwich were armored in a way to serve as ramming devices for barriers and obstacles. Three buses were also armored, one to carry infantry, one to serve as an ambulance, and the third as a makeshift operating room. Another, smaller patrol car, Dingo-type, was also armored. This was to be the main attacking force. The attack was to occur on the night of May 28, 1948, only three days after the intelligence services had decided that such an operation was necessary and informed Palmach Company 3 to prepare.

In the early morning, May 29, 1948, a small diversionary force started up from Israel from Yiftach (above Rosh Pina) and proceeded slowly and directly toward Malkhia to the west where the Lebanese were entrenched. The evening before, the bulk of the force was placed near Misgav Am, far to the north of Yiftach and Malkhia. This larger force started moving at nightfall, May 28, coming down from Misgav Am near Metulla, working its way at night through the hills first in a southwestern direction toward Minrah, Mis-el Gebel, then south toward Belida and Itrun, which was to the west of Malkhia. While the diversionary force approached from the east toward the Lebanese forces in Malkhia, the main Israeli force suddenly attacked from deep inside Lebanon, from the west, from the direction of Itrun, by surprise. The Lebanese were organized for an attack from the east, so they were swiftly defeated, though they outnumbered both of the Israeli forces combined.

This operation's success enabled Israeli forces to again focus on the threat from the east, Iraq and Syria, without concern for the dangers that could emerge from Lebanon, which had been isolated from Syria in this region and unable to help the Arab endeavor.

David Wurmser

OPERATION MEATGRINDER. See ES-SAMU.

OPERATION PEACE FOR GALILEE. See WAR IN LEBANON.

OPERATION ROSE. See KIBYA, UNIT 101.

OPERATION ROTEM (1960). The operation and its aftermath reveal the limits of Israeli red lines for going to war during the period from 1956 to 1967.

Toward the end of December 1959 and in early January 1960, partly in response to gradual Israeli encroachment into the demilitarized zones along the Syria*–Israeli border where the sources of the Jordan River* spring, the Syrians began sporadic shelling of Israeli positions and settlements. The areas of greatest contention were the territories surrounding Tel-Katzir and Tawfiq to the east of the Sea of Galilee.* By the end of January 1960, as artillery exchanges between Syria and Israel intensified, Israel requested an immediate cease-fire and warned of large reprisals if the shelling continued.

Egypt* intervened, apparently prodded by the Soviet Union, by announcing it would aid Syria were the latter attacked, especially since both armies were under the joint command of General Abdel Hakim Amer.*

On January 30, 1960, some United Arab Republic (UAR) infantry forces (Syrians under Amer's command) staged a large attack on Israeli positions in the area, ostensibly to protect Syrian citizens in the disputed zones. This led to Israel's decision to launch a strong reprisal.

Two days later, on the night of February 1, 1960, Israeli forces crossed the border near Tawfiq and destroyed the town and its fortifications, inflicting large casualties. The operation was called Rotem, and it was carried out by Israeli paratroop forces, apparently under Mordechai Gur,* who became the Israeli chief of staff in 1974. The Syrian forces attacked by the Israelis were under the command of General Amer, who later became chief of staff of the Egyptian (then the UAR) army.

The day following the Rotem raid, the Egyptians announced a limited concentration of forces along the Suez Canal.* From this point onward, the events paralleled those events seven years later in May–June 1967.

On February 15, 1960, the UAR army received reliable information from Soviet intelligence services that Israel was massing troops in large numbers near the Syrian border in preparation for a full-scale invasion of Syria. On February 18, the Egyptians announced that they would aid Syria to repel an attack. On the night of February 19, three Egyptian divisions crossed the canal and entered the Sinai Peninsula.* Within a few days, these three divisions, one of them armored, were deployed at El-Arish, Abu Agueila, and Kotzima.

Israel placed its forces on a high state of alert and began mobilization. The tension lasted two weeks without major incident. One month later, Egyptian forces announced they had won and that Israel had been deterred from attacking Syria. Slowly, Egyptian forces withdrew across the Suez Canal toward Cairo.

The Israelis did not launch a strike. Operation Rotem in February 1960 was similar to the operations in May 1967 that led to the Six Day War.*

David Wurmser

OPERATION TESHURA. See BEIRUT AIRPORT RAID.

ORGANIZATION OF AFRICAN UNITY COMMISSION. The Organization of African Unity, at its Summit conference session in June 1971, appointed a commission of ten heads of state to assist in the search for a solution to the Arab–Israeli conflict on the basis of United Nations Security Council Resolution 242.* The Commission of Ten appointed a Subcommission of Four. The subcommittee consisted of Mokttar Ould Dadda, president of the Islamic Republic of Mauritania, Haile Selassie I, emperor of Ethiopia, Leopold Sedar Senghor, president of the Republic of Senegal, and El-Haj Ahmadou Ahidjo, president of the Federal Republic of Cameroon. They held exploratory conversations with the Israeli authorities on November 3, 4, and 5, 1971, and with the Egyptian authorities on November 6 and 7, 1971. They made an urgent appeal to Israel and Egypt* to maintain a positive attitude and to facilitate the resumption of the Jarring mission* and to arrive at a just, lasting, and fraternal peace. No concrete accomplishments could be attributed to this effort.

For further information see: Susan Aurelia Gitelson, ''The OAU Mission and the Middle East Conflict,'' *International Organization* 27 (Summer 1973):413–19; Ran Kochan, ''An African Peace Mission in the Middle East: The One-Man Initiative of President Senghor,'' *African Affairs* 72 (April 1973):186–96.

ORGANIZATION OF ARAB PETROLEUM EXPORTING COUNTRIES (OAPEC). Established in January 1968 and based in Kuwait. Its members include Algeria, Bahrain, Egypt,* Kuwait, Libya, Iraq,* Qatar, Saudi Arabia, Syria,* and the

United Arab Emirates (UAE). Its purpose is to coordinate Arab oil industry activities and promote cooperation among its members. See also OIL WEAPON.

For further information see: Abdelkadir Maachou, *OAPEC: The Organization of Arab Petroleum Exporting Countries* (New York: St. Martin's Press, 1983).

ORGANIZATION OF PETROLEUM EXPORTING COUNTRIES (OPEC). Established in 1960 and headquartered in Vienna. Its members are Algeria, Ecuador (which left the organization in the 1990s), Gabon, Indonesia, Iraq,* Iran, Kuwait, Libya, Nigeria, Qatar, Saudi Arabia, United Arab Emirates (UAE), and Venezuela. See also OIL WEAPON.

For further information see: Fuad Itayim, "The Organization of Petroleum Exporting Countries," *Middle East Forum* 38 (December 1962):13–19, Ian Skeet, *OPEC: 25 Years of Prices and Politics* (New York: Cambridge University Press, 1988).

ORIENT HOUSE. The seat of Palestinian* political activities in East Jerusalem* whose status became an issue in the Israel–Palestine Liberation Organization* (PLO) negotiations to implement the Declaration of Principles* (DOP) despite the fact that the DOP deferred the question of Jerusalem* to the permanent-status talks, scheduled to begin by 1996.

Orient House is one of the buildings in East Jerusalem owned by the Husseini family. After the beginning of the Madrid process,* the Palestinians identified it as the headquarters of their negotiating team. This was an implied challenge to Israel's claim of sole sovereignty over all of Jerusalem. The problem was exacerbated after the signing of the DOP and the recognition of the PLO. Under the terms of the accord, autonomy initially would be restricted to Jericho* and the Gaza Strip.* The DOP also specifically prevented the Palestinian self-government from conducting foreign and defense policy. Nevertheless, Faisal Husseini,* as a member of the Palestinian leadership, continued to host foreign diplomats and visiting officials at Orient House to underscore the Palestinian claim to sovereignty rights in Jerusalem.

On November 5, 1994, Turkish prime minister Tansu Ciller visited Orient House during an official visit to Israel. This caused Yitzhak Rabin* great consternation, and the Israeli government began the process of adopting legislation allowing the police to close Orient House.

OSA MISSILE BOAT. The OSA missile boat is a class of fast attack craft designed and built by the Soviet Union in the 1960s. Two classes were produced: the OSA I in the early 1960s and the OSA II in the late 1960s. The OSA was armed with twin 30mm guns and the Styx ship-to-ship missile. The OSA has a complement of thirty, a maximum speed of thirty-five knots, and a maximum range of 500 miles. Because of its size and range, the OSA is primarily a coastal patrol vessel.

In the Middle East, the OSA was procured by Algeria, Egypt,* Iraq,* Libya,

Syria,* and the former South Yemen. During the Yom Kippur War,* the Israelis sank four Egyptian and two Syrian OSA boats.

See also CHERBOURG GUNBOAT INCIDENT.

For further information see: John E. Moore, ed., *Jane's Fighting Ships* (London: Jane's Yearbook, 1977); Richard Sharpe, ed., *Jane's Fighting Ships,* 95th ed. (Surrey: Jane's Information Group, 1992).

Stephen H. Gotowicki

OSIRAK. See **OSIRAQ.**

OSIRAQ/TAMMUZ REACTOR. Osirak (Osiraq) is the original French* name given to the 70MW nuclear reactor at the Al Tuwaitha nuclear site, located approximately twenty kilometers southeast of Baghdad; the Iraqi* name for the reactor was Tammuz I.

On Sunday, June 7, 1981, eight F-16* single-seat fighter bombers, protected by eight F-15* Eagle single-seat air fighters of the Israeli air force (IAF) took off from the military air base at Etzion, located approximately twenty kilometers from Eilat,* and bombed the Tammuz I reactor in Iraq, destroying it. This IAF mission was code-named Operation Babylon.* The attack was intended to delay, if not halt, Iraqi nuclear weapons ambitions before the reactor was fully operational, at which time an attack would have resulted in the emission of a radioactive dust cloud. This is the first successful preemptive strike on a nuclear installation.

The Iraqis contended that Tammuz I was intended solely for scientific purposes. The Menachem Begin* government, however, was concerned with the ability of the Iraqis to produce weapons-grade plutonium or uranium from the reactor for use in a nuclear bomb directed against Israel, even though Iraq had ratified the Nuclear Nonproliferation Treaty in 1972. Citing remarks by Saddam Hussein* that the nuclear technology derived from Al Tuwaitha was eventually to be used against Israel, the Begin government evoked interpretations of Article 51 of the United Nations Charter regarding ''self-defense'' to justify its actions.

Shimon Peres* and the opposition Labor Party,* while praising the IAF pilots for their performance in the operation, denounced the attack as a political ploy by Prime Minister Begin to win votes in the Knesset* elections to be held later the same month. Begin argued that talks with French officials to suspend assistance on Project Tammuz 17 had come to naught and did not believe that, if elected, Peres would have carried out the operation.

Throughout the Arab world, the official reaction to the attack was condemnation, though some of the moderate Arab states seem to have suggested in private that they were relieved, given Iraqi hegemonic tendencies in the region, which most likely would have been augmented were Iraq to be in possession of nuclear weapons. Further condemnation was directed by many Arabs at Egyptian president Anwar Sadat,* who was looked upon as a collaborator in the attack.

Although Sadat was not given prior notification of any plans to bomb Tammuz I, he had met with Begin three days prior to the raid.

Operation Babylon established Israel's intention to impede progress, by force if necessary, by hostile Arab states in acquiring weapons of mass destruction. For the Arabs, this highlighted Israel's presumed nuclear weapons monopoly in the region, which they see as an unfair military advantage.

For further information see: Shai Feldman, *The Raid on Osiraq: A Preliminary Assessment* (Tel Aviv: Center for Strategic Studies, Tel Aviv University, 1981); Clinton Dan McKinnon, *Bullseye One Reactor* (San Diego: House of Hits, 1987); Shelomoh Nakdimon, *First Strike: The Exclusive Story of How Israel Foiled Iraq's Attempt to Get the Bomb,* trans. Peretz Kidron (New York: Summit Books, 1987); Amos Perlmutter, *Two Minutes over Baghdad* (London: Vallentine, Mitchell, 1982); Hasan Muhammad Tawalibah, *The Aggression on Iraq's Nuclear Reactor—Why?* trans. Namir Abbas Mudhaffer (Baghdad: Dar al-Ma'mum, 1982); *The Iraqi Nuclear Threat—Why Israel Had to Act* (Jerusalem: Ministry of Foreign Affairs, Atomic Energy Commission, Office of the Prime Minister, 1981).

Donald A. Pearson

OSLO DECLARATION. On September 13, 1994, the first anniversary of the signing of the Israel–Palestine Liberation Organization* (PLO) Declaration of Principles* (DOP), Yasser Arafat* and Shimon Peres* met in Oslo, Norway, and issued the Oslo Declaration. They reconfirmed their commitment to fully implement the DOP. In order to promote their economic relationship and the economy of the Palestinian Authority,* the two sides asked the government of Norway to convene an unofficial meeting in Paris to encourage the "donor community to meet the recurrent costs of the Palestinian Authority and its early empowerment." The PLO reaffirmed its commitment to develop the tax collection system of the Palestinian Authority and the hope that emergency donor funds will be needed only until the end of 1994. If funds can be provided to support transitional projects and short-term job creation projects as well as costs of the Palestinian police, the donor community can focus on longer-term development needs of Gaza* and the West Bank.*

Arafat and Peres also expressed their satisfaction with the recent positive developments in the peace process, including those between Jordan* and Israel, the recent statements by Syria* and by Israel, and the upcoming Casablanca Conference.*

OSLO TALKS (1993). The Madrid Conference* launched a series of Washington rounds* of talks between Israel and each of the Arab interlocutors, including the Palestinians.* These talks continued in 1992 and 1993, with little significant results. In the spring of 1993, a parallel channel of discussion between Israelis and Palestinians began in Oslo, Norway, under the aegis and with the facilitation of Johan Jorgen Holst,* the foreign minister of Norway. These talks were kept secret. Crucial decisions by the Palestine Liberation Organization* (PLO), and especially Yasser Arafat,* and by Israel, especially Shimon Peres* and Yitzhak Rabin,* permitted progress in these discussions. They led to an agreement that was initiated in Norway in the summer of 1993. The result of the negotiations, the Declaration of Principles,* was formally signed in Washington, D.C., in September 1993 and paved the way for further Israeli–PLO accords and the establishment of a Palestinian Authority* in the Gaza Strip* and Jericho.*

For further information see: Jane Corbin, *Gaza First: The Secret Norway Channel to Peace between Israel and the PLO* (London: Bloomsbury, 1994); Amos Elon, "The Peacemakers," *New Yorker,* December 30, 1993, pp. 77–85; John King, *Handshake in Washington: The Beginning of Middle East Peace* (London: Ithaca Press, 1994); Mark Perry and Daniel Shapiro, "Navigating the Oslo Channel: How an Unusual Cast of Characters Found Peace in an Unusual Place," *Middle East Insight* 9 (September–October 1993):9–20.

OTTOMAN EMPIRE. The Ottoman Empire was an important regional power for most of its existence. The Ottoman Turks conquered the area of Greater Syria* and Egypt,* which included Palestine,* in 1516–17 and ruled it (at least nominally) until the end of World War I.

During the tenth and eleventh centuries, Turkish tribes migrated from the steppes of Central Asia into the Anatolia region and converted to Islam. At the beginning of the fourteenth century, a member of the predominant Seljuk family, Osman I (1299–1326) won the Battle of Bapheon (1301) and established what was to become the Ottoman Empire.

Administratively and economically, the Ottoman Empire was dependent on continued expansion to maintain its powerful military forces, such as the Janissaries. In 1453, Sultan Mohammed (II) ("the Conqueror") (1451–81) captured Constantinople, effectively ending the Byzantine Empire. Ottoman dominance of the Middle East continued under Selim I ("the Grim") (1512–20) with the capture of Greater Syria and Egypt and the defeat of the Mamluk Empire in 1516–17. This defeat gave the Ottomans control over the heartland of the Islamic world and made it master of the Holy Cities of Mecca, Medina, and Jerusalem.* Geographically, the Ottoman Empire controlled the overland trade routes between Europe and the Far East and therefore was a major player in the valuable commerce between Europe and the East.

The Ottoman Empire was characterized by generally good relations with its non-Muslim subjects. Christian and Jewish communities were legally protected under Islamic law as *dhimmis,* and, though they were second-class citizens, they were allowed to administer their own religious and civil laws.

The pinnacle of the Ottoman Empire's power and expansion into Europe occurred under Suleiman ("the Magnificent") (1520–66) with the first siege of Vienna in 1529. The failure of this siege marked the decline of the Ottoman's military dominance. The loss of revenue gained from military expansion and the growing European sea trade to the East around Africa, via the Cape of Good Hope, resulted in the decline of the Ottoman Empire's economic structure and factored heavily in the slow disintegration of the empire.

A series of disastrous wars with Russia and Austria–Hungary during the eighteenth and nineteenth centuries left the Ottoman Empire further weakened and vulnerable to demands by European powers to represent the interests of the different religious minorities in both Istanbul (Constantinople) and Jerusalem. The Ottoman Empire became known as the "sick man of Europe" as the European powers took advantage of its weakness to both forward their own imperial expansionism and limit that of their rivals. Napoleon Bonaparte's brief foray into Egypt in 1798 marked the first European military move into the heartland of the Middle East since the Crusades and marked the beginning of the eventual European absorption of the Ottoman Empire, which was to conclude with the end of World War I.

In a 1908 military coup, led by Kemal Mustafa Attaturk's Society of Union and Progress (Young Turks), the last reigning Ottoman sultan, Abdul Hamid, was deposed and replaced by a figurehead, Mehmed V.

In August 1914, the empire signed a treaty with Germany and joined the Central Powers against the Entente. Russia, France,* and England* immediately began discussions on how to partition the empire after its defeat. The plans and agreements made by France and England during the war to partition the empire upon its demise included the Hussein–McMahon correspondence,* the Sykes-Picot Agreement,* and the Balfour Declaration.*

For further information see: Amnon Cohen, *Palestine in the 18th Century: Patterns of Government and Administration* (Jerusalem: Magnes Press, Hebrew University, 1973); Sydney Nettleton Fisher, *The Middle East: A History,* 3d ed. (New York: Alfred A. Knopf, 1979); Albert Hourani, *A History of the Arab Peoples* (Cambridge: Belknap Press of the Harvard University Press, 1991); Norman Itzkowitz, *Ottoman Empire and Islamic Tradition* (Chicago: University of Chicago Press, 1972); Moshe Ma'oz, *Ottoman Reform in Syria and Palestine, 1840–1861; The Impact of the Tanzimat on Politics and Society* (London: Oxford University Press, 1968); Moshe Ma'oz, ed., *Studies on Palestine during the Ottoman Period* (Jerusalem: Magnes Press, 1975); Roger Owen, ed., *Studies in the Economic and Social History of Palestine in the Nineteenth and Twentieth Centuries* (Carbondale: Southern Illinois University Press, 1982).

Mark Daryl Erickson

P

PA. See **PALESTINIAN AUTHORITY.**

PALESTINE. The geographical area of which part is occupied by the state of Israel. Palestine is one of the names for the territory that has also been known as the Holy Land* or the Land of Israel* (Eretz Israel*). The name is derived from the fact that it was called Palestina by the Greeks and the Romans because of the Philistines who lived in part of the region. During the period of Ottoman* control it was generally known as the Arabic Filastin, although it was a part of the province of Syria.* The League of Nations Palestine Mandate* awarded to the British included territory on both sides of the Jordan River.* Transjordan* was soon separated, and only the area west of the river was referred to as the Palestine Mandate between 1922 and 1948. With the establishment of Israel and the first Arab–Israeli War,* Palestine ceased to exist as a geographical or political unit.

PALESTINE CONCILIATION COMMISSION (PCC). The United Nations Conciliation Commission for Palestine* was established December 11, 1948, by United Nations General Assembly Resolution 194 (III)* and later modified by Resolution 394 (V) in December 1950 and Resolution 512 (VI) on January 26, 1952, in an attempt to mediate the conflict between Israel and the Arabs and, in that vein, to facilitate the repatriation and resettlement of the Palestine refugees and to deal with the issue of Jerusalem* as an international city. Composed of the United States, France,* and Turkey, the commission established its headquarters in Jerusalem at the former Government House* in late January 1949. The Arabs insisted that there should be no direct contact between them and the Jews and that any exchange of views between the antagonists be done through

United Nations communications or conducted under the Rhodes formula. Nor
did the Arabs believe that general peace negotiations should begin before the
status of refugees* was resolved. Israel was willing to meet with the Arab states
as a collective or separately, but it insisted that peace negotiations should be
viewed in terms of an overall settlement.

On April 27, 1949, the commission met at Lausanne, with the Arabs refusing
to sit at the same negotiating table with Israel. The Arab states also insisted on
negotiating on behalf of the Palestinians. The Lausanne Conference *resulted in
all parties signing a separate protocol in which they agreed to accept a commission proposal as the basis for discussions. Further meetings took place in
1949 and early 1950, but the positions of the two sides remained fixed. The
Arabs insisted that the resolution of the refugee problem was a precondition for
discussions while Israel insisted that this should be discussed as part of the
overall settlement. Israel later altered its position and agreed to discuss the refugee issue separately, but the Arabs remained intransigent.

The Conciliation Commission reconvened in Paris in the summer of 1951 and
presented to the parties a statement of principles whose preamble stated that the
states would solemnly affirm their intention to settle their differences peacefully.
Israel agreed to the principles and proposed that all of the states sign a nonaggression pact. The Arabs rejected the commission's proposal altogether, and the
session ended.

Throughout most of 1952, the Conciliation Commission was based in New
York and dealt with aspects of the Arab refugee issue. That year, Israel agreed
as a gesture of goodwill to transfer 1 million pounds of blocked bank accounts
of Arab refugees, but the Arab states refused to change their position. The
Conciliation Commission was unsuccessful in its efforts to mediate the Arab–
Israeli conflict.

Joseph E. Goldberg

PALESTINE FOUNDATION FUND. See KEREN HAYESOD.

**PALESTINE INTERIM SELF-GOVERNING ARRANGEMENTS (PISGA). See IN-
TERIM SELF-GOVERNING ARRANGEMENTS.**

PALESTINE LIBERATION ARMY (PLA). The second Arab Summit meeting in
September 1964 allocated funds for the establishment of the Palestine Liberation
Army (PLA). It was established after the creation of the Palestine Liberation
Organization* (PLO) and placed under the unified Arab command. It has had a
variable role in the Palestinian effort to achieve a Palestinian state and played
no major role in any of the major Arab–Israeli wars.

PALESTINE LIBERATION FRONT (PLF). A terrorist group that broke away from
the Popular Front for the Liberation of Palestine—General Command* (PFLP—
GC) in the mid-1970s. It later split again into pro-Palestine Liberation Organi-

zation* (PLO), pro-Syrian,* and pro-Libyan factions. The pro-PLO faction was led by Mohammed Abdul Abbas,* who became a member of the PLO Executive Committee in 1984 but left it in 1991. This group was responsible for the October 1985 attack on the cruise ship *Achille Lauro** and the abortive seaborne attack on Israel in May 1990. Since the *Achille Lauro* attack, it has been based in Iraq.*

PALESTINE LIBERATION ORGANIZATION (PLO). At a Cairo Summit in 1964, the Arab League* decided to form an organization that would represent Palestinians* and work for "the liberation of Palestine." Ahmed Shukairy* was chosen to head the new organization. Founded in 1964 as a Palestinian nationalist umbrella organization dedicated to the establishment of an independent Palestinian state, the PLO gained renewed energy after the Six Day War* of 1967. Shukairi was forced to resign as the head of the PLO in December 1967. At the Palestine National Congress held in February 1969, Yasser Arafat* was elected chairman of the PLO's Executive Committee. In the early 1980s, the PLO became fragmented into several contending groups. The United States has considered the PLO an umbrella organization that includes several constituent groups and individuals with differing views on terrorism.

The Palestine National Council* (PNC) is the highest Palestinian policymaking body. In 1970, it established a Central Committee to act on its behalf when it is not in session. The Executive Committee of the PLO is akin to the executive branch of government. It implements PNC decisions and is responsible to it. It speaks for the Palestinian people and represents them internationally. The PLO includes all the Palestinian Armed Resistance (commando) groups, as well as a number of popular organizations, including the General Union of Palestinian Workers, the General Union of Palestinian Students,* the General Union of Palestinian Engineers, the General Union of Palestinian Writers and Journalists, the General Union of Palestinian Doctors, the General Union of Palestinian Teachers, the General Union of Palestinian Lawyers, the General Union of Palestinian Painters and Artists, and other such groups. Additional institutions were developed, over time, by the PLO. These included such groups as the Palestine Red Crescent Society and the Palestinian News Agency (WAFA).

PLO chairman Arafat publicly renounced terrorism in December 1988 on behalf of the PLO. The dialogue between the United States and the PLO was suspended after the PLO failed to condemn the May 30, 1990, Palestine Liberation Front* (PLF) attack on Israeli beaches. The PLO remains based in Tunisia, although Arafat and some of his aides have moved to Gaza* to establish the Palestinian Authority.* See also FATAH.

For further information see: Helena Cobban, *The Palestinian Liberation Organization: People, Power and Politics* (New York: Cambridge University Press, 1984); Kemal Kirisci, *The PLO and World Politics: A Study of the Mobilization and Support for the Palestinian Cause* (London: Francis Pinter, 1986); Neil C. Livingstone and David Halevy, *Inside the PLO* (New York: William Morrow, 1990); Jamal R. Nassar, *The Pal-*

estine Liberation Organization: From Armed Struggle to the Declaration of Independence (New York: Praeger, 1991); Cheryl Rubenberg, *The Palestine Liberation Organization: Its Institutional Infrastructure* (Belmont, MA: Institute of Arab Studies, 1983); Barry Rubin, *Revolution until Victory? The Politics and History of the PLO* (Cambridge: Harvard University Press, 1994).

PALESTINE LIBERATION ORGANIZATION DIALOGUE WITH THE UNITED STATES. See **UNITED STATES–PALESTINE LIBERATION ORGANIZATION DIALOGUE.**

PALESTINE MANDATE. See **BRITISH MANDATE.**

PALESTINE NATIONAL COUNCIL (PNC). This is the Palestinian* "Parliament in exile." A Palestinian congress, attended by more than 400 Palestinians, was convened in Jerusalem* between May 28 and June 2, 1964. Among other actions, it ratified a Palestine National Covenant.* It later became known as the first session of the Palestine National Council (PNC), which is the highest policymaking body within the Palestine Liberation Organization* (PLO). Selected for a three-year term by the PLO Executive Committee, it meets periodically in various Arab capitals. Meetings have been held as follows:

Dates and Venues of the Palestine National Councils (1964–1987)

1	May 28–June 2, 1964	Jerusalem
2	May 31–June 4, 1965	Cairo
3	May 20–May 24, 1966	Cairo
4	July 10–July 17, 1968	Cairo
5	February 1–February 4, 1969	Cairo
6	September 1–September 6, 1969	Cairo
7	May 30–June 4, 1970	Cairo
	August 27–August 28, 1970*	Amman
8	February 28–March 5, 1971	Cairo
9	July 7–July 13, 1971	Cairo
10	April 11–April 12, 1972	Cairo
11	January 6–January 12, 1973	Cairo
12	June 1–June 9, 1974	Cairo
13	March 12–March 20, 1977	Cairo
14	January 15–January 23, 1979	Damascus
15	April 11–April 19, 1981	Damascus
16	February 14–February 22, 1983	Algiers
17	November 22–November 28, 1984	Amman

*Extraordinary session

For the deliberations and outcomes of specific sessions, see the references to those meetings.

For further information see: Muhammad Muslih, *Toward Coexistence: An Analysis of the Resolutions of the Palestine National Council* (Washington, DC: Institute for Palestine Studies, 1990).

PALESTINE NATIONAL COUNCIL, ALGIERS, NOVEMBER 1988. On November 15, 1988, at the nineteenth session of the Palestine National Council* in Algiers, Algeria, Palestine Liberation Organization* (PLO) chairman Yasser Arafat* issued a formal "Declaration of Independence for the State of Palestine."

In his address Arafat asserted that there existed an eternal bond among the land of Palestine,* its people, and their history and that, despite being deprived of their political independence, Palestinian self-determination was rooted in their history as a nation as well as in United Nations (UN) General Assembly Resolution 181 (II),* which partitioned Palestine into one Arab and one Jewish state. Arafat affirmed that this resolution

still provides those conditions of international legitimacy that ensure the right of the Palestinian Arab people to sovereignty and national independence . . . by virtue of natural, historical, and legal rights . . . and relying on the authority bestowed by international legitimacy as embodied in the resolutions of the United Nations since 1947. . . . The Palestine National Council, in the name of God, and in the name of the Palestinian Arab people, hereby proclaims the establishment of the State of Palestine on our Palestinian territory with its capital Jerusalem.*

The declaration maintained that the state of Palestine has a "commitment to the principles and purposes of the United Nations, and to the Universal Declaration of Human Rights." Moreover, the state of Palestine is a "peace-loving state, in adherence to the principles of peaceful co-existence." Arafat also noted that the state of Palestine "believes in the settlement of regional and international disputes by peaceful means . . . it therefore rejects the threat or use of force, violence, and terrorism."

In a political communique issued the same day, the Palestine National Council (PNC) formally committed the PLO to arrive at a comprehensive settlement with Israel that involved a two-state solution. The PNC further affirmed its support for an international peace conference based on UN Security Council Resolutions 242* and 338*; Israeli withdrawal from all Arab territories occupied since 1967, including Arab Jerusalem*; the annulment of all measures instituted by the Israeli government during occupation; questions of Palestinian refugees* to be settled in accordance with relevant United Nations resolutions; and Security Council guarantees for security and peace between all the states concerned, including Palestine.

Other salient points of the political communique were the acknowledgment of "the distinctive relationship between the Jordanian* and Palestinian peoples," which would possibly allow for a future voluntary confederation between the two states; the reiteration of the PNC's rejection of terrorism in all its forms; gratitude to all who have supported the rights of the Palestinian people; and concern for growing extremism in Israel that stressed either the annihilation and/ or expulsion of Palestinians. In closing, the communique called upon the American people to not only recognize the sacred right of Palestinians to self-determination but also conform to conventions and resolutions that serve to establish peace in the Middle East.

The PNC meeting in Algiers occurred as the *intifada** had thrust the Palestinian cause to the forefront of international attention. Then, on July 31, 1988, King Hussein* issued an official renunciation of his claim to the West Bank,* followed a few weeks later by an announcement that Jordan would no longer be party to future joint Palestinian–Jordanian delegations. In the months that followed, Arafat continued to forward the PLO's diplomatic program based upon an international peace conference governed by previous UN resolutions.

The declaration received wide attention, earning within two weeks the recognition of some fifty-five states. Israel and the United States rejected the PNC declaration. Despite pressures to do so, the United States continued to refuse to open a direct dialogue with the PLO. Not until after Arafat's December 13, 1988, address to the UN General Assembly and his subsequent press statement did the United States finally lift its ban on dealing with the PLO, paving the way for a "substantive dialogue with PLO representatives." The dialogue, which continued between the two parties until June 1990, failed to produce any tangible changes in the Israeli–Palestinian conflict.

For further information see: Rashid Khalidi, "The 19th PNC Resolutions and American Policy," *Journal of Palestine Studies* 74 (Winter 1990):20–42; Don Peretz, *Intifada: The Palestinian Uprising* (Boulder, CO: Westview Press, 1990); William B. Quandt, *Peace Process: American Diplomacy and the Arab–Israeli Conflict since 1967* (Washington, DC: Brookings Institution, 1993); Bassam Abu Sharif, "Prospects of a Palestinian–Israeli Settlement," *Journal of Palestine Studies* 74 (Winter 1990):272–75.

Anamika Krishna

PALESTINE NATIONAL COVENANT. The covenant was adopted by the Palestine Liberation Organization* (PLO) in 1964 as the charter for the organization and was amended in Cairo in 1968 by the Palestine National Council.* Its Preamble, speaking on behalf of the Palestinian Arab people, decries the injustice perpetrated upon them by Zionism* and colonialism, which displaced and dispersed them from their homeland. The Palestinian Arab people are asserting their right of self-defense. Article 1 provides: "Palestine* is the homeland of the Arab Palestinian people; it is an indivisible part of the Arab homeland, and the Palestinian people are an integral part of the Arab nation."

The central theme is the elimination of Israel and its replacement by a Palestinian state established in all of Palestine. Palestinians are defined as "those Arab citizens who, until 1947, had normally resided in Palestine, regardless of whether they have been evicted from it or have stayed in it. Anyone born, after that date, of a Palestinian father whether inside Palestine or outside it—is also a Palestinian." Jews of Palestinian origin can be "considered Palestinian if they desire to undertake to live in loyalty and peace in Palestine."

Article 11 states that "Palestinians shall have three mottoes: national unity, national mobilization, and liberation." Once liberation is attained, it adds, the "Palestinian people shall be free to adopt, for its public life, the political, economic or social system of its choice."

The 1968 modification clarifies the importance of Article 20, which is at the heart of the PLO design:

The Balfour Declaration,* the mandate for Palestine* and everything that has been based upon them, are deemed null and void. Claims of historical or religious ties of Jews with Palestine are incompatible with the facts of history and the true conception of what constitutes statehood. Judaism, being a religion, is not an independent nationality. Nor do Jews constitute a single nation with an identity of its own; they are citizens of the states to which they belong.

This article reinforces the view expressed in many of the articles that "[t]he partition of Palestine in 1947 and the establishment of Israel are entirely illegal" (Article 16).

Although various Palestinian leaders have suggested that the covenant has been superseded, in part, by subsequent statements and declarations, the covenant remains formally unchanged as a guide to Palestinian objectives.

PALESTINE NATIONAL FRONT. The Palestine National Front was created in August 1973 in an attempt to establish political influence in the occupied territories.* Much of its early leadership was associated with the Palestine Communist Party, with support from members of the Baath Party. Members of the Palestine Liberation Organization* (PLO) were concerned that the Front would be used by the Communist Party to take control of the movement. From 1973 to 1975, at the height of its influence, the Front adopted many positions advanced by the Soviet Union. Like the USSR, the Front proposed that the PLO participate in the Geneva Peace Conference* after the Yom Kippur War.* The Front's willingness to accept Soviet positions was a constant concern of Fatah* and other PLO factions. To control the movement, the PLO asked that all of the Front's materials be cleared prior to publication. The PLO had been unable to win over the loyalties and mobilize the Arab population in the territories as well as in Israel itself. The Palestine National Front leadership had representation in the Palestine National Council* and other decision-making bodies. In 1975, the Palestine National Front encouraged a list of Palestinians to stand for election in a number of West Bank* towns, and they were successful. Their success, in turn, helped nurture nationalism among the Palestinians. Originally standing for Palestinian cooperation with Jordan,* the Palestine National Front eventually called for the establishment of an independent Palestinian state. Fatah's suspicions of the Front's independence from the Soviet Union was a major reason the organization was not revived in 1975. Fatah feared that the Front's appeal would undermine Fatah influence and promote independent leadership among the Palestinians.

Joseph E. Goldberg

PALESTINE PARTITION PLAN. A plan adopted by the United Nations General Assembly, as United Nations General Assembly Resolution 181 (II),* on November 29, 1947, by a vote of thirty-three in favor, thirteen against, ten abstentions, and one absent. It divided the Palestine Mandate* into an Arab state, a Jewish state, and an internationalized sector, including Jerusalem.* It provided the basis for Israel's independence and for the Arab–Israeli conflict. In general, the Zionists accepted the decision as the best attainable given the political circumstances. The Palestinians and the Arab states rejected the decision as unfair and pledged to restore the rights of the Arabs of Palestine. These reactions ensured that attempts to implement the plan would lead to conflict, and they did. See also WAR OF INDEPENDENCE.

For further information see: Kermit Roosevelt, "The Partition of Palestine: A Lesson in Pressure Politics," *Middle East Journal* 2 (January 1948):1–17.

PALESTINE POPULAR STRUGGLE FRONT (PPSF). Established in 1968, this small organization, numbering between 150 and 200 members, was founded by Bahjat Abu Garbiyya, who had been a member of the Palestine Liberation Organization* (PLO) Executive Council in 1964. It recruited members from the Jordanian* community, as well as from among Palestinians. In 1969, Garbiyya brought the organization into the Palestine Armed Struggle Command, a body established to coordinate the military activities of the various fedayeen* organizations. The PPSF enjoyed support from Iraq* as well as from Libya. See also BLACK SEPTEMBER.

Joseph E. Goldberg

PALESTINE PRESS SERVICE. It was founded in 1977 to provide information in the West Bank* and Gaza Strip* to foreign journalists and diplomats stationed in Israel. The Palestine Press Service published a weekly magazine in English and Arabic that was distributed only within Israel and not allowed to be distributed in the occupied territories.* From its founding to March 1983, the Palestine Press Service also provided a daily translation in English of articles in East Jerusalem* newspapers published in Arabic.

Joseph E. Goldberg

PALESTINE SUMMIT (1974). See **RABAT SUMMIT (1974).**

PALESTINIAN AUTHORITY (PA). The name given to the Palestinian self-governing body established in 1994. The PA was to administer the Gaza Strip* and Jericho* under the agreement negotiated with Israel to implement the Declaration of Principles* (DOP).

Under the terms of Article 4 of the Cairo Agreement* of May 4, 1994, "[t]he Palestinian Authority will consist of one body of 24 members which shall carry out and be responsible for all the legislative and executive powers and responsibilities transferred to it under this Agreement, in accordance with this Article, and shall be responsible for the exercise of judicial functions in accordance with Article VI, subparagraph 1.b. of this Agreement."

Although some of the portfolios and positions were kept open for future appointments, the initial members of the Palestinian Authority and their portfolios are as follows: chairman and interior: Yasser Arafat*; economy and trade: Ahmed Karia* (Abu Alla); planning and international cooperation: Nabil Shaath,* who heads the Palestine Economic Council for Development and Reconstruction (PECDAR)* and serves as chief negotiator in the talks on the Gaza*–Jericho implementation accord; finance: Mohammad Zohdi Nashashibi, a banker from a prominent Jerusalem family; labor: Samir Ghosheh, a member of the Palestine Liberation Organization* (PLO) Executive Committee; social affairs: Intissar al-Wazir,* widow of Khalil al-Wazir* (Abu Jihad), Arafat's second-in-command; education: Yasser Amr, member of the PLO Executive Committee and head of its education department; culture and arts: Yasser Abed-Rabbo,* one of Arafat's aides in the negotiations with Israel; justice: Fraih Abu-Meddain, former head of the Gaza Bar Association and a member of the Palestinian team to the Washington round* of talks with Israel; housing: Zakaria al-Agha, head of the Gaza Medical Association; local government: Saeb Erakat,* an activist in the occupied territories,* lecturer at the West Bank's* an-Najah University, and editorial writer for Palestinian newspapers; tourism and monuments: Elias Freij,* Bethlehem* mayor since 1972; health: Riad Zanoun, chairman of the Health High Council in the Gaza Strip; youth and sports: Azmi Shuaibi, president of the Palestinian Democratic Union; communications and posts: Abdelhafiz Ash'hab, a leader from Hebron* in the West Bank; and transport: Abdelaziz Hajj-Ahmad, a former deportee, head of the dentists' association in the West Bank town of Ramallah.

Yasha Manuel Harari

PALESTINIAN DIASPORA. A reference, derived from the Jewish concept of diaspora,* to the Palestinians located outside Israel and the West Bank* and Gaza Strip.* Their role in the peace process* and especially the post-Madrid* rounds in Washington* and the multilateral talks* has been a constant matter of controversy.

**PALESTINIAN ECONOMIC COUNCIL FOR DEVELOPMENT AND RECON-
STRUCTION (PECDR or PECDAR).** The central economic institution of the Palestinian Authority* in the Gaza Strip* and Jericho,* established in November
1993. It was established to coordinate the program and issue and evaluate ten-
ders for basic infrastructure projects in the areas of transport, power, water,*
and solid waste. Its officials were to work closely with the United Nations Relief
and Works Agency for Palestine Refugees (UNRWA).* In part, its function is
to channel foreign aid and other resources to public sector projects in the West
Bank* and the Gaza Strip.

PALESTINIAN ISLAMIC JIHAD (PIJ). The group originated among militant Palestinian fundamentalists in the Gaza Strip* in the 1970s. It appears to be composed of a number of loosely related factions rather than a cohesive group. It
is committed to the creation of an Islamic Palestinian state and the destruction
of Israel through holy war. It has been involved in terrorist raids against Israeli
targets in Egypt,* the Gaza Strip, and the West Bank.*

PALESTINIAN POPULAR STRUGGLE FRONT (PPSF). See **PALESTINE POP-
ULAR STRUGGLE FRONT.**

PALESTINIAN RIGHTS COMMITTEE. See **COMMITTEE ON THE EXER-
CISE OF THE INALIENABLE RIGHTS OF THE PALESTINIAN PEO-
PLE.**

PALMACH (ACRONYM FOR PLUGOT MAHATZ—ASSAULT COMPANIES).
These were the commando units of the Haganah.* In 1936, Yitzhak Sadeh*
organized night patrols of Jewish youth in Palestine* to protect the areas near
Jewish settlements from Arab marauders and terrorists. Unlike the watchmen
who guarded the settlements, the night patrols ambushed the Arab bands close
to the Arab villages from which they originated. In addition, Sadeh's patrols
scouted for, and guided, British soldiers through the Palestinian mountain passes.
In 1937, Sadeh was given permission to form FOSH (field companies), which
provided greater training. With its headquarters on Tel Aviv's Rothschild Boul-
evard, the field companies provided the Yishuv's* defense with specialized
training. Because the Palestinian Jewish community was poor, funding took
place through a national arms levy to which Jews contributed from their salaries.
It is estimated that by 1938, there were 1,000 men in regional groups.

   Sadeh had been active in the kibbutz movement as well as the left-wing labor
parties in Palestine since his arrival from Russia. When Sadeh formed the Palmach in 1941, he called upon the resources of the United Kibbutz Movement
for volunteers. The members of the Palmach were identified with socialist and
labor principles.

   The Arab Revolt in Palestine in the late 1930s, as well as the rise of the Axis
powers in Europe, influenced the Yishuv's decision to create an offensive ca-

pability or shock platoons from the underground Jewish defense group Haganah. Haganah had followed a policy of restraint, *havlagah,* in which it refrained from initiating action. Unlike the Haganah, Palmach would be trained specifically for offensive warfare.

Established on May 14, 1941, Palmach would provide local defense against Arab attackers as well as defense against a possible Axis invasion. Its members were trained to attack in small units, using guerrilla tactics, and to become expert in the use of munitions for demolition and sabotage. They also engaged in intelligence activities. Recruitment was conducted secretly. Sadeh, the first Palmach commander, personally interviewed and selected company commanders, who, in turn, selected their membership. The Palmach wore no uniforms, were paid no salary, and lived in difficult conditions.

The British agreed to use the Palmach and, as a concession, did not require the Palmach to use their real names or addresses. Some British officials feared that the Palmach would turn eventually on Britain, and, indeed, some Palmach leaders did call for an aggressive policy toward the British. In the summer of 1941, Arabic-speaking Palmach members crossed into Syria* from northern Palestine and conducted sabotage. A later raid against oil refineries near Tripoli that supplied German planes with fuel failed, and twenty-three Palmach were lost at sea.

The Yishuv recognized the importance of the Palmach, but its financial resources were not sufficient to support them. Palmach remained partially mobilized from the summer of 1941 until the summer of 1942. During this period they reported for duty six days a month. They were guided by the motto, ''We must learn to fight with whatever is available rather than with what is theoretically desirable.'' Training was conducted with enemy arms as well.

Because of the worsening military situation, the British agreed in 1942 to give intensive training to 300 Palmach members. Sadeh created three basic groups: an Arabic-speaking platoon, a German-speaking platoon, and a Balkan languages-speaking platoon. From its origins Palmach recruited both men and women.

In addition to their infiltration raids into Syria and Lebanon* on behalf of the Allied war effort, members of the Palmach were dropped behind enemy lines in the Balkans and northern Italy. The intent was to aid captured Allied prisoners, conduct sabotage, and organize resistance. The Palmach hoped, as well, to organize the remnant of the European Jewish community. Thirty-two Palestinian Jews were dropped—nine into Rumania, eight into Yugoslavia, three into Hungary, two into Bulgaria, three into Italy, five into Slovakia, and two into Austria. Seven of those dropped behind enemy lines were killed.

Cooperation with the British ended in 1943 with the British confiscating Palmach's arms, fearing that they would ultimately be used against them.

In June 1948, Israel's prime minister David Ben-Gurion* called upon units of the Palmach to prevent the Irgun Tzvai Leumi* from unloading an arms ship, the *Altalena**, which would have violated the existing truce arrangements and raised questions whether Etzel* would willingly cooperate with the established Jewish authority.

Because of the nature of their operations, all recruits were given amphibious training. The Palmach also established a Naval Officers' Course—the Palyam (the seaborne Palmach).

The courage and skill of the Palmach were appreciated by the British as well as the Yishuv. Its commanders, Yigal Allon,* Yitzhak Sadeh, Yitzhak Rabin,* Shimon Avidan, and Israel Galilee, all made significant contributions to Palestine's safety and Israel's independence. Of the twelve general staff officers during Israel's War of Independence*, three were from the Palmach: Yigal Allon, Moshe Dayan,* and Yitzhak Sadeh. Half of the colonels came from Palmach. Four of Palmach's officers, Moshe Dayan, Yitzhak Rabin, Haim Bar-Lev,* and David Elazar,* were chiefs of Staff of the Israel Defense Forces.*

In 1949, when the Haganah was transformed into the army of Israel, the Palmach was dissolved. First, Prime Minister David Ben-Gurion abolished its Southern Command. Though he had used the Palmach against the Irgun Tzvai Leumi, Ben-Gurion was concerned that the organization was too politicized and attempted to purge a number of its leaders from service. Sadeh was removed from a leadership position, though he was a brigade commander during the War of Independence. He refused to appoint Yigal Allon and Yigael Yadin* as commanders of one of the Fronts. Allon was to come back and lead the Southern Command, but he was replaced by Moshe Dayan. Allon soon resigned, and, with him, hundreds of officers resigned in protest.

The Palmach's special quality as an elite corps is still celebrated in Israel today. One of the lines of its anthem was, "We are always first (Rishonim Tamid Anahnu)." This legacy remained with the officer corps of the Israel Defense Forces as well as the daring of Palmach operations.

For further information see: Yigal Allon, *The Making of Israel's Army* (New York: Bantam Books, 1971); Moshe Pearlman, *The Army of Israel* (New York: Philosophical Library, 1950); Amos Perlmutter, *Military and Politics in Israel: Nation-Building and Role Expansion* (London: Frank Cass, 1969); Ze'ev Schiff, *A History of the Israeli Army (1870–1974)* (New York: Simon and Schuster, 1974).

Joseph E. Goldberg

PARIS PEACE CONFERENCE. At the end of World War I the victorious Allied and Associated Powers sought to negotiate a peace settlement with Germany and the Ottoman Empire* that involved the future of Middle East territories, including Palestine,* that had been under Turkish control. For President Woodrow Wilson,* the Paris Peace Conference presented an opportunity to benefit the populations of the area by enabling them to pursue self-determination through the establishment of independent states. Unlike Wilson, Lloyd George, the British prime minister, saw the Paris Peace Conference as an opportunity to advance British territorial interests through bargaining in much the same way that France's* prime minister, Georges Clemenceau, perceived his country's objectives.

Lloyd George had argued within his Cabinet that Britain's massive commit-ment of forces into the Ottoman territories entitled his country to territorial considerations. At the same time that the British prime minister attempted to increase British territorial presence in the area at the expense of French claims, it was necessary for British diplomacy to counter American anticolonial policies. This diplomatic course was followed skillfully by Lloyd George.

Lloyd George emphasized to Wilson the desire of Italy to gain Anatolia, a piece of Turkish territory to which the Italians believed they had gained claim through the Agreement of St. Jean de Maurienne (1917). When the Italian claim to Anatolia was questioned by the other Allied powers, Italian diplomats left Paris for consultations at home. Greece ultimately gained the seaport of Smyrna, which possessed a large Greek population.

The British prime minister also made sure that Wilson was aware of French designs on Syria.* The British supported Feisal's* claims to rule an independent Syria and thus ensure greater British influence in an area that France had hoped to dominate.

Because of Wilson's concern that the inhabitants in the area be treated justly, he proposed that a commission be created to survey the desires of those who lived in the area. Ultimately, neither Britain nor France would participate, and the King–Crane Commission* was totally an American inquiry.

Britain successfully manipulated the discussions in Paris so that its presence in Egypt* as a protectorate, its concerns in Persia, its control of the Gulf sheikh-doms, and its influence in Arabia came under discussion. At the San Remo Conference* in April 1920, the fruits of the negotiations received international acceptance. France was given Mandatory rights in Lebanon* and Syria and the British Mandatory rights to Palestine and Iraq.* These Mandates were later ratified by the League of Nations.

For further information see: David Fromkin. *A Peace to End All Peace: Creating the Modern Middle East, 1914–1922* (New York: Henry Holt, 1989).

Joseph E. Goldberg

PARTITION PLAN. See **PALESTINE PARTITION PLAN.**

PARTY OF GOD. See **HEZBOLLAH.**

PASSFIELD WHITE PAPER (OCTOBER 1930). The analysis and recommenda-tions of the report by Sir John Hope-Simpson* were incorporated into the Pass-field White Paper. Lord Passfield, then the colonial secretary, criticized the colonization policies and immigration practices of the Histadrut* that focused on Jewish labor. Its recommendations aroused a great furor among the Zionists.* The Cabinet of Prime Minister Ramsay MacDonald* was shaken, and the prime minister issued a letter to Chaim Weizmann* repudiating the Passfield White Paper.

PATTON TANK. See **M-48 "PATTON" TANK.**

PEACE FOR GALILEE. See **WAR IN LEBANON.**

PEACEMAKING. This term entered into Israel's Arab–Israeli conflict lexicon by Israeli prime minister Yitzhak Rabin* during his inaugural speech to the Knesset* in 1992, seeking to replace the term "peace process." It was designed as a more active concept, rather than the passive approach implied by peace process. It foreshadowed compromises and agreements.

PEACE NOW. An interest group in Israel that was founded in Jerusalem* in the spring of 1978 a few months after Egyptian president Anwar Sadat's* dramatic visit to Jerusalem. It was launched by a group of young reserve military officers who wrote to Prime Minister Menachem Begin,* urging him to vigorously pursue peace. It became a "peace" movement that has worked diligently to keep the subject on the public policy agenda with demonstrations and rallies. It has advocated territorial compromise, suggesting that Israel agree to relinquish some of the occupied territories.* It was especially prominent in protests against the War in Lebanon* and the ancillary events, such as the Sabra and Shatila* camp massacres. Among its telling incidents was the killing of one of its young activists, Emil Grunzweig, in February 1983, when a hand grenade was thrown into an antiwar demonstration in Jerusalem.

PECDAR. See **PALESTINIAN ECONOMIC COUNCIL FOR DEVELOPMENT AND RECONSTRUCTION.**

PECDR. See **PALESTINIAN ECONOMIC COUNCIL FOR DEVELOPMENT AND RECONSTRUCTION.**

PEEL COMMISSION. In November 1935, the Arabs in Palestine* petitioned the British Mandatory* authorities to halt land transfers to the Jews, to establish a form of democratic leadership, and to terminate further Jewish immigration until there was an evaluation of the absorptive capacity of the country. Their demands were denied. In April 1936, the Arab Higher Committee* called for a general strike throughout the city. The Arab Revolt* soon escalated into violence as marauding bands of Arabs attacked Jewish settlements, and Jewish paramilitary groups responded. Arab leaders in the surrounding states appealed to the committee to end the strike, offering in return their good offices to mediate with the British government. The committee called off the strike in October 1936.

The British government then appointed a six-member committee under the chairmanship of Lord Robert Peel to assess the situation in Palestine. Its objective was to determine the causes of, and to find a solution for, the Arab Revolt. It began its hearings in Jerusalem* in November 1936. Discouraged and distrustful of previous British promises, the Arabs of Palestine boycotted the hearings. They did not appear until its last week and then only because they had been persuaded by the rulers in the neighboring Arab states.

The Peel report, published as a White Paper in July 1937, opened by stating that the British gained the support of both the Arabs and Jews during World War I and, in return, made promises to each. Each party drew its own expectations from those promises.

Although the British believed that both Arabs and Jews could find a degree of compatibility under the Mandate, this belief had not been justified, nor would it be in the future. However, Britain would not renounce its obligations; it was responsible for the welfare of the Mandate and would strive to make peace.

In the light of experience and of the arguments adduced by the Commission [His Majesty's Government] are driven to the conclusions that there is an irreconcilable conflict between the aspirations of Arabs and Jews in Palestine, that these aspirations cannot be satisfied under the terms of the present Mandate, and that a scheme of partition on the general lines recommended by the Commission represents the best and most hopeful solution to the deadlock.

The commission recognized the conflict between the two national communities. There was no common ground between the Arabs and Jews, only differences of language, culture, and national aspirations. The latter was the greatest barrier to peace. Conflict was inherent from the onset and had grown steadily more bitter; the prognosis was that it would only intensify and grow worse. The commission also recognized that the conflict was primarily political, although the Arabs were concerned about their economic subjection to the Jews. Seeking a way out of the deadlock, the commission realized that there was no resolution that would give both Arabs and Jews what they wanted.

Cantonization was examined as a possible solution and found not to be viable because it would not settle the question of self-government. It would not satisfy the demands of Arab nationalism or raise the status of Palestinian Arabs to the level of the neighboring Arab states. In addition, the Jews would not have the freedom they desired to build up their National Home.

The commission suggested partition. Palestine was to be divided into three zones. The Jewish zone was to incorporate the coastal plain from the area south of Tel Aviv–Jaffa to the Lebanese* border and the complete northern fifth of Palestine, including the towns of Haifa and Nazareth as well as the Sea of Galilee.* The Arab section, about 75 percent of the total, constituted the remainder of Palestine except for a corridor that went from Tel Aviv–Jaffa to Jerusalem and Bethlehem,* which was to be under a continued British Mandate. It was recognized that partition would not be entirely acceptable to either group. However, the commission felt that each would understand the merits of dividing Palestine. The drawbacks of partition, it was believed, would be outweighed by the advantages of peace and security. Each group would have the freedom within its allotted territory to pursue its national aspirations. Southern Palestine, including the Negev* and Dead Sea,* was to be included in the Arab state, in addition to Gaza* and the West Bank.* The Galilee, Tel Aviv–Jaffa, Ramle, half of Lake Tiberias (Sea of Galilee),* and a strip of territory along the northern coastline were to be allotted to the Jewish state. There was also to be a Mandated zone consisting of the area from Tel Aviv–Jaffa to the areas surrounding Jerusalem and Bethlehem.* The protection of the holy places was to be guaranteed by the League of Nations. The Mandate should be dissolved and replaced by a treaty system identical to that of Iraq* and Syria.* Access to the holy places in Jerusalem and Bethlehem would be guaranteed to all. The national principle guiding the partition of Palestine was the separation of Jewish areas of settlement from those completely or mostly occupied by the Arabs.

The commission offered recommendations on how the partitioned states would function—from tariffs, nationality, and civil services to the exchange of land and populations.

In conclusion, the commission found it improbable that the Arabs and the Jews would find the solution satisfactory at first sight. Partition meant compromise. Neither party would achieve all that it wanted. But in the long term, partition offered each party what it wanted most—freedom and security and the prospect of peace.

The partition plan was a reversal of British policy on the Mandate and Balfour Declaration* and engendered anger and protest from both the Arabs and the Zionists.* The Arabs did not want to have to give up any land to the Jews, and the Zionists felt betrayed in their pursuit of all of Palestine as a National Home.

Britain endorsed the Peel plan. After reviewing the Peel Commission report in Geneva in July–August 1937, the Permanent Mandates Commission in Geneva objected to the partition. Most of the Zionist leaders were in favor of the formation of an independent Jewish state. Nevertheless, the Jewish Agency* accepted the plan, even though it was not happy with the exclusion of Jerusalem and the amount of territory allotted to the Jewish state. The Arabs adamantly rejected the plan, and a new and more violent phase of the Arab Revolt began.

A subsequent technical commission, the Woodhead Commission,* was appointed by the British government to work out a detailed program of partition based upon recommendations of the Peel Commission. The commission was unable to agree on a plan that would avoid leaving Arabs in the Jewish state or Jews in the Arab state.

This was the first recommendation for the partition of Palestine. The recommendation was later abandoned, but in 1939, in a new White Paper,* the British dramatically restricted Jewish immigration to Palestine.

For further information see: Great Britain, Colonial Office, *Palestine Royal Commission Report.* Cmnd. 5479. (London: H.M.S.O., July 1937); Great Britain, Parliamentary Papers, *Palestine. Statement by His Majesty's Government in the United Kingdom.* Cmd. 5893. (London: His Majesty's Stationery Office, 1938); Albert M. Hyamson, *Palestine under the Mandate* (Westport, CT: Greenwood Press, 1976).

Nancy Hasanian and Mark Daryl Erickson

PELLETREAU, ROBERT H. (b. Patchogue, New York, July 9, 1935). He earned a bachelor's degree from Yale (1957) and a law degree from Harvard (1961) and served in the Navy Reserve (1957–58). He became assistant secretary of state for Near East affairs in January 1994. Pelletreau had been ambassador of the United States to Egypt* since 1991. He joined the Foreign Service in 1962 and went to Amman as political officer in 1968. He was detailed to the Armed Forces Staff College and then served on the Morocco and Mauritania desks from 1971 to 1973.

After a tour as political officer in Algiers, Pelletreau became deputy chief of mission in Damascus in 1975. He was named ambassador to Bahrain in 1979. Next, he was deputy assistant secretary for the Near East and South Asia at the Department of Defense, 1980–81. In 1981, he became country director for Arabian peninsula affairs. He was deputy assistant secretary for Near Eastern and South Asian affairs, 1983–85. In 1985, he returned to defense as deputy assistant secretary for international security affairs. He served as ambassador to Tunisia, 1987–91. In December 1988, he was designated by Secretary of State George Shultz* to be the sole authorized channel of official dialogue with the Palestine Liberation Organization* (PLO).

PERES, SHIMON (Formerly Persky) (b. Vishneva, Poland, August 16, 1923). Because of British restrictions and the financial burdens associated with immigration, his father, Yitzhak Persky, emigrated to Palestine* in 1931, leaving his wife and two sons behind. The family was reunited in Palestine in 1934. He became involved in the largest of the movements, Hashomer Hatzair (Young Guard), and later joined Hanoar Haoved (Working Youth). By 1941, Peres was a leader in the kibbutz movement in Palestine, and he continued his efforts within Hanoar Haoved. In 1942, Peres joined Kibbutz Alumot, where he remained a member until 1957.

Peres's military career began in the Haganah.* He rose to the rank of position commander by his late teens, and in 1947 he accepted Levi Eshkol's* offer to serve as director of manpower. He was active in the procurement and manufacture of arms for the Israel Defense Forces* (IDF), where his successful efforts to develop and acquire arms both at home and abroad gained him recognition as one of the pioneers of Israel's defense industry. After Israel's War of Independence* in 1949, Peres asked Prime Minister David Ben-Gurion* for a leave of absence to study abroad. Ben-Gurion granted the leave, provided Peres continue his arms acquisition efforts in the United States, where he chose to study at Harvard University and New York University. He returned to Israel and in February 1952 was appointed deputy director general of the Defense Ministry. In October 1952, he became acting director general of the Defense Ministry. As director general of the Defense Ministry, Peres continued his efforts to acquire high-quality weapons for the IDF. Peres spent much of his time fostering Franco–Israeli relations, and France* remained Israel's primary supplier of major weapons systems until after the Six Day War* of 1967. Peres's efforts included gaining French consent to provide Israel with an atomic reactor located at Dimona. Peres was instrumental in the creation of Bedek, which later came to be known as the Israel Aircraft Industries (IAI).

Peres's Knesset* career began in 1959, when he was elected to Parliament as a member of the MAPAI* Party, although he continued to serve as deputy minister of defense. Peres was included in Ben-Gurion's Cabinet, which gave him a larger role in policy debates. In 1963, David Ben-Gurion resigned and was replaced by Levi Eshkol* as prime minister and minister of defense. Ben-Gurion's retirement from politics lasted only two years before he returned to the political arena in June 1965 as the leader of a new political party called RAFI. Peres resigned his position in the government to join Ben-Gurion and become secretary-general of the new party. He managed the party's campaign efforts in the 1965 election, in which it won ten seats. But the government did not include Rafi or any of its members. In 1968, Rafi joined with MAPAI and Ahdut Haavoda to form the Israel Labor Party.* Between 1969 and 1973, Peres held a variety of Cabinet posts, including minister of absorption, minister of transport, minister of information, minister of communications, and minister without portfolio, with responsibility for economic development in the occupied territories.* In April 1974, Golda Meir* submitted her resignation as prime minister. The two candidates who emerged to replace her were Peres, who was serving as minister of information, and Yitzhak Rabin,* minister of labor. Rabin was the preferred choice of the party establishment. Rabin won a close vote over Peres in the Labor Party's Central Committee, but Peres's performance established him as the number two man in the party. The new government was established in June 1974, with Rabin as prime minister and Peres as minister of defense. Relations between Peres and Rabin were strained during the term of the government. Disputes arose over domestic and foreign policy, the selection of personnel, and the scope of their authority. Peres formally announced his intention to challenge Rabin for the party leadership in January 1977. The showdown took place at the Labor Party convention the following month, where Rabin prevailed by a slim majority. However, a series of scandals, including the disclosure that Rabin's wife maintained bank accounts in the United States in violation of Israeli currency laws, led Rabin to resign from the chairmanship of the Labor Party in April 1977, just one month prior to the Knesset elections. Peres became the party's new leader and candidate for the premiership. Despite Peres's efforts, a non-Labor-led government won a plurality of Knesset seats and succeeded in forming the government. In June 1977, Peres was elected Labor Party chairman. The 1981 election was Peres's second loss to Menachem Begin.* In the 1984 election, Labor secured forty-four seats to Likud's* forty-one, and, although he received the mandate to form the government, Peres was unable to form a majority coalition. This led to the formation of a National Unity Government (NUG),* which was a new experiment in Israeli politics. A rotation agreement was adopted that called for Peres to serve as prime minister for the first half of the fifty-month term while Yitzhak Shamir* served as foreign minister. After twenty-five months the two rotated positions for the balance of the term. During his tenure as prime minister, Peres presided over Israel's withdrawal from Lebanon* and confronted the economic problems with austerity measures. He conducted an active foreign policy. Among Peres's successes was a summit meeting with King Hassan* of Morocco in July 1986. Israel's special relationship with the United States improved considerably during Peres's tenure, which was a change from the tension that frequently characterized relations during Begin's and Shamir's tenures in office. The 1988 Knesset election, as in 1984, did not produce a clear victory for either Labor or Likud. Shamir was given the mandate to form a coalition by President Chaim Herzog. The central difference between the 1988 coalition agreement and the 1984 agreement was that Shamir would serve as prime minister for the duration of the government. Peres accepted the position of finance minister. Peres failed to maintain control of leadership of the Labor Party in 1992, losing in an internal election to Yitzhak Rabin. When Rabin succeeded in becoming prime minister as a result of the 1992 Knesset elections, he brought Peres into the Cabinet as foreign minister, where he has represented Israel in negotiations with the Palestine Liberation Organization* (PLO). Peres was the senior figure involved in the Oslo negotiations* with the PLO leading to the Declaration of Principles* (DOP). In 1994, he received the Nobel Peace Prize,* along with Yitzhak Rabin and Yasser Arafat, for his efforts in connection with the DOP. After Yitzhak Rabin's assassination in November 1995, Peres became prime minister and minister of defense.

Peres has written *David's Sling: The Arming of Israel* (New York: Random House, 1970); *From These Men: Seven Founders of the State of Israel,* translated by Philip Simpson (New York: Wyndham Books, 1979); with Arye Naor, *The New Middle East* (New York: Henry Holt, 1993); and *Battling for Peace: A Memoir From Israel's Birth To Today's Struggle for Peace In the Middle East* (New York: Random House, 1995).

For further information see: Matti Golan, *Shimon Peres: A Biography,* trans. Ina Friedman (New York: St. Martin's Press, 1982); Joseph Helman, "Shimon Peres," in Bernard Reich, ed., *Political Leaders of the Contemporary Middle East and North Africa: A Biographical Dictionary* (Westport, CT: Greenwood Press, 1990), pp. 403–12; Bernard Reich and Gershon R. Kieval, eds., *Israel Faces the Future* (New York: Praeger, 1986); Bernard Reich and Gershon R. Kieval, eds., *Israeli National Security Policy: Political Actors and Perspectives* (New York: Greenwood Press, 1988).

PERES–HASSAN SUMMIT (1986). See **HASSAN–PERES SUMMIT.**

PHANTOM F-4 JET AIRCRAFT. See **F-4 PHANTOM AIRCRAFT.**

PHASED PLAN. After the Arab military failure in the Yom Kippur War,* the Palestine Liberation Organization* (PLO) adopted, in June 1974, in Cairo, Egypt,* a two-step or two-stage program to restore the Palestinians to Palestine.* The first step was to create a Palestinian state in any territory vacated by Israel. The second step was to launch a military assault from that state against Israel.

Although formally adopted, there was often contention within PLO ranks concerning this approach. The full text of the political program adopted read:

The Palestinian National Council:

On the basis of the Palestinian National Charter and the Political Programme drawn up at the eleventh session, held from January 6–12, 1973; and from its belief that it is impossible for a permanent and just peace to be established in the area unless our Palestinian people recover all their national rights and, first and foremost, their rights to return and to self-determination on the whole of the soil of their homeland; and in the light of a study of the new political circumstances that have come into existence in the period between the Council's last and present sessions, resolves the following:

1. To reaffirm the Palestine Liberation Organization's previous attitude to Resolution 242,* which obliterates the national right of our people and deals with the cause of our people as a problem of refugees. The Council therefore refuses to have anything to do with this resolution at any level, Arab or international, including the Geneva Conference.*

2. The Liberation Organization will employ all means, and first and foremost armed struggle, to liberate Palestinian territory and to establish the independent combatant national authority for the people over every part of Palestinian territory that is liberated. This will require further changes being effected in the balance of power in favour of our people and their struggle.

3. The Liberation Organization will struggle against any proposal for a Palestinian entity the price of which is recognition, peace, secure frontiers, renunciation of national rights and the deprival of our people of their right to return and their right to self-determination on the soil of their homeland.

4. Any step taken towards liberation is a step towards the realization of the Liberation Organization's strategy of establishing the democratic Palestinian state specified in the resolutions of previous Palestinian National Councils.

5. Struggle along with the Jordanian national forces to establish a Jordanian*–Palestinian national front whose aim will be to set up in Jordan a democratic national authority in close contact with the Palestinian entity that is established through the struggle.

6. The Liberation Organization will struggle to establish unity in struggle between the two peoples and between all the forces of the Arab liberation movement that are in agreement on this programme.

7. In the light of this programme, the Liberation Organization will struggle to strengthen national unity and to raise it to the level where it will be able to perform its national duties and tasks.

8. Once it is established, the Palestinian national authority will strive to achieve a union of the confrontation countries, with the aim of completing the liberation of all Palestinian territory, and as a step along the road to comprehensive Arab unity.

9. The Liberation Organization will strive to strengthen its solidarity with the socialist countries, and with forces of liberation and progress throughout the world, with the aim of frustrating all the schemes of Zionism, reaction and imperialism.

10. In light of this programme, the leadership of the revolution will determine the tactics
    which will serve and make possible the realization of these objectives.

The Executive Committee of the Palestine Liberation Organization will make every
effort to implement this programme, and should a situation arise affecting the destiny
and the future of the Palestinian people, the National Assembly will be convened in
extraordinary session.

PICOT, FRANCOIS GEORGES. A French diplomat primarily remembered for
his negotiation of the Sykes–Picot Agreement.* Picot was a French colonialist
who pursued a campaign at the time of World War I to have France* seek
control over Greater Syria,* "la Syrie intégrale," which included Palestine* and
Jerusalem.* He believed it was one country that France had shaped and that it
was incumbent on France to continue its historical mission there. He also believed that the area was a wealthy one.

He was posted to the French Embassy in London in August 1915 and im-
pressed the ambassador, August Cambon, and was recommended by him to
negotiate with the British to arrange a partition of the Middle East. The first
round of negotiations with the British began on November 23, 1915. Eventually,
Picot and Sykes negotiated the agreement that bears their names. Palestine became a problem, as both sides demanded control of all of it.

For further information see: Christopher M. Andrew and A. S. Kanya-Forstner, *France
Overseas: The Great War and the Climax of French Imperial Expansion* (London:
Thames and Hudson, 1981); David Fromkin, *A Peace to End All Peace: Creating the
Modern Middle East, 1914–1922* (New York: Henry Holt, 1989).

Richard G. R. Schickele

PISGA. See INTERIM SELF-GOVERNMENT ARRANGEMENTS.

PLAN DALET (Plan D). In December 1947, David Ben-Gurion* called for an
aggressive policy in the developing conflict in Palestine.* The nucleus of Plan
Dalet was prepared by Yigael Yadin* in 1944, when he was in charge of planning for the underground. It called for taking control of the key points in the
country and on roads prior to the British departure from Palestine. Key targets
of Plan D were the main Arab villages, in particular, the approximately twenty
Arab villages lying in the corridor between Jerusalem* and Tel Aviv.

Plan Dalet (Plan D) was the master plan for military operations under which
the Zionists* launched successive offensives in April and early May 1948 in
various parts of Palestine. The principal aims of the plan were to enlarge the
Jewish state and to ultimately achieve the military fait accompli upon which the
state of Israel was to be based.

The plan was based on several basic assumptions about the enemy regarding
the composition of forces (the forces of the Arab League* as well as small local
forces operating from "within the borders of the Hebrew state"), actual oper-

ations expected from the enemy, and expected tactical methods. Implementation of the plan would not commence while the British forces (or any international forces) were present in the country.

Provisions were made for defense systems and deployment of armed forces in the major cities and strengthening the defense system in rural areas. Due to the geographical location of settlements, they were organized into local defensive zones. In addition, the main enemy transportation routes would be blocked by any means, for example, acts of sabotage, explosions.

To make the system effective, Zionist forces had to take control of the police stations and government installations and protect secondary transportation arteries.

Operations would be mounted against enemy population centers to prevent their use as bases for the Arab active armed force. These villages were to be destroyed—"setting fire to, blowing up, and planting mines in the debris." If resistance was encountered, the enemy armed forces were to be destroyed, and the population was to be expelled outside the borders of the state. At this point, the villages would be included in the defense system and fortified "as necessary."

The plan included guidelines for enemy cities that were to be besieged. These cities would be isolated from transportation arteries, for example, by laying mines. Vital services, such as electricity and water, would be disrupted. A naval operation against cities capable of receiving supplies by sea would interrupt that capability and would be accomplished by destroying the vessels or carrying out acts of sabotage against the harbor facilities.

Once the targeted cities and villages were contained and controlled, they were to be secured under the guidelines of "counterattacks." Counterattacks were detailed in the list of operational targets of the Strategic Mobile Force (Palmach*).

Plan Dalet is significant because it enabled the Zionists to establish a strong defense perimeter around the land they already occupied and to expand their control over Arab lands (cities, villages), allowing for some depth of security. It also enabled them to establish their claim to land/territory, one of the main prerequisites for statehood.

For further information see: Walid Khalidi, "Plan Dalet: Master Plan for the Conquest of Palestine," *Journal of Palestine Studies* 18 (Autumn 1988):4–70.

Nancy Hasanian

PLAN GIMMEL—PLAN C. "Plan Gimmel" or "Plan C" was the first part of a two-phased strategy developed by the Zionist* leaders to establish a Jewish state in Palestine.* Implemented in May 1946, Plan C contained a detailed series of steps that required collaboration of the Irgun,* the Haganah,* and the Palmach.* These steps would be effected to keep constant pressure on the Palestinian Arabs in every part of Palestine while maintaining contact with the Jewish settlements in the area of the proposed Arab state.

Plan C called for counterattacks and immediate retaliations. The goal was to strike at each source at the beginning of the Arab outbreak so as to deter the instigators from future incidents and to prevent the participation and support of the Arab masses. Retaliatory operations not only targeted the executors of the specific action but also aimed at other active groups or those providing assistance. These counterattacks were to be recounted in complete detail to the Arabs, using all available means of communication.

Counterattacks, whenever possible, would be directed at the Arab rear to undermine the Arab sense of security and would target the Arab political leadership; executors of operations and those who provided shelter to them; high-ranking Arab officers and officials; and villages, neighborhoods, and farms used as a base of operations. There would be two types of counterattacks. The warning operations would come in response to small-scale Arab operations. In this instance, the counterattack would be executed in the particular area in which the Arabs were active—also accompanied by media coverage. The aim of strike operations was to punish those carrying out operations against the Zionists.* The retaliatory strikes were to be more extensive in nature and on a broader level: they would be directed on a regional or countrywide level, the goal being severe punishment.

Plan C is explicit in the aims of these retaliatory strikes against the targets. Each target is individually itemized, with basically the same aims: doing damage to the property; imprisoning members as hostages or to prevent them from performing their activities; and expelling them or physically harming them in some other way.

PLO. See **PALESTINE LIBERATION ORGANIZATION.**

PLO–ISRAEL AGREEMENTS. See **CAIRO AGREEMENT (1994); DECLA-RATION OF PRINCIPLES; EARLY EMPOWERMENT; ISRAEL–PLO ECONOMIC AGREEMENT (1994); SAFE PASSAGE ROUTE.**

PNC. See **PALESTINE NATIONAL COUNCIL.**

PNC, ALGIERS 1988. See **PALESTINE NATIONAL COUNCIL, ALGIERS, NOVEMBER 1988.**

POLITICAL SETTLEMENTS. After again becoming prime minister in 1992, Yitzhak Rabin* distinguished between what he called "political" settlements and others. He based his policy on changed priorities for Israel and therefore did not want to invest government funds in political settlements. He distinguished between those along the lines of confrontation and those in the center of the populated Palestinian areas. Those in the populated areas, the political settlements, did not, in his view, contribute to the security of Israel, and therefore he wanted to stop government money for them. See also SETTLEMENTS.

POLITICAL ZIONISM. Political Zionism is the national movement of the Jewish people that led to the creation of the State of Israel. Theodor Herzl,* who is considered the father of this movement, established the concept of politicizing Jewish efforts to solve the Jewish problem. Herzl was disillusioned by the increasing anti-Semitism in Europe. The Dreyfus affair* in France,* which occurred in 1894, shocked Herzl into believing that the Jews would never be accepted as full citizens in Europe. As Herzl became increasingly aware of the pogroms in Russia, in addition to the Jewish plight in Eastern and Western Europe, he concluded that the only solution to the Jewish problem would be the creation of a separate nation of their own.

Herzl turned Zionism into a political movement. Political Zionism was a response to European civilization and nationalism. In his book, *Der Judenstaat* (*The Jewish State**), first published in 1896, the foundation of Political Zionism was established. Herzl noted that the Jewish Question* was not based on religion; rather, it was a national question. In order to solve the question, the Jews needed to establish their problem as an international political problem to be dealt with and solved by the international community.

The plan of Political Zionism was to establish Jewish sovereignty over a specific territory and allow for the gradual emigration of Jews from Europe to that territory. At first, Herzl was not concerned with where the territory was. However, realizing that the basics of Zionism were rooted in Palestine,* he noted there was more of a likelihood of getting Jews to support returning to the Holy Land* than to another region. Political Zionist values did not demonstrate a preference of territories; it was merely to provide a basis for solving the Jewish Question.

In his book, Herzl suggested that two agencies be created. The first would be the Society of Jews, and it would undertake political negotiations and deal with governments regarding the future Jewish state. In addition, it would investigate land and planning developments and pursue the acquisition of a charter over a specific piece of territory. The second agency would be the Jewish Company, which would be in charge of financial aspects of the entire plan, such as constructing buildings, organizing labor, liquidating emigrants' assets in Europe, and purchasing land in the chosen area. Herzl maintained that the land had to belong to the Jews before they emigrated.

Many Jews questioned Herzl's plan. However, Jewish immigrants who later arrived in Palestine and settled in agricultural colonies often were motivated by political Zionism. Political Zionism was regarded with fear and suspicion by the local Arab inhabitants in Palestine. Arab fear continued to increase after the Second Aliya,* which took place in 1903. This led to the clash between two nationalisms, Arab nationalism and political Zionism/Jewish nationalism. It was here that a foundation for the modern Arab–Israeli conflict was laid.

For further information see: Israel Cohen, *Theodor Herzl: Founder of Political Zionism* (New York: Thomas Yoseloff, 1959); Arthur Hertzberg, ed., *The Zionist Idea: A Historical Analysis and Reader* (Garden City, NY: Doubleday, 1959).

Susan L. Rosenstein

"POLITICIDE." A term coined to describe the destruction of a state, particularly the Arab goal of destroying Israel. Between 1949 and 1967, Israel was prepared for peace with the Arab states on the basis of the 1949 armistice* lines, with minor modifications, but after the events of May and June 1967, including the Six Day War,* the stark reality of "politicide" began to enter into these considerations, and many argued for a need to change the security situation.

POPULAR DEMOCRATIC FRONT FOR THE LIBERATION OF PALESTINE (PDFLP). This organization was established out of a leftist breakaway from the Popular Front for the Liberation of Palestine* (PFLP) in February 1969. It changed its name to Democratic Front for the Liberation of Palestine (DFLP) in August 1974. It proclaims itself to be Marxist–Leninist in nature. Its main leaders are Nayef Hawatmeh* and Yasser Abed-Rabbo.*

POPULAR FRONT FOR THE LIBERATION OF PALESTINE (PFLP). The PFLP emerged from the Arab National Movement (ANM), an organization set up in the 1950s. The PFLP was founded in December 1967 by George Habash,* and it stressed a people's war but also the Arab dimension of the struggle. It pushed the Palestine Liberation Organization* (PLO) into confrontation with Jordan* in 1970.

It has been Fatah's* major rival and has opposed it on many issues, including the attitude toward Arab regimes and the need for political and diplomatic action. In 1974, the PFLP set up the rejection front that attempted to oppose the PLO's participation in any negotiated settlement. The PFLP rejoined the Executive Committee of the PLO in 1981.

It has established its reputation through actions outside the occupied territories,* especially aircraft hijackings, but suspended this type of action in 1972. Wadi Haddad* was its primary terrorist planner in the 1970s until his death in 1977.

The PFLP is one of the many armed factions of Palestinian guerrillas and is technically a branch of the PLO, though on a number of occasions both the PFLP and the PLO have disassociated themselves from each other.

The PFLP is a Marxist–Leninist group. Essentially, it is a group of Palestinian intellectuals who discovered the views of Marx and Lenin at a time of desperation. It was, however, not easy to convince the Palestinian masses that this version of Communism as a political ideology would be the best tool with which to fight Israel. The PFLP secured financial, military, and other forms of support from the USSR and the Communist bloc.

Habash led the PFLP to what he believed was operationally the best anti-Israel group ever assembled. His operational commander, Dr. Wadi Haddad, was known for his bloody, but often innovative, attacks on Israel and on Western targets. He and Habash believed that anything related to Israel or its allies was a legitimate target for terrorism.

The PFLP feels it is the true representation of the majority of Palestinians* and generally believes that the PLO and Yasser Arafat* are too moderate and concede too many points to Israel. This has been the primary reason for tension between the two groups. Furthermore, Habash has often felt that he should be the natural leader of the PLO, since he believes he is a more aggressive negotiator and could best address the needs of the Palestinians when it comes to the question of Israel.

Since the early days of the group, the PFLP followed the Pan-Arab view that President Gamal Abdul Nasser* of Egypt* had instilled in much of the Arab populus. This was the view that Arabs should be fighting together against Israel, rather than against each other. Religion should not be a factor in the war for Palestinian liberation. The PFLP believed that inter-Arab strength would complete the slogan of Habash's view of Pan-Arabism, which was unity, liberty, and revenge. The revenge would be achieved, as far as the PFLP was concerned, only when Israel was completely annihilated.

This group has split several times into splinter groups, each faction claiming to be closer to the original calling of the PFLP. There was the Popular Democratic Front for the Liberation of Palestine* (PDFLP), led by Nayef Hawatmeh.* There was the break into the Popular Front for the Liberation of Palestine—General Command* (PFLP—GC), which was a move supported fully by the government of Syria,* led by Ahmed Jibril.* The Popular Revolutionary Front for the Liberation of Palestine* (PRFLP), led by Abu Shihab, split away in 1972. In 1974, the PFLP joined with the PFLP—GC, the Arab Liberation Front (ALF), and the FPPS to form the Rejection Front—a group of Palestinian guerrillas determined to effectively counter Yasser Arafat as the leader of the PLO.

The PFLP was especially active between 1968 and 1972, hijacking and blowing up commercial jet airliners, shooting at airliners on the runways, taking hostages, killing innocent civilians by the score, and arranging for other groups to act for them (such as the Japanese Red Army's attack on Lod International Airport in 1972). One of the field commanders was Captain Kamal Rafat, who led several of the attacks and was eventually killed by Israeli commandos inside a Sabena airliner that he hijacked with three other terrorists in May 1972. This episode was the culmination of years of operational experience by the PFLP.

The PFLP was outlawed in Egypt in 1974, and many of the members were on the run in other Arab states that same year for having tried to overthrow governments or to assassinate their leaders.

In later years, especially 1983–87, the PFLP broke from the PLO, feeling that Arafat was giving away the Palestinian position to a strong Israel, and not until late 1987, when the *intifada** began, did Habash decide that it would serve his purposes to back up the Palestine Liberation Organization. Nevertheless, the PLO and the PFLP maintain a relation of cautious observation, not getting too close to one another, for fear that too close an alliance might shift the power of their counterpart too far ahead in the popularity contest of the Palestinian-Arabs who support either of the two groups.

For further information see: M. H. Greenberg and A. R. Norton, eds., *The International Relations of the Palestine Liberation Organization* (Carbondale: Southern Illinois

University Press, 1989); David Halevy and Neil C. Livingstone, *Inside the PLO: Covert Units, Secret Funds, and the War against Israel and the United States* (New York: William Morrow, 1990); Raphael Israeli, ed., *PLO in Lebanon Selected Documents* (London: Weidenfeld and Nicolson, 1983); Kemal Kirisci, *The PLO and World Politics: A Study of the Mobilization of Support for the Palestinian Cause* (London: Frances Printers, 1986); A. Yodfat and A. Yuval, *The PLO: Strategy and Tactics* (New York: St. Martin's Press, 1981).

Karin J. England and Yasha Manuel Harari

POPULAR FRONT FOR THE LIBERATION OF PALESTINE—GENERAL COMMAND (PFLP—GC). A small group founded by Ahmed Jibril* that left the Popular Front for the Liberation of Palestine* (PFLP) in 1968, claiming that it wanted to focus more on fighting and less on politics. It is opposed to Arafat's* Palestine Liberation Organization* (PLO). Led by Ahmed Jibril, a former captain in the Syrian army, it is closely linked to Syria* and has carried out numerous cross-border terrorist attacks into Israel. It has been headquartered in Damascus.

POPULAR FRONT FOR THE LIBERATION OF PALESTINE—SPECIAL COMMAND (PFLP—SC). A Marxist–Leninist group formed by Abu Salim in 1979 after breaking away from the Popular Front for the Liberation of Palestine (PFLP)—Special Operations Group. It operates out of southern Lebanon and has received both financial and military support from Syria* and Lebanon.*

POPULAR STRUGGLE FRONT (PSF). A radical Marxist Palestinian terrorist group once closely involved in the Syrian-dominated Palestinian National Salvation Front. Led by Dr. Samir Ghosheh, it rejoined the Palestine Liberation Organization* (PLO) in September 1991. It has been involved in terrorist attacks against Israeli, Arab, and PLO targets. The PSF has received most of its aid from Syria,* though both Iraq* and Libya have also provided assistance.

PRINCIPLES OF PEACE. See **JOHNSON'S FIVE PRINCIPLES OF PEACE.**

PROMISED LAND. Term for the Land of Israel, which was promised to Abraham by God in the Bible. Abraham is told by God to leave Mesopotamia for the Land of Canaan, and, when he enters the land, God promises him, in Genesis 12:7, that "unto thy seed will I give this land." Upon the basis of this divine promise, the Jews are brought out of bondage in Egypt* to inherit the land that God promised them. The frontiers of the Promised Land are outlined in Genesis 15:18–19, where it is stated that the area from the Euphrates River to the river of Egypt, the Shihor, not the Nile, constitutes the land promised to the Jewish people.

Jewish settlement in the land of Israel has continued uninterrupted since the days of Joshua. Despite the destruction of the First and Second Temples* and the exile of the Jewish people from the land, some Jews always remained, and those that did not nevertheless continued to retain a strong emotional and religious attachment to the land.

Jewish tradition emphasizes the inherent sanctity of the land above all other places. The Promised Land remains central in the prayers and customs of Jewish tradition. Jews pray in the direction of Jerusalem,* and their holidays are celebrated throughout the world in conjunction with the agricultural seasons of the Land of Israel.

David Salzberg

PROXIMITY TALKS. Within two weeks after U.S. secretary of state William P. Rogers's* October 4, 1971, speech at the United Nations, the State Department outlined a framework for pursuing the interim agreement for opening the Suez Canal* in an effort to go beyond the cease-fire between Israel and Egypt* of August 1970. The parts of the speech pertaining to the Middle East came to be known as Rogers Plan C,* or the Six-Point Plan, while the framework of negotiation became known as the proximity talks. Similar to the Rhodes* talks, a delegation from Egypt, along with a delegation from Israel, would convene in a New York hotel while a U.S. mediator, Assistant Secretary of State for Near East and South Asian Affairs Joseph Sisco,* would shuttle between their rooms in pursuit of an agreement.

The effort to initiate proximity talks lasted well over a year. On February 2, 1972, Israel, after initial refusal, agreed to the U.S.-sponsored talks, but Egypt, preferring the United Nations-sponsored Jarring mission* as a venue, refused to consent. On February 23, 1973, Hafez Ismail,* Egyptian president Anwar Sadat's* national security adviser, during a visit to Washington, officially declined Egyptian participation in the proposed proximity talks. Although the State Department pursued participation in the talks until the fall of 1973, they never came to fruition.

For further information see: Michael Brecher, *Decisions in Israel's Foreign Policy* (New Haven, CT: Yale University Press, 1975); Henry Kissinger, *White House Years* (Boston: Little, Brown, 1979); William B. Quandt, *Decade of Decisions: American Policy toward the Arab–Israeli Conflict, 1967–1976* (Berkeley: University of California Press, 1977); Bernard Reich, *Quest for Peace: United States–Israel Relations and the Arab–Israeli Conflict* (New Brunswick, NJ: Transaction Books, 1977).

Noah Dropkin

PUBLIC RESOLUTION NO. 73, 67TH CONGRESS, SECOND SESSION, SEPTEMBER 21, 1922.

Resolved by the Senate and House of Representatives of the United States of America in Congress Assembled. That the United States of America favors the establishment in Palestine* of a national home* for the Jewish people, it being clearly understood that nothing shall be done which may prejudice the civil and religious rights of Christian and all other non-Jewish communities in Palestine, and that the holy places and religious buildings and sites in Palestine shall be adequately protected.

PURPLE LINE. An irregular north–south line on the eastern boundary of the Golan Heights* established as the cease-fire line after the Six Day War.* It became known as the purple line between Israel and Syria* because this was the color used to denote the line on United Nations Truce Supervision Organization* (UNTSO) maps.

For further information see: T. N. Dupuy, *Elusive Victory—The Arab–Israeli Wars 1947–74,* 3d ed. (Dubuque, IA: Kendall/Hunt, 1992).

Pamela Rivers

Q

AL-QASSIM, SHEIKH IZZED DIN. Sheikh Izzed Din al-Qassim was an organizer of Arab resistance to British occupation and Zionist* settlement during the Mandate.* He was an Arab nationalist, Syrian* by birth. He studied at Al-Azhar University in Cairo under Mohammed Abdu and later taught at Ibrahim bin Adham University in Damascus. There he was active in uprisings against French* occupation until he fled to Haifa in 1922. In Haifa he attracted a number of followers, with perhaps as many as 200 volunteering for guerrilla action against the British. He and his followers hid in the caves near Ya'id and began raiding Jewish settlements.

In November 1936, the British Palestine police discovered and engaged his irregulars, soundly defeating them. Al-Qassim and two of aides were among the dead. His funeral in Haifa was the cause of large-scale rioting.

For further information see: David Hirst, *The Gun and the Olive Branch: The Roots of Violence in the Middle East* (New York: Harcourt Brace Jovanovich, 1977).

John Fontaine

QASSIM BRIGADES. See HAMAS.

QERIA, AHMED SULEIMAN. See AHMED SULEIMAN KARIA.

QIBYA. See KIBYA.

AL-QUDS. See JERUSALEM.

QUNAITRA. See KUNEITRA.

R

RABAT SUMMIT (1974). At the Arab Summit conference in Rabat, Morocco, in October 1974, the representatives unanimously passed a resolution whereby the Palestine Liberation Organization* (PLO) was recognized "as the sole, legitimate representative of the Palestinian people." This not only was a reaffirmation of the 1973 Algiers Arab Summit, which declared the PLO to be "the sole representative of the Palestinian nation," but provided further delineation of PLO authority. In 1973, King Hussein* of Jordan* objected to the naming of the PLO as the sole representative of the Palestinian people, which weakened his claim to the West Bank,* a territory Jordan considered an integral part of the Hashemite Kingdom. In 1974, the king appeared to alter his position when he joined his fellow delegates in accepting the PLO's claim to negotiate for the West Bank.

The Rabat Summit further affirmed the right of the Palestinians to return to their homeland and self-determination. Additionally, all Arab states pledged to "preserve Palestinian unity and not to interfere in Palestinian internal affairs."

The Rabat declaration solidified the PLO's role as the representative of the Palestinian people.

Its adoption clouded the prospects for Arab–Israeli negotiations, since Israel had declared it would not negotiate with the PLO, and the PLO had consistently refused to recognize Israel's right to exist. It also raised doubts about the viability of Henry Kissinger's* step-by-step* approach.

The resolution adopted on October 28, 1974, reads:

The conference of the Arab Heads of State: 1. Affirms the right of the Palestinian people to return to their homeland and to self-determination. 2. Affirms the right of the Palestinian people to establish an independent national authority, under the leadership of the

PLO in its capacity as the sole legitimate representative of the Palestinian people, over all liberated territory. The Arab States are pledged to uphold this authority, when it is established, in all spheres and at all levels. 3. Supports the PLO in the exercise of its national and international responsibilities, within the context of the principle of Arab solidarity. 4. Invites the Kingdom of Jordan, Syria* and Egypt* to formalize their relations in the light of these decisions and in order that they may be implemented. 5. Affirms the obligation of all Arab States to preserve Palestinian unity and not to interfere in Palestinian internal affairs.

For further information see: Jamal R. Nassar, *The Palestine Liberation Organization: From Armed Struggle to the Declaration of Independence* (New York: Praeger, 1991); Richard H. Ullman, "After Rabat: Middle East Risks and American Roles," *Foreign Affairs* 53 (January 1975):284–96.

Pamela Rivers

RABIN, YITZHAK (b. Jerusalem,* March 1, 1922; d. Tel Aviv, November 4, 1995). His parents were Russian immigrants to Palestine.* He entered the prestigious Kadourie Agricultural School in the Galilee in 1937 and, after graduation in 1940, moved to Kibbutz Ramat Yohanan. Rabin joined the Haganah* in May 1941 and subsequently served in the Palmach.* Later, he was arrested in a massive sweep by British Mandatory* authorities and spent a brief period in a British prison. In October 1947, he was appointed deputy commander of the Palmach. A month before Israel declared its independence, he was put in charge of the Palmach's Harel Brigade and was assigned the task of eliminating Arab strongholds along the Tel Aviv–Jerusalem Road. Rabin's military career included a variety of positions in the Israel Defense Forces* (IDF) during Israel's formative years, including head of the army's tactical operations division from 1950 to 1952, head of the training branch from 1954 to 1956, and commanding officer of the Northern Command from 1956 to 1959. He was then appointed army chief of operations and came into conflict with then deputy defense minister Shimon Peres* over the question of who should determine the priorities in the acquisition and manufacture of arms. Rabin believed that the decision should be made by professional soldiers rather than by civilians in the defense ministry. It developed into a bitter personal feud. Rabin was appointed chief of staff of the IDF in January 1964 and during his tenure focused on the restructuring of the army and on acquiring more advanced weaponry. In the Six Day War* the Israel Defense Forces won a decisive victory over its Arab adversaries, radically transforming the situation in the Middle East. In February 1968, he became Israel's ambassador to the United States and, in March 1973, returned to Israel. After the Knesset* election of December 1973, he was invited by Golda Meir* to join the new Cabinet as defense minister following Moshe Dayan's* refusal to serve in the new government. When Dayan suddenly announced his willingness to join, Rabin became minister of labor. Upon the resignation of Golda Meir following publication of the Agranat Commission's* interim report, Rabin was chosen by the Labor Party* Central Committee, on April 22, 1974, to succeed Golda Meir as prime minister. Peres's strong showing in the vote earned him the post of defense minister, from which he tried to undermine Rabin's authority at almost every turn in the hope of replacing him.

Rabin served as prime minister from June 1974 to May 1977, during which time he concentrated on rebuilding the IDF, to which the successful raid at Entebbe Airport* contributed by restoring the army's and nation's self-confidence. He also successfully negotiated a second disengagement of forces agreement with Egypt* brokered by Henry Kissinger.* Rabin's term as prime minister ended prematurely in 1977 after a Cabinet dispute led to the scheduling of early elections. A month before the election, Rabin was forced to step down after admitting that he and his wife had maintained an illegal bank account in the United States. Peres was designated to head the Labor Party list in the election, but Labor was defeated at the polls. For the next four years, Rabin found himself in Peres's political shadow, and the relationship between the two was highly contentious. Rabin challenged Peres for the party's leadership at its national convention in December 1980 but lost. In 1984, Rabin became minister of defense in the National Unity government* that was formed following the July 1984 election and remained in that position under both Shimon Peres and Yitzhak Shamir.* He once again became minister of defense in the government established in December 1988.

In 1992, Rabin successfully challenged Peres for the leadership of the Labor Party. Labor's victory in the 1992 elections led to the creation of a Labor-dominated government under Rabin as both prime minister and minister of defense.

Rabin launched a new approach to foreign and security policy, emphasizing efforts to achieve negotiations and peace with Israel's neighbors, utilizing the bilateral and multilateral negotiations* tracks established at the Madrid Conference.* But he also pursued a secret channel of negotiations with the Palestine Liberation Organization* (PLO) in Oslo, Norway,* that led to the signing of the Declaration of Principles* (DOP) with the PLO in Washington in September 1993, followed by the Cairo Agreement* and other accords to implement the DOP and establish a Palestinian Authority* in the Gaza Strip* and Jericho.* Rabin recognized the PLO as the legitimate representative of the Palestinians and set in motion a wide range of contacts and negotiations between Israel and the PLO. He also met at the Summit with King Hussein* of Jordan.* They issued a Washington Declaration* in July 1994 and later signed an Israel–Jordan Peace Treaty* in October 1994 that ended the state of war between the two neighbors and began the process toward normalization of relations. During this period he also restored the positive aura of the United States–Israel relationship that had deteriorated during the tenures of George Bush* and Yitzhak Shamir.* In 1994, he received the Nobel Peace Prize,* along with Shimon Peres and Yasser Arafat,* for his efforts in connection with the promotion of peace in the Arab–Israeli conflict and the signing of the DOP. Rabin was assassinated in Tel Aviv on November 4, 1995, by Yigal Amir as he was leaving a rally supporting the Arab-Israeli peace process. Shimon Peres replaced him as Prime Minister and Minister of Defense.

Rabin wrote *The Rabin Memoirs* (Boston: Little, Brown, 1979).

For further information see: Gershon R. Kieval, *Party Politics in Israel and the Occupied Territories* (Westport, CT: Greenwood Press, 1983); Gershon R. Kieval, "Yitzhak Rabin," in Bernard Reich, ed., *Political Leaders of the Contemporary Middle East and North Africa: A Biographical Dictionary* (Westport, CT: Greenwood Press, 1990), pp. 441–48; Robert Slater, *Rabin of Israel: A Biography* (London: Robson Books, 1977).

RABINOVICH, ITAMAR (b. Jerusalem,* 1942). He became head of Israel's delegation to the peace talks with Syria* in Washington in August 1992 and ambassador to the United States in February 1993.

Rabinovich graduated from Hebrew University in 1963 and served in the Israel Defense Forces* (IDF) from 1963 to 1969. He received an M.A. degree from Tel Aviv University and received a Ph.D. in Middle Eastern history from the University of California at Los Angeles (UCLA) in 1971. He joined the faculty of Tel Aviv University in 1971, where he served in a number of positions.

RADIO EL-QUDS. A radio station operated from Syrian* territory by Ahmed Jibril* and devoted to propaganda condemning the Israel–Palestine Liberation Organization* (PLO) peace process and the Palestinian Authority.*

RAMADAN WAR. See **YOM KIPPUR WAR.**

REAGAN, RONALD WILSON (b. Tampico, Illinois, February 6, 1911). He graduated from Eureka College (Illinois) with a B.A. in economics in 1932. After college he became a radio sports announcer. He moved to California and became an actor in 1937 and made more than fifty movies. He married actress Jane Wyman in 1940, and they divorced in 1949. During World War II, he served in the U.S. Army from 1942 to 1945. Reagan was elected president of the Screen Actors Guild in 1947. He became a spokesman for the General Electric Company in the 1950s and traveled nationwide preaching his conservative views. Although raised as a liberal New Deal Democrat, he joined the Republican Party in 1962. In 1952, he married Nancy Davis.

Reagan won the governorship of California in 1966 and served two terms (1967–74). He sought the Republican nomination for president in 1968 and lost. Again in 1976, he narrowly lost the Republican nomination to incumbent President Ford.* Reagan defeated incumbent President Jimmy Carter* in 1980 and became the fortieth president of the United States and was reelected president in 1984, defeating Democratic nominee Walter Mondale in the largest electoral college victory in U.S. history.

President Reagan moved American policy in the Middle East toward recognition of Israel as a strategic asset and as a major non-North Atlantic Treaty Organization (NATO) ally of the United States. The Middle East was viewed as an extension of the U.S.–Soviet rivalry. His administration at first, in 1981, tried to form a strategic consensus between Israel and the pro-Western Arab states under Secretary of State Alexander Haig,* but this effort failed. The Reagan administration sent Philip Habib* to the Middle East in August 1982 to help end the fighting in Lebanon,* after Israel invaded Lebanon in June 1982 to expel the Palestine Liberation Organization* (PLO). Habib arranged the evacuation of PLO fighters from Beirut. American troops were sent as part of an international force to Lebanon to safeguard the PLO departure. Israeli and Syrian* forces still remained lodged in Lebanon, and the conflict there continued.

On September 1, 1982, President Reagan announced the fresh-start initiative,* which was his administration's plan to settle the Israeli–Palestinian conflict. The architect of this plan was the new secretary of state, George P. Shultz,* whose goal was to try to reinvigorate the peace process. Based on Camp David* and the idea of an exchange of land for peace* set forth in United Nations (UN) Resolution 242,* the plan called for a five-year transitional period, during which the Palestinians of the West Bank* and Gaza Strip* would have full autonomy over their own affairs. A successful five-year transitional period would hopefully create the confidence needed for a final resolution and wider participation among other Arab states in these talks. The Reagan administration was looking toward a possible confederation among the West Bank, Gaza,* and Jordan* as a possible solution to the Israeli–Palestinian conflict. By April 1983, the initiative had collapsed.

Reagan's secretary of state Shultz was able to arrange an agreement between Israel and Lebanon, signed on May 17, 1983.* The agreement was abrogated by Lebanon under Syrian pressure. It did result in an Israeli withdrawal from Lebanon, except for a security zone* in the south.

On October 23, 1983, a suicide truck bomb blew up the American Marine compound in Beirut, killing 241 Marines. Within days Reagan signed NSDD 111, reestablishing the strategic cooperation agreement with Israel suspended in 1981. In early 1984, Reagan withdrew the U.S. Marine contingent from Lebanon. Following the October bombing, American policy became one of punishing Syria for its sponsorship of terrorism. At this point, the administration concentrated its energies in the Middle East on the Persian Gulf. There was one last attempt to arrange for talks between Israel and a joint Jordanian–Palestinian delegation, but it fell through.

In 1988, the Reagan administration again tried to attack the Arab–Palestinian conflict head-on. On March 4, 1988, the Shultz Plan* was announced, and it endeavored to reach a comprehensive peace through direct, bilateral Arab–Israeli negotiations. After extensive discussions with the various parties, the Shultz Plan finally broke down by the end of July. The Reagan administration, on December 14, 1988, lifted the ban on United States–PLO dialogue.* It was attained only after diplomatic pressure from the administration on Yasser Arafat.* As a result, Arafat made a statement declaring that he would pursue peace with Israel based on United Nations Security Council Resolution 242 and would forswear terrorism.

For further information see: Juliana Peck, *The Reagan Administration and the Palestinian Question: The First Thousand Days* (Washington, DC: Institute for Palestine Studies, 1984); William B. Quandt, *Peace Process* (Washington, DC: Brookings Institution, 1993); Ronald W. Reagan, *An American Life* (New York: Simon and Schuster, 1990); George P. Shultz, *Turmoil and Triumph* (New York: Charles Scribner's Sons, 1993).

Nolan Wohl

RED EAGLES. Mention of the Palestinian* organization known as the Red Eagles (an-Nisr al-Ahmar) appeared in newspapers beginning in 1989. They were believed to be affiliated with the Popular Front for the Liberation of Palestine* (PFLP), headed by George Habash.* The Red Eagles do not acknowledge the right of the Palestine Liberation Organization (PLO) to represent the Palestinians because they believe that the Fatah* movement (and especially the armed Fatah Hawks*) is too moderate and its ideologies passé.

Very early the group acquired a reputation for its use of violence. Wearing commando-style uniforms with their faces covered to avoid identification by the Israeli Security Services, the Red Eagles used knives, axes, and guns to attack moderate Arabs, Jews, and Palestinians whom they accused of collaborating with the Israelis. To deter collaboration, they confiscated the identity cards of Palestinians and prevented some workers from going into Israel.

The Red Eagles mainly consisted of Palestinians under the age of twenty-one. Ironically, this meant that Palestinians were living in fear of their own children. The group is based in the city of Nablus but has underground cells throughout the Gaza Strip.* Palestinians themselves have viewed the Red Eagles as a ruthless, organized extortion and murder squad, executing their own people over protection fees and sometimes over ideological and moral differences.

Several of their leaders have been killed by Israeli soldiers as well as by Israel's General Security Services, the Shin Bet* or SHABAK. On November 9, 1989, an Israel Defense Forces* (IDF) and SHABAK raid in Shechem led to the arrest of more than ten Red Eagles and the death of their leader, Aiman al-Ruzeh. One of those captured, seventeen-year-old Jaber Hawash, provided detailed information about the terrorist group in an interview on Israel television. Hawash took great pride in his actions and claimed to have murdered eight people by himself. Within the context of the *intifada* (uprising), he held that the Red Eagles were helping to purify the Palestinian people by preventing collaboration with the Israelis. To demonstrate this, they have executed their victims in public places, like the marketplace of Nablus, in order to gain press coverage of their activities.

To protect themselves, many Palestinians have informed the Shin Bet about Red Eagle activities. Many of them have had to leave their native villages and move into secret relocation inside Israel.

More recently, the Red Eagles have attacked Israelis who have worked on behalf of Palestinian human and political rights. Two masked gunmen killed an Israeli lawyer, Ian Feinberg, in his Gaza office. Feinberg supported much of the Palestinian cause.

The Red Eagles have alienated many of the hard-line members of Fatah, and they have relied entirely on Popular Front for the Liberation of Palestine* (PFLP) financial support, as well as money acquired through extortion of local Palestinians to support their cause. Since the signing of the Israeli–PLO Declaration of Principles* (DOP), the Fatah and the Red Eagles have become bitter and violent rivals who have fought in refugee camps.

Yasha Manuel Harari and Joseph E. Goldberg

RED LINE (LEBANON). Syria's* intervention in the Lebanese Civil War during the summer of 1976 and its subsequent pursuit of retreating Palestinian and Muslim leftist forces resulted in Israel's declaration of this line. Geographically, the Red Line ran along the Litani River* from the Zaharani estuary on the Mediterranean Sea to the village of Mashki in the Beka Valley.*

Prime Minister Yitzhak Rabin* asserted that the purpose of the line was to make clear to President Hafez al-Assad* that Syria should not cross the line without expecting an Israeli response. Israel was concerned that Assad might use the civil war as an opportunity to invade Israel through a Lebanese* corridor, bypassing the heavily fortified Golan Heights* region.

The Red Line, later the Red Line Policy, evolved into an agreement between Syria and Israel that was brokered through the good offices of the United States. Specific policy arrangements were negotiated through American special envoy L. Dean Brown during March and April 1976. The negotiations resulted in the tacit understanding that Israel would not object to a strong Syrian presence in Lebanon if Syria limited its involvement to the deployment of ground forces. Assad's use of the air force against ground targets and any deployment of ground-to-air missiles in Lebanon were unacceptable to Israel. The understanding also allowed Israel to freely pursue Palestine Liberation Organization* (PLO) forces that operated in southern Lebanon and to fly reconnaissance missions over the same area.

The Red Line Policy became a subjective monitoring device with which Israel assessed its perceived threat from Syria. This barometer fluctuated with Israel's evaluation of the objectives of Syrian forces and whom they were operating against, the geographical location in which Syria was operating, the strength and composition of its forces, and the duration of their stay in a given area.

In return for its acquiescence, Israel agreed not to interfere with Syrian interests. Syria entered the conflict in 1976 in an attempt to prohibit a victory by Palestinian nationalist and leftist Muslim forces, which was against the interests of Syria's regional concerns. Syrian efforts at checking the PLO and its leftist Muslim allies corresponded with Israel's strong commitment to weakening the political and military determination of the Palestine Liberation Organization. Six weeks after the agreement, Syria deployed approximately 30,000 troops into Lebanon's Beka Valley, the Zogharta region near Tripoli, the southern part of the Shouf Mountains around Jezin, and the cities of Beirut, Sidon, and Tyre.

With few exceptions, both sides adhered to the agreement. The situation remained relatively static until the spring of 1981, when Syria, concerned over the strengthened Israeli-backed Christian Phalangist forces, invaded the Christian city of Zahle near the Beirut–Damascus Highway of the north–central Beka Valley. Israel intervened on behalf of the Phalangists and downed two Syrian helicopters that were being used against the Christian militia.

In response to Israel's actions at Zahle, Syria began deploying Soviet-supplied surface-to-air missiles (SAMs) in the Beka Valley on April 29. By early May, three SA-6 batteries totaling thirty-six missiles had been installed. The SA-6 presence was followed by the deployment of two SA-3 batteries, one SA-2* battery, and one tank brigade. Israeli prime minister Menachem Begin* regarded the SAM presence as a threat to Israel and warned that it might lead to Israel's use of force to remove them. Assad refused to remove the newly introduced missiles, stating that they were defensive weapons needed for the protection of Syrian ground forces.

As the Lebanese situation deteriorated, tensions increased between Syria and Israel. Strengthened Palestinian forces, which had ironically been shielded from Syrian aggression south of the Red Line, also caused much concern. Israel responded to these events with its invasion of Lebanon under Operation Peace for Galilee on June 6, 1982.* On the fourth day of the invasion, Israel's air force attacked the Syrian SAM sites in the Zahle area. Syria responded, and one of the largest modern air battles in history ensued, with the involvement of approximately 200 Syrian and Israeli war planes spread over a 2,500-square-kilometer area. By its conclusion, Israel had downed twenty-nine MiGs and destroyed seventeen of nineteen missile batteries without the loss of a single Israeli plane. Syria and Israel later agreed to an American-negotiated truce on June 11.

Although Israel continued to check Syrian ground movements south of the Red Line, Syrian surface-to-air missiles were again deployed on Lebanese soil in November 1985. These latest deployments, which included SA-6 and SA-8 SAMs, came in response to Syria's objection to Israeli reconnaissance flights that had earlier been accepted. Many of the previous Red Line arrangements originally established in 1976 had disappeared by the mid-1980s.

For further information see: A. I. Dawisha, *Syria and the Lebanese Crisis* (New York: St. Martin's Press, 1980); Trevor Dupuy, *Flawed Victory, the Arab–Israeli Conflict and the 1982 War in Lebanon* (Fairfax, VA: Hero Books, 1986); Yair Evron, *War and Intervention in Lebanon: The Israeli–Syrian Deterrence Dialogue* (Baltimore, MD: Johns Hopkins University Press, 1987); Edward Haley, *Lebanon in Crisis, Participants and Issues* (Syracuse, NY: Syracuse University Press, 1979); Avner Yaniv, *Dilemmas of Security, Politics, Strategy, and the Israeli Experience in Lebanon* (New York: Oxford University Press, 1987); Naomi Weinberger, *Syrian Intervention in Lebanon: The 1975–76 Civil War* (New York: Oxford University Press, 1986).

Robert Crangle, Jr.

RED LINE AGREEMENT. A combination of broader aspirations and strategic competition in Lebanon* between Israel and Syria* led in the early 1970s to the direct extension of the Syrian–Israeli conventional conflict into the periphery, especially Lebanon. Furthermore, this process of geographically expanding the conflict into Lebanon was aggravated by the stalemate that had set in at the core of the Syrian–Israeli conflict on the Golan Heights* following their 1974 Disengagement Agreement.* Not only did the strategic geography of Lebanon make it a convenient extension, but mastery over the country could quickly threaten the defenses of either Syria or Israel.

Lebanon is a land divided into four geographic regions. The dominant direction of this geography is its north–south orientation, with an important divide between the north and south. These two north–south zones, which are actually deep valleys lying between significant mountain ranges (with altitudes of 2,000 to 3,000 meters), are conduits or avenues of strategic movement. Basically, control of the valleys by Syria affords it the opportunity to circumvent Israeli defenses on the Golan Heights and threaten Israel either through the Hula Valley or from along the coast. Since travel along an east–west axis is extremely difficult in Lebanon, Israel's ability to shift forces from the Golan to the west is limited. Furthermore, Israel, through effective exploitation of the strategic geography on the Golan Heights, established a northern defense structure that requires only limited standing forces. Were Israel to have to contemplate a serious threat from Lebanon, which could reach the Israeli border in less than two to three days, it would stretch its defensive abilities in the north beyond their limit. Thus, Israeli territorial defense planning revolves around a perceived need to keep a serious conventional threat from Lebanon at least at two to three days' distance from the northern border at all times and to keep the Lebanese flank from being integrated with the Syrian Golan front. Thus, if Syria were to control the southern quadrants of Lebanon, serious problems would arise in Israel's defense structure, which is nearly exclusively focused on an east–west movement on the Golan Heights.

The overall north–south orientation of Lebanon's geography generally protects Syria from what transpires in Lebanon. However, one gap in the north–south structure makes Lebanon critically important to Syria: the gap corresponding to the Beirut–Damascus Highway. This gap allows any force dominating Lebanon and the Beirut–Damascus Highway to be brought within fifteen to twenty kilometers from Damascus: a potentially fatal problem for Syria.

Israel, on the other hand, feels the need to control the Beka Valley* south of the Rashaya–Karoun–Jezzine–Sidon line, which runs into the Hula Valley, and coastal hills, which run into Israel's heavily populated coast, to be free from threatening forces. Threats needed to be kept at a distance, which represents at least two days' armored movement.

Lebanon, which had been a buffer zone between Israel and Syria, was transformed, following Syria's intervention in Lebanon during the civil war in 1976, into an active competitive zone, resulting in considerable tension. By late March 1976, prior to Syria's invited, official intervention in Lebanon on May 31, 1976, the United States feared that the Israeli–Syrian competition in Lebanon may escalate into direct confrontation and initiated a series of diplomatic exchanges to try to come to a set of understandings demarcating the limits of Syrian and Israeli intervention in advance of Syria's entry. On March 24, Israel sent the United States a series of conditions that it described as "red lines" whose crossing by Syria would cause immediate escalation. There were five Israeli conditions enumerated in the communication: Syria cannot intervene in Lebanon in an open and declared way; Syrian intervention should be limited to one brigade or less; Syrian intervention should not include armor, artillery, or anti-aircraft units; Syrian intervention should not include air or naval forces; Syria units should not move south of a line running approximately ten kilometers south of the Beirut–Damascus Highway.

The actual geographic demarcation was contested the following month and eventually was publicly formulated by Prime Minister Rabin* in June 1976. The line below which Syrian forces were not to deploy was revealed to be along the Rashaya–Jezzine–Sidon axis.

This lack of clarity of demarcation of the vital Syrian and Israeli areas has clearly been the focus of much of the conflict that has existed between Israel and Syria in Lebanon since 1976. Nevertheless, the experience of the first fifteen years after the "understandings" were reached tends to indicate the critical line is approximately the straight line from Rashaya in the east, through Jezzine in the center, to Sidon in the west along the coast, as mentioned earlier. From time to time, this line shifts north to south, as one side or another probes to see how far it can go, but this is usually resolved by a resolute response, such as the Israeli invasion of Lebanon in 1982.

For further information see: Yair Evron, *War and Intervention in Lebanon* (London: Croom Helm, 1987).

David Wurmser

REFUGEES. In general, references to refugees refer to those individuals who fled from what became Israel during Israel's War of Independence.* There are, however, other groups. From the Arab perspective there are also the refugees of the Six Day War* who fled from the West Bank* across the river to Jordan.* These numbered about 220,000 in 1967. From the Israeli perspective there are also the Jewish refugees from Arab and Muslim states who fled their countries of origin to come to Israel, primarily in the late 1940s and early 1950s.

For further information see: Peter Dodd and Halim Barakat, *River Without Bridges: A Study of the Exodus of the 1967 Palestinian Arab Refugees* (Beirut: Institute for Palestine Studies, 1969); Rony E. Gabbay, *A Political Study of the Arab–Jewish Conflict: The Arab Refugee Problem. A Case Study* (Geneva: Librairie E. Droz, 1959); Benny Morris, *The Birth of the Palestinian Refugee Problem, 1947–1949* (New York: Cambridge University Press, 1987); Michael Palumbo, *The Palestinian Catastrophe: The 1948 Expulsion of a People from Their Homeland* (London: Faber and Faber, 1987); Shabtai Teveth, "The Palestine Arab Refugee Problem and Its Origins," *Middle Eastern Studies* 26 (April 1990):214–49.

REFUGEES MULTILATERAL WORKING GROUP. One of the five multilateral negotiations* working groups established as a part of the Madrid Conference peace process.*

REVISIONISTS. A Zionist* political party, founded in 1925 by Vladimir Zeev Jabotinsky,* it reflected the demand for a revision of the Zionist Executive's conciliatory policy toward the British Mandatory* government and of the system and pace of Zionist activity in Palestine.* In the Revisionist conception, the Zionist aim was to provide an integral solution to the worldwide Jewish problem in all its aspects—political, economic, and spiritual. To attain this objective, the Revisionists demanded that the entire Mandated territory of Palestine, on both sides of the Jordan River,* be turned into a Jewish state with a Jewish majority. The contention of the Revisionists was that worldwide political pressure must be exerted in order to induce Britain to abide by the letter and spirit of the Palestine Mandate.* They stressed the imperative necessity of bringing to Palestine the largest number of Jews within the shortest possible time. The financial instrument of the movement was the Keren Tel Hai (Tel Hai Fund). Within the World Zionist Organization* (WZO), Revisionism met with increasingly strong resistance, particularly from the labor groups. The World Union of Zionists–Revisionists was founded in 1925 as an integral part of the WZO, with Jabotinsky as president. The Revisionists strongly opposed expansion of the Jewish Agency* by including prominent non-Zionists, who, they felt, would impair the national character, independence, and freedom of political action of the Zionist movement. From 1929, when the expanded Jewish Agency took over the political prerogatives of the WZO, Jabotinsky consistently urged increasing independence for the Revisionists. In 1935, a referendum held among Revisionists resulted in their seccession from the World Zionist Organization and the establishment of an independent New Zionist Organization* (NZO). Eleven years later, when ideological and tactical differences between the NZO and the WZO had diminished, the NZO decided to give up its separate existence. The United Zionists–Revisionists (the merger of the Revisionist Union and the Jewish State Party) participated in the elections to the twenty-second Zionist Congress in Basle in 1946.

REVOLUTIONARY ORGANIZATION OF SOCIALIST MUSLIMS. See **ABU NIDAL ORGANIZATION.**

RHODES TALKS. On January 13, 1949, armistice talks began between Israel and Egypt* on the island of Rhodes. This was pursuant to the United Nations Security Council Resolution 62 of November 16, 1948, which called for the establishment of a truce "conducted either directly or through the Acting Mediator" between Israel and the Arab states involved in the war. The talks were mediated by Dr. Ralph Bunche,* the United Nations acting mediator on Palestine* at the Hotel des Roses. The location was originally chosen in June 1948 by Count Folke Bernadotte,* Bunche's predecessor, for the purposes of establishing a truce. Rhodes was chosen, among other reasons, for its location close to the war zone.

The talks between Israel and Egypt lasted until February 24, 1949, and resulted in the Egyptian–Israel General Armistice Agreement,* ending Egypt's involvement in the 1948–49 Israeli War of Independence.* After Israel and Egypt concluded their negotiations, talks were held between Israel and Transjordan.* The talks with Transjordan began on March 4, 1949, and were concluded with the signing of an Israeli–Jordanian General Armistice Agreement* on April 3. One glaring difference between the two sets of talks was that the negotiations between Israel and Transjordan in Rhodes were merely a facade for the actual negotiations being conducted in Shuneh, Transjordan. Upon completion of those talks, the wording of the Armistice Agreement was sent to Rhodes, whereupon it was signed on April 3, 1949. The other two Armistice Agreements, with Lebanon* and Syria,* were negotiated along the lines where the fighting ceased.

The structure of the talks in Rhodes was held by the Arab states to be a precedent for later meetings with Israel. In Rhodes the United Nations mediator and his staff occupied one wing of the hotel, the Israeli delegation occupied a floor in the opposite wing, and the Egyptian delegation resided in the floor above the Israeli delegation. Because of the presence of the United Nations mediator, the Egyptians (and the Jordanians) could claim that the talks were not direct. The Israelis, however, could claim that because the parties were under one roof and at times spoke directly, despite the presence of a mediator, the talks were direct. The daily goings-on of the talks were kept secret, which further enhanced the success of the structure.

The Rhodes precedent of indirect negotiations between Israel and the Arab states was insisted upon as the prototype for later discussions by the Arab states.

For further information see: Walter Eytan, *The First Ten Years: A Diplomatic History of Israel* (London: Wiedenfeld and Nicolson, 1958); Shabatai Rosenne, *Israel's Armistice Agreements with the Arab States* (Tel Aviv: International Law Association, 1951); Avi Shlaim, *Collusion across the Jordan: King Abdullah, the Zionist Movement, and the Partition of Palestine* (New York: Columbia University Press, 1988); Saadia Touval, *The Peace Brokers: Mediators in the Arab–Israeli Conflict, 1948–1979* (Princeton, NJ: Princeton University Press, 1982).

Noah Dropkin

RIAD, MAHMOUD (b. Cairo, Egypt,* 1917; d. Cairo, Egypt, January 24, 1992). A highly decorated Egyptian diplomat. He graduated from the Egyptian Military Academy—where he first met President Gamal Abdul Nasser*—in 1936. He attended the General Staff College, where he received his doctorate in engineering in 1943. In August 1948, he was appointed the director of military intelligence in Gaza.* He fought in the 1948 Arab–Israeli War* as an army officer. He was a member of the Egypt–Israel Mixed Armistice Commission*

(1949) that met on Rhodes* and signed the Armistice Agreement.* Holding the rank of colonel, he was a member of the Free Officers organization that overthrew the monarchy in July 1952.

In 1954, he became director of Arab affairs in the Ministry of Foreign Affairs, where he was a principal player in implementing Nasser's Pan-Arab policies during the 1950s. He was a tenacious foe of Israel and an architect of Egypt's diplomatic links with the Soviet Union in the 1960s and the 1970s. He was also a vocal critic of the West, especially Britain, France,* and the United States. In 1955, he was appointed Egypt's ambassador to Syria.* In 1958, he was chosen by Nasser to be his adviser on foreign affairs. In 1961, he was named chairman of the United Arab Republic delegation to the United Nations Economic Commission for Africa. In 1962, he served at the United Nations in New York as Egypt's permanent representative.

Upon his return from his mission in New York in 1964, he was appointed minister of foreign affairs. In June 1972, he was elected to be the secretary-general of the Arab League,* a position he held until 1979, when he resigned shortly before the Arab League was to convene to suspend Egypt's membership as a result of signing the peace treaty with Israel that year. Riad was a critic of the Camp David Accords* and the Egypt–Israel Peace Treaty.*

For further information see: Mahmoud Riad, *The Struggle for Peace in the Middle East* (New York: Quartet Books, 1981).

Ahmed Elbashari

AL-RIFAI, ZAID. Son of Samir al-Rifai, who was prime minister of Jordan* in the 1940s and 1950s and briefly in 1965, Zaid al-Rifai has been a confidant of King Hussein.* He attended college with the king and studied political science and international relations at Columbia and Harvard Universities. In 1969, he was appointed head of the Royal Cabinet. He was in this position during the Jordan–Palestine Liberation Organization* (PLO) crisis of September 1970.

Joseph E. Goldberg

RIGHT OF RETURN. A reference to the right of the Palestinians who became refugees* in 1948 to return to their homes and land in what is now Israel. A component of Palestinian and Arab positions in the Arab–Israeli conflict firmly opposed by Israel.

ROGERS PLAN. On December 9, 1969, U.S. secretary of state William P. Rogers,* in a speech before the 1969 Galaxy Conference on Adult Education entitled, "A Lasting Peace in the Middle East: An American view," publicly presented what later became known as the Rogers Plan (or Rogers Plan A), a policy statement on the situation in the Middle East and the U.S. proposals presented earlier to the Soviet Union on October 28, 1969, as part of the two- and four-power talks* begun in the spring of 1969, in order to aid Ambassador

Gunnar Jarring* in his United Nations-sponsored peace effort as outlined in United Nations Security Council Resolution 242.*

The speech stated four important factors that had guided U.S. policy: an agreement among those parties not directly involved would not substitute for an agreement reached by those parties directly involved; a durable peace must meet the legitimate concerns of both sides; the only framework for negotiations leading to a final settlement is the entire text of United Nations Security Council Resolution 242; and a situation of no war, no peace would serve no one's interests.

The speech further emphasized that U.S. policy was, and would continue to be, a balanced one and called for concessions from both sides. The Arab concession would result in acceptance of a permanent peace based on a binding agreement while the Israeli concession would result in withdrawal from occupied territory gained during the June 1967 war.* The speech went on to enunciate U.S. policy toward Resolution 242. Rogers separated U.S. policy into four areas: peace, security, withdrawal, and territory. A peace agreement should be outlined in specific terms based on clear and understood intentions. In terms of security, it was suggested that demilitarized zones be implemented. In accordance with Resolution 242, the United States supported nonacquisition of territory through war and, therefore, Israeli withdrawal from territories occupied in the 1967 war. The speech did not rule out changes in the 1949 armistice lines, but it did emphasize that any change should be confined to insubstantial alterations* required for mutual security.

U.S. policy viewed a just settlement of the refugee* problem as inseparable from the resolution of the conflict. A settlement must include consideration of their desires and aspirations. Regarding Jerusalem,* U.S. policy was that the future of the city must be decided by an agreement between Jordan* and Israel while considering the views of other involved parties as well as the international community. Rogers stated that the United States preferred the unification of the city with open access for all persons.

The speech outlined three areas of agreement between the United States and the Soviet Union specifically pertaining to a settlement between Israel and the United Arab Republic* (UAR). Both powers agreed upon the pursuit of a binding commitment to peace, the utilization of the Rhodes* negotiating procedures, which facilitated the 1949 Armistice Agreements,* and the withdrawal of Israeli forces from Egyptian* territory in the context of a binding commitment to peace by the UAR. The speech closed by restating that U.S. policy was balanced and fair and that the United States would pursue a course of patient diplomacy in achieving a just and lasting peace.

The Rogers Plan as outlined in the December 9 speech was rejected by Israel, Egypt, and the Soviet Union.

For further information see: Yaacov Bar-Siman-Tov, *The Israeli–Egyptian War of Attrition, 1969–1970* (New York: Columbia University Press, 1980); Michael Brecher, "Israel and the Rogers Peace Initiatives," *Orbis* 18 (1974): 402–26; Michael Brecher,

Decisions in Israel's Foreign Policy (New Haven, CT: Yale University Press, 1975); Henry A. Kissinger, *White House Years* (Boston: Little, Brown, 1979); David A. Korn, "US–Soviet Negotiations of 1969 and the Rogers Plan," *Middle East Journal* 44 (1990): 37–50; William B. Quandt, *Decade of Decisions: American Policy toward the Arab–Israeli Conflict, 1967–1976* (Berkeley: University of California Press, 1977); Bernard Reich, *Quest for Peace: United States–Israel Relations and the Arab–Israeli Conflict* (New Brunswick, NJ: Transaction Books, 1977); U.S. Department of State, "A Lasting Peace in the Middle East: An American View," *Department of State Bulletin* (January 5, 1970): 7–11.

Noah Dropkin

ROGERS PLAN B. In similar letters from U.S. secretary of state William P. Rogers to United Arab Republic* (UAR) foreign minister Mahmoud Riad* and Jordanian* foreign minister Zaid Rifai* dated June 19, 1971, a U.S. initiative toward peace in the Middle East was outlined. (A copy was also presented to Israel.) These letters presented what is known as Rogers Plan B or the Second Rogers Initiative. It also came to be known as the "stop shooting, start talking*" proposal. The letters stated that the United States was interested in a lasting peace, the framework for its establishment being United Nations Security Council Resolution 242,* to be implemented under the auspices of United Nations ambassador Gunnar Jarring.* While the issue of direct negotiations was acknowledged as necessary at a future date, the letters did not call for them at the outset.

In a more detailed fashion, the letters went on to suggest that the first step toward a lasting peace would be the reinstatement of the cease-fire between Israel and the United Arab Republic, to be agreed upon for at least a limited period. The second suggestion was the submission to United Nations (UN) secretary-general U Thant* by Ambassador Jarring of a statement to be agreed upon by the United Arab Republic and Israel. The statement would have three points: that both sides agree on the implementation of UN Security Council Resolution 242 in all its parts and will therefore designate representatives who, under the auspices of Ambassador Jarring, will pursue this end; that both parties agree that the goal of Resolution 242 was the establishment of a just and lasting peace based upon mutual acknowledgment of sovereignty and territorial integrity and Israeli withdrawal from territories occupied in the 1967 June war*; and that both parties agree to observe the cease-fire resolutions of the Security Council beginning July 1, 1970, and ending not earlier than October 1, 1970.

Rogers Plan B was similar to the original Rogers Plan in that it had the same goals, but it departed from the latter's comprehensiveness by primarily seeking the establishment of an interim agreement in the form of a cease-fire in the War of Attrition.* On July 22, 1970, UAR foreign minister Riad accepted Rogers Plan B with qualifications, followed by Jordan on July 26. On July 31, Israel agreed to accept the plan and communicated its intention on August 4, 1970. At 2200 GMT, August 7, 1970, Israel and the United Arab Republic began observing a cease-fire. The talks envisioned by Rogers Plan B began on August 25, 1970. Due to cease-fire violations by Egypt* and U.S. reluctance to support Israeli claims, the Israeli ambassador to the United Nations refused to enter into a second round of talks.

For further information see: Michael Brecher, "Israel and the Rogers Peace Initiatives," *Orbis* 18 (1974):402–26; Henry A. Kissinger, *White House Years* (Boston: Little, Brown, 1979); Robert J. Pranger, *American Policy for Peace in the Middle East, 1969–1971: Problems of Principle, Maneuver, and Time* (Washington, DC: American Enterprise Institute for Public Policy Research, 1971); William B. Quandt, *Decade of Decisions: American Policy toward the Arab–Israeli Conflict, 1967–1976* (Berkeley: University of California Press, 1977); Bernard Reich, *Quest for Peace: United States–Israel Relations and the Arab–Israeli Conflict* (New Brunswick: Transaction Books, 1977); U.S. Department of State, "US Initiative toward Peace in the Middle East," *Department of State Bulletin* (August 10, 1970): 178–79.

Noah Dropkin

ROGERS PLAN C. As part of a general address before the United Nations General Assembly on October 4, 1971, U.S. Secretary of State William P. Rogers* outlined the U.S. position concerning an interim Suez Canal* agreement between Egypt* and Israel. This plan (known as Rogers Plan C, the Third Rogers Initiative, and the Rogers Six-Point Program) capped a summer of diplomatic efforts to achieve this end. In his speech, Rogers stated the ultimate goal of the plan as a lasting peace, to be pursued within the framework of United Nations Security Council Resolution 242,* but for the purposes of establishing an aura of confidence and trust, he urged the immediate acceptance of an interim Suez Canal agreement that would allow the reopening of the canal as well as some kind of disengagement of forces.

The plan stated six areas that must be addressed in order for such an interim agreement to be successful as well as lead further along the road to a lasting peace: the relationship between the interim agreement and a final settlement, the intention being that an interim canal agreement is merely a means toward implementation of Resolution 242 under the auspices of United Nations ambassador Gunnar Jarring*; the maintenance of the cease-fire observed since August 7, 1970; a specified zone of withdrawal from the Suez Canal; the nature of the supervisory arrangements that will ensure adherence to the interim agreement; the question of an Egyptian presence on the East Bank of the Suez Canal, being required in order to reopen the canal; the use of the Suez Canal, it being understood that U.S. policy holds that the canal be open to passage for all nations.

Rogers Plan C continued along the same path as Rogers Plan B in that it continued to pursue interim agreements as opposed to a comprehensive settlement, which had characterized the original Rogers Plan. It did not, however, seek an immediate continuance of the process outlined in Rogers Plan B—discussions under the auspices of Ambassador Jarring. Rogers Plan C continued the trend toward step-by-step diplomacy* that came to characterize the method of U.S. secretary of state Henry Kissinger,* who followed Secretary Rogers.

Israel rejected Rogers Plan C on October 12, 1971, but reversed this decision on February 2, 1972, and agreed to "close-proximity"* talks with Egypt, with the United States acting as mediator. This approach was rejected by Egypt.

For further information see: Michael Brecher, "Israel and the Rogers Peace Initiatives," *Orbis* 18 (1974):402–26; Michael Brecher, *Decisions in Israel's Foreign Policy* (New Haven, CT: Yale University Press, 1975); Henry A. Kissinger, *White House Years* (Boston: Little, Brown, 1979); William B. Quandt, *Decade of Decisions: American Policy toward the Arab–Israeli Conflict, 1967–1976* (Berkeley: University of California Press, 1977); Bernard Reich, *Quest for Peace: United States–Israel Relations and the Arab–Israeli Conflict* (New Brunswick, NJ: Transaction Books, 1977); Robert J. Pranger, *American Policy for Peace in the Middle East, 1969–1971: Problems of Principle, Maneuver, and Time* (Washington, DC: American Enterprise Institute for Public Policy Research, 1971).

Noah Dropkin

ROTHSCHILD, DANNY. A major general in the Israel Defense Forces (IDF).* In June 1994, he became the Israeli coordinator of the negotiations with the Palestinians.* He had been serving as coordinator of government activities in the occupied territories.*

ROUND 1, 2, 3, ETC., OF THE BILATERAL NEGOTIATIONS IN WASHINGTON. See **WASHINGTON ROUNDS.**

ROUNDTABLE CONFERENCE (1939). See **ST. JAMES CONFERENCE.**

RUBINSTEIN, ELYAKIM (Eli) (b. Tel Aviv, 1947). The head of the Israeli delegation for talks with the Jordanian*–Palestinian* delegation in the Washington rounds* of the peace talks. He received a B.A. degree in 1967, an L.L.B. in 1968, and an M.A. in 1974 from the Hebrew University in Jerusalem.* He served in the Israel Defense Forces* from 1966 to 1970. He served in the legal department and as deputy legal adviser in the Ministry of Defense from 1973 to 1977. From 1977 to 1981, he served as chief of bureau and adviser to the minister of foreign affairs. He was a member of the delegation to the peace talks with Egypt* (including Camp David*). From 1981 to 1985, he was legal adviser and assistant director general in the Ministry of Foreign Affairs. He served a brief tour in Washington. He became government secretary in November 1986. In November 1994, Prime Minister Rabin* appointed him to head a committee to oversee implementation of the peace agreement with Jordan.

RUSK, DEAN (b. Cherokee County, Georgia, February 9, 1909; d. Athens, Georgia, December 20, 1994). Rusk grew up in Georgia and attended Davidson College in North Carolina. He spent three years as a Rhodes scholar at Oxford University and later joined the faculty of Mills College in California, where he taught political science.

He joined the Department of State as an assistant chief of the Division of International Security Affairs and then became a special assistant to the secretary of war. In 1947, Rusk returned to the Department of State to head the office of Special Political Affairs.

It was in the office of Special Political Affairs that Dean Rusk encountered the growing issue of the partition of Palestine* and the establishment of the state of Israel. In January 1948, he became director of the Office of United Nations (UN) Affairs and the first assistant secretary of state for United Nations affairs the next year. In March 1950, he became assistant secretary of state for Far Eastern affairs. He left the Department of State in March 1952 to become the president of the Rockefeller Foundation but accepted the invitation of President John F. Kennedy* to be his secretary of state. He served as secretary of state in the Kennedy and Lyndon B. Johnson* administrations from 1961 to 1969.

As secretary of state in the Johnson administration, Dean Rusk was involved in both formulating and implementing U.S. action during the Six Day War* of 1967. When Egyptian* president Gamal Abdul Nasser* closed the Strait of Tiran* to Israeli shipping, the secretary of state, together with other Johnson administration officials, attempted to defuse the situation. Initially, the attempt was to secure a declaration from fifteen maritime powers that the strait was an international waterway that should be open for all shipping. The administration realized that such a declaration would have little significance. Further, a naval operation to open the strait was complicated by the U.S. Sixth Fleet being positioned on the wrong side of the Suez Canal.* Together with Secretary of Defense Robert McNamara, the secretary of state met with members of Congress, who indicated that they did not favor unilateral U.S. action on behalf of Israel.

He participated in meetings with Israeli foreign minister Abba Eban* on May 26, 1967, attempting to persuade Israel that Nasser would not attack. Rusk indicates in his memoirs that the United States thought that Israel had committed itself to the United States not to attack. He indicates that the administration's reaction was to be "shocked as well, and angry as hell." Upon reflection, however, Rusk acknowledged that if Israel had waited for the Arabs to strike first, the situation would have been grim.

Rusk also attempted to persuade King Hussein* of Jordan* not to enter the fighting because it was in his country's interest. Once the fighting started, his efforts were involved in getting an immediate cease-fire.

When the U.S. intelligence ship, USS *Liberty*,* was attacked on June 8 by Israeli fighter jets, Rusk expressed to the Israeli ambassador in Washington his belief that Israel could not have misidentified the ship. He did not accept the Israeli account, though President Johnson and other members of the administration did.

In 1968, the Israeli government of Prime Minister Levi Eshkol* requested the purchase of Phantom jets.* As a guest at the Johnson ranch in January 1968, the prime minister met with the president, Secretary of State Rusk, and Secretary of Defense McNamara. Johnson indicated that Israel would receive the planes. A long bureaucratic struggle within the American government followed. Ultimately, approval for the sale was given, and Israel was promised delivery of the planes in late 1969.

For further information see: Dean Rusk, as told to Richard Rusk, *As I Saw It,* ed. Daniel S. Papp (New York: Penguin Books, 1990).

Joseph E. Goldberg

S

SA-2 MISSILE. The SA-2 is a low-to-high-altitude, surface-to-air missile (SAM)* designed to attack aircraft. It was developed and produced by the Soviet Union in 1957. The SA-2 is a two-staged missile approximately thirty-six feet long and two feet wide. The first stage is a solid-fuel rocket booster, and the second stage is a liquid-fuel sustainer rocket motor. The SA-2 has a maximum range of almost thirty-five miles, a maximum altitude of almost 100,000 feet, and a maximum speed of Mach 3. The SA-2 has a 430-pound, high-explosive fragmentation warhead with proximity, contact, and command-type fusing options. The missile is guided to the target by a missile-control radar with a range of approximately 172 miles and has a target acquisition mode, a target tracking mode, and a missile guidance mode. The radar can track up to six targets simultaneously. When a missile is fired, its onboard computer accepts guidance commands from the radar via a radio link. Once in the vicinity of the target, the missile's fusing system is activated. The entire system is designed to be simple and easy to operate with a minimum of specialized training. A standard battery consists of six launchers, a missile control radar, and a command post.

Countries in the Middle East that have the SA-2 in their inventories include Algeria, Egypt,* Iran, Iraq,* Libya, Syria,* and Yemen. The Egyptians began receiving the SA-2 and had eighteen battalions in service by 1967; however, in the Six Day War* they shot down only two Israeli Mirage* fighters. During the Yom Kippur War,* both Egypt and Syria used the SA-2 and had fourteen kills against Israeli aircraft. Defensive techniques against the SA-2 include ECM (electronic countermeasures), heavy deployment of chaff (strips of aluminum to confuse the missile-control radar), defensive flight maneuvers, and attack of the missile and radar facilities. See also SAM.

For further information see: Tony Cullen and Christopher F. Foss, eds., *Jane's Land-Based Air Defense,* 7th ed. (London: Jane's Information Group, 1994).

Stephen H. Gotowicki

SABRA AND SHATILA. In late July 1982, the Palestine Liberation Organization* (PLO) accepted a plan developed by special U.S. envoy Philip Habib* to leave Lebanon.* The plan was published on August 20, 1982, and implemented the next day. The first units of the PLO departed by sea; the entire evacuation of 8,100 fighters was completed on September 1.

The main concern of the PLO during the negotiations with the United States was securing firm guarantees for the security of the Palestinian and Lebanese civilians left in Beirut and neighboring refugee camps after the PLO's departure.

Habib gave assurances that the civilians would be safe. However, once the PLO was evacuated, U.S. troops were withdrawn, and this was soon followed by the withdrawal of French,* Italian, and British troops as well. No international force was in place with a clear mandate to protect the camps and prevent violations of the arrangement.

On September 14, 1982, a bomb exploded in Ashrafiyeh, Beirut, killing Lebanon's* president-elect Bashir Gemayel.* Immediately, the Israeli army was ordered into Beirut with the stipulation that no troops were to enter the camps.

Evaluations of the motives of the Phalangists regarding the Palestinians* are contradictory. The Kahan Commission* found that in the beginning of the 1982 war, most Mossad* agents who had maintained contact with the Phalangist leadership assessed them as having achieved a stage of political and organizational maturity "that would ensure that atrocities and massacres were a thing of the past." However, the Mossad agents who had met with Bashir Gemayel said that he left no doubt that it was "his intention to eliminate the Palestinian problem in Lebanon when he came to power." Furthermore, experienced Israeli intelligence officers believed that if the Phalangists had the opportunity to massacre Palestinians, they would do so.

The two camps, Sabra and Shatilla, were basically residential areas, containing low structures along narrow alleys and streets. The entire camp was not completely visible from the Phalangist command post. Inexact estimates put the population count at approximately 56,000 people.

On September 16, 1982, the Israelis controlled Beirut. The camps were closed and surrounded. The camps offered resistance. Heavy fire came out of Shatilla and was directed at one Israel Defense Forces (IDF)* battalion.

At 6:00 P.M. on September 16, 1982, the Phalangists entered the Shatilla refugee camp and later moved into the Sabra camp. Under the guise of clearing the camps of Palestinian guerrillas, they proceeded to murder hundreds of Palestinian civilians, including women and children. When they finally were ordered from the camps and left at 8:00 A.M. on September 18, between 700 and 1,000 people had been killed.

The Kahan Commission report concluded that the massacre was the direct responsibility of the Phalangists. However, because the Israeli army controlled their entry into the camps, provided them with services, including illumination at night, and also knew at an early stage that the Phalangists were functioning in violation of human principles, there was an indirect Israeli responsibility.

For further information see: The Beirut Massacre—The Complete Kahan Commission Report (Princeton, NJ: Karz-Cohl, 1983); Yair Evron, *War and Intervention in Lebanon— The Israeli–Syrian Deterrence Dialogue* (London: Croom Helm, 1987); Rashid Khalidi, *Under Siege: P.L.O. Decisionmaking During the 1982 War* (New York: Columbia University Press, 1986).

Nancy Hasanian

AL-SADAT, ANWAR (b. Mit Abul Kom, Egypt, December 25, 1918; d. Cairo, October 6, 1981). Sadat was one of thirteen children. His father was a government clerk, and his mother was part Sudanese. In his early years, prior to his family's moving to Cairo when he was seven, Sadat was educated by an Islamic cleric. He graduated from the Egyptian Royal Military Academy in 1938 and was assigned to the signal corps near Cairo. Sadat became a close associate of those Egyptian military officers who would constitute the Free Officers Corps and would ultimately seize control of the government. Strongly nationalistic and anti-British, Sadat was arrested for anti-British activities, but he escaped from a prison hospital in 1944. Sadat came out of hiding after World War II and assumed his position in the Egyptian army. A member of the Revolutionary Command Council of the Free Officers Corps, Sadat served as secretary-general of an Islamic Congress, editor of newspapers, minister of state in the Egyptian Cabinet, chairman and speaker of the Egyptian National Assembly, and chairman of the Afro–Asian Solidarity Council before Gamal Abdul Nasser* named him vice president. When Nasser died in office, Sadat became president. He succeeded in eliminating his rivals for the presidency in May 1971 and in July declared 1971 to be a year of decision* in the Arab–Israeli conflict. Sadat was intent on eliminating Egypt's dependence on the Soviet Union, in part, because the Soviets had not supplied Egypt with advanced weaponry, because of the Soviet Union's willingness to consider a settlement that would not satisfy Egyptian objectives, and because of friction between Egyptian officers and Soviet advisers. He terminated the Soviet military role in Egypt on July 18, 1972, and hoped that Egypt could turn to the West for aid. Sadat had decided that war with Israel was necessary and launched, with Syria,* the October 6, 1973, attack on Israel that started the Yom Kippur War.* With the assistance of U.S. secretary of state Henry Kissinger's* negotiations, an Egypt–Israel Disengagement Agreement* was signed in January 1974, and a second (Sinai II*) in 1975. Sadat proposed direct negotiations with Israel to resolve the Arab–Israeli conflict, which resulted in his historic visit to Israel in November 1977. Sadat negotiated and signed the Camp David Accords* of 1978 and the Egypt–Israel Peace Treaty* of 1979 and established the process of peace and normalization of relations between Egypt and Israel. He was assassinated* on October 6, 1981, as he was reviewing a military parade.

Sadat wrote *Revolt on the Nile* (New York: John Day, 1957) and *In Search of Identity: An Autobiography* (New York: Harper and Row, 1978).

For further information see: Marius Deeb, ''Anwar Al-Sadat,'' in Bernard Reich, ed., *Political Leaders of the Contemporary Middle East and North Africa: A Biographical Dictionary* (Westport, CT: Greenwood Press, 1990), pp. 453–60; Muhammad Hasanayn Haykal, *Autumn of Fury: The Assassination of Sadat* (London: Deutsch, 1983); Raymond Hinnebusch, Jr., *Egyptian Politics under Sadat: The Post-Populist Development of an Authoritarian-Modernizing State* (London: Cambridge University Press, 1985); David Hirst and Irene Beeson, *Sadat* (London: Faber and Faber, 1981); Raphael Israeli, *Man of Defiance: A Political Biography of Anwar Sadat* (Totowa, NJ: Barnes and Noble Books, 1985); Camelia Sadat, *My Father and I* (New York: Macmillan, 1985); Jihan Sadat, *A Woman of Egypt* (New York: Simon and Schuster, 1987); John Waterbury, *The Egypt of Nasser and Sadat: The Political Economy of Two Regimes* (Princeton, NJ: Princeton University Press, 1983).

SADAT, ANWAR, ASSASSINATION OF. On October 6, 1981, President Anwar Sadat* of Egypt* was assassinated while reviewing a military parade commemorating the eighth anniversary of the Egyptian crossing of the Suez Canal* at the outset of the October War.* Sadat was shot while watching an aerobatics display put on by some of Egypt's Mirage* jet fighters. He and others on the reviewing stand did not see one of the Soviet-made trucks come to a halt, allowing the assassins to disembark and carry out the killing. In the ensuing pandemonium, eight other people were killed, including Fawi Abdel Hafez, Sadat's private secretary, and Bishop Samuel, the leader of the Coptic Christian Church; several persons were wounded.

Upon the announcement of Sadat's death, the nominal mantle of power passed to Parliament speaker Sufi Abu Taleb, who called for elections in sixty days. Vice President Hosni Mubarak* was named president until the election and was chosen as the ruling party's candidate.

In a nationally televised eulogy, President Mubarak promised to uphold the Egypt–Israel Peace Treaty* by stating, ''[W]e are committed to all charters, treaties, and international obligations which Egypt has concluded,'' thus somewhat allaying Israel's fear that the new president would somehow renege on the promises Sadat had made.

There were conflicting reports regarding the identity of the assassins. Anonymous callers to a Beirut newspaper claimed that members of an extremist Egyptian exile group with ties to Libya, the Rejection Front for the Liberation of Arab Egypt, had carried out the attack. The group was formed in 1977 to work for the overthrow of Sadat and blockage of the Egyptian–Israeli peace process. This was of particular concern among the international community, especially the United States, for fear of open war between Libya and Egypt. Sadat had previously made his feelings known about Khaddafi, considering him a ''lunatic'' and most likely his most bitter enemy.

The Libyan conspiracy proved to be unfounded, as two days after the assassination, Defense Minister Abdel Halim Abu Ghazala announced that the assassination was carried out by a group of four men led by an extremist Muslim soldier; there was no outside conspiracy. It was later confirmed that the assassins were members of Takfir Wa Hijra or Repentant and Holy Flight. This confirmed earlier suspicions that members of the rightist Muslim organization, who were targets of the September 1981 crackdown by Sadat were responsible for his death.

Pamela Rivers

SADAT PEACE INITIATIVE (1977). After the breakdown of American efforts to resolve the impasse in Israeli and Egyptian* positions following the Yom Kippur War* and the failure of an October 1977 move by the United States and the U.S.S.R. to revive the Geneva Conference,* President Anwar Sadat* of Egypt decided to make a direct approach. Sadat announced, in the course of an address to the Egyptian Parliament on November 9, 1977, that he would be willing to go to Israel to discuss peace. The Israeli government extended an invitation for a visit by Sadat. Sadat's arrival in Israel on November 19 was without doubt one of the most highly charged moments in recent Arab–Israeli history, and he followed it up with a strong speech to Israel's Parliament. In this speech, Sadat outlined Egypt's conditions for peace: a return to the 1967 borders and justice for the Palestinians.* The cool response of Israel's leaders during the speech was, in its own way, ample forewarning of the difficulties to come. The Israeli prime minister, Menachem Begin,* presented what amounted to Israel's counterproposals at a Summit in Ismailiyya that December—limited Palestinian autonomy in exchange for full Israeli control of security and order in the West Bank* and Gaza.*

The peace initiative signaled a new era in Egyptian–Israeli relations. The lack of consultation with Arab leaders prior to the visit (other than a brief, hostile meeting with President Hafez al-Assad* of Syria*) aroused Arab antagonism. The talks continued with the intervention of various U.S. negotiators, including President Jimmy Carter,* who brought Sadat and Israeli premier Menachem Begin together at Camp David* in September 1978, after the breakdown of bilateral talks and of the Leeds Castle* Summit in July 1978.

SADEH, YITZHAK (Formerly Landsberg) (b. Lublin, Poland, 1890; d. Petah Tikva, Israel, 1952). The son of a respected Jewish family and the grandson of Lublin's rabbi, Yitzhak Landsberg was educated at a Russian gymnasium. He served in the Russian army, rising to the rank of sergeant, the highest rank a Jew could attain in the Czar's army, and distinguished himself in battle during World War I, for which he received the Cross of St. George. Sadeh served in the Soviet army after the 1917 Revolution and became a company commander. During his service, Sadeh met Joseph Trumpeldor, who persuaded him to emigrate to Palestine.* In 1919, Sadeh and Trumpeldor organized the Halutz pioneering movement in the Crimea and left for Palestine in 1920. He became active in various defense activities of the Yishuv.* He participated in Jerusalem's* defense during the Arab riots of 1921 and Safed in the riots of 1929.

Sadeh became active in the Yishuv's defense forces, the Haganah.* In 1937, he attempted to organize a permanent field brigade known as FOSH, but it was disbanded after a year because of the Yishuv's fear that it would become too elite. In 1941, Sadeh helped found the Palmach* and served as its commander until May 1945. His informal manner of leadership was largely responsible for helping to develop its esprit de corps. When the Israel Defense Forces* (IDF) was established, Sadeh served as commander of the eighth Armored Brigade. He was moved out of a senior IDF position primarily because David Ben-Gurion* and other Labor Party* leaders feared that Sadeh's political views were too far to the left, and the leadership was intent on depoliticizing the defense forces.

Following the War of Independence,* Sadeh resigned from the IDF and became a leader of the MAPAM political party and wrote a newspaper column for an Israeli newspaper.

For further information see: Yigal Allon, *Shield of David: The Story of Israel's Armed Forces* (New York: Random House, 1970); Ze'ev Schiff, *A History of the Israeli Army, 1870–1974* (New York: Simon and Schuster, 1974).

Joseph E. Goldberg

SAFE PASSAGE ROUTE. The route to be used by Palestinians* in traveling across Israel between the Gaza Strip* and the Jericho* area under the Palestinian Authority.* Under the terms of the Gaza–Jericho Agreement* (the Cairo Agreement of 1994*) signed in Cairo on May 4, 1994, Israel was obliged to facilitate a "safe passage" between Gaza* and Jericho during daylight hours for residents of those areas. Such passage was to be permitted through the Erez and Vered Jericho crossing points between the territories and Israel. Travelers between the areas were permitted to use limited travel routes and were subjected to specific rules for such travel. The first route opened for use in mid-August 1994.

SAGGER ANTITANK MISSILE. The term *Sagger* is the North Atlantic Treaty Organization (NATO) code name for a small, wire-guided, antitank missile developed and produced in the Soviet Union about 1965. The Soviet designation is PUR-64 Makyutka. The Sagger missile is thirty-four inches long and five inches in diameter and weighs twenty-five pounds. It has a minimum range of 500 meters and a maximum range of 3,000 meters. Its high-explosive warhead can penetrate six inches of steel. When fired, the Sagger trails out a thin wire connected to the gunner's sight. In-flight course corrections are transmitted along this wire from the sight to the missile, allowing the gunner to fly the missile to the target. The Sagger can be launched either vehicle-mounted or man-portable.

The Sagger missile has been extensively deployed among the clients of the Soviet Union in the Middle East. It was frequently used by the Egyptians* and the Syrians* in the Yom Kippur War.* It has also been used occasionally by groups such as Hezbollah* against Israeli personnel in the security zone* in southern Lebanon.

Stephen H. Gotowicki

SAIQA (Arabic: lightning, thunderstorm). As Fatah* increasingly came under Egyptian* influence, Syria* established its own Palestinian organization. In 1968, it renewed Saiqa, which had been an arm of the Syrian army. It initially operated against targets in Lebanon* and later became the principal organization operating along the Israel–Syrian cease-fire line.

SAM (SURFACE-TO-AIR MISSILE) (USSR). Surface-to-air missiles are fired from the ground to destroy targets in the air. SAMs are usually guided to their targets by radio commands from the launch site or internal radar or infrared (heat-seeking) warheads on board the SAM. Mobile SAM systems are usually mounted on vehicles or trailers. There are also man-portable systems such as the SA-7 and the SA-14, which can also be mounted on small vehicles. Between 1967 and 1973, SA-2,* SA-3, SA-6, and SA-7 SAMs were the main SAM systems deployed by the Arab armies. The major differences between different SAM systems involve missile size, range, warhead, and guidance systems.

Surface-to-air missiles employed during the Arab–Israeli wars have demonstrated the vulnerability of combat aircraft to ground troops and the value of the tactics and equipment systems needed to overcome this vulnerability. Israel has conducted extensive research and development of systems to reduce the vulnerability of its aircraft. Countermeasures that are normally employed against SAMs include chaff, canisters with thousands of metallic strips deployed behind the aircraft to deflect and confuse radar-seeking SAMs; flares, high-intensity heat sources deployed beneath the aircraft to attract heat-seeking SAMs away from the target aircraft; electronic countermeasures (ECM) to confuse, jam, or disable radar-guided SAMs; and flight avoidance procedures to avoid SAM target acquisition.

Currently, the Soviet SA-2, SA-3, SA-5, SA-6, SA-7, SA-8, SA-9, SA-13, and SA-14 SAMs are the systems most deployed by the Arab armies of the Middle East.

For further information see: Shelford Bidwell, *Brassey's Artillery of the World* (Oxford: Brassey's, 1981); Neville Brown, "The Real Capabilities of Soviet and U.S. Weapons in the Middle East and How the Two Sides Use Them—A New Approach to Assessing the Aerial Power Balance," *New Middle East,* no. 20 (May 1970): 11–14; Christopher Chant, *A Compendium of Armaments and Military Hardware* (London: Routledge and Kegan Paul, 1987); Chaim Herzog, *The Arab–Israeli Wars: War and Peace in the Middle East from the War of Independence to Lebanon* (London: Arms and Armour, 1984); Steve Zaloga, *Soviet Air Defence Missiles: Design, Development, and Tactics* (Surrey, England: Jane's Information Group, (1989).

Jon J. Peterson and Stephen H. Gotowicki

SAMARIA. Capital of the kingdom of Israel and a term used to refer to the northern kingdom as a whole. Samaria was founded by Omri, the king of Israel in 880 B.C., on a hill owned by one Shemer. From this comes the Hebrew term for the area, "Shomron." In 722–721 B.C., Sargon II of Assyria captured the city, and its inhabitants were deported. In their place, the Assyrians settled people from Babylon, Cutha, and Hanath, and Samaria became the seat of Assyrian government. Samaria was an administrative center in the Persian period and was a Macedonian colony in 331 B.C. It was destroyed by John Hyrcanus in 107 B.C. but was rebuilt by Pompey Herod who renamed the town Sebaste, which means "Augusta" in Greek, in honor of Augustus Ceasar. Samaria became an important center during the Roman period and flourished in the third century A.D. The term Samaria now applies to the northern area of central highlands in the land of Israel. The northern section of the highlands of Palestine,* north of Judea,* it is thirty-one miles long and twenty-three miles wide. The area is very densely populated. It was part of the West Bank* occupied by Jordan* in Israel's War of Independence* and was taken by Israel from Jordan in the Six Day War.*

David Salzberg

ES-SAMU (As-Samu or Samu). A West Bank* Arab town in the southern portion of Mount Hebron five miles north of the 1949 armistice lines,* opposite the Israeli town of Arad. Es-Samu is located atop the site of the biblical town of Eshtemoah. On November 13, 1966, the Israel Defense Forces* (IDF) launched an attack against the village, resulting in hundreds of casualties and fatalities on both sides.

In early 1966, Palestine Liberation Organization* (PLO) factions loyal mostly to Syria* stepped up their campaign against Israel, ending the period of relative quiet that had followed Operation Rotem* in 1960. Syrian-backed factions focused their escalation not along the Syrian border with Israel but in the area of Mount Hebron, because the Syrian regime feared Israeli reprisals, such as those launched in the late 1950s, and wanted to avoid the sort of damage and casualties that would likely ensue. By focusing their efforts in the Hebron* area, the actions executed by pro-Syrian PLO factions also served the dual purpose of destabilizing the Jordanian* regime.

Following nine attacks on Arad in one year and thirteen attacks in the same year that originated from the Mount Hebron area, the Israel Defense Forces determined that Arab villages in the area were providing assistance to the attackers and thus should be held accountable. The government of Israel approved a limited raid on the village of Es-Samu on November 13, 1966. The day prior to the raid, an Israeli command car patrolling near Arad detonated a land mine, killing three and wounding five. The Israeli government cited this incident as the impetus for the raid.

The attack—which turned out to be the largest battle the IDF fought between 1956 and 1967—was planned, in clear departure from tradition, to take place during the day and use NAHAL* forces, armored forces from the seventh Brigade, and elements from Unit 202. The operation was led by Brigadier General Yoav Shaham, who was killed during the operation.

Tactically, this was the first large-scale, combined operation launched by the Israeli army since 1956 and served as something of a trial exercise for the combat doctrine employed during the Six Day War.*

The attack surprised both the villagers and the regular Jordanian forces, who mounted a strong resistance that forced the operation to expand beyond its original scope. This triggered a strong rebuke from Prime Minister Levi Eshkol,* who noted, ''We were trying to wreck the mother-in-law (Syria), but hurt the bride (Jordan) instead.''

While the Israeli government contended that Syria sponsored the raids and was, therefore, ultimately to blame, the attack on Jordan was in accord with Israeli policy to punish the country from which the raids emanated. King Hussein* was concerned that Israel aspired to annex the West Bank* and was attempting to instigate a war with Jordan in order to legitimate a full-scale invasion.

The attack began at 6:45 A.M. with Israeli armored cars firing at a Jordanian police post at Rumj-el-Madfa. From there columns advanced on Es-Samu, as well as two bedouin towns to the east. More than 100 dwellings were destroyed, as well as the local school, clinic, and mosque. Jordanian casualties were over a hundred, with several fatalities; the Israelis had one killed and ten wounded. The attack ended at 10:10 A.M., when the Israeli–Jordanian Mixed Armistice Commission* received word that the Israeli forces had withdrawn.

The incident drew worldwide disapprobation as well as a United Nations resolution condemning it. It is suspected that Israel chose Jordan as the country for its retaliatory strike, rather than Syria, because of the mutual defense agreement* that had been signed between Syria and Egypt* on November 4, nine days prior to the raid. It was also believed by the Arabs that the Israelis were seeking war against a disjointed and weak Arab front.

The United Nations Security Council, acting on Jordan's complaint, considered the matter and on November 25, 1966, warned Israel that any further military reprisals against its Arab neighbors ''cannot be tolerated'' and would lead to ''further and more effective steps'' to end them. It was the strongest rebuke administered by the United Nations to either side since the Armistice Agreements* of 1949. The Security Council, in a vote of fourteen to none, with New Zealand abstaining, adopted United Nations Security Council Resolution 228, on November 25, 1966. It read, in part:

Reaffirming the necessity for strict adherence to the General Armistice Agreement; 1. Deplores the loss of life and heavy damage to property resulting from the action of the Government of Israel on 13 November 1966; 2. Censures Israel for this large-scale military action in violation of the United Nations Charter and of the General Armistice Agreement between Israel and Jordan; 3. Emphasizes to Israel that actions of military reprisal cannot be tolerated and that if they are repeated, the Security Council will have to consider further and more effective steps as envisaged in the Charter to ensure against the repetition of such acts.

Jordan received a flurry of negative propaganda from Syria, Egypt, and the PLO, suggesting that Jordan was unwilling or unable to properly defend the Palestinians in the West Bank and calling for the replacement of King Hussein. Palestinians rioted, and Hussein imposed martial law. It was not until President Gamal Abdul Nasser* of Egypt closed the Strait of Tiran* that Hussein attempted to reconcile their differences. By that time, however, communication between the Arab militaries was virtually nonexistent, and Arab forces were unprepared to coordinate battle plans against Israel in June 1967.

For further information see: Samir A. Mutawi, *Jordan in the 1967 War* (New York: Cambridge University Press, 1987); Eric Rouleau, "Crisis in Jordan," *World Today* (February 1967): 62–70; Peter John Snow, *Hussein: A Biography* (Washington, DC: R. B. Luce, 1972).

Donald A. Pearson and David Wurmser

SAMUEL, HERBERT LOUIS (b. Liverpool, England,* 1870; d. London, 1963). He was active in politics and, with the outbreak of World War I, developed an interest in Zionism* and the creation of a Jewish National Home.*

The British Foreign Office requested that Samuel study the financial and administrative conditions of Palestine.* In 1919, he conducted his inquiry and, upon his return to Britain, stopped at the San Remo Conference* in April 1920. At San Remo Lloyd George asked him to accept appointment as first high commissioner of Palestine. He served from 1920 to 1925, during which time he established the foundations of the civil administration of the Mandate.*

He inaugurated civilian rule in Palestine as of July 1, 1920. Samuel was a Zionist but appeared to believe in the need to take Arab grievances and claims into account. He sought to involve Arab participation in the Mandatory system and to protect their civil and economic rights. However, he also believed in the need to allow Jewish land purchases and immigration to Palestine.

For further information see: Elie Kedourie, "Sir Herbert Samuel and the Government of Palestine," in Elie Kedourie, *The Chatam House Version and Other Middle Eastern Studies* (London: Weidenfeld and Nicholson, 1970), pp. 52–81; M. Mossek, *Palestine Immigration Policy under Sir Herbert Samuel: British, Zionist and Arab Attitudes* (London: Frank Cass, 1978); Herbert L. S. Samuel, *Memoirs* (London: Cresset, 1945); Bernard Wasserstein, "Herbert Samuel and the Palestine Problem," *English Historical Review* 91 (October 1976):753–75.

SAN REMO CONFERENCE. The San Remo Conference was the second international conference convened after the Paris Peace Conference* to settle issues arising from World War I. The London Conference (February 12–23, 1920) was followed by a first conference at San Remo to consider the future of Near Eastern territories that had been under Turkish control. Because the United

States had withdrawn from negotiations after the Paris Conference, Great Britain* and France* decided these issues between themselves.

Meeting in the Italian town of San Remo on April 19–26, 1920, Britain, France, Italy, and Japan* negotiated with Turkey. Their efforts eventually resulted in the Treaty of Sèvres, in which Turkey renounced its claims to its Near Eastern holdings. Two other conferences were required after San Remo to refine the provisions of the agreement signed on August 10, 1920. The treaty, nevertheless, was never implemented, because it was rejected by the new Turkish government led by Mustafa Kemal Ataturk. The demand that these territories be taken from Turkish control and placed under Mandatory authority rested on Article 22 of the Covenant of the League of Nations, which stipulated that some Turkish areas whose population was capable of governing itself should be given sovereign control of their territory after a period of supervision. An Anglo–French statement of November 8, 1918, expressed their intention to fulfill the covenant's expectations.

Three areas were under consideration for Mandatory supervision: Mesopotamia (Britain), Palestine* (Britain), and Syria* and Lebanon* (France). The division of Palestine and Syria between Britain and France, respectively, followed the May 16, 1916 Sykes–Picot Agreement* in splitting "traditional Greater Syria" into a northern region (France) and a southern region (Britain). Syria's border had been discussed during an earlier meeting in London (September 1919), so San Remo focused on Palestine. The Palestine Mandate* was to exclude the region east of the Jordan River* (Transjordan*) in deference to Britain's agreement with Emir Abdullah ibn Hussein* and enunciated in Churchill's 1922 White Paper* on Jewish immigration to Palestine. Britain also prevailed on other issues: Article 95 of the Mandate requiring the Mandatory to implement the terms of the Balfour Declaration* was retained over French objections; France accepted British assurances, rather than codification in the Mandate, that non-Jewish people's political, civil, and religious rights would be guaranteed; and Britain successfully rejected France's desire for a French protectorate over the holy places.

Mesopotamia, consisting of the former Ottoman* *vilayets* of Mosul, Baghdad, and Basra, became a contentious issue due to concerns over oil concessions. An Anglo–French oil agreement was signed at San Remo providing France with a 20–25 percent share of the oil in Mosul in exchange for the district's inclusion in Britain's Mandate. Excepting the Anglo–French oil agreement, each Mandatory power was free to pursue whatever policies it chose within its Mandate. Thus, France was able to operate independently against Emir Feisal ibn Hussein* in Syria and thwart his ambition of ruling Syria (and a Greater Syria) without British interference. On July 25, 1920, French forces entered Damascus, leading to the ouster of Feisal. Britain also established a client state in Mesopotamia, creating the Hashemite Kingdom of Iraq* in a treaty with Feisal on August 10, 1922.

Although San Remo was just another stage in Britain's and France's continuous spheres of influence considerations, the conference did move greatly toward consolidating these issues. A second San Remo Conference, eight months later, further defined the boundaries for Syria, Lebanon, Palestine, and Mesopotamia, with Palestine's boundary shifted north, at the expense of Syria, to contain the headwaters of the Jordan and Litani Rivers.*

The Mandate proposals were approved by the Council of the League of Nations on July 24, 1922, and became official on September 29, 1923. Turkey formally abandoned its claims to the Arab territories in the 1923 Treaty of Lausanne.

For further information see: Norman De Mattos Bentwich, *The Mandate System* (London: Longmans, Green, 1926); Henry H. Cumming, *Franco–British Rivalry in the Post-War Near-East: The Decline of French Influence* (London: Oxford University Press, 1938); M. V. Seton-Williams, *Britain and the Arab States: A Survey of Anglo–American Relations, 1920–1948* (London: Luzac, 1948).

Paul S. Robinson, Jr.

SARTAWI, ISSAM (b. Acre, Palestine,* 1935; d. Albufeira, Portugal, April 10, 1983). An American-trained heart surgeon, he headed the Action Organization for the Liberation of Palestine (AOLP). He formed the organization in February 1969, when he broke away from Fatah.* The AOLP was pro-Nasser.* At the height of its membership, the AOLP consisted of about 700 active members, who were distinguished by the masks they wore as well as their reddish camouflage suits. They were known as the "phantoms of the Jordan Valley."

In July 1970, Yasser Arafat* criticized Egyptian president Gamal Abdul Nasser's acceptance of a U.S. peace proposal for the Middle East. Sartawi rejected Arafat's criticism. Sartawi increasingly became known in the 1980s as an advocate of the recognition of Israel by the Palestine Liberation Organization* (PLO). Sartawi informally was charged with liaison between the Israeli peace movement and the PLO.

Sartawi was assassinated on April 10, 1983, while attending a meeting of the Socialist International. The Abu Nidal* faction claimed responsibility for his assassination, as a move designed to bolster its opposition to any peace with Israel.

Joseph E. Goldberg

SAUNDERS DOCUMENT. On November 12, 1975, U.S. deputy assistant secretary of state for Near Eastern affairs Harold H. Saunders* appeared before the House Subcommittee on the Middle East to make a policy statement concerning the Palestinians.* Just two days before, the United Nations (UN) General Assembly had passed a resolution (UNGA Resolution 3379 [XXX]* defining Zionism* as "a form of racism or racial discrimination." Daniel Patrick Moynihan, then the U.S. ambassador to the UN, voted against the resolution, and his action received strong public support. Israel's supporters were surprised that Saunders issued a statement in which it appeared that the United States was modifying its stance toward the Palestinians.

The Saunders statement came to be called the Saunders Document. He testified that the Palestinians were the "heart" of the Arab–Israeli conflict. "The issue is not whether Palestinian interests should be expressed in a final settlement, but how. There will be no peace unless an answer is found," he stated. Most controversial was his mention of the Palestine Liberation Organization* (PLO); he suggested that "we do not at this point have the framework for a negotiation involving the PLO."

For supporters of Israel a central issue in the conflict had always been Arab refusal to recognize the legitimacy of the Jewish state. The PLO and the Arab League* both renounced the existence of Israel and vowed to establish a Palestinian state. Saunders's mention of a possible negotiating framework with the PLO brought complaints from pro-Israeli groups to Secretary of State Kissinger.* Kissinger denied that he had been involved in preparing the document and downplayed its significance for U.S. foreign policy while referring to it as "an academic exercise." He had, in fact, gone over the draft carefully and cleared it with President Gerald Ford.*

Saunders continued to say that "it is obvious that thinking on the Palestinian aspects of the problem must evolve on all sides. As it does, what is not possible today may become possible." Although by this time the Arab League had sanctioned the PLO's right to speak for Palestinian people, this right was not recognized by the United States so long as the PLO considered terrorism a legitimate means of achieving its goals.

The document contained no new information at the time, but it symbolized the commitment of the administration to work for a peace settlement. Controversy arose mainly because its tone presented the Palestinian question and the PLO in a more positive and central position than any previous statement by a U.S. official. This resulted in an apparent shift in U.S. policy, which raised Arab hopes. When the UN Security Council held a debate on the Middle East in January 1976, the United States allowed the PLO to formally participate. The United States voted against seating the PLO but did not veto the vote to allow the PLO to be present. Israel refused to participate in the debate. This conciliatory move by Kissinger toward the PLO was designed to show it that the United States would listen to its demands, but when a pro-Palestinian resolution emerged, the United States vetoed it, successfully removing Arab hopes for a shifting U.S. policy. Kissinger believed that the veto would restore the credibility with pro-Israel groups and Israeli officials that had been lost when the Saunders Document emerged.

For further information see: William Quandt, *Peace Process: American Diplomacy and the Arab–Israeli Conflict since 1967* (Washington, DC: Brookings Institution, 1993); Steven L. Speigel, *The Other Arab–Israeli Conflict: Making America's Middle East Policy, from Truman to Reagan* (Chicago: University of Chicago Press, 1985).

Erin Z. Ferguson

SAUNDERS, HAROLD HENRY (b. Philadelphia, December 27, 1930). He received his B.A. from Princeton University in 1952 and his Ph.D. from Yale University in 1956. Saunders worked for the Central Intelligence Agency (CIA) from 1959 to 1961. He then joined the National Security Council (NSC) in 1961 and worked there until 1974. He was a member of the Senior Staff of the NSC from 1967 to 1974. Saunders served as deputy assistant secretary for Near Eastern and South Asian Affairs in the State Department from 1974 to 1975.

As deputy assistant secretary, Saunders was at the center of a controversy when, on November 12, 1975, during testimony before the Subcommittee for the Middle East and Europe of the House Foreign Affairs Committee, he called for a ''diplomatic process which will help bring forth a reasonable definition of Palestinians' interests.'' He also stated that the Palestine Liberation Organization* (PLO) was a major element to be dealt with on the Palestine problem and that the aim of the Palestinian organization was to establish a binational secular state. There were indications, as well, that coexistence between separate Palestinian and Israeli states might be considered. These statements became known as the ''Saunders Document''* and were viewed with hostility by the Israelis and many congressmen who saw them as a possible shift in U.S. policy. The Israelis specifically stated that Saunders's statements contradicted previous U.S. policy, which had stated that the Palestinian matter must be negotiated by Israel and Jordan.*

For further information see: Bernard Reich, *The United States and Israel: Influence in the Special Relationship* (New York: Praeger, 1984); Harold Saunders, *The Middle East Problem in the 1980s* (Washington, DC: American Enterprise Institute for Public Policy Research, 1981); Harold Saunders, *Conversations with Harold Saunders: US Policy for the Middle East in the 1980s* (Washington, DC: American Enterprise Institute for Public Policy Research, 1982); *The Other Walls: The Politics of the Arab–Israeli Peace Process* (Washington, DC: American Enterprise Institute for Public Policy Research, 1985).

Donald A. Vogus

SAVIR, URIEL (b. Jerusalem,* 1952). He joined the Israeli Foreign Ministry in 1975 and has held various positions in the legal and press divisions. From 1984 to 1988, he was media adviser and bureau chief for Shimon Peres* in his capacities as prime minister and foreign minister. In November 1988, he assumed the post of consul general of Israel in New York. In May 1993, he was appointed director general of the Foreign Ministry and was involved in the final stages of the negotiation of the Israel–Palestine Liberation Organization* (PLO) Declaration of Principles* (DOP) in Oslo. He participated in the Oslo talks* and subsequent negotiations with the PLO concerning the Gaza and Jericho first* plan.

SAYEGH, FAYEZ ABDULLAH (b. Syria,* January 11, 1922; d. New York, December 10, 1980). Sayegh was one of seven children who grew up in

Tiberias near the Sea of Galilee.* His father was a Presbyterian minister. He
attended school in Safed and studied at the University of Beirut. Later he earned
a Ph.D. from Georgetown University in Washington, D.C. At various times
Sayegh taught at Stanford, Yale, and the American University in Beirut and
published a number of books on Arab political affairs. In the 1950s, he headed
the Information Office of the Arab League* at the United Nations. Sayegh was
the founder of the Palestine Research Center in Beirut, Lebanon.* A political
adviser at the Kuwait mission to the United Nations from 1967 until his death
in 1980, he was a spokesman for the Palestinians and participated in many
United Nations debates on the Arab–Israel conflict. He served on the Executive
Committee of the Palestine Liberation Organization* in 1965 and 1966.

Joseph E. Goldberg

SCOPUS, MOUNT. See **MOUNT SCOPUS.**

SCRANTON MISSION. William Scranton, former governor of Pennsylvania,
the special envoy of President-Elect Richard Nixon,* traveled to the Middle
East after the November 1968 U.S. election on a fact-finding mission. He defined
his mission as informing himself of the opinions of the leaders of the countries
of the area on the Middle East situation and other important world issues, in
order to report to Nixon. He noted that he did not believe there would be any
fundamental change in U.S. Middle East policy. Among other locations, in December 1968, he visited Tehran, Beirut, Cairo, Riyadh, and Jerusalem.* During
the course of remarks he also noted that U.S. policy would be more "evenhanded."*

For further information see: George D. Wolf, *William Warren Scranton, Pennsylvania
Statesman* (University Park: Pennsylvania State University Press, 1981).

SCUD MISSILES. The SS-1 series of Soviet missiles (designated Scuds by the
North Atlantic Treaty Organization [NATO]) are land-mobile, surface-to-
surface, short-range, ballistic missiles. Since the late 1950s, the Soviet Union
has introduced three variants of the Scud missile: Scud A, Scud B, and Scud
C. Introduced in 1957, the Scud A weighed approximately 9,700 pounds, with
an 880 pound high-explosive warhead, and had a range of approximately 81
miles. The Scud B, introduced in 1964, weighed approximately 14,043 pounds,
with a 2,205-pound payload capable of accepting a nuclear, chemical, or high-
explosive warhead. The Scud B has a range to 174 miles. The Scud C was
introduced in the early 1970s, with an extended range of nearly 280 miles. All
of the Scud missiles rely on simplified inertial navigational guidance systems
and are considered significantly inaccurate missiles useful against cities and
other large targets.

Scud missiles first entered the Arab–Israeli conflict before the Yom Kippur
War.* In previous wars, Israeli combat aircraft conducted air strikes deep inside
Egypt* with impunity. Egyptian leaders believed that Scud missiles would serve

as a deterrent against Israeli air strikes by threatening their use against Israeli population centers. However, the Scud missile did not play a major combat role during the Yom Kippur War. Reportedly, only one Scud missile was fired toward the end of the conflict, and it landed in the Sinai Peninsula* without causing damage.

In the late 1980s, Iraq* developed two extended-range variants of the Scud B by decreasing its payload and increasing the missile's fuel capacity. The first Iraqi variant, the Al-Husayn, had a 420-pound payload and a range of approximately 375 miles. The second Iraqi variant, the Al-Abbas, had a 250-pound payload and an expected range of up to 560 miles. The Iraqi modifications induced significant aerodynamic instabilities in both missiles that greatly decreased the Scud's already poor accuracy. During the Persian Gulf War* of 1991, Iraq fired up to thirty-nine of these missiles into Israel and others into Saudi Arabia. These Scuds landed in Israel without causing significant damage or loss of life but did cause significant psychological trauma among the Israeli population. Iraq fired these missiles at Israel in an attempt to fracture the Arab–international coalition opposing its occupation of Kuwait. Saddam Hussein* hoped that if he could goad Israel into combat actions against Iraq, the Arab states would abandon their participation in the coalition against Iraq. Israel, at the strong urging of the United States, refrained from responding to Iraq's attacks.

For further information see: Martin S. Navias, *Going Ballistic: The Build-Up of Missiles in the Middle East* (London: Brassey's, 1993); Edgar O'Ballance, *No Victor, No Vanquished: The Yom Kippur War* (San Rafael, CA: Presidio Press, 1978).

Jon J. Peterson and Stephen H. Gotowicki

SEA OF GALILEE. The Sea of Galilee is a small (fourteen miles long and eight miles across at its broadest point) freshwater lake in northern Israel and is often mentioned in the Bible. It is called the Sea of Kinnereth (Yam Kinneret) in the Old Testament. The name Galilee is used in the New Testament. It is also called Lake Tiberias after a city on its shore. The Sea of Galilee lies on the Jordan* plain in Israel thirty miles from the Mediterranean Sea. It touches the Golan Heights* on the northeast. The Jordan River* flows southward through it.

SECURITY SETTLEMENTS. See **SETTLEMENTS.**

SECURITY ZONE. After the Israeli withdrawal from Lebanon in 1985 of troops that had been there since the 1982 War in Lebanon,* it retained control of a strip of land along the Israel–Lebanon border that Israel referred to as the security zone. Deployed within this zone were Israeli troops as well as components of the South Lebanese Army (SLA).* See also FATAHLAND.

For further information see: Beate Hamizrachi, *The Emergence of the South Lebanon Security Belt: Major Saad Haddad and the Ties with Israel, 1975–1978* (New York: Praeger, 1988).

SEPARATE PEACE. A reference to the charge made against President Anwar Sadat* of Egypt,* accusing him of making a separate peace with Israel in the Egypt–Israel Peace Treaty* and thereby violating principles agreed to by Arab Summit meetings and not taking into account the Palestinian* issue and the rights of the Palestinians. This provided the basis for the decision made at the Baghdad Summit* meeting of November 1978 to send a delegation to try to dissuade Sadat from proceeding with the peace treaty with Israel and, if it failed, to move the headquarters of the Arab League* from Cairo to Tunis. Ultimately, Sadat was accused of acting independently, and Egypt was ousted from the league.

SEPARATION OF FORCES AGREEMENT. Signed by the chiefs of staff of the Israeli and Egyptian* armies on January 18, 1974, the agreement delineated the position of the combatants following the Yom Kippur War.* The Israelis were required to withdraw from forward positions they occupied after the cease-fire. A ten-kilometer buffer zone between the two armies was established, under United Nations supervision. Beyond this, there were zones of "thinned-out" forces where each side was to reduce the number of its troops to parity with the other—eight infantry battalions, thirty tanks, and thirty-six cannons. The signatories were given four weeks to reduce their troop levels in these zones. Behind the thinned-out zones, Egypt and Israel were allowed to station any number of troops, but Egypt was forbidden to install antiaircraft missile batteries in this area. The parties were given seven weeks to position their forces, subject to United Nations (UN) supervision. The agreement followed the mediation of U.S. secretary of state Henry Kissinger* and direct talks between the military chiefs of both sides. It provided a basis for the Israel–Egypt Disengagement of Forces Agreement* of January 1974.

SETTLEMENTS. Over the years since the Six Day War,* Israel has built numerous settlements in the occupied territories.* These settlements have been the subject of significant controversy.

Since shortly after the Six Day War, Israelis have been settling in the occupied territories, although the precise number of settlements, their size, population, importance, and status have not always been easy to determine.

There is no single rationale for the settlements established, but security appears to have been the major factor, especially during the tenure of the Labor Party*-led governments between 1967 and 1977. The Labor policy of land settlement was selective and conditioned by political, as well as strategic, considerations. Labor sought to limit settlements only in particular areas of the most strategic value. Some of the settlements, such as Nahal Yam in the Sinai Peninsula,* served as a means of maintaining the Israeli military presence and was yielded under appropriate circumstances. Others, notably in the Golan Heights* and in the Sinai between the Gaza Strip* and el-Arish, were located in areas Israel would seek to retain for long-range security considerations. But it nev-

ertheless yielded all the settlements in Sinai when it achieved peace with Egypt.*
There were other settlements, such as Kiryat Arba* near Hebron,* where Israel
would seek to ensure a Jewish presence even if the area were ultimately returned
to Arab control.

The utilization of border settlements for the dual purpose of civilian settlements and agriculture, as well as the performance of security functions, is a
historical Israeli–Zionist concept and is reflected in the very existence of the
paramilitary NAHAL* program in which individuals perform their military service by carrying out important settlement-agriculture tasks.

Some settlements were established, at least initially, as a result of private
initiative and against government wishes.

When Yitzhak Rabin* returned to the post of prime minister in 1992, he began
to reassess the settlements and developed a distinction between security settlements* and political settlements. Rabin used the term *security settlements** to
describe those in the Jordan Valley, around Jerusalem,* and in the Golan
Heights. These were essentially areas in which past conflicts took place and that
served as routes of invasion for armies attacking Israel. Rabin used the term
political settlements to describe those that he did not consider vital to Israel's
security and that, therefore, might be subject to negotiation in the discussions
with the Arabs.

SHAATH, NABIL (b. Safed, Galilee, Palestine, 1938). He studied at the Wharton
School of the University of Pennsylvania, where he received his Ph.D., and later
taught economics at the American University of Beirut. Shaath was a member
of Fatah's* Advisory Council and served on its Central Committee. Later, he
headed the Advisory Council. He became the director of the Palestine Liberation
Organization Planning Center. Shaath has served as one of Arafat's* aides and
as a political adviser. He was appointed chief Palestinian delegate in the talks
with Israel at Taba* to work out the details of the Declaration of Principles*
(DOP).

Joseph E. Goldberg

SHAHAK, AMNON (b. Tel Aviv, 1944). Amnon Shahak began serving in the
Israel Defense Forces* (IDF) in 1962. A paratrooper, he rose steadily through
the ranks. During the Six Day War* he commanded a paratroop company and
later, in the Yom Kippur War,* he was deputy commander of a paratroop brigade. Also in 1973, he took part in the operation in Beirut that killed three
Fatah* representatives, most prominent of whom was Kamal Nasir. After the
War in Lebanon,* he commanded the Beirut and Shouf sector as commander
of a standing armored division. In 1983, Shahak was named commanding officer
of the Central Command and was promoted from brigadier general to major
general. He later commanded armored units before being chosen as the director
of military intelligence in February 1986, a position he held until 1991. In 1988,
Shahak oversaw the Israeli raid against the Palestine Liberation Organization*

(PLO) headquarters in Tunisia. In 1991, he was appointed deputy chief of staff and later that year served as the airlift commander for Operation Solomon (the airlift of approximately 15,000 Ethiopian Jews from Addis Ababa to Israel carried out in May 1991).

Shahak served as the chief Israeli delegate to talks with the PLO delegation at Taba* that sought to work out the details for implementation of the Declaration of Principles* (DOP) signed in Washington in September 1993. He began discussions on October 13, 1993, with his Palestinian* counterpart, Nabil Shaath,* concerning Palestinian self-rule in the Gaza Strip* and Jericho.*

On January 1, 1995, Lieutenant General Amnon Lipkin-Shahak began a four-year term as the fifteenth chief of general staff of the Israel Defense Forces.

He began his tenure as the IDF faced new and challenging missions. These included the evacuation of population centers in the West Bank* and the redeployment of forces in the interim stage prior to a permanent solution with the Palestinians. In effect, preparing for the next war had always been the primary mission of the IDF, but now it also had to prepare to preserve and secure peace.

He graduated from the IDF Staff and Command College, the National Security College, and a staff and command course of the U.S. Marine Corps. He holds a bachelor's degree in general history from Tel Aviv University and has twice been decorated—for his role in the Karameh (1968) and Aviv Neurim (1973) operations.

Donald A. Pearson

SHALOM ACHSHAV. See **PEACE NOW.**

SHAMGAR COMMISSION. Following the Hebron Massacre* in the Tomb of the Patriarchs* on February 25, 1994, the government of Israel decided, on February 27, 1994, to appoint a Commission of Inquiry (later it was decided it would be composed of five members). On February 28, the president of the Supreme Court, Justice Meir Shamgar, decided that he would serve as chairman of the commission and that the other members would be Justice Eliezer Goldberg, Judge Abd el-Rahman Zoubai, Professor Menachem Yaari, and Lieutenant General (res.) Moshe Levy. Investigators were appointed to collect information, and the commission heard most of the testimony in public sessions. The commission held thirty-one sessions and heard evidence from 106 witnesses. It also engaged in a thorough and detailed examination of the Tomb of the Patriarchs and the surrounding area.

The Shamgar Commission issued its report on June 26, 1994. It referred to the killings as a "base and murderous act" and said that "the massacre was one of the harshest expressions of the Jewish–Arab conflict." It concluded that Dr. Baruch Goldstein had acted alone and was the only person to blame for the killings. "The evidence presented to us indicates that he acted alone. We were not presented with credible proof that he was helped, while carrying out the killing or prior to that time, by another individual acting as an accomplice. Nor was it proved to us that he had secret partners.'' The commission assigned no blame to either military or political officials but criticized Israeli army and border police procedures, suggesting that they needed to be tightened in Hebron,* especially at the Cave of Machpela.* The commission also suggested that Jewish and Muslim worshipers must be separated at the Cave of the Patriarchs.*

SHAMIR PROPOSAL. Israeli prime minister Yitzhak Shamir* proposed a peace initiative during a visit to Washington between April 12 and 16, 1989, that emphasized Israel's desire for peace and a ''continuation of the political process by means of direct negotiations based on the principles of the Camp David Accords.''* Shamir proposed that all issues be dealt with simultaneously, including a solution to the Palestine* refugee problem.* The initiative was formulated by Shamir and Yitzhak Rabin* and represented the consensus of Israel's National Unity government.* On May 14, 1989, the government formally approved the proposal to initiate negotiations between Israel and Palestinian representatives.

The proposal contained several elements: Israel, Egypt,* and the United States would renew their commitment to Camp David* and peace; the United States and Egypt would ask the Arab states to end their hostility toward Israel and accept negotiations; the United States would lead an international effort to solve the Palestine refugee problem; and Palestinians from the West Bank* and Gaza Strip* would be elected to form a delegation to negotiate an interim agreement and then a final settlement with Israel.

At the core of the proposal was the portion dealing with Israeli–Palestinian negotiations. ''In order to bring about a process of political negotiations and in order to locate legitimate representatives of the Palestinian population, the prime minister proposes that free elections be held among the Arabs of Judea,* Samaria* and Gaza*—elections that will be free of the intimidation and terror of the PLO [Palestine Liberation Organization*].''

The proposal included a two-stage approach. The first would be a transition period of five years. Not later than the third year after the beginning of the transition period, negotiations would begin for achieving a permanent solution.

Israel refused to negotiate with the PLO. ''During the transitional period the Palestinian Arab inhabitants of Judea, Samaria and the Gaza District will be accorded self-rule, by means of which they will, themselves, conduct their affairs of daily life.'' Israel would maintain responsibility for security—including foreign affairs. This period would be a test for coexistence and cooperation and prepare the way for a final settlement.

On May 22, 1989 U.S. secretary of state James Baker,* in a speech before the American Israel Public Affairs Committee,* criticized the ''unrealistic vision of a greater Israel'' articulated by Shamir and others. At the same time, he suggested that the Shamir proposal had ''given us something to work with'' and the details and differences should be discussed among the parties. Nevertheless, despite the attempts to narrow these differences over a ten-month period, the

Israeli objection to negotiating with the PLO or PLO members within the Palestinian delegation proved too much of an obstacle.

SHAMIR, YITZHAK (Formerly Yzernitzky) (b. Rozhinay, eastern Poland, October 15, 1915). He was educated at a Hebrew secondary school in Bialystok, where he became a disciple of Vladimir (Zeev) Jabotinsky* and joined the Revisionist* youth movement, Betar.* He studied law at Warsaw University until 1935, when he emigrated to Palestine* and changed his surname to Shamir. He completed his studies at Hebrew University in Jerusalem.* Shamir joined the Irgun* in 1937 and rose through the ranks of the organization into leadership positions. Menachem Begin* became the commander of the Irgun in 1943 and remained its leader until its dissolution in 1948. In 1940, the Irgun suspended attacks against the British Mandatory* authorities in Palestine and offered its cooperation in the war effort against Germany. This caused a split in the organization and led to the creation of a smaller and more militant group, which Shamir joined. This faction, LEHI* (Lohamei Herut Yisrael—Israel Freedom Fighters), was known as the "Stern gang,"* named after Abraham Stern (Yair), the group's first leader, and viewed the British as the main obstacle to the establishment of a Jewish state in Palestine. After Stern was killed by British police in 1942, Shamir helped to reorganize LEHI, establishing a high command known as LEHI Central, which included Shamir, Nathan Yellin-Mor, and Dr. Israel Scheib (Eldad). Shamir directed LEHI's operations, which became increasingly violent. A terror campaign was conducted against the British that included the assassination in 1944 of Lord Moyne,* Britain's senior Middle East official, who was stationed in Cairo. Two members were captured, tried, convicted, and executed for the crime. The Stern gang was also suspected in the assassination of Swedish Count Folke Bernadotte,* who sought to mediate an end to Israel's War of Independence* on behalf of the United Nations. These charges were never substantiated, and Shamir has refused comment on the matter. He was arrested twice by British authorities, in 1941 and 1946, but managed to escape both times. He was sent to a detention camp in Eritrea, but Shamir escaped and traveled through Ethiopia to Djibouti, ultimately arriving in France,* where he was given political asylum. He remained in France until he returned to the newly established state of Israel in May 1948. Shamir found it difficult to enter Israel's new political system, which was dominated by former Haganah* members and others who had been associated with the Labor Zionist* movement. Shamir sought election to the Knesset* in 1949, with a list of candidates comprising former LEHI members, but his effort failed. Shamir did not pursue elective office again until he joined the Herut Party* of Menachem Begin in 1970. During the period from 1948 to 1955, he remained in private life, where he was active in a number of commercial ventures, including directing an association of cinema owners. These were not particularly successful. Isser Harel, then head of the Mossad,* recruited Shamir into the organization in 1955, where his operational experience from the Mandate period could be put to use.

He spent a decade with the Mossad and rose to a senior position. He was stationed in Paris for a part of that time. Shamir left the Mossad in 1965 and returned to private life, where he pursued commercial interests, but with only moderate success. He remained active in public life primarily through his efforts at increasing Soviet Jewish immigration to Israel. In 1970, Menachem Begin offered him a position in Herut, and he was elected to the Executive Committee and became the director of the Immigration Department. Shamir successfully ran for election to the Knesset for the first time on the Herut list in 1973 and became a member of the State Comptroller Committee and the Defense and Foreign Affairs Committee. He directed the party's Organization Department and in 1975 was elected chairman of Herut's Executive Committee, a post to which he was reelected unanimously two years later. Shamir was elected speaker of the Knesset in June 1977 and continued to be a loyal supporter of Begin, who now was prime minister. Loyalty characterized Shamir's service to Begin both within the party and in the Begin-led governments in which he served. The most significant issue that separated the two was Begin's decision to negotiate and sign the Camp David Accords* and the Egypt–Israel Peace Treaty.* Shamir opposed the treaty, as did other Likud* leaders, including Moshe Arens* and Ariel Sharon,* because he believed Israel was sacrificing too much in return for what he viewed as uncertain guarantees of peace. The withdrawal from the Sinai Peninsula* and the relinquishing of the security buffer it provided, the sophisticated air bases located there, as well as the dismantling of Jewish settlements, were seen as too high a price for Israel to pay. Shamir abstained on the final Knesset vote when the treaty was approved. Begin appointed Shamir his foreign minister in March 1980. Shamir's view of the Camp David process changed during his tenure as foreign minister, as he was responsible for implementing the agreements reached, and he became an advocate of that approach for future negotiations between Israel and the Arab states. Shamir was also active in efforts to reestablish diplomatic relations with several African states that had been severed at the time of the Yom Kippur War.* Shamir also supported legislation declaring united Jerusalem the eternal capital of Israel, as well as the bombing of the Iraqi* nuclear reactor in June 1981* and the "annexation" of the Golan Heights* in December 1981. These actions were seen as contributing to Israel's security. After the 1981 Knesset election, Begin succeeded in establishing a Likud-led coalition that subsequently received the endorsement of the Knesset, and Shamir continued to serve as foreign minister. During this term in office Shamir was criticized by the Kahan Commission* because he failed to pass on to appropriate individuals information he received from Communications Minister Mordechai Zipori suggesting that massacres were taking place in the Sabra and Shatila* camps near Beirut in September 1982. Menachem Begin resigned from office in September 1983. Shamir was the compromise choice to follow Begin, and he formed the new government. On October 10, 1983, the Knesset endorsed the government and its programs, and Yitzhak Shamir became the prime minister of Israel, but many viewed him as an interim leader who would last only until the next Knesset election in 1984. The 1984 Knesset election results were inconclusive, and, after a period of intense, lengthy, and complex negotiations, Labor and Likud formed, in September 1984, a government of National Unity,* the basis of which was a series of compromises and concessions. According to the terms of the agreement, Shamir and Labor's Shimon Peres* each were to serve for twenty-five months as prime minister while the other held the position of vice prime minister and foreign minister. Peres was prime minister during the first period and rotated positions with Shamir, as agreed, in October 1986. The 1988 Knesset election, as in 1984, did not demonstrate a clear preference for either Likud or Labor among the electorate. After weeks of intensive negotiations, Shamir entered into a new coalition agreement with Labor. The agreement placed Labor in an equal position with Likud in the government; however, Shamir would remain the prime minister for the full tenure of the government. The distribution of Cabinet portfolios among the two blocs was equal. In 1992, Likud, headed by Shamir, relinquished parliamentary control to a Labor Party-led government. Soon thereafter, Shamir announced his retirement from active political life.

Shamir wrote "Israel's Role in a Changing Middle East," *Foreign Affairs* 60 (Spring 1982):789–801 and "Israel at 40," *Foreign Affairs* 66:574–90 (America and the World 1987–1988). Shamir's autobiography, *Summing Up: An Autobiography of Yitzhak Shamir,* was published by Little, Brown in 1994.

For further information see: Bernard Reich and Joseph Helman, "Yitzhak Shamir," in Bernard Reich, ed., *Political Leaders of the Contemporary Middle East and North Africa: A Biographical Dictionary* (Westport, CT: Greenwood Press, 1990), pp. 486–94; Bernard Reich and Gershon R. Kieval, *Israel: Land of Tradition and Conflict,* rev. ed. (Boulder, CO: Westview Press, 1993).

AL-SHARAA, FAROUK (b. Dara'a, Syria,* 1938). He received a B.A. in English literature from the University of Damascus in 1953 and later studied international law at London University. He held a number of major posts in Syrian Arab Airlines from 1963 to 1975. He was ambassador to Italy from 1976 to 1980 and was minister of state for foreign affairs from 1980 to 1984. He became minister of foreign affairs in March 1984.

For further information see: Farouk Sharaa, "Serious and Urgent Efforts Are Needed to Achieve a Just and Comprehensive Peace," *Middle East Insight* 9 (September–October 1993):43–46; "Syrian Foreign Minister Farouk al-Sharaa Reaffirms Peace for Golan Withdrawal," *Middle East Insight* 11 (November–December 1994):14–17.

SHARAF, ABDUL (b. Baghdad, 1939; d. July 3, 1980). Abdul Sharaf moved at the age of two to Istanbul with his mother and brother. The British had deported his father to Rhodesia for showing Nazi sympathies. He was a distant cousin of the Jordanian* royal family, and King Abdullah* brought the family to Amman, where Sharaf attended secondary school. He studied at the American University in Beirut, where he joined the Arab Nationalist Movement. At American University Sharaf became acquainted with George Habash,* who was studying medicine. When the Syrian* government outlawed the Arab Nationalist Movement in 1963, Sharaf resigned. Abdul Sharaf joined the Jordanian Foreign Ministry in 1962. During his career he served as the Jordanian ambassador to the United States. As chief of the Jordanian Cabinet, Sharaf advised King Hussein* not to enter the peace negotiations with Israel initiated by President Anwar Sadat* of Egypt. In early 1980, King Hussein appointed him prime minister. He was serving as Jordan's premier at his death due to a heart attack.

Joseph E. Goldberg

SHARETT, MOSHE (Formerly Shertok) (b. Kherson, Russia, 1894; d. Jerusalem,* 1965). Raised in a Zionist* household, Moshe Sharett immigrated with his family to Palestine* in 1906, settling in an Arab village in the Samarian hills. In 1908, the family moved to Jaffa, where his father was a founder of the Ahuzat Bayit quarter, which later became Tel Aviv. After high school, Sharett studied law in Constantinople and then volunteered as an officer in the Turkish army during World War I. In 1920, while studying at the London School of Economics, he joined the British Poalei Zion movement. In 1931, Sharett became secretary of the Jewish Agency's* Political Department and, in 1933, at the Eighteenth Zionist Conference, was elected head of the Political Department after the murder of Chaim Arlosoroff. On June 29, 1946, Sharett and other leaders of the Jewish Agency were arrested by the British in Palestine and were imprisoned in the Latrun camp for four months. During 1947, Sharett sought approval at the United Nations for the United Nations Special Committee on Palestine* partition plan.* Sharett became the state of Israel's first foreign minister in 1948. As foreign minister, he initially sought a nonaligned status for Israel, but after the Korean War he promoted closer ties with Western democratic countries. He sought contacts with developing nations in Asia and Africa. He also signed the Luxembourg Agreement with West Germany's Konrad Adenauer. In January 1954, when Prime Minister David Ben-Gurion* retired from office, Sharett became prime minister but retained the foreign affairs portfolio. With Ben-Gurion's return as prime minister in November 1955 and the subsequent disagreement between the two men, Sharett resigned in 1956. In 1960, Sharett was elected chairman of the Executive of the World Zionist Organization* and Jewish Agency and remained active in MAPAI* party activities.

For further information see: Menachem L. Rosensaft, *Moshe Sharett: Statesman of Israel* (New York: Shengold, 1966).

SHARM EL-SHEIKH. Controlling the Strait of Tiran,* Sharm El-Sheikh (Ophira to Israel) is a strategic harbor on the southern end of the Sinai Peninsula.* It is located west of the Strait of Tiran where the Gulf of Aqaba* meets the Gulf of Suez and the Red Sea.

Sharm El-Sheikh first became an important military objective during the Suez War* when Israeli forces invaded the Sinai Peninsula and attacked the Egyptian* garrison there. At the time, the town had both a harbor and an airport, fortified with 1,500 Egyptian troops. It was primarily a large supply base but also had artillery that could attack ships leaving the Gulf of Aqaba. On November 4, 1956, elements of Israel's Ninth Brigade attacked the Tsafrat-el-At defenses based on a series of hills protecting Sharm El-Sheikh. The next day, the Israelis captured the town. Israel was persuaded by the United States to withdraw from Sharm El-Sheikh in return for assurances of free passage through the Strait of Tiran. In their place a United Nations Emergency Force* occupied the town. Israel also announced that it would regard any future closing of the strait as an act of war against it.

In response to demands made by Egyptian president Nasser,* the United Nations force was withdrawn in May 1967. On May 22, Nasser declared that passage through the Strait of Tiran was closed to Israel. On June 5, Israel attacked, reaching Sharm El-Sheikh on the seventh in a three-pronged attack from land, sea, and air. They discovered that the Egyptian positions were deserted and that the blockade against Israel was nonexistent.

During the October 1973 War,* Israel used the harbor as a base for a blockade of the Gulf of Suez. A force of Egyptian helicopter-borne commandos was shot down trying to reach it. After the war, Israel again wanted to retain control of the area. Israeli general Moshe Dayan* once declared that he would rather have Sharm El-Sheikh than peace with Egypt. Its strategic importance was highlighted by the July 1978 Israeli raid on Entebbe,* which took off from the airport at Sharm El-Sheikh.

In the September 17, 1978, Camp David Accords,* Egypt agreed that Israel would continue to have civilian access to its airfield and passage through the Strait of Tiran. United Nations forces would again be stationed at Sharm El-Sheikh and could not be removed without a unanimous vote of the five permanent members of the United Nations Security Council.

Israel's withdrawal in April 1982 was marked by a ceremony in the resort town. Today Sharm El-Sheikh is Egypt's largest tourist resort on the west coast of the Sinai Peninsula.

For further information see: Chaim Herzog, *The Arab–Israeli Wars: War and Peace in the Middle East from the War of Independence to Lebanon* (London: Arms and Armour, 1984).

David J. Abram

SHARON, ARIEL (Nicknamed Arik) (Formerly Sheinerman) (b. Kfar Malal, Palestine,* 1928). At the age of fourteen he joined the Haganah*; he was wounded during the War of Independence* in 1948 and subsequently rose swiftly in the ranks of the Israel Defense Forces* (IDF). In 1952, Sharon established the "101 Unit"* for special operations (a special commando force known for its daring operations behind enemy lines), and, in 1956, he commanded a paratroop brigade, units of which parachuted at the Mitla Pass* to mark the beginning of the Sinai War.*

Following the Sinai War, he studied at the British Staff College in Camberley and, upon his return, was appointed head of the Israel Defense Forces School of Infantry. In 1962, Sharon became director of military training of the IDF and, that same year, graduated from the law school of the Hebrew University. In the Six Day War* of 1967, he commanded an armored division that fought in the Sinai Peninsula,* and, in 1969, he became commanding officer of the Southern Command. In June 1973, Sharon resigned from the IDF, joined the Liberal Party, and was instrumental in bringing about the alignment of Herut,* the Free Centre, the State List, and the Liberal Party within the framework of the Likud bloc.* The Yom Kippur War* brought him back to active military service in October 1973 as a reserve officer in command of an armored division, units of which were the first to cross the Suez Canal* and establish an Israeli bridgehead on the Egyptian side. In December 1973, Sharon stood for election to the Knesset* and was elected on behalf of the Liberal Party faction of the Likud bloc. In December 1974, Sharon resigned from the Knesset, in order that his reserve commission with the IDF might be reinstated. In June 1975, he was appointed adviser to Prime Minister Yitzhak Rabin* on security affairs and held that position until April 1976, when he resigned to form the Shlomzion Party, which gained two seats in the elections to the Ninth Knesset in May 1977. Immediately following the elections, the Shlomzion Party merged with the Herut Party faction of the Likud bloc, and on this ticket he was reelected to the Tenth Knesset on May 30, 1981.

He was appointed minister of agriculture in June 1977. On August 5, 1981, he was sworn in as minister of defense. Sharon was forced from his position as minister of defense in the spring of 1983 after the Kahan Commission of Inquiry* report concerning the massacre at the Sabra and Shatila* refugee camps in Lebanon,* but he remained in the Cabinet as minister without portfolio. He later became minister of industry and trade, and, in December 1988, he was reappointed to that position. He subsequently served as housing minister. See also KIBYA.

Sharon wrote *Warrior: An Autobiography* (New York: Simon and Schuster, 1989).

For further information see: Uzi Benziman, *Sharon: An Israeli Caesar* (New York: Adama Books, 1985); *Generals of Israel* (Tel Aviv: Hadar Publishing House, 1968).

SHAW COMMISSION. Arab riots in Palestine* in 1928 and 1929 resulted in the death of Jews in Jerusalem,* Hebron,* and Safed, with many more injured. In 1928 and 1929, there were disturbances and riots associated with the Wailing Wall.* The British established a Commission of Inquiry headed by Sir Walter Shaw to investigate the cause of the anti-Jewish riots and to suggest policies that might prevent such occurrences in the future. Shaw had a long career in the colonial service in the West Indies, Ceylon, and the Straits settlements, where he had been chief justice. The commission issued a report on March 31, 1930.

Among other factors it recommended that the land and the immigration issues be studied further. This led to the establishment of the mission of Sir John Hope-Simpson,* which, in turn, led to the Passfield White Paper.* This was followed by the letter of Prime Minister Ramsey MacDonald* effectively nullifying the Passfield White Paper's restrictions on Jewish immigration and land purchases. The latter letter was referred to by the Arabs as the Black Letter. The Shaw Report suggested that Zionist* immigration and land policies were a cause of the riots. The government was uncomfortable with these results and appointed a new commission under Sir John Hope-Simpson to focus on the economic dimension of the land and immigration questions. At the same time, the Cabinet, on May 27, issued a White Paper that reaffirmed the Shaw Commission's conclusions.

The Shaw Commission reported on March 30, 1930, to the British government, but, before it was published, Prime Minister Ramsey MacDonald thought it was too pro-Arab in nature.

The commission made note of the fact that there had been serious attacks by the Arabs on Jews. The commission found that the recent outbreak in 1929 neither was nor was intended to be a revolt against British authority in Palestine.

The commission made several recommendations. The British government should issue a clear statement of policy defining the meanings of the Mandate* provisions that were intended to provide for the rights of the non-Jewish populations, and the government should lay down more explicit directions on the policy of issues such as land tenure and immigration. The government should also make a statement regarding Jewish immigration, with the goal of preventing a repeat of the "excessive immigration of 1925–1926," and a voice should be given to non-Jewish interests on this issue.

The report also called for a special commission to be appointed to determine the rights of Arabs and Jews with regard to the Wailing Wall.

The Zionists were disappointed by the report, as Jewish immigration to Palestine was suspended. The Arabs were disappointed, as they had hoped for a national government with some measure of independence.

The policy statement that the Shaw Commission called for became known as the Passfield Paper of 1930, which called for an end to Jewish immigration and the sale of land only to landless Arabs. Prime Minister Ramsey MacDonald was forced to issue an explanatory letter the following year that virtually nullified the paper and rejected the Shaw Commission Report.

For further information see: Great Britain, Colonial Office. *Report of the Commission on the Palestine Disturbances of August 1929,* Cmd. 3530 (London: His Majesty's Stationery Office, 1930).

Monica M. Boudjouk and Joseph E. Goldberg

SHAZLI, SAAD MUHAMMAD (b. 1922). A highly decorated (twenty-three decorations) Egyptian* army officer and diplomat. He was educated at the University of Cairo and the Egyptian Military College. He holds master's degrees in both military science and political science and studied military tactics in both the United States and the Soviet Union. He was a platoon commander during the Arab–Israeli War of 1948*; commander of the Parachute School from 1954 to 1956 and of the Egyptian Mission in the United Nations forces in the Congo, 1960–61. He served as defense attaché in London from 1961 to 1963 and as brigade commander during the Yemen Civil War (1965–66). He was head of Egypt's Special Forces from 1967 to 1969. In 1971, he was appointed chief of staff of the Egyptian Armed Forces, a position he held until December 12, 1973. Western military experts identify him as the single most important figure in the Egyptian Armed Forces during that period. Lieutenant General Shazli fought in six wars.

Following a major policy disagreement with President Anwar Sadat* concerning Egyptian military strategy during and after the Yom Kippur War,* Shazli was removed from military service by Sadat and appointed Egypt's ambassador to the United Kingdom in 1974. A year later he was transferred to Portugal, where he was Egypt's ambassador until 1978. He frequently criticized Sadat's regime sharply and, as a result, was dismissed from his diplomatic post and forced into exile. He opposed the Camp David Accords* as well as the Egypt–Israel Peace Treaty.* He argued that such agreements would alter the balance of power in the Middle East in Israel's favor and allow for further Israeli territorial expansion. He believes that the military solution is the only option available to the Arabs to solve the Arab–Israeli conflict and should not be discarded by the Arabs. He later resided in Algeria, where he formed the Egyptian National Front Party 1980—a political coalition opposing President Sadat's Middle East peace initiatives.

For further information see: Saad el Shazli, *The Crossing of the Suez* (San Francisco: American Mideast Research, 1980); Saad El Shazli, *The Arab Military Option* (San Francisco: American Mideast Research, 1986).

Ahmed Elbashari

SHEIKH HUSSEIN BRIDGE. See **HUSSEIN BRIDGE.**

SHERIF HUSSEIN. See **HUSSEIN, SHERIF OF MECCA.**

SHERMAN TANK. The Sherman class of tanks is based on the World War II-era American M-4 tank. The original M-4 was armed with a 75mm cannon, weighed about thirty-five tons, and had a road speed of approximately 30 mph and a range of 170 miles. Israel reportedly had two of these M-4 tanks when the state was founded in 1948 and received an additional 100 M-4 tanks from France* in 1956. These tanks were renamed the M-1 Super Sherman and used in the Sinai War* and the Six Day War.* Israel made extensive improvements to its fleet of Sherman tanks, including upgraded armor, improved fire control, improved engines, and cannon upgrades. It also used the basic chassis in a wide variety of tactical uses such as an armored ambulance, a command vehicle, an artillery observation vehicle, an engineering and mine-clearing vehicle, a self-propelled howitzer platform, a multiple rocket launcher platform, and a mortar carriage.

Sherman tanks are no longer in active service with the Israel Defense Forces.* Israel transferred some of its former tanks to the Christian militia in southern Lebanon and sold some to countries such as Chile.

For further information see: Christopher F. Foss, ed., *Jane's Main Battle Tank,* 2d ed. (London: Jane's, 1986).

Stephen H. Gotowicki

SHIHABI, HIKMAT. As part of the negotiations for the disengagement* of Israeli and Syrian* military forces on the Golan Heights* following the Yom Kippur War,* a Syrian delegation came to Washington in April 1974. It was headed by Brigadier General Hikmat al-Shihabi (then chief of military intelligence). They discussed various ideas and proposals for the disengagement of the two opposing forces. This preceded Kissinger's* shuttle diplomacy* of May 1974 that led to the Disengagement Agreement.

SHIN BET (Sheirut Bitachon Klali, SHABAK). Founded on June 30, 1948, in Tel Aviv, the Shin Bet is Israel's General Security Service. By definition it deals with security inside Israel and the occupied territories.* This domestic intelligence community acts directly on orders of the prime minister. From the outset, its goal was to ensure that domestically it had the best possible domestic intelligence network. In order to do this, its directors had to be extremely talented and dedicated to Israel's security. The directors of this organization have been: 1948–52, Isser Harel (also known as the "Memuneh"—the "one in charge"— of Israeli intelligence); 1952–53, Izzy Dorot; 1953–63, Amos Manor; 1964–74, Yosef Harmelin; 1974–81, Avraham Ahituv; 1981–86, Avraham Shalom; 1986–88, Yosef Harmelin; 1988– disclosure forbidden by Israeli law.

In Israel's intelligence community, the Shin Bet is known for its ability to create and maintain a network of informants on all sides of an issue. More controversial has been Shin Bet's assumption that its duties extend to Israelis and Jews all over the world. At times, it has been accused of overstepping its bounds by operating clandestinely in other countries—sometimes without the knowledge of Israel's prime minister.

Harel (who led both Shin Bet and the Mossad*) molded the Shin Bet organization as a nonmilitary intelligence-security team.

After Dorot's interim year of leadership, power was shifted to Amos Manor, under whose guidance the Shin Bet led operations as far away as Moscow. In February 1956, he obtained a copy of a secret speech of Nikita Khrushchev, to be delivered to the twenty-second meeting of the Communist Party, and, on April 17 of that year, Shin Bet gave a copy of it to Allen Dulles of the U.S. Central Intelligence Agency (CIA). This act, more than any other, allied the CIA and the Mossad. This was Shin Bet's "golden era," in which it had a carte blanche on many operations and was very successful.

In 1964, Yosef Harmelin took the helm of the Shin Bet, and, facing a new world of Arab terrorism and international hijackings by Fatah,* he developed Israel's quick-response teams of secret police to handle bus and airplane hijackings. A dozen years after he left the Shin Bet, Harmelin came back in 1986, on special request of the prime minister, to restore confidence in the organization. Under director Avraham Shalom, who was in charge during the 1984 killings and cover-ups of two Palestinian bus hijackers while being held in custody by the Shin Bet, the organization's reputation was tarnished. Harmelin led until mid-1988.

Since the start of the *intifada** in December 1987, SHABAK has rebuilt its network of Arab informants. During the first ten months of the uprising, the Shin Bet successfully exposed no less than 300 terrorist cells, and its human intelligence assets—*humint*—seemed effective. However, Israel neglected to protect its old and reliable paid Arab informants. Many either died in fights with, or at the hands of, other Palestinians. Israel's intelligence was left "blind and deaf" at a time when it needed more informants to quell its newest political and security challenge. See also MOSSAD.

For further information see: Ian Black and Benny Morris, *Israel's Secret Wars—A History of Israel's Intelligence Services* (New York: Grove Weidenfeld Press, 1991); Richard Deacon, *The Israeli Secret Service* (New York: Taplinger, 1977); Dan Raviv and Yossi Melman, *Every Spy a Prince: The Complete History of Israel's Intelligence Community* (Boston: Houghton Mifflin, 1990); Ze'ev Schiff and Ehud Ya'ari, *Intifada* (New York: Simon and Schuster, 1990); Stewart Steven, *The Spymasters of Israel* (New York: Ballantine Books, 1980).

Yasha Manuel Harari

SHLEMUT HAMOLEDET. The concept of the right of the Jewish people to all of Eretz Israel.* The Revisionist Party,* established by Vladimir Jabotinsky* in 1925, and his New Zionist Organization* supported the principle of Shlemut Hamoledet and rejected Arab claims for national and political sovereignty in Palestine.*

SHOAH. See **HOLOCAUST.**

SHUKAIRY, AHMED (Ahmad Al-Shuqayri) (b. Acre, 1908; d. 1980). His father, Assad Shukairy, was part of the Palestine* resistance prior to 1968 and had been a supporter of the Young Turks in 1908. Assad Shukairy was exiled and returned to Acre, where he became a Muslim dignitary. He was trained as a lawyer. Shukairy was a member of the Arab Higher Committee* in 1946 and served on the Syrian* delegation to the United Nations from 1949 to 1950. From 1951 to 1957, he was secretary for political affairs of the Arab League.* Shukairy served as Saudi Arabia's ambassador to the United Nations from 1957 to 1962. When the Congress of Palestinian Representatives met from May 28 to June 2, 1964, in Jerusalem,* he was selected to establish an Executive Committee for the creation of a Palestine Liberation Organization* (PLO). The motivation for the creation of such an organization appeared to come from Egyptian* president Nasser,* who sought a means to control the Palestinians. Shukairy selected fifteen members for the Executive Committee. He became the leader of the PLO.

Shukairy's dictatorial leadership, as well as his irresponsible public statements, generated substantial dissent within the PLO. Furthermore, he was viewed as an extension of Egyptian policy. In an attempt to maintain control of the PLO, Shukairy disbanded the Executive Committee in 1966 and created a Revolutionary Council. His efforts were counterproductive and increased opposition to Shukairy's leadership. On February 27, 1967, Shukairy announced the establishment of a new Executive Committee. He was known for his extremist views and speeches, often calling for the physical elimination of Israel. In December 1967, he was removed from the head of the PLO and replaced by Yasser Arafat.*

Joseph E. Goldberg

SHULTZ, GEORGE P. (b. New York, December 13, 1920). George Pratt Shultz graduated in 1942 from Princeton University with a B.A. in economics. During World War II, Shultz was a Marine officer serving in the Pacific area. He received a Ph.D. from the Massachusetts Institute of Technology (MIT) in 1949 and was then a member of the faculty until 1957. In 1955–56, he was a senior staff economist with President Eisenhower's* Council of Economic Advisers. In 1957, he became a professor of industrial relations at the University of Chicago Graduate School of Business and was dean there from 1962 to 1968. Shultz was secretary of labor (1969–70), chairman of the Office of Management and the Budget (June 1970–June 1972), and secretary of the treasury (June 1972–74) under President Nixon.* In 1974, he joined the Bechtel Corporation and became its president in 1975. In February 1981, Shultz was named head of the new Economic Policy Advisory Board by President Ronald Reagan.* From July 1982 to January 1989, George P. Shultz was secretary of state. Subsequently, he became a professor of economics at Stanford University.

Shultz became secretary of state in the summer of 1982 and helped to arrange the Palestine Liberation Organization's* (PLO) evacuation from Lebanon* and the sending of a multinational force* (MNF) that included U.S. Marines there. Shultz tried to restart the Arab–Israeli peace process through the fresh-start initiative,* which was announced by President Reagan on September 1, 1982. Its goal was to solve the Israel–Palestinian conflict on the basis of the Camp David* format and United Nations Security Council (UNSC) Resolution 242.*

Shultz orchestrated an accord between Israel and Lebanon signed on May 17, 1983.* The accord collapsed because of the failure of Syria* to withdraw from

Lebanon. Still, the Israelis did proceed to engage in a unilateral withdrawal from Lebanon, except for a security zone* in the south.

On October 23, 1984, the American Marine compound in Lebanon was bombed, killing 241 Marines. In early 1984, Reagan withdrew the Marine contingent despite Shultz's objections. After the October bombing, U.S. policy became one of punishing Syria for its support of terrorism, and Shultz concentrated his diplomatic efforts on the Persian Gulf. In 1985, Shultz made one last attempt at arranging peace talks between the Israelis and a joint Jordanian*–Palestinian delegation, but to no avail.

On March 4, 1988, Shultz announced a new initiative to settle the Arab–Israeli conflict that came to be known as the Shultz Plan of 1988.* He again traveled extensively throughout the Middle East, seeing both Arabs and Israelis to organize peace negotiations. His initiative planned to connect discussions on autonomy for the territories with talks on a final settlement. By the end of July, the plan collapsed.

In late 1988, Shultz put pressure on Yasser Arafat* to declare that he would pursue peace with Israel based on UNSC Resolution 242 and would renounce terrorism, in exchange for a United States–PLO dialogue.* On December 14, 1988, after Yasser Arafat stated that he would meet these conditions, Shultz announced the lifting of the ban on United States–PLO dialogue.

For further information see: William B. Quandt, *Peace Process* (Washington, DC: Brookings Institution, 1993); Ronald W. Reagan, *An American Life* (New York: Simon and Schuster, 1990); George P. Schultz, *Turmoil and Triumph: My Years as Secretary of State* (New York: Charles Scribner's Sons, 1993).

Nolan Wohl

SHULTZ PLAN (1988). On March 4, 1988, U.S. secretary of state George Shultz* put forward a plan for resolving the Arab–Israeli conflict. The initiative was designed to produce direct, bilateral Arab–Israeli negotiations to achieve comprehensive peace based on all the provisions and principles of United Nations Security Council (UNSC) Resolution 242.* The United States supported an international conference that would launch a series of bilateral negotiations. All attendees at the conference would be required to accept United Nations Security Council Resolutions 242 and 338* and to renounce violence and terrorism. The conference would be specifically enjoined from intruding in the negotiations, imposing solutions, or vetoing what had been agreed bilaterally.

The Shultz Plan was similar to previous American peace initiatives, given that it aimed to achieve a comprehensive peace through direct, bilateral Arab–Israeli negotiations. During his trip he had discussed ideas for peace negotiations with all the parties concerned, including Israel, Jordan,* Syria,* the Soviet Union, and some individual Palestinians.* The impetus to this initiative was the recent outbreak of the *intifada** in the West Bank* and Gaza Strip.* It was based on UNSC Resolutions 242 and 338 calling for an exchange of land for peace.* While based on the Camp David Accords,* the Shultz Plan would streamline the process and reduce the time period for carrying out the provisions of the accord.

In a letter outlining the elements of his initiative, Shultz described the following elements:

The agreed objective is a comprehensive peace providing for the security of all the states in the region and for the legitimate rights of the Palestinian people. Negotiations will start on an early date certain between Israel and each of its neighbors which is willing to do so. These negotiations could begin by May 1, 1988. Each of these negotiations will be based on United Nations Security Council Resolutions 242 and 338, in all their parts. The parties to each bilateral negotiation will determine the procedure and agenda at their negotiation. All participants in the negotiations must state their willingness to negotiate with one another.

Shultz also discussed details concerning negotiations between Israel and a Jordanian–Palestinian delegation and suggested the holding of an international conference before the opening of negotiations. He noted further that "all participants in the conference must accept United Nations Security Council Resolutions 242 and 338, and renounce violence and terrorism." He also noted that "the conference will not be able to impose solutions or veto agreements reached." "Palestinian representation will be within the Jordanian–Palestinian delegation. The Palestinian issue will be addressed in the negotiations between the Jordanian–Palestinian and Israeli delegations. Negotiations between the Israeli delegation and the Jordanian–Palestinian delegation will proceed independently of any other negotiations."

The distinguishing feature of the initiative was what Shultz described as the "interlock" that connected the negotiations on the transitional period (autonomy*) for the West Bank and Gaza* to the talks on final status. The Palestinians would be represented by a joint Jordanian–Palestinian delegation in its negotiations with an Israeli delegation. The negotiations for transitional arrangements would last for six months. Regardless of the outcome of these talks, the discussions on the final status of the West Bank and Gaza would begin in the seventh month. A goal of one year was set for negotiating the final status of the territories. After an agreement was reached on interim arrangements, a transitional period lasting for three years would start. The United States would take part in both negotiations and present a draft agreement at the beginning of the dialogue for transitional arrangements. An international conference would be held two weeks before the start of the talks with the five permanent members of the United Nations Security Council and the parties involved in the Arab–Israeli conflict invited to take part. The one precondition was that all participants in the conference must accept United Nations (UN) Security Council Resolutions 242 and 338 and renounce violence and terrorism. The conference would not have the power to impose solutions or veto agreements reached.

According to Shultz, the logic behind interlock was that the Arabs would be able to see that self-rule was not a substitute for an outcome on the final status of the territories and thus would be able to accept Camp David-based autonomy talks. On the other hand, the Israelis would see that interlock would convince the Palestinians to negotiate seriously and to renounce violence. The more serious the Palestinians were about autonomy, the more serious the Israelis were likely to be in the final-status talks.

Reaction to the plan was generally negative. Israel's Prime Minister Yitzhak Shamir* opposed the initiative. He was adamantly against the idea of an international conference and felt the interlock concept was contrary to Camp David. The Palestinian leaders were upset that they were given the role of junior partner to Jordan. Jordan's King Hussein* was ambivalent toward the initiative. The Soviet Union thought the international conference was only symbolic and that they did not have a real role in the negotiating process. Syria came out against the Shultz initiative. Only Egypt's* President Hosni Mubarak* outwardly endorsed the plan. On July 31, 1988, the Shultz Plan collapsed when King Hussein officially renounced all Jordanian legal and administrative ties to the West Bank.

For further information see: William B. Quandt, *Peace Process* (Washington, DC: Brookings Institution, 1993); George P. Shultz, "This Is the Plan," *Washington Post* (March 18, 1988), p. A25; George P. Shultz, *Turmoil and Triumph* (New York: Charles Scribner's Sons, 1993).

Nolan Wohl

SHUTTLE DIPLOMACY. In his *Years of Upheaval,* Henry Kissinger* wrote:

"Shuttle diplomacy" has become the catch phrase for my negotiations in the Middle East—as if commuting between capitals had been invented for that special purpose. In fact, the term was coined by the indefatigable Joe Sisco* as we found ourselves flying back and forth between Aswan and Jerusalem* during the second week of January 1974. And the idea of completing the Sinai disengagement negotiation in one continuous assault came from Anwar Sadat,* who suggested that my January trip—conceived as an effort to define principles of disengagement—be turned into the occasion for a definitive agreement.

Kissinger notes that at 8:15 P.M. on January 13, 1974, as he and his team were preparing to fly from Jerusalem to Aswan, Joe Sisco announced to the press accompanying them: " 'Welcome aboard the Egyptian–Israeli shuttle!' " He notes that "thus was shuttle diplomacy named."

Kissinger and his team traveled back and forth among the capitals of Egypt,* Israel, and Syria* to piece together Disengagement Agreements. Kissinger's method of diplomacy was to get proposals from each side, obtain preliminary reactions to these from the parties, identify obstacles, and then engage in the diplomatic process in order to solve the problems. He would explain the tragic consequences to both sides, if an agreement was not reached. Kissinger would then commit his own prestige and shuttle back and forth in order to arrive at an agreement. Finally, the president of the United States would get involved if added pressure were required. Military and economic aid and increased security guarantees were the bargaining tools Kissinger used to make Israel malleable to giving up territory in the Sinai Peninsula* and on the Golan Heights.* Economic aid was used to get Egypt and Syria to acquiesce to the Disengagement Agreements.

Kissinger left for the Middle East on November 5, 1973, on his first venture in shuttle diplomacy. It resulted in the Israeli–Egyptian cease-fire agreement* of November 11, 1973. He returned to the region in both December 1973 and January 1974. Consequently, the first Disengagement Agreement between Israel and Egypt was achieved on January 18, 1974. The next Kissinger undertaking in shuttle diplomacy was between Israel and Syria. It took thirty-four days of back-and-forth negotiating for Kissinger to arrange a Disengagement Agreement on the Golan Heights between Israel and Syria on May 31, 1974. Kissinger's next endeavor in shuttle diplomacy again involved both Egypt and Israel. A second disengagement accord, known as Sinai II,* was signed by the participants on September 4, 1975. This was considered a breakthrough, because for the first time Israel and Egypt agreed to resolve their conflict by peaceful means and not resort to the use of force. It established the preconditions necessary for the eventual negotiations between Israel and Egypt that ultimately led to the Camp David Accords* and the Egypt–Israel Peace Treaty.*

Shuttle diplomacy was also used by United Nations representatives Ralph Bunche* and Gunnar Jarring,* although it was not commonly termed as such. The Shultz Plan of 1988* was negotiated by Secretary of State George Shultz,* traveling throughout the Middle East between the Arabs and Israelis and engaging in a form of shuttle diplomacy. After the Gulf War* of 1991, Secretary of State James Baker* traveled between Middle Eastern capitals and engaged in shuttle diplomacy to organize the Madrid Peace Conference.* Other examples abound, including numerous such trips by Warren Christopher* in the Clinton* administration.

For further information see: Ishaq I. Ghanayem, *The Kissinger Legacy* (New York: Praeger, 1984); Matti Golan, *The Secret Conversations of Henry Kissinger* (New York: Quadrangle/New York Times Book Company, 1976); Walter Issacson, *Kissinger* (New York: Simon and Schuster, 1992); Henry A. Kissinger, *Years of Upheaval* (Boston: Little, Brown, 1982).

Nolan Wohl

SIDQI, ISMAIL (b. 1875; d. 1950). In 1917, Ismail Sidqi created a Committee for Commerce and Industry to promote the establishment of Egyptian* industry. He became president of the Egyptian Federation of Industries in 1930. That same year, as head of the People's Party, he became prime minister. As prime minister, he abolished the Egyptian constitution of 1923. Sidqi's government was characterized by his use of force. One of his major concerns was the development of Egyptian industry, and his administration implemented numerous protectionist policies. He left office in 1935. Sidqi became prime minister again in 1946, when Prime Minister Mahmud Fahmy el-Nokrashy's government brutally repressed a student demonstration in Cairo. Sidqi himself was forced to resign in December 1946 over displeasure about an agreement he signed with Great Britain* to resolve differences between the two countries. The Bevin*–Sidqi Protocol provided for a Joint Defense Board to provide consultation in case of an attack on Egypt or a neighboring country. Bevin agreed, as well, to withdraw all British forces from Egypt by September 1949. What Sidqi failed to obtain from the British was recognition of Egyptian sovereignty over the Sudan. A strong Egyptian nationalist, Sidqi opposed Arab unity. In 1946, while prime minister, Sidqi had meetings with Zionist* envoys toward resolving the issue of Palestine.* He warned the Egyptian Senate against invading the new state of Israel in 1948. Later, Sidqi published a series of articles in which he advocated reconciling Egypt's differences with Israel.

Joseph E. Goldberg

SIILASVUO, ENSIO. Finnish general. He commanded Finnish troops that joined the United Nations Emergency Force* in the Sinai Peninsula* in 1957. At the end of the Yom Kippur War,* United Nations troops under his command facilitated the resupply of the encircled Egyptian Third Army.* He later served as the chairman of the disengagement negotiations between Egypt* and Israel at Kilometer 101* that followed the Yom Kippur War.

For further information see: Ensio Siilasvuo, *In the Service of Peace in the Middle East, 1967–1979* (New York: St. Martin's Press, 1992).

SINAI CAMPAIGN. See **SINAI WAR (1956).**

SINAI FIELD MISSION (SFM). By agreement between Egypt* and Israel in 1975, the United States mounted a unique peacekeeping watch in the Sinai Peninsula.* The role was to detect any movement of military forces and thus to defuse any untoward incident in the Gidi* and Mitla Passes.*

In the Sinai Peninsula, between Israeli and Egyptian lines, the United Nations Emergency Force* patrolled a demilitarized buffer zone. Within that zone, the Sinai Field Mission keeps watch over the entrances to the Gidi and Mitla Passes and monitors the Egyptian and Israeli surveillance stations lodged on the heights at opposite ends of the Gidi Valley. The U.S. tactical early-warning system was designed to complement the Egyptian and Israeli strategic surveillance stations, which collect information about the movements of the other's military forces and provide a broader assessment of military preparations.

In September 1975, at the invitation of Israel and Egypt and to facilitate the Sinai II Agreement,* the United States agreed to assume this new role. The role is to stand watch and alert all parties of any apparent violations of the agreed interim peace terms within its area of surveillance.

P.L. 94-110 of October 13, 1975, authorized the executive branch of the U.S. government to proceed with the task of establishing what became the Sinai Field Mission. By Executive Order 11896 of January 13, 1976, President Gerald Ford* formally established the Sinai Support Mission* (SSM). Both the SSM and the SFM were established in January 1976.

The early-warning system operated until January 25, 1980, when Israel, as part of its staged withdrawal from the Sinai Peninsula under the terms of the Egypt–Israel Peace Treaty,* withdrew from areas east of the passes. According to the terms of the treaty, SFM's role in the Sinai was scheduled to end with this initial Israeli withdrawal, and a United Nations peacekeeping force was to assume responsibility for supervising the security arrangements of the treaty. But the United Nations was unable to fulfill this role. Trilateral talks in Washington resulted in the United States agreeing to verify certain aspects of Egyptian and Israeli adherence to force levels and armament limitations specified in the treaty. SFM soon began to implement this new inspection and verification mission, which formally ended with the completion of Israel's withdrawal from the Sinai in April 1982.

The Washington-based headquarters of this operation is the United States Sinai Support Mission.

For further information see: Watch in the Sinai: The United States Sinai Support Mission (Department of State Publication Number 9131, June 1980).

SINAI PENINSULA. The land bridge between Asia and Africa, some 23,000 square miles in size. It has the shape of a triangle bounded by the Gulf of Suez in the west, the Gulf of Aqaba* in the east, and the Mediterranean Sea in the north. Its highest point is Jebel Musa (the biblical Mount Sinai). The peninsula was occupied by Israel in the 1956–57 Sinai War* and, after its return to Egypt* in 1957, was captured again in the Six Day War.* It was evacuated by Israel and returned to Egypt in accordance with the Egypt–Israel Peace Treaty of 1979.*

The Sinai Peninsula was the main battlefield for three wars between Israel and Egypt. In 1982, Israel returned the Sinai to Egypt under the provisions of their peace treaty.

Primarily desert and barren mountains, the Sinai Peninsula is wedged between Israel and Egypt's Suez Canal,* with a coast along the Mediterranean in the north, the Gulf of Aqaba on the southeast, and the Gulf of Suez on the southwest. The northern plateau is covered with sand dunes and salt flats, with a few inhabited areas such as El-Arish, where roughly half the population of the Sinai resides. In the interior is the extensive plain of Wadi El-Arish, with foothills leading up the steep, sawtooth mountains of the south.

Historically an invasion route between Asia and Africa, the Sinai can be crossed in the north along the coastal plain, through the interior by way of the Gidi* or Mitla* Passes, or along the long narrow southern coastline. Wars in the Sinai have focused around these routes and the heights that control them.

Israel invaded the Sinai during the Suez crisis* of November 1956, withdrawing after the United Nations Emergency Force* was deployed in strategic areas, such as Sharm El-Sheikh,* to guarantee Israeli passage through the Suez Canal and the Strait of Tiran.*

When Egyptian president Gamal Abdul Nasser* removed the United Nations Emergency Force, Israel invaded again in the June 1967 war,* conquering nearly the entire peninsula. Israel then established the Bar-Lev Line* along the Suez Canal to prevent the Egyptians from trying to recapture it. Nasser responded with a War of Attrition* against Israeli forces in the Sinai, which ended with the cease-fire of August 1970.* In the October 1973 war,* Egypt crossed the canal, establishing bridgeheads on the east bank. Israel counterattacked, establishing a bridgehead on the west bank and encircling the Egyptian Third Army.* The Sinai II Accords* of September 1, 1975, provided for Israel to withdraw east of the Mitla and Gidi Passes and for a United Nations force, monitored by an American team, to patrol the El Arish-Ras Mohammad Line. Israel now had free passage for nonmilitary vessels through the Strait of Tiran and the Suez Canal.

The Camp David Accords* and the Egypt–Israel Peace Treaty* provided for Israel to withdraw from the Sinai Peninsula, in return for security guarantees concerning Egyptian troops permitted on the peninsula and the positioning of United Nations forces. Egypt also agreed to sell Israel oil from the Sinai oil wells. In April 1982, Israel withdrew from the Sinai Peninsula, apart from Taba* in the south, which was returned in 1989.

Today the Sinai Peninsula provides Egypt with oil, manganese, and hard currency from tourism.

David J. Abram

SINAI SUPPORT MISSION (SSM). The Washington-based headquarters of the U.S. Sinai Field Mission* (SFM).

Egypt* and Israel concluded negotiations and later signed a basic agreement on September 4, 1975. Major provisions of this agreement called for the establishment of an early-warning system entrusted to U.S. civilian personnel.

The provision for an early-warning system was based on a U.S. proposal made to both parties during the negotiations. The proposal called for an Egyptian and an Israeli surveillance station in the buffer zone supported by an early-warning system operated by U.S. civilians. The proposal was accepted by both parties and became an integral part of the basic agreement.

On October 13, 1975, a joint resolution (H.J. Res. 683, Public Law 94-110) was approved authorizing the president to implement the U.S. proposal but placing certain conditions on U.S. participation.

The U.S. Sinai Support Mission (SSM) was officially established on January 13, 1976, by Executive Order 11896 as a separate government entity. SSM was placed under the guidance of the National Security Council to implement the U.S. proposal. The Sinai Field Mission was later established under SSM to set up and run the early-warning system.

The construction and operation of the early-warning system were contracted to a U.S. firm, E-Systems, Inc., of Dallas. The contractor, together with its subcontractors, has undertaken to install, operate, maintain, and support the early-warning system. Contractor activities in the field are under the overall management and control of the director of SFM. SFM staff include both government and contractor personnel.

SFM became operational on February 22, 1976, when the United Nations Emergency Force (UNEF)* was in place in the buffer zone and Egypt and Israel had completed their redeployment. Movement of SFM from temporary quarters to a permanent base camp was completed by July 4, 1976.

SINAI II ACCORDS (1975). A set of agreements between Israel and Egypt* achieved through the shuttle diplomacy* of U.S. secretary of state Henry Kissinger.* They were signed in Geneva on September 4, 1975, by representatives of Egypt and Israel. They were a significant accomplishment. The agreements consisted of a formal agreement between the two parties, an annex, and a proposal for an American presence in the Sinai Peninsula* in connection with an early-warning system. In addition, there were Memorandums of Agreement between the United States and Israel and U.S. assurances to Israel and to Egypt. This was more than a simple disengagement of military forces because they agreed that "the conflict between them and in the Middle East shall not be resolved by military force but by peaceful means." These were the first steps toward increased accommodation between the parties, and it moved in the direction of a peace settlement. In the Memorandum of Agreement between the United States and Israel regarding the Geneva Peace Conference,* the United States pledged that it "will continue to adhere to its present policy with respect to the Palestine Liberation Organization* [PLO], whereby it will not recognize or negotiate with the Palestine Liberation Organization so long as the Palestine Liberation Organization does not recognize Israel's right to exist and does not accept Security Council Resolutions 242* and 338.*"

After intensive shuttle diplomacy by Kissinger, Egypt and Israel agreed in September 1975 to a partial pullback of Israeli troops in the Sinai Peninsula from the Mitla* and Gidi* Passes, return of the Abu Rudeis* oil fields in exchange for a mutual pledge to refrain from the threat or use of force or military blockade, and the unimpeded passage of nonmilitary cargoes destined for Israel through the Suez Canal.* The American government was to supervise an electronic early-warning system set up in Sinai. To secure Israel's agreement, the United States made a number of concessions, including, most significantly, a pledge not to negotiate directly with the PLO until that organization recognized Israel's right to exist and accepted United Nations Resolutions 242 and 338. For Egypt, the agreement helped consolidate the foothold it had gained in Sinai.

For further information see: Richard H. Ullman, "200 Americans," *New York Times Magazine,* October 12, 1975, pp. 14–15, 90–102.

SINAI WAR (1956). Following the signing of the Rhodes* Armistice Agreements* in 1949, the Arabs maintained a policy of isolating Israel and keeping the war option open. In addition, there was an increase in attacks against Israel, leading in 1951 to more than 150 Israelis killed or wounded, the worst attacks originating in the Gaza Strip.* Israel adopted an active strategy, including a campaign of reprisal raids. These raids and their early failures revealed that the Israeli army had deteriorated on the operational level and that reprisals helped little in reducing the threat of infiltrating terrorists. The Israeli command, especially Moshe Dayan,* head of the General Staff branch of the Israel Defense Forces (IDF) at the time, began to contemplate the occupation of Gaza,* then the key base of operations of Egyptian*-sponsored terrorist groups attacking

Israel. This, he believed, would deny the Arabs a launching zone from which to attack Israeli population centers.

An elite force of paratroop commandos was created to set the operational tempo of the army, establish the esprit de corps lacking among Israeli units, and set the example of quality-based, rather than quantity-based, training and combat style. The most important innovation, developed by Ariel Sharon,* the commander of these special forces, designated "Unit 101,*" was a tactic of step-by-step advance with dedicated fire support and advance teams. They leapfrogged over unvanquished fortified positions to penetrate a command post as soon as possible so as not to lose any of the initial shock effect by being bogged down in the suppression of enemy fire. This tactic placed a premium on decapitation of the enemy's command capabilities. In short, the Israeli army had learned to exploit the adversary's inability to improvise amid confusion, which was to be maximized through initial surprise and sustained momentum.

As the fedayeen* actions became bolder, and more Israelis were killed, tensions grew in 1955. The Lavon affair* and the Czech–Egyptian arms deal* further heightened tensions, and gradually Israel began thinking seriously about striking deeper into Egypt* than Gaza, using a force large enough to deny the Egyptians their base of operations in the Sinai Peninsula* as a whole. The reprisal strategy, however, while increasing Israeli morale and testing the application of the innovative tactics, did little to stop the fedayeen attacks.

By mid-1955, with the return of David Ben-Gurion* to the Cabinet and the decline in the fortunes of Moshe Sharett,* who advocated a more restrained Israeli retaliatory policy, the Israeli government moved toward the war option. Ben-Gurion had already decided that a war was inevitable and, on October 2, 1955, ordered Dayan to prepare for a major military action.

The first step in planning the war was to test the new tactics in a major operation against Egyptian forces that had occupied the al-Auja* demilitarized zone. The commando/paratroops unit under Sharon operated in coordination with regular army forces to attack and evict Egyptian forces with minimal casualties. With the tactical success of this operation, essentially all the conditions and incentives to go to war were in place, and only the immediate trigger was awaited.

Egypt was in an official state of war with Israel and had prevented Israeli shipping from passing through the Strait of Tiran.* Its troops were deployed in the Sinai Peninsula near Israel. The conditions for war with Britain and France* existed as well.

In July 1956, Egypt nationalized the Suez Canal* and other British and French properties in Egypt and supported anti-French rebels in North Africa, creating a congruence of interests between Israel and these two European states. By late October 1956, Britain and France had agreed with Israel to launch a coordinated action against Gamal Abdul Nasser's* Egypt. D-Day was set for October 29, when Israeli forces would invade, to be followed by an Anglo-French ultimatum to both Israel and Egypt to immediately cease fire while Anglo-French troops seized the canal, ostensibly to protect it.

Israel dropped Sharon and his paratroopers at the key line of communication at the western end of the Sinai Peninsula, at the Parker Memorial on the Mitla Pass,* therein severing communications with Egypt's six brigades and two reinforced battalions in the Sinai. This was intended to pave the way for the Anglo-French intervention, whose ostensible goal was to protect the canal and ensure it would remain open. One day after the drop, on October 30, the French and British issued an ultimatum calling on both sides to cease fire and withdraw to positions ten miles on either side of the canal. The ultimatum presented operational challenges to Israel. They did not want to leave their air-dropped forces at the Mitla Pass isolated when the cease-fire took effect. The Egyptians refused the ultimatum on October 30, allowing Israel to continue fighting and consolidate its control over the peninsula and remove the threat of the Egyptian army. Israeli forces reached the Suez Canal and controlled the Sinai Peninsula.

Both the United States and the Soviet Union used diplomatic pressure to force Israel, France, and Britain to cease their actions. U.N. General Assembly Resolutions were passed on November 4, 5, 7, and 24, 1956, calling for the withdrawal of forces.

Eventually, Israel withdrew from all of the captured territory to the prewar frontiers under the weight of United Nations resolutions, but especially Eisenhower* administration pressure. The United States also provided assurances to Israel concerning freedom of navigation through the Strait of Tiran and the Gulf of Aqaba.* The United Nations Emergency Force* (UNEF) was created to patrol the Egyptian side of the Egypt–Israel armistice line, which it did until the days immediately preceding the Six Day War.* The UN force was also to have deployed in the Gaza Strip to keep that area demilitarized and end the threat of further fedayeen raids, but these two provisions were never implemented.

For further information see: Mordechai Bar-On, *The Gates of Gaza: Israel's Road to Suez and Back, 1955–1957* (New York: St. Martin's Press, 1994); Andre Beaufre, *The Suez Expedition 1956* (New York: Praeger, 1969); Erskine Childers, *The Road to Suez: A Study in Western–Arab Relations* (London: Macgibbon and Kee, 1962); Chester L. Cooper, *The Lion's Last Roar, 1956* (New York: Harper and Row, 1978); Moshe Dayan, *Diary of the Sinai Campaign* (New York: Harper and Row, 1966); Mohamed H. Heikal, *Cutting the Lion's Tail: Suez through Egyptian Eyes* (New York: Arbor House, 1987); Robert Henriques, *A Hundred Hours to Suez: An Account of Israel's Campaign in the Sinai Peninsula* (New York: Viking Press, 1957); Kennett Love, *Suez, the Twice-Fought War* (New York: McGraw-Hill, 1969); Donald Neff, *Warriors at Suez: Eisenhower Takes America into the Middle East* (New York: Simon and Schuster, 1981); Anthony Nutting, *No End of a Lesson: The Story of Suez* (New York: Clarkson N. Potter, 1967); Edgar O'Ballance, *The Sinai Campaign* (London: Faber and Faber, 1959); Terence Robertson, *Crisis: The Inside Story of the Suez Conspiracy* (New York: Atheneum, 1965); Hugh Thomas, *Suez* (New York: Harper and Row, 1966).

David Wurmser

SISCO, JOSEPH JOHN (b. Chicago, October 31, 1919). He received his B.A. degree from Knox College in Galesburg, Illinois. Before entering the U.S. Army during World War II, he taught high school briefly. He received a Ph.D. in international relations from the University of Chicago in 1950. Sisco served with the Central Intelligence Agency in 1950–51 and then joined the Department of State, where served as the officer in charge of United Nations political affairs. Sisco was appointed deputy director of the Office of United Nations Affairs in 1958 and became its director in 1960. From 1962 to 1965, Sisco was deputy assistant secretary in the Bureau of International Organization Affairs. On July 1, 1965, he became assistant secretary of state for international organization affairs and served in that capacity until 1969.

In 1969, Sisco became assistant secretary of state for the Near East and South Asia and served in this position until 1974. As assistant secretary, he met with Soviet ambassador Anatoly Dobrynin between March 18 and April 22, 1969, to determine whether there was sufficient agreement on general principles to promote a joint proposal on peace between Israel and the Arabs. Again meeting with Dobrynin from May 6 to May 12, 1969, Sisco explained the major points of the U.S. proposal for a settlement between Egypt* and Israel. In July 1969, he traveled to the Soviet Union, where he presented a modified proposal to attempt to narrow differences over a proposal the Soviets had advanced on June 17. Between September 22 and 30, Sisco and Secretary of State William Rogers* met with the Soviet leadership at the United Nations in New York. These talks were unsuccessful.

President Richard Nixon* sent Sisco to Cairo for direct talks with Egyptian president Gamal Abdul Nasser* from April 10 to 14, 1970. He urged the Egyptian president to give the United States a chance to act as an honest broker. In a speech on May 1, Nasser urged the United States to begin a political initiative to end the fighting between Israel and Egypt. For the next three months, the United States attempted to restore a cease-fire.

After the Rogers Plan* was announced in October 1971, the United States designated Sisco to conduct proximity talks* or hotel talks* as a form of shuttle diplomacy* to see if he might be able to catalyze the parties to reach some form of agreement. The Israelis agreed to participate in February 1972; however, the Egyptians refused.

Sisco continued to play an important role in U.S. policy as an aide to Henry Kissinger* during his tenure as secretary of state.

For further information see: Henry Kissinger, *Years of Upheaval* (Boston: Little, Brown, 1982); Bernard Reich, *The United States and Israel: Influence in the Special Relationship* (New York: Praeger, 1984); Joseph J. Sisco, *Middle East Negotiations: A Conversation with Joseph Sisco* (Washington, DC: American Enterprise Institute, 1980).

SIX DAY WAR (1967). In February 1966, as a consequence of an internal Baathist coup, a new group of leftist army officers with closer ties to the Soviet

Union came into control in Damascus. The new leadership stepped up its war propaganda, and, through Lebanon* and Jordan,* it sent Fatah* guerrillas to step up attacks on Israel. The Israeli government launched a major retaliatory raid (Operation Meatgrinder) on the Jordanian-held West Bank* town of Es-Samu* on November 13, 1966, where the terrorists had crossed into Israel, rather than against a Syrian* target where the terrorists originated and had been trained. The raid into Es-Samu went awry when a Jordanian unit, not known to have been in the area, opened fire on Israeli forces, leaving some Israelis and many Jordanians dead. The damage was done, however. By failing to attack the real culprits, the Israelis encouraged the Syrians to believe that, so long as they had Russian support, they could attack Israeli with impunity.

In November 1966 Egypt* and Syria* entered into a defense agreement* that involved the integration and coordination of their defenses. A joint Soviet–Egyptian communique in April 1967 pledged "friendship and mutual confidence" between the two states. On April 7, 1967, the Syrians suddenly opened fire on Israel's border villages. Israeli aircraft intervened to silence the artillery and also shot down six Syrian aircraft.

On May 13, a Soviet delegation visiting Cairo informed Egypt that Israel had massed some eleven brigades on Syria's border. Though the Israeli government offered the Soviets the opportunity to examine the area themselves to verify that there had been no mobilization, the Soviets refused the offer and continued to back Syria's claim that an Israeli attack was imminent.

Egypt believed Syrian and Russian claims and, on May 17, 1967, proclaimed a state of emergency, mobilized the armed forces, and began moving Egyptian forces across the canal to assume positions along Israel's border. By May 20, 1967, some 100,000 Egyptian troops had already crossed into the border area and deployed.

On May 17, Nasser* demanded the removal of the United Nations (UN) Emergency Force* (UNEF) from the Egypt–Israel frontier area as well. At first, U Thant,* the UN secretary-general, announced that the UN would either remain deployed where it was or leave altogether but that it would not redeploy to rear positions. Within two days, U Thant decided that he should remove the UNEF contingent altogether. Encouraged by the UN withdrawal and the inaction of the international community, Nasser declared the Strait of Tiran* closed to Israeli shipping on May 22.

Israel had withdrawn from the Sinai Peninsula* ten years earlier, following the Sinai War,* under the condition that there would be a UN contingent separating Israeli and Egyptian forces, that Egypt would not remilitarize the Gaza Strip,* that there would be no more fedayeen* raids from Egypt, that Israel would have access to the Suez Canal,* and that Israel would be guaranteed by the Great Powers free passage for Israeli shipping through the Strait of Tiran and Gulf of Aqaba.* By late May 1967, these conditions had been reversed.

On May 26, Nasser declared that his intention was to launch a war of annihilation against Israel. As the week wore on, more Arab states sent contingents to join in the attack. Despite international guarantees to assist Israel were Egypt to violate the 1957 agreements and block Israeli shipping, Israel's Foreign Minister Abba Eban* encountered symbolic and verbal support for Israel's position, but no real help.

After a series of threatening speeches that ridiculed King Hussein* of Jordan and labeled him a coward and traitor, Nasser finally prevailed upon the Jordanian monarch to subordinate his military to Egyptian command to prosecute the impending war of annihilation of Israel. On May 30, 1967, the Jordanian army was placed on alert and was formally subordinated to the command of Egypt's General Abdel Munim Riad.

Israel established a National Unity government with a wall-to-wall coalition to deal with the crisis. Moshe Dayan* was appointed minister of defense.

On June 5, 1967, the Israeli air force struck. In a massive preemptive raid, the Israeli air force destroyed nearly the entire Egyptian air force within an hour and neutralized nearly all its airfields. At first, Israel intended to strike only at Egypt. It had sent numerous messages to Jordan to remain neutral. Israel's air force attacked only Egyptian air bases in the initial assault during the first three hours of the war. After 9:00 A.M. the Syrian and Iraqi* air forces intervened, and at 11:00 the Jordanian air force struck. Syria struck oil refineries in Haifa and air bases around Megiddo; Iraqi aircraft struck Natanya; and Jordanian airplanes attacked an airstrip at Kfar Sirkin.

The Israeli air force, having already destroyed 309 of Egypt's 340 combat aircraft by 9:00 A.M., turned its attention to the other air forces. By that evening, still on the first day of the war, Israel had destroyed the entire Egyptian air force and two-thirds of the Syrian air force and struck hard at the Iraqi air force and facilities within range of Israel (H-3 Airfield). By nightfall, more than 400 Arab combat aircraft had been destroyed, leaving Israel's air force with complete air superiority to conduct ground-support strikes.

The ground war was planned originally as only an Israeli–Egyptian war. Within two hours of the initial air strikes on Egypt and after a series of highly visible Israeli armored movements in the south of the Negev designed to mislead the Egyptians into thinking that was where the main thrust of Israel's offensive would be, Israeli armor crossed the border in the north and central sectors, taking Khan Yunis rapidly and cutting off the Gaza Strip. The Israeli Seventh Armored Division, under General Israel Tal, and the Paratroop Brigade under Eitan captured the rest of Gaza.* By nightfall, Israeli forces under Tal had already reached el-Arish in the northern coast of Sinai.

In the central sector of the front, General Ariel Sharon* broke through on the vital Nitzana–Ismailiya axis, which controlled all the roads between el-Arish in the north and Nakhle in the south. By nightfall, Sharon had managed to surround completely the core of Egypt's army in the Abu-Agheila area and control all the major roads and intersections in the area.

Between these two thrusts, the Israelis launched a third prong under General Yoffe through what had been considered impassable terrain and, therefore, was lightly defended. By nightfall, Yoffe's forces had traveled forty miles, essentially cutting off any possible Egyptian lateral movement between the central and northern sectors.

Still unaware of the magnitude of the Israeli preemptive strike and the extent of Israeli ground advances, in late morning, June 5, Nasser pressured King Hussein and other Arabs to join the war in what he still regarded as an easy, quick victory. In fact, around 11:00 A.M., Nasser telephoned Hussein that his forces had already penetrated deep into the Negev and that he planned to meet Jordanian forces advancing southward from Hebron.* Only at about 2:00 P.M. did Nasser begin to receive information that his plans were in disarray.

The second day of fighting was marked by two trends. The Israelis consolidated their gains, further isolating the Egyptian army from the canal, especially in the north, and pushed farther west along the Sinai's Mediterranean coast. In a two-pronged attack, Tal's and Yoffe's forces joined efforts to capture a central road junction and a main fortification of Egyptian forces in the Sinai, Jebel Libni. When that fortification and junction fell, the only Egyptian forces left in the Sinai at the end of the second day were General Saad el Din Shazli's* armored division in the southern sector and a major armed force east of the Suez Canal near Kantara. The only escape route for Shazli's forces was to pass through both Nakhle, which was Sharon's next objective, and the Mitla Pass, which were Tal's and Yoffe's next objectives.

On the third day of the war, the Egyptian armored force opposite Kantara crossed the canal to move toward the Mitla Pass and secure it for the eventual passage of the retreating armored force under Shazli. Yet, Tal's and Yoffe's forces were advancing rapidly toward the north and began to move onto the canal in the northernmost portions, cutting off any escape route for any lingering Egyptian units in the northern half of the Sinai and beginning the attack on the Egyptian force attempting to cross the canal. Other elements of Tal's and Yoffe's forces swept southwest, heading toward the Mitla Pass to cut off any Egyptian retreat through it. At the same time, Sharon's forces moved southwest as well, heading toward Nakhle in the center of the Sinai to strike at Shazli's forces as they tried to pass through the junction there.

As a result, there were, by the end of the third day of the war, two Israeli divisions racing toward the Mitla Pass from the northeast, an element of which had already reached and begun to secure the pass, another Israeli force moving onto the canal and beginning to turn south with the intent of cutting off the canal bridges should any Egyptian forces manage to pass through Nakhle and the Mitla Pass, and another Israeli division under Sharon converging on Nakhle. Against these forces were an Egyptian force, bidding to cross the canal in the north and head to the Mitla Pass, and a large Egyptian armored force under Shazli trying to rapidly retreat through Nakhle and the Mitla Pass.

Over the fourth day and the following night of fighting, Shazli's forces were entirely destroyed in heavy fighting all along the escape route. General Tal's forces had reached the canal in the north and moved southward along the canal, engaging and defeating the Egyptian tank division trying to cross the canal near Ismailiya into the Sinai in hopes of advancing toward the Mitla Pass to assist Shazli's escape and launch a counterattack. The force was repelled, and, by the beginning of the sixth day of the fighting, Israeli forces had full control of the east bank of the canal. Yoffe's forces began to move along the Sinai's eastern shores toward the southernmost point at Sharm el-Sheikh to link with Israeli paratroopers who had already seized the cape.

Within six days, the entirety of the Sinai Peninsula was under Israeli control, and nearly the entirety of the Egyptian military lay destroyed in the sand or charred on the runways. Egypt lost approximately 15,000 soldiers in this war, and Nasser himself admitted that 80 percent of the entire Egyptian army had been lost in the Sinai battle. In doing this, the Israelis lost only 300 soldiers.

On the morning of June 5, 1967, Prime Minister Levi Eshkol* asked General Odd Bull* of the UN observer force in Jerusalem* to transmit a personal message to King Hussein that Israel had no intention of initiating hostilities and that there would be no war with Jordan if the king also refrained.

Yet, Nassar's euphoric but erroneous reports of Egyptian victories and the fact that Jordanian forces were under Egyptian command rendered Eshkol's pleas futile. At 11:00 A.M. on June 5, the Jordanian army commenced fire with artillery on a number of Israeli border cities, including Tel Aviv and Jerusalem, and its "Hittim" Brigade crossed the armistice lines into the demilitarized zone south of Jerusalem to occupy UN positions at the Government House.* Later that day, Israeli major general Uzi Narkiss ordered the Sixteenth Jerusalem Brigade to counterattack, seize the Government House, and capture Zur Baher, the only passable road from Jordan to the Hebron hills to the south. In effect, this meant that Jordanian forces in the Judean mountains, which had been emplaced to push southward into the Negev to link with Egyptian forces under Shazli, were cut off from Jordan altogether.

Also at 11:00 A.M., the Jordanian army tried in vain to launch an offensive three kilometers northwest of Jerusalem near Maale HaHamisha with the aim, along with the southeastern pincer coming in from Government House, of cutting off Jerusalem from the rest of Israel. The Israeli counterattack in the northwest not only blocked the Jordanian attack but brought the Israeli army two kilometers farther north to take control of the strategic ridge controlling the Jerusalem–Tel Aviv Road.

Having destroyed already most of the Egyptian air force, Israel's air force (IAF) could turn its attention to Jordan. The IAF mission was completed within a few hours, allowing the Israeli air force to concentrate on ground-attack missions against Jordanian positions in Jerusalem and destroy all reinforcements entering the West Bank, the most dangerous of which was a large Iraqi force that was already crossing the Jordan River* and was beginning to make its way up the slopes toward Nablus. By the afternoon of June 5, Israel's elite Fifty-fifth Paratroops Brigade under Colonel Gur* had been diverted back to Jerusalem to reinforce Israeli forces there, arriving in the city by midafternoon. In the early afternoon hours, another Israeli force near Latrun seized the junction from two Jordanian companies, securing the main road between Jerusalem and Tel Aviv.

On the second day of fighting, Israeli units advanced north and west of Jerusalem, linking up with the isolated Israeli enclave on Mount Scopus.* By the end of the day, Colonel Gur's forces had secured positions to the east of the Old City* in preparation for the break-in planned for the next day.

In the northern part of Samaria, which was where the Iraqi troops were headed, Israel managed by the second day to seize the three or four westernmost kilometers and were moving down from the north, seizing Jenin and moving toward Nablus. That afternoon, Israeli forces entered Nablus.

On June 7, the Old City fell to Gur's forces, which had attacked from the east through St. Stephen's gate. By 11:00 A.M., forty-eight hours after the war began in Jerusalem, Israeli forces reached the Wailing Wall.* Also on Wednesday, other units of the Israel Defense Forces* (IDF) captured the entirety of the West Bank, with the exception of a small pocket south of Hebron that was subdued the following day. In this sector of the war, Jordan lost about 6,000 soldiers, and Israel lost 285, slightly less than the number lost in the Sinai.

On the Syrian front, where only a month and a half earlier the Syrians began the chain of events that led to war, the Syrians refrained from large-scale fighting, contenting themselves more with company-sized probing actions into the border kibbutzim and launching massive, continuous artillery barrages along the entire border from the early morning of June 5.

Because of the fear that attacking Syria may provoke Soviet intervention, Israel spent the first four days of the war engaged in a holding action in the north. However, the constant artillery bombardment of the border towns and kibbutzim and the numerous probing actions of the Syrian army began to press the Israeli government to reply in strength. After the bulk of the Egyptian army had been destroyed in the Sinai, and the Jordanian and Iraqi armies completely evicted from the West Bank, Israel went on the offensive on the fifth day of the war, June 9, against Syria.

The Israeli attack proceeded along two main thrusts in the northern sector of the Golan. One Israeli force, under Colonel Bar Kochba, was to attack the Syrian fortifications near Banias at Tel Aziziat, capture Banias, and climb the hills toward Masada and Kuneitra. The second force, under Albert Mandler, departed from Kfar Szold a few kilometers to the south and broke Syrian defenses at Tel Fakher, also then heading east toward Kuneitra. In the central sector, Israeli forces struck at the series of Syrian entrenchments opposite the Bnot Ya'akov Bridge. By the end of June 9, Syrian defenses at Tel Aziziat and Tel Fakher had fallen, leaving the way open for Mandler and Bar Kochba to the interior of the Golan in the northern area. At the same time, Israeli forces under Colonel Ram in the central sector entered the central portions of the Golan and moved onto Nafekh in the geographic center of the plateau.

On June 10, Syrian forces completely broke. Israeli forces moved fast toward

Kuneitra in the north and the Bashan Ridge in the center of the Golan. Another Israeli force under Elad Peled, which included the Fifty-fifth Paratroop Brigade under Colonel Gur, who had just arrived from his Jerusalem victory, passed south of the Sea of Galilee* and moved up in midmorning along the Golan cliffs in the southern portion of the plateau. By late afternoon, Colonel Ram reached Nafekh, and Colonel Peled's forces advanced along a northeast direction toward Fiq, then El-Al, and began to converge with Ram's forces headed toward the volcanic mound known as Tel Faris near Rafid.

In the north on June 10, a Golani paratroop brigade was airlifted by helicopter to the lower peak of Mount Hermon,* some 7,000 feet above sea level. By 2:00 P.M. on June 10, Kuneitra fell to the Israelis, and by the time the cease-fire took effect at 6:30 P.M., Israeli forces had consolidated their hold on the entire perimeter of the Golan Heights* west of Rafid in the south and Kuneitra in the north. Israel lost 141 soldiers in the Golan campaign, mostly in the fierce fighting conducted by Mendler's forces at Tel-Fakher and Bar Kochba's forces at Tel Aziziat near Banias.

As the results of the war became apparent, the Soviets, who had hitherto blocked the United Nations from defusing the crisis, moved to call for a cease-fire at 6:30 P.M. on June 10, six days after the war began. All sides accepted, since Israel had already achieved victory and occupied the entire West Bank, Sinai Peninsula, and Golan Heights, and the Arabs had virtually no forces left with which to continue fighting.

Israel decisively defeated Egypt, Jordan, Syria, and their allies and in six days radically transformed the situation in the Middle East: it was in control of territories stretching from the Golan Heights in the north to Sharm el-Sheikh* in the Sinai Peninsula and from the Suez Canal to the Jordan River. The territories captured included the Sinai Peninsula, the Gaza Strip, the West Bank (referred to by Israel as Judea* and Samaria*), the Golan Heights, and East Jerusalem.*

For further information see: Randolph Churchill and Winston S. Churchill, *The Six Day War* (London: Heinemann, 1967); Chaim Herzog, *The Arab–Israeli Wars* (New York: Random House, 1982); David Kimche and Dan Bawly, *The Six-Day War: Prologue and Aftermath* (New York: Stein and Day, 1971, originally published as *The Sandstorm*); Walter Laqueur, *The Road to War: The Origin and Aftermath of the Arab–Israeli Conflict 1967–8* (Baltimore: Penguin Books, 1969, also published as *The Road to Jerusalem*); Edgar O'Ballance, *The Third Arab–Israeli War* (London: Faber and Faber, 1972).

David Wurmser

SIX-POINT AGREEMENT (1973 Cease-fire agreement). After the adoption of United Nations (UN) Security Council Resolution 338,* Egyptian* and Israeli military officers met at Kilometer 101* on the Cairo-Suez Road. On November 11, 1973, the cease-fire agreement was signed; it took its name from the six points agreed to during the negotiations. These included (1) observance of the UN-sponsored cease-fire; (2) discussions on positions held by each side as of October 22, 1973 (the Israeli forces had advanced beyond these at the time of the first cease-fire); (3) the provision of food, water, and supplies daily to troops trapped in the Sinai* and the evacuation of the Egyptian wounded; (4) the lifting of restrictions on the delivery of nonmilitary supplies to the Egyptian Third Army* in Sinai; (5) the maintenance by UN Emergency Force* troops of checkpoints on the Cairo–Suez Road; and (6) the exchange of prisoners.

SKYHAWK A-4 AIRCRAFT. See **A-4 SKYHAWK.**

SLA. See **SOUTH LEBANESE ARMY.**

SOLE LEGITIMATE REPRESENTATIVE. At the Rabat Arab Summit* meeting in October 1974, the representatives of the Arab states unanimously passed a resolution declaring the Palestine Liberation Organization* ''as the sole legitimate representative'' of the Palestinian people.

SOUTH LEBANESE ARMY (SLA). The SLA, also known as the Free Lebanon Militia* (FLM), also known as the Army of Free Lebanon, is a mostly Christian militia, operating in Israel's small, self-proclaimed security zone* in southern Lebanon,* and it is a small, well-regulated army of a some 2,000–3,000 Lebanese soldiers equipped and trained by the Israel Defense Forces* (IDF).

The SLA has been led by two commanders: Major Saad Georges Haddad,* a Catholic, and Major General Antoine Lahad,* a Maronite Christian from northern Lebanon. It was originally funded officially by the IDF in June 1978 (although ties with Haddad's forces existed as early as 1975).

By this point, Major Saad Haddad was in command of the SLA and was operating within the new Israeli security zone. At first, the SLA officially claimed to have only a few Israeli advisers helping them plan defensive operations, but soon they acknowledged that Israel not only advised and funded, but also equipped, uniformed, trained, and used, the SLA in cooperation with IDF plans. Although the IDF and the SLA had originally been reluctant to become such close allies, they did choose to unite in 1978 in an effort to curb the growth of the Palestine Liberation Organization* (PLO) and other terrorist activity in southern Lebanon. Israeli soldiers, in fact, guarded the commanders' base at Marj Ayoun, and identity cards used to clear all soldiers into the compound (including the Arabic-speaking Lebanese soldiers) were in Hebrew. Even the spokesman for the SLA was an Israeli officer. Despite this support, Haddad was unable to prevent further attacks by the PLO, the Amal militia, Shiite groups, or their development into a conventional army complete with long-range rockets and other weapons.

The exact numbers of the SLA are never clear, but in its first days the number was at about 1,000 militiamen, and, until about early 1987, it is believed that the numbers were at least 1,800. Then the SLA grew to about 6,000, and that number stayed fixed for about five years but then shrank again as the Lebanese

Christians grew tired of the civil war. It has remained at about 3,000 soldiers since 1992 (United Nations and IDF estimates).

Stationed in the security zone, the Lebanese Christians who make up most of the SLA have bases on the low ground of that area, while the Israelis, with their sophisticated equipment, maintain long-range observational and strategic security on the higher grounds, such as the Beaufort Castle (an old Crusader fort), which was captured by the IDF from PLO units.

Time and time again, the SLA has captured or killed terrorists who have tried to infiltrate Israel's northern border and many more who have simply attacked SLA patrols with guns, bombs, and unconventional tactics (i.e., suicide bombings in cars or mules, using even children as the ''martyrs and messengers of Allah''—a militant and fundamentalist Islamic term for terrorists). They also state that the United Nations Interim Forces in Lebanon* (UNIFIL) has been an observer force with no ability to control any of the fighting or attacks. In order to maintain security in the zone, the SLA maintained dawn-to-dusk curfews and required that they be notified of any guests that local residents might be hosting.

On April 4, 1984, Major General Antoine Lahad (formerly of the Lebanese army) was handed control of the Free Lebanon Militia after several names of other potential and likely commanders were reviewed. Immediately, he changed its name to the South Lebanese Army (SLA), for he claimed that it was no longer just for Christians, but for all the freedom-loving peoples of South Lebanon.

In recent years, the SLA has shrunk in size, partly because many of the Shiite supporters have left the area, heading north toward the Muslim-controlled areas of Lebanon, and also due to the fact that Israel has been negotiating successfully with the Lebanese government and has unofficially reached agreements that are waiting to be written, signed, and implemented as soon as the Syrians* agree to such an accord. This makes the SLA slightly less important to Israel's security in the long run. Until agreements are reached, Israel believes it must continue to support the SLA, so that terrorist incursions can be countered effectively. They will most likely do this until the Lebanese government can prevent attacks on northern Israel from its territory.

The SLA has become a main focus of Israelis who contend that they must keep their long-standing relationship with their only ''true friend'' in the region and with those who maintain that peace with Arabs is possible, whether Christian or Muslim.

For further information see: Beate Hamizrachi, *The Emergence of the South Lebanon Security Belt: Major Saad Haddad and the Ties with Israel, 1975–1978* (New York: Praeger, 1988).

Yasha Manuel Harari

SOVIET–EGYPTIAN TREATY OF FRIENDSHIP AND COOPERATION. On May 27, 1971, Soviet president Nikolai Podgorny and Egyptian* president Anwar Sadat* signed a fifteen-year Treaty of Friendship and Cooperation. Consisting

of twelve articles, the treaty declared an unbreakable friendship between the two countries and cooperation in political, economic, scientific, technological, and cultural fields; affirmed their commitment to socialism and rejection of imperialism and colonialism in all forms; pledged the continuation of efforts to establish a lasting and fair peace in the Middle East; promised consultation at different levels on all important questions affecting the interests of both states; guaranteed cooperation in the military fields on the basis of appropriate agreements; ensured that neither party would enter into alliances or take any actions directed against the other party; safeguarded the principles of sovereignty, territorial integrity, and noninterference in each other's internal affairs.

The Soviet–Egyptian Treaty of Friendship and Cooperation was a direct result of Moscow's increasingly strained relationship with Egypt's new president. Following the death of Gamal Abdul Nasser,* President Anwar Sadat directed Egypt through a period of significant challenges and changes. Domestically, Sadat began the gradual de-Nasserization of Egypt's economy. He purged pro-Nasserist and pro-Soviet elements from the government, including Vice President Ali Sabry. Sadat also made overtures in the international arena indicating a change in Egypt's position toward the Arab–Israeli conflict. Throughout 1971, his so-called year of decision,* Sadat's main priority remained the restoration of Egyptian territory occupied by Israel since 1967. While going to war remained a final alternative, Sadat preferred achieving his objectives through negotiation. Subsequently, he proposed an interim agreement on the Suez Canal* and a possible peace settlement with Israel. Despite Israeli rejection, Sadat agreed to American mediation on the issue. In early May, U.S. secretary of state William Rogers* met with Sadat to discuss a possible peace settlement. Though the talks were inconclusive, they represented the highest level of communication between the two countries since 1953.

As a consequence of their inability to control Sadat and their mistrust of his intentions, the Soviets sought to salvage an increasingly tenuous relationship through a formal treaty. Though it was the first treaty with an Arab country, it did not obligate the Soviets to Egypt in the same manner or extent as with the Warsaw Pact countries. Nor did the treaty explicitly promise mutual defense in the face of attack. Rather, it represented a politically expedient maneuver on the part of both parties. Moscow hoped to wage greater influence over Sadat and his actions, while Sadat saw the treaty as a means to acquire the arms necessary for war. Ironically, neither party achieved its greater objectives.

Sensing a deadlock in negotiations with the United States, Sadat began, in late 1971, to express the military option as the only remaining means by which Egypt could recover its territory. Despite his numerous requests, Moscow consistently failed to supply Sadat with aircraft and missiles. Increasingly frustrated, Sadat publicly expelled all Soviet military advisers from Egypt on July 18, 1972. Sadat himself later admitted that his disagreement with the Soviets stemmed from their failure to deliver requested arms, their disapproval over his plans to wage war against Israel, and the existing era of superpower detente. Relations between the Soviet Union and Egypt gradually thawed by the spring of 1973. Moscow ultimately provided the necessary military assistance that enabled Sadat to wage war against Israel later that year. Three years later, in March 1976, Sadat unilaterally abrogated the Soviet–Egyptian Treaty of Friendship and Co-operation. Sadat outlined the following reasons for his decision: the Soviets showed no desire for establishing peace in the Middle East; the Soviets opposed his economic policies and refused to reschedule Egypt's debts; and they refused to overhaul Egyptian aircraft and provide spare parts while simultaneously preventing other states from doing so.

For further information see: Karen Dawisha, *Soviet Foreign Policy towards Egypt* (London: Macmillan Press, 1979); Galia Golan, *Soviet Policies in the Middle East* (Cambridge: Cambridge University Press, 1990); George Lenczowski, *Soviet Advances in the Middle East* (Washington, DC: American Enterprise Institute for Public Policy Research, 1972).

Anamika Krishna

SOVIET PROPOSALS FOR A MIDDLE EAST SETTLEMENT. Soviet proposals for a settlement in the Middle East were put forward on July 29, 1984, during a period characterized by continuing confrontation between the United States and the USSR and an intensified struggle for regional spheres of influence. Striving for a strengthening of its positions in the Middle East and giving impetus to resolving the Middle East conflict, the USSR put forward principles for a settlement and offered a concrete program providing for ways of achieving this aim. Following are the principles for a Middle East settlement.

The principle of inadmissibility of seizure of foreign territories by aggression should be strictly observed. Consequently, Arabs should be given back all the territories occupied by Israel since 1967—the Golan Heights,* the West Bank,* the Gaza Strip,* and the Lebanese* lands. Settlements* set up by Israel in Arab territories after 1967 should be dismantled. The borders between Israel and its Arab neighbors should be declared inviolable.

The inalienable right of the Palestinian* people, with the Palestine Liberation Organization* as its sole legitimate representative,* to self-determination and creation of its own independent state on Palestinian soil liberated from Israeli occupation, in the West Bank of the Jordan River* and the Gaza Strip, should be put into practice. Provided for by the resolution of the general Arab Summit conference at Fez* and by Palestinians' consent, the West Bank and the Gaza Strip should be placed under United Nations (UN) supervision by Israel for a short transitional period not longer than several months. This sovereign, independent Palestinian state would define its own relations with neighboring states, including the possibility of establishing a confederation. Palestinian refugees should be granted the opportunity provided for by UN resolutions to return to their homes or to receive compensation for their property left behind.

East Jerusalem,* occupied by Israel in 1967, is the location of major Muslim sacred sites and should be returned to the Arabs and become an integral part of the Palestinian state. Believers of all religions should be guaranteed free access to the holy sites of Jerusalem.*

The right of all states in the region to a safe and independent existence and development should be realized on the basis of full reciprocity, as it is impossible to ensure genuine security of one state while violating the security of others.

The cessation of the state of war should take place, and peace should be established between Arab states and Israel. All parties to the conflict, including Israel and the Palestinian state, should commit themselves to mutually respecting each other's sovereignty, independence, and territorial integrity and to settling disputes by peaceful means through negotiation.

The permanent members of the UN Security Council or the Security Council as a whole could act to guarantee the peace agreement.

Experience proves convincingly the futility and danger of efforts to solve the Middle East problem by imposing on the Arabs separate agreements with Israel.

The only true and effective way of a cardinal settlement of the Middle East problem is through a collective effort with the participation of all concerned parties within the framework of a specially convened international conference on the Middle East.

The Soviet Union believed that an international conference should be guided by the following concepts.

The conference should aim at finding a solution to all aspects of the Middle East conflict and should result in the signing of a treaty or treaties covering the following integral components of the settlement: withdrawal of Israeli forces from all Arab land occupied since 1967; implementation of lawful national rights of the Arab people of Palestine, including their right to establish their own state; the establishment of peace, which ensures the security and independent development of all the states party to the conflict. International guarantees for maintaining the terms of a settlement must be established. All agreements reached at the conference should be treated as a whole and be approved by all its participants.

All the Arab countries having common borders with Israel—Syria,* Jordan,* Egypt,* Lebanon—and Israel itself should have the right to take part in the conference.

The Palestine Liberation Organization, as the sole legitimate representative of the Palestinian people, should be an equal participant. This is a matter of principle. A Middle East settlement is not possible without solving the Palestine problem, and it cannot be resolved without the PLO participation.

The USSR and the United States, having served as cochairmen at the previous conference and having played an important role in the Middle East, should participate in the conference.

Other states of the Middle East and adjoining areas capable of making a positive contribution to the settlement in the Middle East could take part in the conference by common consent.

The new conference on the Middle East, like the previous one, should be held under UN auspices.

The Soviet proposals constituted for the first time the developed concept of an international conference. Owing to these proposals, the idea of an international forum and collective efforts to attain a settlement began to take concrete shape. Soviet proposals reflected most of the decisions made at the Arab Summit at Fez (September 1982). At the same time the Soviet plan did not receive broad support from all of the concerned parties. A weakness of the Soviet proposals was its excessive detail, which left little room for maneuvering and complicated the search for compromise solutions. Later Soviet approaches were more flexible and balanced.

Simeon Manickavasagam

ST. JAMES CONFERENCE (1939). Also known as the London Conference and the Roundtable Conference. The St. James Conference was opened in London by Colonial Secretary Malcolm MacDonald on February 7, 1939, following the Woodhead Commission* report of November 9, 1938, which found the partition of Palestine* "impracticable." Although the commission was unable to obtain agreement between Arabs and Jews on partition, its report called for "the basis of a settlement by negotiation." The St. James Conference was convened to discuss Britain's future policy toward Palestine. If agreement could not be reached between the two communities, Britain would determine its own course of action.

Arab delegates from Egypt,* Iraq,* Saudi Arabia, Transjordan,* and Yemen participated. The British decided not to allow the mufti of Jerusalem* to attend, but his cousin, Jamal Husseini, did. The participants from Palestine consisted of Fakhr al-Nashashibi* and members of the Arab Higher Committee.*

The Jewish community in Palestine was represented by members of the Jewish Agency* Executive. In addition, there were representatives from the British and American Jewish communities.

The Arab delegates refused to sit with, or meet, the Jewish delegates. As a consequence, the two delegations met separately with the British at sessions chaired by a British delegate, usually Malcolm MacDonald. MacDonald was forced to have two opening sessions.

Because of the threat of war with Germany, Britain was adamant that it did not wish to vacate Palestine. MacDonald hoped to allow Palestine some form of self-government in the Jewish and Arab areas with continued Jewish immigration into specified sectors. The future of Palestine, he believed, rested in an eventual federation with other Arab states. Arab demands going into the conference did not change. They sought to prohibit Jewish immigration and land sales to Jews and to create an independent state. Arab control of an independent state would give them total control over Jewish immigration and land purchases. Both the British Foreign Office and Colonial Office agreed that Britain could not grant independence, but there was disagreement between the two over the extent to which they could limit Jewish immigration and land sales.

Jamal Husseini pushed for independence, the end of the Mandate,* the end of the Mandate policy of establishing a Jewish National Home* in Palestine, and the creation of an independent Arab state. The Arab delegation denied that Britain had an obligation to the Jews, and they based their claim on an interpretation of the Hussein–McMahon correspondence,* in which the Arabs claimed that Britain intended Palestine to be included in the area specified for Arab independence. Britain disputed this, though it did grant to the Arabs a reading of the correspondence in which McMahon agreed not to "dispose of Palestine without regard for the wishes and interests of the inhabitants" of the country.

MacDonald then said to the Jewish delegation that their right to Palestine rested on the consent of the Arab population in Palestine. MacDonald's argument, Chaim Weizmann* and others recognized, abrogated the Balfour Declaration* and raised their concern that the British would grant the Arabs a veto on their Palestine policy. The colonial secretary then emphasized the strategic concerns of the British in Palestine because of the possibility of war. The Zionists* argued in vain that the Arabs exaggerated their threats in order to obtain greater leverage over British policy.

Various plans were introduced, but no solution was acceptable to both sides. MacDonald called for further discussions in the autumn about a constitutional structure for a proposed independent state. Palestinians and Jews were to be on the Executive Council. The Jewish delegation discovered later that the ratio of Arabs to Jews on the council was not to be equal, as originally promised, but three to two in the Arabs' favor. Further, the Zionists discovered by receiving the wrong documents that the Colonial Office had formulated different proposals to the two sides. They had proposed to the Arabs that in five years, not ten years as specified in the proposal given to the Jews, the Arab veto on Jewish immigration and land purchases would come into effect.

Although the British persuaded the Zionists to stay at the conference and continue negotiations, the St. James Conference ended by March 7. The White Paper of May 17, 1939, which was the outcome of the conference, granted the Arabs their veto over immigration after five years. During that five-year period, 15,000 Jews per year would be allowed to enter Palestine. An additional 25,000 Jewish refugees would be allowed to enter as well. Land transfers to Jews would be restricted to specified coastal areas. It was anticipated that an independent Palestinian state with a population that consisted of no more than one-third Jews would come into existence within ten years. Britain would aid its constitutional development. The White Paper was rejected by both the Arabs and the Jews.

For further information see: Michael J. Cohen, *Palestine: Retreat from the Mandate— The Making of British Policy, 1936–45* (New York: Holmes and Meier, 1978); Christopher Sykes, *Crossroads to Israel* (Cleveland: World, 1965).

Joseph E. Goldberg

STEADFASTNESS FRONT. After Egyptian* president Anwar Sadat* visited Jerusalem* in November 1977, Syria* initiated opposition to the Egyptian–Israeli peace negotiations. Known as the Pan-Arab Front of Steadfastness and Resistance, Syria, Libya, Algeria, the Peoples Democratic Republic of Yemen (South Yemen), and the Palestine Liberation Organization* (PLO) issued a declaration in Tripoli on December 5, 1977. Speaking in the name of Pan-Arabism, the Tripoli statement described the Sadat initiative as an American–Zionist* plan ''aimed at imposing capitulatory settlements on the Arab nation, prejudicing the established national rights of the Palestinian people, liquidating the national Arab accomplishments and striking at the Arab liberation movement.'' Sadat's visit was said to have constituted a ''departure from the unity of the Arab ranks and thus a violation of the Arab League Charter.'' A later Summit of the Steadfastness and Confrontation Front was held in Damascus on September 23, 1978, and agreed to four basic points: economic and political relations with Egypt were to be severed, and encouragement was to be given to ''progressive and nationalist forces'' to overthrow the Sadat government; the headquarters of the Arab League* was to be moved from Cairo; greater cooperation with the Soviet Union was to be sought; and a joint political and military command was to be established to coordinate action against Israel and Egypt.

Joseph E. Goldberg

STEERING COMMITTEE (Steering Group). Established by the Madrid Conference peace process* to coordinate the work of the five multilateral negotiations* working groups (arms control and regional security, economic development, environment, refugees, water resources) also established by the Madrid Conference.

STEP-BY-STEP DIPLOMACY. The concept of step-by-step diplomacy emerged after the Yom Kippur War,* when Secretary of State Henry Kissinger* made the decision that an attempt for a permanent, comprehensive settlement of the Arab–Israeli conflict was not possible. Thus, despite criticism for not seizing the opportunity to try for an overall solution, Kissinger believed that a step-by-step approach would be more fruitful. He calculated that the quest for a comprehensive solution was too full of risks for unattainable goals. The more ambitious effort, if it failed, would lead Israelis, Arabs, and allies to criticize U.S. efforts and would provide the Soviet Union with an opportunity to exploit the situation. He launched a series of diplomatic efforts, beginning with the Egypt–Israel Disengagement of Forces Agreement* of January 1974, each designed to deal with a piece of the problem, thereby building a settlement step by step.

For further information see: Henry Kissinger, *Years of Upheaval* (Boston: Little, Brown, 1982).

STERN (GANG) GROUP. Also known as LEHI-Lohamei Herut Yisrael—Fighters for the Freedom of Israel; Jewish underground fighting force in Palestine,*

formed by Abraham Stern (Yair) in 1940 after a split in the Irgun Tzvai Leumi.*
At the outbreak of World War II, Vladimir Jabotinsky,* supreme commander
of the Irgun,* ordered the cessation of hostile activities against the British Mandatory* government in Palestine. Stern, insisting that British involvement in the
war presented the Jewish national movement with the opportunity to force Great
Britain* to honor its obligations toward the Jewish people, advocated the intensification of anti-British activities. LEHI's activities were strongly opposed and
condemned by the majority of the Yishuv,* including the Haganah,* and its
policies were in contradiction even to those of the Irgun. In February 1942,
British police officers found Stern and shot him, and, subsequently, many leaders
and members of the group were arrested. A command composed of Nathan
Friedmann-Yellin, Yitzhak Yzernitsky (Shamir),* and Dr. Israel Scheib (Eldad)
took over responsibility for the military and political activities of the organization, which became known as the Stern gang. LEHI adopted a policy of individual acts of terrorism. In the summer of 1944, the LEHI command decided
to extend anti-British hostilities beyond Palestine. In November 1944, Lord
Moyne* was assassinated in Cairo. LEHI attacked the oil refineries in Haifa and
various British military installations, businesses, government offices, British military and police personnel, and army trains and other vehicles, increasingly ha-
rassing the administration. Following the United Nations Palestine partition*
decision of November 1947, LEHI fought the Arab irregulars who attacked the
Yishuv. After the proclamation of Israel's independence, LEHI was disbanded
as an independent fighting force, and its units were incorporated in the Israel
Defense Forces.* Friedmann-Yellin was elected on a LEHI slate to the First
Knesset,* but attempts to develop a cohesive political program and to form a
political party proved ineffectual.

   For further information see: ''Avner,'' *Memoirs of an Assassin* (London: Anthony
Blond, 1959); J. Bowyer Bell, *Terror out of Zion: Irgun Zvai Leumi, LEHI and the
Palestine Underground, 1919–1949* (New York: St. Martin's Press, 1977); Gerold Frank,
The Deed (New York: Simon and Schuster, 1963); Miriam Getter, ''The Arab Problem
in the Ideology of Lehi,'' *Zionism* 1 (Spring 1980): 129–39; Giora Goldberg, ''Haganah,
Irgun and 'Stern'; Who Did What?'' *Jerusalem Quarterly,* no. 25 (Fall 1982): 116–20.

STOCKHOLM DECLARATION (1988). In an attempt to initiate discussions
between the Palestine Liberation Organization* (PLO) and American Jews,
Swedish foreign minister Sten Anderson contacted the International Center for
Peace in the Middle East in Tel Aviv and arranged for a group of five American
Jews to meet with the chairman of the PLO's Foreign Affairs Committee, Khalid
al-Hassan.* The intent of the American Jewish group was to demonstrate to the
American government that there was little reason not to enter into talks with
the PLO. The group agreed upon a statement for release. Yasser Arafat* met
with them in Stockholm, and the statement was made public on December 7,
1988. The text of the joint declaration read as follows:

The Palestine National Council [PNC] met in Algiers from 12–15 November 1988, and announced the Declaration of Independence which proclaimed the State of Palestine,* and issued a political statement.

The following explanation was given by the representatives of the PLO of certain important points in the Palestinian Declaration of Independence and the political statement adopted by the PNC in Algiers.

Affirming the principle incorporated in those UN resolutions, which call for a two-state solution of Israel and Palestine, the PNC: 1. Agree to enter into peace negotiations at an international conference under the auspices of the U.N. with the participation of the permanent members of the Security Council and the PLO as the sole legitimate representative* of the Palestinian people, on an equal footing with the other parties to the conflict; such an international conference to be held on the basis of UN Resolutions 242* and 338* and the right of the Palestinian people to self-determination, without external interference as provided in the UN Charter, including the right to an independent state, which conference should resolve the Palestinian problem in all its aspects. 2. Established the independent State of Palestine and accepted the existence of Israel as a state in the region. 3. Declared its rejection and condemnation of terrorism in all its forms, including state terrorism. 4. Called for a solution to the Palestinian refugee* problem in accordance with international law and practices and relevant UN resolutions (including right of return or compensation).

The American personalities strongly supported and applauded the Palestinian Declaration of Independence and the Political Statement adopted in Algiers and felt there was no further impediment to a direct dialogue between the United States Government and the PLO.

The chairman of the Conference of Presidents of Major American Jewish Organizations, Morris Abram, accused the American Jews who signed the Stockholm Declaration of being ''willing dupes'' who were used by Arafat. The U.S. secretary of state, George Shultz,* stated that his government still did not believe that the PLO had met the conditions necessary for discussions.

Joseph E. Goldberg

STOP SHOOTING, START TALKING INITIATIVE. On June 25, 1970, Secretary of State William Rogers announced: ''The United States has undertaken a political initiative, the objective of which is to encourage the parties to stop shooting and start talking under the auspices of Ambassador Jarring in accordance with the resolution of the Security Council. Our objective in launching this initiative has been to encourage the parties to move toward a just and lasting peace.'' The proposal was designed to end the hostilities of the War of Attrition* and foster negotiations for peace under the aegis of the Jarring mission.* Among other factors, the growing Soviet military presence and activity in Egypt* was an element in generating the initiative that was sometimes referred to as Rogers Plan B.* Ultimately, a cease-fire* was agreed to and came into effect on August 7, 1970.

STRAIT OF TIRAN. Connects the Red Sea and the Gulf of Aqaba* (Gulf of Eilat*). The strait is narrow and constricted by islands (Tiran and Sanafir) and reefs. From the Egyptian Sinai Peninsula* to Tiran Island, the distance is approximately five miles. Coral formations constrict the seaway into two navigable channels—Enterprise Passage, which borders the Sinai coast, is 1,300 yards wide, while Grafton Passage, about one mile from the island of Tiran, is about 900 yards wide. Israel has argued that the Gulf of Aqaba should be treated as an international waterway and that no state has the right to deny passage through the Strait of Tiran. The Arab argument is that the Gulf of Aqaba consists of Arab territorial waters and that passage through it and the Strait of Tiran therefore cannot be undertaken without the consent of the Arab states. Until 1956, Egypt prevented shipping to Israel by military positions along the shore of the Sinai Peninsula. These were destroyed by Israel during the Sinai War* of 1956. The announcement by President Nasser* of Egypt in May 1967 that the strait was blockaded was a proximate cause of the Six Day War.* See also GULF OF AQABA; SHARM EL-SHEIKH.

STRATEGIC PARITY WITH ISRAEL. A policy of the Syrian* government under President Hafez al-Assad.* From the time he came to power in Syria in 1971, Assad had two principal goals: Arab unity and the struggle against Israel. According to Assad, the problems that face the Arab nation can be successfully resolved only through Arab unity. Inherent in this is the struggle of the Arab nation against Israel. The Arab nation can redress the Arab–Israeli conflict only through a position of strategic parity with Israel.

Assad long held the view that Israel's domination of the region is due to its military superiority. By overcoming their own inferiority, the Arab states can not only deter Israel's perceived expansionist aims but also enable them to negotiate or impose a settlement with Israel from a position of strength. Hence, strategic parity serves as both a military and a political weapon.

Prior to 1978, the strategic balance in the Middle East consisted of a larger Arab coalition, primarily Egypt* and Syria, against Israel. Regional circumstances such as the Camp David Accords* and the Iran–Iraq War left Syria to challenge Israel on its own. Accordingly, Assad embarked on a program of achieving strategic parity, or balance, with Israel, independent of other Arab states. While political and economic factors also play a role, the foundation of strategic parity involves the building up of a military capable of either deterring or effectively defending against attack.

Consequently, throughout the 1980s, Assad, with massive Soviet* assistance, embarked on the systematic buildup of Syria's military capability. The result was Syria's emergence as a powerful regional actor and direct challenger to Israel's security doctrine. While Assad's achievements have been formidable and impressive, Israel has maintained a qualitative edge, primarily through U.S. assistance and support. The Soviet Union, however, failed to provide Syria with similar unwavering commitments, culminating in Gorbachev's statement that Assad was to no longer assume Soviet support for his policy of strategic parity.

Without his strategic lifeline, Assad's attempt to effect change through strategic parity reached an impasse.

Beginning with the Madrid Conference* in 1991, Syria has been involved in bilateral and multilateral negotiations with Israel on various aspects of the Arab–Israeli conflict, and the concept of strategic parity has receded from the center of rhetoric and policymaking.

For further information see: Efraim Karsh, *Soviet Policy toward Syria since 1970* (New York: St. Martin's Press, 1991); Moshe Maoz, *Asad: The Sphinx of Damascus: A Political Biography* (New York: Weidenfeld and Nicolson, 1988); Patrick Seale, *Asad of Syria: The Struggle for the Middle East* (Los Angeles: University of California Press, 1988).

Anamika Krishna

STRAUSS, ROBERT (b. Lockhart, Texas, October 19, 1918). He received his undergraduate education and law degree from the University of Texas at Austin. He served as a special agent for the Federal Bureau of Investigation (FBI) from 1941 to 1945. From 1968 to 1970, Strauss was a member of the Democratic National Committee (DNC); he served as the DNC treasurer from 1970 to 1972 and as its chairman from 1972 to 1977. On April 24, 1979, President Carter* appointed Strauss special presidential envoy to the Middle East with the title of ambassador at large.

In this position, Strauss served as the head of the U.S. team of negotiators discussing the implementation of the Camp David Accords* with the Egyptians and Israelis. These negotiations, which were to be the first in a multistage process, began on May 25, 1979, in Beersheba, Israel. The goal of the negotiations was "full autonomy for the inhabitants of the West Bank* and Gaza* under a freely elected, self-governing authority that would serve for a transitional period of not more than five years." The negotiations, which were boycotted by both the Jordanians* and the Palestinians,* were soon stalled because of the differences between the Egyptians and Israelis. Ambassador Strauss, who stated he "would not invest much time or effort on the detailed negotiating sessions," became personally active in the negotiations only in the summer of 1979. At this time he proposed that the negotiators break down into smaller committees to discuss the technicalities for electing an autonomous Palestinian council and to decide what powers that council would possess. After continued stalemates, the United States proposed a United Nations solution; however, this was rejected by the Israelis, and the United States refused to support any other proposals. Strauss ended his tenure as special presidential envoy when he became President Carter's campaign chairman.

Strauss received the Presidential Medal of Freedom in 1981. He later served as the U.S. ambassador to Russia.

For further information see: Department of State Bulletin 79, no. 2031 (October 1979); Elizabeth Drew, "Profiles: Equations," *New Yorker,* May 7, 1979, pp. 50–129; Bernard

Reich, *The United States and Israel: Influence in the Special Relationship* (New York: Praeger, 1984).

Donald A. Vogus

SUEZ CANAL. The Suez Canal is a partially artificial waterway connecting the Mediterranean Sea and the Red Sea. Port Said is the northern outlet, and Suez the southern.

The idea of connecting the Red Sea and the Mediterranean Sea by a waterway through the Isthmus of Suez to facilitate communications and increase trade can be traced to antiquity. A canal connecting the two seas and utilizing the Nile River and its branches was dug in the reign of Senusret III. Subsequently, other canals were dug connecting the Mediterranean and the Red Seas indirectly through the Nile and its branches. In the nineteenth century, the idea was put forward of connecting the two seas by a direct canal, with a view to facilitating trade between Europe and its colonies in India and the Far East.

Ferdinand de Lesseps, a French engineer, was the driving force behind the project. On April 25, 1859, the project was begun with the breaking of ground near what has become Port Said. The project was completed on August 18, 1869, and the canal was officially inaugurated on November 17, 1869. The Suez Canal is the shortest navigable route between Europe and the East because it allows the bypassing of the long loop around Africa.

The Suez Canal has been an economic and strategic keystone in the Middle East since its opening. The canal, located between the Gulf of Suez and the Mediterranean Sea, extends 114 miles (184 kilometers), with seven miles (11 kilometers) of channel approaches at each end. The canal can handle approximately sixty vessels a day with a maximum draft of 53 feet (16.2 meters) and maximum width of 197 feet (60 meters). Between 1975 and 1980, the canal was widened and deepened to accommodate larger vessels. Petroleum accounts for about one-third of the freight through the canal.

Britain became the largest shareholder in the commercial Suez Maritime Company when Khedive Ismail Pasha could no longer afford to finance his loans and sold his stock to Britain in 1875. The company owned and operated the canal until Egyptian* president Gamal Abdul Nasser* nationalized it on July 26, 1956, twelve years before the ninety-nine-year contract with the Suez Company was to end. For Nasser, the nationalization served as a symbol of his quest for legitimacy to lead the Pan-Arabism movement as well as a move to restore the dignity he believed they lost. Nasser's decision resulted, in part, from the withdrawal of offers to finance the building of the Aswan Dam by the United States and Britain. This, combined with strong Arab nationalist sentiments and pervasive anticolonial attitudes throughout the Arab world, gave him added legitimacy. From Nasser's perspective, the nationalization had two objectives: to provide foreign exchange for Egypt to build the Aswan Dam and other development projects and to demonstrate that small countries need no longer accept public insult and degradation from Great Powers. The reaction of the Great

Powers to Nasser's nationalization permanently altered the political landscape of the Arab–Israeli conflict.

The British government of Anthony Eden* wished to preserve great power status in the Middle East. Egypt, because of its neutrality, was of particular importance since British control depended on the support of pro-Western regimes in the Middle East such as Iraq,* Jordan,* and the Arabian Peninsula. The United States supported, but was not active in, British Middle East policies, which included attempts to sway Egypt in favor of the West. After the nationalization of the canal, Anthony Eden altered Britain's policy to one of eliminating the Nasser regime. Also, oil was a significant factor in the recovery of postwar European economies.

French* foreign minister Christian Pineau was instrumental in designing the French plan for Israel to attack Egypt, followed by British and French intervention. He, along with Anthony Eden and the Israeli prime minister David Ben-Gurion,* feared Nasser's political ambitions. Since Nasser supported the Algerian insurrection against the French, it was advantageous for Pineau and Prime Minister Guy Mollet to get rid of him.

Ben-Gurion sought to secure Israel's existence in the Middle East by demonstrating to the Arabs the ''insuperable strength'' of the Jews in Palestine,* but he recognized that it would be easier with legitimate international diplomatic and military support. The agreement gave Israel the assurance that France would provide military support and that Britain would not be hostile, as it would if Israel had attacked Jordan.

The Sinai War* transformed the Arab–Israeli conflict. Britain and France, instead of regaining regional influence, were severely weakened, while the United States and the Soviet Union began to establish direct relationships with Middle East nations and to play a larger role in influencing their policy. As a result, the conflict no longer centered on border and refugee problems between Israel and its neighbors but, because of the strategic significance of the canal, included the interests of the two emerging superpowers. The war also resulted in the first United Nations Emergency Force* patrolling the Sinai Peninsula,* where it remained until 1967. Nasser maintained control of the canal and closed it to Israeli shipping, a situation that continued until Sadat reopened the canal on June 5, 1975, the eighth anniversary of the Six Day War.*

Since the independence of Israel, Egypt had blocked the Suez Canal to navigation by Israeli ships and denied its use to vessels coming from, or bound to, Israel. Israel argued that this was an illegal and arbitrary position. The Constantinople Convention of 1888 noted, ''The Suez Maritime Canal shall always be free and open, in time of war as in time of peace, to every vessel of commerce or of war without distinction of flag.'' Egypt was ordered by the United Nations Security Council on September 1, 1951, ''[t]o terminate the restriction on the passage of international commercial shipping and goods through the Suez Canal wherever bound.'' Israel gained access to the canal as a result of the Sinai II Accords.*

For further information see: Chester L. Cooper, *The Lion's Last Roar: Suez, 1956* (New York: Harper and Row, 1978); Chaim Herzog, *The Arab–Israeli Wars* (New York: Random House, 1982); William Roger Louis and Roger Owen, eds., *Suez 1956: The Crisis and Its Consequences* (New York: Oxford University Press, 1989); Hugh Thomas, *Suez* (New York: Harper and Row, 1966).

Erin Z. Ferguson

SUEZ CRISIS (1956). See **SINAI WAR (1956).**

SUEZ WAR (1956). See **SINAI WAR (1956).**

SYKES–PICOT AGREEMENT. In the late fall of 1914, Turkey entered World War I on the side of the Central Powers. Soon thereafter, Great Britain,* France,* and Russia began to contemplate the disposition of the Ottoman Empire's* territory in the Middle East. As early as 1915, the British government of Lord Herbert Asquith formulated a secret plan with regard to the territories. Palestine* was distinguished from other Turkish-held areas. Its determination required special negotiations because both belligerents and neutrals were interested in Palestine's fate. Britain and France began secret negotiations over the disposition of the Ottoman territory in 1915, which were completed in January 1916. Britain's negotiator was Sir Mark Sykes, a member of Parliament, an Arabist, and assistant secretary to the British War Cabinet. France was represented in the negotiations by Francois-Georges Picot,* a French diplomat who had served as consul general in Beirut. The two countries officially ratified the agreement in May 1916 in an exchange of letters from British foreign secretary Sir Edward Grey to France's ambassador to Great Britain, Paul Cambon.

The Sykes–Picot Agreement defined areas of British and French control as well as spheres of interest. Britain's authority was to extend in southern Iraq* (Mesopotamia) and from the Egyptian border to Iraq. The agreement identified this as the "red zone." In addition, the ports of Acre and Haifa on the Mediterranean Sea were to be under British control. The French authority was to include a coastal strip of Syria* and Lebanon* as well as a portion of Palestine west of the Jordan River.* The agreement identified this as the "blue zone." A "brown zone" was established as well. This territory was to be administered internationally. Palestine, including Jerusalem,* was part of the internationalized area.

The Sykes–Picot negotiations were not the only negotiations that the British were engaged in over the future disposition of the Ottoman territories. Sir Henry McMahon,* British high commissioner in Cairo, had begun a correspondence with the Sherif of Mecca. McMahon had hoped to nurture an Arab Revolt* against the Turks, which would aid in the British war effort. In return, the British were willing to entertain Arab aspirations for an independent state. When the details of the secret Sykes–Picot Agreement were made public, Arab distrust of British intentions increased.

Although the Sykes–Picot Agreement was an understanding between Britain and France, the distribution of Ottoman Empire territories under the League of Nations Mandate system was along the lines of the agreement.

For further information see: Roger Adelson, *Mark Sykes: Portrait of an Amateur* (London: Jonathan Cape, 1975); Elie Kedourie, "Sir Mark Sykes and Palestine 1915–16," *Middle Eastern Studies* 6 (October 1970):340–45; Rashid Ismail Khalidi, *British Policy towards Syria and Palestine 1906–1914: A Study of Antecedents of the Hussein–McMahon Correspondence, the Sykes–Picot Agreement and the Balfour Declaration* (London: Ithaca Press [for The Middle East Centre, St. Antony's College], 1980); Aaron Klieman, "Britain's War Aims in the Middle East in 1915," *Journal of Contemporary History* 3 (July 1968):237–51; Shane Leslie, *Mark Sykes: His Life and Letters* (London: Cassess, 1923); Jukka Nevakivi, *Britain, France and the Arab Middle East, 1914–1920* (New York: Oxford University Press, 1969).

Joseph E. Goldberg

SYRIA. Syria is Israel's neighbor to the northeast and a major antagonist since the independence of Israel. They fought in the War of Independence,* the Six Day War* (during which Israel captured the Golan Heights*), the Yom Kippur War* (in which there were some additional Israeli territorial gains), and the War in Lebanon.* U.S. secretary of state Henry Kissinger* brokered a disengagement of forces agreement* between the two states in the spring of 1974. No further progress toward peace between the two states was made, and Syria sought to achieve "strategic parity"* between the two states. This policy became unachievable with the demise of the Soviet Union, Syria's principal arms supplier.

Syria joined in the Madrid Peace Conference* and subsequently participated in the Washington rounds* of bilateral talks and the multinational negotiations.* Ambassador's talks* in Washington and Clinton* administration efforts to bring the parties to a conclusion of their negotiations focused on the question of trading peace for Israeli withdrawal from the Golan Heights.

SYRIA–EGYPT DEFENSE PACT (1966). See **EGYPT–SYRIA DEFENSE PACT.**

SYRIA–ISRAEL DISENGAGEMENT OF FORCES AGREEMENT. See **ISRAEL–SYRIA DISENGAGEMENT OF FORCES AGREEMENT.**

T

T-54/55 AND T-62 TANKS. The T-54/55 tank is a main battle tank produced originally in the Soviet Union in 1949. The T-62 is a variant of the T-54/55 produced in the late 1950s. The T-54/55/62 tanks are manned by a crew of four. They weigh approximately thirty-seven tons, have a maximum road speed of 30 mph, and can travel unrefueled up to 400 miles. T-54/55 tanks are armed with a 100mm cannon, and the T-62 has a 115mm cannon. T-54/55/62 tanks have onboard storage for thirty-four, forty-three, and forty cannon rounds, respectively. All three variants also come armed with a 7.62mm machine gun with 3,000–3,500 rounds of ammunition and a 14.5mm antiaircraft machine gun with 250–500 rounds.

Since the Six Day War,* the T-54/55 main battle tank has been the primary tank used by Arab armies. The T-62 was introduced in the Middle East following the Six Day War. Israel also employs T-54/55/62 in the Israel Defense Forces* from serviceable T-54/55/62 tanks it recovered on the battlefield. In 1994, the armies of the Middle East and North Africa collectively deployed well over 6,000 T-54/55 and 2,800 T-62 tanks.

The human engineering of the T-55 and T-62 is regarded as relatively poor. The crew compartments are small, and crews find little room to maneuver. This inhibits a rapid loading and firing sequence, which results in a major tactical drawback. The T-54/55 tanks employed external fuel tanks, which proved easy to set afire with small arms or artillery. These tanks were also not optimized for the Middle Eastern environment so they tended to overheat and break down frequently. Despite these drawbacks, the 115mm cannon was found to have excellent armor penetration at ranges to 1,600 meters, and Israeli armored forces discovered that the silhouettes and turret shapes of these tanks made them difficult to target and hit.

For further information see: Christopher Chant, *A Compendium of Armaments and Military Hardware* (London: Routledge and Kegan Paul, 1987); David Eshel, *Chariots of the Desert: The Story of the Israeli Armoured Corps* (London: Brassey's Defence, 1989).

Jon J. Peterson and Stephen H. Gotowicki

T-72 TANK. The T-72 is a Soviet-designed and -manufactured main battle tank that entered production in 1971 and became fully operational in 1973. The main armament on the T-72 is a 125mm cannon firing either APFSDS (armor-piercing, fin-stabilized discarding sabot), HEAT (high-explosive antitank) or HE (high-explosive) projectiles. Maximum effective range for the APFSDS and HEAT rounds is claimed to be 4,000 meters. The main cannon of the T-72 is stabilized, which allows it to be fired while the tank is moving, with a high probability of a first-round hit. Thirty-nine projectiles are stored in the tank's turret. The T-72 is also equipped with coaxial 7.62mm and turret-mounted 12.5mm machine guns. The T-72 has a maximum road speed of 38 miles per hour, with a range of 300 miles. The T-72 has a crew of three. Poland and Czechoslovakia also produced and exported variants of the T-72.

The T-72 was exported to Algeria, Iraq,* Libya, and Syria* in the early 1980s. In the late 1980s, a small number were purchased by Iran. The Israel Defense Forces* first encountered the T-72 in the War in Lebanon,* where they were employed by the Syrian army.

For further information see: Christopher F. Foss, ed., *Jane's Armour and Artillery,* 14th ed. (London: Jane's Information Group, 1994).

Stephen H. Gotowicki

TABA. A small, 1.2-square-kilometer (0.48 square-mile) enclave in the Sinai Peninsula* on the border between Egypt* and Israel located south of Eilat* on the Gulf of Aqaba* that remained in dispute when the international boundary was established between the two countries following the Egypt–Israel Peace Treaty* of 1979. Israel had retained the area after withdrawing from Sinai in 1982, arguing that the maps showed incorrect lines.

Although it is an insignificant piece of land, it became symbolic of a number of difficulties in the relations between the two countries following the signing of the peace treaty. When Israel withdrew from the Sinai Peninsula under the terms of the peace treaty, it questioned Egypt's claim that Taba was a part of Sinai. But for Egypt, it was not a conventional dispute; rather, it was a technical dispute to demarcate international borders. Once bitter enemies that fought five costly wars, both countries had to settle the dispute through peaceful means. The resulting dispute lasted six years and assumed an importance out of proportion to its size.

While Egypt's possession of Taba dates back to pharaonic times, its legal claim is based on Ottoman* decrees issued in 1841. In a test designed to determine British might and influence in Egypt, Ottoman Turkey seized Taba and attempted to annex it to the Hejaz province in 1906. With British influence, the crisis ended in October, with the 1906 border agreement reestablishing Egyptian sovereignty. Border markers were emplaced defining the eastern border from Rafah in the north to Taba in the south.

With the conclusion of the Egypt-Israel Peace Treaty in March 1979, Israel agreed to withdraw from Sinai behind the international borders between Egypt and Mandate Palestine.* Between the second and third stages of the Israeli withdrawal, Israel questioned the placing of some border markers, claiming that Taba was not included. Under the provisions of the agreement—the Temporary Method for Settling the Dispute regarding the Borderline between Egypt and Israel—the two sides agreed on April 25, 1982, to station multinational peace-keeping forces and observers in the disputed area, that Israel would undertake no new construction, and that the dispute would be resolved through conciliation or arbitration.

On November 1, 1982, Israel opened the 326-room Sonesta Hotel and a tourist village, which prompted charges from Egypt that Israel had violated the April agreement. Egypt pressed for arbitration in order to get a binding decision. President Hosni Mubarak's* insistence on not sending Egypt's ambassador back to Israel until it submitted to arbitration won the Israeli inner Cabinet's consent for arbitration in January 1986.

A five-arbiter international panel—with a representative from both Egypt and Israel—was appointed and asked to place fourteen disputed markers along the Egyptian–Israeli border based on the boundaries of the 1949 Egyptian–Israeli Armistice Agreement in making their final decision.

On April 2, 1988, the panel sided with Israel in the placement of four markers and with Egypt in the placement of ten, including marker 91, which placed the Taba area in Egypt. Egypt and Israel signed a series of agreements on February 26, 1989, to turn Taba back to Egypt. When it was returned to Egypt on March 15, 1989, Taba was inhabited by 600 people and featured a tourist cafeteria, a desalination station, a security post, a television transmission station, and telephone exchange facilities. As part of the settlement, Egypt agreed to pay $37 million for the hotel and $150,000 for the village.

For further information see: Ann Mosely Lesch and Mark Tessler, *Israel, Egypt and the Palestinians* (Bloomington: Indiana University Press, 1989); *Taba Liberating Egyptian Territories Completed Negotiation for Peace* (Arab Republic of Egypt, Ministry of Information, State Information Service, n.d.); *Taba—The Dispute and Its Solution* (Washington, DC: Embassy of Egypt, March 1990).

Ahmed Elbashari

TABA TALKS. Talks in Taba* between Israeli and Palestinian* delegations designed to work out the details of the Declaration of Principles* signed in Washington on September 13, 1993. The Israeli team was headed by Major General Amnon Shahak.* The Palestinian team was chaired by Nabil Shaath.*

AL-TAL, WASFI (b. Irbid, Jordan,* 1920; d. Cairo, November 1971). He graduated from the American University in Beirut. During World War II, he served in the British army. He fought in the Arab–Israeli War of 1948* and afterward joined the Jordanian diplomatic service. He served as ambassador to Iraq* in 1961–62. He became prime minister and minister of defense of Jordan in 1962 for one year and later in 1965–67 and 1970–71. He was prime minister during the conflict with the Palestine Liberation Organization* (PLO) and was assassinated by Palestinians* in Cairo—the first act by Black September.*

For further information see: Asher Susser, *On Both Banks of the Jordan: A Political Biography of Wasfi Al-Tall* (Newbury Park, United Kingdom: Frank Cass, 1994).

Joseph E. Goldberg

TALAL IBN ABDULLAH, KING (b. Mecca, 1909; d. 1972). Talal was the son of King Abdullah* of Jordan* and acceded to the throne upon his father's assassination in 1951. He suffered from schizophrenia and was removed from office in 1952. He spent his remaining years in a Turkish nursing home. He abdicated in favor of his son Hussein* in 1953. He had three sons: Hussein, Muhammad, and Hassan.*

TAMMUZ REACTOR. See **OSIRAQ/TAMMUZ REACTOR.**

TAWIL, SUHA (b. Jerusalem,* July 1963). She comes from a prominent Christian family and is the daughter of Daoud Tawil and Raymonda Hawa Tawil, a Palestinian* activist who supported Arab–Israeli coexistence. Suha spent her childhood in Ramallah and Nablus and was educated by French nuns. In the fall of 1981, she left the West Bank* for Paris and studied at the Sorbonne, from which she received a double M.A. degree in political science and linguistics. Her thesis was on the image of the Arabs in the American mass media. In October 1989, she left Paris for Tunis. In 1990, on her twenty-seventh birthday, she and Yasser Arafat* were secretly married. The ceremony was officially registered two years later.

For further information see: Mary Anne Weaver, ''The Chairman and His Wife,'' *The New Yorker,* May 16, 1994, pp. 72–85.

TEHIYA (Renaissance). Founded in 1979, Tehiya is an Israeli political party of ''true believers'' focusing on the Land of Israel with an ideological fervor reminiscent of Israel's political parties in the early years of independence and before. It is composed of both religious and secular elements and appeals strongly to Israel's youth. It has a component from Gush Emunim* (Bloc of the Faithful), but various secularists and secular-oriented groupings are also involved. Tehiya includes old associates of Menachem Begin* from the anti-British underground and former Herut Knesset* members such as Geula Cohen, as well as Land of Israel Movement* personalities. Included among its prominent members were Moshe Shamir, Aluf Avraham Yoffe, Dr. Zeev Vilnay, and Dr. Israel Eldad.

Tehiya's origins are in the Camp David Accords* (which they wanted to see revised in favor of a more hard-line stance) and the Egypt*–Israel Peace Treaty,* which called for total withdrawal from the Sinai Peninsula* and commitment to autonomy for the Palestinians.* They believe that Begin sold out and that the occupied territories* must remain in Israel's hands. The party's head is Professor Yuval Neeman, a physicist from Tel Aviv University, who is a leading nuclear scientist with a long-standing role in the defense establishment. In July 1982, Tehiya joined the ruling coalition of Menachem Begin's Likud.* This move seemed to help ensure Tehiya's future as well as strengthen the opposition in the government to concessions concerning Palestinian autonomy in the West Bank.* Neeman became minister of science and technology. Rafael Eitan,* former chief of staff of the Israel Defense Forces,* assumed the leadership of the combined Tehiya-Tsomet. Tehiya campaigned in the 1988 election on a platform that called for peace for peace, without Israel yielding any portion of the Land of Israel, and for increasing settlement in the territories as a guarantee of peace. It supported the application of Israeli sovereignty to Judea,* Samaria,* and Gaza.* It joined the government established by Yitzhak Shamir* in June 1990 but resigned from the government in January 1992 to protest Shamir's willingness to discuss an interim agreement on self-rule for West Bank and Gaza Palestinians. It lost all three of its Knesset seats in the June 1992 Knesset election.

TEL CHAI. A Jewish settlement founded in 1918 by the members of the Hashomer organization as a shepherd camp and an outpost to guard the Jewish lands in the surrounding area. When the Huleh Valley was to become part of the French Mandate in Syria,* the Arabs of the region objected and resorted to violence. The Jewish settlements in the area also became targets for attack. In 1920, the Arabs attacked Tel Chai and other Jewish settlements in the Upper Galilee on the edge of the Huleh Valley, and anti-Jewish riots broke out in Jerusalem.* Among the defenders of the settlement against Arab attackers was Joseph Trumpeldor, who became a legendary hero, as he and seven others were killed. The battle and Trumpeldor's reported last words, "It is good to die for our land," subsequently became legendary examples of self-sacrifice and heroism in Israeli folklore that symbolized the Jewish determination to settle and defend the land. In 1926, Tel Chai merged with the neighboring settlement of Kfar Giladi. The Revisionist* youth movement and its sports organization are named (Betar-Brit Yosef Trumpeldor) after Trumpeldor. The violence contributed to the decision to create the Haycraft Commission.*

David Salzberg

TEMPLE. The central building for the worship of God in Israel. The wanderings of the Ark of the Covenant were brought to a halt with the capture of Jerusalem* by King David. It was decided that a central place for the ark would be built in the new capital of the Jewish kingdom. The First Temple was completed by

King Solomon but was destroyed in 586 B.C. by the Babylonian conquest. King Cyrus of Persia allowed the Jews to return from exile in Babylon and to rebuild the Temple. In 538 B.C., the construction of the Second Temple was completed. This Temple stood until A.D. 70, when it was razed by the Roman legions under Titus.

The Temple was considered the national center of the Jewish people and kingdom. It was the site where the ark was stored, and, as such, the Temple was believed to be the location of the divine presence on earth. It served as a place of assembly and prayer for the people of ancient Israel, and sacrifices and prayers of repentance and thanksgiving in accordance with Jewish law were conducted there.

With the destruction of the Second Temple, Judaism emphasized the study of Torah and the religious structure of the synagogue. However, Jews continued to hope and pray for the restoration of the Temple, which it is believed would be achieved with the arrival of the Messiah.

David Salzberg

TEMPLE MOUNT. An area in the southeastern corner of the Old City* of Jerusalem* located on Mount Moriah. It is regarded as the site of the binding of Isaac and the location of the two Temples.* In Arabic, the area is known as the Haram al-Sharif* (the Noble Sanctuary). Muslims believe that the Prophet Mohammed was transported to the Temple Mount by his winged horse, al-Buraq, and ascended to heaven from this location.

In A.D. 638, the Caliph Omar conquered Jerusalem. In 684, the Ummayyad Caliph Abd al-Malik began to build the Dome of the Rock* on the ruins of the Jewish Temple. The work was completed in 690–91. In 700, the al-Aksa Mosque* was built on the spot where it was believed that Mohammed offered his prayers. After the Crusader conquest of Jerusalem, the Temple Mount came under Christian control, and the Dome of the Rock was converted into a church with the name Templum Domini (Temple of the Lord). In 1187, Saladin's victory in Jerusalem restored Muslim control of the Temple Mount, and the Dome of the Rock was restored as a mosque.

In 1967, Israel took control of the Temple Mount when it captured East Jerusalem* from Jordan.* Israel did not interfere with the administration of the Muslim holy places and left a Muslim council and *waqf* administration in charge. See also HARAM AL-SHARIF.

David Salzberg

TEMPLE MOUNT CRISIS (1990). See **AL-AKSA MOSQUE INCIDENT (1990).**

TEMPORARY INTERNATIONAL PRESENCE IN HEBRON (TIPH). In the wake of the Hebron Massacre,* it was agreed to establish a temporary international presence in Hebron.* This would consist of international observers from Norway, Italy, and Denmark. The force, consisting of 117 unarmed foreign observers, entered Hebron on May 8, 1994. Israel and the Palestine Liberation Organization* (PLO) agreed to set up the force after the United Nations Security Council passed a resolution after the Hebron Massacre that called for "a temporary international or foreign presence" in Hebron. The observers have no military or police powers and cannot intervene in violent confrontations. They are supposed to monitor events and report to a committee composed of the Israeli military governor of Hebron, the town's Palestinian* mayor, and their assistants. The observers are supposed to give Palestinians in Hebron a sense of security and to monitor their safety and restore calm and promote conditions for economic development.

In the aftermath of the Hebron Massacre in 1994, delegations representing Israel and the PLO agreed to take measures to provide for greater security throughout the West Bank* and Gaza Strip.* On March 31, 1994, an agreement was signed in Cairo between Israel and the Palestinians that, among other matters, established a temporary international presence in Hebron. The agreement provided:

In response to the unique situation created in Hebron in the aftermath of the massacre, a temporary international presence will be established in the city of Hebron ("TIPH"). . . . the TIPH will assist in promoting stability and in monitoring and reporting the efforts to restore normal life in the city of Hebron, thus creating a feeling of security among Palestinians in the city of Hebron. . . . The two sides shall request the donor countries to provide 160 persons, citizens of Norway, Denmark and Italy, as TIPH personnel, consisting of field observers, office staff and support personnel, as agreed by the two sides. . . . Consistent with its stated tasks, the TIPH personnel shall have no military or police functions. . . . The tasks of TIPH personnel will be: a. to provide by their presence a feeling of security to the Palestinians of Hebron; b. to help promote stability and an appropriate environment conducive to the enhancement of the well-being of the Palestinians of Hebron and their economic development; c. to monitor the efforts to restore the safety of Palestinians and events affecting it and the return to normal life in the city of Hebron.

The agreement also provided for the resumption of the Gaza–Jericho* negotiations and their acceleration to make up for lost time.

TEN-POINT PLAN. A plan put forward by Egyptian* president Hosni Mubarak* in July 1989 for holding Palestinian* elections in the occupied territories.* The points were that all Palestinians in the West Bank,* the Gaza Strip,* and East Jerusalem* should be allowed to vote and run for office. Candidates should be free to campaign without interference from the Israeli authorities. Israel should allow international supervision of the election process. Construction or expansion of Jewish settlements* would be frozen during this period. The army would withdraw from the area of polling places on election day. Only Israelis who live or work in the occupied territories would be permitted to enter them on election day. Preparation for the elections should not take longer than two months; Egypt and the United States would help form the Israeli–Palestinian committee doing that work. The Israeli government should agree to negotiate the exchange of land for peace, while also protecting Israel's security. The United States and Israel should publicly guarantee Israel's adherence to the plan. Israel should publicly agree in advance to accept the outcome of the elections.

For further information see: Sanford R. Silverburg, "The Bush Administration and the Middle East," *JIME Review,* no. 9 (Spring 1990): 60–71.

TERRITORIAL COMPROMISE. The idea that Israel would agree to compromise on its position of retaining all of the territories occupied in the Six Day War* and relinquish some of the territory. See also LAND FOR PEACE.

TERRITORIES. See OCCUPIED TERRITORIES.

TERRITORY FOR PEACE. See LAND FOR PEACE.

THIRD ARMY. During the Yom Kippur War,* the Egyptian Third Army, as of October 23, 1973, found itself encircled on the east bank of the Suez Canal* by the Israeli military and virtually cut off from all supplies, including food, water, and medicine. The situation became a point of contention between the two sides on the issue of war prisoners. The Egyptians* conditioned the return of all Israeli prisoners of war on an Israeli withdrawal to the canal's west bank, whereas the Israelis refused to remove their forces until the prisoners had been exchanged. Israel had allowed limited humanitarian supplies to reach the Third Army; however, it was not until the six-point* Egyptian–Israeli accord went into effect that Israel allowed unimpeded nonmilitary supplies to reach the Third Army.

On several occasions the Third Army attempted to breach the Israeli perimeter but was forced back. The Egyptian government complained that the Israelis were forcing the Third Army into unacceptable conditions, but Israel responded that the Third Army's situation was not as desperate as suggested. However, on October 25, the Israelis allowed the Red Cross to supply the Third Army with plasma, and, on October 29, the first 30 of 125 United Nations trucks were permitted to deliver relief supplies; an additional 50 supply trucks were later added.

The Egyptian government had also protested the continued encirclement of its Third Army by Israeli forces because this violated United Nations Security Council Resolution 339,* which stated that both armies return to their positions as of 6:55 P.M., October 22, which was alleged to have been before the Third Army had been completely surrounded. On November 12, United Nations Emergency Force* (UNEF) troops were stationed at Kilometers 101 and 119 to assist in the supply of the Third Army.

For further information see: Avraham Adan, *On the Banks of the Suez: An Israeli General's Personal Account of the Yom Kippur War* (Jerusalem: Edanim, 1980); Matti Golan, *The Secret Conversations of Henry Kissinger: Step-by-Step Diplomacy in the Middle East,* trans. Ruth Geyra Stern and Sol Stern (New York: Quadrangle/New York Times Book Company, 1976), Lester A. Sobel, ed., and Hal Kosut, contrib. ed., *Israel and the Arabs, The October 1973 War* (New York: Facts on File, 1974).

Donald A. Pearson

THREE NOES. The Fourth Arab Summit Conference, also known as the Khartoum Summit Conference* (August 29–September 1, 1967), was the first Arab Summit to be held after the 1967 Six Day War.* The result of the meeting was a formula of three negative statements or "three noes" that established and clarified the general Arab position toward Israel and the gains that it had made in the Six Day War. The Arab states put forth their decision to unite in order to secure an Israeli withdrawal from Arab lands occupied in the war. In achieving such a withdrawal, it was stated that the Arab states would be governed by the main principles agreed upon: "no peace with Israel, no recognition of Israel, and no negotiations with Israel."

The resolution states, in part:

The Arab heads of state have agreed to unite their political efforts on the international and diplomatic level to eliminate the effects of the aggression and to ensure the withdrawal of the aggressive Israeli forces from the Arab lands which have been occupied since the 5 June aggression. This will be done within the framework of the main principles to which the Arab states adhere, namely: no peace with Israel, no recognition of Israel, no negotiations with it and adherence to the rights of the Palestinian* people in their country.

The Arab states' pledge for no negotiation, no recognition, and no peace with Israel reflected the post-1967 feeling of inability to negotiate with Israel on a level of equality in the wake of the humiliating and devastating defeat in the 1967 war. The Arab resolve underlying the "three noes" formula created substantial obstacles to efforts designed to resolve the conflict until the early 1970s and the Yom Kippur War.*

Mark Daryl Erickson

TIBI, AHMED. An Israeli Arab, citizen of Israel, and a physician. He serves as a special adviser and sometime spokesman for Yasser Arafat* on Israeli affairs. In effect, he has served as a liaison between Israelis and Palestinians.* In January 1995, the Knesset* considered legislation, apparently aimed at Tibi, that prohibits Israeli citizens from advising terrorist groups and bodies that the government of Israel is negotiating with. Prime Minister Yitzhak Rabin* expressed strong negative views about this effort.

TIPH. See **TEMPORARY INTERNATIONAL PRESENCE IN HEBRON.**

TIRAN, STRAIT OF. See **STRAIT OF TIRAN.**

TOMB OF THE PATRIARCHS. The tomb, in Hebron,* was the site of the Hebron Massacre* in 1994.

The Tomb of the Patriarchs is referred to by Jews as the Cave of Machpela.* In this cave are believed to be the tombs of Abraham, Sarah, Isaac, Rebecca, Jacob, and Leah. The Bible refers to the cave where the tomb is housed as the first purchase made by Abraham, from whom all three monotheistic religions claim to be descended, as a symbol of his intention to settle in the new land. For Orthodox Jews, this first real estate purchase by the first Jew symbolizes the indisputable Jewish sovereignty over the site. For both Muslims and Christians, it bestows a universal sense of religious sanctity upon the site, the degree of which varies depending on individual religious beliefs.

Abraham's purchase of a piece of property specifically for use as a family tomb indicates that his wandering had ended and that elaborate burial had become a factor in sedentary life. The tomb has a fourth couple, whose names are a mystery but whose presence gave Hebron the biblical name of Kiryat Arba,* or Town of the Four. Today, Kiryat Arba is a settlement established first by squatters in 1968 and later sanctioned by the Israeli government.

Although Jews lived in the West Bank* city of Hebron for thousands of years and were later joined by Christians and Muslims, the cave was not routinely accepted as the actual burial site of the patriarchs until the late nineteenth century. Protestants and Zionists* desired to reestablish pilgrimage and settlement in the Holy Land* during this time, and their efforts gave renewed prominence to the Tomb of the Patriarchs. The shrine was closed to non-Muslims throughout the nineteenth century.

The political significance of the tomb became apparent when, after the 1967 war, ultraright religious groups such as the Gush Emunim* (Block of the Faithful) and the Temple Mount Faithful Movement were formed and declared the victory a sign from God. They interpreted it as God's hand in human affairs based on the overwhelming odds against Israel, the resulting reunification of Jerusalem,* and the retaking of historically Jewish land in the West Bank.

The Arab–Israeli conflict is always present at the tomb, the only major religious site where Muslims and Jews could both pray after the 1967 war. This arrangement worked until clashes between Arab youths and Jewish extremists in October 1976 brought the Israeli military, which placed the Arabs under day-and-night curfew. Another incident occurred in 1980, when six Jews from Kiryat Arba were ambushed and killed on their way from the cave. The incident of February 25, 1994, in which Dr. Baruch Goldstein, a far-right religious extremist from Brooklyn, New York, killed nearly thirty Arabs exemplifies both the religious reverence with which the site is viewed and the strong Jewish nationalism felt by the settlers in their attempts to establish undisputed administration over the West Bank.

The city of Hebron and the West Bank region represent the reestablishment

of Jewish rights over sacred Jewish monuments for the various extremist religious movements. The West Bank is also claimed by many Arabs as the site of
a future Palestinian state.

For further information see: Albert Hourani, *A History of the Arab Peoples* (Cambridge: Belknap Press of Harvard University Press, 1991); F. E. Peters, *Jerusalem, the
Holy City in the Eyes of Chroniclers, Visitors, Pilgrims, and Prophets from the Days of
Abraham to the Beginnings of Modern Times* (Princeton, NJ: Princeton University Press,
1985).

                                                                                                      Erin Z. Ferguson

TRANSJORDAN. See **JORDAN.**

**TREATY OF PEACE BETWEEN THE ARAB REPUBLIC OF EGYPT AND THE
STATE OF ISRAEL.** See **EGYPT–ISRAEL PEACE TREATY.**

TRIPARTITE AGGRESSION. An Arab reference to the Sinai War* and the Israeli, British, and French "aggression" against Egypt.

TRIPARTITE DECLARATION. A declaration by the United States, France,* and
England* on May 25, 1950, in which they proposed limiting arms supplies to
the region to those needed for local security.

The Tripartite Declaration refers to the U.S. joint declaration with the United
Kingdom and France made on May 25, 1950. These three powers reviewed the
situation in the Near East regarding security and stability of the area. These
states were concerned about the free flow of oil as well as containing the threat
of Soviet encroachment. By neutralizing the Arab–Israeli conflict, they hoped
to create a regional defense against the Soviet Union. This resulted in a declaration for the sale of arms and military equipment to the Middle East.

This declaration recognized the need for the Arab states and Israel to maintain
their armed forces at certain levels for internal and external security. It was
agreed, however, that all applications for arms and military matériel would be
considered within the light of several principles. All agreed that the development
of an arms race between the Arab states and Israel should be opposed. They
declared that assurances should be gained by the states that supply arms to the
region that the states in the region requesting arms did not intend to use such
arms to undertake acts of aggression against any other state. The three states
further declared their opposition to the use of force or threat of force between
any states in the region. Finally, they agreed that, should it be found that any
state was intending and preparing to violate the frontiers or armistice lines established in the region, they would immediately take action to prevent such a
violation within and outside the United Nations.

Another aim was to create a status quo between the Arab states and Israel
until a real peace could be obtained. The declaration is seen as one of the earliest
arms control documents regarding arms proliferation in the Middle East. Al-

though the declaration aimed at stemming arms proliferation in the region, it was largely ineffective. The clause stressing that the powers sell arms only with the assurance that the purchasing states would not use them for acts of aggression against other states was not enforceable. Another factor that led to the inevitable arms race was the Soviet Union's arms transfers via Czechoslovakia to Egypt* after 1955.

Susan L. Rosenstein

TRUMAN, HARRY S (b. Lamar, Missouri, May 8, 1884; d. Kansas City, Missouri, December 26, 1972). Truman grew up in Independence, Missouri, and served in the U.S. Army during World War I. After some years in private business, he was elected a U.S. senator in 1934 and was reelected in 1940. In 1944, with President Franklin Roosevelt's backing, he was nominated for vice president and elected. He became president on Roosevelt's death in 1945 and was reelected in 1948.

President Roosevelt did not formulate a precise American policy regarding the Palestine* problem; the matter was left to Truman on his succession to office in 1945. Initially, U.S. involvement centered on the emigration of displaced persons from Europe to Palestine. While the United States and England* were in substantial agreement on many aspects of the postwar Middle East, there was a divergence with regard to Palestine. Although both sought a solution that would safeguard and protect the rights and interests of the Jews and Arabs of Palestine, the differing perspectives affected their policies and generated considerable discord. Britain remained concerned with the future of its imperial position and, in particular, its relations with Jordan,* Iraq,* and Egypt.* A central element in Truman's approach to the Palestine question was the humanitarian problem of aiding displaced European Jewry. Britain sought to restrict the influx of Jews to Palestine; the United States pressed for increased Jewish immigration to provide for the remnants of the Jewish communities of Europe. Truman also believed in the need to redeem the pledges concerning the establishment of a Jewish homeland in Palestine. The Anglo-American Committee of Inquiry* was established to sort out the differing approaches.

When, in the spring of 1947, the Palestine problem was turned over to the United Nations, Truman believed in the need to redeem the pledge of the Balfour Declaration* and to support the establishment of a Jewish homeland in Palestine and access to it for the displaced Jews of Europe. The United States supported the partition plan* adopted in November 1947, although it proposed a temporary trusteeship over Palestine in March 1948, when it believed that partition could not be achieved by peaceful means at that time. When Israel declared its independence in May 1948, the United States was the first country to recognize it. Subsequently, the Truman administration sought to reduce tensions in the region, focusing, in part, on the Tripartite Declaration of 1950,* which sought to reduce arms supplies to the region and thereby the arms race in the Middle East.

In addition to its support of the partition resolution and immediate recognition of the new state, the United States supported Israel's applications for membership in the United Nations. U.S. aid programs for Israel were inaugurated, and efforts to achieve a solution to the Arab–Israeli conflict continued, with many of the efforts channeled through the Palestine Conciliation Commission,* which submitted proposals to Israel and the Arab states for a political, territorial, and economic settlement.

For further information see: John Snetsinger, *Truman, the Jewish Vote, and the Creation of Israel* (Stanford, CA: Hoover Institution Press, 1974); Harry S Truman, *The Memoirs of Harry S Truman,* 2 vols. (New York: Doubleday, 1956); Evan M. Wilson, *Decision on Palestine: How the U.S. Came to Recognize Israel* (Stanford, CA: Hoover Institution Press, 1979).

TUNIS TALKS. Dialogue between U.S. ambassador to Tunisia, Robert Pelletreau,* and Palestine Liberation Organization* (PLO) representatives in Tunis, authorized by the Reagan* administration in December 1988. These followed Yasser Arafat's* meeting the conditions placed on such a dialogue by a succession of U.S. administrations.

TUPOLEV TU-16 BOMBER. The Tu-16 is a twin-engined, subsonic, intermediate-range bomber designed and produced in the Soviet Union beginning in 1953. The Tu-16 has a maximum speed of 616 mph and a maximum altitude of 40,350 feet. The Tu-16 is armed with seven 23mm guns and can carry a 19,800-pound bomb load. It has a maximum range of 3,680 miles and an unrefueled combat radius of 1,955 miles. The Tu-16 has a crew of six and is air-refuelable.

In the Middle East, Tu-16s were acquired by Egypt,* Syria,* Iraq,* Libya, and Algeria. The Tu-16 did not play a major role in the Arab–Israeli Wars. In 1967, thirty of Egypt's Tu-16 bombers were destroyed on the ground during Israel's initial air strike. In 1973, two Egyptian Tu-16s unsuccessfully attempted to bomb a target near Eilat. One of these bombers crashed, and the other returned to Egypt.

For further information see: Chaim Herzog, *The Arab–Israeli Wars* (Tel Aviv: Steimatzky, 1984); Michael J. H. Taylor, ed., *Jane's World Combat Aircraft* (Surrey: Jane's Information Group, 1988).

Stephen H. Gotowicki

TWO-TRACK PROCESS. At Madrid,* a two-track system of peace process negotiations was established. There were bilateral, face-to-face talks between Israel and the Arab states as well as talks with the Palestinians* on the question of autonomy.

TZVAH HAGANAH LE YISRAEL. See **ISRAEL DEFENSE FORCES.**

U

U THANT (b. Panpanaw, Burma, January 22, 1909; d. New York, November 25, 1974). On November 30, 1962, U Thant, Burma's permanent representative to the United Nations and a teacher by training, was elected the third secretary-general of the United Nations following the untimely death of Dag Hammarskjold.* His election was supported by both the United States and the Soviet Union. His life was rooted in Buddhism, and his capacity for subdued and delicate diplomacy enabled him to survive ten years as secretary-general. When he announced in 1971 that, due to failing health, he would not be a candidate for a third five-year term, the United States tried to dissuade him before reluctantly joining in the search for a successor.

U Thant became personally involved in the Arab–Israel conflict in May 1967. Since 1957, the United Nations Emergency Force* (UNEF) had been stationed along the border with Israel in the Sinai Peninsula* and the Gaza Strip.* On May 13, in response to rumors that the Israeli army was gathering on the Syrian* border, President Gamal Abdul Nasser* of the United Arab Republic* (UAR) began moving troops into the Sinai Peninsula. On May 16, a message was sent to the commander of the UNEF to withdraw his troops from the border as the UAR wished to move its troops up to face Israel. Three hours later, U Thant confronted the UAR permanent representative to the United Nations. U Thant stated that the UAR request was unacceptable; the UNEF would remain precisely where it was, or it would withdraw from the Middle East entirely, but it would not merely retreat. U Thant indicated that if the UAR made a formal request to the secretary-general for the UNEF's withdrawal, he would comply. On May 18, 1967, the UAR formally requested the UNEF's withdrawal, and he promptly complied with the request.

U Thant justified his action by explaining that once the Egyptian* troops had deployed themselves between Israel and the UNEF, the UNEF had no further useful function. He added that "if the force was no longer welcome it could not as a practical matter remain in the United Arab Republic since the friction which would almost inevitably have arisen with the United Arab Republic Government, armed forces and the local population would have made the situation of the force both humiliating and untenable." U Thant believed that he had no alternative to complete withdrawal. Before he issued the withdrawal order, Nasser had interposed UAR troops between the UNEF and the Israeli border, and the countries that had contributed soldiers to the UNEF had informed him of their intention of withdrawing their troops.

U Thant also believed that the history of the establishment of the UNEF required his action. He noted that (1) negotiations on the issue of Egypt's right to terminate the UNEF's presence had delayed its arrival in November 1956; (2) the peacekeeping force had been established by the General Assembly, not the Security Council; and (3) the General Assembly had intended that UNEF take up positions on the Israeli, as well as the Egyptian, side of the border, but Israel had refused to have members of the territorial force on its territory on the grounds that it would mean a surrender of some degree of sovereignty.

Although U Thant personally continued to seek diplomatic resolutions to the crisis, the Six Day War* broke out on June 5, 1967, seventeen days after the withdrawal of the UNEF.

He was criticized for having given the UAR an "ultimatum" without consulting with any of the involved or interested governments. From the beginning, the presence of the UNEF in the Sinai* and the Gaza* had been intended to inhibit open conflict. A crisis in the Middle East in 1967 may have been inevitable, but U Thant's uncharacteristic sudden "ultimatum" ended whatever slim prospect there had been for negotiating with Nasser on the future of the UNEF. Furthermore, U Thant's precipitous action denied the parties the opportunity to gradually adjust to the change while the withdrawal of the UNEF was negotiated.

U Thant steadfastly maintained that he had acted within the letter of his mandate and that he had no choice but complete withdrawal. He noted that "not one member of the council expressed the view that my decision to comply with the demand of the United Arab Republic was unjustified, or that a decision of the question of the withdrawal of UNEF should have been taken by the Security Council or the General Assembly." U Thant believed that he had done his best to negotiate, but when that failed, political considerations as well as concern for the welfare of the troops mandated their withdrawal.

Richard G. R. Schickele

UAR. See **UNITED ARAB REPUBLIC.**

AL-UMARI, MUHAMMAD. See **15 MAY ORGANIZATION.**

UMM JIHAD. See **INTISSAR AL-WAZIR.**

UNDOF. See **UNITED NATIONS DISENGAGEMENT OBSERVER FORCE.**

UNEF. See **UNITED NATIONS EMERGENCY FORCE.**

UNIFIED NATIONAL COMMAND. See **INTIFADA.**

UNIFIL. See **UNITED NATIONS INTERIM FORCE IN LEBANON.**

UNION OF PALESTINIAN STUDENTS. See **GENERAL UNION OF PALESTINIAN STUDENTS.**

UNIT 101. This unit—a successor to the elite, pre-independence Palmach* (Plugot Mahatz) units that followed in the tradition of Britain's armed forces captain Orde Wingate* and his "special night squads"—is generally credited for being the origin of the Israeli army-based elite commando units. The unit is also credited with providing the model of tactical style and proficiency that was to broadly mark other elite Israeli infantry units.

In response to numerous Arab infiltrations into Israeli territory, almost all of which originated from Jordanian* territory and which resulted in a steady rise in the number of Israelis killed between 1950 and 1953, Jerusalem brigade commander Colonel Michael Shaham advised the Israeli army and Moshe Dayan* to establish a special elite unit. Shaham suggested this unit should be generally removed from the army structure and unfettered by regular army discipline and generally not wear uniforms or rank insignia. The strategic purpose of this unit was to carry out a persistent campaign of reprisal raids that would force Arab armies surrounding Israel to deploy in more heavily fortified positions and remain static and defensive.

Chief of Staff Mordechai Makhleff decided, against Dayan's preference, in August 1953, to draw from the ranks of retired junior officers about forty promising, skilled fighters for the purpose of carrying out these irregular raids. Shaham chose a battalion commander in the reserves, Ariel Sharon,* who had returned to the university to pursue Oriental studies, to lead this unit, which was to be designated Unit 101. Sharon himself was allowed to travel around the country to handpick the members of the unit. Dayan initially opposed the creation of Unit 101 because he believed that all units should have these special cross-border raiding skills and capabilities. Dayan became a staunch advocate of the unit by late 1953 and became a close personal admirer of Sharon's deputy, Meir Har-Zion.

Unit 101 never engaged in a large-scale battle during its existence but instead focused on smaller raids and perfected unique skills: night fighting and silent infiltration.

Following an attack on Lod in early October 1953, in which three Israelis were killed, Unit 101 was tasked to enter Kibya,* an Arab town close to the Israeli border near the Israeli city of Rosh Haayin, and demolish several houses. Because the village was thought to be heavily defended, the Israel Defense Forces* (IDF) sent a cover force along with Unit 101 during this operation, called Operation Rose.* Forty-five houses were demolished in this operation, but Unit 101 failed to ensure that all the houses were vacated prior to the attack. Sixty-six villagers were killed during the assault and demolition activities.

The brutality of the raid led Prime Minister David Ben-Gurion,* who faced an international outcry and censure from the United Nations, to ask for the dismemberment of Unit 101. Moshe Dayan, rather than dismantle the unit, instead decided to unite it with Paratroops Unit 890, which had been responsible for numerous cross-border operations between 1950 and 1953. The new combined paratroop unit was redesignated Unit 202. With retraining—some of which was designed to avoid the sort of catastrophe that marked the Kibya operation—and expansion, Unit 202's raids were generally larger and more surgical than those of Unit 101, though the tactics remained the same as before. The character of the new unit followed much more closely the unregimented character of Unit 101 than it did the more disciplined character of Paratroop Unit 890.

The most innovative tactic employed by this unit, developed by Sharon while recuperating from being wounded on a raid into Egypt, regarded the method of attacking a fortified stronghold. Rather than sequentially employing two teams, one "fire" and the other "assault," to storm a fortified position, Sharon retrained his unit to silently approach the fortification without firing a shot until an actual breach of fortification was made. Then the entire unit would storm, exploiting the shock effect of relentless movement. This later became a standard commando tactic.

Units 101 and 202 effectively monopolized all Israeli combat operations between 1953 and 1955. While Unit 202 engaged in only eight major raids in its first year, 1954, these operations were so spectacular that the unit became the model for training and deployment of numerous other infantry divisions in the Israeli army. By late 1955, other infantry units, such as the Golani Infantry Brigade, had been retrained with Unit 202's tactics and began to assume more responsibility for cross-border raids, such as the second Kibya raid in November 1955. The second Kibya raid was executed so successfully by Golani brigade elements that it finally became standard practice to task several different units with cross-border raiding responsibilities. Unit 202 itself gradually expanded until it became a brigade, playing a central role in the 1956 war* by seizing the Mitla* and Gidi* Passes well in advance of Israeli armor.

For further information see: Uzi Benziman, *Sharon, an Israeli Caesar* (New York: Adama Books, 1985); Dan Horowitz and Edward Luttwak, *The Israeli Army* (New York: Harper and Row, 1975); Ze'ev Schiff, *A History of the Israeli Army: 1874 to the Present* (New York: Macmillan, 1985).

David Wurmser

UNIT 202. See **UNIT 101.**

UNITED ARAB KINGDOM PROPOSAL OF KING HUSSEIN (1972). See HUS-SEIN'S UNITED ARAB KINGDOM PLAN.

UNITED ARAB REPUBLIC (UAR). In November 1957, the Syrian* National Assembly passed a resolution supporting union with Egypt.* President Gamal Abdul Nasser* of Egypt had long advocated Arab unity as well as a desire to lead the movement. Within Syria, the Baath Party held as a central principle the creation of an Arab state and emphasized its concern for "overall Arab interests." It led the drive for union and saw union with Egypt not only as advancing its political goals but also as a means of promoting its own influence. The union of Egypt and Syria was formally announced on February 1, 1958, with the Syrian National Assembly ratifying it on February 5, 1958. On February 21, President Nasser became the first head of the UAR, and he opened the first National Assembly on July 21, 1960. Though the first assembly did not convene until 1960, a central Cabinet and two regional Executive Councils were established, one in Egypt and one in Syria, in 1958. In March 1960, the assembly was modified, and a single legislature for the UAR was established. Egypt was allocated 400 deputies, and Syria 200 deputies. Syrian officials believed that Egyptian influence had become too dominant, and their dissatisfaction was the major cause of a military coup d'état that took place in Syria on September 28, 1961, which resulted in the dissolution of the United Arab Republic. Egypt continued to use the full title of United Arab Republic until it became the Arab Republic of Egypt in 1971.

Joseph E. Goldberg

UNITED ISRAEL APPEAL (UIA). Successor organization to the United Palestine Appeal.* See also **UNITED JEWISH APPEAL.**
   For further information see: Ernest Stock, *Partners & Pursestrings: A History of the United Israel Appeal* (Lanham, MD: University Press of America, 1987).

UNITED JEWISH APPEAL (UJA). A fund-raising campaign in the United States for the development of the Jewish National Home* in Palestine* and, later, Israel, as well as for Jewish communities and concerns worldwide. It began to function as a permanent organization in 1938.
   For further information see: Marc Lee Raphael, *A History of the United Jewish Appeal, 1939–1982* (Chico, CA: Scholars Press, 1982).

UNITED NATIONS CONCILIATION COMMISSION. See **PALESTINE CONCILIATION COMMISSION.**

UNITED NATIONS DISENGAGEMENT OBSERVER FORCE (UNDOF). After the Yom Kippur War,* there were periodic clashes between Israeli and Syrian* forces on the Golan Heights.* These became increasingly serious during April

1974. A Disengagement Agreement* between Israel and Syria was concluded in May 1974. In accordance with that agreement, an "area of separation" was created on the Golan Heights between Israeli and Syrian military forces. The parties also agreed to limit their forces and armaments to two equal "areas of limitation" on either side of the area of separation. UNDOF was established by the United Nations Security Council on the day the agreement was signed and was deployed in the area of separation. UNDOF also monitors compliance by the parties with the agreed limitations on forces and armaments. It is headquartered in Damascus, Syria.

On May 29, 1974, following days of intensive negotiations, an Agreement on Disengagement between Israeli and Syrian forces was concluded. On the next day, the secretary-general transmitted to the Security Council the text of this agreement, with an attached protocol concerning the United Nations Disengagement Observer Force. The agreement was signed on May 31, 1974, at Geneva. On the basis of a joint United States–USSR draft resolution, the Security Council welcomed the agreement and decided to set up the UNDOF immediately, as called for by the agreement. On May 31, 1973, the United Nations Security Council adopted resolution 350, which established the UNDOF along the same lines as the United Nations Emergency Force II* stationed in the Sinai Peninsula.* Under the agreement and the accompanying protocol, Israeli and Syrian forces were to be separated by a buffer zone manned by a UNDOF of about 1,250. The secretary-general drew troops from the existing forces in the area, especially United Nations Emergency Force II* (UNEF II). They included troops from Austria, Peru, Canada,* and Poland. In addition to the contingents from UNEF, approximately ninety of the United Nations Truce Supervision Organization* (UNTSO) military observers already deployed in the area were transferred to UNDOF. Israel and Syria agreed that UNDOF's function would be to use its best efforts to maintain the cease-fire and to see that it is scrupulously observed and to supervise the agreement with regard to areas of separation and limitation of forces and armament.

The Israeli withdrawal took place in stages that were completed on June 26, 1974. UNDOF troops were deployed into the void produced by the Israel Defense Forces* (IDF) withdrawal and maintained the separation between the Israeli and the returning Syrian troops.

The Israeli–Syrian disengagement proceeded as planned and was completed on June 25. On June 5, they signed the detailed plan of the separation of forces.

The UNDOF area of operations extends eighty miles from Mount Hermon* in the north to the Jordan River* in the south. It consists of an area of separation (a buffer zone varying in width from less than a kilometer to eight kilometers) and three zones of limitation established at ten, twenty, and twenty-five kilometers on each side of the area of separation. Only UNDOF forces are authorized in the area of separation. Each of the areas of limitations places restrictions on numbers of soldiers and quantities and types of equipment allowed. The restrictions are more stringent closer to the area of separation.

UNDOF's original mandate was for six months. This mandate has been extended every six months since 1974. UNDOF is widely considered one of the most effective and successful United Nations peacekeeping forces operating in the Middle East. Factors that have contributed to its success have been the continued observance of both Israel and Syria of the Disengagement Agreement, the narrow scope and requirements of UNDOF's mandate, and the reasonably unrestricted freedom of movement enjoyed by the force.

For further information see: Robert B. Houghton and Frank G. Trinka, *Multinational Peacekeeping in the Middle East* (Washington, DC: Foreign Service Institute, U.S. Department of State, 1985); John Mackinlay, *The Peacekeepers: An Assessment of Peacekeeping Operations at the Arab–Israeli Interface* (London: Unwin Hyman, 1989); United Nations, *The Blue Helmets: A Review of United Nations Peace-Keeping* (New York: United Nations Department of Public Information, 1985).

Stephen H. Gotowicki and Matthew Dorf

UNITED NATIONS EMERGENCY FORCE (UNEF). UNEF was established in direct response to the Sinai War.* The United Nations (UN) Security Council was deadlocked when trying to pass a resolution calling for compliance with UN Resolution 997 (ES-I) of November 2, 1956. Member states sought a cease-fire and the withdrawal of Israeli, British, and French* forces from Egyptian territory. Deadlock was created in the Security Council by the use of the veto power by Britain and France. This led to the calling of a special session of the General Assembly on November 5, 1957, under the Uniting for Peace Resolution of 1950.

There was a reluctance on the part of several states in the General Assembly to condemn Israel as the aggressor. Israel maintained that it was acting in retaliation for acts of Egyptian* aggression committed against it. Britain and France had declared that they sought only to ensure and protect the rights of Suez Canal* users. Western European states were also hesitant in placing complete blame on Britain and France. On the other hand, the Soviet bloc, along with several Asian and African states, wanted the UN to take strong measures to oppose the aggression taken against Egypt.*

Because the disagreement generated in the General Assembly hindered taking action, members of the assembly sought to find a common ground. In November, Lester Pearson of Canada* introduced a plan to authorize the secretary-general to create a UN international peacekeeping force with the capabilities of keeping the borders at peace until a political settlement could be reached. The plan requested the secretary-general to set up an emergency international force within forty-eight hours to secure and supervise compliance with Resolution 997(ES-I), which called for the cessation of hostilities. This plan was adopted as Resolution 998(ES-I) on November 4. The same day, Secretary-General Dag Hammarskjold* submitted his first report. He requested that the General Assembly create a UN Command for the force and appoint Major General E.L.M. Burns,* who was then the chief of staff of the United Nations Truce Supervision

Organization* (UNTSO), as its chief. Burns was to be allowed immediately to organize a staff and officers to be drawn from various members of the UN, excluding the permanent members of the Security Council.

Hammarskjold's report was adopted by the General Assembly as Resolution 1000(ES-I) on November 5. The resolution established a UN command for an international emergency force and authorized Burns to commence immediately in organizing a staff. It also invited the secretary-general to provide administrative measures for the prompt execution of the creation of a UN force.

UNEF was created as an armed police and patrol force, in contrast to the existing UNTSO, which was primarily an observer force. It was authorized to use force only in self-defense. At its maximum strength UNEF numbered some 6,000 soldiers from ten contributing countries.

UNEF's mandate directed four major objectives: secure the cessation of hostilities and supervise the cease-fire; ensure the orderly withdrawal of French, British, and Israeli forces; patrol the border between Israel and Egypt; and oversee the observance of the Egypt–Israel armistice. UNEF forces were deployed along the 145 miles of the international frontier in a combination of manned observation posts and mobile ground and aerial patrols on the Egyptian side only. The Israeli government never consented to the stationing of UNEF forces in Israel.

UNEF was to be temporary, with the length of its term to be decided by the needs arising out of the conflict. It was to be directly responsible to the UN. It would be allowed to function only to the extent of the consent of the states concerned. It was the first time such a force would be created. To secure the cessation of hostilities, UNEF would have to be more than an observer force, but not a UN military force.

Israel refused to allow UNEF to station itself on its soil, but Egypt agreed. UNEF was to enter Egypt only after a cease-fire was established in order to maintain quiet at the time of withdrawal of the non-Egyptian forces and to obtain compliance with Resolution 997(ES-I). At first, UNEF was to be placed at the Suez Canal and later moved to the armistice lines agreed to by Israel and Egypt in 1949.

Resolution 1001(ES-I), adopted November 7, dealt further with aspects regarding the composition and organization of the force and created an advisory committee to deal with issues not yet addressed by the assembly. It also approved the basic financing of the operation. Troops from ten member states were authorized to contribute forces to UNEF: Brazil, Canada, Colombia, Denmark, Finland, India, Indonesia, Norway, Sweden, and Yugoslavia. The General Assembly passed Resolution 1089(XI) on December 21, 1956, which decided that UNEF was to be financed by the UN, which would apportion the cost among member states according to each state's assessment for the 1957 fiscal year.

The first UNEF unit was deployed to the Suez Canal on November 15. Between January 28 and February 6, UNEF assisted in the exchange of Israeli and Egyptian prisoners of war. By February 1957, some 6,000 troops were deployed in the area. On March 7, the force became operational in the Gaza Strip* with the permission of Egypt following the Israeli withdrawal.

The UNEF operation was widely considered a success until it was withdrawn on May 18, 1967, at Egypt's request, for which United Nations secretary-general U Thant* was widely criticized. UNEF forces were stationed in Egypt with Egypt's consent. When the consent was withdrawn, the secretary-general ordered the evacuation of UN troops, leaving no buffer zone or troops between Israel and Egypt.

For ten years UNEF served its function. On May 16 and 17, 1967, however, various UN commanders in Egypt were asked to withdraw their UNEF units. Two Egyptian shells exploded in the vicinity of two UNEF camps on May 18. That same day, Secretary-General U Thant was requested by Egypt to terminate UNEF's presence. Following the request, the secretary-general issued a special report to the General Assembly regarding the withdrawal of UNEF from the Sinai Peninsula* and the Gaza Strip.

Israel was asked on May 18 to allow UNEF onto its soil, but it refused. After consultations, the secretary-general felt there was no choice but to remove the force since consent was lost. The beginning of UNEF's withdrawal commenced.

The UNEF force was re-created between Egypt and Israel following the Yom Kippur War* and referred to as UNEF II.

For further information see: Michael Comay, *U.N. Peacekeeping in the Israeli–Arab Conflict, 1948–1975: An Israeli Critique* (Jerusalem: Hebrew University, 1974); Elihu Lauterpacht, *The United Nations Emergency Force: Basic Documents* (New York: Praeger, 1960); Istvan S. Pogany, *The Security Council and the Arab–Israeli Conflict* (New York: St. Martin's Press, 1984); Indar Jit Rikhye, *The Sinai Blunder: Withdrawal of the United Nations Emergency Force Leading to the Six-Day War of June 1967* (London: Frank Cass, 1980); Indar Rikhye, Michael Harbottle, and Bjorn Egge, *The Thin Blue Line* (New Haven, CT: Yale University Press, 1974); Gabriella Rosner, *The United Nations Emergency Force* (New York: Columbia University Press, 1963); Ensio Siilasvuo, *In the Service of the Middle East, 1967–1979* (New York: Hurst, 1992); Bertil Stjernfelt, *The Sinai Peace Front: UN Peacekeeping Operations in the Middle East, 1973–1980* (New York: St. Martin's Press, 1992); United Nations, *The Blue Helmets: A Review of United Nations Peace-Keeping* (New York: United Nations Department of Public Information, 1985); David W. Wainhouse, *International Peace Observation: A History and Forecast* (Baltimore: Johns Hopkins Press, 1966); David W. Wainhouse, *International Peacekeeping at the Crossroads: National Support—Experience and Prospects* (Baltimore: Johns Hopkins Press, 1973); David W. Wainhouse, *International Peace Observation* (Baltimore: Johns Hopkins Press, 1977).

Susan L. Rosenstein, Stephen H. Gotowicki, and Matthew Dorf

UNITED NATIONS EMERGENCY FORCE II. United Nations Emergency Force II (UNEF II) was established by United Nations Security Council Resolution 340* on October 25, 1973, in response to the Yom Kippur War.* For the first time in the history of United Nations peacekeeping operations, the resolution creating the force had almost unanimous support of the council. China did not participate in the voting, for political reasons, while the other members of the council approved the resolution. Unlike the United Nations Emergency Force* (UNEF), this force could not be withdrawn unilaterally and without action by the Security Council.

UNEF II supervised the withdrawal of Israel's troops to a line east of the Suez Canal.* Under the terms of the Disengagement Agreement* signed at Kilometer 101* on the Cairo–Suez Road on January 18, 1974, UNEF was to occupy the buffer zone of disengagement between Egyptian* and Israeli forces and supervise the deployment lines of the forces and the areas of limited forces and armaments. The latter was an area where each side was allowed to station only limited forces, tanks, artillery, and air defense weapons. At its maximum strength, UNEF II consisted of nearly 7,000 soldiers from twelve contributing countries.

UNEF II's mandate was for a period of six months but was extended eight times. On July 24, 1979, the Security Council refused to extend UNEF's mandate, and its term of service ended on that day. Responsibility to monitor the area was returned to the United Nations Truce Supervision Organization* (UNTSO).

When the Yom Kippur War broke out on October 6, 1973, the only United Nations forces in the area were assigned to UNTSO and were stationed along the Suez Canal and at observer posts in the Golan Heights.* The posts on the Syrian* Front were overrun and evacuated until the fighting ceased, and the posts along the east bank of the Suez were evacuated after they came under direct fire. Those located on the west bank of the Suez became obsolete because of advances along the east bank.

Major General Ensio Siilasvuo,* a Finnish officer who was serving as the chief of staff for UNTSO, was appointed the interim commander of UNEF II and held that post until returning to Finland in 1980. Troops for UNEF II were dispatched within twenty-four hours from the United Nations Force in Cyprus (UNFICYP). This rapid deployment has been attributed not only to the initial success of the force but its subsequent success in carrying out its mandate.

The first UNEF II troops were deployed October 27 on the west bank of the Suez. That same day senior Israeli and Egyptian officers met to discuss evacuating wounded and supplying food, water, and medical supplies to the Egyptian Third Army.* Israeli troops had surrounded the Third Army but had been pressured to allow the passage of necessary supplies to the Egyptian troops. By December 1, UNEF II consisted of 3,174 troops from Austria, Canada,* Finland, Indonesia, Ireland, Panama, Peru, Poland, and Sweden.

Although UNEF II forces were deployed rapidly and with the support of the member states, fighting continued in the region. Despite the renewed hostilities, supplies were able to pass through to the Egyptian Third Army, and, by October 29, the Israelis permitted UNEF II troops to occupy positions on the canal's east bank.

No agreement was reached to return to the positions held on October 22, the date that the Security Council first declared a cease-fire. In large part through U.S. secretary of state Henry Kissinger's* diplomacy, a six-point agreement* was reached between Israel and Egypt and signed on November 11 at Kilometer 101,* laying the foundation for the ensuing peace negotiations.

For further information see: The Blue Helmets (New York: United Nations Department of Public Information, 1985); Istvan S. Pogany, *The Security Council and the Arab–Israeli Conflict* (New York: St. Martin's Press, 1984); Indar Rikhye, Michael Harbottle, and Bjorn Egge, *The Thin Blue Line* (New Haven, CT: Yale University Press, 1974); Ensio Siilasvuo, *In the Service of the Middle East, 1967–1979* (New York: Hurst, 1992); David W. Wainhouse, *International Peace Observation* (Baltimore: Johns Hopkins Press, 1977).

UNITED NATIONS GENERAL ASSEMBLY RESOLUTION 181 (II). On November 29, 1947, the United Nations (UN) General Assembly, by a vote of thirty-three in favor, thirteen against, and ten abstaining, adopted Resolution 181, the partition plan for Palestine.* In favor: Australia, Belgium, Bolivia, Brazil, Byelorussian S.S.R., Canada,* Costa Rica, Czechoslovakia, Denmark, Dominican Republic, Ecuador, France,* Guatemala, Haiti, Iceland, Liberia, Luxemburg, Netherlands, New Zealand, Nicaragua, Norway, Panama, Paraguay, Peru, Philippines, Poland, Sweden, Ukrainian S.S.R., Union of South Africa, United States, USSR, Uruguay, Venezuela. Against: Afghanistan, Cuba, Egypt,* Greece, India, Iran, Iraq,* Lebanon,* Pakistan, Saudi Arabia, Syria,* Turkey, Yemen. Abstained: Argentina, Chile, China, Colombia, El Salvador, Ethiopia, Honduras, Mexico, United Kingdom, Yugoslavia.

The partition plan was placed before the international body after the United Nations Special Committee on Palestine* (UNSCOP) Report in August 1947 called for the end of the British Mandate* and for partition of Palestine into Jewish and Arab State, with Jerusalem* an internationalized city and with an economic union for all three entities. The report called for British withdrawal no later than August 1, 1948.

Arab and Jewish residents of Jerusalem were free to choose becoming citizens of either the Arab or Jewish state and were entitled to vote in that state. Each state's Constituent Assembly was entrusted with drafting a democratic constitution and choosing a provisional government. Each state was expected to guarantee to all persons equal and nondiscriminatory rights in civil, political, economic, and religious matters. The resolution guaranteed "freedom of transit and visit for all residents and citizens of the other State in Palestine and the City of Jerusalem." It was also guaranteed that there should be liberty of access to holy places, the preservation of holy places, and freedom to worship in holy places.

The resolution called for an "Economic Union of Palestine," which would provide a customs union; a joint currency system and a single foreign exchange rate; railroads, telephones, and ports; joint economic development; and water and power facilities. A Joint Economic Board composed of representatives from both states as well as foreign members would supervise the economic activities.

Part II of the resolution stated in great detail the boundaries of both states. Jerusalem, which is the subject of Part III, would have a governor, appointed by the UN Trusteeship Council, and an administrative staff. The governor would not be from either the Arab or Jewish state. Jerusalem would have a Legislative Council, elected by adult residents based on proportional representation. Both Arabic and Hebrew were declared official languages of the city.

The decision to partition Palestine was followed by the first Arab–Israeli War,* as a consequence of which the UN-proposed boundaries and the status of Jerusalem were changed. The Jewish State came into existence as Israel, while the proposed Arab state in Palestine did not declare its independence.

UNITED NATIONS GENERAL ASSEMBLY RESOLUTION 194 (III). On December 11, 1948, the General Assembly adopted this resolution, which delineated the way to resolve the Palestine* problem. The assembly declared that refugees* wishing to return to their homes and live at peace with their neighbors should be permitted to do so, and those choosing not to return should be compensated. It also called for the demilitarization and internationalization of Jerusalem* and for the protection of, and free access to, the holy places. The resolution provided for the establishment of a three-member United Nations Conciliation Commission for Palestine* to assist the parties in achieving a final settlement on outstanding questions. Subsequently, the United States, France,* and Turkey were named as members of the commission.

UNITED NATIONS GENERAL ASSEMBLY RESOLUTION 2672c (XXV). The General Assembly adopted this resolution on December 8, 1970, by a vote of forty-seven to twenty-two, with fifty abstentions. It spoke of the "inalienable rights of the people of Palestine.*" The full text follows:

The General Assembly, Recognizing that the problem of the Palestinian Arab refugees has arisen from the denial of their inalienable rights under the Charter of the United Nations, and the Universal Declaration of Human Rights, Recalling its resolution 2535B (XXIV) of 10 December 1969, in which it reaffirmed the inalienable rights of the people of Palestine, Bearing in mind the principle of equal rights and self-determination of peoples enshrined in Articles 1 and 55 of the Charter and more recently reaffirmed in the Declaration on Principles of International Law concerning Friendly Relations and Co-operation among States in accordance with the Charter of the United Nations, 1. Recognizes that the people of Palestine are entitled to equal rights and self-determination, in accordance with the Charter of the United Nations; 2. Declares that full respect for the inalienable rights of the people of Palestine is an indispensable element in the establishment of a just and lasting peace in the Middle East.

UNITED NATIONS GENERAL ASSEMBLY RESOLUTION 3210 (XXIX). On October 14, 1974, the United Nations General Assembly adopted Resolution 3210 (XXIX) by a vote of 105 in favor, 4 against, and 20 abstaining, inviting the

Palestine Liberation Organization* to participate in the deliberations of the General Assembly. The full text: "The General Assembly, Considering that the Palestinian people is the principal party to the question of Palestine,* Invites the Palestine Liberation Organization, the representative of the Palestinian people, to participate in the deliberations of the General Assembly on the question of Palestine in plenary meetings."

UNITED NATIONS GENERAL ASSEMBLY RESOLUTION 3236 (XXIX). United Nations (UN) General Assembly Resolution 3236 (XXIX) was adopted, by a vote of eighty-nine in favor, seven against, and thirty-seven abstentions, on November 22, 1974, in response to discussion of the Palestinian* problem. It reaffirmed the inalienable rights of the Palestinian people, including the right of self-determination without external interference, the right to national independence and sovereignty, and the right to return to their homes and property. The General Assembly heard a statement by Yasser Arafat,* the chairman of the Palestine Liberation Organization* (PLO) Executive Committee, on November 13. Following numerous statements by various UN delegates, there was wide agreement that without a settlement of the Palestinian problem, no lasting peace could be obtained in the Middle East. The U.S. delegate's position on the subject stipulated that a solution could be obtained only through a negotiation process in which Palestinian interests were incorporated.

Resolution 3236 was one of two resolutions adopted on this issue. This resolution recognized that the Palestinian problem endangers the peace and security of the region and affirmed the inalienable rights of the Palestinian people in Palestine and their right to national independence and sovereignty. The Palestinian people were recognized as the "principal party" to negotiate with to establish peace, and the secretary-general was requested to establish contact with the PLO on matters concerning the Palestinian problem. The resolution also reaffirmed the right of Palestinian refugees to return home. The text follows:

The General Assembly, Having considered the question of Palestine, Having heard the statement of the Palestine Liberation Organization, the representative of the Palestinian people, Having also heard other statements made during the debate, Deeply concerned that no just solution to the problem of Palestine has yet been achieved and recognizing that the problem of Palestine continues to endanger international peace and security, Recognizing that the Palestinian people is entitled to self-determination in accordance with the Charter of the United Nations, Expressing its grave concern that the Palestinian people has been prevented from enjoying its inalienable rights, in particular its right to self-determination, 1. Reaffirms the inalienable rights of the Palestinian people in Palestine, including: (a) The right of self-determination without external interference; (b) The right to national independence and sovereignty; 2. Reaffirms also the inalienable right of the Palestinians to return to their homes and property from which they have been displaced and uprooted, and calls for their return; 3. Emphasizes that full respect for and the realization of these inalienable rights of the Palestinian people are indispensable for the solution of the question of Palestine; 4. Recognizes that the Palestinian people is a principal party in the establishment of a just and durable peace in the Middle East; 5. Further recognizes the right of the Palestinian people to regain its rights by all means in accordance with the purposes and principles of the Charter of the United Nations; 6. Appeals to all States and international organizations to extend their support to the Palestinian people in its struggle to restore its rights, in accordance with the Charter; 7. Requests the Secretary-General to establish contacts with the Palestine Liberation Organization on all matters concerning the question of Palestine; 8. Requests the Secretary-General to report to the General Assembly at its thirtieth session on the implementation of the present resolution; 9. *Decides* to include the item ''Question of Palestine'' in the provisional agenda of its thirtieth session.

Susan L. Rosenstein

UNITED NATIONS GENERAL ASSEMBLY RESOLUTION 3237 (XXIX). In November 1974, the United Nations General Assembly (UNGA), by a vote of ninety-five in favor, seventeen opposed (including the United States and Israel), and nineteen abstentions, passed resolution 3237 (XXIX) granting observer status to the Palestine Liberation Organization* (PLO).

The resolution stressed a previous United Nations (UN) resolution, UNGA 3102 (XXVIII), which stated that the Palestinians are entitled to equal rights and self-determination and to membership in several other UN organizations, like the World Population Council and World Food Conference. The operative clauses called for PLO participation in all sessions and workings of all international conferences convened under the auspices of the UN.

During debate on the resolution, Israel, represented by Ambassador Yosef Tekoah, held to its position that it would not negotiate or otherwise recognize an organization committed to the destruction of Israel. Additionally, it cited as a possible violation of the UN Charter the acceptance of a nongovernmental group to participate in UN activities, as the charter calls for participation by member states. For its part, the Arab side argued that it was not possible to solve the Palestinian* question without the participation of the Palestinian people, and, because the PLO is recognized as the legitimate representative of the Palestinian people, it is only logical to allow the organization to become an observer at the UN. Additionally, because the PLO was already a participant in other specialized UN agencies, it follows that the PLO be allowed to participate in assembly debates.

The outcome of the debate was not in question, as votes for passage were ensured by the Third World's support of liberation movements.

Although observer status did not necessarily mean formal recognition, it can be considered a form of implied recognition. By granting observer status to the PLO, the United Nations granted an aura of legitimacy to the organization's claim to be the sole representative of the Palestinian people and thereby further boosted the organization's status.

For further information see: Murray Gordon, ''The UN, Israel and the PLO'' *Midstream* 21 (March 1975):37–50; Jamal R. Nassar, *The Palestine Liberation Organization:*

From Armed Struggle to the Declaration of Independence (New York: Praeger, 1991); UN Resolution 3237 (XXIX), Observer Status for Palestine Liberation Organization, *UN Monthly Chronicle* 9 (December 1974):37; Abraham Yeselson and Anthony Gaglione, "What Really Happened When Arafat Spoke at the UN," *Worldview* 18 (March 1975): 49–55.

Pamela Rivers

UNITED NATIONS GENERAL ASSEMBLY RESOLUTION 3376 (XXX). On November 10, 1975, the United Nations General Assembly adopted this resolution by a vote of ninety-three in favor, eighteen against, with twenty-seven abstentions. It created the Committee on the Exercise of the Inalienable Rights of the Palestinian* People.*

UNITED NATIONS GENERAL ASSEMBLY RESOLUTION 3379 (XXX). On November 10, 1975, the United Nations General Assembly, by a vote of seventy-two in favor, thirty-five against, with thirty-two abstentions, adopted resolution 3379, in which it declared: "*Determines* that zionism* is a form of racism and racial discrimination."

On December 16, 1991, the United Nations General Assembly, with 111 countries voting in the affirmative, repealed its November 10, 1975, resolution (number 3379) equating Zionism with racism; there were twenty-five against, thirteen abstentions, and seventeen absent or not voting. The Arab states opposed the repeal, arguing that revocation would hinder the Middle East peace process. The Palestinian*-born Saudi Arabian president of the General Assembly refused to chair the session.

U.S. deputy secretary of state Lawrence Eagleburger introduced the one-sentence resolution: "The General Assembly decides to revoke the determination contained in its resolution 3379 (XXX) of 10 November 1975." The Soviet Union was among the eighty-five cosponsors of the resolution.

Israel welcomed the decision and saw it as correcting a historic distortion. Although most of the Arab states voted against the repeal measure, some (including Egypt,* Kuwait, Bahrain, Oman, Morocco, and Tunisia) decided not to vote on the issue.

UNITED NATIONS GENERAL ASSEMBLY RESOLUTION 48/58. On December 14, 1993, the United Nations General Assembly adopted a resolution endorsing the Israel–Palestine Liberation Organization* (PLO) Declaration of Principles* and supporting the Middle East peace process. The resolution endorsed the peace process without criticizing Israel. The vote was 155 in favor, 3 opposed, 1 abstention, and 25 absent. The text of the resolution noted:

The General Assembly, Stressing that the achievement of a comprehensive, just and lasting settlement of the Middle East conflict will constitute a significant contribution to strengthening international peace and security, Recalling the convening of the Peace

Conference on the Middle East at Madrid on 30 October 1991, on the basis of Security Council resolutions 242* (1967) of 22 November 1967 and 338* (1973) of 22 October 1973, and the subsequent bilateral negotiations, as well as the meetings of the multilateral working groups, and noting with satisfaction the broad international support for the peace process, Noting the continuing positive participation of the United Nations as a full extraregional participant in the work of the multilateral working groups, Bearing in mind the Declaration of Principles on Interim Self-Government Arrangements, signed by Israel and the Palestine Liberation Organization in Washington, D.C., on 13 September 1993, Also bearing in mind the Agreement between Israel and Jordan* on the Common Agenda,* signed in Washington, D.C., on 14 September 1993, 1. Welcomes the peace process started at Madrid and supports the subsequent bilateral negotiations; 2. Stresses the importance of, and need for, achieving a comprehensive, just and lasting peace in the Middle East; 3. Expresses its full support for the achievements of the peace process thus far, in particular the Declaration of Principles on Interim Self-Government Arrangements signed by Israel and the Palestine Liberation Organization, and the Agreement between Israel and Jordan on the Common Agenda, which constitute an important initial step in achieving a comprehensive, just and lasting peace in the Middle East, and urges all parties to implement agreements reached; 4. Stresses the need for achieving rapid progress on the other tracks on the Arab–Israeli negotiations within the peace process; 5. Welcomes the results of the International Donors Conference to Support Middle East Peace,* convened in Washington, D.C., on 1 October 1993, and the establishment of the high-level United Nations task force to support the economic and social development of the Palestinian* people, and urges Member States to provide economic, financial and technical assistance to the Palestinian people during the interim period; 6. Calls upon all Member States also to extend economic, financial and technical assistance to States in the region, and to render support for the peace process; 7. Considers that an active United Nations role in the Middle East peace process and in assisting in the implementation of the Declaration of Principles can make a positive contribution; 8. Encourages regional development and cooperation in the areas where work has already begun within the framework of the Madrid Conference.

UNITED NATIONS INTERIM FORCE IN LEBANON (UNIFIL). The United Nations Interim Force in Lebanon (UNIFIL) was created on March 19, 1978, by United Nations Security Council Resolution 425* in response to the 1978 Israeli invasion of southern Lebanon known as Operation Litani.* It is head-quartered in Lebanon.* The Security Council called for an end to Israel's military action and on March 19, 1978, set up UNIFIL to confirm the withdrawal of Israeli forces, restore international peace and security, and assist the Lebanese government in ensuring the return of its effective authority in the area.

An advanced party was assembled from existing forces in the area and deployed on March 22, 1978. By May 5, 1978, there were 4,000 United Nations troops in southern Lebanon, and the force grew to 6,000.

UNIFIL's mandate was to be an interim force. The secretary-general provided terms of reference for the force, including the appointment of Major General E. A. Erskine as the force commander and Lieutenant General Ensio Siilasvuo* as the chief coordinator for peacekeeping operations in the Middle East.

UNIFIL comprises approximately 14,000 soldiers from contributing countries. At one time or another, these included Fiji, Finland, France,* Ghana, Ireland, Iran, Italy, Nepal, the Netherlands, Norway, Senegal, and Sweden. The force is organized into infantry battalions deployed throughout the area, a support battalion, and support companies. The battalions control their assigned areas by roving patrols and fixed checkpoints along the roads where civilians and vehicles are searched for arms. Any arms found are confiscated.

The UNIFIL area of operations was originally envisioned as bounded by the Israel–Lebanon border in the south, the Litani River* in the north, the Mediterranean Sea in the west, and the Lebanon–Syria* border on the east. UNIFIL has never been allowed by Israel to deploy forces into its southernmost operational area—the Christian enclave, which in 1985 became Israel's self-declared security zone.* This area is five to eight kilometers deep, running parallel to the Israeli–Lebanese border. Control of this area has been maintained by the Israel Defense Forces* (IDF) and the Christians of South Lebanon organized into an Israeli-supported militia called the South Lebanese Army* (SLA). Because the government of Lebanon does not recognize the SLA, UNIFIL does not recognize any legitimacy or authority for the South Lebanese Army and officially refers to it only as a de facto force.

The original UNIFIL mandate was for six months. This mandate has been renewed every six months since 1978. UNIFIL has been unable to fulfill its mandate over the years for a variety of reasons: the mandate was formulated too broadly; Israel has not allowed UNIFIL to exercise its full mandate; UNIFIL has been subject to frequent armed opposition from extrastate players such as the South Lebanese Army, the Palestine Liberation Organization,* and Hezbollah,* as well as clashes with the IDF; faced with this opposition, UNIFIL has usually not exercised its authority with sufficient strength; and the Lebanese government has not been unified or strong enough to reestablish sovereignty in the south. After the War in Lebanon,* UNIFIL remained in the area with the same mandate.

For further information see: Robert B. Houghton and Frank G. Trinka, *Multinational Peacekeeping in the Middle East* (Washington, DC: Foreign Service Institute, U.S. Department of State, 1985); Ensio Siilasvuo, *In the Service of Peace in the Middle East, 1967–1979* (London: C. Hurst, 1992); Ramesh Thakur, *International Peacekeeping in Lebanon* (Boulder, CO: Westview Press, 1987); United Nations, *The Blue Helmets: A Review of United Nations Peace-Keeping* (New York: United Nations Department of Public Information, 1985).

Stephen H. Gotowicki and Matthew Dorf

UNITED NATIONS MIDDLE EAST MISSION. See **JARRING MISSION.**

UNITED NATIONS PALESTINE COMMISSION. Shortly after the Palestine* partition plan* vote of November 1947, the United Nations established a Palestine Commission, composed of five member states appointed by the General Assembly to effect the transfer from the Mandatory power to the proposed Arab and Jewish states. The commission was abolished on May 14, 1948, by General Assembly Resolution 189(S-2), and its responsibilities transferred to Count Folke Bernadotte,* the first United Nations mediator on Palestine.

UNITED NATIONS PARTITION PLAN. See **PALESTINE PARTITION PLAN.**

UNITED NATIONS RELIEF AND WORKS AGENCY FOR PALESTINE REFUGEES (UNRWA). UNRWA is the United Nations (UN) agency set up in the aftermath of the 1948–49 Arab–Israeli War* with a mandate to give assistance to the Palestinian refugees.* It provides schooling and health and welfare services for Palestinian refugees registered with UNRWA, as well as housing for those who live in official refugee camps administered by UNRWA. It provides education to the children, takes care of basic health needs, and provides relief and social welfare services. It operates in the Gaza Strip,* Jordan,* Lebanon,* Syria,* and the West Bank.* It is funded by voluntary contributions. During its initial years, most of its resources were used for providing emergency relief—food, shelter, clothing. As the need for basic assistance diminished, food aid was gradually phased out. At present, 70 percent of the resources go for education, 20 percent for health services, and 10 percent for relief and welfare. Since the beginning of the *intifada,** it has been providing special emergency assistance.

By 1991–92 UNRWA was providing assistance to some 2.6 million registered Palestinian refugees in Jordan, Lebanon, Syria, the West Bank, and the Gaza Strip. Elementary and preparatory education was provided to 374,000 pupils in 636 schools, and health services were delivered through a network of 117 health points. There were also women's program centers and community rehabilitation centers for the disabled.

UNITED NATIONS RELIEF FOR PALESTINE REFUGEES (UNRPR). The UNRPR was created in 1948 to provide emergency assistance to the Palestine refugees.* In December 1949, United Nations Relief and Works Agency for Palestine Refugees* was established in its place.

UNITED NATIONS SECURITY COUNCIL RESOLUTION 228 (NOVEMBER 25, 1966). See **ES-SAMU.**

UNITED NATIONS SECURITY COUNCIL RESOLUTION 242. The United Nations Security Council, on November 22, 1967, adopted a British-sponsored resolution designed to achieve a solution to the Arab–Israeli conflict that was deliberately vague but emphasized an exchange of land for peace.* The full text of the resolution follows:

The Security Council, Expressing its continuing concern with the grave situation in the Middle East. Emphasizing the inadmissibility of the acquisition of territory by war and the need to work for a just and lasting peace in which every State in the area can live in security. Emphasizing further that all Member States in their acceptance of the Charter of the United Nations have undertaken a commitment to act in accordance with Article 2 of the Charter. 1. Affirms that the fulfillment of Charter principles requires the establishment of a just and lasting peace in the Middle East which should include the application of both the following principles: (i) Withdrawal of Israeli armed forces from territories occupied in the recent conflict; (ii) Termination of all claims or states of belligerency and respect for and acknowledgement of the sovereignty, territorial integrity and political independence of every State in the area and their right to live in peace within secure and recognized boundaries free from threats or acts of force; 2. Affirms further the necessity (a) For guaranteeing freedom of navigation through international waterways in the area; (b) For achieving a just settlement of the refugee* problem; (c) For guaranteeing the territorial inviolability and political independence of every State in the area, through measures including the establishment of demilitarized zones; 3. Requests the Secretary-General to designate a Special Representative to proceed to the Middle East to establish and maintain contacts with the States concerned in order to promote agreement and assist efforts to achieve a peaceful and accepted settlement in accordance with the provisions and principles in this resolution; 4. Requests the Secretary-General to report to the Security Council on the progress of the efforts of the Special Representative as soon as possible.

The resolution has been the basis of all subsequent peace efforts. Gunnar Jarring, then Sweden's ambassador to Moscow, was appointed by the United Nations secretary-general in November 1967 to implement the resolution, but ultimately he failed to secure meaningful movement toward peace.

For further information see: Eugene V. Rostow, "The Illegality of the Arab Attack on Israel of October 6, 1973," *American Journal of International Law* 69 (April 1975): 272–89; Eugene V. Rostow, "Letter from Washington: A Question to Settle," *Hadassah Magazine,* December 1991, pp. 11–12; *UN Security Council Resolution 242: The Building Block of Peacemaking* (Washington, DC: Washington Institute for Near East Policy, 1993).

UNITED NATIONS SECURITY COUNCIL RESOLUTION 262 (DECEMBER 31, 1968). See BEIRUT AIRPORT RAID.

UNITED NATIONS SECURITY COUNCIL RESOLUTION 338. On October 22, 1973, the United Nations Security Council adopted Resolution 338, which called for an immediate cease-fire in the Yom Kippur War,* the implementation of United Nations Security Council Resolution 242,* and explicitly required negotiations "between the parties." The full text follows:

The Security Council 1. Calls upon all parties to the present fighting to cease all firing and terminate all military activity immediately, no later than 12 hours after the moment of the adoption of this decision, in the positions they now occupy; 2. Calls upon the parties concerned to start immediately after the cease-fire the implementation of Security Council resolution 242 (1967) in all of its parts; 3. Decides that, immediately and concurrently with the cease-fire, negotiations start between the parties concerned under appropriate auspices aimed at establishing a just and durable peace in the Middle East.

This provided the basis for the initial postwar military disengagement negotiations.

The resolution was submitted as a joint United States–Soviet Union resolution and was adopted by a vote of fourteen to none, with China not participating in the vote, on October 22, 1973. The text had been agreed upon by the United States and the USSR on October 21 in Moscow after Henry Kissinger* had flown to Moscow on October 20. China did not partake in the voting (but did not cast a veto), citing the fact that the text failed to condemn Israel, and it was formulated by the United States and the Soviet Union without reference to the Security Council.

For further information see: Henry Kissinger, *Years of Upheaval* (Boston: Little, Brown, 1982); Istvan S. Pogany, *The Security Council and the Arab–Israeli Conflict* (New York: St. Martin's Press, 1984).

Matthew Dorf

UNITED NATIONS SECURITY COUNCIL RESOLUTION 339.

The Security Council, Referring to its resolution 338* (1973) of 22 October 1973, 1. Confirms its decision on an immediate cessation of all kinds of firing and of all military action, and urges that the forces of the two sides be returned to the positions they occupied at the moment the cease-fire became effective; 2. Requests the Secretary-General to take measures for immediate dispatch of United Nations observers to supervise the observance of the cease-fire between the forces of Israel and the Arab Republic of Egypt,* using for this purpose the personnel of the United Nations now in the Middle East and first of all the personnel now in Cairo.

At Egypt's request the Security Council convened on October 23, 1973, because of the breakdown of the cease-fire agreed to one day earlier in United Nations Security Council (UNSC) Resolution 338. Like 338, the draft resolution was sponsored jointly by the United States and USSR, causing concern among some council members that the Security Council was becoming a superpower forum to enact bilateral policies. China did not take part in the voting, and 339, like 338, was adopted fourteen-none.

October 21, the night before 338 was adopted, Israel launched two major offensives. In the Golan,* Israel sought to regain Mount Hermon,* which was captured by the Syrian* army early in the fighting. On the Egyptian Front, Israeli ground forces crossed the Suez Canal,* resulting in an encirclement of the Egyptian Third Army.* Fighting continued on both fronts after the appointed cease-fire time, 6:58 P.M. Israel time, twelve hours after 338 was passed.

UNSC Resolution 339 not only confirms the cease-fire but also calls for the "immediate dispatch of United Nations observers." The United States, among others, felt an urgent need for up-to-the-minute reports to the Security Council and therefore included operative clause 2 in the draft. Observations had ceased after the hostilities broke out when United Nations observers were forced to evacuate their posts because of heavy fighting in their zones.

Egypt had already told the Soviets on October 22 that they would accept a cease-fire. Israel set an exchange of prisoners as a prerequisite to a cease-fire. Egyptian president Anwar Sadat* proposed that the United States should intervene, using force in order to ensure compliance. U.S. secretary of state Henry Kissinger* was clear that no U.S. force would be used. Instead, President Richard Nixon* sent a communiqué to Egyptian president Anwar Sadat, ensuring him that the United States would not allow the Israeli forces to eliminate the encircled Third Army.

Syria accepted 339 on the condition that Israel would return to pre-1967 boundaries, as well as the safeguarding of the legitimate national rights of the Palestinians.

UNSC Resolution 339 did not secure a cease-fire. On October 24, fighting continued as Israeli forces completed the encirclement of Egypt's Third Army and launched a direct assault on Suez City. The fate of the Third Army and resulting impasse resulted in a difficult diplomatic situation. Nonetheless, a compromise position and cease-fire were secured through Security Council Resolution 340* (1973).

Matthew Dorf

UNITED NATIONS SECURITY COUNCIL RESOLUTION 340.

The Security Council, Recalling its resolution 338* (1973) of 22 October 1973 and 339* (1973) of 23 October 1973, Noting with regret the reported repeated violation of the cease-fire in non-compliance with resolutions 338 (1973) and 339 (1973), Noting with concern from the Secretary-General's report that the United Nations military observers have not yet been enabled to place themselves on both sides of the cease-fire line, 1. Demands that immediate and complete cease-fire be observed and that the parties return to the positions occupied by them at 1650 GMT on 22 October 1973; 2. Requests the Secretary-General, as an immediate step, to increase the number of military observers on both sides; 3. Decides to set up immediately under its authority a United Nations Emergency Force to be composed of personnel drawn from States Members of the United Nations except the permanent members of the Security Council, and requests the Secretary-General to report within 24 hours on the steps taken to this effect; 4. Requests the Secretary-General to report to the Council on an urgent and continuing basis on the state of the implementation of the present resolution, as well as resolution 338 (1973) and 339 (1973); 5. Requests all Member States to extend their full cooperation to the United Nations in the implementation of the present resolution, as well as resolutions 338 (1973) and 339 (1973).

The Security Council failed to secure a cease-fire through its prior resolutions concerning the October War,* 338 (1973) and 339 (1973). Resolution 340

(1973) was adopted by a fourteen to none vote on October 25, with China not participating in the voting.

Israeli forces launched two major offensives on October 21, the night before 338 (1973) was adopted, in an effort to regain Mount Hermon* in the Golan, which was captured by the Syrian* army early in the fighting, and reverse losses on the Egyptian* front as well. Israeli ground forces crossed the Suez, resulting in an encirclement of the Egyptian Third Army. Egyptian president Anwar Sadat* proposed that the United States intervene, using force in order to ensure compliance with the cease-fire. U.S. secretary of state Henry Kissinger* was adamant that no U.S. or Soviet forces would be used, but President Nixon* sent a communique to Sadat ensuring him that the United States would not allow the Israeli forces to eliminate the Third Army, which they had encircled on the banks of the Suez. A draft of 340 (1973), submitted by the nonaligned members of the Security Council, called for the establishment of a United Nations Emergency Force. The United States threatened to veto any resolution that included forces from either or both superpowers. The fate of the Third Army and resulting impasse created a difficult diplomatic situation, but nonetheless a compromise position facilitated the eventual cease-fire secured through Security Council resolution 340 (1973).

The Soviet Union, at Egypt's request, strongly supported the use of superpower troops to secure a cease-fire. The Soviet Union, in a communiqué to Kissinger, threatened unilateral action, causing much concern in the Nixon administration. The Soviets eventually backed down and instead sent seventy observers to the region. However, the Third Army remained surrounded by Israeli troops, which prevented the passage of food and medical supplies.

On October 26, the Third Army resumed hostilities in an attempt to break out of their encirclement. The attempt failed, and Egypt filed an urgent request with the Security Council accusing Israel of cease-fire violations. Israel denied the accusations, blaming Egypt for the renewed hostilities. Under strong pressure from the United States, the Israeli government allowed an Egyptian convoy carrying food, medicine, and water to pass through to the Third Army.

Resolution 339 (1973) called for the "immediate dispatch of United Nations observers." Resolution 340 (1973), in stronger language, requested in operative clause 2 the secretary-general "as an immediate step, to increase the number of United Nations military observers on both sides"; and in operative clause 3 established a United Nations Emergency Force [UNEF] to consist of troops from member states except the permanent members of the United Nations, that is, United States, Soviet Union, France,* Great Britain,* and China. This force became known as UNEF II, as UNEF I was stationed until the outbreak of the 1967 war.

Although 340 (1973) secured a cease-fire, it was unstable at best. Kissinger, through talks with President Sadat and Prime Minister Meir,* facilitated a six-point agreement* signed on November 11, 1993, in which both sides agreed they would "observe scrupulously" the cease-fire.

Matthew Dorf

UNITED NATIONS SECURITY COUNCIL RESOLUTION 350. See **UNITED NATIONS DISENGAGEMENT OBSERVER FORCE.**

UNITED NATIONS SECURITY COUNCIL RESOLUTION 425. On March 14, 1978, Israel sent troops into southern Lebanon* in response to a major attack by the Palestine Liberation Organization* (PLO). On March 11, 1978, a terrorist attack against two Israeli buses near Tel Aviv (in which thirty-seven Israelis were killed and more than seventy-five injured), the Israel Defense Forces* (IDF) entered southern Lebanon in order to eliminate PLO bases and staging areas south of the Litani River.* This was Operation Litani.* By March 19, 1978, Israel was in control of all of Lebanon south of the Litani River, and Israeli prime minister Menachem Begin* stated that withdrawal of Israeli forces would be contingent upon the removal of Palestinian* guerrillas from the area. The United States, meanwhile, proposed that Israeli troops be replaced by an international force and that in time these troops would be replaced by the Lebanese army. The United Nations Security Council thus adopted Resolution 425 on March 19, 1978.

The resolution passed with the support of Bolivia, Canada,* France,* Gabon, Federal Republic of Germany (FRG), India, Kuwait, Mauritius, Nigeria, United Kingdom, United States, and Venezuela. Czechoslovakia and the Soviet Union abstained. The resolution created the United Nations Interim Force in Lebanon* (UNIFIL).

The nations that initially contributed forces to UNIFIL in 1978 were Canada, Fiji, France, Iran, Ireland, Nepal, Nigeria, Norway, and Senegal; and the total force composition was 5,900 soldiers.

The UNIFIL troops first arrived in southern Lebanon on March 22, 1978, to take up positions between the Israelis and Palestinians. They have remained in southern Lebanon since 1978, even during the 1982 invasion of Lebanon by Israel.

Two of the three original goals—confirming the Israeli troop withdrawal and reestablishing Lebanese government authority in the area—have not been achieved. The troops have, however, proved to be a stabilizing factor in reducing the chances of war and have received widespread support for their efforts.

The resolution called "for strict respect for the territorial integrity, sovereignty and political independence of Lebanon within its internationally recognized boundaries." It also called "upon Israel immediately to cease its military action against Lebanese territorial integrity and withdraw forthwith its forces from all Lebanese territory."

The council also decided "to establish immediately under its authority a

United Nations interim force for Southern Lebanon for the purpose of confirming the withdrawal of Israeli forces, restoring international peace and security and assisting the Government of Lebanon in ensuring the return of its effective authority in the area, the Force to be composed of personnel drawn from Member States.''

For further information see: Ramesh Thakur, *International Peacekeeping in Lebanon: United Nations Authority and Multinational Force* (Boulder, CO: Westview Press, 1967).

Donald A. Vogus

UNITED NATIONS SECURITY COUNCIL RESOLUTION 672 (1990). On October 8, 1990, violence broke out at the al-Aksa Mosque* in Jerusalem,* in which Palestinians* were shot and killed by Israeli border police. A combination of Palestinian provocation and what Israeli judge Ezra Kama was to call police negligence resulted in the violence. The situation became an international incident, which resulted in the United Nations Security Council considering the matter. On October 12, 1990, the United Nations Security Council unanimously adopted Resolution 672, which read:

1. Expresses alarm at the violence which took place on 8 October at the Al Haram Al Sharif* and other Holy Places of Jerusalem resulting in over twenty Palestinian deaths and the injury of more than one hundred and fifty people, including Palestinian civilians and innocent worshippers; 2. Condemns especially the acts of violence committed by the Israeli security forces resulting in injuries and loss of human life; 3. Calls upon Israel, the occupying Power, to abide scrupulously by its legal obligations and responsibilities under the Fourth Geneva Convention relative to the Protection of Civilian Persons in Time of War, of 12 August 1949, which is applicable to all the territories occupied by Israel since 1967.

It also called on the secretary-general to report to the council concerning his findings and conclusions based on a mission that he planned to send to the area. See also AL-AKSA MOSQUE INCIDENT.

Joseph E. Goldberg

UNITED NATIONS SECURITY COUNCIL RESOLUTION 726. On January 6, 1992, the United Nations Security Council adopted unanimously Resolution 726, condemning Israel's decision to deport twelve Palestinians* subsequent to a series of Palestinian terrorist actions against Israelis. The resolution contained a strong condemnation of Israel's action and noted the applicability of the Fourth Geneva Convention ''to all the Palestinian territories occupied by Israel since 1967, including Jerusalem.*'' This is the first time that the territories were designated as Palestinian.

The core of the resolution stated:

Having been apprised of the decision of Israel, the occupying power, to deport 12 Palestinian civilians from the occupied Palestinian territories, 1. Strongly condemns the decision of Israel, the occupying power, to resume deportations of Palestinian civilians; 2. Reaffirms the applicability of the Fourth Geneva Convention of 12 August 1949 to all the Palestinian territories occupied by Israel since 1967, including Jerusalem; 3. Requests Israel, the occupying power, to refrain from deporting any Palestinian civilians from the occupied territories*; 4. Also requests Israel, the occupying power, to insure the safe and immediate return to the occupied territories of all those deported.

UNITED NATIONS SECURITY COUNCIL RESOLUTION 904. On March 18, 1994, the United Nations Security Council adopted Resolution 904 in response to the Hebron Massacre* and its effects on the Arab–Israeli peace process. The text of the resolution follows:

The Security Council, Shocked by the appalling massacre committed against Palestinian* worshippers in the Mosque of Ibrahim in Hebron,* on 25 February 1994, during the holy month of Ramadan, Gravely concerned by the consequent Palestinian casualties in the occupied Palestinian territory as a result of the massacre, which underlines the need to provide protection and security for the Palestinian people, Determined to overcome the adverse impact of the massacre on the peace process currently under way, Noting with satisfaction the efforts undertaken to guarantee the smooth proceeding of the peace process and calling upon all concerned to continue their efforts to this end, Noting the condemnation of this massacre by the entire international community, Reaffirming its relevant resolutions, which affirmed the applicability of the Fourth Geneva Convention of 12 August 1949 to the territories occupied by Israel in June 1967, including Jerusalem,* and the Israeli responsibilities thereunder, 1. Strongly condemns the massacre in Hebron and its aftermath which took the lives of more than 50 Palestinian civilians and injured several hundred others; 2. Calls upon Israel, the occupying Power, to continue to take and implement measures, including, inter alia, confiscation of arms, with the aim of preventing illegal acts of violence by Israeli settlers; 3. Calls for measures to be taken to guarantee the safety and protection of the Palestinian civilians throughout the occupied territory, including, inter alia, a temporary international or foreign presence, which was provided for in the declaration of principles,* within the context of the ongoing peace process; 4. Requests the co-sponsors of the peace process, the United States of America and the Russian Federation, to continue their efforts to invigorate the peace process, and to undertake the necessary support for the implementation of the above-mentioned measures; 5. Reaffirms its support for the peace process currently under way, and calls for the implementation of the declaration of principles, signed by the Government of Israel and the Palestine Liberation Organization* on 13 September 1993 in Washington D.C. without delay.

UNITED NATIONS SPECIAL COMMITTEE ON PALESTINE (UNSCOP). Unable to satisfy the conflicting views of the Arab and Jewish communities of Palestine* and to ensure public safety because of the conflicts between them and faced with the heavy burden entailed in retaining the Palestine Mandate (British Mandate*), which compounded the extensive costs of World War II, the British conceded that the Mandate was unworkable and turned the Palestine problem over to the United Nations in the spring of 1947. The United Nations Special Committee on Palestine (UNSCOP) examined the issues and recommended that the Mandate be terminated and that the independence of Palestine be achieved without delay. However, it was divided on the future of the territory. The majority proposed partition into a Jewish state and an Arab state linked in an economic union, with Jerusalem* and its environs established as an international enclave. The minority suggested that Palestine become a single federal state, with Jerusalem as its capital and with Jews and Arabs enjoying autonomy in their respective areas. The majority proposal was adopted by the United Nations General Assembly on November 29, 1947. See also PALESTINE PARTITION PLAN.

UNITED NATIONS SPECIAL REPRESENTATIVE IN MIDDLE EAST. See **JAR-RING MISSION.**

UNITED NATIONS TRUCE SUPERVISION ORGANIZATION (UNTSO). Headquartered in Jerusalem,* the UNTSO was established in 1948, initially to supervise the truce called for in Palestine* by the United Nations Security Council during the first Arab–Israeli War.* Its personnel have monitored the observance of cease-fire arrangements, acted as go-between, and ensured that isolated incidents were contained and prevented from escalating into major conflicts. They have also been available to form the nucleus of other peacekeeping operations at short notice. They continue to assist the United Nations Disengagement Observer Force* (UNDOF) and United Nations Interim Force in Lebanon* (UN-IFIL) in their activities.

United Nations Truce Supervision Organization (UNTSO) has been in continuous existence along various armistice and cease-fire lines since 1949. Its basic mandate remains a 1948 Security Council resolution calling for an armistice in the first Arab–Israeli War, a 1949 resolution that declares that UNTSO should play a continuing role in "observing and maintaining the cease-fire," and the four 1949 General Armistice Agreements* between Israel and its Arab neighbors. Aside from observation and supervision of the Armistice Agreements following the first Arab–Israeli War, UNTSO officers also served as neutral chairmen of the Mixed Armistice Commissions.* The latter were intended to oversee full implementation of each of the 1949 Armistice Agreements and resolve disputes that might arise between the parties.

UNTSO is one of the few United Nations (UN) peacekeeping operations in which the United States has participated directly, and the first (after the 1973 war*) to boast active Soviet support and participation.

The mission of UNTSO military observers (UNMOs) is perhaps best described by UN Undersecretary General Brian Urquhart in a document provided to the U.S. government in April 1974.

The function of United Nations observers is to observe and report breaches of cease-fires which include firing, movement forward of the forward defended localities (FDLs) and overflights by aircraft forward of the FDLs. The observers also receive complaints from the parties on violations of the cease-fire alleged to have been committed by the other side, and they may conduct inquiries on these complaints if so requested by the parties. When an outbreak of violence threatens, observers seek to prevent it by appealing to the parties for restraint, and when firing occurs they will endeavor to arrange an immediate cease-fire. Because of their training, experience and rank (usually Captains and Majors), United Nations observers are well equipped to report on military matters.

The observers, who are always unarmed, are usually stationed in groups of two or three at static observation posts, but mobile patrols are often available. Observers operate with the consent of the parties and are dependent on the co-operation of the parties for their effectiveness. Thus they have no power to prevent violations of cease-fires or to enforce any decisions. Observers are stationed with the forces on each side and are usually accompanied by liaison officers from the respective armies. They are not inter-posed between the armies, nor, by virtue of their small numbers, can they exercise control or authority over a given stretch of territory.

UNTSO is commanded by a chief of staff headquartered in Jerusalem who, until the 1973 war,* reported directly to the UN secretary-general as well as to the concerned parties in the area. Since the 1973 war, the UNTSO operation on the Syrian* and Sinai* fronts has been informally integrated with the United Nations Emergency Force* (UNEF) and UNDOF operations. Overall command and control are exercised on a de facto basis by the UNEF commander, who also provides supervision of UNDOF.

UNTSO is funded from the regular budget of the UN (i.e., from regular assessments on member states).

UNTSO was the first United Nations peacekeeping operation established in the Middle East. It was originally constituted by Security Council Resolution 50 on May 29, 1948, to provide military advisers and observers to support the Palestine Truce Commission. In August 1949, the Truce Commission observers were reorganized formally as UNTSO by Security Council Resolution 73 and assigned the mission of supervising the Armistice Agreements* signed between Israel and Egypt,* Lebanon,* Syria,* and Jordan.*

UNTSO's role is peacekeeping rather than peacemaking. Its military observer functions have been directed at observing compliance with established cease-fires, truces, and Armistice Agreements, reporting violations, and mediating dis-putes. It has not been tasked, nor does it have the military resources, to enforce the agreements.

UNTSO remains in service today with 177 unarmed military observers from eighteen countries. UNTSO maintains observer groups in southern Lebanon, Beirut, the Golan Heights,* and the Sinai Peninsula.* It also maintains liaison groups in Amman and Damascus. In southern Lebanon and on the Golan Heights, UNTSO observers cooperate with, and assist, UNIFIL and UNDOF, respectively.

UNTSO's original mission was to supervise the 1949 Arab–Israeli Armistice Agreements; however, after each of the Arab–Israeli Wars, UNTSO's functions have been modified to accommodate its continued presence. In 1956, Israel declared the Israeli–Egyptian Armistice Agreement dead, citing Egypt's deliberate support of the fedayeen* raids into Israel as a fundamental breech of the agreement. The United Nations maintained that the Armistice Agreements could not be unilaterally abridged, and UNTSO continued to operate in the Sinai. UNTSO served as an experience pool for the creation of UNEF, which was established after the 1956 war* and unofficially assumed many of UNTSO's supervisory functions between Israel and Egypt. After the 1967 Arab–Israeli War,* Israel declared the remaining three Armistice Agreements void. UNTSO remained in place to supervise the resulting cease-fire agreements. After the 1973 war, two additional United Nations observer missions were constituted: the second implementation of the United Nations Emergency Force (UNEF II) along the Suez Canal* and UNDOF on the Golan Heights. UNTSO observers were again used as a manpower and experience pool to form the initial ranks of UNDOF, and UNTSO headquarters at Government House* in Jerusalem became a coordinating agency for UNEF II and UNDOF.

For further information see: Rosalyn Higgins, United Nations Peacekeeping 1946–1967: Documents and Commentary (London: Oxford University Press, 1969); Ensio Siilasvuo, In the Service of Peace in the Middle East, 1967–1979 (New York: St. Martin's Press, 1992); United Nations, The Blue Helmets: A Review of United Nations Peace-Keeping (New York: United Nations Department of Public Information, 1985); David W. Wainhouse, International Peace Observation: A History and Forecast (Baltimore: Johns Hopkins Press, 1966).

UNITED PALESTINE APPEAL (UPA). An American organization established in 1925 to coordinate the various Zionist* fund-raising efforts primarily to support the establishment of Jewish settlements in Palestine.* In 1950, it was renamed the United Israel Appeal.*

Stephen H. Gotowicki

UNITED STATES–PALESTINE LIBERATION ORGANIZATION DIALOGUE. On December 14, 1988, President Ronald Reagan* issued a statement concerning U.S. relations with the Palestine Liberation Organization* (PLO):

The Palestine Liberation Organization today issued a statement in which it accepted United Nations Security Council Resolutions 242* and 338,* recognized Israel's right to exist, and renounced terrorism. These have long been our conditions for a substantive dialogue. They have been met. Therefore, I have authorized the State Department to enter into a substantive dialogue with P.L.O. representatives. The Palestine Liberation Organization must live up to its statements. In particular it must demonstrate that its renunciation of terrorism is pervasive and permanent.

Secretary of State George Shultz* issued a similar statement and then noted: ''I am designating our Ambassador to Tunisia [Robert Pelletreau*] as the only authorized channel for that dialogue.'' He went on to note: ''Nothing here may be taken to imply an acceptance or recognition by the United States of an independent Palestinian* state.''

UNITED STATES–SOVIET UNION JOINT COMMUNIQUE (1977). See **JOINT COMMUNIQUE BY THE GOVERNMENTS OF THE UNITED STATES AND THE UNION OF SOVIET SOCIALIST REPUBLICS, OCTOBER 1, 1977.**

UNRPR. See **UNITED NATIONS RELIEF FOR PALESTINE REFUGEES.**

UNRWA. See **UNITED NATIONS RELIEF AND WORKS AGENCY.**

UNSCOP. See **UNITED NATIONS SPECIAL COMMITTEE ON PALESTINE.**

UNTSO. See **UNITED NATIONS TRUCE SUPERVISION ORGANIZATION.**

USS LIBERTY. See *LIBERTY.*

USSR AND THE ARAB–ISRAELI CONFLICT. USSR policy on the Middle East in general and the Arab–Israeli conflict in particular was determined by its global and regional interests. For a long period, Soviet Middle East policy was subordinated to concerns over Soviet–American rivalry. The Middle East policy of the USSR was an integral part of the cold war. At the same time, Soviet policy had its own specific features that distinguished it from the course pursued by the USSR in other regions. First, the geographical proximity of the Middle East to the USSR gave it particular importance from the standpoint of national security interests. Because the main military threat was perceived to be the United States, Soviet leadership focused on American actions in the region that would strengthen American influence and undermine the influence of the USSR. Mutual distrust, long a burden of Soviet–American relations, contributed to the Middle East's being an arena of struggle for spheres of influence. One of the instruments in this struggle became the Arab–Israeli conflict, where the antagonists became Soviet and American clients. These circumstances hindered the achievement of settlement, contributed new sources of conflict, and further undermined the possible normalization of Soviet–American relations.

Apart from the goals of strengthening its security, the USSR pursued economic interests in the Middle East. Because the USSR was a leading producer and exporter of oil, the Soviet concern was mainly in the development of trade.

Ideologically, the conflicts in the Middle East were perceived as a continuation of the class struggle throughout the world. Its manifestation was the struggle between capitalism, led by the United States, and socialism, led by the USSR. The allies of socialism were the ''world working-class movement and national liberation movement,'' forming together three revolutionary flows. The Arab national liberation movement was held to be an intricate ally of socialism. Which regimes the Soviets would align with was dictated by pragmatic considerations: the alignment of political forces within the Arab world.

The Arab–Israeli conflict also serves as a good example of the Soviet approach to the Middle East situation. The USSR supported the United Nations (UN) partition plan for Palestine.* Speaking at the UN in May 1947, Andrei Gromyko* stressed that ''the interests of both the Jews and the Arabs of Palestine can be properly protected only by the creation of a democratic independent Judeo–Arab state: but ''due to increasingly strained relations between Jews and Arabs . . . the partition of the country into two independent states'' would be called for. The USSR was one of the first to recognize the state of Israel and rendered it armed assistance during the war of 1948–49 through Czechoslovakia. The main factor that determined Soviet policy during this period was the desire to weaken the positions of Great Britain* in the region and to strike a blow at its Arab allies. ''Pro-imperialist'' Arab regimes were considered to be the greater evil than Israeli Zionists,* though the Soviet leadership long had held ideological enmity and mistrust toward them too. The social Zionists were considered enemies of the international struggle of the working class and, as ''backsliders,'' were viewed by Stalin and his entourage as no better than the imperialists themselves. Due to the foreign-policy priorities of the USSR at that time, however, the desire to speed up the collapse of British colonialism outweighed the ideological contradictions that the Soviets had with the leadership of Israel.

Aid to Israel was motivated by the requirements of the moment and could not be lasting. Soon this became evident. The USSR inspired anti-Semitic trials in Hungary of Jewish physicians, and the increased development of Israeli–American ties added sharp tension in relations between the USSR and Israel. Even until the official rupture in 1967, political contacts were of limited character, and cooperation was practically nonexistent.

Possibilities for strengthening the Soviet position in the region appeared after the Egyptian Revolution of 1952. The course of the new Egyptian* leadership, their aspiration for political and economic independence, and their association of social justice with socialism as the alternative to capitalism created favorable conditions for the development of relations between the USSR and Arab nationalists. In September 1955, Egyptian president Gamal Abdul Nasser* announced an arms deal with Czechoslovakia* that was to supply large quantities of military equipment, including Soviet tanks and aircraft, in return for cotton and rice. The activation of Soviet–Egyptian relations was due more to external factors than to the orientation of the Egyptian regime. Gaza* was a target of regular Israeli retaliatory raids. U.S. policy gave Cairo little alternative except to turn to the Soviet Union. The American policy in the region at that time was watchful and distrustful of the Arab nationalists.

The United States refused to provide aid, including military support, while it did provide support to Israel. This was especially clear after the Suez War* of 1956, during which Egypt still hoped it could cooperate with the United States.

The attack on Egypt by Great Britain, France,* and Israel created a unique situation where Soviet and American interests in the region coincided or at least did not contradict one another. The Soviet Union and the United States, for different reasons, were interested in forcing Great Britain and France to withdraw. Their interaction in the UN put an end to aggression. Washington pressured Israel to withdraw from the Gaza Strip* and Sharm el-Sheikh,* which its army continued to hold even after its forces evacuated the Sinai.*

After 1956, the struggle between the two superpowers for spheres of influence developed with new force, coinciding in time with increased radicalization in Arab countries. Nasser, having withstood the aggression, became the recognized leader of the Arab world and was viewed as an example to follow for many Arab political leaders. All of this contributed to the Soviets' developing a special relationship with Egypt. The orientation toward Arab nationalism required correcting the ideological guidelines that no longer corresponded to the new conditions. During the long postrevolutionary period, Soviet leadership believed that the only staunch allies of the USSR were Communists. This did not prevent Stalin and his entourage from crushing the Comintern, subjecting members of foreign Communist parties to repression while paying lip service to the thesis about the historical role of the Communist movement. The national patriotic forces were considered petty bourgeois and consequently hostile to the idea of liberation of the working class. The initial assessment of Arab nationalism carried all signs of ideological dogmatism. The real situation in the Middle East required party theoreticians to revise their approach, in order to conform to Marxist–Leninist theory. Thus, Lenin's thesis about the dual nature of "the nationalism of the oppressed nations" was reanimated so that, along with the reactionary elements, the democratic elements were also said to exist. The regimes that emerged in Egypt, Syria,* Iraq,* South Yemen, Libya, and some other Arab states were called revolutionary democratic ones, and these states themselves, in the 1960s, were put on a list of the noncapitalist way of development or socialist orientation. In the context of the Arab–Israeli conflict, the USSR, in its support for the Arab side, stressed assisting radical regimes. Israel's military threat was examined through the prism of serving U.S. interests that aimed to overthrow "progressive" forces in the Arab world. Soviet–American competition made such assumptions not so groundless. At the same time, the conflict, as it was considered in Moscow, gave additional impetus for Arab cooperation with the Soviet Union in the military-political field. Anxious about their security, the Arab radical regimes willingly bought Soviet weapons and used the services of military experts and advisers. By the end of the 1960s, the list of Soviet allies in the Middle East also included the Palestine Liberation Organization* (PLO).

Supporting the development of left-radical tendencies and movements, the USSR was obliged to follow them. Soviet policy in the conflict sometimes took maximalistic positions. On their part, its Arab allies, whose interests and goals did not fully coincide with the interests of the USSR, tried to obtain from the Soviet Union more direct involvement in the conflict itself. In several instances when this occurred, for example, the Soviet military took part in combat operations on the Suez front during the War of Attrition* in 1970.

The 1967 war* brought serious changes in the Middle East that could not but affect the Soviet approach. The military victory of Israel and the defeat of Egyptian and Syrian armies demonstrated the danger of the conflict for Soviet interests in the region. The Soviet task was to strengthen its position in the Middle East, though this was still seen as part of a global confrontation between two systems. The decision of the CPSU Central Committee plenum on July 21, 1967, stated: "The aggression of Israel is the result of a plot of the most reactionary forces of international imperialism (first of all of the USA) directed against one of the groups of the national liberation movement." The perception of the conflict as class conflict was preserved in official assessments nearly till the late 1980s. However, the practical policy of the USSR did not remain stark. A Soviet peace plan for the Middle East was worked out in 1969. It suggested the withdrawal of Israeli forces in two stages: the guarantee of the inviolability of borders and the establishment of demilitarized zones. These proposals were defined precisely and later modified. They were based on the triple formula: the withdrawal of Israeli forces from all occupied territories,* the self-determination for the Palestinian people, ensuring the right for independent existence; and security for all of the states directly involved in the conflict.

The thaw in the international climate and the aggravation of the regional situation focused attention on finding a settlement. Detente, which meant the beginning of the retreat from the cold war, led to greater cooperation between the USSR and United States. At the beginning of the 1970s, detente developed on a narrow basis, affecting only the limitation of the arms race. There was no new philosophy of international relations as a whole that predetermined the weakness and fragility of the processes of detente. At the same time, the positive trends in Soviet–American relations were perceived by both parties as of paramount importance, and both powers aspired in the mid-1970s to preserve these improved developments. In this connection, the next crisis in the Middle East— the war of 1973*—placed the USSR and the United States on the brink of confrontation. The destabilizing effects of the conflict threatened detente. Simultaneously, the necessity of joint USSR–United States action in order to find a political settlement became apparent. In December 1973, the Geneva Peace Conference* on the Middle East was called and cochaired by the USSR and the United States. The conference showed some progress in searching for a solution to the Arab–Israeli conflict but did not bring the expected results. First, the lack of confidence between both powers limited their cooperation; competition continued to dominate. Second, the parties to the conflict themselves were not ready for compromise. Syria refused to take part in the conference. The government of Israel remained hard-line on the Palestine problem. Secretary of State Henry

Kissinger's* diplomacy was perceived in Moscow as a U.S. attempt to force the USSR out of the Middle East. Kissinger openly said this was one of his goals. The deadlock on the way to Geneva and the debarring of the USSR from the talks led to the growth of mutual suspicion. The unsuccessful experience of Soviet–American cooperation in the search for a settlement had consequences for later developments. The Soviet Union categorically denounced Camp David,* believing that the United States wanted to sanctify the achieved agreements with its authority but did not want at all to see the USSR as an equal party to the peace process.

Soviet negativism toward Camp David was based on the position of most of the Arab states. They castigated Egypt for capitulating. At the same time, the USSR in its approach was more inclined toward the radical regimes that created the Steadfastness Front* than to side with the more reserved reaction of moderate Arab states that were considered American allies. This explained its cool attitude to the Fahd Plan,* strongly opposed by Syria, which did not want the Saudis to assume leadership of the Arab world. Linking itself with the Arab left-radicals, the USSR found itself in a difficult situation. Interested in reducing the conflict after 1967, the Soviet Union, acting through its own channels, encouraged Arab moderation—especially the PLO. Soviet diplomacy continued to support Arab demands. None of this contributed to finding political solutions.

Though Soviet policy in the conflict was not balanced, its support of the Arabs had limits. Politically, though Soviet relations with Israel had been severed in 1967, the USSR never questioned Israel's right to exist and was critical of extremist calls for Israel's demise. In military terms, the USSR was one of the main arms suppliers to the Middle East, but the Soviet Union never supplied its allies with its most sophisticated and destructive types of weapons, despite repeated requests for such deliveries. Also, acts of terrorism were not backed by the Soviet Union, although at times they underestimated their destabilizing effect.

The failure of detente in the late 1970s put an end to limited Soviet–American cooperation to resolve the conflict. The concepts of the cold war returned, largely because of the invasion of Afghanistan. At this time the USSR proposed a number of settlement plans (1982, 1984), but they were never realized. Despite this, in the mid-1980s the idea of an international conference as a settlement mechanism began to win increasing recognition. The accession to power in the Soviet Union of new political leaders had long-term consequences for international relations. Soviet policy in the Middle East was also seriously transformed during *perestroika*. The deideologization of interstate relations promoted the gradual liberation of the region from the influence of Soviet–American rivalry. Soviet policy had become more balanced. Consular relations with Israel were established, and contacts with that country expanded into full diplomatic relations. The process of democratization of the Soviet society has helped to solve the emigration problem. Paradoxically, the mass inflow of Soviet Jews to Israel has had an ambiguous influence on the situation, which is still unsettled.

Diplomatic relations were established with the United Arab Emirates (UAE), Oman, and Qatar and restored with Saudi Arabia.

Soviet interests in the Middle East have become more diversified. Besides national security interests, the situation in the region affects the internal political situation in the country. The presence of 55 million Muslims in the USSR having ethnocultural ties with peoples of the Middle East determines the significance of good neighborly relations with Arab states, Iran, and Turkey. The acquisition of sovereignty by the former Soviet republics is realized in the form of their more independent course on the international scene. It applies equally to the republics of Central Asia and Transcaucasia, developing their own relations with the nations of the region. The economic significance of the Middle East has also grown for the USSR, which is more interested in trade, economic exchange, and obtaining credits and investments. The USSR may become an importer of Middle East oil, as its oil production is dropping because of technological backwardness. Finally, because Russia and the other former republics depend on cooperation with the West for economic support, it is essential for Moscow that the Middle East not become again an arena of rivalry and confrontation.

The coordination of Soviet efforts with the United States and other states of the coalition that halted Iraqi aggression against Kuwait provided more favorable opportunities for joint action aimed at settling the Arab–Israeli conflict within the framework of the peace conference.

After the Gulf War* the Soviet Union (now Russia) acted as the cochair of the Madrid Peace Conference* and was a participant in the subsequent efforts to achieve peace in the conflict.

Irina Zviagelskaia

V

VANCE, CYRUS (b. Clarksburg, West Virginia, March 27, 1917). He received his B.A. in economics from Yale University (1939) and his L.L.B. from Yale (1942). In 1962, he served as secretary of the army, and from 1964 to 1967 he was deputy secretary of defense under Robert McNamara. During 1968–69 he served as the chief delegate to the Vietnam peace talks in Paris.

Vance's career in international affairs began in November 1967, when he was appointed special envoy by Lyndon Johnson* to the negotiations to resolve the Cyprus dispute. The plan that emerged affirmed Cypriot independence, removed unauthorized troops from the island, and increased the role of United Nations (UN) resident forces in the area. The same year, he was Johnson's special representative during the Detroit riots. The report that emerged from the committee of which Vance was a member is considered a primer for quelling urban unrest with a minimum of bloodshed. For his outstanding service, Vance was awarded the Medal of Freedom, the nation's highest civilian honor, in 1969.

In 1977, President Jimmy Carter* appointed Vance his secretary of state. During his tenure, Vance was a part of the negotiating team that successfully brought about the Camp David Accords* and the peace treaty between Egypt* and Israel in 1979. He remained in this position until 1980, when he resigned in protest over a disagreement with President Carter and National Security Adviser Brzezinski on the military operation to rescue the Americans held hostage in Iran.

For further information see: David S. McLellan, *Cyrus Vance* (Totowa, NJ: Rowman and Allanheld, 1985); Cyrus R. Vance, *Hard Choices: Critical Years in America's Foreign Policy* (New York: Simon and Schuster, 1983).

Pamela Rivers

VENICE DECLARATION. In June 1980, the nine members of the European Community met in Venice, Italy, to exchange views on the Middle East, among other subjects. They believed "that the traditional ties and common interests" that linked Europe to the Middle East "oblige[d] them to play a special role" to work for peace based on Security Council Resolutions 242* and 338.* On June 13, they issued a declaration that called for

[t]he right to existence and to security of all the states in the region, including Israel, and justice for all the peoples, which implies the recognition of the legitimate rights of the Palestinian* people. . . . All of the countries in the area are entitled to live in peace within secure, recognized and guaranteed borders. [Necessary guarantees should be provided by the United Nations (UN).] The Nine declare that they are prepared to participate within the framework of a comprehensive settlement in a system of concrete and binding international guarantees. . . . A just solution must finally be found to the Palestinian problem, which is not simply one of refugees.* The Palestinian people . . . must be placed in a position . . . to exercise fully its right to self-determination. [The Palestine Liberation Organization (PLO)] will have to be associated with the negotiations. . . . The Nine recognize the special importance of the role played by the question of Jerusalem* for all the parties concerned. The Nine stress that they will not accept any unilateral initiative designed to change the status of Jerusalem and that any agreement on the city's status should guarantee freedom of access for everyone to the Holy Places. . . . The Nine stress the need for Israel to put an end to the territorial occupation which it has maintained since the conflict of 1967, as it has done for part of Sinai.* They are deeply convinced that the Israeli settlements* constitute a serious obstacle to the peace process in the Middle East. The Nine consider that these settlements . . . are illegal under international law.

The declaration was a European effort to advance its own political unity and to adopt a consensus approach to the Arab–Israeli conflict.

The declaration was rejected by Israel and the PLO, and it was overshadowed by the Reagan fresh-start initiative* in September 1992.

VILLAGE LEAGUES. An alternative political structure in the occupied territories* that claimed to represent the rural areas. Israel supported these units as alternative representation for the Palestinians* in dealing with the Israelis.

When Israel captured the West Bank* from Jordan* in the Six Day War,* an Israeli military administration replaced the former Jordanian government. The Israeli military commander issued a proclamation in June 1967 by which he vested powers of legislation, appointment, and administration in himself and those who exercised authority through his appointment. Israel's Supreme Court contended that the legislative power of the military administration was limited to changing only those conditions necessary for law and order, for military necessity, and for the well-being of the civilian population. Defense Minister Moshe Dayan* described the military government's occupation policy as non-interventionist, meaning that Israel would not become involved in local affairs. Jordanian law, which had been in effect when Israel captured the territory, continued to determine local matters, including local elections and school and public administration.

By the late 1970s, significant social and political changes were taking place within the West Bank population, and the traditional West Bank elite no longer dominated local politics. Much of the Palestinian population now identified the Palestine Liberation Organization* (PLO) as their representative and sought the establishment of an independent Palestinian state, as advocated by the PLO, as their goal. Jordanian influence was being replaced by PLO influence. This support for the PLO was evidenced in the 1976 municipal elections in the West Bank in which candidates supporting the PLO were elected mayors of Ramallah, Al-Birah, Nablus, and Anabta.

The political authority of those sympathetic to the Palestine Liberation Organization was itself challenged in the early 1980s by candidates representing other factions of the PLO. In addition, when Ariel Sharon* became Israeli defense minister in the summer of 1981, he decided to abolish the military government, and, in November 1981, a civilian administration was established. Menahem Milson,* a professor of Arabic languages and literature at the Hebrew University and an adviser on Arab affairs to the military government, was appointed West Bank–Gaza* civilian administrator. Milson had come to the attention of the Likud* government through an article he had published in the May 1981 issue of *Commentary* entitled, ''How to Make Peace with the Palestinians,'' in which he argued that the Dayan policy of noninvolvement, which liberalized the right of political expression, had only encouraged the rise of radicalism. This, he contended, posed a danger to Israel's security. Milson wanted to nurture conditions where the moderates in the territories would be able to express their views openly. This required that the Palestinian moderates be given ''moral and political support against the extremists.'' New political and social conditions must be created in the territories by rewarding moderates with moral and financial support while inhibiting West Bank leaders who openly support the PLO. Milson contended that the politics in the Arab world were governed through rewards and punishments.

Demographically, Milson contended, 60 percent of the West Bank's 800,000 Arabs are from rural areas. They are less politically oriented and more ambivalent toward the PLO than are city residents. To address the majority of the population, he proposed the creation of village leagues, which would provide a political alternative to rival the dominance of pro-PLO mayors of the larger towns. Those villages that joined and cooperated with the league would benefit from financial patronage as well as housing and development programs through a Regional Development Fund, while those villages and mayors that did not cooperate would not receive such benefits and, in fact, could face the loss of jobs, as well as other pressures.

The first village league was founded in the Hebron* hill region in 1978, when Milson was an adviser for the military governor. With Sharon's support, new village leagues were established in the districts of Bethlehem,* Ramallah, Nablus, Tulkarm, and Jenin. In Hebron, Milson had negotiated with Mustafa Dudeen, a sixty-seven-year-old farmer and former Jordanian minister of social welfare who advocated ties with the Palestinian population in Jordan and opposed the PLO. The Hebron League, constituting seventy-four villages in the area, received $15 million for the development of roads, clinics, and schools. The leagues published a newspaper in Tel Aviv.

The mayor of Al-Bireh, Ibrahim a-Tawil, was invited to meet with Milson for a working session and declined. The Civil Administration dismissed the mayor and the municipal council on March 18, 1982, on the grounds that a-Tawil's refusal to cooperate with the administration harmed the local inhabitants. Milson's action was in accord with Jordanian law, but the message was clear to other West Bank mayors. Other mayors were arrested for disturbances, and disorders continued to develop throughout the territories. Nablus, Ramallah, and Al-Bireh called for a three-day strike.

Yusuf al-Khatib, the Ramallah Village League head, and his twenty-three-year-old son had been assassinated by the PLO in November 1981, and attempts were made on the lives of others. On March 16, 1982, Jordan condemned Palestinian cooperation with the village leagues under a threat of property confiscation as well as trying members in absentia for treason. About fifty village league members resigned. Bir Zeit University* became a center of protest. As the protests increased, so did the firmness of the defense minister's reactions. This constituted a significant departure from Sharon's policy of relaxing controls.

After the Israeli invasion of Lebanon* in June 1982* and the disclosures of the Phalangist massacres at Sabra and Shatila,* Milson resigned.

For further information see: Michael Oren, "A Horseshoe in the Glove: Milson's Year on the West Bank," *Middle East Review* 16 (Fall 1983): 17–29; Don Peretz, *The West Bank: History, Politics, Society, and Economy* (Boulder, CO: Westview Press, 1986); Emile Sahliyeh, "Jordan and the Palestinians," in William B. Quandt, ed., *The Middle East: Ten Years after Camp David* (Washington, DC: Brookings Institution, 1988); Salim Tamari, "Israel's Search for a Native Pillar: The Village Leagues," in Naseer H. Aruri, ed., *Occupation: Israel over Palestine* (Belmont, MA: Association of Arab–American University Graduates, 1983), pp. 377–90.

Joseph E. Goldberg

VOICE OF PEACE. Abie Nathan* decided in the summer of 1967 to bridge the gap between Egypt* and Israel by starting an independent radio station to broadcast beyond governmental control. He bought a ship in Holland and outfitted it with radio transmitters. The "Voice of Peace" was soon transmitting from "somewhere in the Mediterranean." It appealed for "no more war, no more bloodshed." It concluded its broadcasting in September 1993. Nathan then said that the ship had fulfilled his goal of establishing dialogue between enemies.

W

WACHSMAN, NAHSHON. See **NAHSHON WAXMAN.**

WAILING WALL. See **WESTERN WALL.**

WAILING WALL INCIDENT (AUGUST 1929). On August 16, 1929, a crowd of several thousand Arab Moslems pressed their way to the Wailing Wall* at the Temple Mount* in Jerusalem,* where Jews were concluding Tishah Be-Av ceremonies. The Arabs attacked the worshipers and desecrated or destroyed sacred objects and prayer books. As a result of the attack, riots ensued for several days throughout Palestine* between Arabs and Jews, in which several hundred Arabs, Jews, and others were killed or injured. The British government eventually imposed martial law and dispatched additional troops to Palestine in order to quell the riots.

The events drew their impetus from a decision made by the British government to permit the Moslem Supreme Council to commence construction at the site of the Wailing Wall. The Jews complained that this would defile their most sacred shrine, the only remaining part of Solomon's Temple, and was also in violation of the status quo between Arabs and Jews. The Arabs countered by saying that the Jews were attempting to extend their rights to the site.

On the day of the incident, the British had blockaded all streets leading to the Wailing Wall but had stationed only three Arab policemen and a Jewish officer at the wall itself. The Arab Moslems, who had been celebrating the eve of Mohammed's birthday, entered the Wailing Wall area through a newly built gate leading from the Mosque of Omar, which the British had not been guarding.

The bloodiest clashes between Arabs and Jews in the aftermath of August 16 took place in Jerusalem, Safed, and Hebron.* In Hebron virtually all of the Jewish inhabitants were either killed or fled.

As a result of the events surrounding the Wailing Wall incident, the British ordered an investigation, the result of which was the Passfield White Paper.* Recommendations from the Passfield White Paper included restrictions on Jewish immigration as well as land purchases.

For further information see: Paul L. Hanna, *British Policy in Palestine* (Washington, DC: American Council on Public Affairs, 1942); International Commission for the Wailing Wall, *Report of the Commission Appointed by His Majesty's Government in the United Kingdom of Great Britain and Northern Ireland, with the Approval of the Council of the League of Nations, to Determine the Rights and Claims of Moslems and Jews in Connection with the Western or Wailing Wall at Jerusalem* (London: His Majesty's Stationery Office, 1930); Martin Kolinsky, *Law, Order and Riots in Mandatory Palestine, 1928–1935* (London: St. Martin's Press, 1993); Office of the Secretary of State for the Colonies, *Commission on the Palestine Disturbances of August, 1929* (London: His Majesty's Stationery Office, 1930); Herbert Sidebotham, *Great Britain and Palestine* (London: Macmillan, 1937).

Donald A. Pearson

WAR IN LEBANON (1982). Also known as "Operation Peace for Galilee." On June 6, 1982, Israel began a major military action against the Palestine Liberation Organization* (PLO) in Lebanon.* The announced immediate goal was to put the Galilee out of range of PLO shelling. It sought to reduce the PLO military and terrorist threat to Israel and to reduce the PLO's political capability. It was described as a major response to years of PLO terror attacks against Israel and its people. The 1982 war was the culmination of a series of events and trends beginning in the late 1950s that involved not only the PLO but also Syria* and Israel.

After the War of Independence,* Israel faced few serious threats to its existence from Lebanon. The border region remained quiet until the 1960s.

In 1964, the first signs that Lebanon could no longer remain isolated from the Arab–Israeli conflict appeared. Controversy over Israel's diversion of Jordan River* water* led Syria to threaten to poison or divert all the sources of the Jordan River. The river's sources were primarily in either Syria or Lebanon. In the ensuing crisis and at the Arab summit to plan a response to the Israeli water diversion plan, Syria pressed Lebanon to help. By engaging in Arab–Israeli hostilities, Lebanon understood that its fragile internal structure, which relied on a delicate internal sectarian balance and included one of the largest Palestinian* refugee populations, could become a source of manipulation for all sides.

In the mid-1960s, the large Palestinian refugee community became a source for recruiting and even hosting some of the radical Palestinian organizations emerging. The Six Day War* left Lebanon as the only country bordering Israel close to Israeli population centers. All the other borders had been pushed away from the towns and cities that Arab forces and fedayeen* had targeted in the previous twenty years. The logistics of undertaking terror attacks, except against the more isolated Israeli settlements along the northernmost Jordanian–Israeli border, became difficult. This was even more true of the PLO's and Egyptian-based fedayeen's previously most important area of deployment: the Gaza Strip.* There, the strip had been occupied, and 200 miles of desert lay between the Palestinian population and the new border.

Israel's capture of the Golan Heights* created a buffer zone between Israeli settlements along the old Syrian–Israeli border and the new deployment.

The Six Day War forced the PLO out of the West Bank.* It deployed among the Palestinians in Jordan,* a matter of much graver danger for the Hashemite monarch. After a series of PLO attacks and Israeli retaliations, coupled with PLO leadership demands to establish PLO bases in sensitive areas of Jordan as well as the removal of pro-Western defense advisers, the Hashemite regime saw little alternative but to expel the Palestinians. In September 1970, the Jordanian Royal Armed Force struck against the Palestinians. Syria intervened in the conflict but was forced to withdraw under Israeli threats. The PLO lost and was expelled and joined an already established, though still limited, infrastructure in Lebanon.

Some of the Muslim leaders of Lebanon saw in the Palestinian presence and in the emerging PLO an opportunity to enhance their position in the delicate internal balance and began to encourage PLO elements to deploy in Lebanon. By 1969, the number of PLO operatives, as well as the frequency of attacks against Israel from Lebanon, posed a danger that Lebanon would be dragged into the Arab–Israeli conflict and that its internal balance would be upset.

After the first major Israeli retaliation into Lebanon against the Beirut International Airport* on December 28, 1968, Christians in the Lebanese government sought to reverse the trend, but to no avail. The Cairo Agreement* specified that PLO elements were to be concentrated in specific areas and barred from launching operations against Israel directly from Lebanese territory. This agreement was unenforceable by the Lebanese government, lest it risk open civil war.

The PLO expulsion from Jordan in September 1970 ended Lebanon's attempt to remain insulated from the Arab–Israeli conflict. The PLO shifted its infrastructure to Lebanon and began to establish, under the protection of the Muslims, a massive presence—"a state within a state." It also presented Syria with the first real avenue of intervention in Lebanon.

Through terrorism, Lebanon was dragged into the Arab–Israeli conflict, upsetting its internal balance and offering Syria a venue through which to enter and increase its presence in Lebanon. Syria's presence in Lebanon, in turn, led to a strategic change in the area, presenting Israel with a problem larger than just protecting itself from Lebanese-based terrorists. Lebanon, in the early 1970s, therefore, began to become both a terrorism and security problem for Israel.

From 1970 to 1975, the number, intensity, and effectiveness of the terror attacks on Israel increased, and Lebanon was becoming one of the central bases of training and launching terror operations not only locally against Israel (e.g., the PLO raid at the Maalot* schoolhouse) but globally against Israeli interests (e.g., the attack on Israeli athletes in the Munich Olympics*).

After the death of President Gamal Abdul Nasser* in Egypt* and Hafez al-Assad's* rise to power in Syria, there emerged a growing split between the top PLO leadership under Yasser Arafat* and Syria.

A civil war erupted in Lebanon in 1975. After the Christians began to lose the war in 1976, the Lebanese government invited Syria to intervene to stabilize the situation. The Syrians, eager for a direct role in Lebanon, obliged, effectively beginning the process of bringing Lebanon directly under Syrian tutelage. The PLO remained an important force, not under Syrian control and even opposed to Assad. Israel realized that the situation in Lebanon represented a danger far greater than the threat from the PLO.

The Yom Kippur War* shifted the locus and reduced the scale of the conventional Arab–Israeli conflict. The military stalemate that had set in on the Golan Heights forced Syria to extend the conflict into the periphery, namely, Lebanon. Israeli defenses on the Golan Heights, set up in the months and years following the 1973 Yom Kippur War, defined the front and potential strike axes into narrowly defined corridors by use of natural obstacles and tactical fortifications. These corridors had been reinforced by an intricate network of defenses, all of which were designed to absorb an attack without prior mobilization. This represented the implementation of the lessons learned from the Yom Kippur War. It allowed Israel to withstand without difficulty a first strike or a two-front war. Under these circumstances, Israel remained interested in restricting Syrian forces to the Golan Heights to force them to advance into the heart of this intricate defense apparatus, rather than threaten a large-scale circumvention of the theater as a whole through Lebanon.

By the end of the 1970s, eastern Lebanon had become a strategic pivot that could be used to circumvent Israeli forces and defense structures. Israel's invasion of Lebanon refocused the Syrian–Israeli competition on the Golan Heights, away from Lebanon. The Syrians also used the terrain of Lebanon to gather valuable strategic and tactical intelligence data regarding Israeli deployments, vulnerabilities, and defense structures. The Lebanon War, therefore, was part of the ongoing geostrategic competition between the Israelis and the Syrians. Operating under the proper geographic conditions, Syria exploited its numerical manpower and weapon advantage to circumvent Israel's Golan defenses. Israel, thus, intended the war not to fight Syria by proxy in Lebanon, but the opposite—to deny Syria a broad, strategic outflanking maneuver and, instead, concentrate a future war back into the narrowest space possible: the Golan Heights and the lower part of the Beka Valley* near Damascus.

After a series of terror attacks, including one on a bus traveling on the coastal road between Haifa and Tel Aviv in Israel that claimed forty-seven lives, Israel invaded Lebanon in 1978 (Operation Litani*) and established a security zone* in the south to serve as a buffer. The security zone, however, was not wide enough to push PLO Katyusha rockets* out of range of Israeli towns. PLO rocket attacks in the late 1970s led to a series of Israeli retaliatory raids, leading eventually to an extremely tense standoff by 1981, when an unofficial cease-fire was arranged through the offices of American mediator Philip Habib.* The cease-fire held nearly a year.

When Israel entered Lebanon on June 6, 1982, following an assassination attempt on an Israeli diplomat in London, it intended to destroy Syria's increasingly dangerous deployment in Lebanon and to remove the PLO threat once and for all times. To accomplish both, Israel sought not only to expel the PLO and Syria from the south and central parts of the country but to forestall the possibility of their returning. Israel attempted to use Bashir Gemayel* to reassert Lebanese sovereignty and transcend the factional violence that enabled both the PLO and Syria to occupy Lebanon.

Israel's invasion plan, called "Tall Pines," was based primarily on the dictates of Lebanese geography. There are few lateral roads in Lebanon. Most roads run north–south.

The key point is Shtoura, a town just south of Zahle, at the junction of two roads: the major road linking Beirut to Damascus and the major road linking Zahle to the south. To control this town is to control all of South Lebanon, with the exception of one other intersection: the intersection of the Beirut–Damascus Highway and the road to Marj-Ayoun running through Sultan Jacob (the eastern arm of the "V"). This intersection lies close to the Syrian border where the Syrians had located its Second Division. To enter Lebanon, Syrian troops had to pass through narrow mountain corridors that functioned as choke points exploited by the IDF.

These sectors are all separated by high mountain chains and generally impassable ridges. The valleys divided by these mountains, however, all converge near Marj-Ayoun, only a few kilometers from Metulla in Israel, a town that lies farther down in the continuation of the deep valley (called the Hula Valley in Israel), which extends all the way to Eilat* and the Red Sea (and the Great African Rift Valley beyond).

Syria had deployed SAM* missiles along the Beka Valley, and its forces held the two most important observation platforms in Lebanon, Jebel Baruch and Jebel Arva. The Syrians also held an observation post on the Syrian Hermon* on the Golan. Until 1976, this peak had little significance, and hence Israel conceded it as part of the Syrian–Israeli Disengagement Agreement in 1974. While this peak does not afford any view of the Israeli Golan, it does provide an excellent view of all the eastern sector of Lebanon toward Rachaiye and the Beka.

Zahle was the key to dominating the region near the Beirut–Damascus Highway. The fall of the Phalange "fortress" in Zahle signaled not the end of the Phalange but the beginning of Syrian strategic dominance of all of Lebanon. This development drove Israel and the Phalange together. Israel's downing of a Syrian helicopter in Zahle in 1981 signaled the Syrians that the fall of Zahle was a strategic advance that Israel could not tolerate.

The Syrians retaliated by emplacing missiles in the Beka Valley. This signaled Syrian irritation with Israel for violating Syria's "rights" under the unwritten agreement—to dominate the ground and to consolidate Syria's hold on strategic areas.

The missiles Syria deployed were seen in 1982 as a major strategic challenge to Israel, given the experience Israel had with SAM missiles in the Yom Kippur War.* In deploying missiles, Syria must have assumed it would curtail, if not stop, Israeli aerial activity over most of Lebanon. This would have all but removed direct Israeli military presence from all of Lebanon, except for the areas near the coastlines and the border region near Israel. Syria's deployment of missiles, therefore, would have consolidated Syrian strategic superiority over virtually all of Lebanon. The extent of Syria's missile deployment required a major strike if there was to be any strike at all.

The Israeli invasion of Lebanon came suddenly, and without full mobilization. Israeli forces moved swiftly north of the border, destroying and capturing numerous PLO strongholds and positions within hours. Within a week, Israel controlled much of the southern portion of the country, and thousands of PLO fighters were either killed or captured. By the middle of June, Israel had virtually laid siege to Beirut.

But the way the war unfolded did not match exactly the way in which it had been planned. The basic objective Israel hoped to achieve by invading Lebanon to the north of the Har Dov region (known more commonly as Fatahland*) was to make Syria's presence in Lebanon untenable.

Israel viewed this eastern zone of activity as a strategic theater isolated from the rest of the war. The delineation of command was not between Lebanon and the Golan but between western Lebanon, on the one side, and eastern Lebanon and the Golan Heights on the other, indicating that at this period in Israeli military thought, the Golan Heights and eastern Lebanon must therefore be viewed as a unified front to emphasize Israel's advantages and Syria's weaknesses. By threatening Damascus from the north, the Syrians were forced to withdraw forces from eastern Lebanon and consolidate them around their capital.

This would force the Syrians to deploy primarily in the territory east of the Golan Heights, across from which the Israelis had meticulously prepared to engage the Syrians with minimal forces ever since the mid-1970s.

Israel considered the destruction and expulsion of Syrian forces from the southern half of Lebanon to be a major objective. Certain topographic features dictated a particular advance and deployment after cease-fire. Israel would primarily focus on capturing the Beirut-Damascus Highway near Shtoura and threatening Syria's position in Zahle. To accomplish this, the Israelis would first have to outflank the Syrians by moving up the valleys without engagement.

The history of the Syrian facet of the Lebanese invasion must focus on the central thrust of Colonels Peled and Einan up the center of Lebanon to separate from each other strong Syrian deployments (Syrian Eighty-Fifth Brigade) in Beirut and Aleii, and Behamdoun; the Syrian forces in Zahle; those in Jub

Jennin; and the First Division in Yanta and Rachaiye. This could be done by capturing the key territories dividing them: Sofer, Ain Dera, Shtoura, and the cutting of the Beirut–Damascus Highway. Israel sought to deny the Syrians any ability to save their Eighty-Fifth Brigade. All Syrian forces in western Lebanon would have to be resupplied and reinforced through the Shtoura junction on the Beirut–Damascus Highway. Arriving at Shtoura, Israeli forces could have linked with Phalange forces north and east of Beirut. Alone and isolated from any relief and denied air reinforcement, Syrian forces in Beirut and Zahle would have been without supply and reinforcement against a major attack launched by the Phalange under Bashir Gemayel.

By the second week of the war, Israel had set the stage for the Phalange to destroy Syrian forces in the areas around Zahle, Bahamdoun, and Beirut by leaving the Syrian First Divisional command in Rachaiye and Jub Jennin in wholly untenable, isolated positions.

The Israeli plan hinged on the ability to seize a considerable part of their objectives in and around Shtoura before commencing major combat with the Syrians. This required outflanking the Syrians before they realized what had taken place.

Israel planned a feigned attack westward into Damour and Aleii—which eventually came from the sea rather than the east—to cultivate the impression that they were moving into Beirut. During the fighting, Israeli radio constantly noted the "pivot" that was creating a major thrust into Beirut from the west, when in fact, these forces turned east toward Shtoura after reaching Bahamdoun.

The bulk of the forces in the west reverted to the coastal command, leaving the rest of the force to concentrate its energies on the eastward objective— Syria—and were placed under Ben-Gal's command. The move to the west by forces detached from Einan's division was a cover for the ultimate objective of seizing the area around Ain Dera and Sofer, slightly to the west of Shtoura. When the purpose of the cover was no longer needed and the thrust had to move east, those forces moving west toward Beirut were jettisoned from Einan's command, making it clear that Einan's prime objective had been Shtoura.

The other prong of this thrust attempted to avoid contact with Syrians until the northern objectives near Shtoura had been seized. This force (under Peled) proceeded alongside the Syrian forces near Maschara, went around the far side of Lake Karoun, and passed Jub Jennin under Jebel Baruch and Kab Elias without engaging the enemy. A force was detached from the main thrust and began to fight the Syrians near lake Karoun and Jub Jennin, almost as a strategic diversion, while the main thrust of Peled's forces hastened toward the critical Shtoura intersection.

The Israelis relied on more than just a frontal thrust in the eastern valley. The ridge separating Lebanon's two eastern valleys is difficult and slow to traverse. While Israeli forces moved toward Sultan Yacob, another Israeli force proceeded to attack Jub Jennin. After accomplishing this task, the force crossed the mountain ridge and converged on Sultan Yacob from the west.

By the middle of June, Israel had virtually laid siege to Beirut. The war occasioned major debate and demonstration within Israel, resulted in substantial casualties, and led to Israel's increased international political and diplomatic isolation. It also brought about major political and diplomatic clashes with the United States. An agreement of May 17, 1983,* between Israel and Lebanon providing for the withdrawal of Israeli forces from Lebanon noted that "they consider the existing international boundary between Israel and Lebanon inviolable." Although it was signed and ratified by both states, Lebanon, under Syrian pressure, abrogated the agreement in March 1984. Except for a security zone* in southern Lebanon along the border with Israel, all Israeli forces were withdrawn from Lebanon by 1985.

For further information see: Dan Bavly and Eliahu Salpeter, *Fire in Beirut: Israel's War in Lebanon with the PLO* (New York: Stein and Day, 1984); Richard A. Gabriel, *Operation Peace for Galilee: The Israeli–PLO War in Lebanon* (New York: Hill and Wang, 1984); Itamar Rabinovich, *The War for Lebanon, 1970–1985* (Ithaca, NY: Cornell University Press, 1985); Jonathan C. Randall, *Going All the Way: Christian Warlords, Israeli Adventurers, and the War in Lebanon* (New York: Viking Press, 1983); Ze'ev Schiff and Ehud Ya'ari, *Israel's Lebanon War* (New York: Simon and Schuster, 1984).

David Wurmser

WAR OF ATTRITION (1969–70). In the first years after the Six Day War,* Israel retained control of the occupied territories,* and, despite various efforts, no significant progress was made toward the achievement of peace. The Palestinians* became more active—initially gaining publicity and attention through terrorist acts against Israel, some of which were spectacular in nature. However, the most serious threat to Israel came from Egypt,* which embarked on a series of military actions that together constituted a War of Attrition, which was declared in the spring of 1969 in an effort, as President Gamal Abdul Nasser* put it, "to wear down the enemy."

Within three weeks after the cease-fire in 1967, the first incidents occurred, leading to a chain of events that eventually came to be known as the War of Attrition.

On July 1, 1967, Egypt sent out a small party in the northern canal near Ras el-Aish, ambushed an Israeli company, and shelled it, killing its commander and wounding thirteen. The fighting that ensued eventually involved Israeli naval vessels along the northern coast of the Sinai Peninsula* and, two weeks later, heavy air force interventions. On July 14, 1967, the Israeli air force downed seven Egyptian aircraft operating near the canal. Though it was the bloodiest single day since the 1967 war, two months of calm followed.

On September 1, 1967, the Arab leaders met for a Summit in Khartoum,* at which they decided not to enter negotiations with Israel. Egyptian president Nasser formulated and announced a three-phased Egyptian strategy of dealing with Israel: a "defensive rehabilitation" phase, an "offensive defense" stage, and a "liberation" phase. Soon after Nasser's speech describing this strategy, the second major eruption of hostilities began, marking the beginning of the "defensive rehabilitation" phase of Nasser's strategy of attrition. Egyptian forces opened fire on Israeli vessels in the northern portion of the Gulf of Suez and quickly escalated their attacks to a general artillery barrage along the entire Suez Canal.* Israel responded in kind, shelling Egyptian border cities and creating a mass exodus of some 750,000 Egyptians from Suez and Ismailiya. These heavy exchanges were followed by a lull in the fighting at the end of September.

On October 21, 1967, an Israeli naval vessel, the *Eilat,** while operating near Port Said, was struck and sunk with a loss of forty-seven personnel by three Soviet-manufactured STYX surface-to-surface missiles launched from Egyptian vessels still tied to the dock and unnoticed by Israeli radar. This incident was of importance because it was the first time in which a ship was sunk by missiles, thereby ushering in a new era in naval warfare.

Israel's response, four days later, was severe. Israeli artillery opened up along the entire length of the canal, striking particularly at Egyptian refineries, petroleum depots, and petrochemical installations in Suez, causing heavy physical and economic damage.

After Israel's response, a lull in fighting set in, which lasted nearly a year. During that year, the Soviets replaced weaponry Egypt lost in 1967 with modern equipment. With Soviet equipment came Soviet advisers, who soon began to involve themselves in every aspect of Egypt's military, even operational, command.

By September 1968, Egypt had again concentrated some 150,000 troops along the Suez Canal. Nasser, in order to reverse the psychological effects of the Six Day War and the ensuing emphasis on defense, which had caused low morale among the troops, moved to a more aggressive campaign of harassment of Israeli forces. On September 8, 1968, Egypt fired over 1,000 artillery pieces in a massive barrage that killed twenty-eight Israeli soldiers. A few weeks later, a similar offensive was launched, killing forty-nine Israelis.

Unable to respond in kind, Israeli commandos on October 31, 1968, struck deep into the heart of the Nile Valley, embarrassing the Egyptian government for its inadequate security measures. Again a lull set in, this time exploited by the Israelis, who fortified their positions to reduce the effects of Egyptian artillery. This defensive line later was dubbed the "Bar-Lev Line"* after the Israel Defense Forces* (IDF) chief of staff at the time, Haim Bar-Lev.*

The work was completed by March 15, 1969. As the construction of the Bar-Lev Line neared completion, Egypt resumed its artillery barrages, breaking the general quiet that had existed since September 1968. Nasser announced at that time that the "offensive defense" phase of the war was over, and the "liberation" phase had begun.

In March 1969, Egyptian aircraft penetrated Israeli air space on reconnaissance missions, resulting in one of them being shot down. The next day, on March 17, 1969, a concentrated artillery exchange ensued. During the Egyptian offensive, Israeli artillery struck back, hitting the forward position from which the Egyptian chief of staff and several of his aides were observing the progress. All those in the position were killed, therein silencing the guns, but only for a few weeks.

In April, the Egyptians resumed the heavy, constant artillery barrages until August 1970. On May 1, 1969, Nasser formally announced that the cease-fire that had ended the Six Day War was no longer in effect.

Egypt's strategy was to pin Israel down in a static war, denying Israel the ability to wage a war of maneuver and speed. A static war would be decided primarily by concentrated artillery power, an area neglected at the time by the IDF. Such constant bombardment of Israeli lines would lead, Egypt believed, to a point where rising sensitivity to casualties and insufficient Israeli artillery to respond in kind would combine to cause Israeli forces along one point or another of the canal to slacken. The Egyptian army could seize the advantage, cross the canal at an opportune moment, and establish a limited bridgehead on the east bank.

Israel's fortifications enabled it to withstand Egypt's artillery barrages; but this came at the expense of mobility. To blind Egyptian forces from choosing targets of opportunity on the Israeli side, Israel built a large wall of piled earth to hide all activity from Egyptian view. This led Egypt to more constant and severe artillery barrages at all signs of movement on Israel's side.

Israel once again attacked Egypt deep in its interior. Egypt reacted by launching indirect attacks on Israeli targets, using commandos in the Sinai to ambush IDF patrols and laying mines along roads.

By the summer of 1969, Israel was aware that it had lost the initiative. Israel reacted in three ways: it began to employ Hawk* antiaircraft missiles against Egyptian planes; it launched a series of high-profile, spectacular raids or even two-day incursions deep into Egypt and along Egypt's northern Red Sea coast; and it began to employ its air force, including newly delivered F-4 Phantoms,* but especially A-4 Skyhawks,* as flying artillery* for canal zone and deep-penetration raids.*

In the ensuing dogfights and ground fire, Israel lost three aircraft by the end of the summer, but Egypt lost twenty-one. Israel's use of airpower further reinforced the notion held by many in the IDF's high command that Israel could dispense with developing a truly modern and effective artillery force and instead continue to rely on armor and air assets to function as long-, medium-, and short-range artillery.

Israel also launched spectacular raids in this period. In "Operation Raviv" in September 1969, Israel landed tank and armor forces far to the south of Suez near the Egyptian Red Sea cape of Za'afrana, rampaging there for over two days and returning via landing craft safely to the Israeli-held Sinai Peninsula. Some have argued that this was planned, in part, as a test for eventual use in war, wherein an Israeli counterattack would circumvent the heavily fortified canal and embark on landing craft to the south of Suez and broadly outflank and surround the Egyptian army along the canal. This essentially repeated the strategy of the 1967 war—except in Egyptian Africa rather than in the Sinai.

This did little to quiet the front. The Egyptians, too, had become daring and persistent. At one point Israel captured a complete, late-model Russian P-12 radar and airlifted all seven tons of it to Israel.

By the fall of 1969, constant Israeli air raids, commando raids, and artillery attacks succeeded in pushing the Egyptians onto the defensive, forcing the Egyptian army to begin using Russian-supplied surface-to-air missiles (SAMs*) to neutralize the Israeli air force. By January 1970, Israel had, through persistent raids, succeeded in destroying a considerable portion of the Egyptian air defense structure and even eliminating part of the Egyptian air force. Between July 1969 and January 1970, forty-eight Egyptian aircraft had been shot down, compared to a loss of only five for the Israelis. Israel sensed it was beginning to achieve an advantage and stepped up its raids to seize the initiative for the first time in a year. On January 7, to emphasize the vulnerability of Egypt's position, Israel launched a series of fierce raids on Cairo, hitting supply depots, military headquarters, and training facilities. Israel also launched a number of commando raids in the following weeks. The result of the Israeli offensive was evident: Israel suffered fewer casualties in January than in any other month prior to that.

Egypt appealed to its East-bloc allies for help in countering these attacks. Nasser himself traveled to Moscow in January 1970, exacting a Soviet promise to send 1,500 more advisers with the latest Soviet antiaircraft system: SAM-3s. These missiles were manned by Soviet troops. By the spring, Soviet forces in Egypt had increased in number to 15,000. They not only manned missile installations but assumed overall responsibility for protecting Egyptian assets in depth and even piloted aircraft in combat.

In the spring of 1970, the Israeli initiative was reined in for fear of provoking a direct Israeli–Soviet clash. Egypt again seized the initiative and leveled heavy artillery barrages on Israeli positions along the canal and launched a series of commando raids on Israeli positions in February, one even as distant as Eilat. Egyptian commandos crossed the canal frequently, some reaching as deep into the Sinai as the Mitla Pass.* Egypt's air force also began to use the Soviet defensive cover to launch hit-and-run air raids against Israeli positions and then scramble back rapidly under Soviet cover when Israel's air force responded. By April 1970, Soviet involvement had become so heavy that Israel halted all deep-penetration air sorties for fear of directly confronting the Soviets. This led the Egyptians to further escalate the ground fighting and launch more commando raids into the Sinai.

The Egyptians launched a heavy offensive in March, April, and May 1970, and Israel suffered so many casualties that, at the end of May, Israel began a series of intense, continuous air raids in the canal area, sometimes with sustained bombing strikes that lasted fourteen hours. Israel also launched a series of effective and destructive canal crossings with forces.

By late June 1970, the deployment and concentration of Soviets and their equipment altered the situation. The Soviets managed, in effect, to create an impenetrable wall of missiles in two areas of the canal zone, downing a number of Israeli aircraft. The Soviets deployed missiles in ''boxes'' where each missile battery was protected by dozens of others surrounding it. This was a major innovation in Soviet tactics and marked a dramatic challenge to Western air forces, as became evident to Israel in 1973.

Still, the Israelis escalated their attacks, slowly eroding the air defense system throughout July. By July 25, what the Israelis had tried to avoid happened: Soviet pilots tangled with Israeli pilots. Soviet pilots fared much worse than their Egyptian comrades in combat, losing all their aircraft in these encounters (eleven on July 30, 1970) without damaging a single Israeli plane.

In late July, Nasser traveled to the Soviet Union. It was agreed to use diplomatic means to halt the exchanges and develop, under the cover of the cease-fire, a defense structure for the purpose of eventually launching a general war.

The War of Attrition was ended by a cease-fire proposed by U.S. secretary of state William Rogers* that came into effect in August 1970, and talks under Ambassador Gunnar Jarring's auspices were restarted, but no significant progress toward peace followed.

For further information see: Yaacov Bar-Siman-Tov, *The Israeli–Egyptian War of Attrition, 1969–1970: A Case-Study of Limited Local War* (New York: Columbia University Press, 1980); Chaim Herzog, *The Arab–Israeli Wars* (New York: Random House, 1982); David A. Korn, *Stalemate: The War of Attrition and Great Power Diplomacy in the Middle East, 1967–1970* (Boulder, CO: Westview Press, 1992); Eli Landau, *Suez: Fire on the Water* (Tel Aviv: Otpaz, 1970); Edgar O'Ballance, *The Electronic War in the Middle East, 1968–70* (London: Faber and Faber, 1974); Ezer Weizman, *On Eagles' Wings* (New York: Macmillan, 1976); Lawrence L. Whetten, *The Canal War: Four Power Conflict in the Middle East* (Cambridge: MIT Press, 1974).

David Wurmser

WAR OF INDEPENDENCE (1948–49). The first Arab–Israeli War—Israel's War of Independence—began before Israel officially declared the establishment of the state. Following the adoption of the United Nations (UN) General Assembly partition plan* on November 29, 1947, and the commencement of Britain's withdrawal, hostilities erupted between the Israelis and local Arab forces.

As early as October 1947, the Arab League* requested that its member states establish voluntary units to send into Palestine* to fight. The Arab Liberation Army* had its headquarters northeast of Nablus. At the same time, the Yishuv* began to prepare more actively for the impending hostilities.

The first phase of conflict began immediately after the UN partition plan vote when passengers on an Israeli bus from Netanya to Jerusalem* were attacked. Similar attacks occurred elsewhere across Palestine. The Yishuv organized a territorial defense, dividing the country into several zones. The Palmach* protected the settlements in the Negev* but also served as a floating reserve to be used anywhere in the country.

In December 1947, Arab forces strove to eliminate small Jewish enclaves in large population centers, to attack larger Jewish communities in mixed settlements (such as Jerusalem and Haifa), and to secure lines of communication and strategic high ground and deny these to the Yishuv's forces. The first major skirmishes took place on December 10, 1947. Arab forces opened fire on Israeli traffic in the Negev and along the Jerusalem–Gush Etzion corridor, other Arab forces struck at vulnerable points, and in mixed communities Arab forces detonated a series of carbombs near major Jewish institutions.

As the skirmishing continued, Arab forces isolated Jewish-held territory and dominated major lines of communication. In Jerusalem, Arab forces severed the connections between various Jewish neighborhoods. By the end of March 1948, Jewish forces in the Negev were cut off from the central part of the country; Jerusalem was cut off from the coast; Gush Etzion was cut off from Jerusalem; the Western Galilee was cut off from Haifa. The lines of communication between Haifa and Tel Aviv remained in Jewish hands but were frequently under attack. Israel's emerging army and defense industry began to take shape. A general draft had increased the Yishuv's forces. The Jewish community was successfully producing some submachine guns, tank obstacles, and gunpowder and acquired some weapons abroad, especially from Czechoslovakia.

Based upon intelligence about the Arab plan of attack in Palestine, the Yishuv hoped to seize strategic territory in advance. The Arab plan reportedly would have the Lebanese* thrust down the coast and in the central part of the Galilee. The Syrians* would thrust just north and south of the Sea of Galilee. The Iraqis* would thrust north to link with Lebanese forces in the Jezreel Valley, strike west into Netanya to cut off Haifa from Tel Aviv, directly assault Tel Aviv, and push south into Latrun to link with the Egyptians, cutting off the south of Israel from the north. They also were to assist the Jordanian* forces in isolating Jerusalem from the west. The Jordanians would move around Jerusalem in a pincer to the west of the city, cutting it off from the coast, and frontally assault the Jewish pockets in the Gush Etzion* region, cutting off Jerusalem from any southern or southwestern approach. The Egyptian forces in Gaza* would go north along the coast to assault Tel Aviv directly and northeast toward Latrun to join the Iraqi forces. Egyptian forces in Beer Sheva would move north toward Hebron* and Gush Etzion to link with Jordanian forces and also join a small Jordanian force that was to move into Palestine from just south of the Dead Sea.*

The Yishuv formulated Plan Dalet (Plan D).* The first major operation under Plan D was Operation Nachshon, which was designed to open a corridor to Jerusalem from Tel Aviv. The Yishuv's forces managed to take key strategic territory to the west of Jerusalem at Kastel and, farther west, the town of Zerifim near Ramle. The operation opened a corridor to the south that linked Tel Aviv and Jerusalem, albeit in rough, nearly impassable terrain. The capture of Kastel marked the first time the Jewish forces had managed to take and hold territory.

At the same time, the Arab Salvation Front Army launched an offensive in the Galilee but failed to take any territory.

In the second week of April, the Yishuv's forces took Tiberias and Haifa and on April 22, opened the corridor to the Upper Galilee for the Jewish forces. Accordingly, the Haganah* launched Operation Yiftach to capture the central and northeastern parts of the Galilee, including Zefat on May 10. Jewish thrusts in the south of the Sea of Galilee established links among Beth Shean, Ein Gev, Tiberias, Zefat, and most of the Hula Valley. In the second week of May, the link between this pocket and Haifa was reestablished. Operation Ben Ami, launched from north of Haifa, resulted in the capture of Acre, Achziv, and Shlomi (on the Lebanese border) and moved the Haganah into the Galilee near Hanita by independence day. Jaffa fell to Etzel forces on May 13.

LEHI* and Etzel* forces on April 9, 1948, attacked Deir Yassin.* In the ensuing combat against the Iraqi forces, 254 Arab civilians were killed at the hands of LEHI forces. The news of the massacre spread in the Arab community in Palestine, causing panic and helping trigger a mass exodus of Arab refugees* from Palestine. The attack was also condemned by the Jewish Agency.* On April 13, a Jewish convoy of ambulances in northern Jerusalem was ambushed, and seventy-seven doctors and nurses were killed as British forces, still present, watched. As the situation in Jerusalem deteriorated, the Jewish High Command pulled Harel forces away from the Tel Aviv–Jerusalem corridor into the city itself to help protect it. Consequently, the corridor was again cut, and Jerusalem was isolated by the third week of April. Operation Yabusi, intended to open corridors to unify isolated Jewish sections in the eastern and southern parts of the city, failed. By the end of April, the Jewish presence in Jerusalem as a whole was increasingly tenuous. On May 4, a major Jordanian attack was launched against Gush Etzion south of Jerusalem, and by May 14, the bloc fell to the Jordanian Legion. Jewish forces also suffered losses north of Jerusalem in the areas of the airport in Atarot and Neve Yaakov. On May 14, the last British troops left Jerusalem, whereupon the Eztioni division launched Operation Kilshon to seize the strong points being vacated by the British. The operation successfully established Jewish control over contiguous territory south of the city. Operation Kilshon failed, however, to open a corridor to the Jewish Quarter of the Old City* and to consolidate the Yishuv's hold on the northern approaches to Jerusalem before the Jordanian Legion arrived in full force on May 18.

As Israel declared its independence on midnight May 14, 1948, the armies of Egypt, Syria, Jordan, Iraq, and Lebanon, with assistance from some other Arab states, entered Palestine and engaged in open warfare with defense forces of the new state with the stated goals of destroying the Jewish state and ensuring the liberation of all Palestine and its return to Arab hands. Because of the implementation of the first phases of Plan D, key strategic territory from which many of the Arab thrust axes were to have been launched had fallen already to Jewish forces, and territorial contiguity had been established between many of the Jewish enclaves. Cooperation among the Arab states was in question from the beginning of their invasion. The Arab states appeared to be as interested in competing for influence and territory with each other as they were committed to preventing a partition of Palestine. Furthermore, there was little operational coordination among Arab troops to exploit the weakness of the still much smaller and ill-equipped Jewish army.

On May 15, Syrian forces crossed into Palestine south of the Sea of Galilee.* Due to intense Israeli resistance, the mainstay of Israel's defense in the north, Degania, held, causing the Syrians to reconsider a lightning advance toward Haifa and focus, instead, on seizing land near the Mandatory border, a task at which they registered some successes by the second week of June when they captured Mishmar HaYarden.

Also on May 15, Lebanese units in the northeast crossed the border into the northern Galilee. But by May 18, the Palmach had successfully outmaneuvered Lebanese forces, seized territory in Malkhia (Operation Malkhia B),* and cut the main supply route between Lebanon and Lebanese forces operating along the Israeli–Lebanese border in the northeast. The Carmeli Brigade in the western part of the Galilee held firm control of the coast. On June 6, the same day that Mishmar HaYarden fell to Syrian forces, another Syrian force counterattacked near Malchia, pushing the Israelis back into the central part of the Galilee by the time the cease-fire on June 11 took effect.

On May 28, the Iraqi army launched an offensive toward the coastal city of Netanyah, held by the Alexandroni Brigade, and threatened to slice the Jewish state in half. The Alexandroni forces stopped the offensive that night and advanced rapidly toward Jenin, to the flank of the Iraqi army. The Alexandroni Brigade failed to press a counteroffensive against the Iraqis from the west. As a result, the Iraqis retreated and launched a counteroffensive against the encroaching Golani Brigade. While the coastal area around Netanyah was secured, the areas north of Jenin fell back to the Iraqi army, which had secured its position. An opportunity to force surrender through a coordinated pincer movement on the entire Iraqi contingent in the northern part of Samaria had thus been lost by the Jewish forces.

On May 29, the Egyptian forces, located south of Ashkelon, launched a major offensive toward Tel Aviv. The first Israeli fighters, Messerschmidt aircraft from Czechoslovakia, raided the columns and, with a coordinated ground assault, forced an Egyptian retreat. While other Israeli towns nearby fell to Egyptian forces, as did Gezer on the route between Tel Aviv and Jerusalem, the decisive victory of the war had been won. The heart of the Jewish Yishuv, Tel Aviv, was attacked and defended, and the Egyptian thrust was halted, therein securing the core of the nascent Jewish state.

Failing to take Tel Aviv, it became clear to all warring sides that the UN was about to step in, and cease-fire was imminent. The fighting between the end of May and the first truce on June 11 resulted in the Arabs' capturing the territory designated as Arab Palestine. Jerusalem was a bitter loss for the Israelis. While the new part of Jerusalem had been secured, the Old City fell to the Jordanian Legion on May 28 despite repeated Israeli attempts to relieve the siege.

After the truce took effect on June 11, Israel faced three serious problems. First, the established road to Jerusalem remained in Arab hands, even though territory to the south did establish a corridor, albeit without roads, to Jerusalem. Second, the Negev still was isolated from the rest of the country. Third, the Syrians had penetrated in the north in Mishmar HaYarden and in the Central Galilee along the Lebanese border.

The Israeli army built a major road, "the Burma Road,"* in the rugged terrain on the route to Jerusalem in order to bypass Latrun, which had remained in Jordanian hands.

Abdul Rahman Azzam, secretary-general of the Arab League, informed Count Bernadotte* of the UN that they rejected an extension of the cease-fire ending July 6. In part, the Arab states believed their own propaganda and were misled. Sir John Glubb* described this as an "incredible folly." Israel went on the offensive and, in the Ten-Day Battle, captured two sectors near Nazareth and also Lydda and Ramle. By July 18, the Israelis opened a corridor, albeit tenuous, to the Negev and, in the central region, to the east of Tel Aviv, widened the corridor to Jerusalem. Around Jerusalem itself, the Israelis consolidated their hold of the western part of the city and even advanced north and west of the city.

A second truce took effect at nightfall on July 18, 1948. During this truce, heavy fighting did stop, but there were reported violations by both sides. Based on a claimed Egyptian truce violation, the Israeli army launched a massive attack in the south against Egyptian forces, named Operation Yoav. Beersheva fell to Israel on October 21. The Harel division launched an attack, Operation Hahar, cutting off Egyptian forces near Bethlehem* and Hebron and expanding the Jerusalem corridor along its southern part, therein beginning to cut off Egyptian forces in the Negev from those in Gaza and Sinai.

The British, worried about the effect the fighting would have on their Jordanian allies, pressed the UN Security Council to order a cease-fire into effect on October 22, though isolated, but important, skirmishes took place as late as November. Israel captured Bet Guvrin and Iraq-Sueidan, therein surrounding Egyptian forces in Faluja on November 8.

On October 22, the day the cease-fire was to have taken effect in Palestine, the Arab Salvation Army, which had held parts of the Central Galilee near Lebanon and the Lebanese and Syrian armies along the Mandatory border, opened an offensive. While Israel at first sustained considerable losses in this attack, by October 28, the Israeli army launched its counteroffensive, named Operation Hiram. Not only did the Israeli army recapture the entire Galilee in this operation within sixty hours, but Israeli forces thrust deep into Lebanon, with some units reaching as far north as the Litani River.*

The cease-fire that finally took effect in November required the sides to immediately enter truce negotiations. Nevertheless, fighting continued. The Israelis contended the Arabs were engaged in guerrilla operations against Israel. Israel, in turn, improved its position through Operations Horev and Ayin, which were designed to expel the Egyptian army from Palestine and push them across the international border. By December 26, Egyptian forces were in a rout, and Israeli forces entered the Sinai and started a long arc toward El-Arish, along the Sinai's northern coast, in an attempt to cut off all Egyptian forces in Gaza. By December 29, they were within a few kilometers south of El-Arish. Some Israeli forces even penetrated as deep as 110 kilometers into the heart of the Sinai, near Bir Hama. Yet, as the Israelis advanced deeper into the Sinai, international pressure grew on Israel to cease combat. By December 30, the British threatened Israel directly, presenting it with an ultimatum that, were the country to remain in the Sinai, Britain would enact a 1936 Anglo-Egyptian defense treaty and attack Israel with its might. Israel ceased operations in the Sinai but continued its offensive in the Gaza Strip.* Fearing a complete defeat, the Egyptians agreed to a cease-fire on January 4, 1949, which was to take effect on January 7, and to commence truce negotiations in Rhodes over the following week.

The War of Independence was Israel's most costly war, claiming more than 4,000 soldiers and 2,000 civilians, about 1 percent of the Jewish population in Palestine at the time. For the Palestinian Arabs, the war left much of the designated Arab Palestine in the control of Transjordan,* the Gaza Strip in Egypt's control, and Israel in possession of more territory than that allocated by the partition plan. No Palestine state emerged. Palestinian refugees* who fled the fighting were in need of assistance. Armistices had been signed between Israel and four Arab states, but no peace agreement followed.

For further information see: Lynne Reid Banks, *Torn Country: An Oral History of the Israeli War of Independence* (New York: Franklin Watts, 1982); Jon Kimche and David Kimche, *Both Sides of the Hill: Britain and the Palestine War* (London: Secker and Warburg, 1960); Netanel Lorch, *The Edge of the Sword: Israel's War of Independence, 1947–1949* (New York: G. P. Putnam's Sons, 1961).

David Wurmser

WAR OF RAMADAN. See **YOM KIPPUR WAR.**

WASHINGTON DECLARATION. On July 25, 1994, King Hussein* of Jordan* and Prime Minister Yitzhak Rabin* of Israel signed the Washington Declaration in Washington, D.C.

The full text of the declaration reads as follows:

A. After generations of hostility, blood and tears and in the wake of years of pain and wars, His Majesty King Hussein and Prime Minister Yitzhak Rabin are determined to bring an end to bloodshed and sorrow. It is in this spirit that His Majesty King Hussein of the Hashemite Kingdom of Jordan and Prime Minister and Minister of Defense, Mr. Yitzhak Rabin of Israel, met in Washington today at the invitation of President William J. Clinton* of the United

States of America. This initiative of President William J. Clinton constitutes an historic landmark in the United States' untiring efforts in promoting peace and stability in the Middle East. The personal involvement of the President has made it possible to realize agreement on the content of this historic declaration.

The signing of this declaration bears testimony to the President's vision and devotion to the cause of peace.

B. In their meeting, His Majesty King Hussein and Prime Minister Yitzhak Rabin have jointly reaffirmed the five underlying principles of their understanding on an Agreed Common Agenda* designed to reach the goal of a just, lasting and comprehensive peace between the Arab States and the Palestinians, with Israel.

1. Jordan and Israel aim at the achievement of just, lasting and comprehensive peace between Israel and its neighbors and at the conclusion of a Treaty of Peace between both countries.

2. The two countries will vigorously continue their negotiations to arrive at a state of peace, based on Security Council Resolutions 242* and 338* in all their aspects, and founded on freedom, equality and justice.

3. Israel respects the present special role of the Hashemite Kingdom of Jordan in Muslim Holy shrines in Jerusalem.* When negotiations on the permanent status will take place, Israel will give high priority to the Jordanian historic role in these shrines. In addition the two sides have agreed to act together to promote interfaith relations among the three monotheistic religions.

4. The two countries recognize their right and obligation to live in peace with each other as well as with all states within secure and recognized boundaries. The two states affirmed their respect for and acknowledgment of the sovereignty, territorial integrity and political independence of every state in the area.

5. The two countries desire to develop good neighborly relations of cooperation between them to ensure lasting security and to avoid threats and the use of force between them.

C. The long conflict between the two states is now coming to an end. In this spirit the state of belligerency between Jordan and Israel has been terminated.

D. Following this declaration and in keeping with the Agreed Common Agenda, both countries will refrain from actions or activities by either side that may adversely affect the security of the other or may prejudice the final outcome of negotiations. Neither side will threaten the other by use of force, weapons, or any other means, against each other and both sides will thwart threats to security resulting from all kinds of terrorism.

E. His Majesty King Hussein and Prime Minister Yitzhak Rabin took note of the progress made in the bilateral negotiations within the Jordan–Israel track last week on the steps decided to implement the sub-agendas on borders, territorial matters, security, water, energy, environment and the Jordan Rift Valley.

In this framework, mindful of items of the Agreed Common Agenda (borders and territorial matters) they noted that the boundary sub-commission has reached agreement in July 1994 in fulfillment of part of the role entrusted to it in the sub-agenda. They also noted that the sub-commission for water, environment and energy agreed to mutually recognize, as the role of their negotiations, the rightful allocations of the two sides in Jordan River* and Yarmuk River waters and to fully respect and comply with the negotiated rightful allocations, in accordance with agreed acceptable principles with mutually acceptable quality. Similarly, His Majesty King Hussein and Prime Minister Yitzhak Rabin expressed their deep satisfaction and pride in the work of the trilateral commission in its meeting held in Jordan on Wednesday, July 20th 1994, hosted by the Jordanian Prime Minister, Dr. Abdessalam al-Majali, and attended by Secretary of State Warren Christopher* and Foreign Minister Shimon Peres.* They voiced their pleasure at the association and commitment of the United States in this endeavor.

F. His Majesty King Hussein and Prime Minister Yitzhak Rabin believe that steps must be taken both to overcome psychological barriers and to break with the legacy of war. By working with optimism towards the dividends of peace for all the people in the region, Jordan and Israel are determined to shoulder their responsibilities towards the human dimension of peace making. They recognize imbalances and disparities are a root cause of extremism which thrives on poverty and unemployment and the degradation of human dignity. In this spirit His Majesty King Hussein and Prime Minister Yitzhak Rabin have today approved a series of steps to symbolize the new era which is now at hand:

1. Direct telephone links will be opened between Jordan and Israel.

2. The electricity grids of Jordan and Israel will be linked as part of a regional concept.

3. Two new border crossings will be opened between Jordan and Israel—one at the southern tip of Aqaba-Eilat and the other at a mutually agreed point in the north.

4. In principle free access will be given to third country tourists traveling between Jordan and Israel.

5. Negotiations will be accelerated on opening an international air corridor between both countries.

6. The police forces of Jordan and Israel will cooperate in combating crime with emphasis on smuggling and particularly drug smuggling. The United States will be invited to participate in this joint endeavor.

7. Negotiations on economic matters will continue in order to prepare for future bilateral cooperation including the abolition of all economic boycotts.

All these steps are being implemented within the framework of regional infrastructural development plans and in conjunction with the Jordan–Israel bilaterals on boundaries, security, water and related issues and without prejudice to the final outcome of the negotiations on the items included in the Agreed Common Agenda between Jordan and Israel.

G. His Majesty King Hussein and Prime Minister Yitzhak Rabin have agreed to meet periodically or whenever they feel necessary to review the progress of the negotiations and express their firm intention to shepherd and direct the process in its entirety.

H. In conclusion, His Majesty King Hussein and Prime Minister Yitzhak Rabin wish to express once again their profound thanks and appreciation to President William J. Clinton and his Administration for their untiring efforts in furthering the cause of peace, justice and prosperity for all the peoples of the region. They wish to thank the President personally for his warm welcome and hospitality. In recognition of their appreciation to the President, His Majesty King Hussein and Prime Minister Yitzhak Rabin have asked President William J. Clinton to sign this document as a witness and as a host to their meeting.

The declaration was signed by His Majesty King Hussein, Prime Minister Yitzhak Rabin, and President William J. Clinton.

WASHINGTON ROUNDS. The Madrid Peace Conference* set in motion a series of bilateral discussions of Arab–Israeli issues between Israel and Arab interlocutors (Syria,* Lebanon,* Jordan,* and the Palestinians*). These discussions began with a first round in Madrid on November 3, 1991, and with subsequent rounds in Washington, D.C., beginning in December 1991. These negotiations continued over the ensuing months. Round 1 took place in November 1991 in Madrid, Spain. Round 2 and subsequent rounds took place in Washington, D.C.: Round 2, December 10–18, 1991; Round 3, January 7–16, 1992; Round 4, February 24–March 4, 1992; Round 5, April 27–30, 1992; Round 6, Session 1: August 24–September 3, 1992; Session 2: September 14–24, 1992; Round 7, Session 1: October 21–29, 1992; Session 2: November 9–19, 1992; Round 8, December 7–17, 1992; Resumption of Talks: April 27–May 13, 1993; June 15–July 1, 1993; August 31–September 14, 1993; January 24–February 3, 1994; February 15–25, 1994.

WATER. Water has been an issue in the Arab–Israeli conflict virtually from the outset. Among its many elements is the question of the division and use of the waters of the Jordan River* system. Allocating the waters of the Jordan and Yarmuk* Rivers was a focus of Syria,* Jordan,* and Israel in the 1950s and was dealt with in the Johnston Plan,* among other efforts. The construction of Israel's National Water Carrier* and Arab League* plans to divert the headwaters of the Jordan to prevent Israeli use of them became matters of controversy in the 1960s. Access to, and use of, water was an important issue in the Israel–Jordan peace negotiations and an important element in the Israel–Jordan Peace Treaty of 1994.*

For further information see: A Strategy for Managing Water in the Middle East and North Africa (Washington, DC: World Bank, 1994).

WATER RESOURCES. One of the five multilateral negotiations* working groups established as a part of the Madrid Conference peace process.*

WAXMAN (WACHSMAN), NAHSHON (d. 1994). Waxman, an Israel Defense Forces (IDF)* corporal, was kidnapped by HAMAS* on October 9, 1994, as part of an Islamic fundamentalist terrorist campaign against Israel and its citizens as well as against Yasser Arafat* for signing an agreement with Israel. HAMAS threatened to kill him unless Israel freed HAMAS's founder and spiritual leader, Sheikh Ahmed Yassin,* and other imprisoned Palestinians. The Israeli government stressed Yasser Arafat's complete responsibility for the welfare and return of Waxman, alive and healthy, to Israel. Waxman was killed during a rescue attempt by IDF commandos in the West Bank* village of Bir Nabala. An Israeli officer and three HAMAS captors were also killed in the attempt.

AL-WAZIR, INTISSAR (Known as Umm Jihad). She is the widow of Abu Jihad.* Umm Jihad was sworn in, in July 1994, as minister of social affairs in the Palestinian Authority* established in Jericho* and the Gaza Strip.*

AL-WAZIR, KHALIL IBRAHIM (ABU JIHAD—father of the struggle) (b. Ramleh, October 10, 1935; d. Tunis, April 16, 1988). His family fled to Gaza* when Israel declared its independence in 1948. He became active in politics at a young age and became the leader of the Palestinian Students Union in Gaza. He was arrested in 1954 by the Egyptian* authorities after a raid against Israel but was released. He was responsible for a large raid against Israel in 1955.

He was cofounder, with Yasser Arafat,* of the first Fatah* cell, formed in 1957, and later served as Arafat's second-in-command as deputy commander of the Palestine Liberation Organization* (PLO) forces. He was regarded by some as Arafat's heir apparent. He was the military chief of the PLO. After the start of the *intifada,** he became responsible for coordinating the uprising in the West Bank* and Gaza Strip.*

The PLO and others accused Israel of his killing, arguing that the attack was carried out so professionally that it could only have been the work of the Mossad.*

Nancy Hasanian and Joseph E. Goldberg

WEIZMAN, EZER (b. Tel Aviv, 1924). A nephew of Chaim Weizmann*; he deliberately spelled his name with one *n* to avoid benefiting from the family connection. He was educated at the Reali School in Haifa and joined the Haganah* in 1939. In 1942, he enlisted in the British Royal Air Force and in 1948 served as a squadron commander in the Israel Defense Forces* (IDF), where he rose through the ranks. Weizman studied with the British Royal Air Force from 1951 to 1953, and in 1958 he became commander in chief of the Israel air force. From 1966 to 1969, he served as chief of the General Staff Branch of the IDF. Weizman resigned from the IDF in December 1969, apparently convinced that he would not be made chief of staff, and immediately entered political life. In 1969–70, he served as minister of transport in the national unity government

led by Golda Meir* in one of the six seats allocated to GAHAL. He served as
minister of defense (as a Likud* member) but resigned in 1980. From 1980 to
1984, he was in private business. He was minister in the prime minister's office
(as a Labor Alignment member) in the 1984 National Unity government,* shifting from the Right to the Left in Israel's political spectrum. He became minister
of science and development in the government established in December 1988.
In 1992, he resigned from the Knesset* and from party politics. He was elected
president of Israel in 1993.

He wrote *The Battle for Peace* (New York: Bantam, 1981).

For further information see: Generals of Israel (Tel Aviv: Hadar Publishing House,
1968).

WEIZMANN, CHAIM (b. Motol, near Pinsk, Russia, November 27, 1874; d.
November 9, 1952). The Weizmann family were ardent Zionists* and belonged
to the Hovevei Zion.* He was educated in Germany, where he received a doctor
of science degree from the University of Freiburg in 1900. In 1904, Weizmann
moved to England,* where he began his career as a faculty member in bio-
chemistry at the University of Manchester. As director of the Admiralty Labo-
ratories during 1916–19, he discovered a process for producing acetone, thus
helping the war effort. Weizmann became the leader of the English Zionist
movement and was instrumental in securing the Balfour Declaration.* In 1918,
he became chairman of the Zionist Commission to Palestine.* Following World
War I, Weizmann emerged in the 1920s as the leader of the World Zionist
Organization* and built a home in Palestine* near Rehovot. He served as president of the World Zionist Organization from 1920 to 1946, except for the years
1931–35. He helped found the Jewish Agency,* the Hebrew University at Jerusalem,* and the Sieff Research Institute at Rehovot (now the Weizmann Institute of Science). In 1919, Weizmann headed the Zionist delegation to the
Paris Peace Conference,* and in the fall of 1947 he addressed the United Nations
General Assembly to plead for the establishment of a Jewish state. Weizmann
also appealed to U.S. president Harry Truman* for assistance in the effort to
secure a Jewish state. When the U.S. State Department seemed willing to omit
the Negev* from the proposed Jewish state, Truman overrode them, and the
American delegate supported the plan that included the Negev. On the day Israel
declared its independence, the United States immediately extended recognition
to the new Jewish state. With the declaration of Israel's independence and the
establishment of a provisional government in May 1948, Weizmann became
president of Israel's provisional government, and, in February 1949, the first
elected Israeli Knesset* selected Weizmann as the first president of Israel. He
was reelected in November 1951.

Weizmann wrote *Trial and Error* (New York: Harper and Brothers, 1949)
and *The Letters and Papers of Chaim Weizmann. Series A: Letters,* 23 vol.,
Series B: Papers, 2 vol. (Oxford: Oxford University Press, 1968–84).

For further information see: Isaiah Berlin, *Chaim Weizmann* (London: Weidenfeld and Nicolson, 1958); Barnet Litvinoff, *Weizmann: Last of the Patriarchs* (New York: G. P. Putnam's, 1976); Jehuda Reinharz, *Chaim Weizmann: The Making of a Zionist Leader* (New York: Oxford University Press, 1985); Norman Rose, *Chaim Weizmann* (New York: Viking, 1986); Samuel Shihor, *Hollow Glory: The Last Days of Chaim Weizmann, First President of Israel* (New York: Yoseloff, 1960); Melvin Urofsky, ''Chaim Weizmann,'' in Bernard Reich, ed., *Political Leaders of the Contemporary Middle East and North Africa: A Biographical Dictionary* (Westport, CT: Greenwood Press, 1990), pp. 495–502.

WEST BANK. The West Bank, a part of historical Palestine,* lies to the west of the Jordan River* and the Dead Sea.* It came into political existence in 1948, when Jordanian* troops occupied it during the Arab–Israeli War of 1948–49.* Some include Arab East Jerusalem* in their definition of the West Bank; others do not. Many Israelis refer to the West Bank by its biblical designation, Judea* and Samaria.*

After the West Bank was occupied by Jordanian forces during the 1948–49 Arab–Israeli fighting, a series of political steps led to its inclusion in the Hashemite Kingdom of Jordan. Two key meetings of Palestinian notables were held—one in Amman and one in Jericho*—during which the participants called for union of the East and West Banks. Despite the strong objections of a number of Arab countries, King Abdullah* proceeded to act upon this request. He withdrew the military administration and replaced it with a civilian one. He also dissolved the Parliament elected from only the East Bank and called for the election of a Parliament whose members would be equally drawn from both banks. These elections were held in April 1950, and the Parliament met later that month. On April 24, 1950, this body voted for the union of the West and East Banks under the kingship of Abdullah. The text of the resolution read:

First, [Parliament's] support of complete unity between the two sides of the Jordan and their union into one state, which is the Hashemite Kingdom of Jordan, at whose head reigns King Abdullah Ibn al Husain, on a basis of constitutional representative government and equality of the rights and duties of all citizens.

Second, its reaffirmation of its intent to preserve the full Arab rights in Palestine, to defend those rights by all lawful means in the exercise of its natural rights but without prejudicing the final settlement of Palestine's just case within the sphere of national aspirations, inter-Arab cooperation and international justice.

By these actions, Jordan tripled its population and added about 2,100 square miles, or 5,440 square kilometers, to its territory. It also became directly involved in the Arab–Israeli conflict.

In the Six Day War,* Jordan lost the West Bank to Israel. Despite this change of status, the government of Jordan maintained administrative and political ties to the West Bank, and the people maintained social and economic relations. In the summer of 1988, King Hussein* announced that Jordan would disengage

politically and administratively from the West Bank. This was in response to
the political opinion expressed in the Palestinian *intifada,** whereby the Palestinians of the West Bank and Gaza,* inter alia, manifested their loyalty to the
Palestine Liberation Organization* and Palestinian nationalism and showed that
they did not want Jordan to represent them. See also HUSSEIN'S RENUNCI-
ATION OF THE CLAIM TO THE WEST BANK; JUDEA and SAMARIA.

For further information see: Said K. Aburish, *Cry Palestine: Inside the West Bank*
(Boulder, CO: Westview Press, 1993); Geoffrey Aronson, *Creating Facts: Israel, Pales-
tinians, and the West Bank* (Washington, DC: Institute for Palestine Studies, 1987);
Meron Benvenisti, *Legal Dualism: The Absorption of the Occupied Territories into Israel*
(Boulder, CO: Westview Press, 1990); Meron Benvenisti, *The West Bank Data Project:
A Survey of Israel's Policies* (Washington, DC: American Enterprise Institute for Public
Policy Research, 1984); Meron Benvenisti and Shlomo Khayat, *The West Bank and Gaza
Atlas* (Jerusalem: West Bank Data Base Project, 1988); Vivian A. Bull, *The West Bank—
Is It Viable?* (Lexington, MA: Lexington Books, [1975]); William W. Harris, *Taking
Root: Israeli Settlement in the West Bank, the Golan and Gaza–Sinai* (Chichester,
England: Research Studies Press, 1980); David J. Schnall, *Beyond the Green Line: Israeli
Settlements West of the Jordan* (New York: Praeger, 1984); Shabtei Teveth, *The Cursed
Blessing: The Story of Israel's Occupation of the West Bank* (New York: Random House,
1971).

WESTERN WALL/WAILING WALL. For the Jews, the Western Wall (Kotel ha-
Maarvi) is the most sacred of holy places. It is all that remains of the western
exterior of the Temple of Herod, which was built on the site of the Temple of
Solomon. Since the Middle Ages, Jews have come to the wall to pray and to
mourn the destruction of the Temple* and the greatness of ancient Israel.

The Western Wall (al-Buraq) is also the outer containing wall of the Haram
al-Sharif,* the third holiest site of Islam. It is part of the rectangular area that
encloses the al-Aksa Mosque* and the Dome of the Rock.* From the latter, the
Prophet Mohammed ascended into heaven ''on a nocturnal journey.'' The wall
is also known as ''al-Buraq'' by the Arabs, so named for the prophet's horse,
which he tethered to the wall on the evening of his ascension.

In the early 1920s, soon after the British occupation of Palestine,* there was
a series of disputes and confrontations over the wall. On one occasion, the Jews
offered the Moslems a trade of land for part of the *waqf* properties. The sale of
waqf land was forbidden, but an exchange could be approved by a Moslem
religious court. Negotiations were abandoned because the Moslem population
grew apprehensive that the Jews would intrude on their holy places.

In 1920, there was difficulty about the repair of certain courses of stone in
the wall. In the end, the government did the work. In 1922, Muslims protested
that the Jews had brought benches to the wall on the Day of Atonement. This
was in contradiction to an order given by the Turks, an order that was still in
force as part of the status quo. A proposal was made to hold a judicial inquiry
into the practices at the wall, but it never came about. The Mandatory administration, not knowing how to deal with the question, restricted its action to

preserving the status quo. There was no written record regarding the wall as to the practice observed by the Turks.

In the late 1920s, the dissension turned violent, so much so that, in November 1928, the British secretary of state published a White Paper* that defined the policy of His Majesty's government regarding the wall. Further disturbances provoked the high commissioner to issue instructions in regard to the use of the Wailing Wall. When he returned from his leave on August 29, 1929, the country was in a state of disorder. When order was restored, over a hundred Jews had been killed, many were seriously wounded, and half a dozen settlements had been destroyed. The British estimated the Arabs' losses as even greater.

The British government sent a Commission of Inquiry, headed by Sir Walter Shaw,* to report on the events leading up to the disturbances and to formulate measures that would prevent a recurrence. The report was published in December 1930. The commission interviewed witnesses, and extensive testimony was taken from all parties.

The commission, citing Article 13 of the provisions of the Mandate, established that the Mandatory power alone bore the responsibility for the holy places, including other religious buildings and sites in Palestine. Two restrictions applied: the Mandatory must ensure the preservation of public order, and it would "have no authority to interfere with the management of any of the purely Moslem sacred shrines." Immunity of the latter was guaranteed by the Mandate.

The commission concluded that, although the ownership of the wall, including those parts of its surroundings, belonged to the Moslems (under the *waqf*), the wall itself and the pavement were not "Moslem sacred shrines" from the Moslem point of view. It found evidence that, for many centuries, the Western Wall of the Temple had been an object of religious veneration to the Jews.

In an effort to be just, the commission prescribed a number of provisions that would allow both Jews and Arabs access to the holy places. The Jews would have the right to observe their religious rites, with certain restrictions. The Moslems were entitled to construct or build any desired erection and to tear down or restore any existing building in the *waqf* properties adjacent to the wall; however, no work could encroach on the pavement area or prevent access of the Jews to the wall.

For further information see: Fannie Fern Andrews, *The Holy Land under Mandate,* 2 vols. (Boston: Houghton Mifflin, 1931); Meir Ben-Dov, Mordechay Naor, and Zeev Aner, *The Western Wall,* trans. Raphael Posner (New York: Adama Books, 1983); Philip Mattar, "The Role of the Mufti of Jerusalem in the Political Struggle over the Western Wall, 1928–1929," *Middle Eastern Studies* 19 (January 1983):104–18.

Nancy Hasanian

WHITE PAPER OF 1922 (Churchill White Paper). The 1922 Churchill White Paper is an official British statement of policy regarding the geographical boundaries of Palestine* and a more restrictive definition of the phrase "a Jewish National Home* in Palestine." It represents a step in the evolution and fulfillment of both the Balfour Declaration* and the Hussein–McMahon correspondence.* The Churchill White Paper was published by the British government on July 1, 1922, and was accepted on July 6 by the House of Commons and by the Council of the League of Nations on September 29, 1922.

The phrase "a Jewish National Home in Palestine," as used in the 1917 Balfour Declaration, was vague in its definition of both the geographical boundaries of Palestine and what was meant in political terms by "a Jewish National Home." As the League of Nations was in the process of assigning Palestine as a Mandated territory to Great Britain* and since the Balfour Declaration apparently was in contradiction of promises made by McMahon to Sherif Hussein* regarding the future of Palestine, a clarification of British policy was necessary.

In the face of growing Arab tensions over increased Jewish immigration into Palestine and the Zionist* perception that the British were reneging on the promises established in the Balfour Declaration, the British colonial secretary, Winston Churchill,* drafted a new statement of British policy in June 1922. The Churchill White Paper restricted the geographical borders of the Jewish National Home to the area west of the Jordan River,* avoided the idea of creating a primarily Jewish political entity, and limited Jewish immigration into Palestine to the "economic capacity of the country."

Regarding Zionist concerns, the White Paper states, in part:

The tension which has prevailed from time to time in Palestine is mainly due to apprehensions, which are entertained both by sections of the Arab and by sections of the Jewish population. These apprehensions, so far as the Arabs are concerned, are partly based on exaggerated interpretations of the meaning of the [Balfour] Declaration favouring the establishment of a Jewish National Home in Palestine, made on behalf of His Majesty's Government on 2nd November, 1917. . . . Phrases have been used such as that Palestine is to become "as Jewish as England is English." His Majesty's Government regard any such expectation as impracticable and have no such aim in view. . . . They would draw attention to the fact that the terms of the [Balfour] Declaration referred to do not contemplate that Palestine as a whole should be converted into a Jewish National Home, but that such a home should be founded *in Palestine*. . . . When it is asked what is meant by the development of a Jewish National Home in Palestine, it may be answered that it is not the imposition of a Jewish nationality upon the inhabitants of Palestine as a whole but the further development of the existing Jewish community, with the assistance of Jews in other parts of the world, in order that it may become a centre in which the Jewish people as a whole may take, on grounds of religion and race, an interest and a pride.

Regarding Arab claims to the whole of Palestine, the White Paper states:

In the first place, it is not the case, as has been represented by the Arab Delegation, that during the war His Majesty's Government gave an undertaking that an independent national government should be at once established in Palestine. This representation mainly rests upon a letter dated the 24th October, 1915, from Sir Henry McMahon, then His

Majesty's High Commissioner in Egypt, to the Sherif of Mecca, now King Hussein of the Kingdom of the Hejaz. That letter is quoted as conveying the promise to the Sherif of Mecca to recognize and support the independence of the Arabs within the territories proposed by him. But this promise was given subject to a reservation made in the same letter, which excluded from its scope, among other territories, the portions of Syria* lying to the west of the district of Damascus. This reservation has always been regarded by His Majesty's Government as covering the vilayet of Beirut and the independent Sanjak of Jerusalem. The whole of Palestine west of the Jordan was thus excluded from Sir H. McMahon's pledge.

The Zionists, though unhappy with the new restrictions on the Jewish National Home, accepted the 1922 White Paper because it ultimately guaranteed them a role in the Mandate of Palestine. The Arabs, on the other hand, rejected the White Paper because it gave the Zionists assurances of a future in Palestine and deprived the Arabs of their population and economic base west of the Jordan River.

For further information see: Howard M. Sachar, *The Emergence of the Middle East: 1914–1924* (New York: Alfred A. Knopf, 1969).

Mark Daryl Erickson

WHITE PAPER OF 1939. The White Paper issued by the British government on May 17, 1939, called for severe restrictions on Jewish immigration. The paper followed the Woodhead Commission* report and the St. James Conference.* Both Arabs and Jews rejected the White Paper.

Not long after the Peel Commission* and the Woodhead Commission gave their reports, the British government issued a statement of policy (White Paper) in 1939 known as the MacDonald Paper (Ramsey MacDonald was prime minister at this time). This paper acknowledged the Woodhead Commission's findings that the partition of Palestine* was not feasible for economic reasons; there were not enough resources for two viable states. Woodhead had also noted the difficulties of getting Arab agreement to the division of the country. This paper demonstrated a break in British policy of the past twenty years and was a direct repudiation of the Balfour Declaration.* After conferences with both Jewish and Arab delegations in London, the policy was issued on May 17, 1930, and identified under three headings.

The first part outlined the constitution of the territory of Palestine. While the paper referred to Churchill's* words in 1922 to offer the prospect of a National Home* in Palestine for Jewish people, it clarified that such a state should not result in the subordination of the Arab people living there. Britain would now support and work toward the development of one independent state (an ally, of course) in ten years. The transitional period would allow for the gradual increase in responsibility of the people in Palestine in government. If, in ten years, an independent state was not possible, Britain would consult with the people of Palestine, the League of Nations, and neighboring Arab states.

The second section discussed immigration. The paper acknowledged that Jewish immigration had been to the benefit of the economy and the population of Palestine, but it called for it to be curtailed. Over the next five years Jewish immigration could continue at a maximum rate of 15,000 persons per year, but, unless there was Arab agreement, it would cease. These quotas would be flexible so that if one year did not see the entrance of the entire 15,000, it could be carried over until the end of the five-year period. During these early years of the war, transportation of Jews out of Germany and Eastern Europe was desired by most, but logistics posed a problem. The restrictions of the White Paper were ignored continually by the Europeans; even the Third Reich was alleged to be aiding illegal immigration to Palestine. Restrictions were placed on the purchase of land by Jewish immigrants to avoid the growth of a landless class of Arabs.

The House of Commons debated the White Paper on May 22, 1939, and it was approved by a vote of 268 to 179. The House of Lords approved it. There was outrage in both Arab and Jewish communities. The Arabs wanted an immediate end to all Jewish immigration and the review of all immigrants who had entered Palestine since 1918. The Zionists* felt that the British had backed out of any and all previous agreements to work toward a Jewish homeland. This was the beginning of the Jewish rebellion in Palestine that resulted in the partition of Palestine and driving the British out of the country. A possible explanation for British policy was their desire to stabilize their base in the Middle East to entrench themselves for the rest of the war. Adherence to the White Paper would secure Arab compliance and help Britain through the war. They needed to maintain their global bases. However, shock rang through Eastern Europe and America. European Jews had few places to go, and they were becoming desperate. The official reaction of the United States was not that strong. However, the State Department was pressed by American Zionists to come out in strong opposition, citing that American interests in the region could be in jeopardy. President Roosevelt felt that the White Paper could not be approved by the United States and informed the British government of American disappointment. The White Paper became a rallying flag around which Zionists could unite and organize. The Jewish community refused to cooperate. David Ben-Gurion* proclaimed that they would ''fight the White paper as if there were no war!''

The Zionist reaction to the White Paper appeared in a statement by the Jewish Agency* in 1939. It said that the Jewish people regarded this policy as a breach of faith and a surrender to Arab terrorism. The prospect of peace in the area was now impossible. The British government was accused of being cruel for betraying the Jewish people in their ''darkest hour,'' when they were in desperate need of a homeland. The Zionists vowed to continue defending Jewish immigration, the Jewish home, and Jewish freedom with the same strength they had in rebuilding Palestine.

The White Paper declared: ''His Majesty's Government believe that the framers of the Mandate in which the Balfour Declaration was embodied could not have intended that Palestine should be converted into a Jewish State against the will of the Arab population of the country.'' It called therefore for the establishment of a Jewish National Home in an independent Palestinian state. Jewish immigration would be restricted, as would land transfers. The White Paper foresaw an independent Palestinian state within ten years. Both the Arabs and the Jews rejected the White Paper.

For further information see: Michael J. Cohen, ''Appeasement in the Middle East: The British White Paper on Palestine, May 1939,'' *Historical Journal* 16 (1973):571–96; Great Britain, Colonial Office, *Palestine: Statement of Policy by His Majesty's Government,* Cmd. 6019 (London: His Majesty's Stationery Office, 1939).

Monica M. Boudjouk

WILSON, THOMAS WOODROW (b. Staunton, Virginia, December 28, 1856; d. Washington, D.C., February 3, 1924). Woodrow Wilson served as president of the United States from 1912 to 1919. In May 1917, British foreign secretary Lord Arthur James Balfour sought to gain his endorsement of a pro-Zionist* statement. Under the influence of Louis D. Brandeis and other prominent American Zionists, Wilson gave his approval to the draft declaration proposed by the British government. Wilson expressed his explicit support for the Zionist movement and for the Balfour Declaration* in a letter to the former president of the Provisional Zionist Committee, Rabbi Stephen S. Wise, on August 31, 1918.

Earlier that year, on January 8, Wilson had delivered a fourteen-point speech to a joint session of Congress, outlining the elements upon which world peace could be achieved. The following aspects of Wilson's speech had significant bearing on the Middle East:

Open covenants of peace, openly arrived at, after which there shall be no private international understandings of any kind but diplomacy shall proceed always frankly and in the public view. . . . A free, open-minded, and absolutely impartial adjustment of all colonial claims, based upon a strict observance of the principle that in determining all such questions of sovereignty the interests of the populations concerned must have equal weight with the equitable claims of the government whose title is to be determined. . . . The Turkish portions of the present Ottoman Empire* should be assured a secure sovereignty, but the other nationalities which are now under Turkish rule should be assured an undoubted security of life and an absolutely unmolested opportunity of autonomous development. . . . A general association of nations must be formed under specific covenants for the purpose of affording mutual guarantees of political independence and territorial integrity to great and small nations alike.

Wilson later proclaimed on February 11, 1918, that a permanent peace settlement must ensure that ''[p]eoples are not to be handed about from one sovereignty to another by an international conference or an understanding between rivals and antagonists.''

Whereas the principles of sovereignty and national self-determination as enunciated by Wilson were welcomed by the Arabs, his pronouncements proved incompatible and contradictory to the plans and agreements made by Britain

and France.* Wilson attended the Paris Peace Conference* in 1919 in the hope
of bringing his ideas to fruition. Faced with stiff opposition, Wilson proposed
the Mandate system as a compromise between self-determination and the intent
of the colonial powers to maintain their interests and control in the region. As
a means to determine who was to exercise Mandatory functions and where,
Wilson proposed sending a British, French, and American delegation to the
region to determine the will of those concerned. Lacking British and French
participation, Wilson dispatched the all-American King–Crane Commission* to
Palestine and the Harbord Commission to Armenia.

The recommendations of the King–Crane Commission attempted to reflect the
nationalist desires and aspirations of the peoples whose destinies were being
decided by Western powers. The report, however, was ignored at the Paris Peace
Conference and remained unpublished until 1922.

Wilson was forced to return from the Paris Peace Conference to the United
States in mid-1919 due to growing domestic opposition to the Treaty of Versailles, including the League of Nations Covenant. Wilson's postwar positions
were officially repudiated when the U.S. Senate refused to ratify the Treaty of
Versailles, compelling the United States out of an effective role in the final
peace settlement. The American delegation played no part in the San Remo
Conference,* where Wilson's principle of self-determination was rejected, as
the Mandates were officially assigned. Having collapsed on September 26, 1919,
Wilson remained an invalid until his death in 1924.

For further information see: Ray Stannard Baker and William E. Dodd, *The Public
Papers of Woodrow Wilson* (New York: Harper and Brothers, 1927); Lawrence Evans,
United States Policy and the Partition of Turkey, 1914–1924 (Baltimore: Johns Hopkins
University Press, 1965); Harry N. Howard, *The King–Crane Commission: An American
Inquiry in the Middle East* (Beirut: Khayat, 1963); H.W.V. Temperly, ed., *A History of
the Peace Conference of Paris,* vol. 4 (London: Henry Frowde and Hodder and Stough-
ton, 1924).

Anamika Krishna

WINGATE, ORDE CHARLES (b. India, 1903; d. Burma, 1944). Major General
Orde Charles Wingate was a British army officer who was sent to Palestine* in
1936 and remained there until 1939, where he served in the British intelligence
staff as a captain. Though not Jewish, he was a strong supporter of the Zionist*
cause. At the time of his service, the British were very concerned about the
smuggling of weaponry and contraband into Palestine from Syria* and Transjordan.* The British wanted to find a way to put a stop to this action. Wingate
provided a solution by training Jewish settlers (many of whom belong to the
underground Haganah*). These trainees were used in his Special Night Squads
for use against Arab smugglers, bandits, and rebels.

Wingate's military tactics, such as surprise, mobility, and use of captured
enemy resources, became characteristic of the later Israel Defense Forces.* His
use of offensive warfare as a means of defense has been utilized successfully

by the Jewish state. Wingate has been called the grandfather of the Israeli military, and he is called "the friend" in Israel.

Wingate's Zionist sympathies eventually made the Mandatory authorities consider him a liability, and he was sent to action in Burma. He dreamed of returning to Palestine, though, and even had fantasies of leading the Israeli army. He died in 1944 in a plane crash in Burma. At his death he had been promoted to a major general.

For further information see: Leonard Mosley, *Gideon Goes to War* (London: A. Barker, [1955]); Christopher Sykes, *Orde Wingate: A Biography* (Cleveland, OH: World, 1959); Derek Tulloch, ed., *Wingate in Peace and War* (London: Macdonald, 1972).

John Fontaine

WOJAC. See **WORLD ORGANIZATION OF JEWS FROM ARAB COUNTRIES.**

WOODHEAD COMMISSION (1938). In June 1937, the Peel Commission* recommended that Palestine* be partitioned into a Jewish state, an Arab state, and an area to remain under British Mandatory* control. In December 1937, a four-member technical commission was appointed to investigate the feasibility of the recommendations. Headed by Sir John Woodhead, who had served in the Indian Civil Service and was later to be the governor of Bengal, the Woodhead Commission arrived in Palestine in April 1938. The commission was subjected to pressures from within the British government concerning the proper direction for British policy. The Colonial Office, headed by Secretary William Ormsby-Gore, who was known for his pro-Zionist* positions, contended that the British had to demonstrate resolve not to succumb to the pressures of terrorist threats and that any policy statement should help moderate Arab leadership. Furthermore, Britain had a responsibility to maintain its promises to the Jews. The Foreign Office, however, contended that Britain's major concern was strategic. It feared that a pro-Zionist policy would increase Arab support for the Axis powers.

The Woodhead Report was published in October 1938. It held that the Peel Commission's proposals were not feasible—primarily because it would leave a large Arab minority within the boundaries of a Jewish state that also would be surrounded by other Arab states. The commission offered two alternative proposals for partition. One would have reduced the size of the Jewish state by annexing an area south of Jerusalem* to the Arab state and including Galilee in a Mandatory territory. The second alternative would have left a Jewish state as a coastal strip. Because the commission could not reach agreement, it stated that it could not recommend boundaries for states created from the Mandatory territory. Its primary conclusion was that there were no feasible boundaries for self-supporting Arab and Jewish states in Palestine. Nevertheless, it suggested a number of partition plans. The Zionists rejected these ideas, and the government issued a White Paper on November 9, 1938, noting that partition was impracticable. On February 7, 1939, the British government convened the St. James Conference* in London to see if a solution could be developed through negotiations with the Arabs and the Jews. The St. James Conference convened in February 1939 but was unsuccessful. This led to a British White Paper of May 17, 1939.*

For further information see: Great Britain, Colonial Office, *Palestine Partition Commission Report* (London: H.M.S.O., October 1938). [Cmd. 5854]

Joseph E. Goldberg

WORLD ORGANIZATION OF JEWS FROM ARAB COUNTRIES (WOJAC). The World Organization of Jews from Arab Countries was founded by the leaders of immigrants' associations and communities of Jews originating from Arab countries in Israel and worldwide, headed by former Israeli Cabinet minister and member of Knesset* Mordechai Ben-Porat and by Leon Tamman, then chairman of the Sephardi Federation in Great Britain.* Delegates of Jews from Arab countries, Israel, and other states convened in Paris in November 1975 and passed a resolution to establish a roof-organization of Jews from Arab countries and their descendants living in Israel and throughout the world. Their aim was to raise the long-neglected issue of Jews from Arab countries and representing their interests before national and international forums, governments, and organizations and world public opinion to gain recognition of their rights and claims against their countries of origin.

It is an international, nongovernmental, and nonprofit organization. Membership is open to Jews originating from an Arab country and their descendants, as well as to any person identifying with the aims of the organization and participating in its activities.

Its main objectives are to focus attention on the recognition of the rights and claims of Jews from Arab countries for compensation from their countries of origin for the loss of spiritual, cultural, and material assets and significant private and communal property left behind in those countries when the Jews left the Arab countries, primarily to immigrate to Israel.

WORLD ZIONIST ORGANIZATION (WZO). The official organization of the Zionist* movement founded at the initiative of Theodor Herzl* at the First Zionist Congress in Basel, Switzerland, in August 1897. The World Zionist Organization conducted the political, economic, and settlement activities leading to the establishment of Israel. The right of membership in the Zionist organization was accorded to every Jew who subscribed to the organization's program—the Basle Program*—and who paid the shekel, the required dues payment. (The shekel was a biblical measure of weight by which pieces of silver and gold were used for money.) Each shekel holder who was at least eighteen years of age was entitled to elect delegates to the Zionist Congress or to be elected to Congress once having attained the age of twenty-four. Over the years, the center of the Zionist movement was shifted from place to place until it was transferred to Jerusalem.* Since 1952, the Zionist organization has functioned in the framework of the Status Law. In 1960, various changes were introduced in its constitution (which had been in force since 1899). In 1951, the Jerusalem Program* was adopted in addition to the Basle Program. This Jerusalem Program was subsequently superseded by the new Jerusalem Program of 1968.

The Zionist Congress is the supreme body of the Zionist organization. The Congress is empowered to elect the president, the chairman, the General Council and the members of the Zionist Executive, the Congress attorney, and the comptroller. The Congress deals with, and determines, all basic matters relating to the activities of the World Zionist Organization. It is composed of delegates elected in all countries, except Israel, where the Zionist parties in the country receive their representation in Congress on the basis of elections to the Knesset.* The Congress receives and discusses reports from the Zionist General Council and the Executive. The Congress met annually until 1901, when it was resolved to meet every two years. Subsequently, until 1939, it met every other year (except in the period of World War I). According to the constitution adopted in 1960, the Zionist Congress convenes every four years.

The Zionist General Council, which is elected by the Zionist Congress, functions in the period between Congresses and is empowered to deliberate and decide on all matters affecting the Zionist organization and its institutions, including the budget, with the exception of matters relegated solely to the authority of Congress. Its composition reflects the relative strength of forces in the Congress. The Zionist General Council supervises the activities of the Zionist Executive by means of its various committees.

The Zionist Executive is the executive arm of the World Zionist Organization and is elected by Congress for a period of four years. Some of its members are placed in charge of the various departments of the Executive; others serve as members without portfolio. The Executive reflects the relative strength of forces in the Congress.

The Zionist Executive is composed of thirty-one members, of whom twenty are in Israel and eleven in New York. The latter are known as ''the American Section.''

WZO. See **WORLD ZIONIST ORGANIZATION.**

Y

YAD VASHEM (THE HEROES' AND MARTYRS' AUTHORITY). The official Israeli authority to commemorate the heroes and martyrs who died in the Holocaust.* The name, meaning "monument" and "memorial," is derived from the Bible. The authority was created by an act of the Knesset* in 1953. It has archives and a library on the Nazi era and publishes material on the Holocaust. Among its buildings is a memorial hall, dedicated in 1961, in which there is a memorial flame, and on the floor are inscribed the names of the most notorious of the extermination camps.

YADIN, YIGAEL (Formerly Sukenik) (b. Jerusalem,* March 21, 1917; d. June 28, 1984). He was the son of the noted archaeologist Eliezer Lipa Sukenik. He joined the Haganah* at age fifteen. He left the Haganah in 1945 to pursue his education at the Hebrew University but returned at the time of preparations for Israel's independence. Yadin became chief of General Staff Branch of Haganah headquarters in 1947 and chief of operations of the Israel Defense Forces* (IDF) General Staff in 1948, a post he held during the War of Independence.* In 1949, he became chief of staff of the IDF at age thirty-two and began to develop the foundations for the reorganization of the IDF into a regular army. He served as one of Israel's negotiating team in the armistice negotiations at Rhodes.* Yadin resigned in December 1952 in protest over cuts in the military budget and to resume his research as an archaeologist. He received his Ph.D. in archaeology from the Hebrew University and later became professor of archaeology at that institution. From 1955 to 1958, Yadin directed the excavations at Hazor, and, from 1960 to 1961, he led explorations of the Judean Desert caves, where the Bar Kochba* documents were discovered. From 1963 to 1965, he directed the Masada* Expedition. Yadin was awarded the Israel Prize in Jewish Studies in

1956 and the Rothschild Science Prize in 1964. He is the author of numerous publications in the field of archaeology. After the Yom Kippur War,* he served as one of the members of the Agranat Commission,* appointed to look into Israel's state of readiness at the time of the outbreak of the war. In 1976, he decided to reenter public life and seek the position of prime minister, arguing that Israel urgently needed political and economic reforms. His announcement was greeted with popular enthusiasm since he was not of the group of politicians that Israelis had been forced to choose from for decades, nor had he been involved in the scandals that seemed to affect public figures. Yadin seemed to appeal to the Israeli public as a trusted and untainted, but fresh, political face. In 1976, he helped to form a new political party—Democratic Movement for Change. The party did well in the 1977 Knesset* election and joined the government coalition. Yadin served as deputy prime minister from 1977 to 1981 in the government led by Menachem Begin.*

For further information see: Moshe Ben-Shaul, *Generals of Israel* (Tel Aviv: Hadar Publishing House, 1968).

YAMIT. A settlement on the northern coast of the Sinai Peninsula,* close to the Gaza Strip,* built in the 1970s by the Israeli government as part of a string of settlements erected in the occupied territories* after the Six Day War.* The Labor government saw it as a major population center in Sinai. The towns and the farms in the area grew and flourished, in part, because of cheap labor and lack of crime. It was abandoned and leveled in 1982 in accord with the Egypt–Israel Peace Treaty.*

After the treaty was signed, there was considerable opposition to the withdrawal from Yamit. The first group to protest were businessmen and farmers living in Yamit who originally settled there in the 1970s with the encouragement and financial support of the government. Much to the chagrin of Gush Emunim,* their organized opposition dissolved, however, after the Israeli government offered them generous relocation and compensation benefits. Gush Emunim ("bloc of the faithful") was a group that believed settlement in the occupied territories ensured that those territories would remain part of the greater Land of Israel.

A group called the Movement to Halt the Retreat at Sinai, related to Gush Emunim, arose in the spring of 1981. The leadership of this movement consisted of Gush activists fearful that evacuation of settlements in the Sinai in return for peace would set a dangerous precedent for the West Bank* and the Gaza Strip. A number of rabbis committed to the idea that Yamit was an integral part of the Land of Israel believed the abandonment would interrupt the process of the messianic redemption.

The movement's primary objective was to halt withdrawal by appealing to public opinion. If this failed, they were prepared to engineer a clash between the government and the settlers opposing the withdrawal, the ramifications of which would inhibit the government from considering future evacuation of other settlements.

During the autumn of 1981, hundreds of settlers from the West Bank settled in Yamit, replacing those who had left. In September, the movement launched a countrywide petition campaign to prevent evacuation. It declared a goal of obtaining a million signatures. The goal was not met. In March 1982, a rally at the Western Wall* in Jerusalem* drew more than 40,000 opponents of evacuation.

The final stage in the fight to prevent the evacuation of Yamit was an attempt to concentrate 100,000 opponents in Yamit itself on April 22, the day the Israel Defense Forces* (IDF) were scheduled to complete the evacuation of the city. This attempt failed, as only several thousand people (mostly religious seminary, or yeshiva, students) appeared in Yamit to offer resistance to the army. Despite reports that extremist groups were ready to resist with arms if the operation was not terminated, the evacuation was completed by unarmed soldiers without serious injury.

Many of the evacuees formed a new movement called Shvut Sinai (Return to Sinai), dedicated to returning Jewish rule to the Sinai. Several groups belonging to this movement resettled across the border in the Gaza Strip.

The evacuation of Yamit had profound effects on movements like Gush Emunim. Two viewpoints arose out of this episode. Some militants believed their failure in preventing the evacuation lay in their failure to integrate their efforts with the views of the Israeli mainstream. They advocated a public outreach campaign to educate the general public concerning the fundamentalist ideology. The other view held that the fault lay in the undependability of the Israeli government and public in matters concerning redemption of the Land of Israel. This view advocated direct action and violence to achieve its goals. Both these viewpoints found their expression in the ensuing years.

For further information see: Gadi Wolfsfeld, "Collective Political Action and Media Strategy: The Case of Yamit," *Journal of Conflict Resolution* 28 (September 1984):363–81.

Monica M. Boudjouk

YARIV–SHEMTOV FORMULA. In 1975, Aharon Yariv and Victor Shemtov proposed what became known as the Yariv–Shemtov formula. The heart of the proposal was that "Israel is prepared to conduct negotiations with any Palestinian element that recognizes the State of Israel and United Nations Security Council Resolution 242,* and disavows actions of terror and sabotage." Yariv interpreted this to mean that proclaiming a halt to terrorism would be accompanied by practices that followed this statement. It would also have to declare that the articles of the Palestinian Covenant* that speak of the destruction of Israel are null and void.

YARMUK RIVER. The river originates in Syria* and flows westward between Jordan* and Syria for forty kilometers and joins the Jordan River* ten kilometers south of Lake Tiberias (Sea of Galilee*). Below the junction of the Yarmuk and the Jordan Rivers are the boundaries between Israel and Jordan and, farther below, between Jordan and the West Bank.*

The Yarmuk is a major source of water in the region. Given the salinity of the Jordan River and Lake Tiberias, the Yarmuk is a good source of fresh water for Jordan and has figured prominently in Jordan's plans to exploit the freshwater resources of the Jordan River basin. Jordan has long planned to construct a dam on the Yarmuk, called the Maqarin Dam, or the Al Waheda Dam (Unity Dam), as it is called now. Despite an agreement between Syria and Jordan concluded in 1953, later replaced by another agreement in 1987, no progress was made, as there was no agreement with Israel. The United States attempted to bring about an improvement in the general situation in the Middle East and, to this end, sent Eric Johnston* in 1953 to discuss with Israel and some Arab states the development of the water resources of the Jordan River valley. After several visits to the Middle East and discussions with Arab and the Israeli governments, Johnston revised his earlier-presented plan known as the Unified Plan. The revised Unified Plan was reported to provide water to Lebanon* from the Hasbani, to Syria from the Banias, the Jordan, and the Yarmuk, to Jordan from the Yarmuk and the Jordan, and to Israel from all waters of the Jordan River except said withdrawals for its "unconditional use." The revised Unified Plan was never formally accepted by any of the parties.

In 1966, Yugoslavian consultants recommended the construction of the Maqarin Dam. In 1978, a feasibility study of the Maqarin was carried out by Harza Overseas Engineering Company. This project could not receive funding from international financial agencies due to lack of satisfactory agreements on water sharing. The project was revived again in the 1980s under the name of Al Waheda (Unity) Dam, but by this time a new actor, the West Bank, entered the picture. Once again no progress could be made due to lack of agreement among the riparians.

For further information see: Samir N. Saliba, *The Jordan River Dispute* (The Hague: Marinus Nijhoff, 1968); Georgiana G. Stevens, *Jordan River Partition* (Stanford: Stanford University, Hoover Institute of War, Revolution and Peace, 1965).

YASIN, ALI. A member of Fatah,* he was considered a moderate in the Palestinian movement. He resided in Kuwait from 1965 to 1978, where he was the Palestine Liberation Organization* (PLO) representative. He came to Kuwait from Egypt,* where he had earned a law degree from Cairo University.

Ali Yasin was shot to death on June 15, 1978, in Kuwait when he answered his door. Fatah accused "elements in Iraq" of being responsible for the murder.

Joseph E. Goldberg

YASSIN, SHEIK AHMED ISMAIL (b. Ashkelon). Founder of the militant Islamic group HAMAS.* He is a quadriplegic. In 1984, he was sentenced to thirteen years in prison for possession of arms but was released a year later in a prisoner exchange. He began serving a life term in 1989 for issuing orders to kidnap and kill four Israeli soldiers.

Nancy Hasanian

YEAR OF DECISION. A term used to refer to the fact that the year 1971 might be a year of decision in the Arab–Israeli conflict. In a press conference, on December 23, 1970, U.S. secretary of state William Rogers* noted: "We think 1971 may be a year of decision in the Middle East. We think the climate is very good."

Generally, the reference is to Egyptian president Anwar Sadat's* proclamation of 1971 as a year of decision. In a July 23, 1971, speech, delivered at the inaugural meeting of the General National Congress of the Arab Socialist Union meeting in Cairo, Sadat declared 1971 as a "year of decision" that would end with peace or war and said that, if war was necessary, he was prepared to sacrifice 1 million men. He repeated this theme on a number of occasions later in the year.

Sadat's proclaimed year of decision ended quietly with no action on his war-or-peace deadline. In a speech on January 13, 1972, he explained that the lack of concrete action was a result of the Indo–Pakistani War, which had created a "fog" requiring a reassessment since the Soviet Union was distracted by its assistance to India. Thus, the planned military action against Israel had to be canceled.

YESHA. Acronym of Yehuda, Shomron, and Aza, the Hebrew for Judea,* Samaria,* and Gaza.* Yesha also translates as "salvation." Name adopted by the YESHA Council of Jewish Communities in Judea, Samaria, and Gaza.

YISHUV. The Jewish community in Palestine* in the period of the British Mandate.* The term means "settlement." The *yishuv* was an autonomous political body that gained valuable experience in political procedures and self-rule. A political elite developed, civil servants gained experience, and political parties were established and developed procedures for working together. An educational system was established. The Histadrut* was founded and became a major political, economic, and social force. A self-defense capability was created and became the basis of the Israel Defense Forces.* The Yishuv provided the foundation for the governmental institutions and political processes of Israel after independence.

For further information see: Y. Barnai, *The Jews of Palestine in the Eighteenth Century: Under the Patronage of the Istanbul Committee of Officials for Palestine* (Tuscaloosa: University of Alabama Press, 1992); Sherman Lieber, *Mystics and Missionaries: The Jews in Palestine, 1799–1840* (Salt Lake City: University of Utah Press, 1992).

YOM KIPPUR WAR (1973). On October 6, 1973 (Yom Kippur), Egypt* and Syria* launched a coordinated attack on Israeli positions on the Suez Canal* and Golan Heights.* Taking Israel by surprise, the Arab armies crossed the Suez Canal, secured a beachhead in the Sinai Peninsula,* and advanced into the Golan Heights while—during the first three days of combat—a skeletal Israeli force sought to withstand the invasion until additional troops could be mobilized.

On October 6, 1973, Syrian and Egyptian forces began a massive artillery barrage along both fronts, followed within five minutes by the first crossings of the Suez Canal and tank ditches on the Golan Heights.

In the final hours before the war, Israel had detected the scale of the buildup and began to mobilize, but a plan to launch a preemptive air strike was halted.

Egypt crossed the Suez Canal with five infantry divisions, three mechanized divisions, two armored brigades, 150 missile batteries, and a number of independent brigades, and the first bridgehead on the Israeli side was emplaced within fifteen minutes. The Egyptian artillery barrage was at the rate of 175 shells per second launched from 2,000 artillery pieces. The Egyptian Second Army struck in the northern part of the canal, and the Third Army* in the southern portion. Against this force, Israel had only 208 tanks in three brigades, although most were held farther east as a reserve.

Egypt not only penetrated the Bar-Lev Line* but managed to seize almost the entire length on the east bank of the canal and proceeded to move further into the Sinai, all with a loss of only 208 soldiers.

Not all Israeli fortifications along the line fell instantly; indeed, some resisted for nearly seven days, such as the "Quay" fortification near Port Tewfiq. Only one fortification far in the north, known as "Budapest," held out for the entire war.

By the second day of the war, Defense Minister Moshe Dayan* ordered Israeli forces to retreat to higher ground and pass through the mountains of Jebel Maara and Jebel Yalek. General Shmuel Gonen accepted the order but withdrew far less extensively. Reserve Major General Ariel Sharon,* activated and already in place in the central sector of the Sinai Peninsula front by the second day, unsuccessfully requested an immediate counterattack—to cross to the west bank of the canal in the unguarded seam between the Second and Third Egyptian Armies.

While the Israelis regrouped to the east, the Egyptians consolidated their positions on the two banks of the canal. On the third day, October 8, Israel launched its first counterattack, which was unsuccessful. Reserve Major General Avraham Adan, activated and already in place in the northern sector of the canal by the second day, launched the counterattack with Sharon's forces in the central sector. Adan's counterattack ran directly into the bulk of the massing Egyptian Second Army's armor bridgehead and suffered heavy casualties and was forced to withdraw farther to the east. Sharon's force was ordered first south and then, when Adan's offensive failed, to the north in reserve. With Adan's forces depleted and Sharon's forces in reserve, Israel's defense positions were in disarray. Command problems arose between Gonen and Sharon.

As a result, on October 9, against orders, Sharon launched a counterattack in the south against the Third Army in the area of the Chinese Farm,* the vulnerable gap that divided command between the Egyptian Second and Third Armies. Adan, farther to the north, successfully regrouped and began to stabilize the line. October 9, then, was the day of farthest Egyptian penetration and the day that Israel's counterattack began. Sharon's actions on this occasion led the temporary commander of the Southern Command, Lieutenant General Bar-Lev,* who replaced Gonen on October 9, to request the dismissal of Sharon.

There was also controversy on the Egyptian side. On October 10, the First Egyptian Mechanized Brigade advanced south toward Ras Sudar, out of range of the protective surface-to-air-missile (SAM)* umbrella. Israeli major general Yeshayahu Gavish, in command of the southern sector, understood the vulnerability of the Egyptian unit and ordered an Israeli air attack, which obliterated the Egyptian force. The Egyptian chief of staff, Saad El-Shazli,* used this incident to oppose a precipitous advance in the Sinai that would outrace the missile umbrella. In opposition, the minister of war, Ahmed Ismail Ali, pressed Shazli to move faster and farther.

By October 10, Israeli forces began to contemplate the crossing of the canal. Early Egyptian gains in the war had emplaced 1,000 Egyptian tanks on the eastern side of the canal. For this reason, Israel's General Staff hesitated to push to the canal and to cross for fear of not leaving enough Israeli forces between Egypt's army and Israel. By October 12, a crossing plan was formulated that entailed logistical risks that defied accepted military doctrine. Still, the General Staff, aware of the massing of Egyptian armor on the east bank in preparation for a new thrust, postponed the counterattack plan and instead ordered Israeli forces to assume defensive positions to block the expected Egyptian attack. Only after repelling a new Egyptian thrust would the Israelis begin a counteroffensive. Egypt's attack was planned for the central sector, the most protected by the SAM umbrella, opposite Sharon's forces. On October 14, the Egyptian attack began, but the Israelis had prepared and were waiting. The canal zone became the site of the largest tank-against-tank battle ever fought, and, as the day wore on, the tide of battle turned, and the Israelis began to assume the initiative for the first time. Israel lost 10 tanks that day, and Egypt lost nearly 300, revealing the extent to which the Israeli army had been able to recover from the disarray of the first days of the war.

A day later, on the night of October 15, Israeli forces under Sharon pushed through to the Chinese Farm in the seam between the Second and Third Armies and began to approach the canal in the area of Deversoir on the northern coast of the Great Bitter Lake, the location where Israeli forces had chosen to cross. By early morning of October 16, the first Israeli forces crossed the canal. By 8:00 A.M. on the sixteenth, the Israeli bridgehead already included some tanks and extended three miles inward on the west bank of the canal. However, the tenuous Israeli hold on the east bank corridor near the Chinese Farm between the Egyptian Second and Third Armies led the General Staff to conclude that the crossing operation was too vulnerable to greatly expand the bridgehead and ordered Israeli forces on the east bank of the canal to widen the axes and wait for the arrival of a pontoon bridge to cross the canal with greater force, rather than precipitously expand along the west bank. At this point, the conflict between Generals Shazli and Ali again erupted, with Shazli demanding a withdrawal of the bulk of the forces to the west bank of the canal, while Ali believed Egyptian forces should stay where they were.

A dispute also raged at the same time on the Israeli side of the line. Sharon continued to expand the bridgehead on the west bank, while the General Staff believed that the corridor supplying the bridgehead was irresponsibly narrow and needed first to be widened before committing too many troops to the west bank efforts. Sharon continued to build up forces on the west bank of the canal. He sought and destroyed SAM batteries to reopen the skies for Israeli airpower and exploited the confusion of the Egyptians. Sharon expanded the bridgehead in contravention of orders. Finally, on the night of October 17, Adan's forces also crossed the canal, but only after they had spent an extra day widening the corridor, which Adan claims was to have been Sharon's task. Because of the controversy, Bar-Lev again requested Sharon's removal but was again turned down.

By October 21, Adan's force had moved far south, taking territory near Suez City and encircling the Egyptian Third Army. Sharon's forces were moving north and west, reaching Ismailiya in the north and threatening to cut off the Egyptian Second Army and reaching Kilometer post 101 on the road to Cairo. Sharon's advance forces had already taken positions as close as sixty-six kilometers to Cairo.

Realizing the magnitude of the loss, understanding that the Third and, almost, the Second Armies were cut off, and sensing that Israeli forces were advancing rapidly without resistance toward Cairo, Egypt and the Soviet Union rapidly moved diplomatically to install a cease-fire before the remaining Egyptian footholds on the east bank of the canal were endangered. This was psychologically important for Egypt. The cease-fire went into effect on the evening of October 22. The Third Army, attempting to break out of its isolation in the south, tried to rush across the canal after the cease-fire, but the ensuing fighting only worsened their situation, letting Sharon move farther north and Israeli forces farther south of Suez. The final cease-fire took effect on October 24. Israel held 1,000 square miles in Africa.

Israeli forces in the north were caught by surprise as well on October 6. With 1,500 tanks and 1,000 artillery pieces, Syria launched the war at the same moment the Egyptians did. Within hours, Israel's position on Mount Hermon* fell to the Syrians. Because Israel was without aerial surveillance, due to Syria's thick wall of SAMs, the loss of electronic surveillance left Israel blind.

Several days before the war, Israel's northern commander, Yitzhak Hofi, had sensed trouble and independently began mobilizing some of his reserve forces. As a consequence, the Israeli army on the Golan Heights numbered two brigades, with about 170 tanks, instead of the usual 60.

Within one day of the start of the war, 90 percent of the Israeli brigade holding the southern portion of the Golan was destroyed, and its commander was killed. On the night of October 7, Syrian forces captured all but a small salient of the entire southern portion of the Golan Heights. In the north, the Israeli Seventh Brigade faced the Syrian Third Armored Division. The 100 Israeli tanks fared slightly better than the force to the south, but by October 10, the Israeli brigade, reduced to a mere 7 tanks, was preparing to withdraw.

On October 9, the first Israeli reserve forces mobilized and moved into position in the north, with one battalion moving to join the beleaguered Seventh Brigade. At dawn of October 11, Israeli forces surveyed the valley and discovered that while they were left with seven tanks, they had eliminated more than 500 Syrian tanks in the process.

Also on October 9, Israeli forces began to reestablish themselves in the southern sector, under Colonel Ori Orr and Major General Moshe Peled. The Syrian southern sector commander, General Jehani, realized that his flank to the north was vulnerable as long as Israel continued to hold its positions. Thus, he chose to consolidate his hold and pull back so as not to expose his logistics line. This move allowed Israel to rapidly regain territory in the south. By midday on October 10, only two days after Israel was reduced to a defending force of seven tanks in the north, Israel had moved so rapidly that it began to reestablish its hold over the entirety of the territory Syria held only four days earlier. The Israeli counteroffensive took the Syrians by such surprise that Syrian president Assad* called President Sadat* of Egypt to plead for a counteroffensive in the Sinai to place pressure on the Israel Defense Forces* (IDF). This plea explains why Ali and Sadat refused to accede to Shazli's demands that the Egyptian army move back to the west bank of the canal and secure proper defensive positions and why, despite the lack of sufficient SAM protection, the Egyptian army launched the counteroffensive on October 14 that eventually brought the entire Egyptian army to the brink of disaster.

On the night of the October 10, the Israeli General Staff decided to launch a counteroffensive into Syria the next morning. By early October 14, Syrian positions were beginning to collapse, and Assad issued pleas to Iraq* and Jordan* to help. One Iraqi division was quickly loaded onto transports and brought to bear in the southern sector of the fighting near Tel al Mal and Tel Maschara. In addition to Syrian armor, hundreds of Iraqi and, later, Jordanian tanks littered the battlefield. The Iraqis tried three offensives, but the stiffness of their tactics and lack of coordination with other units led them to disaster. Another Iraqi division was also damaged in eastern Syria by the Israeli air force as it tried to cross Syria to join the war.

By October 20, the Syrians were retreating to their capital as Israeli forces approached within twelve kilometers of Damascus. The next day, Israeli forces recaptured a series of Syrian peaks on Mount Hermon, and, by the twenty-second, the highest Syrian peak of the Hermon had been captured. The Golani forces tasked with taking the Israeli peak of Hermon fared far worse, and it was not recaptured until October 22, at a cost of fifty-one killed.

On the evening of October 22, a cease-fire went into effect. It had been a costly war. In two weeks, Syria had lost 1,150 tanks and nearly 3,500 troops. Israel lost 772 troops and 250 tanks.

Ultimately, Israel stopped the Arab forces and reversed the initial Arab successes; it retook the Golan Heights and some additional territory, while Egypt and Israel traded some territory along the Suez Canal following Israel's crossing of the canal and its advance toward Cairo. The United Nations Security Council adopted Resolution 338,* which called for an immediate cease-fire and the implementation of United Nations Security Council Resolution 242* and explicitly required negotiations "between the parties." Subsequently, U.S. secretary of state Henry Kissinger* negotiated the Israel–Egypt Disengagement of Forces Agreement* of 1974 and the Sinai II Accords* of 1975 between Egypt and Israel, as well as the Israel–Syria Disengagement of Forces Agreement of 1974.* These agreements involved Israeli withdrawals from territory in the Suez Canal zone in the two agreements with Egypt and in the Golan Heights in the arrangement with Syria. The Yom Kippur War resulted in an Israeli military victory, but that victory was accompanied by significant political and diplomatic disappointments and by domestic economic, psychological, and political stress. In purely tangible terms, the 1973 war had perhaps the most far-reaching effects on Israel of any conflict to that time. Personnel losses and overall casualty rates were substantial. The mobilization of the largest part of the civilian reserve army of several hundred thousand caused dislocations in agriculture and industry. Tourism and diamond sales fell, and the sea passage to Eilat* was blockaded at the Bab el Mandeb.* Numerous other aspects of the war added to the economic costs of the conflict, and austerity was the logical result. At the same time, Israel's international position deteriorated. Although it was not the initiator of the war, Israel was condemned, and numerous states (particularly in Africa) broke diplomatic relations. The ruptures with Africa were a disappointment, but a shift in the attitudes and policies of the European states and Japan* was perhaps more significant. The Arab oil weapon* was utilized and proved successful in altering the political and diplomatic situation. The war also increased Israel's dependence on the United States. No other country could provide Israel—or was prepared to do so—with the vast quantities of modern and sophisticated arms required for war or the political and moral support necessary to negotiate peace. The cease-fire of October 22, 1973, was followed by what Israelis often refer to as the "wars of the Jews"—internal political conflicts and disagreements. The initial domestic political effect of the war was to bring about the postponement to December 31 of the elections originally scheduled for October 30 and the suspension of political campaigning and electioneering for the duration of the conflict. The war not only interrupted the campaign for the Knesset* elections but also provided new issues for the opposition to raise, including the conduct of the war and the "mistakes" that preceded it. In November 1973, the government appointed a Commission of Inquiry,* headed by Chief Justice Shimon Agranat* of the Supreme Court, to investigate the events leading up to the hostilities (including information concerning the enemy's moves and intentions), the assessments and decisions of military and civilian bodies in regard to this information, and the Israel Defense Forces deployments, preparedness for battle, and actions in the first phase of the fighting.

For further information see: Frank Aker, *October 1973: The Arab–Israeli War* (Hamden, CT: Archon Books, 1985); Peter Allen, *The Yom Kippur War* (New York: Charles Scribner's Sons, 1982); Arab Republic of Egypt, *International Symposium on the 1973 October War* (Cairo, 1975); Hassan el Badri, Taha el Magdoub, and Mohammed Dia el din Zohdy, *The Ramadan War, 1973* (Dunn Loring, VA: T. N. Dupuy Associates, 1978); Uri Dan, *Sharon's Bridgehead* (Tel Aviv: E. L. Special Edition, 1975); Trevor N. Dupuy, *Elusive Victory: The Arab–Israeli Wars, 1947–1974* (New York: Harper and Row, 1978); Mohamed Heikal, *The Road to Ramadan* (New York: Quadrangle, 1975); Chaim Herzog, *The War of Atonement* (Boston: Little, Brown, 1974); Edgar O'Ballance, *No Victor, No Vanquished: The Yom Kippur War* (San Rafael, CA: Presidio, 1978); Dan Ofry, *The Yom Kippur War* (Tel Aviv: Zohar, 1974); Ze'ev Schiff, *October Earthquake: Yom Kippur 1973* (Tel Aviv: University Publishing Projects, 1974); Saad El Shazly, *The Crossing of the Suez* (San Francisco: American Mideast Research, 1980); "Sunday Times" Insight Team, *The Yom Kippur War* (London: Andre Deutsch, 1975); "The October War and Its Aftermath," *Journal of Palestine Studies,* 3, no. 2 (Winter 1974); Louis Williams, ed., *Military Aspects of the Israeli–Arab Conflict* (Tel Aviv: University Publishing Projects, 1975).

David Wurmser

YOUNG AFFAIR. On July 26, 1979, Andrew Young, Jr., the U.S. representative to the United Nations, met with a representative of the Palestine Liberation Organization* (PLO) in contravention of the expressed U.S. policy to have no dealings with the PLO until and unless it accepted Israel's right to exist and right to secure, recognized borders.

In January 1977, Andrew Young, a fourth-term congressman from Georgia and a close adviser to President Jimmy Carter,* accepted President Carter's nomination to be U.S. ambassador to the United Nations. Ambassador Young proved to be an outspoken interpreter of U.S. policy.

In July 1979, the Security Council was considering a resolution dealing with Palestinian* rights that included a reference to United Nations Security Council Resolution 242* and language on the right of Palestinians to practice self-determination and to have an independent state. Ambassador Young was scheduled to assume the presidency of the Security Council on behalf of the United States for the month of August. The United States sought a consensus to postpone debate on the resolution in order to avoid having to cast a veto over the statehood issue, in the hope that a milder resolution could be produced, to allow Robert Strauss,* the special U.S. negotiator, more time with the intensive peace negotiations he was conducting and because the White House was preoccupied with domestic matters.

Ambassador Young discussed the issue with Kuwait's permanent representative to the United Nations, Abdulla Yaccoub Bishara, because Kuwait at that time was a member of the Security Council. Bishara indicated that the PLO's position on a postponement was critical and suggested that Young meet directly with a representative of the PLO, Zehdi Labib Terzi. Young responded that this was not possible in light of official policy but apparently agreed to "drop by the house" in the evening to learn what Arab League* members had decided in the course of the day.

On July 26, 1979, Young visited Bishara's apartment in New York and, finding Terzi present, met with him. The meeting lasted fifteen to thirty minutes, and, toward the end of the session, they were joined by the Syrian* delegate, Hammoud el-Choufi. As a result of this and other efforts, the United States succeeded in obtaining a postponement of debate until August 23, 1979.

On August 13, 1979, when news of the meeting was leaked, Young stated that he had not known that Terzi would be at Bishara's apartment, that he "arrived unexpectedly," and that they had "an exchange of courtesies, no more."

Later in the day, however, Young went to see the Israeli ambassador, Yehuda Blum, and gave him a more complete account of his meeting with Terzi. Young explained, "I didn't want them [the Israelis] to blame the State Department for what I had done and which they might fit into a conspiracy theory." He further stated that "I didn't tell State because the less they knew, the less they would be responsible."

Young's report to Blum led to Israel's lodging a formal protest on the ground that the meeting violated the United States' repeated pledge to Israel, first given in 1975 at the time of the Sinai II Accords,* not to have any dealings with the PLO unless and until the PLO accepted Israel's right to exist and right to secure, recognized borders. Secretary of State Cyrus Vance* immediately assured Israel that Young had acted on his own and that there was no change in U.S. policy.

Secretary Vance expressed his "displeasure" to Young for his action, noting that it violated long-standing American policy toward the PLO. His criticism was joined by a number of powerful voices, including that of Senator Robert C. Byrd, the majority leader, who demanded Young's removal from office.

On August 15, 1979, Young bowed to the furor and tendered his resignation to President Carter. In his letter, Young stated that he had "always acted in behalf of what [he] felt was the best interest of our nation, though often it has been interpreted to the contrary," and that it was "extremely embarrassing that my actions, however well intended, may have hampered the peace process."

Reaction to the meeting and Young's resignation was predictable. Israel said that it had considered itself offended by Young's action but had not demanded his resignation. Israel was more concerned that the meeting might mark a "serious shift in U.S. policy." Yasser Arafat* said that Young was "pushed to resign" because "he believed in the just cause of the Palestinian people." Terzi stated that the United States, by "succumbing to Zionist* pressure," had proved that it "does not enjoy freedom of action at the United Nations" and had "disqualified itself from playing an even-handed role in the Middle East."

Richard G. R. Schickele

Z

ZINGER, YOEL. A legal adviser in Israel's Ministry of Foreign Affairs who was involved in the Oslo talks* and subsequent negotiations concerning the Gaza and Jericho first* plan.

ZION. A term used by the Hebrew prophets to refer to Jerusalem* as a spiritual symbol. As a symbol of all of the Land of Israel, of the Holy Land,* it became central in the religious life of Jews outside Israel in the Diaspora* and eventually became the basis of Zionism.*

ZIONISM. A term coined by Nathan Birnbaum* in 1890 for the movement seeking the return of the Jewish people to Palestine.* After 1896, Zionism referred to the political movement founded by Theodor Herzl* seeking a Jewish National Home* in Palestine. The term is derived from Mount Zion,* one of the hills of Jerusalem.* Zion came to symbolize for the Jews their desire to return to their homeland at least as far back as the Babylonian exile in the sixth century B.C. Psalm 137 says: "By the waters of Babylon, there we sat down and wept, when we remembered Zion." In the latter part of the nineteenth century, the Eastern European movement that promoted settlement in the Land of Israel called itself Hibbat Zion* (Love of Zion). Theodor Herzl adopted it to refer to his political movement, which sought the return of the Jews to the Holy Land.* See also POLITICAL ZIONISM.

For further information see: Shlomo Avineri, *The Making of Modern Zionism: The Intellectual Origins of the Jewish State* (New York: Basic Books, 1986); Ben Halpern, *The Idea of the Jewish State,* 2d ed. (Cambridge: Harvard University Press, 1970); David Vital, *The Origins of Zionism* (New York: Oxford University Press, 1980); David Vital,

Zionism: The Formative Years (New York: Oxford University Press, 1982); David Vital, *Zionism: The Crucial Phase* (New York: Oxford University Press, 1987).

ZIONISM IS RACISM. See **UNITED NATIONS GENERAL ASSEMBLY RESOLUTION 3379.**

ZIONIST CONGRESS. See **WORLD ZIONIST ORGANIZATION.**

Chronology

1800 B.C.E.	Abraham (Ibrahim) migrated from Mesopotamia to Canaan. Jewish and Islamic traditions hold Abraham to be the father of the Jews and the Arabs through his sons Isaac (Isak) and Ishmael (Ismail).
70 C.E.	Destruction of the second Jewish Commonwealth by the Roman Empire. Beginning of the Jewish Diaspora.
135	Failure of Bar Kochba revolt against Rome; Jews are expelled from "Palestine," a name given to Judea by Rome.
632	Mohammed dies. Muslim Umayyad Dynasty begins conquests of vast territories from Spain to Central Asia.
691	Mosque of Omar, the Dome of the Rock, constructed in Jerusalem.
1099	Coastal Palestine seized by the Crusaders; "Latin Kingdom of Jerusalem" established.
1187	Battle of Hittin; Saladin takes Jerusalem from the Crusaders.
1516–1918	Ottoman rule over Palestine.

1860–1904		Life of Theodor Herzl.
1882		Beginning of first aliyah to Palestine. First group of Hibbat Zion arrive at Jaffa. Britain occupies Egypt.
1888		Constantinople Treaty provides for international transit of Suez Canal.
1894		Dreyfus trial in France.
1896		Theodore Herzl publishes *Der Judenstaat.*
1897		The First Zionist Congress meets in Basle, Switzerland. The World Zionist Organization is created.
1901		Jewish National Fund is established.
1904		Herzl dies.
1909		Founding of Tel Aviv.
1914		World War I begins. Egypt declared a British Protectorate.
1915	July–1916 March	Hussein–McMahon correspondence promises Sherif Hussein an independent Arab state in return for Arab support against Ottoman Turkey in World War I.
1916	May 16	Sykes–Picot Agreement, dividing Ottoman lands among Allied powers. Palestine to be internationalized under British supervision.
	June 5	Arab Revolt, led by Amir Feisal, with the aid of T. E. Lawrence, begins.
1917	November 2	Balfour Declaration published, suggesting a "national home" for the Jewish people in Palestine.
	December	British forces conquer Palestine from Ottoman Empire. Allenby captures Jerusalem.
1918	June	Declaration to the Seven.
1919		Weizmann–Feisal correspondence. Paris Peace Conference. Palestine to become a British Mandate. King–Crane Commission sent to region.
1920		San Remo Conference grants British Mandate for Palestine.

	July	Feisal expelled from Syria by French; Arab Nationalist Congress proclaims Feisal king of Greater Syria.
1920–21		Arab attacks on Jewish areas of Jerusalem and Jaffa.
1921	March	Transjordan becomes separate entity within Palestine Mandate; Abdullah established as emir.
	March	Haganah formed.
	April	Hajj Amin al-Husseini appointed grand mufti and head of the Supreme Moslem Council by British high commissioner, Sir Herbert Samuel.
1921–22		Cairo Conference.
		Haycraft investigation.
1922		Britain gives Egypt internal independence.
	June	British (Churchill) White Paper reaffirms Balfour Declaration; limits Jewish immigration.
1922	July	Palestine Mandate ratified by League of Nations. Includes Balfour Declaration.
1922	September	Transjordan exempted from Balfour Declaration provisions.
1924		Adolf Hitler writes *Mein Kampf.*
1925	June	Hebrew University opens.
1929		Arab riots in Hebron and Jerusalem against Jews.
1930		Shaw Commission Report. Hope-Simpson Report. British issue Passfield White Paper limiting Jewish immigration into Palestine and Jewish land sales.
1931	February	MacDonald letter negates White Paper provisions.
1936		Outbreak of Arab Revolt in Palestine. Farouk becomes king of Egypt.
1936	April	Arab Higher Committee formed.
1937		Peel Commission Report; first proposal to partition Palestine.

1939	May 17	British White Paper further limits Jewish immigration and Zionist land purchases; signals shift of Britain's Palestine policy toward a pro-Arab orientation.
1942	May	Biltmore Program promulgated by Zionists at Biltmore Conference in New York.
1944	February	Menachem Begin, commander of Irgun Zvai Leumi, proclaims revolt against Britain.
	November 6	Lord Moyne assassinated in Cairo.
1945	March 22	Arab League founded.
	November	Anglo-American Committee of Inquiry established.
1945–46		Sharp increase in Jewish–Arab communal tensions in Palestine; resumption of British–Jewish conflict over immigration and other Mandatory policies.
1946	May	Report of the Anglo-American Committee of Inquiry. Independent Kingdom of Transjordan created; Abdullah becomes king.
	July 22	British headquarters in King David Hotel, Jerusalem, bombed.
1947	February 14	British foreign secretary announces that his government has decided to turn the Palestine problem over to the United Nations.
	April 28	Opening of United Nations General Assembly special session on Palestine.
	May	United Nations Special Committee on Palestine (UNSCOP) created.
	August 31	UNSCOP reports to General Assembly.
	November 29	United Nations (UN) adopts Palestine partition plan in General Assembly Resolution 181 (II), which calls for the establishment of both Jewish and Arab states in Palestine. Arabs are opposed; United States and USSR are in support.

1947–1948	December 1947–May 1948	Intense Jewish–Arab communal warfare in Palestine.
1948	January	Arab Liberation Army enters Palestine.
	March 19	United States proposes UN trusteeship in Palestine.
	April 9	Jewish attack on Deir Yassin.
	April 13	Arab attack on bus convoy to Mount Scopus.
	May	Termination of British Mandate over Palestine.
	May 14	Israel proclaims its independence. Truman extends de facto recognition. David Ben-Gurion becomes first prime minister of Israel. Beginning of first Arab–Israeli War.
	May 17	USSR extends full recognition to Israel.
	September 17	UN mediator Count Folke Bernadotte is assassinated in Jerusalem.
	December 11	UN General Assembly adopts Resolution 194.
1949		Israel signs Armistice Agreements with Transjordan, Egypt, Syria, and Lebanon.
	January 29	Great Britain extends de facto recognition to Israel.
	January 31	United States extends full recognition to Israel and Transjordan.
	February 24	Egypt and Israel sign Armistice Agreement at Rhodes.
	March 23	Israel and Lebanon sign armistice.
	April 3	Israel and Jordan sign armistice.
	May 11	Israel admitted to the United Nations.
	July 20	Israel and Syria sign armistice.
	December	Abdullah annexes that part of Palestine occupied by Arab Legion (West Bank) and East Jerusalem and changes Transjordan to Jordan.
1950	April 24	Jordanian Parliament ratifies annexation of West Bank and East Jerusalem.

	April 27	Great Britain recognizes Jordanian annexation of West Bank and East Jerusalem.
	May 25	Tripartite Declaration (Britain, France, and United States) regulates arms to the Middle East.
	July 5	Knesset approves Law of Return.
1951	July 20	King Abdullah assassinated in Jerusalem by Palestinian nationalist; his son Talal becomes king.
1952		Arafat among the organizers of Palestinian Students' Union in Cairo.
	July 23	Free Officers coup overthrows Egyptian monarchy; Muhammad Naguib becomes leader; Farouk abdicates on July 26, 1952.
	August 11	King Talal is removed from the throne and replaced by his son Hussein in Jordan.
1953		David Ben-Gurion resigns as prime minister and moves to Sde Boker in the Negev.
	May	Hussein formally assumes throne of Jordan.
	June 18	Republic of Egypt declared.
	October 14	Israeli troops attack Kibya, Jordan.
	November	Moshe Sharett becomes prime minister of Israel, replacing David Ben-Gurion.
1954		Johnston Plan for sharing Jordan River water proposed. Moshe Dayan appointed chief of staff of Israel Defense Forces (IDF). Nasser becomes prime minister and president of Egypt.
	July	Lavon affair.
1955	February 28	Israel raids Gaza Strip in retaliation for guerrilla activity against Israel.
	August 26	Secretary of State John Foster Dulles proposes plan to end Arab–Israeli conflict.
	September	Announcement of Czechoslovakia–Egypt arms deal.

	November	David Ben-Gurion again becomes prime minister of Israel.
1956	March 1	King Hussein of Jordan dismisses British general Glubb.
	July	Nasser declares nationalization of the Suez Canal Co.; Suez crisis begins.
	October 29	Israel invades Sinai Peninsula.
	October 31	British and French bomb Egyptian airfields.
	November 5	Britain and France invade Suez Canal zone.
	November 6–7	Britain, France, and Israel agree to cease-fire.
	December	Anglo-French withdrawal from Suez completed. Replaced by United Nations Emergency Force (UNEF) troops.
1957	January 5	Eisenhower Doctrine announced.
	January 9	Anthony Eden resigns as British prime minister.
	March	Egypt agrees to deployment of UNEF on border between Gaza Strip and Israel and at Sharm el-Sheikh. Congress approves Eisenhower Doctrine.
1958	February	United Arab Republic (UAR) of Egypt and Syria created.
	July	Civil war in Lebanon.
	July 14	Revolution in Iraq.
1961	September 29	Syria withdraws from UAR.
1962	September	United States announces first direct sale of American weapons (Hawk missiles) to Israel.
1963	June	Ben-Gurion retires; Levi Eshkol becomes prime minister of Israel.
1964	January	Palestine Liberation Organization (PLO) is created in Cairo; Ahmed Shukairi becomes first chairman.
	May	First Palestine National Council (PNC) meets in Jerusalem.

	June	Israel's National Water Carrier begins operation; crisis erupts over Jordan River waters.
1965	January 1	Fatah is established and launches its first attack against Israel.
	May 31–June 4	Second PNC is held in Cairo.
1966	January	Golda Meir resigns as Israel's foreign minister; succeeded by Abba Eban.
	February	General Jadid leads coup in Syria.
	April	Clashes between Syria and Israel.
	May 20–24	Third PNC meets in Gaza.
	November	Egypt and Syria sign defense pact.
	November 13	Israel responds to killing of Israelis with attack at es-Samu.
1967	May 13	USSR tells Egypt of impending Israeli attack on Syria.
	May 17	Nasser declares alert, remilitarizes Sinai.
	May 18	Nasser ends UNEF presence in Sinai.
	May 22	Nasser asks for withdrawal of UNEF troops.
	May 23	Nasser announces blockade of Strait of Tiran, thereby closes Gulf of Aqaba to Israeli shipping.
	May 30	Egypt and Jordan sign defense pact. Arabs and Israel mobilize for war.
	June	Moshe Dayan becomes defense minister of Israel.
	June 5–10	Six Day War. Israel captures West Bank and East Jerusalem from Jordan, the Sinai Peninsula and Gaza Strip from Egypt, and the Golan Heights from Syria.
	August	Arab Summit at Khartoum declares "three noes"—no recognition, no negotiation, no peace with Israel.
	November 22	UN Security Resolution 242 is adopted.
	November 23	Gunnar Jarring appointed UN special representative.
	December	Jarring mission begins.

	December 24	Ahmed Shukairi resigns as head of PLO.
1968		PLO charter redrafted.
	March 21	Israel attacks Karameh.
	July	Coup in Iraq. President Abd al-Salam Arif ousted. Ahmed Hasan al-Bakr becomes president.
	July 10	Fourth PNC meeting; PLO Covenant revised.
	July 23	First PLO airplane hijacking.
	October	Hafez al-Assad becomes leader of Syria following a coup.
	December	Israel raids Beirut International Airport in retaliation for Palestinian aircraft hijackings.
1969	January	Death of Levi Eshkol; Golda Meir becomes Israeli prime minister.
	February	Yasser Arafat becomes head of the PLO. Assad takes direct control of the Syrian government.
	February 1–4	Fifth PNC meets in Cairo. Arafat is elected chairman of the PLO Executive Committee.
	March–August	War of Attrition begins along the Suez Canal and continues until cease-fire of August 1970; maturation of PLO state-within-a-state in Jordan.
	April 3	Four-power talks open in New York.
	September 1–16	Sixth PNC is held in Cairo.
	December 9	Rogers speech outlining plan for resolution of conflict.
1970	February 13	A bomb destroys a Swissair plane bound from Zurich to Tel Aviv.
	March 15	Bar-Lev Line completed by Israel.
	May 30–June 4	Seventh PNC meets in Cairo.
	June 25	Rogers announces initiative for Egypt–Israel cease-fire.
	August 7	Cease-fire along Suez Canal.
	September	Jordanian Civil War between armed forces and the PLO. PLO is ousted from Jordan by Hussein's army.

	September 28	Nasser dies; Anwar al-Sadat becomes Egyptian president.
1971	February 28–March 5	Eighth PNC meets in Cairo.
	March	Hafez al-Assad endorsed as president of Syria.
	May	Sadat solidifies power as leader of Egypt.
	May 27	Soviet–Egyptian Treaty of Friendship.
	July 7–13	Ninth PNC meets in Cairo.
	November 28	Black September assassinates Jordanian prime minister Wasfi Tell in Cairo.
1972	March	Jordan proposes United Kingdom Plan for confederation of the West Bank with Jordan.
	April	Soviet–Iraqi Treaty of Friendship signed.
	April 6–12	Tenth PNC meets in Cairo.
	May 30	Japanese gunmen, acting for the Popular Front for the Liberation of Palestine (PFLP), shoot up Lod Airport in Israel, killing at least twenty-five.
	July	Sadat expels Soviet advisers from Egypt.
	September 5	Munich Olympic massacre of Israeli athletes by Black September.
1973	January 6–12	Eleventh PNC meets in Cairo.
	October 6–22	The Yom Kippur/Ramadan War.
	October 17	Organization of Arab Petroleum-Exporting Countries (OAPEC) imposes oil embargo.
	October 22	United Nations Security Council (UNSC) Resolution 338 passes.
	October 25	U.S. DEFCON 3 alert. Convening of Geneva Conference.
	October 28	Arab Summit at Rabat recognizes PLO as sole legitimate representative of Palestinian people.
	November 11	Israel–Egypt cease-fire signed at Kilometer 101.
	December 21	Geneva Peace Conference convenes.

1974	January 17	Israeli–Egyptian Disengagement Agreement brokered by U.S. secretary of state Henry Kissinger, signed in a tent at Kilometer 101.
	January 18	Israeli–Egyptian disengagement accord.
	February 28	United States and Egypt resume full diplomatic relations.
	April	Golda Meir resigns as prime minister of Israel.
	April 11	Palestinians infiltrate Kiryat Shmona and kill sixteen civilians.
	May 15	Palestinian infiltrators hold schoolchildren hostage in Maalot. Twenty-one children are killed.
	May 31	Israeli–Syrian disengagement brokered by Kissinger is signed in Geneva.
	June	Yitzhak Rabin becomes Israeli prime minister.
	June 1–9	Twelfth PNC meets in Cairo.
	June 12	President Richard Nixon visits the Middle East.
	June 16	United States and Syria resume diplomatic relations.
	October	PLO adopts phased program for liberation of Palestine, and Arab League invests PLO as "sole legitimate representative of the Palestinian people" at the Rabat Summit.
	October 28	Arab League summit meeting at Rabat recognizes PLO as sole legitimate representative of Palestinians.
	November 13	Yasser Arafat addresses UN General Assembly. PLO later granted observer status.
1975	April	Lebanese Civil War begins.
	June 5	Suez Canal reopens.

	September 4	Sinai II, second Israeli–Egyptian Disengagement Agreement reached; United States pledges to Israel that it will not deal with the PLO unless it affirms United Nations Security Council Resolution 242 and ceases to engage in terrorism.
	November 8	Soviets call for reconvening of Geneva Peace Conference.
	November 10	United Nations General Assembly resolution declares Zionism to be a form of racism.
	December 4	United Nations Security Council allows PLO to participate in debate on Arab–Israeli question.
1976		Massive Syrian armed intervention in Lebanon.
	April 12	West Bank municipal elections under Israeli occupation are held.
	July 4	Israeli commandos raid airport at Entebbe, Uganda, freeing hostages of hijacked jetliner.
1977	March 12–22	Thirteenth PNC meets in Cairo.
	March 16	Carter endorses a Palestinian "homeland" in address at Clinton, Massachusetts.
	May	Israeli Knesset elections; Likud Party forms Israeli government for the first time in Israeli history; Menachem Begin becomes prime minister.
	May 9	Carter meets Syrian president Assad in Geneva.
	May 17	Menachem Begin and his Likud coalition win Israeli general elections.
	June	Shamir elected speaker of the Knesset.
	July 16	Egyptian president Anwar Sadat announces willingness to accept Israel after signing of a peace treaty.
	September	Dayan meets secretly in Morocco with Sadat's adviser Hassan Tuhamy.
	October 1	U.S.–Soviet communique on the Middle East issued.

	November	Sadat travels to Jerusalem and addresses Knesset.
	November 9	Sadat states he is prepared to speak to Israeli Knesset if necessary to obtain peace.
	November 19–20	Sadat meets Israeli leaders in Jerusalem.
	November 19	Sadat addresses Israeli Knesset.
	December 25–26	Begin meets Sadat in Ismailia, Egypt.
1978	January 4	Carter issues Aswan Declaration, calling for solution to Palestinian problem "in all its aspects."
	March 11	Palestinians attack an Israeli bus on the coastal highway, killing thirty-seven. Israel launches Operation Litani into southern Lebanon on March 14.
	June 13	Israel completes withdrawal from Lebanon.
	July 17–19	Vance, Dayan, and Egyptian foreign minister Mohammed Ibrahim Kamel meet at Leeds Castle, England.
	September 5–17	Carter, Begin, and Sadat meet at Camp David.
	September 17	Begin and Sadat sign the Camp David Accords at the White House. Carter is a witness.
	October 12	Blair House talks begin.
	November 5	Arab Summit in Baghdad criticizes Camp David Accords.
	December 10	Nobel Peace Prize awarded jointly to Sadat and Begin.
	December 25	Begin and Sadat meet in Ismailia, Egypt. Summit fails to produce Egypt–Israel agreement.
1979	January 15–22	Fourteenth PNC meets in Damascus.
	March 7–13	Carter travels to Egypt and Israel to conclude the negotiations.
	March 8	Carter visits Middle East.
	March 26	Signing of Egypt–Israel Peace Treaty in Washington.

	March 31	Egypt expelled from Arab League, which moves headquarters to Tunis. League and PLO break diplomatic relations with Egypt and impose boycotts.
	April 30	First Israeli freighter since independence passes through Suez Canal.
	May 9	Egypt expelled from Islamic Conference.
	May 25	Israel begins withdrawal from Sinai Peninsula.
	October	Moshe Dayan resigns as foreign minister.
	November 2–5	Baghdad Arab Summit denounces Camp David and Egypt.
	December	Soviet Union invades Afghanistan.
1980	March	Shamir appointed foreign minister of Israel.
	June 13	European Community issues Venice Declaration.
	July 30	Israel adopts Basic Law: Jerusalem, Capital of Israel.
	September	Beginning of the Iran–Iraq War.
	October	Soviet–Syrian Treaty of Friendship and Cooperation signed.
1981	April 11–19	Fifteenth PNC meets in Damascus.
	June	Menachem Begin leads Likud to victory in Israeli elections. Ariel Sharon becomes minister of defense.
	June 7	Israel bombs Iraqi nuclear reactor at Osirak near Baghdad.
	August	Crown Prince Fahd of Saudi Arabia proposes peace plan.
	October 6	Anwar Sadat assassinated in Cairo by Islamic fundamentalists; Hosni Mubarak becomes president of Egypt.
	December 14	Israel extends its law and jurisdiction to the Golan Heights.
1982	February	Fundamentalist Muslim opposition to Assad regime in Syria leads to massacre in Hama; thousands killed.

	April 25	Israel completes withdrawal from Sinai Peninsula.
	June 6	Israel invades Lebanon (Operation Peace for Galilee).
	July–August	Israeli siege of Beirut.
	August	Multinational peacekeeping force enters Beirut to oversee evacuation of PLO from Lebanon. PLO forces withdraw from Beirut and disperse in a number of Arab countries with Arafat and his leadership team established in Tunisia.
	September 1	Reagan announces an initiative for peace in the Middle East.
	September 9	Fez Peace Plan.
	September 14	President-elect Bashir Gemayal of Lebanon is assassinated.
	September 15	After President-elect Bashir Gemayel's assassination, Israel breaks cease-fire and enters Beirut.
	September 17–18	Christian Phalange attack Sabra and Shatila camps outside Beirut and kill hundreds of Palestinians.
	September 20	Amin Gemayel becomes president of Lebanon.
	September 28	Multinational Force reenters Lebanon; aims to keep peace and speed reassertion of Lebanese government's authority in all of Lebanon.
	October 9	King Hussein and Yasser Arafat begin talks to investigate possibilities for a joint Palestinian–Jordanian response to the Reagan proposals.
1983	February 8	Israel's Kahan Commission of Inquiry releases its report concerning the massacres at Sabra and Shatilla. Among other recommendations, it calls for the resignation of Ariel Sharon as defense minister.
	February 11	Ariel Sharon resigns as defense minister.
	February 14	Moshe Arens becomes Israel's defense minister.

February 14–22	Sixteenth PNC convenes in Algiers.
April 10	PLO–Jordanian negotiations break down. Jordan's King Hussein announces the failure to reach agreement with Arafat on a joint role under the Reagan proposals.
April 18	The U.S. Embassy in Beirut is bombed, and more than fifty people are killed.
April 24	A draft agreement is reached between Israel and Lebanon focusing on troop withdrawals.
April 28	Secretary of State Shultz begins to shuttle between Israel and Lebanon to work out the final details of their accord.
May	Israeli–Lebanese agreement signed. The agreement is later abrogated by Lebanon under intense pressure from Syria. Syria supports a mutiny within Arafat's al-Fatah.
May 4	Lebanon accepts draft agreement for withdrawal of Israeli troops in Lebanon.
May 13	Syria rejects the May 4 withdrawal agreement "in form and substance."
May 17	Lebanon and Israel sign an agreement for the withdrawal of all foreign troops from Lebanon.
September 16	Begin resigns as prime minister of Israel. Israel begins first phase of withdrawal from Lebanon.
October 10	Yitzhak Shamir's new government is formally confirmed by the Knesset.
October 23	U.S. Marine compound, part of Multinational Force, is destroyed by truck bomb; 241 U.S. Marines and naval personnel killed in truck-bomb attack in Beirut; United States evacuates forces from Lebanon.
December 20	PLO leaders depart Lebanon to establish headquarters in Tunis.
1984 January 14	Saad Haddad dies of cancer.

	January 19	Islamic Conference readmits Egypt.
	February 21	U.S. peacekeeping force departs Lebanon.
	March 5	Lebanon formally abrogates May 17, 1983, agreement with Israel.
	June	Israeli National Unity government formed.
	September	Shimon Peres begins term as prime minister while Shamir remains foreign minister.
	November	Seventeenth PNC meets in Amman.
1985		Hafez al-Assad reelected president of Syria.
	January	Israel announces intent to withdraw unilaterally from Lebanon.
	February 11	Agreement between King Hussein and Yasser Arafat to move together toward achievement of a peaceful and just settlement of the Middle East crisis.
	February 13	PLO and Jordan announce political accord. Hussein and Arafat agree on a framework for peace.
	February 22	Jordanian–PLO peace plan.
	July	Israel completes evacuation of Lebanon except for security zone astride Israeli–Lebanese frontier.
	September	Israeli air force raids PLO headquarters in Tunis.
	October 1	Israel bombs PLO headquarters in Tunis.
	October	*Achille Lauro* incident.
1986	March	Jordan's King Hussein formally breaks relations with PLO chairman Yasser Arafat.
	July	Israeli prime minister Shimon Peres visits King Hassan II in Morocco.
	October	Shamir becomes prime minister; Peres assumes position of foreign minister.
1987	April	Arafat abrogates agreement with King Hussein of Jordan.
	April 20–25	Eighteenth PNC meets in Algiers.

	October	Hosni Mubarak reelected president of Egypt.
	December 8	Israeli truck hits a Palestinian car in Gaza, killing four people. Anti-Israeli violence erupts throughout Gaza.
	December 9	*Intifada* begins.
	December 10	Israeli soldiers fire on crowd of Palestinians leaving a refugee camp mosque.
1988	February	HAMAS is created in Gaza.
	April 16	Khalil al-Wazir (Abu Jihad) is assassinated in Tunis.
	May 13	The Unified Leadership of the Uprising (UNLU) publishes its demands.
	July 31	Jordan's King Hussein announces severing of most Jordanian administrative and legal ties to the West Bank and declares, "Jordan is not Palestine."
	September 29	Taba is awarded to Egypt by international arbitration panel.
	November 15	Palestine National Council in Algiers declares independent Palestinian state and issues ambiguous statements concerning acceptance of UNSC Resolutions 242 and 338.
	December	Shamir forms coalition government after November Israeli elections. Yasser Arafat, in Geneva, amplifies PLO conciliation, and the United States, in recognition, agrees to open one-channel dialogue with the PLO through the U.S. ambassador in Tunis.
	December 13	Arafat addresses United Nations in Geneva; says PNC accepts UNSC Resolutions 242 and 338 and rejects terrorism.
	December 14	Arafat, at press conference, recognizes Israel's right to exist, accepts UNSC Resolutions 242 and 338, renounces terrorism; United States announces it will begin a dialogue in Tunisia with PLO.

1989	April 6	Shamir announces election plan for the occupied territories.
	May	Israeli prime minister Yitzhak Shamir unveils Israeli elections proposal; United States accepts it as basis for peace process, but Palestinians are noncommittal.
	May 22	Egypt readmitted to Arab League.
	June 27	European Community issues Madrid statement on peace process.
	September	Egyptian president Hosni Mubarak introduces ten-point plan to clarify and advance Israel's Palestinian election proposal.
	December 27	Syria reestablishes diplomatic relations with Egypt.
1990	January	Soviet Jews begin to arrive in Israel in large numbers; Arabs begin campaign to limit migration.
	February	Meeting of Israeli and Egyptian foreign ministers with U.S. secretary of state, designed to break impasse in peace process, fails to materialize.
	March	Shamir government falls after vote of no confidence.
	June	Shamir forms new government.
	June 20	President Bush suspends U.S. dialogue with PLO.
	August	Iraq invades Kuwait. PLO chairman Arafat declares support for Iraqi president Saddam Hussein.
	October 8	Palestinians are killed in clashes with Israeli police after a stone-throwing incident at the Western Wall.
	October 12	United Nations Security Council unanimously adopts Resolution 672, condemning the Israeli action.
1990–91		PLO chairman Arafat sides with Saddam Hussein after Saddam's invasion of Kuwait and in the Gulf crisis and war that follow.

1991	January 16	Allied forces launch a massive air campaign against Iraq (Operation Desert Storm). Iraq launches Scud missiles against Israel and Saudi Arabia.
	February 23	Allied ground attack against Iraq commences.
	February 27	President Bush announces the liberation of Kuwait and the suspension of allied attacks.
	March–September	U.S. secretary of state Baker makes a series of visits to the region, partly to pursue an Arab–Israeli settlement.
	October 18	Soviet Union reestablishes diplomatic relations with Israel.
	October 30	Arab–Israeli peace conference begins in Madrid.
	December 10	Beginning of Washington rounds of bilateral Arab–Israeli negotiations.
	December 16	United Nations General Assembly repeals "Zionism is racism" resolution.
1992	April 7	Arafat is injured in plane crash in Libyan desert.
	June 23	Labor Party wins plurality in Knesset election.
	July	Yitzhak Rabin forms coalition government.
1993	Spring	Secret negotiations between Israel and PLO in Oslo, Norway.
	July	Israel launches Operation Accountability into Lebanon.
	September 13	Israel–PLO Declaration of Principles signed in Washington, D.C., to bring self-rule for Palestinians in Gaza and Jericho and eventually all of the West Bank.
	September 14	Israel and Jordan sign a Common Agenda for future negotiations.
	October	Negotiations between Israel and PLO to implement Declaration of Principles (DOP) begin.

	October 1	The Conference to Support Middle East Peace (the Donors Conference) meets in Washington.
	October 13	Israel and the PLO open talks in Egypt on how to carry out self-rule.
	October–December	Israel and the PLO continue negotiations on implementation of DOP.
1994	January	President Bill Clinton meets with President Assad in Geneva to further the Arab–Israeli negotiations.
	February 25	Jewish settler kills Palestinian worshipers in Hebron Massacre. Israel–PLO talks suspended.
	March 31	Israel–PLO talks resume.
	April 29	An agreement is signed in Paris establishing a framework for economic ties between Israel and the areas under Palestinian autonomy.
	May 4	Agreement on the details of self-rule for the Gaza Strip and Jericho is signed by Rabin and Arafat in Cairo.
	May 11	First Palestinian police enter the Gaza Strip.
	May 18	Last Israeli troops withdraw from Palestinian towns and refugee camps in Gaza.
	May 20	Two Israeli soldiers are killed in an attack on their Gaza Strip checkpoint.
	June 26	Shamgar Commission issues its report on the Hebron Massacre.
	July 2	Two Palestinians and an Israeli policeman are killed during riots by Palestinians protesting delays at the main crossing point between the Gaza Strip and Israel.
	July 25	Summit meeting in Washington, D.C., between Prime Minister Yitzhak Rabin and King Hussein of Jordan. Washington Declaration is issued.
	July 26	Rabin and Hussein address a joint session of the U.S. Congress.

August 29	Israel and the Palestinians sign an agreement on early empowerment providing for the transfer of some civil responsibilities to the Palestinians. Israel hands over education services to the Palestinians.
September 13	Oslo Declaration issued in Oslo, Norway, by Yasser Arafat and Shimon Peres.
October 1	The Cooperation Council of the Arab States of the Gulf (Gulf Cooperation Council—GCC) announces the end of the secondary and tertiary boycotts of Israel.
October 9	Two Arab gunmen kill two and wound thirteen in Jerusalem. HAMAS takes responsibility. Members of HAMAS kidnap an Israeli soldier, Corporal Nachshon Waxman, and threaten to kill him unless Israel frees the group's spiritual leader and other imprisoned Palestinians. He dies in a rescue attempt five days later. The Palestinian Authority, under pressure from Israel, triggers anger as it rounds up hundreds of Palestinian militants.
October 14	Rabin, Peres, and Arafat share the Nobel Peace Prize.
October 19	A HAMAS suicide-bomber detonates explosives on a crowded bus in Tel Aviv, killing twenty-two people and himself and wounding twenty-six.
October 26	Israel and Jordan sign a Treaty of Peace.
November 2	A member of Islamic Jihad, Hani Abed, whom Israel has accused of being behind the May 20 attack on Israeli soldiers in Gaza, is killed by a car bomb. Islamic Jihad blames the Israeli secret service and vows revenge.
November 10	King Hussein of Jordan and Israeli prime minister Yitzhak Rabin exchange ratified copies of the Israel–Jordan Peace Treaty on the shores of the Sea of Galilee during King

	Hussein's first official public visit to Israel.
November 11	An Islamic Jihad suicide bomber kills three Israeli officers at a military checkpoint. Islamic Jihad says the bombing is the first reprisal for Abed's assassination. The Palestinian Authority rounds up nearly 200 Islamic Jihad campaigners.
November 18	Palestinian police fire on demonstrators near a mosque in Gaza City, killing at least 12 people and wounding up to 200.
November 27	Israel and Jordan declare the establishment of diplomatic relations at ambassadorial level.
December	Israeli and Syrian chiefs of staff, Ehud Barak and Hikmat Shihabi, and their aides meet in Washington.
December 10	Yitzhak Rabin, Shimon Peres, and Yasser Arafat receive the 1994 Nobel Peace Prize in Oslo, Norway.
December 26	Israeli prime minister Rabin visits Oman and meets with Sultan Qaboos. Rabin was thus the first Israeli prime minister to visit an Arab state in the Persian Gulf. The Knesset passes a measure that bans political activity by "the Palestinian Authority and other Palestinians" in Jerusalem.
December 29	At the end of a two-day Summit meeting in Alexandria, Egypt, Egyptian president Hosni Mubarak, Saudi Arabia's king Fahd, and Syrian president Hafez al-Assad issue a joint statement expressing support for "Syria's valid demand for a full Israeli withdrawal from the Golan Heights as a condition to a peace treaty with Israel." They also said that peace in the Middle East should be based on the principle of "land for peace" and United Nations Security Council Resolutions 242, 338, and 425. The leaders also called for Israel to withdraw from Arab

		lands occupied in 1967, including East Jerusalem.
1995	January 22	In an Islamic Jihad terrorist strike at the Beit Lid junction, nineteen Israelis are killed, and sixty-two are wounded.
	January–June	Continued high-level meetings take place to achieve implementation of the Israel-PLO Declaration of Principles. Israel-Syria negotiations are resumed after a hiatus.
	February 2	Rabin, King Hussein, Arafat, and Mubarak meet at the summit in Cairo to discuss the peace process. In a joint statement they ''reaffirmed their determination to continue the Middle East peace process towards the fulfillment of a just, lasting and comprehensive peace in the region.''
	February 12	After a follow-up meeting in Washington, at which Egypt, Israel, Jordan and the Palestinian Authority were joined by United States representatives, the Blair House Joint Communique was issued in which ''the five participants reaffirmed their determination to consolidate the breakthroughs achieved in the Arab-Israeli peace process, to overcome obstacles and disputes, and to push forward toward a just, lasting and comprehensive peace in the region based on United Nations Security Council Resolutions 242 and 338.''
	June 27–29	Israeli and Syrian Chiefs of Staff meet in Washington to continue discussions of the security arrangements on the Golan Heights and related issues.
	September 28	An Israeli-Palestinian interim agreement is signed in Washington.
	October 29–31	The second Middle East/North Africa Economic Summit is held in Amman, Jordan.
	November 4	Prime minister Yitzhak Rabin is assassinated in Tel Aviv at the end of a rally supporting the peace process. He is succeeded by Shimon Peres.

Bibliographical Note

The Arab-Israeli conflict has been the subject of a vast literature, just the listing of which would take several volumes. Thus, this is a selected listing, primarily of reference works. The reader who wishes to pursue further the subjects of the entries in this volume is referred to the "for further information" listing at the end of each entry in which the author has listed the most valuable English-language works on the subject. The reader may also wish to consult the bibliographical notes of related entries.

For a collection of the most salient documents that illustrate the core of the dispute as well as the efforts at conciliation and peace, see Bernard Reich, ed., *Arab-Israeli Conflict and Conciliation: A Documentary History* (Westport, CT: Greenwood Press, 1995; Praeger, 1995).

General histories that provide an introduction to the development of the conflict and the efforts to resolve it include Ian J. Bickerton and Carla L. Klausner, *A Concise History of the Arab-Israeli Conflict,* Second Edition (Englewood Cliffs, NJ: Prentice Hall, 1995); Charles D. Smith, *Palestine and the Arab-Israeli Conflict,* 2nd ed. (New York: St. Martin's Press, 1992); and Mark Tessler, *A History of the Israeli-Palestinian Conflict* (Bloomington and Indianapolis: Indiana University Press, 1994). J. C. Hurewitz, *The Struggle for Palestine* (New York: W.W. Norton, 1950) provides an overview of the mandate period.

Several bibliographical works will be of value to the reader seeking a path through the massive collection of works available on this subject: Ronald M. De Vore, ed., *The Arab-Israeli Conflict: A Historical, Political, Social and Military Bibliography* (Santa Barbara, California: CLIO Books, 1976); Walid Khalidi and Jill Khadduri, eds., *Palestine and the Arab-Israeli Conflict: An Annotated Bibliography* (Beirut: Institute for Palestine Studies; Kuwait, University of Kuwait, 1974); and Sanford R. Silverburg, *Middle East Bibliography* (Metuchen, N.J.: The Scarecrow Press, 1992).

Martin Gilbert, *Atlas of the Arab-Israeli Conflict,* sixth edition (New York: Oxford University Press, 1993) is an historical atlas tracing the evolution of the conflict in maps and text.

The Arab-Israeli conflict has generated thousands of documents, both official and unofficial. Some of the more useful, albeit outdated, collections include Charles L. Geddes, ed., *A Documentary History of the Arab-Israeli Conflict* (New York: Praeger, 1991); Walter Laqueur and Barry Rubin, eds., *The Israel-Arab Reader: A Documentary History of the Middle East Conflict,* revised and updated edition (New York: Penguin Books, 1984); Yehuda Lukacs, ed., *The Israeli-Palestinian Conflict: A Documentary Record, 1967–1990* (Cambridge: Cambridge University Press, 1992); and John Norton Moore, ed., *The Arab-Israeli Conflict, Volume III: Documents* (Princeton, NJ: Princeton University Press, 1974), sponsored by the American Society of International Law.

The United States government has published several documentary collections that often have the added benefit of useful chronologies and commentaries. *The Quest For Peace* (Washington, D.C.: Department of State, 1984) (Department of State Publication 9373) incorporates the principal United States public statements and related documents on the Arab-Israeli peace process between 1967 and 1983. Among the Congressional publications are United States Senate, Committee on Foreign Relations, *A Select Chronology and Background Documents Relating to the Middle East* (Washington, D.C.: U.S. Government Printing Office, 1967); United States Senate, Committee on Foreign Relations, *A Select Chronology and Background Documents Relating to the Middle East,* First Revised Edition (Washington, D.C.: U.S. Government Printing Office, 1969); United States Senate, Committee on Foreign Relations, *A Select Chronology and Background Documents Relating to the Middle East,* Second Revised Edition (Washington, D.C.: U.S. Government Printing Office, 1975); United States House of Representatives, Committee on Foreign Affairs, *The Search for Peace in the Middle East: Documents and Statements, 1967–79* (Washington, D.C.: U.S. Government Printing Office, 1979); United States House of Representatives, Committee on Foreign Affairs, *Documents and Statements on Middle East Peace, 1979–82* (Washington, D.C.: U.S. Government Printing Office, 1982); United States House of Representatives, Committee on Foreign Affairs, *Documents on Middle East Peace, 1982–88* (Washington, D.C.: U.S. Government Printing Office, 1989).

The United Nations Committee on the Exercise of the Inalienable Rights of the Palestinian People has produced a large number of publications that include documents and studies that will be of utility to the student of the themes in this volume.

The Journal of Palestine Studies (a quarterly on Palestinian Affairs and the Arab-Israeli Conflict) published by The University of California Press for the

Institute for Palestine Studies and Kuwait University, is an invaluable source for the study of the conflict despite its strong bias toward the Palestinian position.

Index

Editor's Note: This index does not include individuals, places, events, and other terms that are mentioned only peripherally in the book. Also, terms such as Egypt, Iraq, Jordan, Lebanon, Palestine, Palestine Liberation Organization, and Syria (and variations of them) appear with such frequency that, except for main entries, they are similarly excluded from this index. **Boldface** numbers indicate the location of the main entries in the text.

235, 238, 242, 244, 256, 262, 264,
283, 286, 298, 314, 315, 324, 325,
326, 328, 351, 369, 370, 378, 388,
390, 391, 395, 400, 401, 402, 408,
425, 427, 428, 434, 446, 447, 458,
460, 461, 473, 474, 480, 481, 482,
484, 485, 489, 493, 501, 510, 512,
519, 520, 526, 536, 549, 555, 559,
569, 572, 573, 577, 580, 591, 594

Gaza–Jericho agreements. *See* Cairo
agreements, 1994; early empowerment;
Israel–PLO Economic Agreement
(1994); Safe Passage Route

Gemayel, Amin, **183,** 253

Gemayel, Bashir, 107, 108, **183–84,** 220,
288, 361, 443, 561, 563

General Union of Palestinian Students,
41, **184–85,** 211, 288, 298, 395

Geneva Conference (1973), 84, 101, 102,
157, **185,** 194, 244, 251, 279, 280,
302, 306, 399, 412, 446, 480, 550, 551

Gidi Pass, 8, 180, **185,** 477, 478, 479,
480, 522

Glassboro, New Jersey, Summit Meeting
(1967), **185–86**

Glubb, John Bagot, 37, 38, **186–87,** 281,
316, 317, 572

Golan Heights, 47, 48, 81, 97, 98, 99,
141, 145, 152, 167, 179, 184, **187–89,**
242, 254, 256, 281, 283, 306, 311,
340, 345, 353, 354, 377, 378, 385,
421, 429, 431, 457, 458, 459, 463,
470, 475, 476, 488, 489, 493, 505,
523, 524, 528, 538, 540, 546, 559,
560, 561, 562, 595, 597, 598, 599

Goldmann, Nahum, **189–90**

Goldstein, Baruch, 217, 241, 291, 460,
515

good fence, **190–91**

Goren, Shlomo, **191**

Government House, **191,** 393, 487, 546;
of Sidon, **191–92**

Government of National Unity, 45, **192,**
197, 252, 314, 325, 327, 342, 344,
410, 425, 461, 464, 577, 578

Great Britain. *See* England

Green Line, **192,** 381

Gromyko, Andrei Andreyevich, **192–94,**
279, 548

Guinness, Walter Edward. *See* Moyne,
Lord

Gulf of Aqaba, 13, 79, 141, **194–95,** 372,
465, 466, 478, 482, 484, 499, 500, 507

Gulf War, 58, 113, 155, 173, **196,** 246,
262, 265, 337, 374, 457, 476, 552

Gur, Mordechai, **197,** 386, 487, 488, 489

Gush Emunim, **197–98,** 311, 314, 325,
509, 515, 591, 592

Habash, George, 2, 65, **199–201,** 203,
214, 276, 417, 428, 465

Habib, Philip Charles, 48, **201–2,** 360,
427, 443, 561

Haddad, Saad Georges, 174, 190, **202–3,**
313, 490

Haddad, Wadi, 166, **203,** 417

Hadera, **203–4,** 208

Haganah, 21, 26, 27, 39, 41, 59, 69, 87,
88, 122, 128, 149, 150, 191, 197, **204–
5,** 247, 271, 280, 314, 316, 329, 340,
402, 403, 409, 414, 424, 447, 462,
466, 498, 570, 577, 586, 590

Haig, Alexander, **205–6,** 427

HAMAS, 11, 24, 43, 160, 203, **206–8,**
577, 593

HAMAS Charter, **208–9**

Hammarskjold, Dag, 51, **209–10,** 356,
519, 525

Haram al-Sharif, 14, 15, **210,** 267, 511,
542, 580. *See also* al-Aksa Mosque;
Dome of the Rock

Hasbani River, 161, **210–11,** 284

Hassan, Hani, **211**

al-Hassan, Khalid, 159, **211,** 498

Hassan ibn Talal, H.R.H. Crown Prince,
116, **211–12,** 227

Hassan II, 103, 133, 165, 174, **212–13,**
323, 352, 509

Hassan–Peres Summit (1986), 212, **213,**
323, 411

Hawari Group, 159, **213–14**

Hawatmeh, Nayef, 6, 129, 131, 200, **214,**
417, 418

Hawk missile, **214–15,** 566

Haycraft Commission, **215–16,** 510

Hebron, 20, 25, 33, 38, 104, 148, 149,
150, 160, **216–17,** 241, 285, 295, 306,
325, 369, 372, 401, 449, 459, 461,

About the Editors and Contributors

BERNARD REICH (Editor) is Professor of Political Science and International Affairs and former Chairman of the Department of Political Science at The George Washington University in Washington, D.C. He is the author of *Quest for Peace: United States-Israel Relations and the Arab-Israeli Conflict, The United States and Israel: Influence in the Special Relationship, Israel: Land of Tradition and Conflict, Securing the Covenant: United States-Israel Relations After the Cold War;* editor and co-author of *The Powers in the Middle East: The Ultimate Strategic Arena* and *Political Leaders of the Contemporary Middle East and North Africa: A Biographical Dictionary;* co-editor and co-author of *Government and Politics of the Middle East and North Africa* (3 editions), co-editor and co-author of *Israel Faces the Future* and of *Israeli National Security Policy: Political Actors and Perspectives;* as well as the author of numerous articles and monographs on the Arab-Israeli conflict and on the politics and foreign policy of the Middle East and North Africa.

JOSEPH E. GOLDBERG (Associate Editor), Ph.D., is Professor of Political Science and Director of Research at the Industrial College of the Armed Forces at the National Defense University in Washington, D.C. He previously was Director of Research at the Institute for National Strategic Studies at the National Defense University. He has published widely on Middle Eastern politics, terrorism, strategic issues, and political theory.

STEPHEN H. GOTOWICKI (Military Editor) is a Lieutenant Colonel in the U.S. Army assigned as a Politico-Military Planner in the Strategic Plans and Policy Directorate (J-5), the Joint Chiefs of Staff. He is a Field Artillery Officer and a Middle East Foreign Area Officer and has served in Southern Lebanon as a United Nations Military Observer. He holds an M.A. in National Security Affairs and Middle East studies from the United States Naval Postgraduate School and is a Ph.D. candidate in Political Science at The George Washington University.

SANFORD R. SILVERBURG (Bibliographic Editor) is Professor of Political Science and Chairman of the Department of Political Science at Catawba College in Salisbury, North Carolina. Among his numerous publications are *Middle East Bibliography, U.S. Foreign Relations with the Middle East and North Africa: A Bibliography, United States Foreign Policy and the Middle East/North Africa: A Bibliography of Twentieth Century Research,* and *Asian States' Relations with the Middle East and North Africa: A Bibliography, 1950–1993.*

MARK DARYL ERICKSON (Assistant Editor) has a B.A. in Middle Eastern Studies and an M.A. in International Affairs from The George Washington University. He has lived and traveled extensively in the Middle East.

DAVID J. ABRAM holds a B.A. in Political Science and an M.A. in Security Policy, the latter from The George Washington University. He studied at the American University in Cairo, has travelled widely in the region, and is a Middle East foreign area officer in the United States Army Reserve.

MONICA M. BOUDJOUK received her M.A. in Political Science with a Middle East concentration from The George Washington University.

ROBERT CRANGLE, JR., holds an M.A. in International Affairs from The George Washington University.

MATTHEW DORF, a journalist, is the Washington Bureau Chief of the Jewish Telegraphic Agency.

NOAH DROPKIN has an M.A. in Political Science from The George Washington University.

AHMED ELBASHARI is a Ph.D. candidate in the Department of Politics at The Catholic University of America. He holds an M.A. in Middle East politics from the George Washington University. He has worked as a journalist for a number of Middle Eastern newspapers and serves as a radio journalist for the Arab Network of America and as a news reporter for Abu Dhabi TV of the United Arab Emirates.

GALINA EMELYANOVA holds a Ph.D. in History and is a Senior Researcher of the Institute of Oriental Studies of the Russian Academy of Sciences with a specialization in Middle East history, the Arab countries, and the Arab-Israeli conflict.

KARIN J. ENGLAND is a student of International Relations at Georgetown University.

ERIN Z. FERGUSON holds an M.A. in International Affairs from The George Washington University and a B.A. in Near Eastern Languages and Literatures from New York University. She works for *The New Yorker* magazine.

JOHN FONTAINE holds a B.A. in Middle Eastern Studies from The George Washington University. He has travelled, studied and worked in the region.

DAVID H. GOLDBERG holds a Ph.D. in Political Science from McGill University and is Director of Research for the Foundation for Middle East Studies, Toronto. He is the author or co-editor of three books, two of which deal principally with the formulation of Canada's Middle East policy.

YASHA MANUEL HARARI is a graduate of The George Washington University, where he specialized in Middle Eastern politics. He has lived in the Middle East and has covered the Arab-Israeli peace process as a photojournalist.

NANCY HASANIAN holds an M.A. in International Affairs with a Middle East concentration. She was a Wolcott Fellow during her graduate studies.

KOHEI HASHIMOTO holds a BA degree from American University of Beirut and an M.Phil and D.Phil from St. Antony's College, Oxford. He has published widely on various aspects of the Middle East and international relations. He is currently a Senior Research Associate at PHP Research Institute in Kyoto, Japan.

YEVGENI KOZLOV holds a Ph.D. in History. He is a Senior Researcher for the Institute of Oriental Studies of the Russian Academy of Sciences, where he is an expert on Arab affairs.

ANAMIKA KRISHNA has a B.A. with Honours in Political Science from the University of Western Ontario, Canada, and an M.Sc. in the Politics of Asia and Africa with special reference to the Near and Middle East from the School of Oriental and African Studies of the University of London, England. She lectures on Comparative Asian Politics at Roanoke College, Roanoke, Virginia.

SIMEON MANICKAVASAGAM holds a B.A. in Political Science and an M.A. in International Affairs, the latter from Catholic University.

DONALD A. PEARSON holds an M.A. in Security Policy Studies with a concentration in Middle East history and politics from The George Washington University.

JON J. PETERSON is completing an M.A. in Security Policy Studies from The George Washington University and is a staff associate with the Committee on International Relations of the United States House of Representatives.

TIMOTHY J. PIRO holds a Ph.D. in Political Science from The George Washington University. He has lived and studied in the Middle East. Among his publications are articles and book chapters on contemporary Arab world politics and France's role in the Middle East and North Africa.

PAMELA RIVERS holds an M.A. in Middle Eastern Studies from The George Washington University and a B.A. in Political Science and International Relations.

PAUL S. ROBINSON, JR., has lived in Saudi Arabia and holds an M.A. in International Affairs from The George Washington University.

SUSAN L. ROSENSTEIN holds a B.A. in Political Science with a concentration in Middle Eastern Affairs from Hofstra University and is completing an M.A. at the University of Hartford.

DAVID SALZBERG is a graduate student in international affairs at The George Washington University and holds a B.A. in International Affairs and Political Science with a concentration in Middle East Studies.

RICHARD G. R. SCHICKELE, Counsel of the Supreme Court of the United States, received his law degree from Boalt Hall, University of California, Berkeley. He also has an M.A. in Political Science from The George Washington University.

DONALD A. VOGUS is a Defense Analyst at Science Applications International Corporation, where he works on arms control and related issues. He holds an M.A. in Security Policy Studies from The George Washington University.

NOLAN WOHL holds an M.A. in International Affairs from The American University, where he concentrated in Middle East Studies. He has also served as a Research Associate at The Heritage Foundation in Washington, D.C.

DAVID WURMSER holds a Ph.D. from Johns Hopkins University and is Director of Institutional Grants at the Washington Institute for Near East Policy and served previously (1988–1994) as a project officer at the United States Institute of Peace. He is the author of numerous articles, book chapters, and United States Institute of Peace Reports on various aspects of Middle East and international politics.

IRINA ZVIAGELSKAIA is a Dr.Sc. and a Senior Researcher of the Institute of Oriental Studies of the Russian Academy of Sciences. She is also Vice President of the Russian Center for Strategic Research and International Studies. Her specializations include the international relations of the Middle East.